GREGORIAN MISSAL

THE GREGORIAN MISSAL
FOR SUNDAYS

*NOTATED IN GREGORIAN CHANT
BY THE MONKS OF SOLESMES*

SOLESMES

1990

*Concordat cum originalibus approbatis;
imprimatur:*
Die 16 novembris 1989,
† Georgius Gilson,
Cenomanensis episcopus.

© 1990, St. Peter's Abbey, Solesmes.
© 1990, Desclée, Paris · Tournai.

The English translation of the prayers, the eucharistic prayers, prefaces, and other texts from the Order of Mass from The Roman Missal © *1973, International Committee on English in the Liturgy, Inc. All rights reserved.*

La loi du 11 mars 1957 interdit les copies ou reproductions destinées à une utilisation collective. Toute représentation ou reproduction intégrale ou partielle faite par quelque procédé que ce soit, sans le consentement des auteurs, est illicite et constitue une contrefaçon sanctionnée par les articles 425 et suivants du code pénal.

Abbaye Saint-Pierre,
F-72300 Solesmes, France.

ISBN 2-85274-133-4

FOREWORD

The *Gregorian Missal* is intended for the faithful who participate in Mass sung in Gregorian chant. It is useful both for choirs and for the people in general, since the proper chants of the Gregorian repertory, as presented in the post-Vatican II edition of the Roman Gradual approved by Pope Paul VI, do not, as a rule, correspond to the song texts proposed in the present-day Roman Missal.

Vatican II declared: "The musical tradition of the universal Church is a treasure of inestimable value, greater even than that of any other art. The main reason for this pre-eminence is that, as sacred song united to the words, it forms a necessary or integral part of the solemn liturgy." (Constitution on the Sacred Liturgy, n° 112). In addition, "the Church acknowledges Gregorian chant as specially suited to the Roman liturgy; therefore, other things being equal, it should be given pride of place in liturgical services." (ibid, n° 116). And thus, to ensure "the preservation and careful fostering of this treasure of sacred music" (ibid, n° 114), the collection of Gregorian melodies for Mass was renovated by the *Ordo Cantus Missæ* of June 24, 1972, and made available for use by publication of the new, above mentioned, *Graduale Romanum*, (Solesmes, 1974), in order to promote "full, conscious and active participation of the faithful." (Ibid, n° 14).

This *Graduale Romanum*, which our present *Gregorian Missal* follows, re-distributes the chants in accordance with the renewed liturgical cycle and in order to accompany the new lectionary with its wide choice of readings. Furthermore, it enriches the Gregorian repertory itself, since it puts back into circulation certain authentic pieces which were not used for centuries while setting aside many inauthentic neo-Gregorian compositions of the 19th or early 20th centuries.

The *Gregorian Missal* contains the Latin and English texts for the complete celebration of Mass, with masses for all Sundays and solemnities and for those feasts which take precedence over a Sunday. In order to limit the size of this volume, it was necessary to omit the text of the readings. Only the references have been given.

Foreword

All chant melodies – both for the Ordinary of Mass and for the Propers – are presented in the traditional square Gregorian notation with the added rhythmical signs.

Alongside the Latin prayers, in a second column, have been placed the corresponding texts of the official liturgical translation for English speaking countries. These were created for the needs of the vernacular liturgy and they are printed here in conformity with official directives, even though they do not always constitute a literal, word for word rendering of the Latin. The notated Gregorian chant pieces proper to each Mass, are generally followed by our own translation, printed across the full width of the page. Its only function is to facilitate comprehension of the sung Latin text, and it is in no way intended for use in the Liturgy.

The Introits and Communion antiphons of each Mass, as well as the Offertory chants and other antiphons, are refrains meant to be alternated with sung verses taken, generally, from a psalm. Except for the Introit, these verses have not been indicated since they concern only the cantors.

The mode of execution for the various chants is defined in the course of the celebration of Mass. A distinction is made between the choir (which can eventually be divided in two) and one or several cantors. The choir consists either of a schola or of all the people, according to the nature of each particular piece and the capacities of the singers. And, in the words of Vatican II, it is important to "take steps so that the faithful may also be able to say or sing together in Latin those parts of the Ordinary of Mass which pertain to them." (ibid, n° 54).

We hope to complete the *Gregorian Missal* by the publication of Vespers and Compline, as soon as it becomes possible to do so. As for the chants of Mass during the week, they can be found in the *Graduale Romanum*.

THE ORDER OF MASS

INTRODUCTORY RITES

Introit *proper to each day. It is sung by the choir, and repeated after each psalm verse chanted by cantors, while the celebrant enters and venerates the altar. (At the beginning of the chant pieces, an asterisk indicates the end of those intonations which are not made by the entire choir but by one or several cantors.) Then, the priest and the faithful, who remain standing, make the sign of the Cross:*

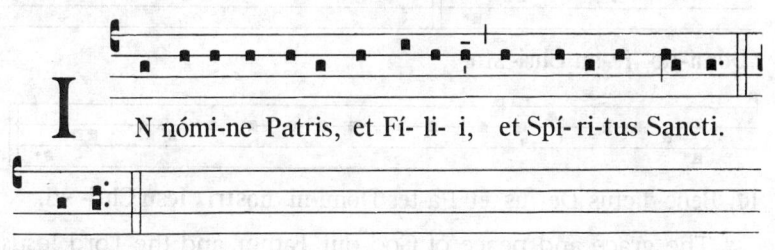

I N nómi-ne Patris, et Fí- li- i, et Spí- ri-tus Sancti.

℟. Amen.

℣. In the name of the Father, and of the Son, and of the Holy Spirit.
℟. Amen.

The priest welcomes the people in the name of the Lord:

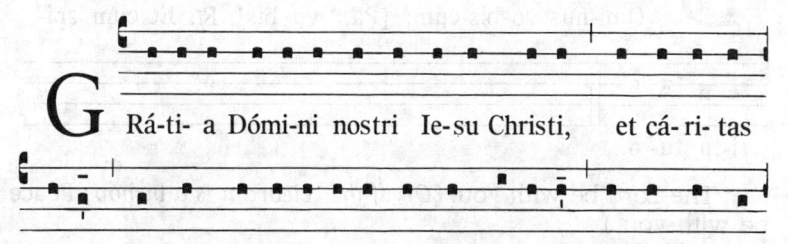

G Rá-ti- a Dómi-ni nostri Ie-su Christi, et cá- ri- tas De- i, et commu-ni-cá-ti- o Sancti Spí- ri-tus sit cum ómnibus vo- bis. ℟. Et cum spí-ri-tu tu- o.

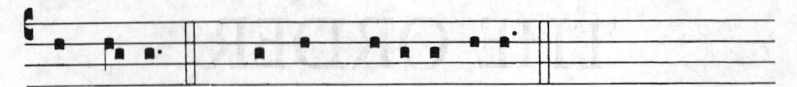

℣. The grace of our Lord Jesus Christ and the love of God and the fellowship of the Holy Spirit be with you all.

℟. And also with you.

Or:

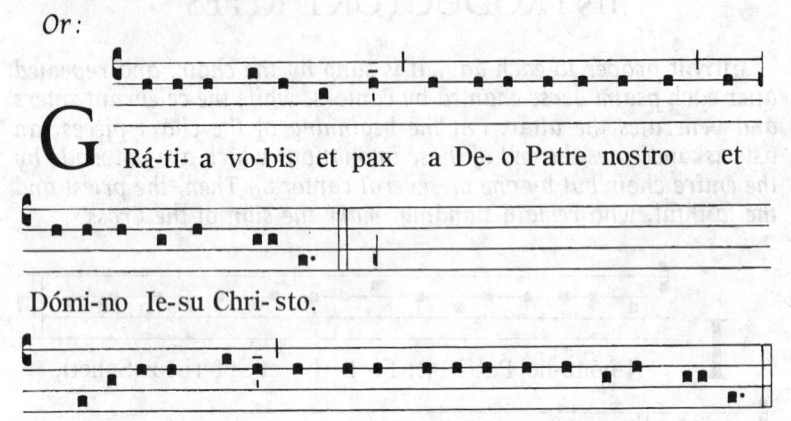

GRá-ti- a vo-bis et pax a De- o Patre nostro et Dómi-no Ie-su Chri- sto.

℟. Bene-díctus De- us et Pa-ter Dómi-ni nostri Iesu Chri- sti.

℣. The grace and peace of God our Father and the Lord Jesus Christ be with you.

℟. Blessed be God, the Father of our Lord Jesus Christ.

Or:

DOmi-nus vo-bís-cum. [Pax vo- bis]. ℟. Et cum spí-ri-tu tu- o.

℣. The Lord be with you. (*Or, if the celebrant is a bishop*: Peace be with you.)

℟. And also with you.

Alternative tone:

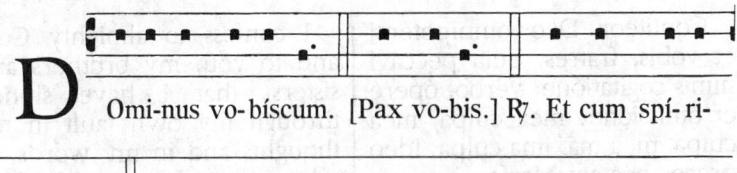

D Omi-nus vo-bíscum. [Pax vo-bis.] ℟. Et cum spí-ri-tu tu-o.

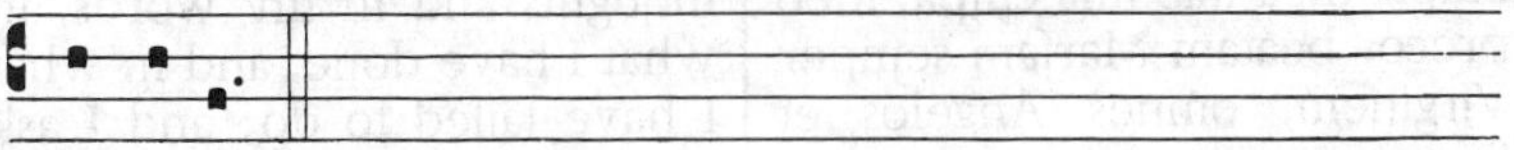

Penitential rite

The priest invites the people to repentance:

| Fratres, agnoscámus peccáta nostra, ut apti simus ad sacra mystéria celebránda. | My brothers and sisters, to prepare ourselves to celebrate the sacred mysteries, let us call to mind our sins. |

After a pause for silent prayer he continues:

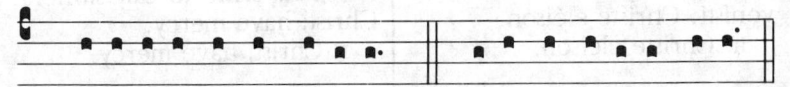

℣. Mi-se-ré-re nostri, Dómine. ℟. Qui-a peccávimus ti-bi.

℣. Lord, we have sinned against you: Lord, have mercy.
℟. Lord, have mercy.

℣. Osténde no-bis, Dómine, mi-se-ricórdi-am tu-am. ℟. Et sa-lu-tá-re tu-um da no-bis.

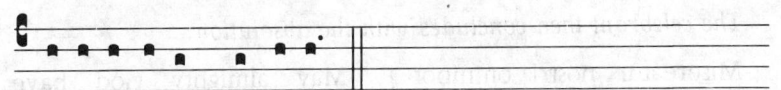

℣. Lord, show us your mercy and love.
℟. And grant us your salvation.

Order of Mass

Or, all say together:

Confíteor Deo omnipoténti et vobis, fratres, quia peccávi nimis cogitatióne, verbo, ópere et omissióne: mea culpa, mea culpa, mea máxima culpa. Ideo precor beátam Maríam semper Vírginem, omnes Angelos et Sanctos, et vos, fratres, oráre pro me ad Dóminum Deum nostrum.	I confess to almighty God, and to you, my brothers and sisters, that I have sinned through my own fault in my thoughts and in my words, in what I have done, and in what I have failed to do; and I ask blessed Mary, ever virgin, all the angels and saints, and you, my brothers and sisters, to pray for me to the Lord our God.

Or:

℣. Qui missus es sanáre contrítos corde: Kýrie eléison.
℟. Kýrie eléison.

℣. Qui peccatóres vocáre venísti: Christe eléison.
℟. Christe eléison.

℣. Qui ad déxteram Patris sedes, ad interpellándum pro nobis: Kýrie, eléison.
℟. Kýrie, eléison.

℣. You were sent to heal the contrite: Lord, have mercy.
℟. Lord, have mercy.

℣. You came to call sinners: Christ, have mercy.
℟. Christ, have mercy.

℣. You plead for us at the right hand of the Father: Lord, have mercy.
℟. Lord, have mercy.

For the response, Kyrie XVI, p. 128, or XVIII, p. 132, may be used.

The celebrant then concludes with the absolution:

Misereátur nostri omnípotens Deus et, dimíssis peccátis nostris, perdúcat nos ad vitam ætérnam. *People:* Amen.	May almighty God have mercy on us, forgive us our sins, and bring us to everlasting life.

Order of Mass

The sprinkling of holy water. *When this rite is celebrated, it replaces the penitential preparation. See p. 68.*

Kýrie.

Next, the Kýrie is sung. The invocations can be alternated between the two sides of the choir or between the cantors and the entire choir. The Kýrie is omitted if it has already been sung as part of the penitential rite, or when Mass is preceded by some other ceremony (such as the procession of Candlemas, Palm Sunday or the Easter Vigil). All chants for the ordinary of Mass are found in this book starting on page 73. Some of the melodies require that each invocation be repeated three times.

Kýrie, eléison.	Lord, have mercy.
Kýrie, eléison.	Lord, have mercy.
Christe, eléison.	Christ, have mercy.
Christe, eléison.	Christ, have mercy.
Kýrie, eléison.	Lord, have mercy.
Kýrie, eléison.	Lord, have mercy.

Gloria.

The Gloria is sung on solemnities and feasts and on Sundays outside of Advent and Lent. It can be alternated between cantors and choir or between the two sides of the choir. The intonation is given by the celebrant. Melodies are found in the chants for the Ordinary starting on p. 73.

GLÓRIA in excélsis Deo Et in terra pax homínibus bonæ voluntátis.
   Laudámus te, benedícimus te, adorámus te,
   Glorificámus te, grátias ágimus tibi propter magnam glóriam tuam,

GLORY to God in the highest, and peace to his people on earth.
   Lord God, heavenly King, almighty God and Father,
   we worship you, we give you thanks, we praise you for your glory.

Dómine Deus, Rex cæléstis, Deus Pater omnípotens.
Dómine Fili unigénite, Iesu Christe,
Dómine Deus, Agnus Dei, Fílius Patris,
Qui tollis peccáta mundi, miserére nobis ;
Qui tollis peccáta mundi, súscipe deprecatiónem nostram.
Qui sedes ad déxteram Patris, miserére nobis.
Quóniam tu solus Sanctus,
Tu solus Dóminus,
Tu solus Altíssimus, Iesu Christe, cum Sancto Spíritu:
In glória Dei Patris. Amen.

Lord Jesus Christ, only Son of the Father, Lord God, Lamb of God,
you take away the sin of the world: have mercy on us;
you are seated at the right hand of the Father: receive our prayer.
For you alone are the Holy One,
you alone are the Lord,
you alone are the Most High, Jesus Christ, with the Holy Spirit,
in the glory of God the Father. Amen.

Opening prayer

After an invitation to pray (orémus), *the celebrant sings the opening prayer, ending with one of the following long conclusions:*

When addressing the Father:

Per Dóminum nostrum Iesum Christum, Fílium tuum, qui tecum vivit et regnat in unitáte Spíritus Sancti, Deus, per ómnia sǽcula sæculórum.
℟. Amen.

We ask this (We make our prayer) (Grant this) through our Lord Jesus Christ, your Son, who lives and reigns with you and the Holy Spirit, one God, for ever and ever.
℟. Amen.

When addressing the Father while invoking the Son:

Qui tecum vivit et regnat in unitáte Spíritus Sancti, Deus, per ómnia sǽcula sæculórum.
℟. Amen.

Who lives and reigns with you and the Holy Spirit, one God, for ever and ever.
℟. Amen.

Order of Mass

When addressing the Son:

| Qui vivis et regnas cum Deo Patre in unitáte Spíritus Sancti, Deus, per ómnia sǽcula sæculórum. ℟. Amen. | You live and reign with the Father and the Holy Spirit, one God, for ever and ever. ℟. Amen. |

... per ómni- a sǽcu-la sæcu-ló- rum. ℟. Amen.

Alternative tone.

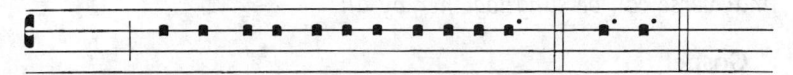

... per ómni- a sǽcu- la sæcu-ló-rum. ℟. Amen.

LITURGY OF THE WORD

First reading. *The assembly sits during this reading. The lector may conclude as follows.*

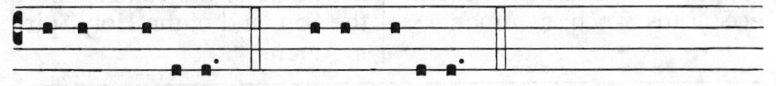

Verbum Dómi-ni. ℟. De- o grá-ti- as.

℣. This is the Word of the Lord.
℟. Thanks be to God.

Gradual *proper to each day. The first part is sung by the choir and the verse is given by the cantors. The choir then repeats the first part. During Eastertide, a first Alleluia is sung in place of the Gradual. When there is only one Mass reading, it is followed by either the Gradual or the Alleluia except in Lent, when the Alleluia is always omitted, and during the Easter season, when there is a choice between two Alleluias.*

Second reading *on Sundays and Solemnities.*

The lector may conclude as follows:

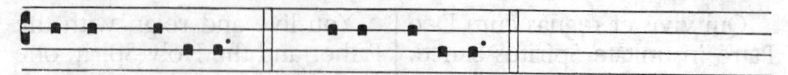

Verbum Dómi-ni.   ℟. De- o grá-ti- as.

℣. This is the Word of the Lord.
℟. Thanks be to God.

Alleluia *proper to each day. The choir sings the* Alleluia *or repeats it after the cantors; then the cantors sing the verse and all repeat the* Alleluia. *In Lent, the* **Tract** *is sung, with alternation between the two sides of the choir or between cantors and choir. The final verse can be sung together by all.*

Gospel

Meanwhile, the priest puts incense into the censer. Then, the deacon who is to proclaim the Gospel bows to the priest and says:

Iube, domne, benedícere.	Father, give me your blessing.

The priest replies:

Dóminus sit in corde tuo et in lábiis tuis: ut digne et competénter annúnties Evangélium suum: in nómine Patris, et Fílii, et Spíritus Sancti. ℟. Amen.	The Lord be in your heart and on your lips that you may worthily proclaim his gospel. In the name of the Father, and of the Son, and of the Holy Spirit. ℟. Amen.

The priest, if it is he who is to read the Gospel, prays as follows:

Munda cor meum ac lábia mea, omnípotens Deus, ut sanctum Evangélium tuum digne váleam nuntiáre.	Almighty God, cleanse my heart and my lips that I may worthily proclaim your gospel.

The deacon or the priest then goes to the pulpit. He may be accompanied by a procession of acolytes with candles and thurible. He says:

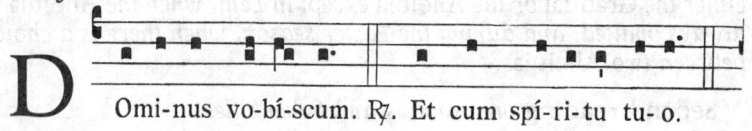

DOmi-nus vo-bí-scum. ℟. Et cum spí-ri-tu tu- o.

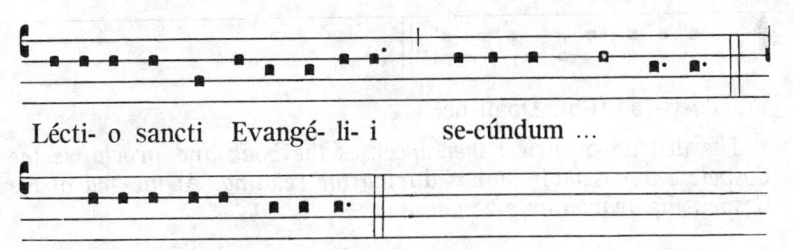

Order of Mass

[chant notation]

Lécti- o sancti Evangé- li- i se-cúndum ...

[chant notation]

℟. Gló-ri- a ti-bi, Dómi-ne.
℣. The Lord be with you.
℟. And also with you.
℣. A reading from the holy gospel according to N.

He makes the sign of the cross on the open book, and on his forehead, lips and breast.

℟. Glory to you, Lord.

Alternative tone:

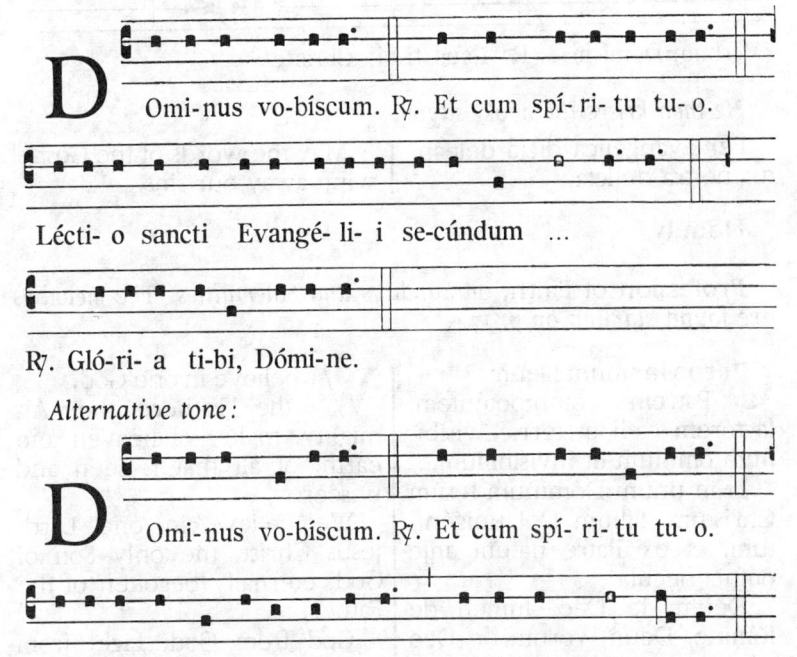

[chant notation]

D Omi-nus vo-bíscum. ℟. Et cum spí- ri- tu tu- o.

[chant notation]

Lécti- o sancti Evangé- li- i se-cúndum ...

[chant notation]

℟. Gló-ri- a ti-bi, Dómi-ne.

Alternative tone:

[chant notation]

D Omi-nus vo-bíscum. ℟. Et cum spí- ri- tu tu- o.

[chant notation]

Lécti- o sancti Evangé- li- i se-cúndum ...

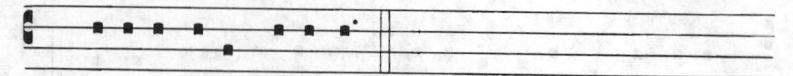

℟. Gló-ri-a ti-bi, Dómi-ne.

The deacon or priest then incenses the book and proclaims the Gospel. The assembly stands during the reading. At the end of the Gospel, the deacon or priest says:

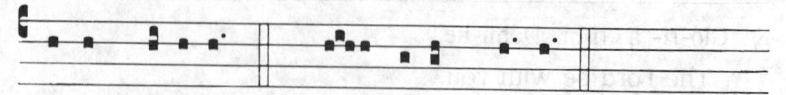

Verbum Dómi-ni.   ℟. Laus   ti-bi, Chri-ste.

℣. This is the Gospel of the Lord.
℟. Praise to you, Lord Jesus Christ.

Alternative tone:

Verbum Dómi-ni.   ℟. Laus ti-bi, Christe.

He then kisses the book, saying:

| Per evangélica dicta deleántur nostra delícta. | May the words of the Gospel wipe away our sins. |

Homily

Profession of Faith, *on Sundays and Solemnities. The melodies are found starting on p. 134.*

Credo in unum Deum, Patrem omnipoténtem, factórem cæli et terræ, visibílium ómnium et invisibílium.	We believe in one God, the Father, the Almighty, maker of heaven and earth, of all that is seen and unseen.
Et in unum Dóminum Iesum Christum, Fílium Dei unigénitum, et ex Patre natum ante ómnia sǽcula.	We believe in one Lord, Jesus Christ, the only Son of God, eternally begotten of the Father,
Deum de Deo, lumen de lúmine, Deum verum de Deo vero,	God from God, Light from Light, true God from true God,

Génitum, non factum, consubstantiálem Patri: per quem ómnia facta sunt.
Qui propter nos hómines et propter nostram salútem descéndit de cælis.
Et incarnátus est de Spíritu Sancto ex María Vírgine, et homo factus est.
Crucifíxus étiam pro nobis sub Póntio Piláto; passus et sepúltus est,
Et resurréxit tértia die, secúndum Scriptúras, et ascéndit in cælum, sedet ad déxteram Patris.
Et íterum ventúrus est cum glória, iudicáre vivos et mórtuos, cuius regni non erit finis.

Et in Spíritum Sanctum, Dóminum et vivificántem : qui ex Patre Filióque procédit.

Qui cum Patre et Fílio simul adorátur et conglorificátur: qui locútus est per prophétas.

Et unam, sanctam, cathólicam et apostólicam Ecclésiam.

Confíteor unum baptísma in remissiónem peccatórum.
Et exspécto resurrectiónem mortuórum et vitam ventúri sæculi.
Amen.

begotten, not made, one in Being with the Father. Through him all things were made.
For us men and for our salvation he came down from heaven:
by the power of the Holy Spirit he was born of the Virgin Mary, and became man.
For our sake he was crucified under Pontius Pilate; he suffered, died, and was buried.
On the third day he rose again in fulfillment of the Scriptures; he ascended into heaven and is seated at the right hand of the Father.
He will come again in glory to judge the living and the dead, and his kingdom will have no end.
We believe in the Holy Spirit, the Lord, the giver of life, who proceeds from the Father and the Son.
With the Father and the Son he is worshipped and glorified. He has spoken through the Prophets.
We believe in one holy catholic and apostolic Church.
We acknowledge one baptism for the forgiveness of sins.
We look for the resurrection of the dead, and the life of the world to come.
Amen.

Prayer of the Faithful. *The celebrant invites the assembly to pray for all the intentions of the Church and the world.*

LITURGY OF THE EUCHARIST

The Offertory Antiphon *proper to each day is sung by the choir.*

Meanwhile, the ministers prepare the altar, a procession of the faithful brings the gifts for the eucharistic celebration, and the priest offers the bread and the wine.

The priest offers the bread saying:

Benedíctus es, Dómine, Deus univérsi, quia de tua largitáte accépimus panem, quem tibi offérimus, fructum terræ et óperis mánuum hóminum, ex quo nobis fiet panis vitæ.	Blessed are you, Lord, God of all creation. Through your goodness we have this bread to offer, which earth has given and human hands have made. It will become for us the bread of life.

If the Offertory antiphon is not sung, the assembly may respond:

Benedíctus Deus in sǽcula.	Blessed be God for ever.

The deacon or the priest pours a drop of water into the chalice, saying:

Per huius aquæ et vini mystérium eius efficiámur divinitátis consórtes, qui humanitátis nostræ fíeri dignátus est párticeps.	By the mystery of this water and wine may we come to share in the divinity of Christ, who humbled himself to share in our humanity.

The priest then offers the wine saying:

Benedíctus es, Dómine, Deus univérsi, quia de tua largitáte accépimus vinum, quod tibi offérimus, fructum vitis et óperis mánuum hóminum, ex quo nobis fiet potus spiritális.	Blessed are you, Lord, God of all creation. Through your goodness we have this wine to offer, fruit of the vine and work of human hands. It will become our spiritual drink.

If the Offertory antiphon is not sung, the assembly may respond:

Benedíctus Deus in sǽcula.	Blessed be God for ever.

Order of Mass

The priest bows and says in a low voice:

In spíritu humilitátis et in ánimo contríto suscipiámur a te, Dómine; et sic fiat sacrifícium nostrum in conspéctu tuo hódie, ut pláceat tibi, Dómine Deus.	Lord God, we ask you to receive us and be pleased with the sacrifice we offer you with humble and contrite hearts.

He may incense the gifts and the altar. The deacon or minister then incenses the priest and the people.

The priest washes his hands.

Lava me, Dómine, ab iniquitáte mea, et a peccáto meo munda me.	Lord, wash away my iniquity; cleanse me from my sin.

Then, standing at the altar, facing the people, he says:

℣. Oráte, fratres, ut meum ac vestrum sacrifícium acceptábile fiat apud Deum Patrem omnipoténtem.

℟. Suscípiat Dóminus sacrifícium de mánibus tuis ad laudem et glóriam nóminis sui, ad utilitátem quoque nostram totiúsque Ecclésiæ suæ sanctæ.

℣. Pray, brethren, that our sacrifice may be acceptable to God, the almighty Father.

℟. May the Lord accept the sacrifice at your hands for the praise and glory of his name, for our good, and the good of all his Church.

Prayer Over the Gifts *proper to each day. The priest ends with one of the following short conclusions:*

When addressing the Father:

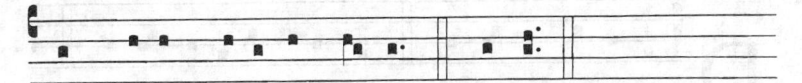

Per Christum Dómi-num nostrum. ℟. Amen.

We ask this (Grant this) through Christ our Lord. ℟. Amen.
Or:
We ask this (Grant this) in the name of Jesus the Lord.
℟. Amen.

When addressing the Father while invoking the Son:

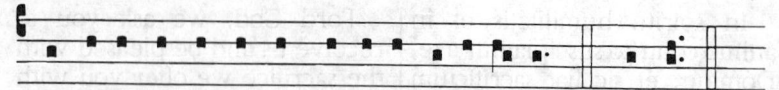

Qui vi-vit et regnat in sǽ-cu-la sæcu-ló- rum. ℟. Amen.
Who lives and reigns with you for ever and ever. ℟. Amen.

When addressing the Son:
Qui vivis et regnas in sǽcula sæculórum. ℟. Amen.
You live and reign for ever and ever. ℟. Amen.

Alternative tone:

Per Christum Dómi-num nostrum. ℟. Amen.

Qui vi-vit et regnat in sǽ-cu-la sæcu-ló-rum. ℟. Amen.

EUCHARISTIC PRAYER

Preface.
The text of the prefaces can be found either in the formularies of individual Masses, or grouped together according to liturgical season, starting on p. 49. Eucharistic Prayers II and IV each have a proper preface. The preface is introduced by the following dialogue between the celebrant and the assembly.

Tone for Sundays, Solemnities, Feasts and Memorials:

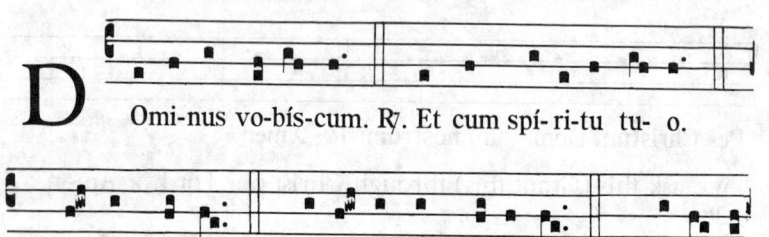

D Omi-nus vo-bís-cum. ℟. Et cum spí- ri-tu tu- o.

℣. Sur-sum corda. ℟. Habé-mus ad Dómi- num. ℣. Grá- ti- as

Order of Mass

agá-mus Dómi-no De- o nostro. ℟. Dignum et iustum est.

Tone for ferial days and for Masses of the dead:

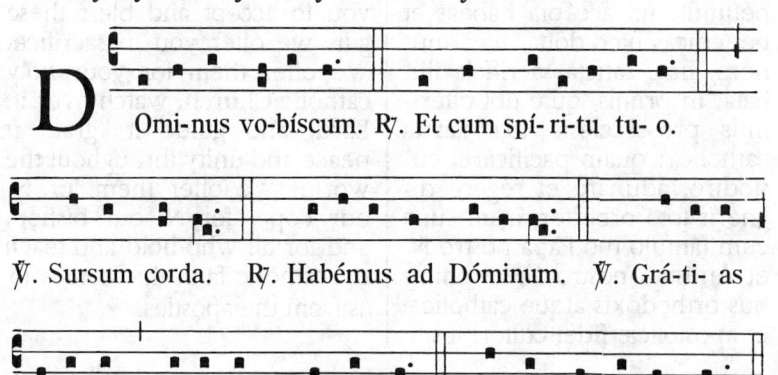

Dómi-nus vo-bíscum. ℟. Et cum spí- ri-tu tu- o.

℣. Sursum corda. ℟. Habémus ad Dóminum. ℣. Grá-ti- as

agámus Dómi-no De- o nostro. ℟. Dignum et iustum est.

℣. The Lord be with you.
℟. And also with you.
℣. Lift up your hearts.
℟. We lift them up to the Lord.
℣. Let us give thanks to the Lord our God.
℟. It is right to give him thanks and praise.

The **Sanctus** *is sung by all at the end of the preface. Its melodies are found among the chants of the Ordinary of Mass, starting on p. 73.*

Sanctus, Sanctus, Sanctus, Dóminus Deus Sábaoth. Pleni sunt cæli et terra glória tua. Hosánna in excélsis. Benedíctus qui venit in nómine Dómini. Hosánna in excélsis.

Holy, holy, holy Lord, God of power and might, heaven and earth are full of your glory. Hosanna in the highest. Blessed is he who comes in the name of the Lord. Hosanna in the highest.

EUCHARISTIC PRAYER I

Te igitur, clementíssime Pater, per Iesum Christum, Fílium tuum, Dóminum nostrum, súpplices rogámus ac pétimus, uti accépta hábeas et benedícas hæc dona, hæc múnera, hæc sancta sacrifícia illibáta, in primis, quæ tibi offérimus pro Ecclésia tua sancta cathólica: quam pacificáre, custodíre, adunáre et régere dignéris toto orbe terrárum: una cum fámulo tuo Papa nostro N. et Antístite nostro N. et ómnibus orthodóxis atque cathólicæ et apostólicæ fídei cultóribus.

Meménto, Dómine, famulórum famularúmque tuárum N. et N. et ómnium circumstántium, quórum tibi fides cógnita est et nota devótio, pro quibus tibi offérimus: vel qui tibi ófferunt hoc sacrifícium laudis, pro se suísque ómnibus: pro redemptióne animárum suárum, pro spe salútis et incolumitátis suæ: tibíque reddunt vota sua ætérno Deo, vivo et vero.

Communicántes, et memóriam venerántes, in primis gloriósæ semper Vírginis Maríæ, Genetrícis Dei et Dómini nostri Iesu Christi: † sed et beáti Ioseph, eiúsdem Vírginis Sponsi, et beatórum Apostolórum ac

We come to you, Father, with praise and thanksgiving, through Jesus Christ your Son. Through him we ask you to accept and bless these gifts we offer you in sacrifice. We offer them for your holy catholic Church, watch over it, Lord, and guide it; grant it peace and unity throughout the world. We offer them for N. our Pope, for N. our bishop, and for all who hold and teach the catholic faith that comes to us from the apostles.

Remember, Lord, your people, especially those for whom we now pray, N. and N. Remember all of us gathered here before you. You know how firmly we believe in you and dedicate ourselves to you. We offer you this sacrifice of praise for ourselves and those who are dear to us. We pray to you, our living and true God, for our well-being and redemption.

In union with the whole Church we honour Mary, the ever-virgin mother of Jesus Christ our Lord and God. † We honour Joseph, her husband, the apostles and martyrs Peter and Paul, Andrew, (James,

Eucharistic Prayer I

Mártyrum tuórum, Petri et Pauli, Andréæ, (Iacóbi, Ioánnis, Thomæ, Iacóbi, Philíppi, Bartholomǽi, Matthǽi, Simónis et Thaddǽi: Lini, Cleti, Cleméntis, Xysti, Cornélii, Cypriáni, Lauréntii, Chrysógoni, Ioánnis et Pauli, Cosmæ et Damiáni) et ómnium Sanctórum tuórum; quórum méritis precibúsque concédas, ut in ómnibus protectiónis tuæ muniámur auxílio. (Per Christum Dóminum nostrum. Amen.)

John, Thomas, James, Philip, Bartholomew, Matthew, Simon and Jude; we honour Linus, Cletus, Clement, Sixtus, Cornelius, Cyprian, Lawrence, Chrysogonus, John and Paul, Cosmas and Damian) and all the saints. May their merits and prayers gain us your constant help and protection. (Through Christ our Lord. Amen.)

The beginning of this prayer varies on major feast days. Continuation p. 25.

PROPER COMMUNICANTES

During the octave of Christmas
Communicántes, et (noctem sacratíssimam) diem sacratíssimum celebrántes, (qua) quo beátæ Maríæ intemeráta virgínitas huic mundo édidit Salvatórem: sed et memóriam venerántes, in primis eiúsdem gloriósæ semper Vírginis Maríæ, Genetrícis eiúsdem Dei et Dómini nostri Iesu Christi: †

In union with the whole Church we celebrate that day (night) when Mary without loss of her virginity gave the world its Saviour. We honour Mary, the ever-virgin mother of Jesus Christ our Lord and God. †

On the feast of the Epiphany
Communicántes, et diem sacratíssimum celebrántes, quo Unigénitus tuus, in tua tecum glória coætérnus, in veritáte carnis nostræ visibíliter corporális appáruit: sed et memóriam venerántes, in primis gloriósæ semper Vírginis Maríæ, Genetrícis eiúsdem Dei et Dómini nostri Iesu Christi: †

In union with the whole Church we celebrate that day when your only Son, sharing your eternal glory, showed himself in a human body. We honour Mary, the ever-virgin mother of Jesus Christ our Lord and God. †

From the Easter Vigil until the second Sunday of Easter

Communicántes, et (noctem sacratíssimam) diem sacratíssimum celebrántes Resurrectiónis Dómini nostri Iesu Christi secúndum carnem: sed et memóriam venerántes, in primis gloriósæ semper Vírginis Maríæ, Genetrícis eiúsdem Dei et Dómini nostri Iesu Christi: †	In union with the whole Church we celebrate that day (night) when Jesus Christ, our Lord, rose from the dead in his human body. We honour Mary, the ever-virgin mother of Jesus Christ our Lord and God. †

On the feast of the Ascension

Communicántes, et diem sacratíssimum celebrántes, quo Dóminus noster, unigénitus Fílius tuus, unítam sibi fragilitátis nostræ substántiam in glóriæ tuæ déxtera collocávit: sed et memóriam venerántes, in primis gloriósæ semper Vírginis Maríæ, Genetrícis eiúsdem Dei et Dómini nostri Iesu Christi: †	In union with the whole Church we celebrate that day when your only Son, our Lord, took his place with you and raised our frail human nature to glory. We honour Mary, the ever-virgin mother of Jesus Christ our Lord and God. †

On the feast of Pentecost

Communicántes, et diem sacratíssimum Pentecóstes celebrántes, quo Spíritus Sanctus Apóstolis in ígneis linguis appáruit: sed et memóriam venerántes, in primis gloriósæ semper Vírginis Maríæ, Genetrícis Dei et Dómini nostri Iesu Christi: †	In union with the whole Church we celebrate the day of Pentecost when the Holy Spirit appeared to the apostles in the form of countless tongues. We honour Mary, the ever-virgin mother of Jesus Christ our Lord and God. †

Eucharistic Prayer I

Hanc ígitur oblatiónem servitútis nostræ, sed et cunctæ famíliæ tuæ, quǽsumus, Dómine, ut placátus accípias: diésque nostros in tua pace dispónas, atque ab ætérna damnatióne nos éripi et in electórum tuórum iúbeas grege numerári. (Per Christum Dóminum nostrum. Amen).

Father, accept this offering from your whole family. Grant us your peace in this life, save us from final damnation, and count us among those you have chosen. (Through Christ our Lord. Amen.)

From the Easter Vigil until the second Sunday of Easter

Hanc ígitur oblatiónem servitútis nostræ, sed et cunctæ famíliæ tuæ, quam tibi offérimus pro his quoque, quos regeneráre dignátus es ex aqua et Spíritu Sancto, tríbuens eis remissiónem ómnium peccatórum, quǽsumus, Dómine, ut placátus accípias: diésque nostros in tua pace dispónas, atque ab ætérna damnatióne nos éripi et in electórum tuórum iúbeas grege numerári. (Per Christum Dóminum nostrum. Amen.)

Father, accept this offering from your whole family and from those born into the new life of water and the Holy Spirit, with all their sins forgiven. Grant us your peace in this life, save us from final damnation, and count us among those you have chosen. (Through Christ our Lord. Amen.)

Quam oblatiónem tu, Deus, in ómnibus, quǽsumus, benedíctam, adscríptam, ratam, rationábilem, acceptabilémque fácere dignéris: ut nobis Corpus et Sanguis fiat dilectíssimi Fílii tui, Dómini nostri Iesu Christi.

Qui, prídie quam paterétur, accépit panem in sanctas ac venerábiles manus suas, et elevátis óculis in cælum ad te

Bless and approve our offering; make it acceptable to you, an offering in spirit and in truth. Let it become for us the body and blood of Jesus Christ, your only Son, our Lord.

The day before he suffered he took bread in his sacred hands and looking up to heaven, to you, his almighty Father,

Deum Patrem suum omnipoténtem, tibi grátias agens benedíxit, fregit, dedítque discípulis suis, dicens:

«Accípite et manducáte ex hoc omnes: hoc est enim corpus meum, quod pro vobis tradétur.»

Símili modo, postquam cenátum est, accípiens et hunc præclárum cálicem in sanctas ac venerábiles manus suas, item tibi grátias agens benedíxit, dedítque discípulis suis, dicens:

« Accípite et bíbite ex eo omnes: hic est enim calix sánguinis mei, novi et ætérni testaménti, qui pro vobis et pro multis effundétur in remissiónem peccatórum.

Hoc fácite in meam commemoratiónem. »

he gave you thanks and praise. He broke the bread, gave it to his disciples, and said:

"Take this, all of you, and eat it: this is my body which will be given up for you."

When supper was ended, he took the cup. Again he gave you thanks and praise, gave the cup to his disciples, and said:

"Take this, all of you, and drink from it: this is the cup of my blood, the blood of the new and everlasting covenant. It will be shed for you and for all so that sins may be forgiven.

Do this in memory of me."

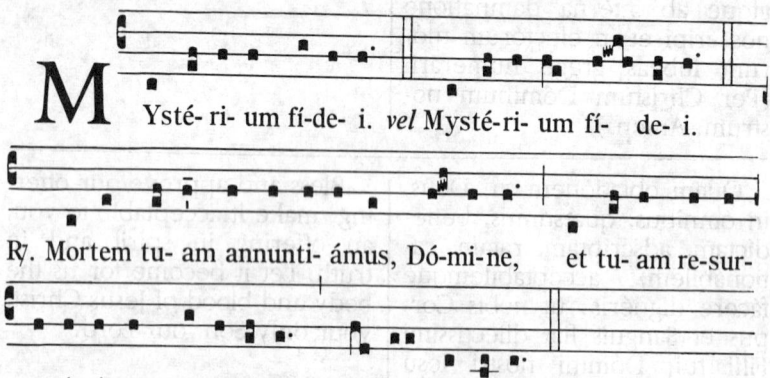

M Ysté-ri- um fí-de- i. *vel* Mysté-ri- um fí- de- i.

℟. Mortem tu- am annunti- ámus, Dó-mi-ne, et tu- am resurrecti- ó-nem confi-témur, do- nec vé-ni- as.

℣. Let us proclaim the mystery of faith:
℟. Christ has died, Christ is risen, Christ will come again.

This is the only form of the acclamation presently set to Gregorian chant.

Eucharistic Prayer I

Unde et mémores, Dómine, nos servi tui, sed et plebs tua sancta, eiúsdem Christi, Fílii tui, Dómini nostri, tam beátæ passiónis, necnon et ab ínferis resurrectiónis, sed et in cælos gloriósæ ascensiónis: offérimus præcláræ maiestáti tuæ de tuis donis ac datis hóstiam puram, hóstiam sanctam, hóstiam immaculátam, panem sanctum vitæ ætérnæ et cálicem salútis perpétuæ.

Supra quæ propítio ac seréno vultu respícere dignéris: et accépta habére, sícuti accépta habére dignátus es múnera púeri tui iusti Abel, et sacrifícium Patriárchæ nostri Abrahæ, et quod tibi óbtulit summus sacérdos tuus Melchísedech, sanctum sacrifícium, immaculátam hostiam.

Súpplices te rogámus, omnípotens Deus: iube hæc perférri per manus sancti Angeli tui in sublíme altáre tuum, in conspéctu divínæ maiestátis tuæ; ut, quotquot ex hac altáris participatióne sacrosánctum Fílii tui Corpus et Sánguinem sumpsérimus, omni benedictióne cælésti et grátia repleámur. (Per Christum Dóminum nostrum. Amen.)

Meménto étiam, Dómine, famulórum famularúmque tuárum N. et N., qui nos præ-

Father, we celebrate the memory of Christ, your Son. We, your people and your ministers, recall his passion, his resurrection from the dead, and his ascension into glory; and from the many gifts you have given us we offer to you, God of glory and majesty, this holy and perfect sacrifice: the bread of life and the cup of eternal salvation.

Look with favour on these offerings and accept them as once you accepted the gifts of your servant Abel, the sacrifice of Abraham, our father in faith, and the bread and wine offered by your priest Melchisedech.

Almighty God, we pray that your angel may take this sacrifice to your altar in heaven. Then, as we receive from this altar the sacred body and blood of your Son, let us be filled with every grace and blessing. (Through Christ our Lord. Amen.)

Remember, Lord, those who have died and have gone before us marked with the sign of

cessérunt cum signo fídei, et dórmiunt in somno pacis. Ipsis, Dómine, et ómnibus in Christo quiescéntibus, locum refrigérii, lucis et pacis, ut indúlgeas, deprecámur. (Per Christum Dóminum nostrum. Amen.)

Nobis quoque peccatóribus fámulis tuis, de multitúdine miseratiónum tuárum sperántibus, partem áliquam et societátem donáre dignéris cum tuis sanctis Apóstolis et Martýribus: cum Ioánne, Stéphano, Matthía, Bárnaba, (Ignátio, Alexándro, Marcellíno, Petro, Felicitáte, Perpétua, Agatha, Lúcia, Agnéte, Cæcília, Anastásia) et ómnibus Sanctis tuis: intra quorum nos consórtium, non æstimátor mériti, sed véniæ, quǽsumus, largítor admítte. Per Christum Dóminum nostrum.

Per quem hæc ómnia, Dómine, semper bona creas, sanctíficas, vivíficas, benedícis, et præstas nobis.

Per ipsum, et cum ipso, et in ipso, est tibi Deo Patri omnipoténti, in unitáte Spíritus Sancti, omnis honor et glória per ómnia sæcula sæculórum.

faith, especially those for whom we now pray, N. and N. May these, and all who sleep in Christ, find in your presence light, happiness, and peace. (Through Christ our Lord. Amen.)

For ourselves, too, we ask some share in the fellowship of your apostles and martyrs, with John the Baptist, Stephen, Matthias, Barnabas, (Ignatius, Alexander, Marcellinus, Peter, Felicity, Perpetua, Agatha, Lucy, Agnes, Cecilia, Anastasia) and all the saints. Though we are sinners, we trust in your mercy and love. Do not consider what we truly deserve, but grant us your forgiveness.

Through Christ our Lord you give us all these gifts. You fill them with life and goodness, you bless them and make them holy.

Through him, with him, in him, in the unity of the Holy Spirit, all glory and honour is yours, almighty Father, for ever and ever.

...per ómni- a sæ-cu-la sæ-cu-ló- rum. ℟. Amen.

All respond: Amen. *Continuation p. 41.*

EUCHARISTIC PRAYER II

There is a special preface for this eucharistic prayer but any other preface may be used.

VERE dignum et iustum est, æquum et salutáre, nos tibi, sancte Pater, semper et ubíque grátias ágere per Fílium dilectiónis tuæ Iesum Christum, Verbum tuum per quod cuncta fecísti.

Quem misísti nobis Salvatórem et Redemptórem, incarnátum de Spíritu Sancto et ex Vírgine natum.

Qui voluntátem tuam adímplens et pópulum tibi sanctum acquírens exténdit manus cum paterétur, ut mortem sólveret et resurrectiónem manifestáret.

Et ídeo cum Angelis et ómnibus Sanctis glóriam tuam prædicámus, una voce dicéntes: Sanctus...

VERE Sanctus es, Dómine, fons omnis sanctitátis. Hæc ergo dona, quæsumus, Spíritus tui rore sanctífica, ut nobis Corpus et Sanguis fiant Dómini nostri Iesu Christi.

Qui cum Passióni voluntárie traderétur, accépit panem et

FATHER, it is our duty and our salvation, always and everywhere to give you thanks through your beloved Son, Jesus Christ.

He is the Word through whom you make the universe, the Saviour you sent to redeem us. By the power of the Holy Spirit he took flesh and was born of the Virgin Mary.

For our sake he opened his arms on the cross; he put an end to death and revealed the resurrection. In this he fulfilled your will and won for you a holy people.

And so we join the angels and the saints in proclaiming your glory as we sing: Holy...

LORD, you are holy indeed, the fountain of all holiness. Let your Spirit come upon these gifts to make them holy, so that they may become for us the body and blood of our Lord, Jesus Christ.

Before he was given up to death, a death he freely accept-

grátias agens fregit, dedítque discípulis suis, dicens:

«ACCÍPITE ET MANDUCÁTE EX HOC OMNES: HOC EST ENIM CORPUS MEUM, QUOD PRO VOBIS TRADÉTUR.»

Símili modo, postquam cenátum est, accípiens et cálicem, íterum grátias agens dedit discípulis suis, dicens:

«ACCÍPITE ET BÍBITE EX EO OMNES: HIC EST ENIM CALIX SÁNGUINIS MEI, NOVI ET ÆTÉRNI TESTAMÉNTI, QUI PRO VOBIS ET PRO MULTIS EFFUNDÉTUR IN REMISSIÓNEM PECCATÓRUM.

HOC FÁCITE IN MEAM COMMEMORATIÓNEM.»

℣. Mystérium fídei:
℟. Mortem tuam annuntiámus, Dómine, et tuam resurrectiónem confitémur, donec vénias.

Melody, p. 26.

Mémores ígitur mortis et resurrectiónis eius, tibi, Dómine, panem vitæ et cálicem salútis offérimus, grátias agéntes qui nos dignos habuísti astáre coram te et tibi ministráre.

Et súpplices deprecámur ut Córporis et Sánguinis Christi partícipes a Spíritu Sancto congregémur in unum.

ed, he took bread and gave you thanks. He broke the bread, gave it to his disciples, and said:
"TAKE THIS, ALL OF YOU, AND EAT IT: THIS IS MY BODY WHICH WILL BE GIVEN UP FOR YOU."

When supper was ended, he took the cup. Again he gave you thanks and praise, gave the cup to his disciples, and said:
"TAKE THIS, ALL OF YOU, AND DRINK FROM IT: THIS IS THE CUP OF MY BLOOD, THE BLOOD OF THE NEW AND EVERLASTING COVENANT. IT WILL BE SHED FOR YOU AND FOR ALL SO THAT SINS MAY BE FORGIVEN.
DO THIS IN MEMORY OF ME."

℣. Let us proclaim the mystery of faith:
℟. Christ has died, Christ is risen, Christ will come again.

In memory of his death and resurrection, we offer you, Father, this life-giving bread, this saving cup. We thank you for counting us worthy to stand in your presence and serve you.

May all of us who share in the body and blood of Christ be brought together in unity by the Holy Spirit.

Eucharistic Prayer II

Recordáre, Dómine, Ecclésiæ tuæ toto orbe diffúsæ, ut eam in caritáte perfícias una cum Papa nostro N. et Epíscopo nostro N. et univérso clero.

Lord, remember your Church throughout the world; make us grow in love, together with N. our Pope, N. our bishop, and all the clergy.

In masses for the dead, there may be added:

Meménto fámuli tui (fámulæ tuæ) N. quem (quam) (hódie) ad te ex hoc mundo vocásti. Concéde, ut, qui (quæ) complantátus (complantáta) fuit similitúdini mortis Fílii tui, simul fiat et resurrectiónis ipsíus.

Remember N., whom you have called from this life. In baptism he (she) died with Christ: may he (she) also share his resurrection.

Meménto étiam fratrum nostrórum, qui in spe resurrectiónis dormiérunt, omniúmque in tua miseratióne defunctórum, et eos in lumen vultus tui admítte. Omnium nostrum, quǽsumus, miserére, ut cum beáta Dei Genetríce Vírgine María, beátis Apóstolis et ómnibus Sanctis, qui tibi a sǽculo placuérunt, ætérnæ vitæ mereámur esse consórtes, et te laudémus et glorificémus, per Fílium tuum Iesum Christum.

Remember our brothers and sisters who have gone to their rest in the hope of rising again; bring them and all the departed into the light of your presence. Have mercy on us all; make us worthy to share eternal life with Mary, the virgin Mother of God, with the apostles, and with all the saints who have done your will throughout the ages. May we praise you in union with them, and give you glory through your Son, Jesus Christ.

Per ipsum, et cum ipso, et in ipso, est tibi Deo Patri omnipoténti, in unitáte Spíritus Sancti, omnis honor et glória per ómnia sǽcula sæculórum.

Through him, with him, in him, in the unity of the Holy Spirit, all glory and honour is yours, almighty Father, for ever and ever.

All respond: Amen.
Melody, p. 28. Continuation p. 41.

EUCHARISTIC PRAYER III

Vere Sanctus es, Dómine, et mérito te laudat omnis a te cóndita creatúra, quia per Fílium tuum, Dóminum nostrum Iesum Christum, Spíritus Sancti operánte virtúte, vivíficas et sanctíficas univérsa, et pópulum tibi congregáre non désinis, ut a solis ortu usque ad occásum oblátio munda offerátur nómini tuo.

Súpplices ergo te, Dómine, deprecámur, ut hæc múnera, quæ tibi sacránda detúlimus, eódem Spíritu sanctificáre dignéris, ut Corpus et Sanguis fiant Fílii tui Dómini nostri Iesu Christi, cuius mandáto hæc mystéria celebrámus.

Ipse enim in qua nocte tradebátur accépit panem et tibi grátias agens benedíxit, fregit, dedítque discípulis suis, dicens:

«Accípite et manducáte ex hoc omnes: hoc est enim Corpus meum, quod pro vobis tradétur.»

Símili modo, postquam cenátum est, accípiens cálicem, et tibi grátias agens benedíxit, dedítque discípulis suis, dicens:

Father, you are holy indeed, and all creation rightly gives you praise. All life, all holiness comes from you through your Son, Jesus Christ our Lord, by the working of the Holy Spirit. From age to age you gather a people to yourself, so that from east to west a perfect offering may be made to the glory of your name.

An so, Father, we bring you these gifts. We ask you to make them holy by the power of your Spirit, that they may become the body and blood of your Son, our Lord Jesus Christ, at whose command we celebrate this eucharist.

On the night he was betrayed, he took bread and gave you thanks and praise. He broke the bread, gave it to his disciples, and said:

"Take this, all of you, and eat it: this is my body which will be given up for you."

When supper was ended, he took the cup. Again he gave you thanks and praise, gave the cup to his disciples, and said:

Eucharistic Prayer III

«Accípite et bíbite ex eo omnes: hic est enim calix sánguinis mei, novi et ætérni testaménti, qui pro vobis et pro multis effundétur in remissiónem peccatórum.

Hoc fácite in meam commemoratiónem.»

℣. Mystérium fídei:
℟. Mortem tuam annuntiámus, Dómine, et tuam resurrectiónem confitémur, donec vénias.

Melody, p. 26

Mémores ígitur, Dómine, eiúsdem Fílii tui salutíferæ passiónis necnon mirábilis resurrectiónis et ascensiónis in cælum, sed et præstolántes álterum eius advéntum, offérimus tibi, grátias reveréntes, hoc sacrifícium vivum et sanctum.

Réspice, quæsumus, in oblatiónem Ecclésiæ tuæ et, agnóscens Hóstiam, cuius voluísti immolatióne placári, concéde, ut qui Córpore et Sánguine Fílii tui refícimur, Spíritu eius Sancto repléti, unum corpus et unus spíritus inveniámur in Christo.

Ipse nos tibi perfíciat munus ætérnum, ut cum eléctis tuis

"Take this, all of you, and drink from it: this is the cup of my blood, the blood of the new and everlasting covenant. It will be shed for you and for all so that sins may be forgiven. Do this in memory of me."

℣. Let us proclaim the mystery of faith.
℟. Christ has died, Christ is risen, Christ will come again.

Father, calling to mind the death your Son endured for our salvation, his glorious resurrection and ascension into heaven, and ready to greet him when he comes again, we offer you in thanksgiving this holy and living sacrifice.

Look with favour on your Church's offering, and see the Victim whose death has reconciled us to yourself. Grant that we, who are nourished by his body and blood, may be filled with his Holy Spirit, and become one body, one spirit in Christ.

May he make us an everlasting gift to you and enable us to

hereditátem cónsequi valeámus, in primis cum beatíssima Vírgine, Dei Genetríce, María, cum beátis Apóstolis tuis et gloriósis Martýribus (cum Sancto N.) et ómnibus Sanctis, quorum intercessióne perpétuo apud te confídimus adiuvári.

share in the inheritance of your saints, with Mary, the virgin Mother of God; with the apostles, the martyrs, (Saint N.) and all your saints, on whose constant intercession we rely for help.

Hæc Hóstia nostræ reconciliatiónis profíciat, quæsumus, Dómine, ad totíus mundi pacem atque salútem. Ecclésiam tuam, peregrinántem in terra, in fide et caritáte firmáre dignéris cum famulo tuo Papa nostro N. et Epíscopo nostro N., cum episcopáli órdine et univérso clero et omni pópulo acquisitiónis tuæ.

Lord, may this sacrifice, which has made our peace with you, advance the peace and salvation of all the world. Strengthen in faith and love your pilgrim Church on earth; your servant, Pope N., our bishop N., and all the bishops, with the clergy and the entire people your Son has gained for you.

Votis huius famíliæ, quam tibi astáre voluísti, adésto propítius. Omnes fílios tuos ubíque dispérsos tibi, clemens Pater, miserátus coniúnge.

Father, hear the prayers of the family you have gathered here before you. In mercy and love unite all your children wherever they may be.

† Fratres nostros defúnctos et omnes qui, tibi placéntes, ex hoc sǽculo transiérunt, in regnum tuum benígnus admítte, ubi fore sperámus, ut simul glória tua perénniter satiémur, per Christum Dóminum nostrum, per quem mundo bona cuncta largíris.

† Welcome into your kingdom our departed brothers and sisters, and all who have left this world in your friendship. We hope to enjoy for ever the vision of your glory, through Christ our Lord, from whom all good things come.

Eucharistic Prayer III

At masses for the dead the following prayer may replace the preceding paragraph.

† Meménto fámuli tui (fámulæ tuæ) N., quem (quam) (hódie) ad te ex hoc mundo vocásti. Concéde, ut, qui (quæ) complantátus (complantáta) fuit similitúdini mortis Fílii tui, simul fiat et resurrectiónis ipsíus, quando mórtuos suscitábit in carne de terra et corpus humilitátis nostræ configurábit córpori claritátis suæ. Sed et fratres nostros defúnctos, et omnes qui, tibi placéntes, ex hoc sǽculo transiérunt, in regnum tuum benígnus admítte, ubi fore sperámus, ut simul glória tua perénniter satiémur, quando omnem lácrimam abstérges ab óculis nostris, quia te, sícuti es, Deum nostrum vidéntes, tibi símiles érimus cuncta per sǽcula, et te sine fine laudábimus, per Christum Dóminum nostrum, per quem mundo bona cuncta largíris.

† Remember N. In baptism he (she) died with Christ: may he (she) also share his resurrection, when Christ will raise our mortal bodies and make them like his own in glory. Welcome into your kingdom our departed brothers and sisters, and all who have left this world in your friendship. There we hope to share in your glory when every tear will be wiped away. On that day we shall see you, our God, as you are. We shall become like you and praise you for ever through Christ our Lord, from whom all good things come.

Per ipsum, et cum ipso, et in ipso, est tibi Deo Patri omnipoténti, in unitáte Spíritus Sancti, omnis honor et glória per ómnia sǽcula sæculórum.

Through him, with him, in him, in the unity of the Holy Spirit, all glory and honour is yours, almighty Father, for ever and ever.

All respond: Amen.

Melody, p. 28. Continuation p. 41.

EUCHARISTIC PRAYER IV

This eucharistic prayer always takes its own proper preface.

VERE dignum est tibi grátias ágere, vere iustum est te glorificáre, Pater sancte, quia unus es Deus vivus et verus, qui es ante sǽcula et pérmanes in ætérnum, inaccessíbilem lucem inhábitans; sed et qui unus bonus atque fons vitæ cuncta fecísti, ut creatúras tuas benedictiónibus adimpléres multásque lætificáres tui lúminis claritáte.

Et ídeo coram te innúmeræ astant turbæ angelórum, qui die ac nocte sérviunt tibi et, vultus tui glóriam contemplántes, te incessánter gloríficant.

Cum quibus et nos et, per nostram vocem, omnis quæ sub cælo est creatúra nomen tuum in exsultatióne confitémur, canéntes:

FATHER in heaven, it is right that we should give you thanks and glory: you alone are God, living and true. Through all eternity you live in unapproachable light. Source of life and goodness, you have created all things, to fill your creatures with every blessing and lead all men to the joyful vision of your light.

Countless hosts of angels stand before you to do your will; they look upon your splendour and praise you, night and day. United with them, and in the name of every creature under heaven, we too praise your glory as we sing: Holy...

CONFITÉMUR TIBI, Pater sancte, quia magnus es et ómnia ópera tua in sapiéntia et caritáte fecísti. Hóminem ad tuam imáginem condidísti, eíque commisísti mundi curam univérsi, ut, tibi soli Creatóri sérviens, creatúris ómnibus imperáret. Et cum amicítiam tuam, non obœ́diens, amisísset, non eum dereliquísti in mortis império. Omnibus enim miseri-

FATHER, we acknowledge your greatness: all your actions show your wisdom and love. You formed man in your own likeness and set him over the whole world to serve you, his creator, and to rule over all creatures. Even when he disobeyed you and lost your friendship you did not abandon him to the power of death, but helped all men to seek and find

Eucharistic Prayer IV

córditer subvenísti, ut te quæréntes invenírent. Sed et fœdera plúries homínibus obtulísti eósque per prophétas erudísti in exspectatióne salútis.

Et sic, Pater sancte, mundum dilexísti, ut, compléta plenitúdine témporum, Unigénitum tuum nobis mítteres Salvatórem. Qui, incarnátus de Spíritu Sancto et natus ex María Vírgine, in nostra condiciónis forma est conversátus per ómnia absque peccáto; salútem evangelizávit paupéribus, redemptiónem captívis, mæstis corde lætítiam. Ut tuam vero dispensatiónem impléret, in mortem trádidit semetípsum ac, resúrgens a mórtuis, mortem destrúxit vitámque renovávit.

Et, ut non ámplius nobismetípsis viverémus, sed sibi qui pro nobis mórtuus est atque surréxit, a te, Pater, misit Spíritum Sanctum primítias credéntibus, qui, opus suum in mundo perfíciens, omnem sanctificatiónem compléret.

Quǽsumus ígitur, Dómine, ut idem Spíritus Sanctus hæc múnera sanctificáre dignétur, ut Corpus et Sanguis fiant Dómini nostri Iesu Christi ad hoc magnum mystérium celebrándum, quod ipse nobis relíquit in fœdus ætérnum.

you. Again and again you offered a covenant to man, and through the prophets taught him to hope for salvation.

Father, you so loved the world that in the fullness of time you sent your only Son to be our Saviour. He was conceived through the power of the Holy Spirit, and born of the Virgin Mary, a man like us in all things but sin. To the poor he proclaimed the good news of salvation, to prisoners, freedom, and to those in sorrow, joy. In fulfilment of your will he gave himself up to death; but by rising from the dead, he destroyed death and restored life.

And that we might live no longer for ourselves but for him, he sent the Holy Spirit from you, Father, as his first gift to those who believe, to complete his work on earth and bring us the fullness of grace.

Father, may this Holy Spirit sanctify these offerings. Let them become the body and blood of Jesus Christ our Lord as we celebrate the great mystery which he left us as an everlasting covenant.

Ipse enim, cum hora venísset ut glorificarétur a te, Pater Sancte, ac dilexísset suos qui erant in mundo, in finem diléxit eos: et cenántibus illis accépit panem, benedíxit ac fregit, dedítque discípulis suis, dicens:

«ACCÍPITE ET MANDUCÁTE EX HOC OMNES: HOC EST ENIM CORPUS MEUM, QUOD PRO VOBIS TRADÉTUR.»

Símili modo accípiens cálicem, ex genímine vitis replétum, grátias egit, dedítque discípulis suis, dicens:

«ACCÍPITE ET BÍBITE EX EO OMNES: HIC EST ENIM CALIX SÁNGUINIS MEI, NOVI ET ÆTÉRNI TESTAMÉNTI, QUI PRO VOBIS ET PRO MULTIS EFFUNDÉTUR IN REMISSIÓNEM PECCATÓRUM.

HOC FÁCITE IN MEAM COMMEMORATIÓNEM.»

℣. Mystérium fídei:
℟. Mortem tuam annuntiámus, Dómine, et tuam resurrectiónem confitémur, donec vénias.
Melody, p. 26.

Unde et nos, Dómine, redemptiónis nostræ memoriále nunc celebrántes, mortem Christi eiúsque descénsum ad ínferos recólimus, eius resurrectiónem et ascensiónem ad

He always loved those who were his own in the world. When the time came for him to be glorified by you, his heavenly Father, he showed the depth of his love. While they were at supper, he took bread, said the blessing, broke the bread, and gave it to his disciples, saying:
"TAKE THIS, ALL OF YOU, AND EAT IT: THIS IS MY BODY WHICH WILL BE GIVEN UP FOR YOU."

In the same way, he took the cup, filled with wine. He gave you thanks, and giving the cup to his disciples, said:
"TAKE THIS, ALL OF YOU, AND DRINK FROM IT: THIS IS THE CUP OF MY BLOOD, THE BLOOD OF THE NEW AND EVERLASTING COVENANT. IT WILL BE SHED FOR YOU AND FOR ALL SO THAT SINS MAY BE FORGIVEN.
DO THIS IN MEMORY OF ME."

℣. Let us proclaim the mystery of faith.
℟. Christ has died, Christ is risen, Christ will come again.

Father, we now celebrate this memorial of our redemption. We recall Christ's death, his descent among the dead, his resurrection, and his ascension to your right hand; and, look-

Eucharistic Prayer IV

tuam déxteram profitémur, et, exspectántes ipsíus advéntum in glória, offérimus tibi eius Corpus et Sánguinem, sacrifícium tibi acceptábile et toti mundo salutáre.

ing forward to his coming in glory, we offer you his body and blood, the acceptable sacrifice which brings salvation to the whole world.

Réspice, Dómine, in Hóstiam, quam Ecclésiæ tuæ ipse parásti, et concéde benígnus ómnibus qui ex hoc uno pane participábunt et cálice, ut, in unum corpus a Sancto Spíritu congregáti, in Christo hóstia viva perficiántur, ad laudem glóriæ tuæ.

Lord, look upon this sacrifice which you have given to your Church; and by your Holy Spirit gather all who share this bread and wine into the one body of Christ, a living sacrifice of praise.

Nunc ergo, Dómine, ómnium recordáre, pro quibus tibi hanc oblatiónem offérimus: in primis fámuli tui, Papæ nostri N., Epíscopi nostri N. et Episcopórum órdinis univérsi, sed et totíus cleri, et offeréntium, et circumstántium, et cuncti pópuli tui, et ómnium, qui te quærunt corde sincéro.

Lord, remember those for whom we offer this sacrifice, especially N. our Pope, N. our bishop, and bishops and clergy everywhere. Remember those who take part in this offering, those here present and all your people, and all who seek you with a sincere heart.

Meménto etiam illórum, qui obiérunt in pace Christi tui, et ómnium defunctórum, quorum fidem tu solus cognovísti.

Remember those who have died in the peace of Christ and all the dead whose faith is known to you alone.

Nobis ómnibus, fíliis tuis, clemens Pater, concéde, ut cæléstem hereditátem cónsequi valeámus cum beáta Vírgine,

Father, in your mercy grant also to us, your children, to enter into our heavenly inheritance in the company of the

Dei Genetríce, María, cum Apóstolis et Sanctis tuis in regno tuo, ubi cum univérsa creatúra, a corruptióne peccáti et mortis liberáta, te glorificémus per Christum Dóminum nostrum, per quem mundo bona cuncta largíris.

Virgin Mary, the Mother of God, and your apostles and saints. Then, in your kingdom, freed from the corruption of sin and death, we shall sing your glory with every creature through Christ our Lord, through whom you give us everything that is good.

Per ipsum, et cum ipso, et in ipso, est tibi Deo Patri omnipoténti, in unitáte Spíritus Sancti, omnis honor et glória per ómnia sǽcula sæculórum.

Through him, with him, in him, in the unity of the Holy Spirit, all glory and honour is yours, almighty Father, for ever and ever.

All respond: Amen.

Melody, p. 28.

COMMUNION RITE

Præcéptis salutáribus móniti, et divína institutióne formáti, audémus dícere:

Let us pray with confidence to the Father in the words our Saviour gave us:

All sing: (this tone may be used on Sundays.)

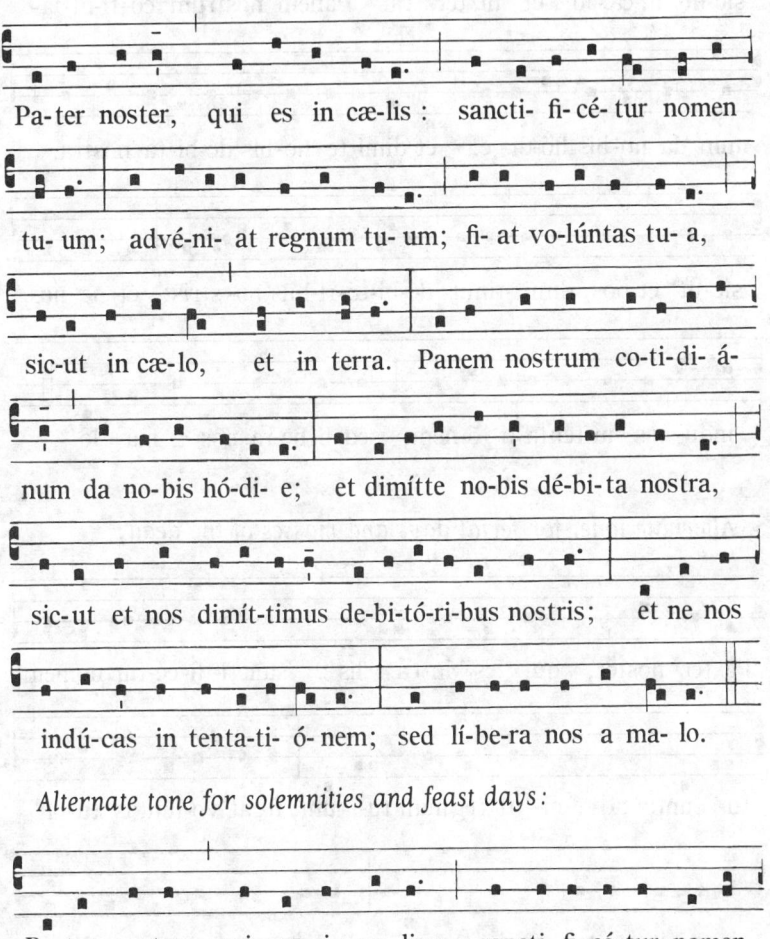

Pa-ter noster, qui es in cæ-lis : sancti- fi- cé- tur nomen tu- um; advé-ni- at regnum tu- um; fi- at vo-lúntas tu- a, sic-ut in cæ-lo, et in terra. Panem nostrum co-ti-di- á- num da no-bis hó-di- e; et dimítte no-bis dé-bi- ta nostra, sic-ut et nos dimít-timus de-bi-tó-ri-bus nostris; et ne nos indú-cas in tenta-ti- ó- nem; sed lí-be-ra nos a ma- lo.

Alternate tone for solemnities and feast days:

Pa-ter noster, qui es in cæ- lis : sancti- fi- cé-tur nomen

tu- um; advé-ni- at regnum tu- um; fi- at vo-lúntas tu- a,

sic-ut in cæ-lo, et in ter- ra. Panem nostrum co-ti-di- á-

num da no-bis hó-di- e; et dimítte no-bis dé-bi-ta nostra,

sic-ut et nos dimít-timus de-bi-tó-ri-bus no- stris; et ne nos

indú- cas in tenta-ti- ó-nem; sed lí-be-ra nos a ma- lo.

Alternate tone, for ferial days and masses of the dead:

Pa- ter noster, qui es in cæ- lis : sancti- fi-cé-tur nomen

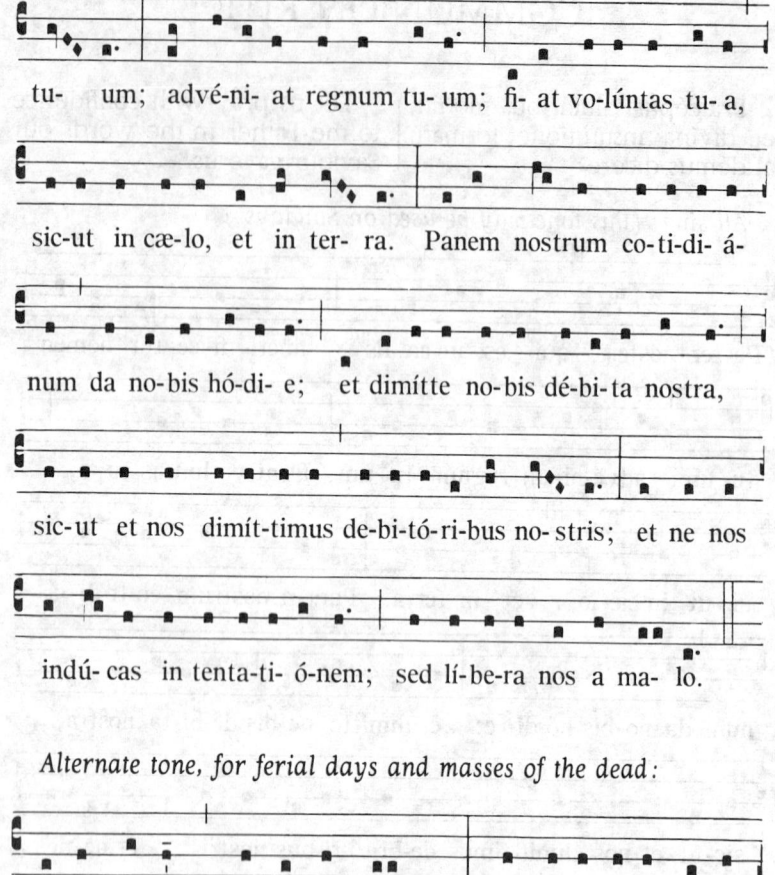

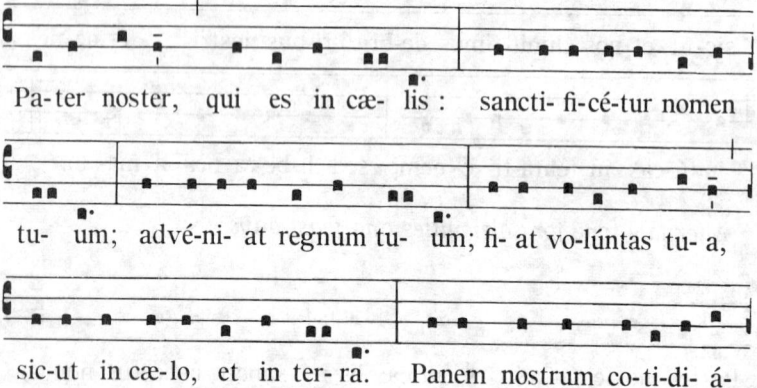

tu- um; advé-ni- at regnum tu- um; fi- at vo-lúntas tu- a,

sic-ut in cæ-lo, et in ter- ra. Panem nostrum co-ti-di- á-

Communion

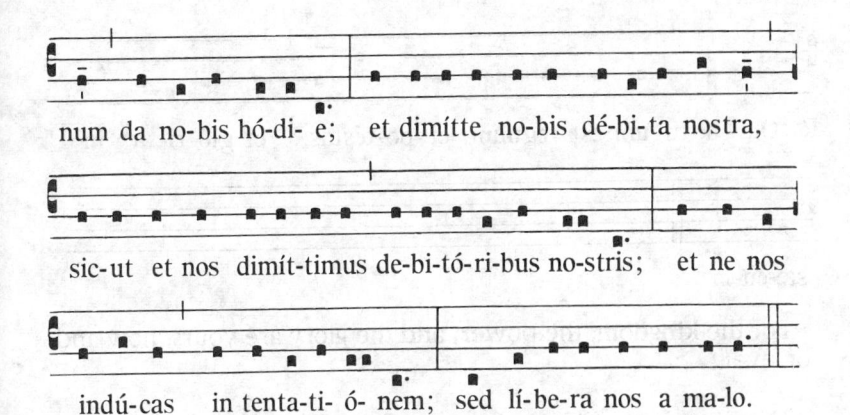

num da nobis hódie; et dimítte nobis débita nostra, sicut et nos dimíttimus debitóribus nostris; et ne nos indúcas in tentatiónem; sed líbera nos a malo.

Our Father, who art in heaven,
hallowed be thy name.
Thy kingdom come.
Thy will be done on earth, as it is in heaven.
Give us this day our daily bread,
and forgive us our trespasses,
as we forgive those who trespass against us,
and lead us not into temptation,
but deliver us from evil.

The priest continues:

Líbera nos, quǽsumus, Dómine, ab ómnibus malis, da propítius pacem in diébus nostris, ut, ope misericórdiæ tuæ adiúti, et a peccáto simus semper líberi et ab omni perturbatióne secúri: exspectántes beátam spem et advéntum Salvatóris nostri Iesu Christi.

Deliver us, Lord, from every evil, and grant us peace in our day. In your mercy keep us free from sin and protect us from all anxiety as we wait in joyful hope for the coming of our Saviour, Jesus Christ.

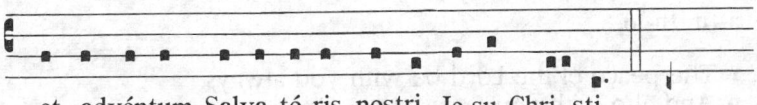

et advéntum Salvatóris nostri Iesu Christi.

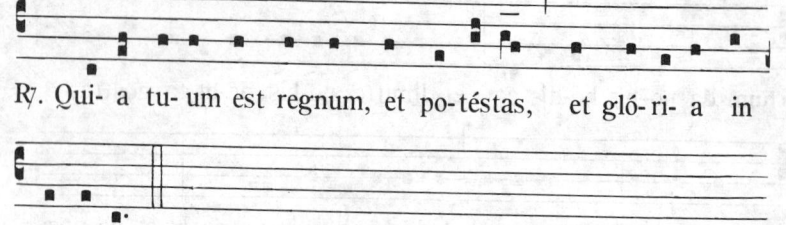

℟. Qui- a tu- um est regnum, et po- téstas, et gló- ri- a in sǽ-cu- la.

For the kingdom, the power, and the glory are yours, now and for ever!

| Dómine Iesu Christe, qui dixísti Apóstolis tuis: «Pacem relínquo vobis, pacem meam do vobis», ne respícias peccáta nostra, sed fidem Ecclésiæ tuæ; eámque secúndum voluntátem tuam pacificáre et coadunáre dignéris. Qui vivis et regnas in sǽcula sæculórum. | Lord Jesus Christ, you said to your apostles: "I leave you peace, my peace I give you." Look not on our sins, but on the faith of your Church, and grant us the peace and unity of your kingdom where you live for ever and ever. |

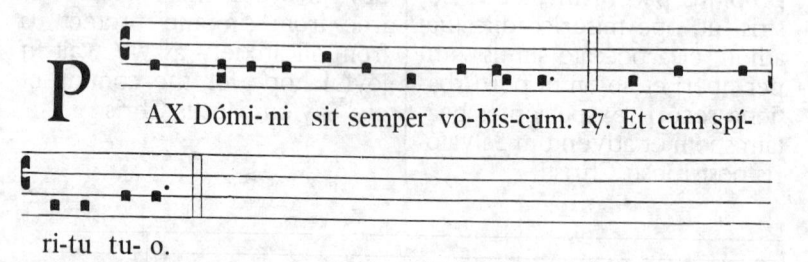

in sǽcu- la sæcu-ló- rum. ℟. Amen.

PAX Dómi- ni sit semper vo-bís-cum. ℟. Et cum spí-ri-tu tu- o.

℣. The peace of the Lord be with you always.
℟. And also with you.

Communion

The deacon, or priest, may now say:

Offérte vobis pacem.	Let us offer each other the sign of peace.

The sign of peace is then given.

The priest breaks the host and drops a particle into the chalice saying:

Hæc commíxtio Córporis et Sánguinis Dómini nostri Iesu Christi fiat accipiéntibus nobis in vitam ætérnam.	May this mingling of the body and blood of our Lord Jesus Christ bring eternal life to us who receive it.

Meanwhile the following is sung:

Agnus Dei, qui tollis peccáta mundi: miserére nobis.	Lamb of God, you take away the sins of the world: have mercy on us.
Agnus Dei, qui tollis peccáta mundi: miserére nobis.	Lamb of God, you take away the sins of the world: have mercy on us.
Agnus Dei, qui tollis peccáta mundi: dona nobis pacem.	Lamb of God, you take away the sins of the world: grant us peace.

The melodies for the Agnus Dei *are found among the chants of the Mass Ordinary, starting on p. 73.*

The priest continues:

Dómine Iesu Christe, Fili Dei vivi, qui ex voluntáte Patris, cooperánte Spíritu Sancto, per mortem tuam mundum vivificásti: líbera me per hoc sacrosánctum Corpus et Sánguinem tuum ab ómnibus iniquitátibus meis et univérsis malis: et fac me tuis semper inhærére mandátis, et a te numquam separári permíttas.	Lord Jesus Christ, Son of the living God, by the will of the Father and the work of the Holy Spirit your death brought life to the world. By your holy body and blood free me from all my sins and from every evil. Keep me faithful to your teaching, and never let me be parted from you.

Or:

Percéptio Córporis et Sánguinis tui, Dómine Iesu Christe, non mihi provéniat in iudícium et condemnatiónem: sed pro tua pietáte prosit mihi ad tutaméntum mentis et córporis, et ad medélam percipiéndam.

Lord Jesus Christ, with faith in your love and mercy I eat your body and drink your blood. Let it not bring me condemnation, but health in mind and body.

The priest genuflects, and raising the host says:

Ecce Agnus Dei, ecce qui tollit peccáta mundi. Beáti qui ad cenam Agni vocáti sunt.

This is the Lamb of God who takes away the sins of the world. Happy are those who are called to his supper.

All say with him:

Dómine, non sum dignus, ut intres sub tectum meum, sed tantum dic verbo et sanábitur ánima mea.

Lord, I am not worthy to receive you, but only say the word and I shall be healed.

The priest receives the host, saying:

Corpus Christi custódiat me in vitam ætérnam.

May the body of Christ bring me to everlasting life.

He then receives the chalice, saying:

Sanguis Christi custódiat me in vitam ætérnam.

May the blood of Christ bring me to everlasting life.

Communion Antiphon *proper to each day. The choir sings it during the distribution of Holy Communion. The cantors can add on verses; after each of these, the choir repeats the Communion antiphon.*

The communion of the people follows, the priest holding up a host to each one and saying:

Corpus Christi. ℟. Amen. | The body of Christ. ℟. Amen.

When communion is given from the chalice, the priest says:

Sanguis Christi. ℟. Amen. | The blood of Christ. ℟. Amen.

After the communion, the priest purifies the sacred vessels, saying:

Quod ore súmpsimus, Dómine, pura mente capiámus, et

Lord, may I receive these gifts in purity of heart. May

Communion

de múnere temporáli fiat nobis remédium sempitérnum. | they bring me healing and strength, now and forever.

A pause for silent prayer is fittingly observed.

Prayer After Communion *proper to each day. It is terminated by the short conclusion, like the Prayer Over the Gifts (p. 19). All respond:* Amen.

Concluding rite

After any possible announcements, the priest blesses the assembly:

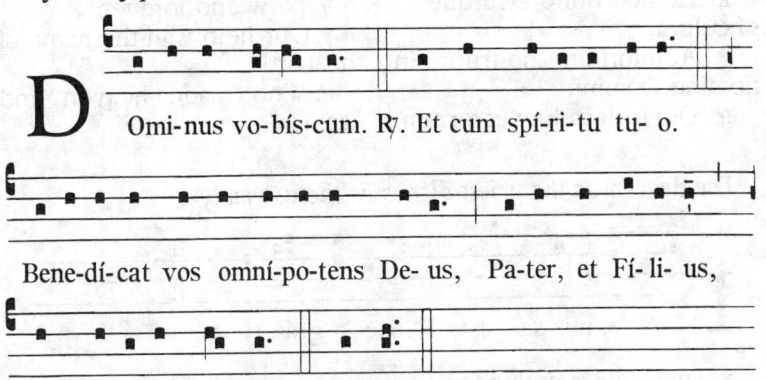

Dómi-nus vo-bís-cum. ℟. Et cum spí-ri-tu tu-o.

Bene-dí-cat vos omní-po-tens De-us, Pa-ter, et Fí-li-us,

et Spí-ri-tus Sanctus. ℟. Amen.

℣. The Lord be with you.
℟. And also with you.
May almighty God bless you, the Father, and the Son, and the Holy Spirit.
℟. Amen.

Alternate tone:

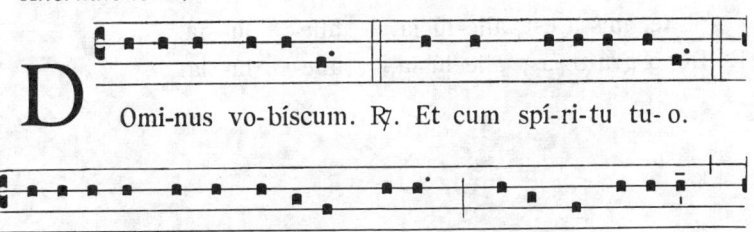

Dómi-nus vo-bíscum. ℟. Et cum spí-ri-tu tu-o.

Bene-dí-cat vos omní-po-tens De-us, Pa-ter, et Fí-li-us,

et Spí-ri-tus Sanctus. ℟. Amen.

When a bishop gives his blessing, it is preceded by the following dialogue:

℣. Sit nomen Dómini bene-díctum.
℟. Ex hoc nunc et usque in sǽculum.
℣. Adiutórium nostrum in nómine Dómini.
℟. Qui fecit cælum et terram.

℣. Blessed be the name of the Lord.
℟. Now and forever.
℣. Our help is in the name of the Lord.
℟. Who made heaven and earth.

The deacon or the priest dismisses the assembly:

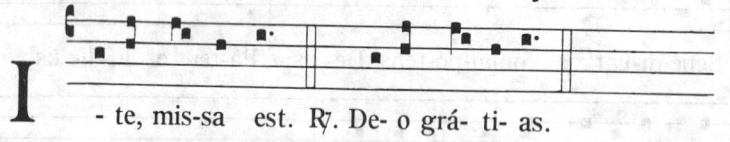

I - te, mis-sa est. ℟. De- o grá- ti- as.

℣. The Mass is ended, go in peace.
℟. Thanks be to God.

From the Easter Vigil to the Second Sunday of Easter inclusive, and on the day of Pentecost:

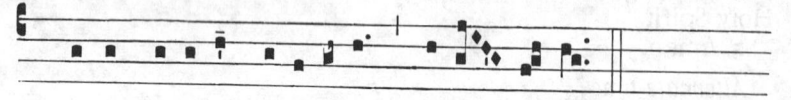

I- te, missa est, alle-lú-ia,   alle- lú- ia.
℟. De- o grá-ti- as, alle-lú-ia,   alle- lú- ia.

PREFACES

Prefaces proper to a single Mass are given in the formulary of that Mass. This Missal's table of contents contains a listing of all prefaces. Changeable prefaces are used with the First and Third Eucharistic Prayers, and sometimes with the Second Eucharistic Prayer.

Advent Preface I
Before December 17: The two comings of Christ

VERE dignum et iustum est, æquum et salutáre, nos tibi semper et ubíque grátias ágere : Dómine, sancte Pater, omnípotens ætérne Deus: per Christum Dóminum nostrum.

Qui, primo advéntu in humilitáte carnis assúmptæ, dispositiónis antíquæ munus implévit, nobísque salútis perpétuæ trámitem reservávit: ut, cum secúndo vénerit in suæ glória maiestátis, manifésto demum múnere capiámus, quod vigilántes nunc audémus exspectáre promíssum.

Et ídeo cum Angelis et Archángelis, cum Thronis et Dominatiónibus, cumque omni milítia cæléstis exércitus, hymnum glóriæ tuæ cánimus, sine fine dicéntes:

FATHER, all-powerful and ever-living God, we do well always and everywhere to give you thanks through Jesus Christ our Lord.

When he humbled himself to come among us as a man, he fulfilled the plan you formed long ago and opened for us the way to salvation. Now we watch for the day, hoping that the salvation promised us will be ours when Christ our Lord will come again in his glory.

And so, with all the choirs of angels in heaven we proclaim your glory and join in their unending hymn of praise: Holy...

Advent Preface II
Starting on December 17: Waiting for the two comings of Christ

VERE dignum et iustum est, æquum et salutáre, nos tibi semper et ubíque grátias ágere: Dómine, sancte Pater, omnípotens ætérne Deus: per Christum Dóminum nostrum.

FATHER, all-powerful and ever-living God, we do well always and everywhere to give you thanks through Jesus Christ our Lord.

Quem prædixérunt cunctórum præcónia prophetárum, Virgo Mater ineffábili dilectióne sustínuit, Ioánnes cécinit affutúrum et adésse monstrávit.

Qui suæ nativitátis mystérium tríbuit nos prævenire gaudéntes, ut et in oratióne pervígiles et in suis invéniat láudibus exsultántes.

Et ídeo cum Angelis et Archángelis, cum Thronis et Dominatiónibus, cumque omni milítia cæléstis exércitus, hymnum glóriæ tuæ cánimus, sine fine dicéntes:

His future coming was proclaimed by all the prophets. The virgin mother bore him in her womb with love beyond all telling. John the Baptist was his herald and made him known when at last he came. In his love Christ has filled us with joy as we prepare to celebrate his birth, so that when he comes he may find us watching in prayer, our hearts filled with wonder and praise.

And so, with all the choirs of angels in heaven we proclaim your glory and join in their unending hymn of praise: Holy...

Christmas Preface I
Christ the light

VERE dignum et iustum est, æquum et salutáre, nos tibi semper et ubíque grátias ágere: Dómine, sancte Pater, omnípotens ætérne Deus:

Quia per incarnáti Verbi mystérium nova mentis nostræ óculis lux tuæ claritátis infúlsit: ut, dum visibíliter Deum cognóscimus, per hunc in invisibílium amórem rapiámur.

Et ídeo cum Angelis et Archángelis, cum Thronis et Dominatiónibus, cumque omni milítia cæléstis exércitus, hymnum glóriæ tuæ cánimus, sine fine dicéntes:

FATHER, all-powerful and ever-living God, we do well always and everywhere to give you thanks through Jesus Christ our Lord.

In the wonder of the incarnation your eternal Word has brought to the eyes of faith a new and radiant vision of your glory. In him we see our God made visible and so are caught up in love of the God we can not see.

And so, with all the choirs of angels in heaven we proclaim your glory and join in their unending hymn of praise: Holy...

Christmas Preface II

Christ restores unity to all creation

Vere dignum et iustum est, æquum et salutáre, nos tibi semper et ubíque grátias ágere: Dómine, sancte Pater, omnípotens ætérne Deus: per Christum Dóminum nostrum.

Qui, in huius venerándi festivitáte mystérii, invisíbilis in suis, visíbilis in nostris appáruit, et ante témpora génitus esse cœpit in témpore; ut, in se érigens cuncta deiécta, in íntegrum restitúeret univérsa, et hóminem pérditum ad cæléstia regna revocáret.

Unde et nos, cum ómnibus Angelis te laudámus, iucúnda celebratióne clamántes:

Father, all-powerful and ever-living God, we do well always and everywhere to give you thanks through Jesus Christ our Lord.

Today you fill our hearts with joy as we recognize in Christ the revelation of your love. No eye can see his glory as our God, yet now he is seen as one like us. Christ is your Son before all ages, yet now he is born in time. He has come to lift up all things to himself, to restore unity to creation, and to lead mankind from exile into your heavenly kingdom.

With all the angels of heaven we sing our joyful hymn of praise: Holy...

Christmas Preface III

Divine and human exchange in the Incarnation of the Word

Vere dignum et iustum est, æquum et salutáre, nos tibi semper et ubíque grátias ágere: Dómine, sancte Pater, omnípotens ætérne Deus: per Christum Dóminum nostrum.

Per quem hódie commércium nostræ reparatiónis effúlsit, quia, dum nostra fragílitas a tuo Verbo suscípitur, humána mortálitas non solum in perpétuum transit honórem, sed nos

Father, all-powerful and ever-living God, we do well always and everywhere to give you thanks through Jesus Christ our Lord.

Today in him a new light has dawned upon the world: God has become one with man, and man has become one again with God. Your eternal Word has taken upon himself our

quoque, mirándo consórtio, reddit ætérnos.

Et ídeo, choris angélicis sociáti, te laudámus in gáudio confiténtes:

Lenten Preface I

Lent, a time for conversion

VERE dignum et iustum est, æquum et salutáre, nos tibi semper et ubíque grátias ágere: Dómine, sancte Pater, omnípotens ætérne Deus: per Christum Dóminum nostrum.

Qui fidélibus tuis dignánter concédis quotánnis paschália sacraménta in gáudio purificátis méntibus exspectáre: ut, pietátis offícia et ópera caritátis propénsius exsequéntes, frequentatióne mysteriórum, quibus renáti sunt, ad grátiæ filiórum plenitúdinem perducántur.

Et ídeo cum Angelis et Archángelis, cum Thronis et Dominatiónibus, cumque omni milítia cæléstis exércitus, hymnum glóriæ tuæ cánimus, sine fine dicéntes:

Lenten Preface II

The spirit of penance

VERE dignum et iustum est, æquum et salutáre, nos

human weakness, giving our mortal nature immortal value. So marvelous is this oneness between God and man that in Christ man restores to man the gift of everlasting life.

In our joy we sing to your glory with all the choirs of angels: Holy...

FATHER, all-powerful and ever-living God, we do well always and everywhere to give you thanks through Jesus Christ our Lord.

Each year you give us this joyful season when we prepare to celebrate the paschal mystery with mind and heart renewed. You give us a spirit of loving reverence for you, our Father, and of willing service to our neighbor. As we recall the great events that gave us new life in Christ, you bring the image of your Son to perfection within us.

Now, with angels and archangels, and the whole company of heaven, we sing the unending hymn of your praise: Holy...

FATHER, all-powerful and ever-living God, we do

Prefaces

tibi semper et ubíque grátias ágere: Dómine, sancte Pater, omnípotens ætérne Deus:

Qui fíliis tuis ad reparándam méntium puritátem, tempus præcípuum salúbriter statuísti, quo, mente ab inordinátis afféctibus expedíta, sic incúmberent transitúris ut rebus pótius perpétuis inhærérent.

Et ídeo, cum Sanctis et Angelis univérsis, te collaudámus sine fine dicéntes:

well always and everywhere to give you thanks.

This great season of grace is your gift to your family to renew us in spirit. You give us strength to purify our hearts, to control our desires, and so to serve you in freedom. You teach us how to live in this passing world, with our heart set on the world that will never end.

Now, with all the saints and angels, we praise you for ever: Holy...

Lenten Preface III
Motivation for doing penance

VERE dignum et iustum est, æquum et salutáre, nos tibi semper et ubíque grátias ágere: Dómine, sancte Pater, omnípotens ætérne Deus:

Qui nos per abstinéntiam tibi grátias reférre voluísti, ut ipsa et nos peccatóres ab insoléntia mitigáret, et, egéntium profíciens aliménto, imitatóres tuæ benignitátis effíceret.

Et ídeo, cum innúmeris Angelis, una te magnificámus, laudis voce dicéntes:

FATHER, all-powerful and ever-living God, we do well always and everywhere to give you thanks.

You ask us to express our thanks by self-denial. We are to master our sinfulness and conquer our pride. We are to show to those in need your goodness to ourselves.

Now, with all the saints and angels, we praise you for ever: Holy...

Lenten Preface IV
The effects of Lent

VERE dignum et iustum est, æquum et salutáre, nos

FATHER, all-powerful and ever-living God, we do

tibi semper et ubíque grátias ágere: Dómine, sancte Pater, omnípotens ætérne Deus:

Qui corporáli ieiúnio vítia cómprimis, mentem élevas, virtútem largíris et prǽmia: per Christum Dóminum nostrum.

Per quem maiestátem tuam laudant Angeli, adórant Dominatiónes, tremunt Potestátes. Cæli cælorúmque Virtútes, ac beáta Séraphim, sócia exsultatióne concélebrant. Cum quibus et nostras voces ut admítti iúbeas, deprecámur, súpplici confessióne dicéntes:

well always and everywhere to give you thanks.

Through our observance of Lent you correct our faults and raise our minds to you, you help us grow in holiness, and offer us the reward of everlasting life through Jesus Christ our Lord.

Through him the angels and all the choirs of heaven worship in awe before your presence. May our voices be one with theirs as they sing with joy the hymn of your glory: Holy...

Preface of Our Lord's Passion I

The power of the cross

VERE dignum et iustum est, æquum et salutáre, nos tibi semper et ubíque grátias ágere: Dómine, sancte Pater, omnípotens ætérne Deus:

Quia per Fílii tui salutíferam passiónem totus mundus sensum confiténdæ tuæ maiestátis accépit, dum ineffábili crucis poténtia iudícium mundi et potéstas émicat Crucifíxi.

Unde et nos Dómine, cum Angelis et Sanctis univérsis, tibi confitémur, in exsultatióne dicéntes:

FATHER, all-powerful and ever-living God, we do well always and everywhere to give you thanks.

The suffering and death of your Son brought life to the whole world, moving our hearts to praise your glory. The power of the cross reveals your judgment on this world and the kingship of Christ crucified.

We praise you, Lord, with all the angels and saints in their song of joy: Holy...

Easter Preface I
The paschal mystery

Vere dignum et iustum est, æquum et salutáre: Te quidem, Dómine, omni témpore confitéri, sed in hac potíssimum (nocte) die (*extra octavam:* in hoc potíssimum) gloriósius prædicáre, cum Pascha nostrum immolátus est Christus. Ipse enim verus est Agnus qui ábstulit peccáta mundi. Qui mortem nostram moriéndo destrúxit, et vitam resurgéndo reparávit.

Quaprópter, profúsis paschálibus gáudiis, totus in orbe terrárum mundus exsúltat. Sed et supérnæ virtútes atque angélicæ potestátes hymnum glóriæ tuæ cóncinunt, sine fine dicéntes:

Father, all-powerful and ever-living God, we do well always and everywhere to give you thanks through Jesus Christ our Lord. We praise you with greater joy than ever on this Easter night (day), when Christ became our paschal sacrifice.

He is the true Lamb who took away the sins of the world. By dying he destroyed our death; by rising he restored our life.

And so, with all the choirs of angels in heaven we proclaim your glory and join in their unending hymn of praise: Holy...

Easter Preface II
New life in Christ

Vere dignum et iustum est, æquum et salutáre: Te quidem, Dómine, omni témpore confitéri, sed in hoc potíssimum gloriósius prædicáre, cum Pascha nostrum immolátus est Christus.

Per quem in ætérnam vitam fílii lucis oriúntur, et fidélibus regni cæléstis átria reserántur. Quia mors nostra est eius morte redémpta, et in eius resurrectióne vita ómnium resurréxit.

Father, all-powerful and ever-living God, we do well always and everywhere to give you thanks through Jesus Christ our Lord. We praise you with greater joy than ever in this Easter season, when Christ became our paschal sacrifice.

He has made us children of the light, rising to new and everlasting life. He has opened the gates of heaven to receive his faithful people. His death is our ransom from death; his resurrection is our rising to life.

Quaprópter, profúsis paschálibus gáudiis, totus in orbe terrárum mundus exsúltat. Sed et supérnæ virtútes atque angélicæ potestátes hymnum glóriæ tuæ cóncinunt, sine fine dicéntes:

The joy of the resurrection renews the whole world, while the choirs of heaven sing for ever to your glory: Holy...

Easter Preface III
Christ lives and intercedes for us for ever

VERE dignum et iustum est, æquum et salutáre: Te quidem, Dómine, omni témpore confitéri, sed in hoc potíssimum gloriósius prædicáre, cum Pascha nostrum immolátus est Christus.

Qui se pro nobis offérre non désinit, nosque apud te perénni advocatióne deféndit; qui immolátus iam non móritur, sed semper vivit occísus.

Quaprópter, profúsis paschálibus gáudiis, totus in orbe terrárum mundus exsúltat. Sed et supérnæ virtútes atque angélicæ potestátes hymnum glóriæ tuæ cóncinunt, sine fine dicéntes:

FATHER, all-powerful and ever-living God, we do well always and everywhere to give you thanks through Jesus Christ our Lord. We praise you with greater joy than ever in this Easter season, when Christ became our paschal sacrifice.

He is still our priest, our advocate who always pleads our cause. Christ is the victim who dies no more, the Lamb, once slain, who lives for ever.

The joy of the resurrection renews the whole world, while the choirs of heaven sing for ever to your glory: Holy...

Easter Preface IV
The restoration of the universe through the paschal mystery

VERE dignum et iustum est, æquum et salutáre: Te quidem, Dómine, omni témpore confitéri, sed in hoc potíssimum gloriósius prædicáre, cum Pascha nostrum immolátus est Christus.

FATHER, all-powerful and ever-living God, we do well always and everywhere to give you thanks through Jesus Christ our Lord. We praise you with greater joy than ever in this Easter season, when Christ became our paschal sacrifice.

Quia, vetustáte destrúcta, renovántur univérsa deiécta, et vitæ nobis in Christo reparátur intégritas.
Quaprópter, profúsis paschálibus gáudiis, totus in orbe terrárum mundus exsúltat. Sed et supérnæ virtútes atque angélicæ potestátes hymnum glóriæ tuæ cóncinunt, sine fine dicéntes:

In him a new age has dawned, the long reign of sin is ended, a broken world has been renewed, and man is once again made whole.
The joy of the resurrection renews the whole world, while the choirs of heaven sing for ever to your glory: Holy...

Easter Preface V
Christ is priest and victim

VERE dignum et iustum est, æquum et salutáre: Te quidem, Dómine, omni témpore confitéri, sed in hoc potíssimum gloriósius prædicáre, cum Pascha nostrum immolátus est Christus.

Qui, oblatióne córporis sui, antíqua sacrifícia in crucis veritáte perfécit, et, seípsum tibi pro nostra salúte comméndans, idem sacérdos, altáre et agnus exhíbuit.

Quaprópter, profúsis paschálibus gáudiis, totus in orbe terrárum mundus exsúltat. Sed et supérnæ virtútes atque angélicæ potestátes hymnum glóriæ tuæ cóncinunt, sine fide dicéntes:

FATHER, all-powerful and ever-living God, we do well always and everywhere to give you thanks through Jesus Christ our Lord. We praise you with greater joy than ever in this Easter season, when Christ became our paschal sacrifice.
As he offered his body on the cross, his perfect sacrifice fulfilled all others. As he gave himself into your hands for our salvation, he showed himself to be the priest, the altar, and the lamb of sacrifice.
The joy of the resurrection renews the whole world, while the choirs of heaven sing for ever to your glory: Holy...

Ascension Preface I
Christ, the Lord of heaven, remains close to us

VERE dignum et iustum est, æquum et salutáre: nos

FATHER, all-powerful and ever-living God, we do

tibi semper et ubíque grátias ágere: Dómine, sancte Pater, omnípotens ætérne Deus:

Quia Dóminus Iesus, Rex glóriæ, peccáti triumphátor et mortis, mirántibus Angelis, ascéndit (hódie) summa cælórum, Mediátor Dei et hóminum, Iudex mundi Dominúsque virtútum; non ut a nostra humilitáte discéderet, sed ut illuc confiderémus, sua membra, nos súbsequi, quo ipse, caput nostrum principiúmque, præcéssit.

Quaprópter, profúsis paschálibus gáudiis, totus in orbe terrárum mundus exsúltat. Sed et supérnæ virtútes atque angélicæ potestátes hymnum glóriæ tuæ cóncinunt, sine fine dicéntes:

well always and everywhere to give you thanks.

(Today) the Lord Jesus, the king of glory, the conqueror of sin and death, ascended to heaven while the angels sang his praises. Christ, the mediator between God and man, judge of the world and Lord of all, has passed beyond our sight, not to abandon us but to be our hope. Christ is the beginning, the head of the Church; where he has gone, we hope to follow.

The joy of the resurrection and ascension renews the whole world, while the choirs of heaven sing for ever to your glory: Holy...

Ascension Preface II
The mystery of the Ascension.

V ERE dignum et iustum est, æquum et salutáre, nos tibi semper et ubíque grátias ágere: Dómine, sancte Pater, omnípotens ætérne Deus: per Christum Dóminum nostrum.

Qui post resurrectiónem suam ómnibus discípulis suis maniféstus appáruit, et ipsis cernéntibus est elevátus in cælum, ut nos divinitátis suæ tribúeret esse partícipes.

Quaprópter profúsis paschálibus gáudiis, totus in orbe terrárum mundus exsúltat. Sed

F ATHER, all-powerful and ever-living God, we do well always and everywhere to give you thanks through Jesus Christ our Lord.

In his risen body he plainly showed himself to his disciples and was taken up to heaven in their sight to claim for us a share in his divine life.

And so, with all the choirs of angels in heaven we proclaim your glory and join in their

et supérnæ virtútes atque angélicæ potestátes hymnum glóriæ tuæ cóncinunt, sine fine dicéntes:

unending hymn of praise: Holy...

Preface For Sundays In Ordinary Time I
The paschal mystery and the people of God

VERE dignum et iustum est, æquum et salutáre, nos tibi semper et ubíque grátias ágere: Dómine, sancte Pater, omnípotens ætérne Deus: per Christum Dóminum nostrum.

Cuius hoc miríficum fuit opus per paschále mystérium, ut de peccáto et mortis iugo ad hanc glóriam vocarémur, qua nunc genus eléctum, regále sacerdótium, gens sancta et acquisitiónis pópulus dicerémur, et tuas annuntiarémus ubíque virtútes, qui nos de ténebris ad tuum admirábile lumen vocásti.

Et ídeo cum Angelis et Archángelis, cum Thronis et Dominatiónibus, cumque omni milítia cæléstis exércitus, hymnum glóriæ tuæ cánimus, sine fine dicéntes:

FATHER, all-powerful and ever-living God, we do well always and everywhere to give you thanks through Jesus Christ our Lord.

Through his cross and resurrection he freed us from sin and death and called us to the glory that has made us a chosen race, a royal priesthood, a holy nation, a people set apart. Everywhere we proclaim your mighty works for you have called us out of darkness into your own wonderful light.

And so, with all the choirs of angels in heaven we proclaim your glory and join in their unending hymn of praise: Holy...

Preface For Sundays In Ordinary Time II
The mystery of salvation

VERE dignum et iustum est, æquum et salutáre, nos tibi semper et ubíque grátias ágere: Dómine, sancte Pater, omnípotens ætérne Deus: per Christum Dóminum nostrum. Qui, humánis miserátus erróribus, de Vírgine nasci dignátus est. Qui, crucem passus, a per-

FATHER, all-powerful and ever-living God, we do well always and everywhere to give you thanks through Jesus Christ our Lord.

Out of love for sinful man, he humbled himself to be born of the Virgin. By suffering on the

pétua morte nos liberávit et, a mórtuis resúrgens, vitam nobis donávit ætérnam.

Et ídeo cum Angelis et Archángelis, cum Thronis et Dominatiónibus, cumque omni milítia cæléstis exércitus, hymnum glóriæ tuæ cánimus, sine fine dicéntes:

cross he freed us from unending death, and by rising from the dead he gave us eternal life.

And so, with all the choirs of angels in heaven we proclaim your glory and join in their unending hymn of praise: Holy...

Preface For Sundays In Ordinary Time III
Salvation of our humanity through the humanity of Christ

VERE dignum et iustum est, æquum et salutáre, nos tibi semper et ubíque grátias ágere: Dómine, sancte Pater, omnípotens ætérne Deus:

Ad cuius imménsam glóriam pertinére cognóscimus, ut mortálibus tua deitáte succúrreres; sed et nobis providéres de ipsa mortalitáte nostra remédium, et pérditos quosque unde períerant, inde salváres, per Christum Dóminum nostrum.

Per quem maiestátem tuam adórat exércitus Angelórum, ante conspéctum tuum in æternitáte lætántium. Cum quibus et nostras voces ut admítti iúbeas, deprecámur, sócia exsultatióne dicéntes:

FATHER, all-powerful and ever-living God, we do well always and everywhere to give you thanks.

We see your infinite power in your loving plan of salvation. You came to our rescue by your power as God, but you wanted us to be saved by one like us. Man refused your friendship, but man himself was to restore it through Jesus Christ our Lord.

Through him the angels of heaven offer their prayer of adoration as they rejoice in your presence for ever. May our voices be one with theirs in their triumphant hymn of praise: Holy...

Preface For Sundays In Ordinary Time IV
The history of salvation

VERE dignum et iustum est, æquum et salutáre, nos tibi semper et ubíque grátias

FATHER, all-powerful and ever-living God, we do well always and everywhere to

ágere: Dómine, sancte Pater, omnípotens ætérne Deus: per Christum Dóminum nostrum.
Ipse enim nascéndo vetustátem hóminum renovávit, patiéndo delévit nostra peccáta, ætérnæ vitæ áditum præstitit a mórtuis resurgéndo, ad te Patrem ascendéndo cæléstes iánuas reserávit.
Et ídeo, cum Angelórum atque Sanctórum turba, hymnum laudis tibi cánimus, sine fine dicéntes:

give you thanks through Jesus Christ our Lord.
By his birth we are reborn. In his suffering we are freed from sin. By his rising from the dead we rise to everlasting life. In his return to you in glory we enter into your heavenly kingdom.
And so, we join the angels and the saints as they sing their unending hymn of praise: Holy...

Preface For Sundays In Ordinary Time V

Creation

VERE dignum et iustum est, æquum et salutáre, nos tibi semper et ubíque grátias ágere: Dómine, sancte Pater, omnípotens ætérne Deus:
Qui ómnia mundi eleménta fecísti, et vices disposuísti témporum variári; hóminem vero formásti ad imáginem tuam, et rerum ei subiecísti univérsa mirácula, ut vicário múnere dominarétur ómnibus quæ creásti, et in óperum tuórum magnálibus iúgiter te laudáret, per Christum Dóminum nostrum.
Quem cæli et terra, quem Angeli et Archángeli confiténtur et proclámant, incessábili voce dicéntes:

FATHER, all-powerful and ever-living God, we do well always and everywhere to give you thanks.
All things are of your making, all times and seasons obey your laws, but you chose to create man in your own image, setting him over the whole world in all its wonder. You made man the steward of creation, to praise you day by day for the marvels of your wisdom and power, through Jesus Christ our Lord.
We praise you, Lord, with all the angels in their song of joy: Holy...

Preface For Sundays In Ordinary Time VI
The pledge of an eternal Easter.

VERE dignum et iustum est, æquum et salutáre, nos tibi semper et ubíque grátias ágere: Dómine, sancte Pater, omnípotens ætérne Deus:

In quo vívimus, movémur et sumus, atque in hoc córpore constitúti non solum pietátis tuæ cotidiános experímur efféctus, sed æternitátis étiam pígnora iam tenémus. Primítias enim Spíritus habéntes, qui suscitávit Iesum a mórtuis, paschále mystérium sperámus nobis esse perpétuum.

Unde et nos tibi grátias ágimus, et tuas virtútes cum Angelis prædicámus, dicéntes:

FATHER, all-powerful and ever-living God, we do well always and everywhere to give you thanks.

In you we live and move and have our being. Each day you show us a Father's love; your Holy Spirit, dwelling within us, gives us on earth the hope of unending joy. Your gift of the Spirit, who raised Jesus from the dead, is the foretaste and promise of the paschal feast of heaven.

With thankful praise, in company with the angels, we glorify the wonders of your power: Holy...

Preface For Sundays In Ordinary Time VII
Salvation through the obedience of Christ

VERE dignum et iustum est, æquum et salutáre, nos tibi semper et ubíque grátias ágere: Dómine, sancte Pater, omnípotens ætérne Deus:

Quia sic mundum misericórditer dilexísti, ut ipsum nobis mítteres Redemptórem, quem absque peccáto in nostra voluísti similitúdine conversári, ut amáres in nobis quod diligébas in Fílio, cuius obœdiéntia sumus ad tua dona reparáti, quæ per inobœdiéntiam amisérámus peccándo.

FATHER, all-powerful and ever-living God, we do well always and everywhere to give you thanks.

So great was your love that you gave us your Son as our redeemer. You sent him as one like ourselves, though free from sin, that you might see and love in us what you see and love in Christ. Your gifts of grace, lost by disobedience, are now restored by the obedience of your Son.

Unde et nos, Dómine, cum Angelis et Sanctis univérsis tibi confitémur, in exsultatióne dicéntes:

We praise you, Lord, with all the angels and saints in their song of joy: Holy...

Preface For Sundays In Ordinary Time VIII
The Church united in the mystery of the Trinity.

VERE dignum et iustum est, æquum et salutáre, nos tibi semper et ubíque grátias ágere: Dómine, sancte Pater, omnípotens ætérne Deus:

Quia fílios, quos longe peccáti crimen abstúlerat, per sánguinem Fílii tui Spiritúsque virtúte, in unum ad te dénuo congregáre voluísti: ut plebs, de unitáte Trinitátis adunáta, in tuæ laudem sapiéntiæ multifórmis Christi corpus templúmque Spíritus noscerétur Ecclésia.

Et ídeo, choris angélicis sociáti, te laudámus in gáudio confiténtes:

FATHER, all-powerful and ever-living God, we do well always and everywhere to give you thanks.

When your children sinned and wandered far from your friendship, you reunited them with yourself through the blood of your Son and the power of the Holy Spirit. You gather them into your Church, to be one as you, Father, are one with your Son and the Holy Spirit. You call them to be your people, to praise your wisdom in all your works. You make them the body of Christ and the dwelling-place of the Holy Spirit.

In our joy we sing to your glory with all the choirs of angels: Holy...

Preface of the Holy Eucharist I

VERE dignum et iustum est, æquum et salutáre, nos tibi semper et ubíque grátias ágere: Dómine, sancte Pater, omnípotens ætérne Deus: per Christum Dóminum nostrum.

Qui, verus æternúsque Sacérdos, formam sacrifícii perénnis instítuens, hóstiam tibi se primus óbtulit salutárem, et

FATHER, all-powerful and ever-living God, we do well always and everywhere to give you thanks through Jesus Christ our Lord.

He is the true and eternal priest who established this unending sacrifice. He offered himself as a victim for our

nos, in sui memóriam, præcépit offérre. Cuius carnem pro nobis immolátam dum súmimus, roborámur, et fusum pro nobis sánguinem dum potámur, ablúimur.

Et ídeo cum Angelis et Archángelis, cum Thronis et Dominatiónibus, cumque omni milítia cæléstis exércitus, hymnum glóriæ tuæ cánimus, sine fine dicéntes:

deliverance and taught us to make this offering in his memory. As we eat his body which he gave for us, we grow in strength. As we drink his blood which he poured out for us, we are washed clean.

Now, with angels and archangels, and the whole company of heaven, we sing the unending hymn of your praise: Holy...

Preface of the Holy Eucharist II

VERE dignum et iustum est, æquum et salutáre, nos tibi semper et ubíque grátias ágere: Dómine, sancte Pater, omnípotens ætérne Deus: per Christum Dóminum nostrum.

Qui cum Apóstolis suis in novíssima cena convéscens, salutíferam crucis memóriam prosecutúrus in sǽcula, Agnum sine mácula se tibi óbtulit, perféctæ laudis munus accéptum. Quo venerábili mystério fidéles tuos aléndo sanctíficas, ut humánum genus, quod cóntinet unus orbis, una fides illúminet, cáritas una coniúngat. Ad mensam ígitur accédimus tam mirábilis sacraménti, ut, grátiæ tuæ suavitáte perfúsi, ad cæléstis formæ imáginem transeámus.

Propter quod cæléstia tibi atque terréstria cánticum no-

FATHER, all-powerful and ever-living God, we do well always and everywhere to give you thanks through Jesus Christ our Lord.

At the last supper, as he sat at table with his apostles, he offered himself to you as the spotless lamb, the acceptable gift that gives you perfect praise. Christ has given us this memorial of his passion to bring us its saving power until the end of time. In this great sacrament you feed your people and strengthen them in holiness, so that the family of mankind may come to walk in the light of one faith, in one communion of love. We come then to this wonderful sacrament to be fed at your table and grow into the likeness of the risen Christ.

Earth unites with heaven to sing the new song of creation as

vum cóncinunt adorándo, et nos cum omni exércitu Angelórum proclamámus, sine fine dicéntes:

we adore and praise you for ever: Holy...

Preface for the Dead I
Sorrow and hope in the face of death

VERE dignum et iustum est, æquum et salutáre, nos tibi semper et ubíque grátias ágere: Dómine, sancte Pater, omnípotens ætérne Deus: per Christum Dóminum nostrum.

In quo nobis spes beátæ resurrectiónis effúlsit, ut, quos contrístat certa moriéndi condício, eósdem consolétur futúræ immortalitátis promíssio. Tuis enim fidélibus, Dómine, vita mutátur, non tóllitur, et, dissolúta terréstris huius incolátus domo, ætérna in cælis habitátio comparátur.

Et ídeo cum Angelis et Archángelis, cum Thronis et Dominatiónibus, cumque omni milítia cæléstis exércitus, hymnum glóriæ tuæ cánimus, sine fine dicéntes:

FATHER, all-powerful and ever-living God, we do well always and everywhere to give you thanks through Jesus Christ our Lord.

In him, who rose from the dead, our hope of resurrection dawned. The sadness of death gives way to the bright promise of immortality. Lord, for your faithful people life is changed, not ended. When the body of our earthly dwelling lies in death we gain an everlasting dwelling place in heaven.

And so, with all the choirs of angels in heaven we proclaim your glory and join in their unending hymn of praise: Holy...

Preface for the Dead II
Christ died so that we might live

VERE dignum et iustum est, æquum et salutáre, nos tibi semper et ubíque grátias ágere: Dómine, sancte Pater, omnípotens ætérne Deus: per Christum Dóminum nostrum.

FATHER, all-powerful and ever-living God, we do well always and everywhere to give you thanks through Jesus Christ our Lord.

Ipse enim mortem unus accépit, ne omnes nos morerémur; immo unus mori dignátus est, ut omnes tibi perpétuo viverémus.

Et ídeo, choris angélicis sociáti, te laudámus in gáudio confiténtes:

He chose to die that he might free all men from dying. He gave his life that we might live to you alone for ever.

In our joy we sing to your glory with all the choirs of angels: Holy...

Preface for the Dead III

Christ, our life and our resurrection

VERE dignum et iustum est, æquum et salutáre, nos tibi semper et ubíque grátias ágere: Dómine, sancte Pater, omnípotens ætérne Deus: per Christum Dóminum nostrum.

Qui est salus mundi, vita hóminum, resurréctio mortuórum.

Per quem maiestátem tuam adórat exércitus Angelórum, ante conspéctum tuum in æternitáte lætántium. Cum quibus et nostras voces ut admítti iúbeas, deprecámur, sócia exsultatióne dicéntes:

FATHER, all-powerful and ever-living God, we do well always and everywhere to give you thanks through Jesus Christ our Lord.

In him the world is saved, man is reborn, and the dead rise again to life.

Through Christ the angels of heaven offer their prayer of adoration as they rejoice in your presence for ever. May our voices be one with theirs in their triumphant hymn of praise: Holy...

Preface for the Dead IV

God our Creator will raise us up

VERE dignum et iustum est, æquum et salutáre, nos tibi semper et ubíque grátias ágere: Dómine, sancte Pater, omnípotens ætérne Deus:

Cuius império náscimur, cuius arbítrio régimur, cuius

FATHER, all-powerful and ever-living God, we do well always and everywhere to give you thanks.

By your power you bring us to birth. By your providence

præcépto in terra, de qua sumpti sumus, peccáti lege absólvimur. Et, qui per mortem Fílii tui redémpti sumus, ad ipsíus resurrectiónis glóriam tuo nutu excitámur.

Et ídeo, cum Angelórum atque Sanctórum turba, hymnum laudis tibi cánimus, sine fine dicéntes:

you rule our lives. By your command you free us at last from sin as we return to the dust from which we came. Through the saving death of your Son we rise at your word to the glory of the resurrection.

Now we join the angels and the saints as they sing their unending hymn of praise: Holy...

Preface for the Dead V
Redeemed by Christ, we will rise with him.

VERE dignum et iustum est, æquum et salutáre, nos tibi semper et ubíque grátias ágere: Dómine, sancte Pater, omnípotens ætérne Deus:

Qui, etsi nostri est mériti quod perímus, tuæ tamen est pietátis et grátiæ quod, pro peccáto morte consúmpti, per Christi victóriam redémpti, cum ipso revocámur ad vitam.

Et ídeo, cum cælórum Virtútibus, in terris te iúgiter celebrámus, maiestáti tuæ sine fine clamántes:

FATHER, all-powerful and ever-living God, we do well always and everywhere to give you thanks through Jesus Christ our Lord.

Death is the just reward for our sins, yet, when at last we die, your loving kindness calls us back to life in company with Christ, whose victory is our redemption.

Our hearts are joyful, for we have seen your salvation, and now with the angels and saints we praise you for ever: Holy...

THE SPRINKLING OF HOLY WATER

Invitation to prayer:

Dóminum Deum nostrum, fratres caríssimi, supplíciter precémur, ut hanc creatúram aquæ benedícere dignétur, super nos aspergéndam in nostri memóriam baptísmi. Ipse autem nos adiuváre dignétur, ut fidéles Spirítui, quem accépimus, maneámus.

Dear friends, this water will be used to remind us of our baptism. Let us ask God to bless it and to keep us faithful to the Spirit he has given us.

After a moment of silence, the priest says one of the following prayers:

Omnípotens sempitérne Deus, qui voluísti ut per aquam, fontem vitæ ac purificatiónis princípium, étiam ánimæ mundaréntur ætérnæque vitæ munus excíperent, dignáre, quæsumus, hanc aquam benedícere, qua vólumus hac die tua, Dómine, communíri. Fontem vivum in nobis tuæ grátiæ renovári et ab omni malo spíritus et córporis per ipsam nos deféndi concédas, ut mundis tibi córdibus propinquáre tuámque digne salútem valeámus accípere. Per Christum Dóminum nostrum. ℟. Amen.

God our Father, your gift of water brings life and freshness to the earth; it washes away our sins and brings us eternal life. We ask you now to bless this water, and to give us your protection on this day which you have made your own. Renew the living spring of your life within us and protect us in spirit and body, that we may be free from sin and come into your presence to receive your gift of salvation. We ask this through Christ our Lord. ℟. Amen.

Or:

Dómine Deus omnípotens, qui es totíus vitæ córporis et ánimæ fons et orígo, hanc aquam, te quæsumus, benedícas, qua fidénter útimur ad nostrórum implorándam véniam peccatórum et advérsus omnes morbos inimicíque insí-

Lord God almighty, creator of all life, of body and soul, we ask you to bless this water: as we use it in faith forgive our sins and save us from all illness and the power of evil. Lord, in your mercy give us living water, always springing up as a

dias tuæ defensiónem grátiæ consequéndam. Præsta, Dómine, ut misericórdia tua interveniénte, aquæ vivæ semper nobis sáliant in salútem, ut mundo tibi corde appropinquáre possímus, et omnis córporis animǽque perícula devitémus. Per Christum Dóminum nostrum. ℟. Amen.

fountain of salvation: free us, body and soul, from every danger, and admit us to your presence in purity of heart. Grant this through Christ our Lord. ℟. Amen.

During the Easter season:

Dómine Deus omnípotens, précibus pópuli tui adésto propítius; et nobis, mirábile nostræ creatiónis opus, sed et redemptiónis nostræ mirabílius, memorántibus, hanc aquam benedícere tu dignáre. Ipsam enim tu fecísti, ut et arva fecunditáte donáret, et levámen corpóribus nostris munditiámque præbéret. Aquam étiam tuæ minístram misericórdiæ condidísti; nam per ipsam solvísti tui pópuli servitútem, illiúsque sitim in desérto sedásti; per ipsam novum fœdus nuntiavérunt prophétæ, quod eras cum homínibus initúrus; per ipsam dénique, quam Christus in Iordáne sacrávit, corrúptam natúræ nostræ substántiam in regeneratiónis lavácro renovásti. Sit ígitur hæc aqua nobis suscépti baptísmatis memória, et cum frátribus nostris, qui sunt in Páschate baptizáti, gáudia nos tríbuas sociáre. Per Christum Dóminum nostrum. ℟. Amen.

Lord God almighty, hear the prayers of your people: we celebrate our creation and redemption. Hear our prayers and bless this water which gives fruitfulness to the fields, and refreshment and cleansing to man. You chose water to show your goodness when you led your people to freedom through the Red Sea and satisfied their thirst in the desert with water from the rock. Water was the symbol used by the prophets to foretell your new covenant with man. You made the water of baptism holy by Christ's baptism in the Jordan: by it you give us a new birth and renew us in holiness. May this water remind us of our baptism, and let us share the joy of all who have been baptized at Easter. We ask this through Christ our Lord.

℟. Amen.

Sprinkling of Holy Water

If salt is to be added to the holy water, the priest says:

Súpplices te rogámus, omnípotens Deus, ut hanc creatúram salis benedícere tua pietáte dignéris, qui per Eliséum prophétam in aquam mitti eam iussísti, ut sanarétur sterílitas aquæ. Præsta, Dómine, quæsumus, ut, ubicúmque hæc salis et aquæ commíxtio fúerit aspérsa, omni impugnatióne inimíci depúlsa, præséntia Sancti tui Spíritus nos iúgiter custódiat. Per Christum Dóminum nostrum. ℟. Amen.

Almighty God, we ask you to bless this salt as once you blessed the salt scattered over the water by the prophet Elisha. Wherever this salt and water are sprinkled, drive away the power of evil, and protect us always by the presence of your Holy Spirit. Grant this through Christ our Lord.
℟. Amen.

The priest then pours the salt into the water.
He then goes through the church sprinkling the assembly, while one of the following antiphons is sung:

Ps 50: 9 and 3

VII

A-SPERGES me, *Dómine, hyssópo, et mundábor: lavábis me, et super nivem dealbábor. Ps. 50. Miserére mei, Deus, secúndum magnam misericórdiam tuam.

You will sprinkle me with hyssop, O Lord, and I shall be cleansed; you will wash me and I shall be made whiter than snow.

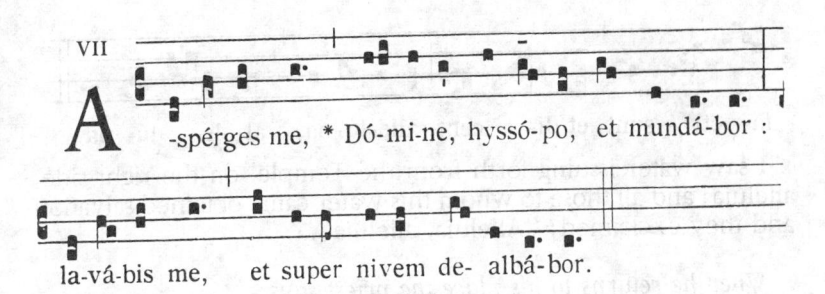

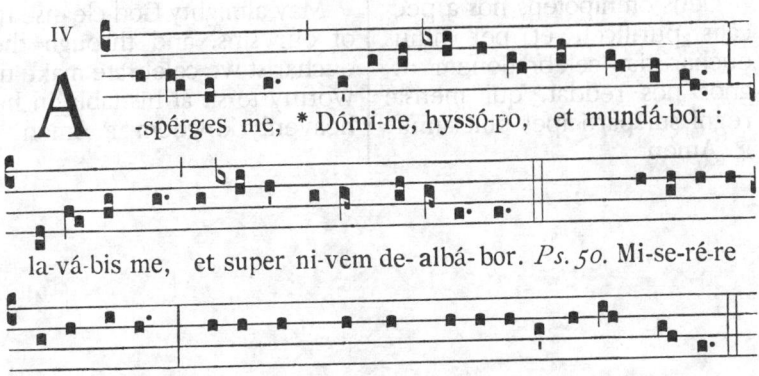

Sprinkling of Holy Water

VII

A-spérges me, * Dó-mi-ne, hyssó-po, et mundá-bor : la-vá-bis me, et super nivem de- albá-bor.

IV

A-spérges me, * Dómi-ne, hyssó-po, et mundá-bor : la-vá-bis me, et super ni-vem de- albá- bor. *Ps. 50.* Mi-se-ré-re me- i De- us, secúndum magnam mi-se-ri-córdi- am tu- am.

During the Easter season:

Ezek 47 : 1, 9

VIII

VI- di a- quam * egre- di- én- tem de tem- plo, a lá- te- re dex- tro, alle- lú- ia : et omnes, ad quos pervé-nit a- qua i-sta, sal- vi

Sprinkling of Holy Water

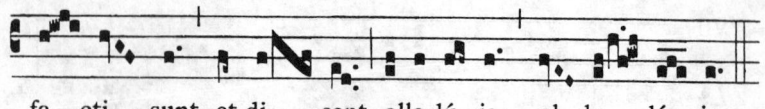

fa- cti sunt, et di- cent, alle-lú- ia, al- le- lú- ia.

I saw water issuing forth from the Temple, on the right side, alleluia; and all those to whom this water came obtained salvation and they exclaimed: "Alleluia, alleluia".

When he returns to his place the priest says:

Deus omnípotens nos a peccátis puríficet, et per huius eucharístiæ celebratiónem dignos nos reddat, qui mensæ regni sui partícipes efficiámur. ℟. Amen.

May almighty God cleanse us of our sins, and through the eucharist we celebrate make us worthy to sit at his table in his heavenly kingdom. ℟. Amen.

CHANTS OF THE MASS ORDINARY

I
EASTER SEASON

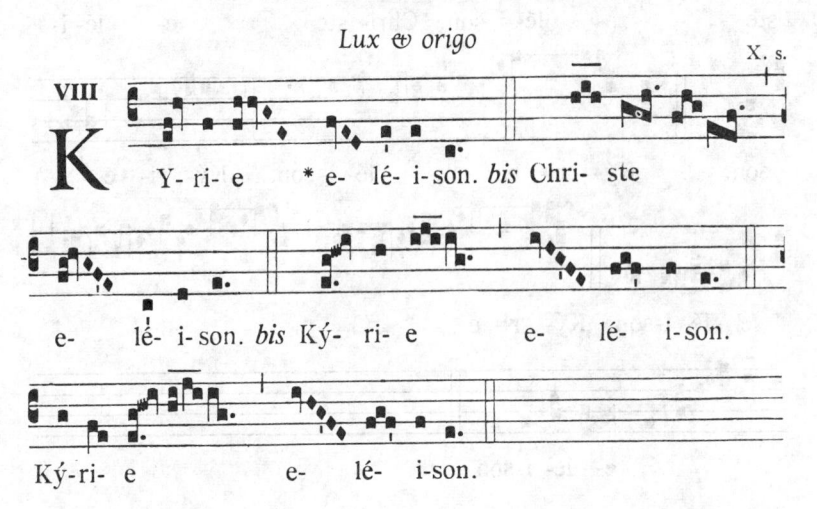

Lux & origo

VIII Ký-ri-e * e-lé-i-son. *bis* Chri-ste e-lé-i-son. *bis* Ký-ri-e e-lé-i-son. Ký-ri-e e-lé-i-son.

A
SUNDAYS

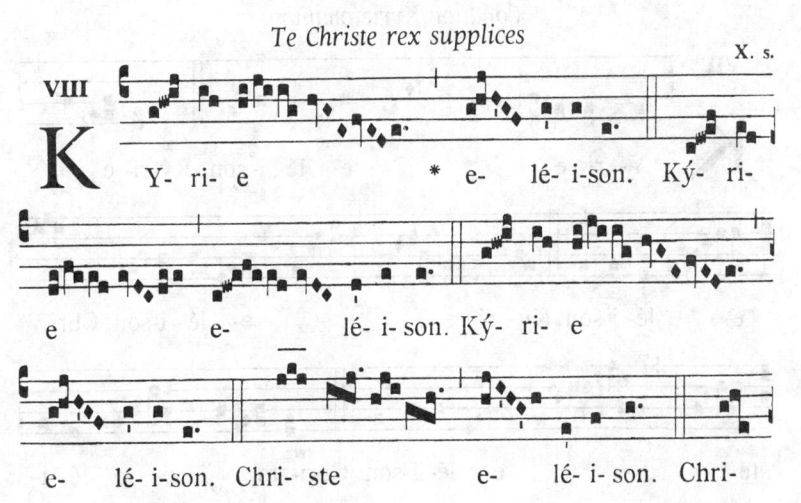

Te Christe rex supplices

VIII Ký-ri-e * e-lé-i-son. Ký-ri-e e-lé-i-son. Ký-ri-e e-lé-i-son. Chri-ste e-lé-i-son. Chri-

76 Chants of the Mass Ordinary I

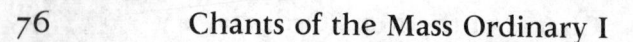

ste   e- lé- i- son. Chri- ste   e- lé- i-

son.   Ký- ri- e   e- lé- i- son.   Ký- ri- e

e- lé- i-son. Ký- ri- e   *   **

e- lé- i-son.

B
ON FEAST DAYS & MEMORIALS

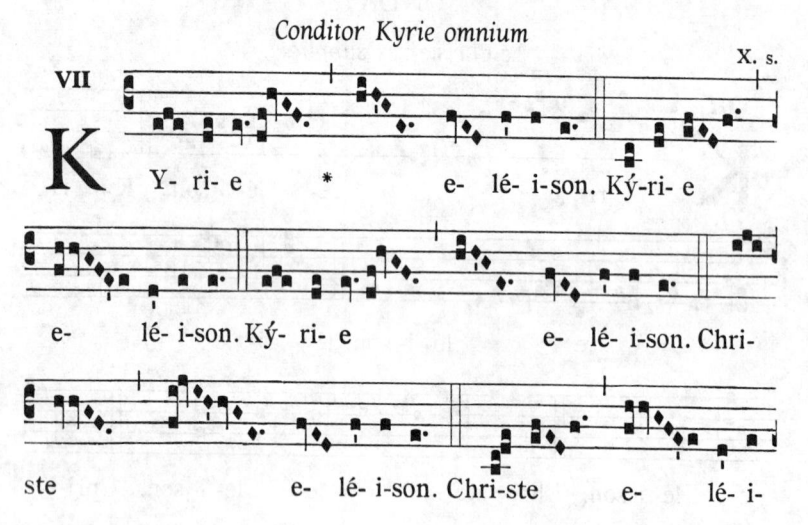

Conditor Kyrie omnium

VII   X. s.

K Y- ri- e   *   e- lé- i- son. Ký-ri- e

e- lé- i-son. Ký- ri- e   e- lé- i-son. Chri-

ste   e- lé- i-son. Chri-ste   e- lé- i-

Chants of the Mass Ordinary I

son. Chri- ste　　　　　　　e- lé- i-son. Ký- ri- e

e- lé- i-son. Ký- ri- e　　　　e- lé- i-son. Ký-

ri- e　　　*　　　　**

e- lé- i-son.

IV　　　　　　　　　　　　　　　　　　X. s.

G Ló- ri- a in excél-sis De- o.　Et in ter- ra pax

ho-mí-ni-bus bonae vo-luntá- tis. Laudámus te. Be-ne-dí-ci-

mus te.　Ado-rámus te.　Glo-ri- fi-cá-mus te.　　Grá-ti- as

á-gimus ti- bi propter magnam gló- ri- am tu- am. Dó-mi-ne

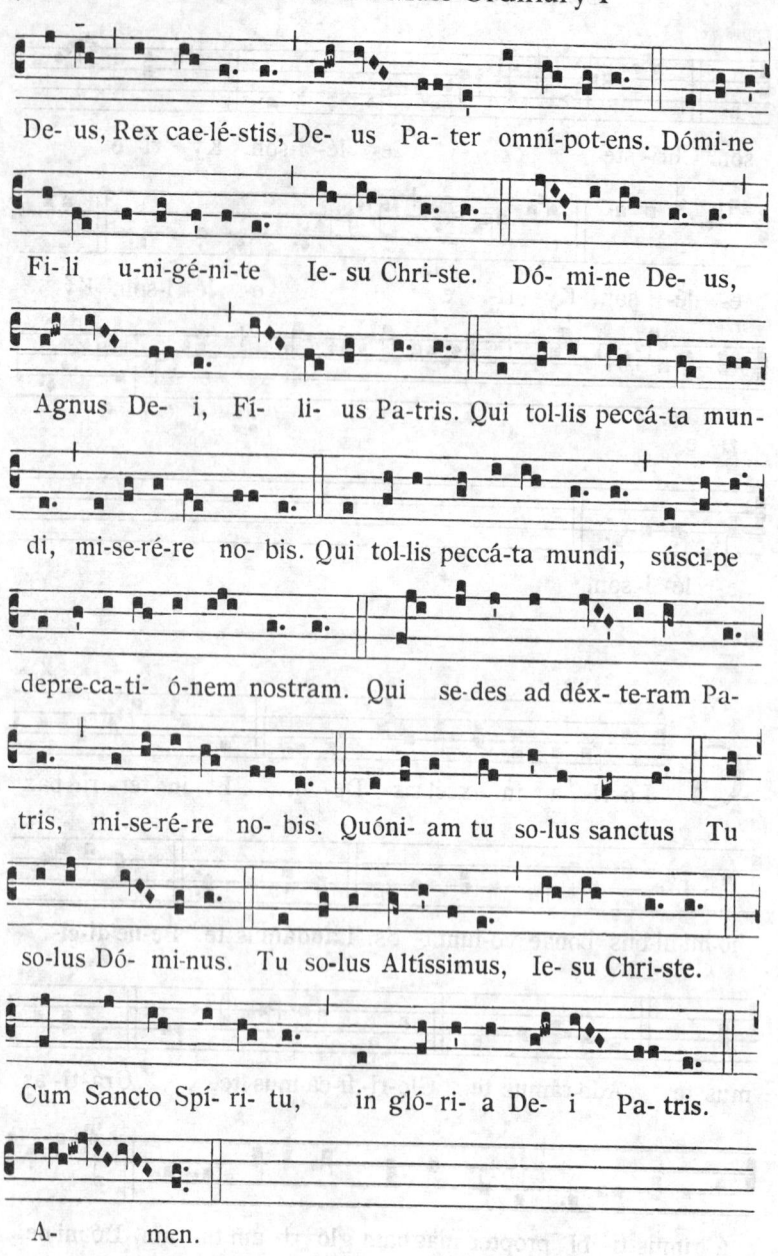

Deus, Rex caeléstis, Deus Pater omnípotens. Dómine Fili unigénite Iesu Christe. Dómine Deus, Agnus Dei, Fílius Patris. Qui tollis peccáta mundi, miserére nobis. Qui tollis peccáta mundi, súscipe deprecatiónem nostram. Qui sedes ad déxteram Patris, miserére nobis. Quóniam tu solus sanctus Tu solus Dóminus. Tu solus Altíssimus, Iesu Christe. Cum Sancto Spíritu, in glória Dei Patris.

Amen.

Chants of the Mass Ordinary I

IV. Sanctus, * Sanctus, Sanctus Dómi-nus De- us Sá-ba- oth. Ple-ni sunt cae- li et ter-ra gló- ri- a tu- a. Ho-sánna in ex-cél-sis. Be-ne-díctus qui ve-nit in nó-mi-ne Dó-mi-ni. Ho- sánna in excél- sis.

IV. A-gnus De- i, * qui tol-lis peccá- ta mun- di : mi-se-ré- re no- bis. Agnus De- i, * qui tol-lis peccá-ta mun-di : mi-se-ré- re no- bis. Agnus De- i, * qui tol-lis peccá- ta mun- di : dona no- bis pa- cem.

Chants of the Mass Ordinary II

From the Easter Vigil to the Second Sunday of Easter inclusive, and on the day of Pentecost:

VIII

I - te, missa est, alle-lú-ia, alle- lú- ia.
De-o grá-ti- as, alle-lú-ia, alle- lú- ia.

II

Kyrie fons bonitatis

III   X. s.

KYrie * e-lé- i-son. *bis*

Chri-ste e-lé- i-son. *bis*

Ký-ri-e e-lé- i-son. Ký-ri-

e * ** e-lé- i-son.

I   XIII. s.

Gló-ri-a in excélsis De-o. Et in terra pax ho-

mí- ni- bus bonae vo-luntá-tis. Laudámus te. Be-ne-

Chants of the Mass Ordinary II

dí-cimus te.   Ado- rámus te.   Glo- ri- fi-cá- mus te.   Grá- ti- as

á-gimus ti- bi   propter ma- gnam gló- ri- am tu- am.

Dómi-ne De- us, Rex cae-léstis, De- us Pa- ter omní-pot- ens.

Dó- mi-ne Fi- li u-ni- gé-ni- te Ie- su Chri- ste. Dómi-

ne De- us,   Agnus De- i,   Fí- li- us Pa-tris.   Qui tol-

lis peccá-ta mundi, mi-se- ré- re no- bis. Qui tol- lis pec-

cá-ta mundi,   súsci-pe depre-ca-ti- ó-nem nostram. Qui se-

des ad déx-te-ram Pa- tris, mi-se- ré- re no- bis. Quó-ni- am tu so- lus sanctus. Tu so-lus Dómi-nus. Tu so-lus Al- tís-

simus, Ie- su Chri-ste. Cum Sancto Spí- ri- tu in gló-

ri- a De- i Pa- tris. A- men.

XII-XIII. s.

S Anctus, * Sanctus, Sanctus

Dómi-nus De- us Sába- oth. Ple-ni sunt caeli et ter- ra

gló- ri- a tu- a. Ho-sánna in ex-cél-sis. Be-ne-

díctus qui ve- nit in nó- mi-ne Dómi-ni. Ho-sánna

in ex-cél-sis.

Chants of the Mass Ordinary III

I   X. s.

A-gnus De- i, * qui tol- lis pec-cá-ta mun- di : mi-se-ré- re no- bis. Agnus De- i, * qui tol-lis peccá-ta mun- di : mi-se-ré- re no- bis. Agnus De- i, * qui tol- lis pec-cá-ta mun- di : do-na no- bis pa- cem.

III

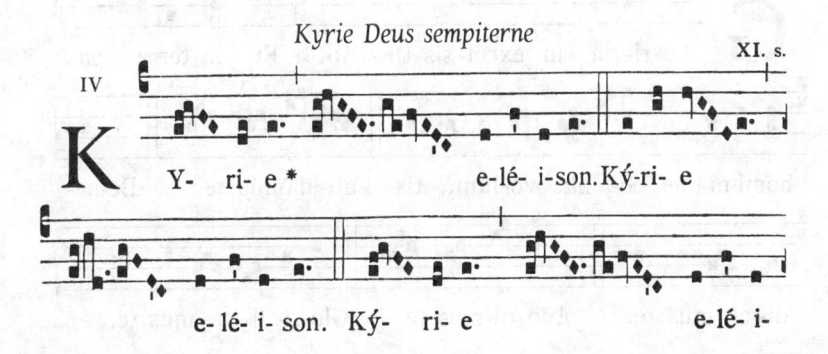

Kyrie Deus sempiterne

IV   XI. s.

KY- ri- e * e-lé- i-son. Ký-ri- e e-lé- i- son. Ký- ri- e e-lé- i-

Chants of the Mass Ordinary III

son. Chri- ste e-lé- i-son. Christe

e-lé- i-son. Chri- ste e- lé- i-

son. Ký- ri- e e- lé- i- son. Ký-ri-

e e- lé- i- son. Ký- ri- e

* **

e-lé- i-son.

VIII XI. s.

G Ló-ri- a in excél- sis De- o. Et in terra pax

homí- ni-bus bo- nae vo-luntá- tis. Lau- dámus te. Bene-

dí- ci- mus te. Ado- rá-mus te. Glo-ri- fi- cá- mus te.

Chants of the Mass Ordinary III

Grá-ti- as á-gimus ti-bi propter ma-gnam gló-ri- am tu- am.

Dómi-ne De- us, Rex cae-léstis, De- us Pa- ter o-mní- pot-ens.

Dómi-ne Fi- li u-ni- gé-ni-te Ie- su Chri-ste. Dómi-ne

De- us, Agnus De- i, Fí- li- us Patris. Qui tol-lis pec- cá- ta

mundi, mi-se-ré- re no- bis. Qui tol-lis pec- cá-ta mundi,

súscipe depre-ca- ti- ó-nem nostram. Qui se- des ad déxte-ram

Pa- tris, mi- se- ré-re no- bis. Quó-ni- am tu so-lus sanctus.

Tu so-lus Dómi-nus. Tu so-lus Altíssimus, Ie- su Chri-

ste. Cum Sancto Spí- ri-tu in gló-ri- a De- i Pa- tris.

A- men.

Chants of the Mass Ordinary III

Or:

A

Rector cosmi pie

XI. s.

II

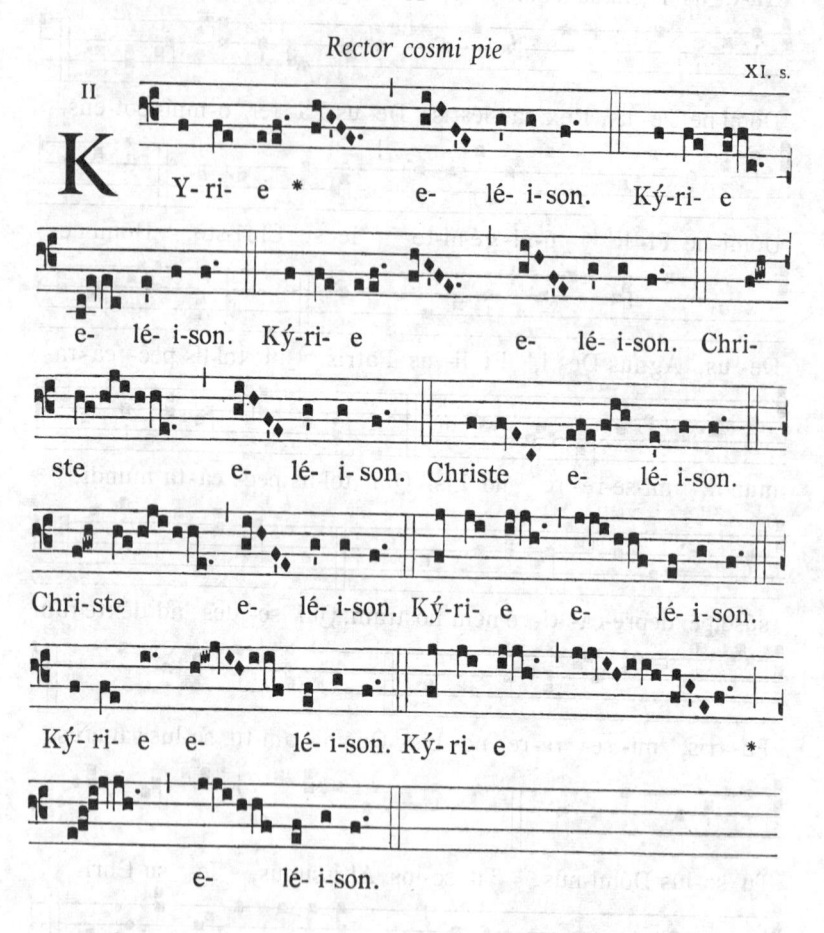

KY-ri- e * e- lé- i-son. Ký-ri- e

e- lé- i-son. Ký-ri- e e- lé- i-son. Chri-

ste e- lé- i-son. Christe e- lé- i-son.

Chri-ste e- lé- i-son. Ký-ri- e e- lé- i-son.

Ký- ri- e e- lé- i-son. Ký-ri- e *

e- lé- i-son.

B

X-XI. s.

II

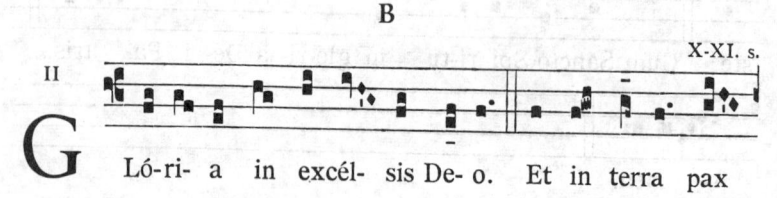

GLó-ri- a in excél- sis De- o. Et in terra pax

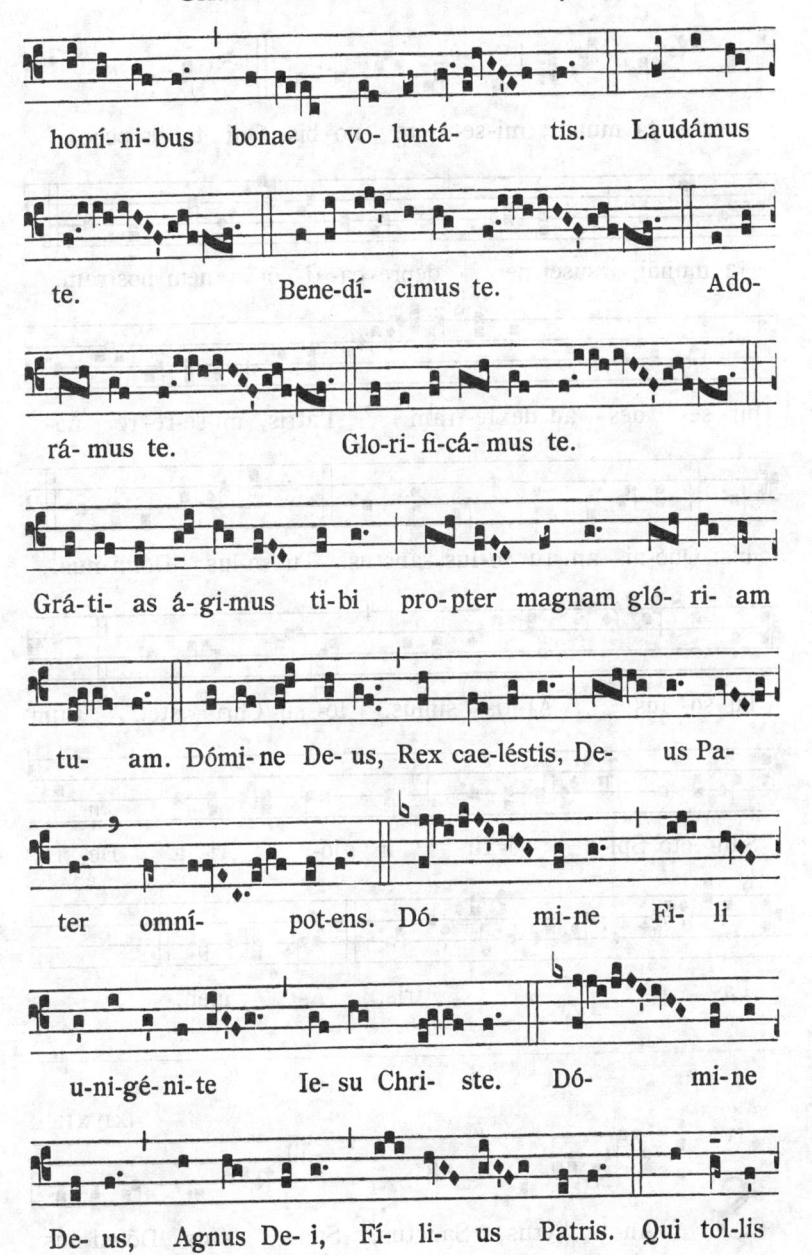

Chants of the Mass Ordinary III

homí- ni- bus bonae vo- luntá- tis. Laudámus

te. Bene-dí- cimus te. Ado-

rá- mus te. Glo-ri- fi-cá- mus te.

Grá-ti- as á- gi-mus ti-bi pro-pter magnam gló- ri- am

tu- am. Dómi- ne De- us, Rex cae-léstis, De- us Pa-

ter omní- pot-ens. Dó- mi-ne Fí- li

u-ni-gé-ni-te Ie- su Chri- ste. Dó- mi-ne

De- us, Agnus De- i, Fí- li- us Patris. Qui tol-lis

peccá- ta mundi, mi-se-ré-re no-bis. Qui tol-lis peccá-

ta mundi, súsci-pe depre-ca-ti-ó- nem nostram.

Qui se- des ad déxte- ram Patris, mi-se-ré-re no-

bis. Quó-ni- am tu so-lus sanctus. Tu so-lus Dómi-nus.

Tu so-lus Al-tís-simus, Ie-su Chri-ste. Cum

San-cto Spí- ri-tu in gló- ri-a De-i

Pa- tris. A- men.

IV (XI) XII. s.

S An-ctus, * Sanctus, San- ctus Dó-mi-nus

De- us Sá-ba- oth. Ple-ni sunt cae-li et terra gló- ri- a tu- a. Ho- sánna in excél-sis. Be-ne-dí-ctus qui ve-nit in nó-mi-ne Dó-mi-ni. Ho- sánna in excél-sis.

IV

XI-XII. s.

A- gnus De- i, *qui tol- lis peccá- ta mun- di : mi- se- ré- re no- bis. Agnus De- i, *qui tol- lis peccá- ta mun- di : mi- se- ré- re no- bis. A- gnus De- i, *qui tol- lis peccá- ta mun- di : do- na no-bis pa- cem.

IV
ON THE FEASTS OF APOSTLES

Cunctipotens genitor Deus

KY-ri- e * e- lé- i-son. *bis* Chri- ste e- lé- i-son. *bis* Ký- ri- e e- lé- i-son. Ký-ri- e * ** e- lé- i-son.

GLó- ri- a in excélsis De- o. Et in terra pax ho- mí-ni- bus bonae vo-luntá- tis. Laudámus te. Be-ne-dí-cimus te. Ado-rá- mus te. Glo- ri- fi-cá- mus te. Grá-ti- as á-gimus ti-bi propter magnam gló- ri- am tu- am. Dómi-ne

De- us, Rex cae-léstis, De- us Pa- ter omní- pot-ens.

Dómi-ne Fi- li u-ni- gé-ni- te Ie- su Chri- ste.

Dómi-ne De- us, Agnus De- i, Fí- li- us Pa- tris. Qui

tol-lis peccá- ta mundi, mi- se- ré-re no- bis. Qui tol-lis pec-

cá-ta mundi, súsci-pe depre-ca-ti- ónem nostram. Qui se-

des ad déx-te-ram Patris, mi- se- ré-re no- bis. Quó-ni- am

tu so-lus sanctus. Tu so-lus Dó-mi-nus. Tu so-lus Altíssi-

mus, Ie- su Chri- ste. Cum San-cto Spí- ri- tu

in gló-ri- a De- i Pa- tris. A- men.

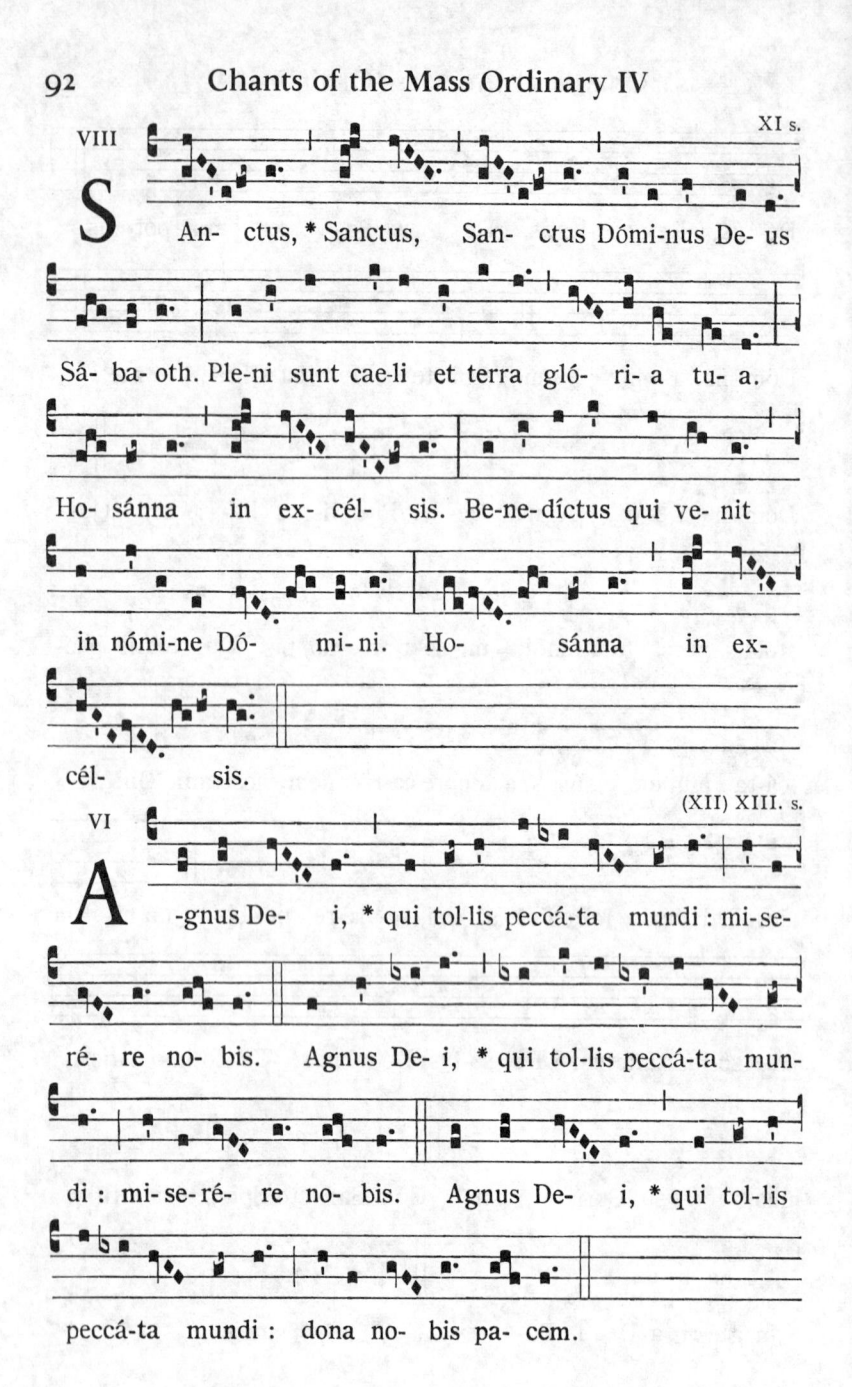

Chants of the Mass Ordinary IV

VIII   XI s.

SAnctus, * Sanctus, Sanctus Dóminus Deus Sábaoth. Pleni sunt caeli et terra glória tua. Hosánna in excélsis. Benedíctus qui venit in nómine Dómini. Hosánna in excélsis.

VI   (XII) XIII. s.

Agnus Dei, * qui tollis peccáta mundi : miserére nobis. Agnus Dei, * qui tollis peccáta mundi : miserére nobis. Agnus Dei, * qui tollis peccáta mundi : dona nobis pacem.

Chants of the Mass Ordinary V

V

Kyrie magnæ Deus potentiæ — XIII. s.

VIII

KY-ri- e * e- lé- i-son. *bis*

Chri- ste e- lé- i-son. *bis* Ký-ri- e

e- lé- i-son. *bis*

XII. s.

VIII

GLó- ri- a in excél-sis De- o. Et in terra pax

ho- mí- ni- bus bonae vo-lun- tá- tis. Laudámus te.

Be-ne- dí- cimus te. Ado-rámus te. Glo-ri- fi- cá-mus

te. Grá- ti- as á- gimus ti- bi propter magnam

gló- ri- am tu- am. Dó- mi- ne De- us, Rex cae-léstis, De-us Pa-ter o-mní-pot-ens. Dó-mi-ne Fi-li

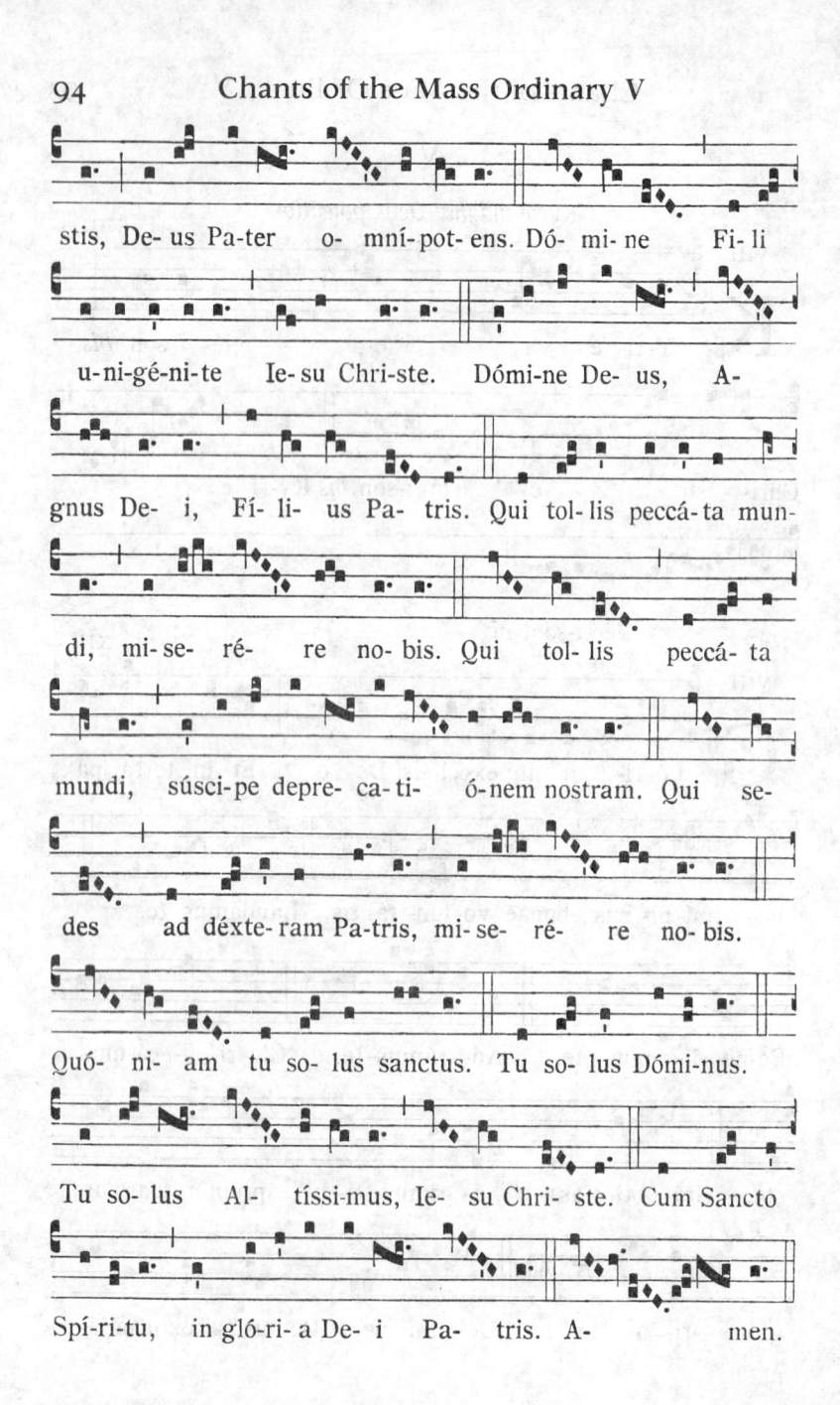

u-ni-gé-ni-te Ie-su Chri-ste. Dómi-ne De-us, A-

gnus De-i, Fí-li-us Pa-tris. Qui tol-lis peccá-ta mun-

di, mi-se-ré-re no-bis. Qui tol-lis peccá-ta

mundi, súsci-pe depre-ca-ti-ó-nem nostram. Qui se-

des ad déxte-ram Pa-tris, mi-se-ré-re no-bis.

Quó-ni-am tu so-lus sanctus. Tu so-lus Dómi-nus.

Tu so-lus Al-tíssi-mus, Ie-su Chri-ste. Cum Sancto

Spí-ri-tu, in gló-ri-a De-i Pa-tris. A- men.

Chants of the Mass Ordinary V

XII. s.

Sanctus, * Sanctus, Sanctus Dóminus Deus Sábaoth. Pleni sunt caeli et terra glória tua. Hosánna in excélsis. Benedíctus qui venit in nómine Dómini. Hosánna in excélsis.

XII. s.

Agnus Dei, * qui tollis peccáta mundi: miserére nobis. Agnus Dei, * qui tollis peccáta mundi: miserére nobis. A- gnus De- i, * qui tol- lis pec- cá- ta mun- di : dona no- bis pa- cem.

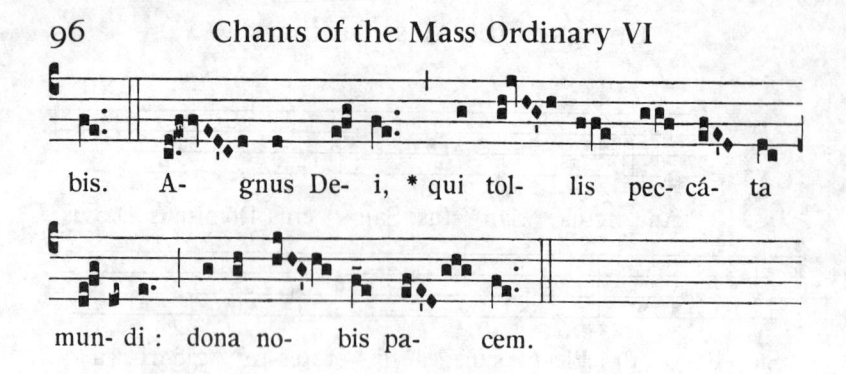

VI

Kyrie rex genitor

X. s.

VII

KY-ri- e * e- lé- i- son. Ký-ri- e e- lé- i- son. Ký-ri- e e- lé- i- son. Chri- ste e- lé- i-son. Chri- ste e- lé- i-son. Chri- ste e- lé- i-son. Ký-ri- e e- lé- i-son. Ký- ri- e e- lé- i- son. Ký-ri-

Chants of the Mass Ordinary VI

e　　　　　　*　　　　　　**

e- lé- i-son.

X. s.

G Ló- ri- a in excél-sis De- o. Et in ter- ra pax homí- ni-bus bonae vo-luntá- tis. Laudámus te. Bene-dí- cimus te. Ado-rámus te. Glo-ri- fi- cámus te. Grá-ti- as ágimus ti-bi propter ma-gnam gló- ri- am tu- am. Dómi- ne De- us, Rex caelé- stis, De- us Pa- ter omní- pot- ens. Dómi- ne Fi- li u-nigé-ni- te Ie- su Christe. Dó- mi-ne De- us, Agnus De- i, Fí- li- us Pa- tris. Qui tol- lis pec- cá- ta mundi, mi- se- ré- re no- bis. Qui tol- lis pec-

cá- ta mun- di, sús- ci- pe depreca- ti- ó-nem nostram.

Qui se- des ad déxte-ram Pa- tris, mi- se- ré-re no- bis.

Quóni- am tu so-lus sanctus. Tu so-lus Dó-mi-nus. Tu so-lus

Altíssimus, Ie-su Chri- ste. Cum San-cto Spí-ri- tu, in

gló- ri- a De- i Pa-tris. A- men.

XI. s.

III

SAnctus, * Sanctus, Sanctus Dóminus De- us Sá-

ba- oth. Ple-ni sunt cae- li et ter-ra gló- ri- a tu- a.

Ho- sánna in ex- cél- sis Be-ne-díctus qui ve-nit

in nó- mi- ne Dómi- ni. Ho- sánna in ex-

cél- sis.

XI. s.
VIII
A- gnus De- i, * qui tol- lis pec- cá- ta mun-

di : mi-se- ré- re no- bis. A- gnus De- i, * qui tol-

lis pec- cá-ta mun-di : mi-se- ré- re no- bis. A- gnus

De- i, * qui tol- lis pec- cá- ta mun-di : dona no-

bis pa- cem.

VII

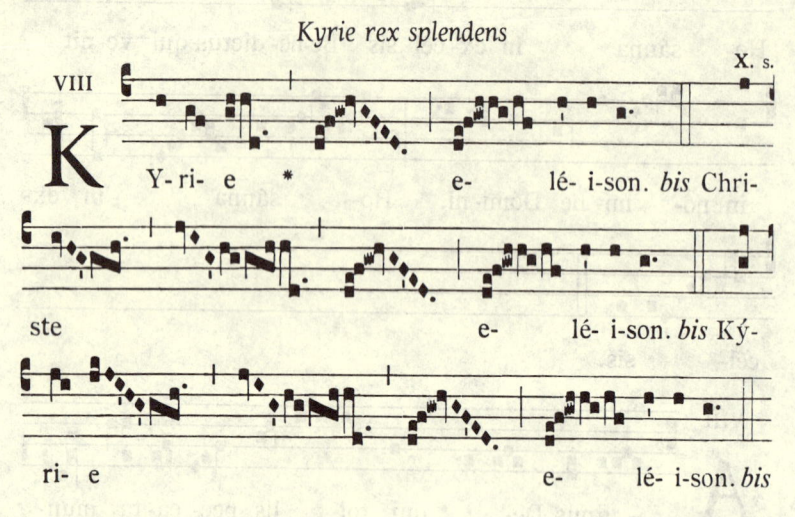

Kyrie rex splendens

X. s.

KY-ri- e * e- lé- i-son. *bis* Chri-ste e- lé- i-son. *bis* Ký-ri- e e- lé- i-son. *bis*

Or Additional Kýrie I, p. 150.

XII. s.

GLó-ri- a in excélsis De- o. Et in ter-ra pax ho-mí-ni-bus bonae vo-luntá- tis. Laudámus te. Be-ne-dí-cimus te. Ado-rámus te. Glo-ri- fi-cámus te. Grá-ti- as á- gi-mus ti-bi propter magnam gló-ri- am tu- am. Dómi-ne De- us,

Chants of the Mass Ordinary VII

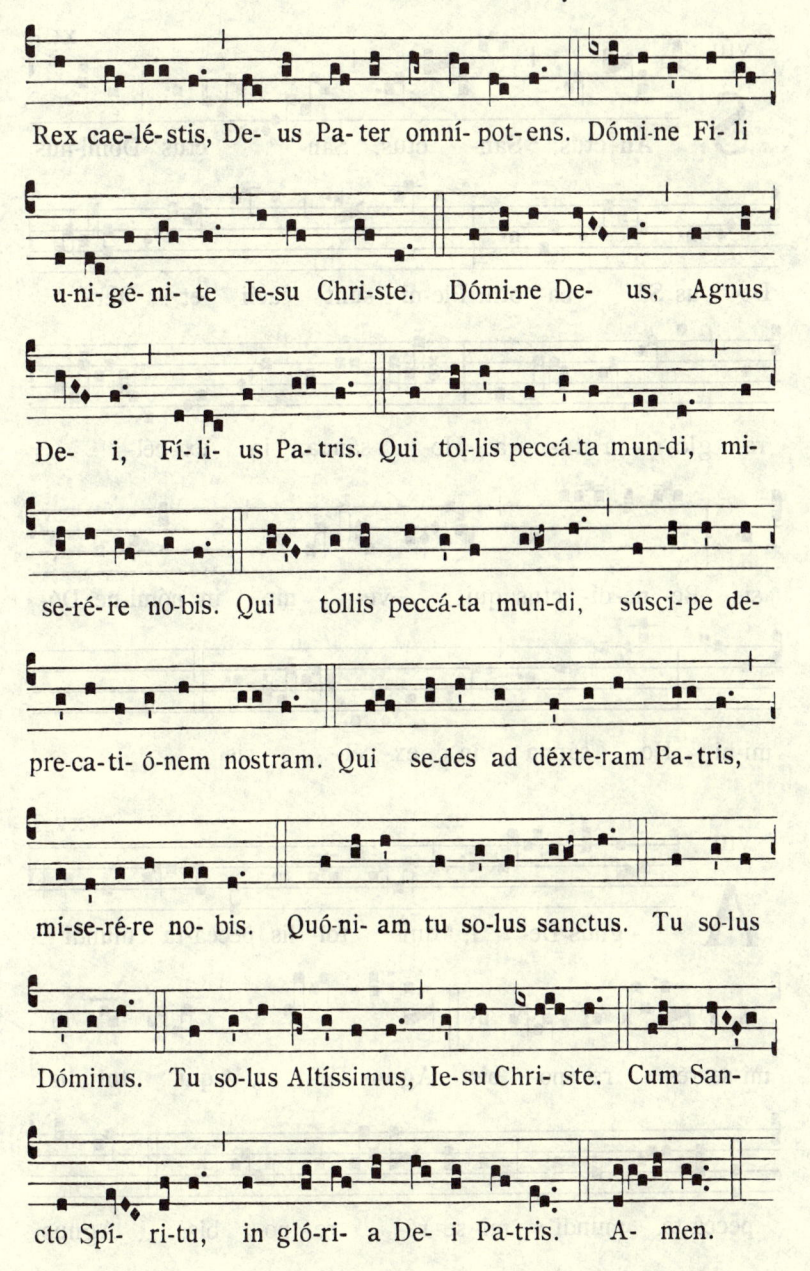

Rex cae-lé-stis, De- us Pa- ter omní- pot- ens. Dómi-ne Fi- li

u-ni- gé- ni- te Ie-su Chri-ste. Dómi-ne De- us, Agnus

De- i, Fí- li- us Pa- tris. Qui tol-lis peccá-ta mun-di, mi-

se-ré- re no-bis. Qui tollis peccá-ta mun-di, súsci- pe de-

pre-ca-ti- ó-nem nostram. Qui se-des ad déxte-ram Pa-tris,

mi-se-ré-re no- bis. Quó-ni- am tu so-lus sanctus. Tu so-lus

Dóminus. Tu so-lus Altíssimus, Ie-su Chri- ste. Cum San-

cto Spí- ri-tu, in gló-ri- a De- i Pa-tris. A- men.

Chants of the Mass Ordinary VII

VIII — XI. s.

SAnctus, *Sanctus, Sanctus Dóminus Deus Sábaoth. Pleni sunt caeli et terra glória tua. Hosánna in excélsis. Benedíctus qui venit in nómine Dómini. Hosánna in excélsis.

VIII — XV. s.

Agnus Dei, *qui tollis peccáta mundi: miserére nobis. Agnus Dei, *qui tollis peccáta mundi: miserére nobis. Agnus

Chants of the Mass Ordinary VIII

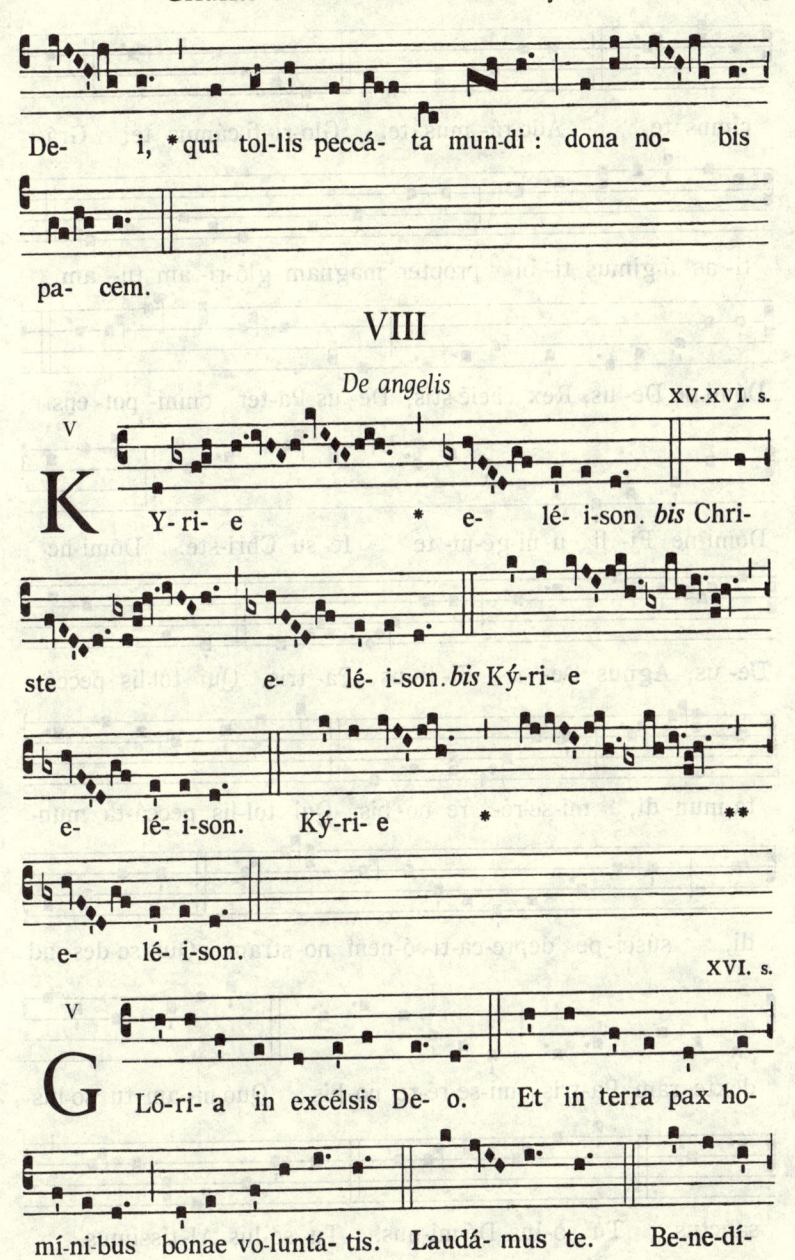

De- i, *qui tol-lis peccá- ta mun-di : dona no- bis pa- cem.

VIII

De angelis

XV-XVI. s.

KY- ri- e * e- lé- i-son. *bis* Chri- ste e- lé- i-son. *bis* Ký-ri- e e- lé- i-son. Ký-ri- e * ** e- lé- i-son.

XVI. s.

GLó-ri- a in excélsis De- o. Et in terra pax ho- mí-ni-bus bonae vo-luntá- tis. Laudá- mus te. Be-ne-dí-cimus te. Adorámus te. Glorificámus te. Grátias ágimus tibi propter magnam glóriam tuam. Dómine Deus, Rex caeléstis, Deus Pater omnípotens. Dómine Fili unigénite Iesu Christe. Dómine Deus, Agnus Dei, Fílius Patris. Qui tollis peccáta mundi, miserére nobis. Qui tollis peccáta mundi, súscipe deprecatiónem nostram. Qui sedes ad déxteram Patris, miserére nobis. Quóniam tu solus sanctus. Tu solus Dóminus. Tu solus Altíssimus,

Chants of the Mass Ordinary VIII

Ie-su Chri-ste. Cum Sancto Spí-ri-tu, in gló-ri-a De-i Pa-tris. A-men.

VI (XI) XII. s.

SAnctus, * Sanctus, San-ctus Dó-mi-nus De-us Sá-ba-oth. Ple-ni sunt cae-li et ter-ra gló-ri-a tu-a. Ho-sánna in excél-sis. Bene-dí-ctus qui ve-nit in nómi-ne Dó-mi-ni. Ho-sán-na in excél-sis.

VI XV. s.

A-gnus De-i, * qui tol-lis peccá-ta mun-di : mi-se-ré- re no- bis. Agnus De- i, * qui tol- lis peccá-ta mun-di : mi-se-ré- re no- bis. A-gnus De- i, * qui tol-lis peccá-ta mun-di : dona no- bis pa- cem.

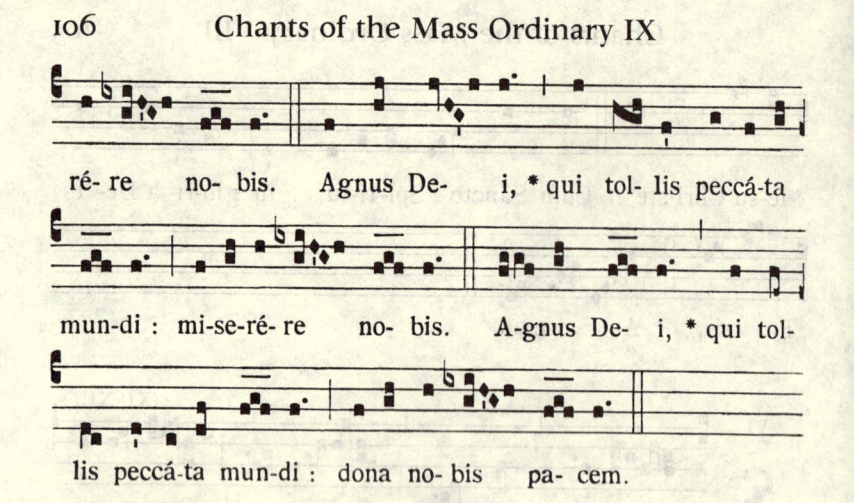

IX
ON SOLEMNITIES & FEASTS OF OUR LADY

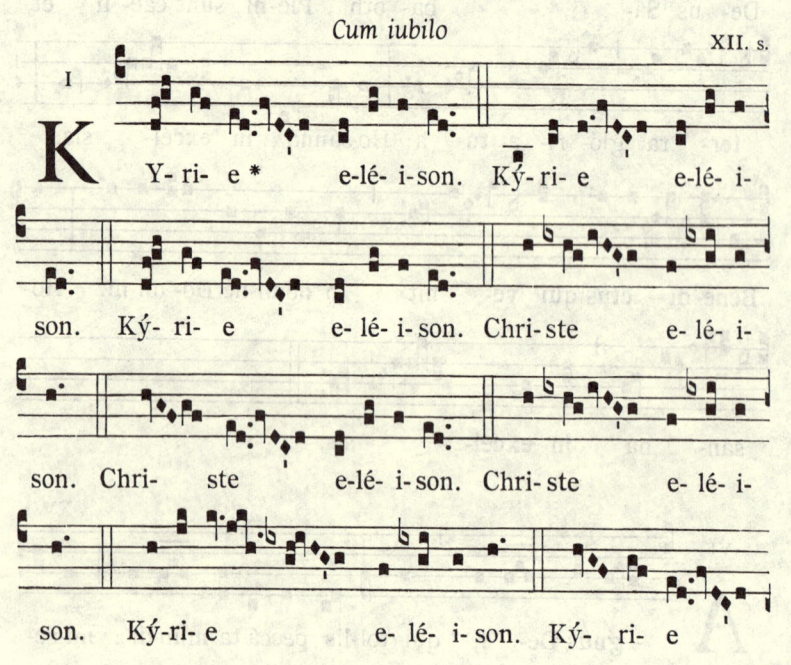

Cum iubilo

XII. s.

KÝ- ri- e * e-lé- i-son. Ký-ri- e e-lé- i-son. Ký-ri- e e-lé- i-son. Chri-ste e-lé- i-son. Chri- ste e-lé- i-son. Chri-ste e-lé- i-son. Ký-ri- e e-lé- i-son. Ký- ri- e

Chants of the Mass Ordinary IX

e-lé- i- son.   Ký-ri- e   *   **

e-lé- i- son.

XI. s.

VII

G Ló- ri- a in excélsis De- o. Et in ter-ra pax ho-mí- ni- bus bonae vo-luntá- tis. Laudá- mus te. Bene-dí-cimus te. Ado- rá- mus te. Glo-ri-fi-cá-mus te. Grá-ti- as á-gimus ti- bi propter magnam gló- ri- am tu- am. Dómi-ne De- us, Rex cae- léstis, De- us Pa- ter omní-pot- ens. Dómi-ne Fi-li u-ni-gé-ni-te Ie-su Chri- ste.

Chants of the Mass Ordinary IX

Dó- mi-ne De- us, Agnus De- i, Fí- li- us Pa-tris. Qui tol-lis peccá-ta mundi, mi-se-ré- re no-bis. Qui tol-lis pec- cá- ta mundi, sús- ci- pe depre-ca-ti- ó- nem nostram. Qui se-des ad déxte-ram Patris, mi-se-ré- re no-bis. Quóni- am tu so-lus sanctus. Tu so-lus Dómi-nus. Tu so-lus Altíssi- mus, Ie-su Chri- ste. Cum Sancto Spí-ri-tu, in gló-ri- a De- i Pa- tris. A- men.

XIV. s.

V

S An- ctus, * San-ctus, San- ctus Dómi-nus

Chants of the Mass Ordinary IX

De- us Sá- ba- oth. Ple-ni sunt cae-li et ter- ra gló- ri- a tu- a. Ho-sán-na in excél- sis. Be- ne-díctus qui ve- nit in nó- mi- ne Dó- mi- ni. Ho- sánna in ex- cél- sis.

(X) XIII. s.

V. A-gnus De- i, * qui tol- lis peccá-ta mun- di : mi- se- ré-re no- bis. Agnus De- i, * qui tol- lis peccá-ta mundi : mi- se- ré- re no- bis. Agnus De- i, * qui tol- lis peccá-ta mun- di : do-na no- bis pa- cem.

X
ON FEASTS & MEMORIALS OF OUR LADY

Alme Pater   XI. s.

KY- ri- e * e- lé- i-son. Ký-ri- e e- lé- i-son.

Ký- ri- e e- lé- i-son. Christe e- lé- i-son. Chri-

ste e- lé- i-son. Christe e- lé- i-son. Ký- ri- e

e- lé- i-son. Ký- ri- e e- lé- i-son. Ký-ri- e *

** e- lé- i-son.

XV. s.

GLó-ri- a in excélsis De- o. Et in terra pax ho-

mí-ni-bus bonae vo-luntá- tis. Laudámus te. Be-ne-dí-cimus

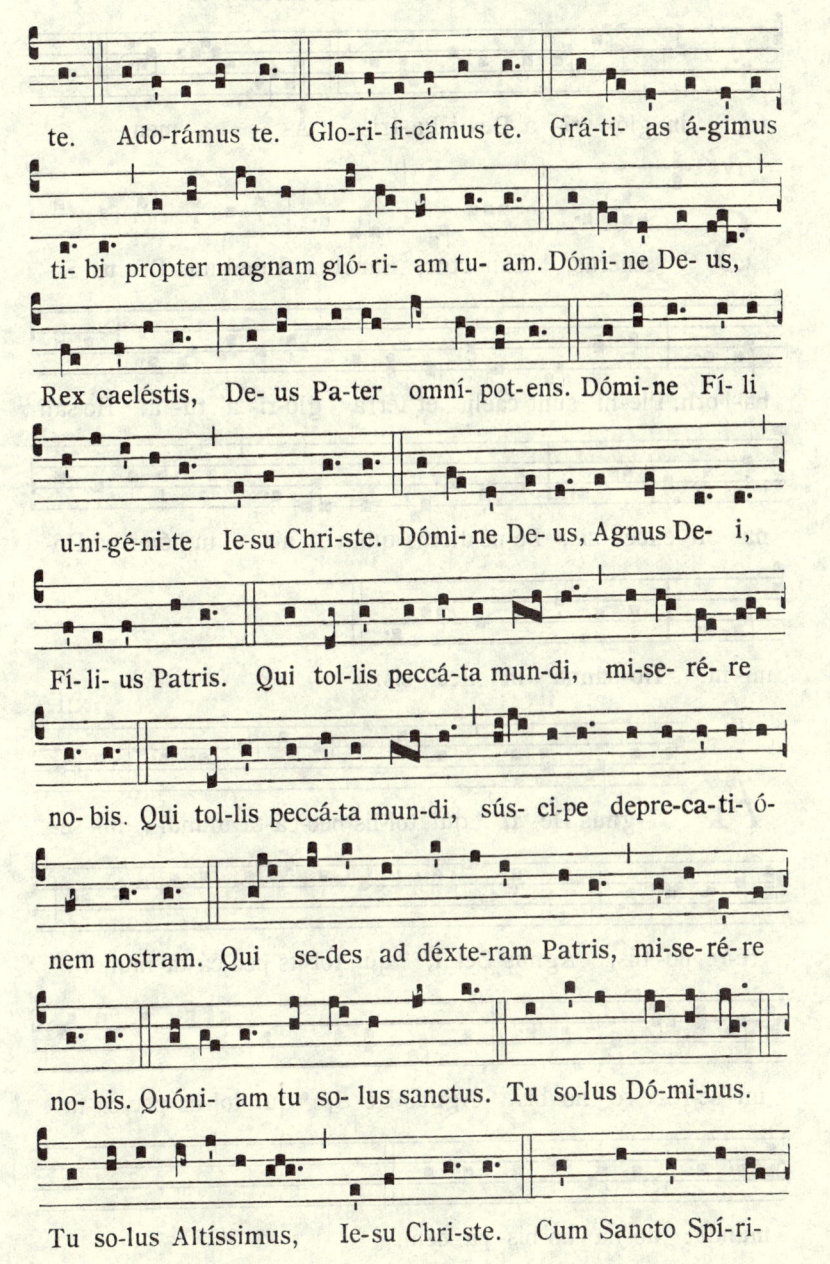

Chants of the Mass Ordinary X

te. Ado-rámus te. Glo-ri- fi-cámus te. Grá-ti- as á-gimus

ti- bi propter magnam gló- ri- am tu- am. Dómi- ne De- us,

Rex caeléstis, De- us Pa-ter omní- pot-ens. Dómi-ne Fí- li

u-ni-gé-ni-te Ie-su Chri-ste. Dómi- ne De- us, Agnus De- i,

Fí- li- us Patris. Qui tol-lis peccá-ta mun-di, mi-se- ré- re

no- bis. Qui tol-lis peccá-ta mun-di, sús- ci-pe depre-ca-ti- ó-

nem nostram. Qui se-des ad déxte-ram Patris, mi-se-ré-re

no- bis. Quóni- am tu so- lus sanctus. Tu so-lus Dó-mi-nus.

Tu so-lus Altíssimus, Ie-su Chri-ste. Cum Sancto Spí-ri-tu, in gló- ri- a De- i Pa-tris. A- men.

IV

Sanctus, * San-ctus, Sanctus Dómi-nus De- us Sába- oth. Ple-ni sunt caeli et terra gló-ri- a tu- a. Hosánna in excél- sis. Be-ne-díctus qui ve- nit in nómi-ne Dómi- ni. Ho-sánna in excél- sis.

IV   XII. s.

Agnus De- i, * qui tol-lis pec-cá-ta mundi : mi-se-ré-re no- bis. Agnus De- i, * qui tol-lis pec-cá-ta mundi : mi-se-ré- re no- bis. Agnus De- i, * qui tol-lis pec-cá-ta mundi : do-na no-bis pa- cem.

XI
ORDINARY SUNDAYS

Orbis factor

A   X. s.

Ký-ri-e * e- lé- i-son. *bis* Chri-ste e- lé- i-son. *bis* Ký-ri- e e- lé- i-son. Ký- ri- e e- lé- i-son.

B   (X) XIV-XVI. s.

Ký-ri-e * e- lé- i-son. *bis* Chri-ste e- lé- i-son. *bis* Ký-ri- e e- lé- i-son. Ký- ri- e e- lé- i-son.

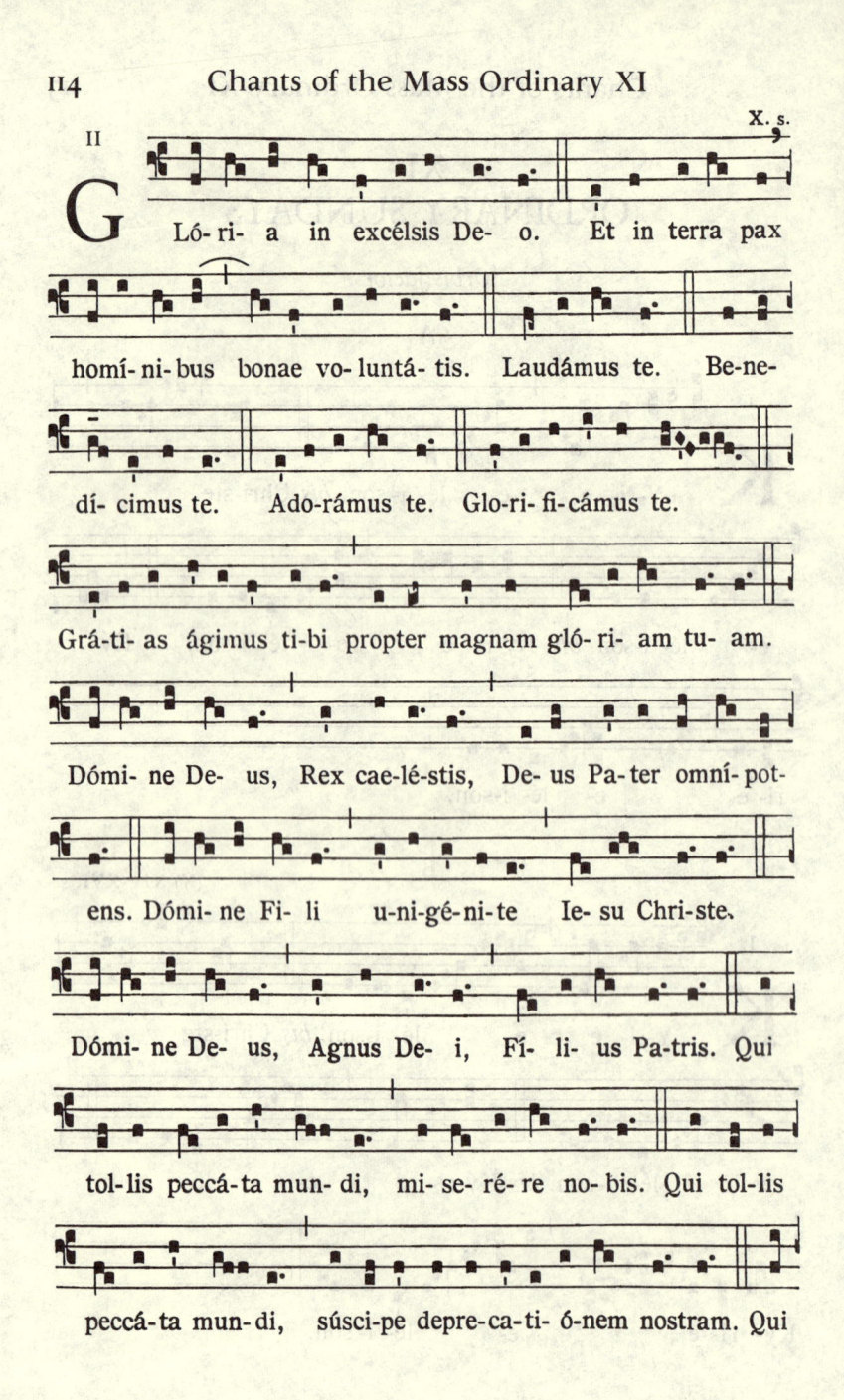

Chants of the Mass Ordinary XI

G Ló- ri- a in excélsis De- o. Et in terra pax homí- ni- bus bonae vo- luntá- tis. Laudámus te. Bene- dí- cimus te. Ado-rámus te. Glo-ri- fi-cámus te. Grá-ti- as ágimus ti-bi propter magnam gló- ri- am tu- am. Dómi- ne De- us, Rex cae-lé-stis, De- us Pa- ter omní- potens. Dómi- ne Fi- li u-ni-gé-ni-te Ie- su Chri-ste. Dómi- ne De- us, Agnus De- i, Fí- li- us Pa-tris. Qui tol-lis peccá-ta mun- di, mi- se- ré- re no- bis. Qui tol-lis peccá-ta mun- di, súsci-pe depre-ca-ti- ó-nem nostram. Qui

Chants of the Mass Ordinary XI

se-des ad déx-teram Pa-tris, mi-se-ré-re no-bis. Quóni- am tu so-lus sanctus. Tu so-lus Dómi-nus. Tu so- lus Altís-simus, Ie- su Chri-ste. Cum Sancto Spí- ri- tu, in gló- ri- a De- i Pa- tris. A- men.

XI. s.

S Anctus, * San-ctus, Sanctus Dó-mi-nus De- us Sá-ba-oth. Ple- ni sunt cae- li et ter- ra gló- ri- a tu- a Ho-sánna in ex- cél-sis. Be-ne-díctus qui ve-nit in nó- mi- ne Dó-mi- ni. Ho-sánna in ex- cél-sis.

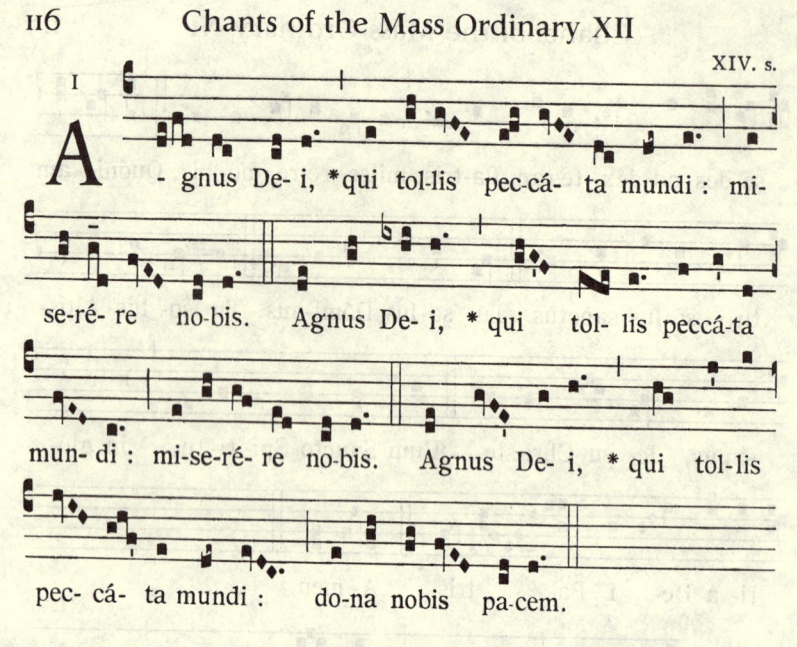

Chants of the Mass Ordinary XII

I   XIV. s.

A-gnus De- i, *qui tol-lis pec-cá- ta mundi : mi-se-ré- re no-bis. Agnus De- i, * qui tol- lis peccá-ta mun- di : mi-se-ré- re no-bis. Agnus De- i, * qui tol-lis pec- cá- ta mundi : do-na nobis pa-cem.

Other chants for Sundays: XIII & XIV.

XII

Pater cuncta

VIII   XII. s.

K Y-ri- e * e- lé- i-son. *bis* Christe e-lé- i-son. *bis* Ký-ri- e e- lé- i-son. Ký-ri- e e-lé- i-son.

Or Additional Kýrie IX, *p. 154.*

Chants of the Mass Ordinary XII

XII. s.

IV

Gló-ri-a in excélsis De- o. Et in terra pax homí-ni-bus bonae volunta- tis. Laudámus te. Bene-dí-ci-mus te. Ado-rámus te. Glo-ri-fi-cámus te. Grá-ti-as ági-mus ti-bi propter magnam gló-ri-am tu-am. Dómi-ne De-us, Rex caeléstis, De-us Pa-ter omní-pot-ens. Dómi-ne Fi-li u-ni-gé-ni-te Ie-su Chri-ste. Dómi-ne De-us, Agnus De-i, Fí-li-us Pa-tris. Qui tol-lis peccá-ta mundi, mi-se-ré-re no-bis. Qui tol-lis peccá-ta mundi, súsci-pe depre-ca-ti-ó-nem nostram. Qui se-des ad déxte-ram Patris, mi-se-ré-re no-bis. Quó-ni- am tu so- lus sanctus. Tu so-lus Dómi-nus.

Tu so-lus Altíssi-mus, Ie-su Christe. Cum Sancto Spí- ri-

tu, in gló-ri- a De- i Patris. A- men.

II   XIII. s.

S An- ctus, * Sanctus, San- ctus Dómi-nus

De- us Sá-ba- oth. Ple-ni sunt caeli et ter-ra gló-ri- a

tu- a. Ho-sánna in excél- sis. Be-ne-díctus qui ve-

nit in nó-mi-ne Dómi-ni. Ho-sánna in excél- sis.

II   XI. s.

A -gnus De- i, * qui tol- lis peccá- ta mundi:

Chants of the Mass Ordinary XIII

mi- se- ré- re no- bis. Agnus De- i, * qui tollis peccá-ta mun-di : mi-se- ré-re no- bis. Agnus De- i, * qui tol- lis peccá- ta mundi : do-na no-bis pa- cem.

XIII

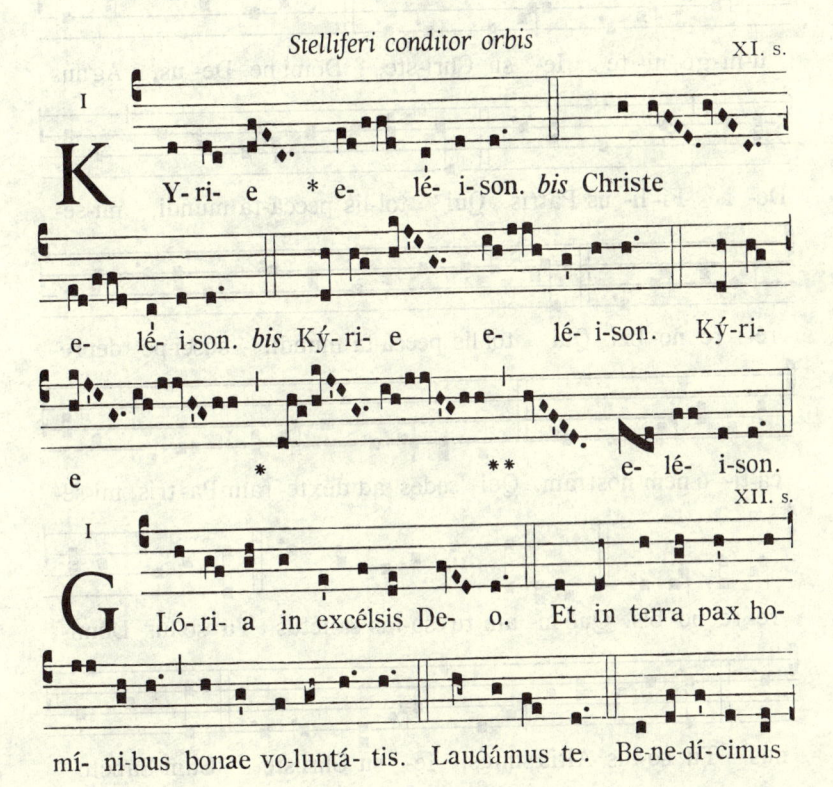

Stelliferi conditor orbis

XI. s.

KY-ri- e * e- lé- i-son. *bis* Christe e- lé- i-son. *bis* Ký-ri- e e- lé- i-son. Ký-ri- e * ** e- lé- i-son.

XII. s.

GLó-ri- a in excélsis De- o. Et in terra pax ho- mí- ni-bus bonae vo-luntá- tis. Laudámus te. Be-ne-dí-cimus

Chants of the Mass Ordinary XIII

te. Ado-rámus te. Glo-ri-fi-cámus te. Grá-ti-as á-gimus ti-bi propter magnam gló-ri-am tu-am. Dómi-ne De-us, Rex cae-lé-stis, De-us Pa-ter omní-pot-ens. Dómi-ne Fi-li u-ni-gé-ni-te Ie-su Chri-ste. Dómi-ne De-us, Agnus De-i, Fí-li-us Patris. Qui tol-lis peccá-ta mundi, mi-se-ré-re no-bis. Qui tol-lis peccá-ta mundi, súsci-pe depre-ca-ti-ó-nem nostram. Qui sedes ad déxte-ram Pa-tris, mi-se-ré-re no-bis. Quó-ni-am tu so-lus sanctus. Tu so-lus Dómi-nus. Tu so-lus Altís-simus, Ie-su Chri-ste. Cum Sancto

Chants of the Mass Ordinary XIII

Spí-ri-tu, in gló-ri- a De- i Pa-tris. A- men.

XIII. s.

VIII

SAnctus, * Sanctus, Sanctus Dóminus De- us Sá- ba- oth. Ple-ni sunt caeli et terra gló-ri- a tu- a. Ho-sán-na in ex- cél-sis. Be-ne-díctus qui ve- nit in nómi-ne Dómi- ni. Ho-sánna in ex-cél-sis.

I

A-gnus De- i, * qui tol-lis pec- cá-ta mun- di : mi-se-ré-re 'no-bis. Agnus De- i, * qui tol- lis pec- cá-ta mundi : mi-se-ré- re no- bis. Agnus De- i, * qui tol-lis pec- cá-ta mun- di : do-na no-bis 'pa-cem.

XIV

Iesu redemptor

VIII   Ký-ri-e * e-lé-i-son. *bis* Chri-ste e-lé-i-son. *bis* Ký-ri-e e-lé-i-son. Ký-ri-e e-lé-i-son.

III   Gló-ri-a in excélsis De-o. Et in ter-ra pax ho-mí-ni-bus bonae vo-luntá-tis. Laudámus te. Bene-dí-cimus te. Ado-rámus te. Glo-ri-fi-cá-mus te. Grá-ti-as á-gimus ti-bi propter magnam gló-ri-am tu-am.

Chants of the Mass Ordinary XIV

Dómi-ne De- us, Rex cae- lé- stis, De-us Pa-ter omní-pot-ens. Dómi-ne Fi-li u-ni-gé-ni-te Ie-su Chri-ste. Dó-mi-ne De-us, Agnus De-i, Fí-li-us Pa-tris. Qui tol-lis peccá-ta mun-di, mi-se- ré- re no-bis. Qui tol-lis peccá-ta mun-di, sús-ci-pe depre-ca-ti-ó-nem no-stram. Qui se-des ad déxte-ram Pa-tris, mi-se- ré-re no-bis. Quóni-am tu so-lus sanctus. Tu so-lus Dómi-nus. Tu so-lus Altíssi-mus, Ie-su Chri-ste. Cum Sancto Spí-ri-tu, in gló-ri-a De-i Pa-tris. A- men.

Chants of the Mass Ordinary XIV

XII. s.

SAnctus, * Sanctus, Sanctus Dómi- nus De- us Sá- ba- oth. Pleni sunt cae- li et ter- ra gló-ri- a tu- a. Ho- sánna in excél- sis. Be- ne- dí- ctus qui ve- nit in nómi- ne Dó- mi- ni. Ho- sánna in excél- sis.

XIII s.

A-gnus De- i, * qui tol- lis peccá- ta mundi : mi- se-ré- re no- bis. Agnus De- i, * qui tol-lis peccá- ta mun- di : mi-se-ré- re no- bis. Agnus De- i, * qui tol- lis pec-

Chants of the Mass Ordinary XV

cá- ta mundi : do-na no- bis pa- cem.

XV

Dominator Deus

XI-XIII. s.

IV

KY-ri- e * e- lé- i-son. Ký-ri- e e- lé- i- son.

Ký-ri- e e- lé- i-son. Christe e- lé- i-son. Chri- ste

e- lé- i-son. Christe e- lé- i-son. Ký-ri- e

e- lé- i-son. Ký-ri- e e- lé- i-son. Ký-ri- e e-

lé- i-son.

X. s.

IV

GLó-ri- a in excélsis De- o. Et in terra pax homí-

ni-bus bonae vo-luntá-tis. Laudámus te. Be-ne-dí-cimus te.

Adorámus te. Glorificámus te. Grátias ágimus tibi propter magnam glóriam tuam. Dómine Deus, Rex caeléstis, Deus Pater omnípotens. Dómine Fili unigénite Iesu Christe. Dómine Deus, Agnus Dei, Fílius Patris. Qui tollis peccáta mundi, miserére nobis. Qui tollis peccáta mundi, súscipe deprecatiónem nostram. Qui sedes ad déxteram Patris, miserére nobis. Quóniam tu solus sanctus. Tu solus Dóminus. Tu solus Altíssimus, Iesu Christe. Cum Sancto Spíritu, in gló-ri- a De- i Pa- tris. A- men.

X. s.

SAnctus, * Sanctus, Sanctus Dómi-nus De- us Sá-ba- oth. Ple-ni sunt cae-li et ter-ra gló- ri- a tu- a. Ho- sánna in excél- sis. Be-ne-díctus qui ve- nit in nómi-ne Dó-mi-ni. Ho- sánna in excél-sis.

(XII) XIV. s.

A-gnus De- i, * qui tol-lis peccá-ta mundi : mi-se-ré- re no- bis. Agnus De- i, * qui tol- lis peccá-ta mun-di : mi-se-ré- re no- bis. Agnus De- i, * qui tol-lis peccá-ta mundi : dona no- bis pa- cem.

XVI
IN ORDINARY TIME DURING THE WEEK

XI-XIII. s.

III

KY-ri- e * e-lé- i-son. *bis* Christe e-lé- i-son. *bis* Ký-ri- e e-lé- i-son. Ký-ri- e e-lé- i-son.

XIII. s.

II

SAnctus, * Sanctus, Sanctus Dómi-nus De- us Sába- oth. Ple-ni sunt cae-li et terra gló-ri- a tu- a. Hosán- na in excél- sis. Bene-díctus qui ve- nit in nó-mi- ne Dómi-ni. Ho-sánna in excél- sis.

X-XI. s.

I

A-gnus De- i, * qui tol-lis peccá-ta mun- di : mi-se-ré- re no- bis. Agnus De- i, * qui tol-lis peccá-ta mundi : mi-se-ré-re no-bis. Agnus De- i, * qui tol-lis pec-

cá-ta mun- di : do-na no- bis pa- cem.

XVII
SUNDAYS
IN ADVENT & IN LENT

A
Kyrie salve

X. s.

KY-ri- e * e- lé- i-son. *bis* Chri- ste

e- lé- i-son. *bis* Ký-ri- e e- lé- i-son.

Ký-ri- e * ** e- lé- i-son.

B

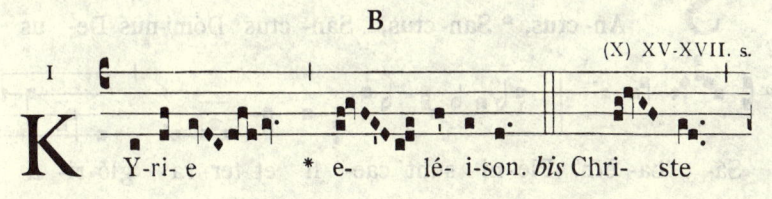

(X) XV-XVII. s.

KY-ri- e * e- lé- i-son. *bis* Chri- ste

Chants of the Mass Ordinary XVII

e- lé- i-son. *bis* Ký-ri- e e- lé- i-son.

Ký- ri- e * ** e- lé- i-son.

C

VI   XIV. s.

KY-ri- e * e- lé- i-son. *bis* Christe e- lé- i-son. *bis* Ký-ri- e e- lé- i-son. Ký-ri- e * ** e- lé- i-son.

V   XI. s.

SAn- ctus, * San- ctus, San- ctus Dómi-nus De- us Sá- ba- oth. Ple-ni sunt cae- li et ter-ra gló-ri- a

Chants of the Mass Ordinary XVII

tu- a. Ho- sánna in excél- sis. Be- ne- díctus qui ve- nit in nó- mi-ne Dómi- ni. Ho- sánna in excél- sis.

XIII. s.

A-gnus De- i, * qui tol- lis peccá- ta mundi : mi- se-ré-re no- bis. Agnus De- i, * qui tol- lis peccá- ta mun- di : mi-se-ré-re no- bis. Agnus De- i, * qui tol- lis pec- cá- ta mundi : do-na no-bis pa- cem.

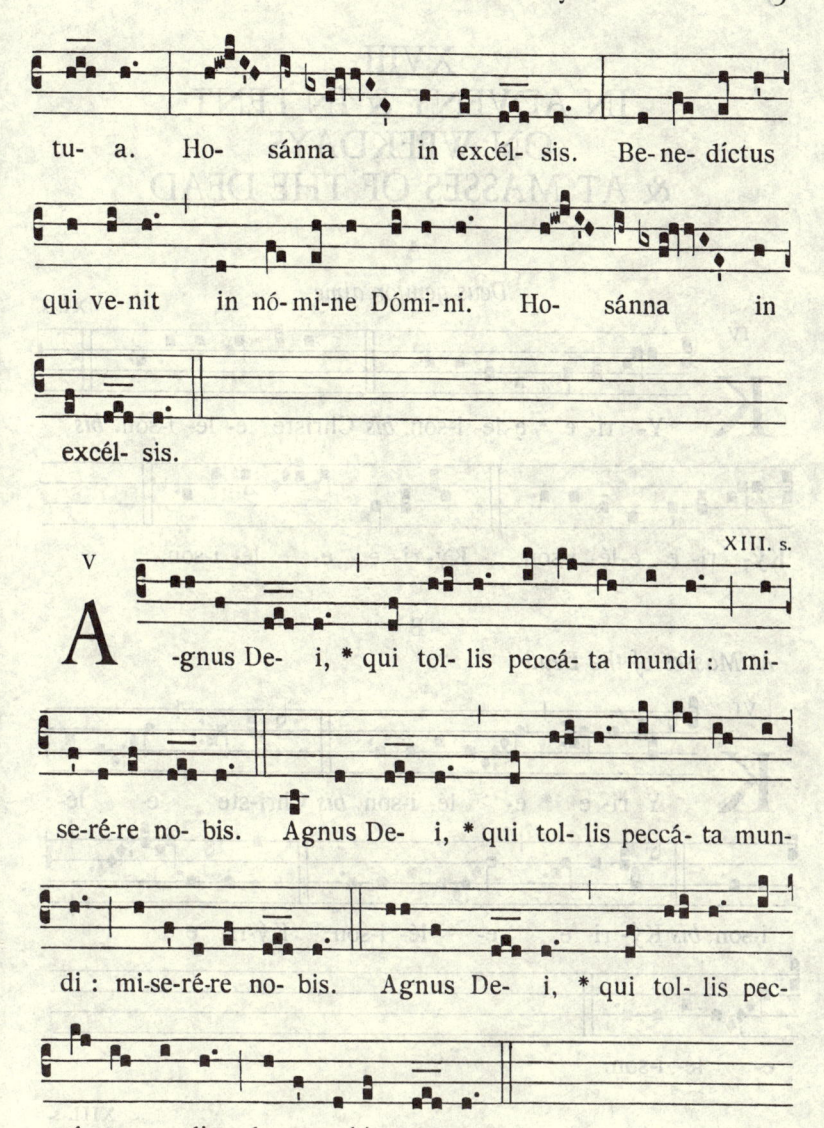

XVIII
IN ADVENT & IN LENT
ON WEEKDAYS
& AT MASSES OF THE DEAD

A

Deus genitor alme

XI. s.

KYrie * eléison. *bis* Christe eléison. *bis* Kýrie eléison. Kýrie eléison.

B

At Masses of the Dead:

KYrie * eléison. *bis* Christe eléison. *bis* Kýrie eléison. Kýrie eléison.

XIII. s.

SAnctus, * Sanctus, Sanctus Dóminus Deus Sá-

Chants of the Mass Ordinary XVIII

ba-oth. Ple-ni sunt caeli et terra gló-ri-a tu-a. Ho-sánna in excélsis. Be-ne-díctus qui ve-nit in nómine Dómi-ni. Ho-sánna in excélsis.

XII. s.

A-gnus De-i, *qui tol-lis peccá-ta mundi : mi-se-ré-re no-bis. Agnus De-i, *qui tol-lis peccá-ta mundi : mi-se-ré-re no-bis. Agnus De-i, *qui tol-lis peccá-ta mun-di : do-na no-bis pa-cem.

CREDO

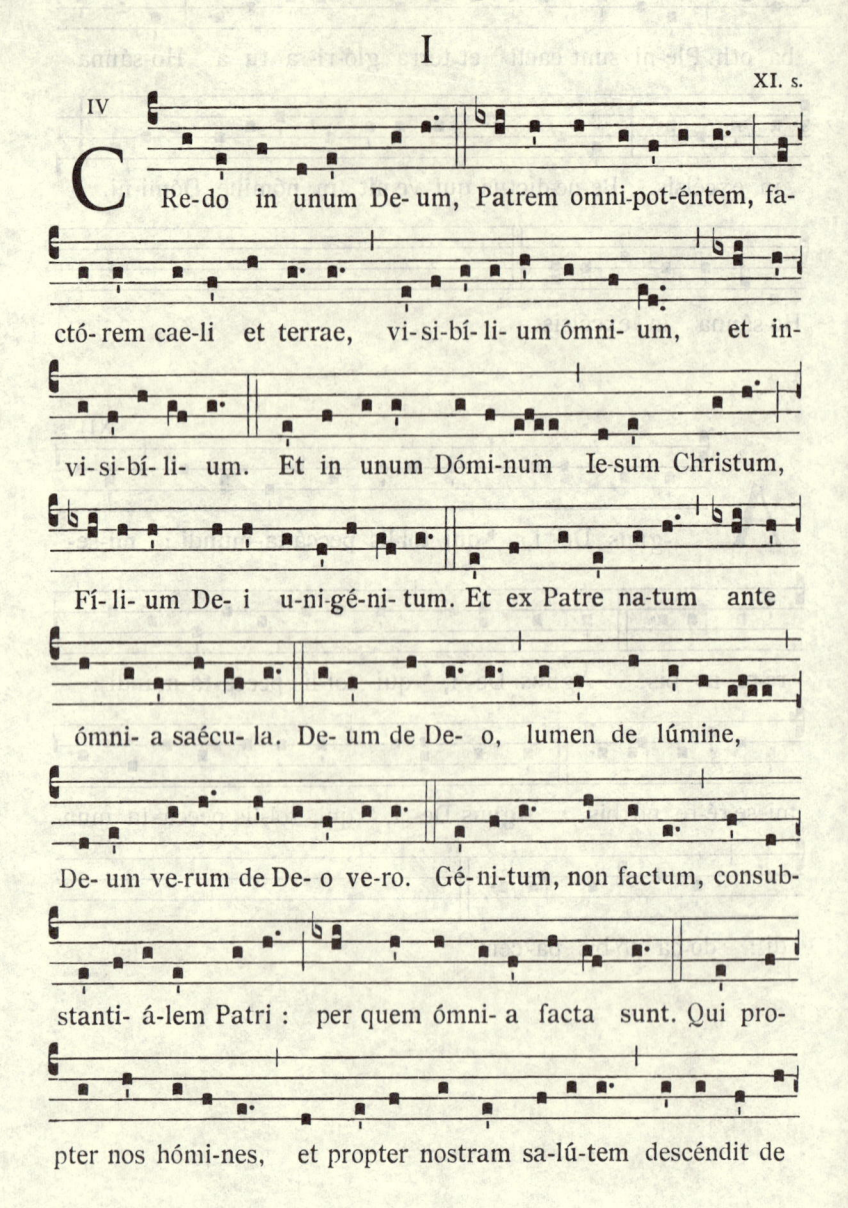

I

IV   XI. s.

Credo in unum Deum, Patrem omni-pot-éntem, factórem caeli et terrae, vi-si-bí-li-um ómni-um, et in-vi-si-bí-li-um. Et in unum Dómi-num Ie-sum Christum, Fí-li-um De- i u-ni-gé-ni-tum. Et ex Patre na-tum ante ómni-a saécu-la. De-um de De-o, lumen de lúmine, De-um ve-rum de De-o ve-ro. Gé-ni-tum, non factum, consubstanti-á-lem Patri : per quem ómni-a facta sunt. Qui propter nos hómi-nes, et propter nostram sa-lú-tem descéndit de

Credo I

cae-lis. Et incarná-tus est de Spí-ri-tu Sancto ex Ma-rí- a

Vírgi- ne : Et homo factus est. Cru-ci- fí-xus ét-i- am pro

no-bis : sub Pónti- o Pi- lá-to passus, et sepúl-tus est. Et

re-surréxit térti- a di- e, se-cúndum Scriptú-ras. Et ascén-

dit in caelum : se-det ad déxte-ram Patris. Et í-te-rum ven-

tú-rus est cum gló-ri- a, iu-di-cá-re vivos et mórtu- os :

cu-ius regni non e- rit fi- nis. Et in Spí- ri- tum Sanctum,

Dómi-num, et vi-vi- fi-cántem : qui ex Patre Fi- li- óque pro-

cé- dit. Qui cum Patre et Fí- li- o simul ad-o-rá-tur, et

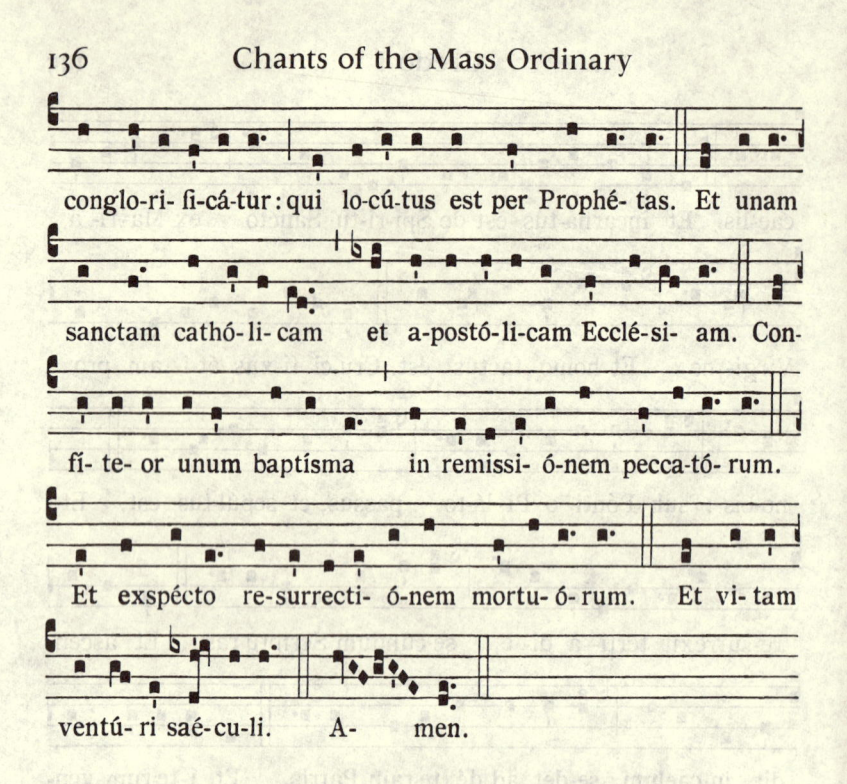

conglo-ri- fi-cá-tur : qui lo-cú-tus est per Prophé- tas. Et unam

sanctam cathó- li- cam et a-postó-li-cam Ecclé-si- am. Con-

fí- te- or unum baptísma in remissi- ó-nem pecca-tó- rum.

Et exspécto re-surrecti- ó-nem mortu- ó- rum. Et vi- tam

ventú- ri saé-cu-li. A- men.

II

IV

CRe-do in unum De- um, Patrem omni-pot-éntem,

factó-rem cae-li et terrae, vi- si- bí- li- um ómni- um, et

invi-si-bí-li- um. Et in unum Dómi-num Ie-sum Christum,

Credo II

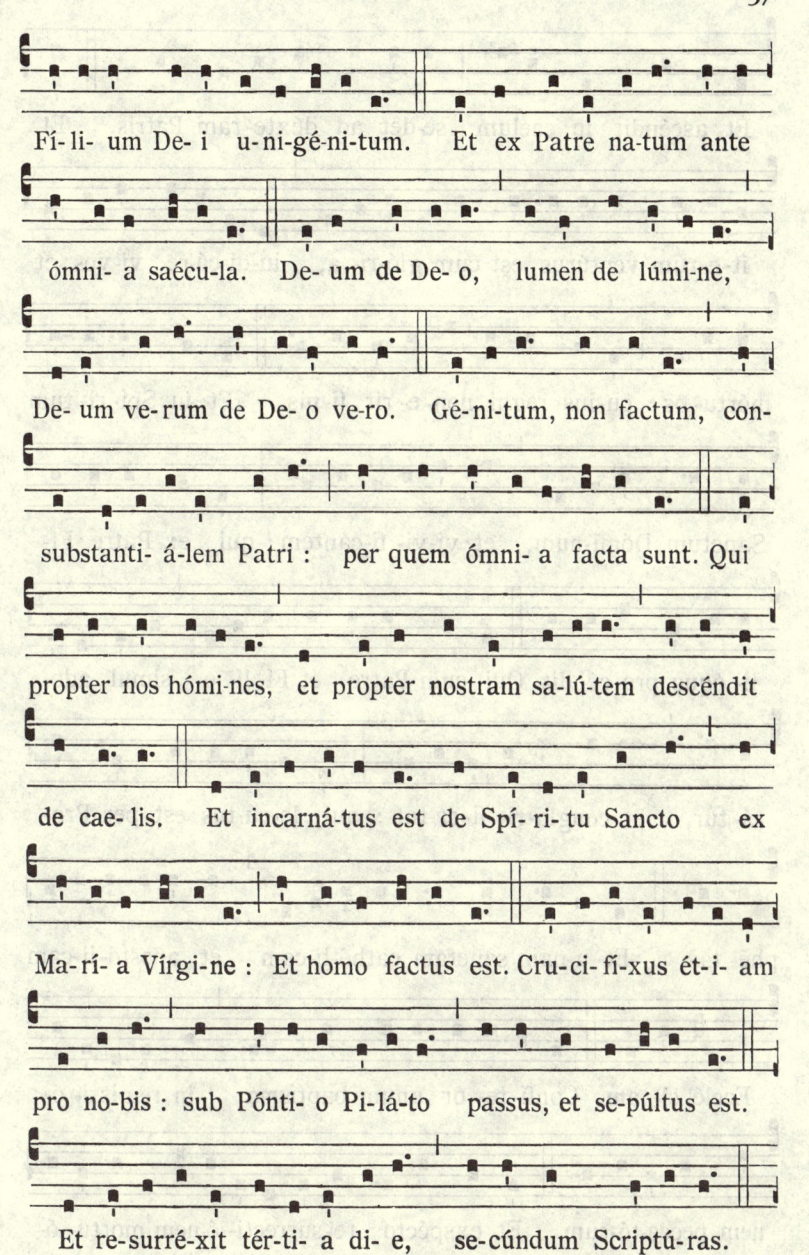

Fí-li-um De-i u-ni-gé-ni-tum. Et ex Patre na-tum ante ómni-a saécu-la. De-um de De-o, lumen de lúmi-ne, De-um ve-rum de De-o ve-ro. Gé-ni-tum, non factum, consubstanti-á-lem Patri : per quem ómni-a facta sunt. Qui propter nos hómi-nes, et propter nostram sa-lú-tem descéndit de cae-lis. Et incarná-tus est de Spí-ri-tu Sancto ex Ma-rí-a Vírgi-ne : Et homo factus est. Cru-ci-fí-xus ét-i-am pro no-bis : sub Pónti-o Pi-lá-to passus, et se-púltus est. Et re-surré-xit tér-ti-a di-e, se-cúndum Scriptú-ras.

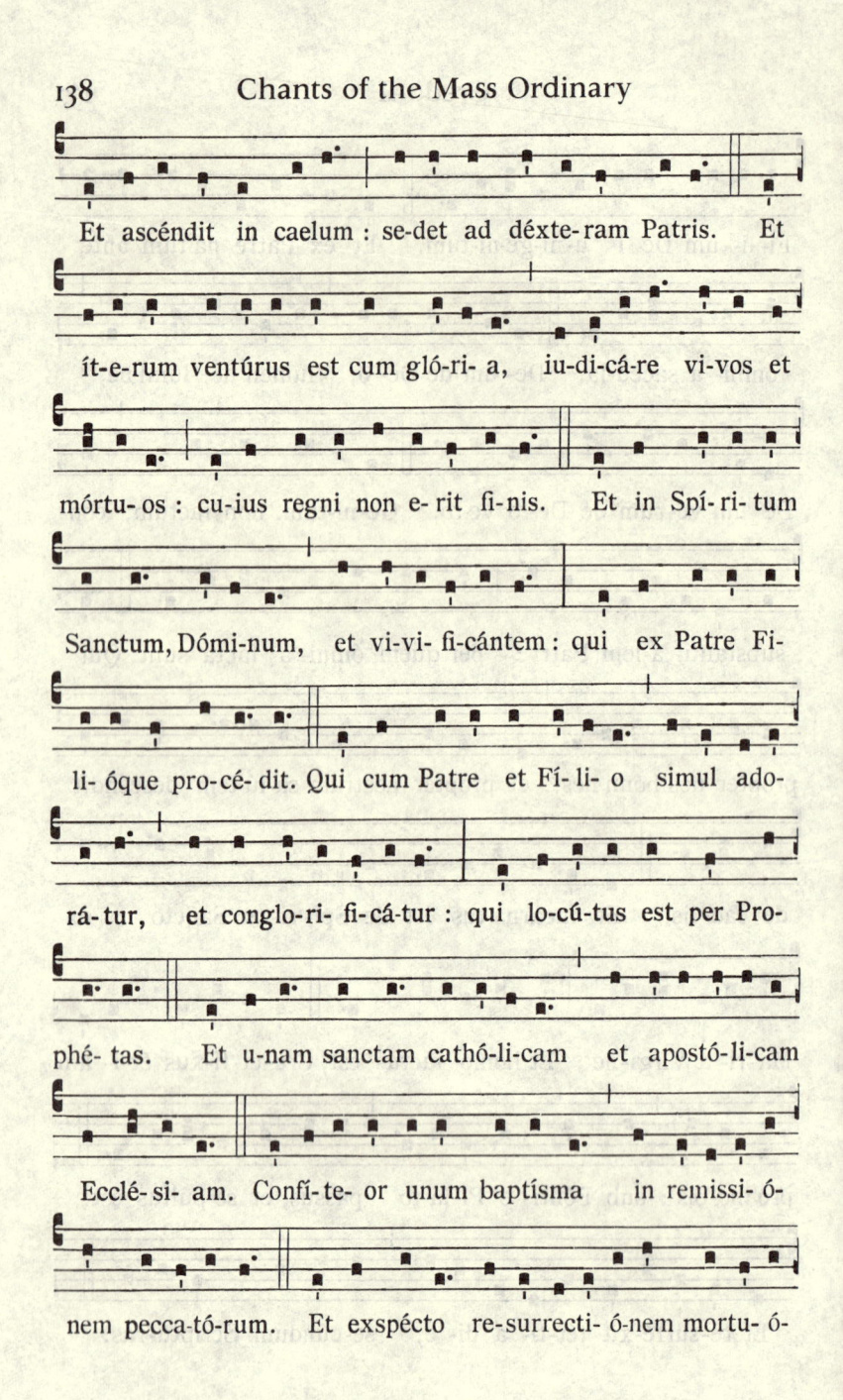

Et ascéndit in caelum : se-det ad déxte-ram Patris. Et ít-e-rum ventúrus est cum gló-ri- a, iu-di-cá-re vi-vos et mórtu- os : cu-ius regni non e- rit fi-nis. Et in Spí- ri- tum Sanctum, Dómi-num, et vi-vi- fi-cántem : qui ex Patre Fí- li- óque pro-cé- dit. Qui cum Patre et Fí- li- o simul ado-rá- tur, et conglo-ri- fi-cá-tur : qui lo-cú-tus est per Pro-phé- tas. Et u-nam sanctam cathó-li-cam et apostó-li-cam Ecclé- si- am. Confí- te- or unum baptísma in remissi- ó-nem pecca-tó-rum. Et exspécto re-surrecti- ó-nem mortu- ó-rum. Et vi-tam ventú-ri saécu-li. A- men.

III

XVII. s.

CRedo in unum De- um, Patrem omni-pot-éntem, factó- rem caeli et terrae, vi- si-bí-li- um ó-mni- um, et in- vi- si- bí- li- um. Et in unum Dómi-num Ie- sum Christum, Fí- li- um De- i u-ni-gé-ni-tum. Et ex Patre na- tum ante ómni- a saé- cu- la. De- um de De- o, lumen de lúmi-ne, De- um ve-rum de De- o ve- ro. Gé-ni-tum, non fa- ctum, con- substanti- á-lem Patri : per quem ómni- a fa-cta sunt. Qui propter nos hómines, et propter nostram sa- lú- tem descén-

dit de cae-lis. Et incarná-tus est de Spí-ri-tu Sancto ex

Ma- rí- a Vírgi-ne : Et homo factus est. Cru- ci- fí- xus

ét-i- am pro no-bis : sub Pónti- o Pi-lá-to passus, et se-púl-

tus est. Et re-surré-xit térti- a di- e, se-cúndum Scri-

ptú-ras. Et ascéndit in cae- lum : se-det ad déxte- ram Pa-

tris. Et í-te-rum ventú-rus est cum gló-ri- a, iu-di-cá-re

vi-vos et mórtu- os : cu-ius regni non e- rit fi- nis. Et in

Spí- ri- tum Sanctum, Dómi-num, et vi- vi- fi-cántem : qui ex

Credo IV

... Patre Fi- li- óque pro- cé-dit. Qui cum Patre et Fí- li- o simul ad-o-rá-tur, et conglo- ri- fi-cá-tur : qui lo-cú-tus est per Prophé-tas. Et unam sanctam cathó- li-cam et a-po- stó- li- cam Ecclé- si- am. Confí- te- or unum ba-ptísma in remissi- ó-nem pecca-tó- rum. Et exspécto re-surre- cti- ó-nem mortu- ó-rum. Et vi- tam ventú-ri saé-cu- li. A- men.

IV

XV. s.

Credo in unum De- um, Patrem omni-pot-én- tem, factó-rem cae-li et ter- rae, vi-si-bí- li- um ómni- um, et invi-si-bí-li-um. Et in unum Dómi-num Ie-sum Chri-stum,

Fí-li-um De- i u-ni-gé-ni-tum. Et ex Patre na-tum ante

ómni-a saécu-la. De-um de De-o, lumen de lúmi-ne,

De-um ve-rum de De-o ve-ro. Gé-ni-tum, non factum, con-

substanti-á-lem Pa-tri : per quem ómni-a facta sunt. Qui

propter nos hómi-nes, et propter nostram sa-lú-tem descéndit

de cae- lis. Et incarná-tus est de Spí-ri-tu Sancto ex

Ma-rí-a Vírgi-ne : Et homo factus est. Cru-ci-fí-xus ét-i-am

pro no- bis: sub Pónti-o Pi-lá- to passus, et se-púl-tus est.

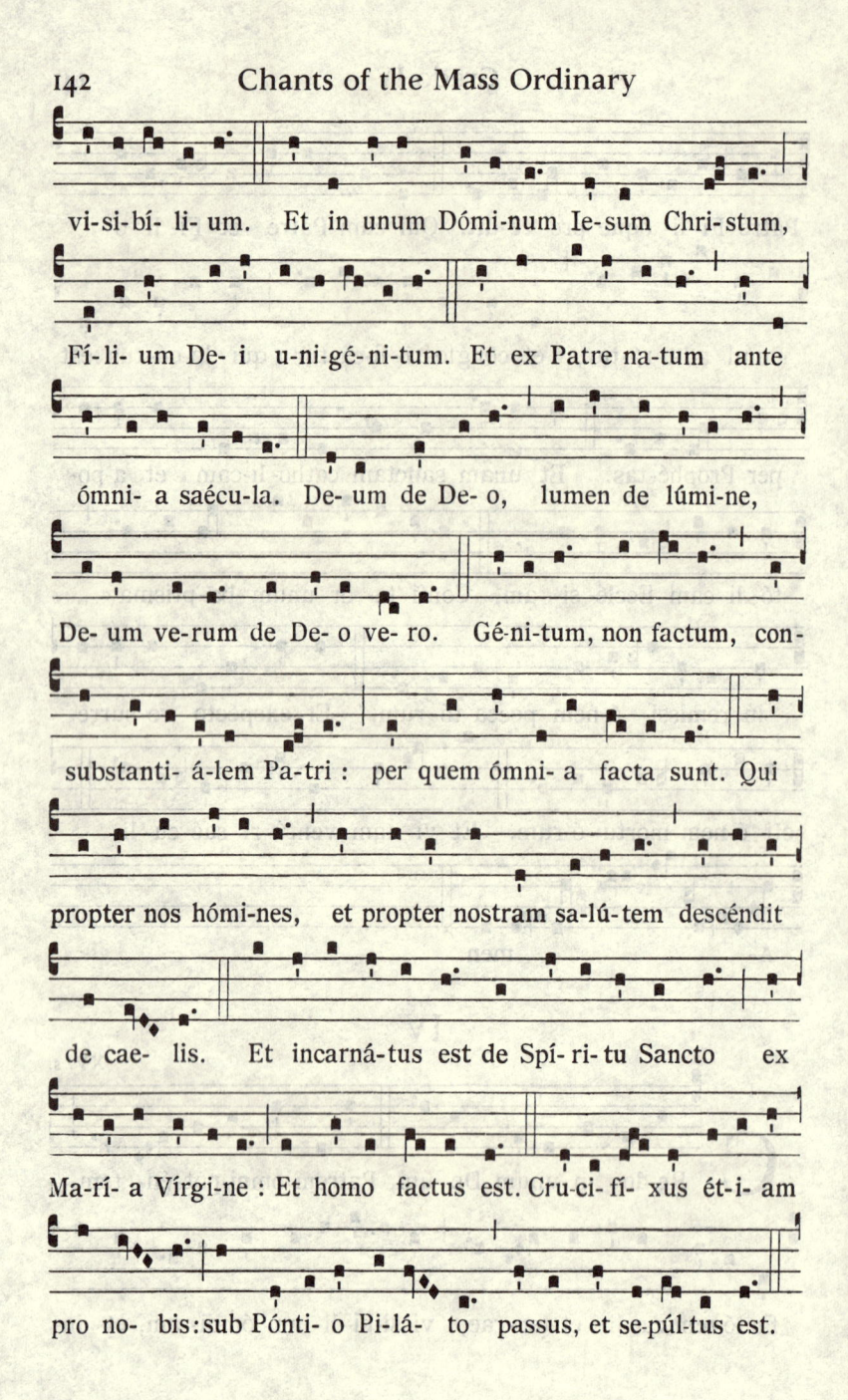

Credo IV

Et re-surréxit térti- a di- e, se-cúndum Scriptú- ras. Et ascéndit in caelum : se-det ad déxte-ram Patris. Et í-te-rum ventúrus est cum gló-ri- a, iu-di-cá- re vi-vos et mórtu- os : cu-ius regni non e-rit fi- nis. Et in Spí- ri-tum Sanctum, Dó-mi-num, et vi-vi- fi-cántem : qui ex Patre Fi- li- óque pro-cé-dit. Qui cum Patre et Fí- li- o simul ad-o-rá-tur, et con-glo-ri- fi-cá-tur : qui lo-cú-tus est per Prophé- tas. Et unam sanctam cathó-li-cam et apostó- li-cam Ecclé-si- am. Confi-te- or unum baptísma in remissi- ónem pecca-tó- rum.

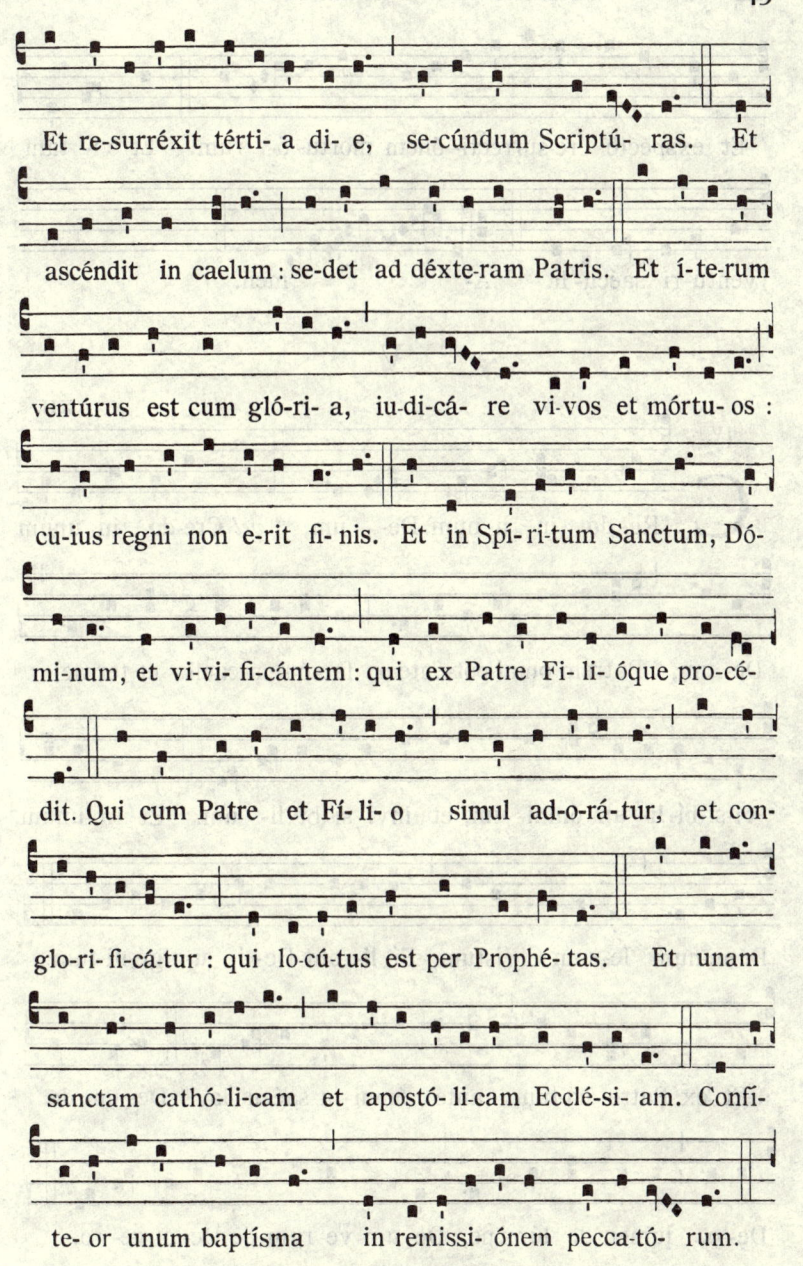

Et exspécto re-surrecti- ónem mortu- ó- rum. Et vi- tam ventú-ri saécu- li. A- men.

V

IV — XII. s.

Credo in unum Deum, * *vel* Credo in unum Deum, * Patrem omni-pot-éntem, factó-rem caeli et terrae, vi-si-bí-li- um ómni- um, et invi- si-bí-li- um. Et in unum Dómi-num Ie-sum Christum, Fí- li- um De- i u-nigé-ni-tum. Et ex Patre na-tum ante ómni- a saécu- la. De- um de De- o, lumen de lúmi-ne, De- um ve-rum de De- o ve- ro.

Credo V

Génitum, non factum, consubstanti- á-lem Patri : per quem ómni- a facta sunt. Qui propter nos hómi-nes et propter nostram sa-lú- tem descéndit de cae- lis. Et incarnátus est de Spí- ri-tu Sancto ex Ma-rí- a Vírgi- ne : Et ho-mo factus est. Cru-ci-fí-xus ét-i- am pro no-bis : sub Pónti- o Pi-lá-to passus, et se-púltus est. Et re-surré-xit térti- a di- e, se-cúndum Scriptú- ras. Et ascéndit in caelum : se-det ad déxte-ram Patris. Et í-te-rum ventú-rus est cum gló-ri- a, iu-di-cá-re vi-vos et mórtu- os : cu-ius regni non e-rit fi- nis. Et in Spí- ri-tum Sanctum, Dómi-num, et vi-vi-fi-cántem : qui ex Patre Fi- li- óque pro- cé- dit. Qui cum Patre et Fí- li- o simul ado-rá-tur, et conglo-ri- fi- cá-tur : qui lo-cú-tus est per Prophé- tas. Et unam sanctam cathó-li-cam et apostó- li-cam Ecclé-si- am. Confí-te- or unum baptísma in remissi- ó-nem pecca- tó- rum. Et ex-spécto re- surrecti- ó-nem mortu- ó-rum. Et vi-tam ventú-ri saécu-li. A- men.

VI

Credo in unum Deum, * vel Credo in unum Deum * Patrem omnipoténtem, factórem caeli et terrae, visibílium ómnium, et invisibílium. Et in unum Dóminum Iesum Christum, Fílium Dei unigénitum. Et ex Patre natum ante ómnia saécula. Deum de Deo, lumen de lúmine, Deum verum de Deo vero. Génitum, non factum, consubstantiálem Patri: per quem ómnia facta sunt. Qui propter nos hómi-nes, et propter nostram sa-lú- tem descéndit de cae- lis.

Et incarná-tus est de Spí-ri-tu Sancto ex Ma-rí- a Vír-

gi- ne : Et homo factus est. Cru-ci- fí-xus ét- i- am pro

no- bis : sub Pónti- o Pi-lá- to passus, et sepúltus est.

Et re-surré-xit térti- a di- e, se-cúndum Scriptú- ras.

Et ascéndit in cae-lum : se-det ad déxte-ram Pa- tris.

Et í-te-rum ventú-rus est cum gló-ri- a iu-di-cá- re vi-vos et

mórtu- os : cu-ius regni non e-rit fi- nis. Et in Spí-

ri-tum Sanctum, Dómi-num, et vi-vi-fi-cán- tem : qui ex

Credo VI

Pa-tre Fi-li-óque pro-cé- dit. Qui cum Pa-tre et Fí-li-o simul ado-rá-tur, et conglo-ri-fi-cá- tur : qui lo-cú-tus est per Prophé- tas. Et u-nam sanctam cathó-li-cam et apo-stó-li-cam Ecclé-si- am. Confí-te- or u-num baptísma in remissi- ó-nem pecca-tó- rum. Et exspé-cto re-surrecti-ó-nem mortu- ó- rum. Et vi- tam ventú-ri saécu- li.

Amen.

150

Chants of the Mass Ordinary

A CHOICE OF ADDITIONAL CHANTS

KYRIE

I
Clemens rector

X. s.

Ký-ri-e * e- lé-i-son. Ký-ri-e e- lé- i-son. Ký-ri-e e- lé-i-son. Chri-ste e- lé-i-son. Chri-ste e- lé-i-son. Chri-ste e- lé-i-son. Ký-ri-e e- lé-i-son. Ký-ri-e

Additional Chants – Kyrie

e- lé- i-son. Ký- ri- e * *

* ** e- lé- i-son.

II

Summe Deus

KY-ri- e * e- lé- i-son. Ký-ri- e

e- lé- i-son. Ký-ri- e e- lé- i-son. Chri-

ste e- lé- i-son. Christe e- lé- i-son.

Christe e- lé- i-son. Ký- ri- e e-

lé- i-son. Ký-ri- e e- lé- i-son. Ký- ri-

Chants of the Mass Ordinary

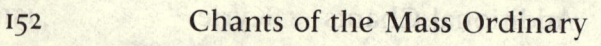

e　　　　*　　　　　**　e- lé- i-son.

III

Cf. III A, p. 86.

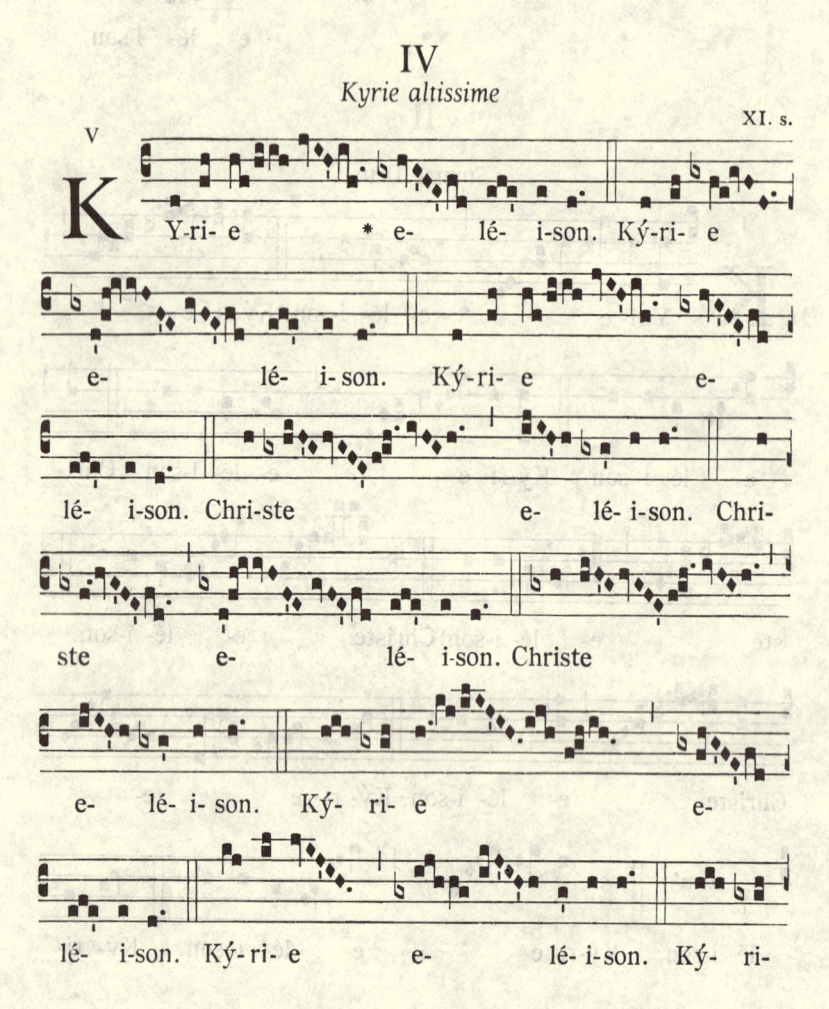

IV
Kyrie altissime

V   XI. s.

Ký-ri- e　　*　e- lé- i-son. Ký-ri- e

e- lé- i-son. Ký-ri- e　　　　　e-

lé- i-son. Chri-ste　　　　e- lé- i-son. Chri-

ste　　　e- 　　lé- i-son. Christe

e- lé- i-son. Ký- ri- e　　　　　　e-

lé- i-son. Ký-ri- e　　　e- 　　lé- i-son. Ký- ri-

Additional Chants – Kyrie

e　　　　　　　　*　　　　** e- lé- i-son.

V. Cf. I B, p. 76.
VI. Cf. I A, p. 75.

VII

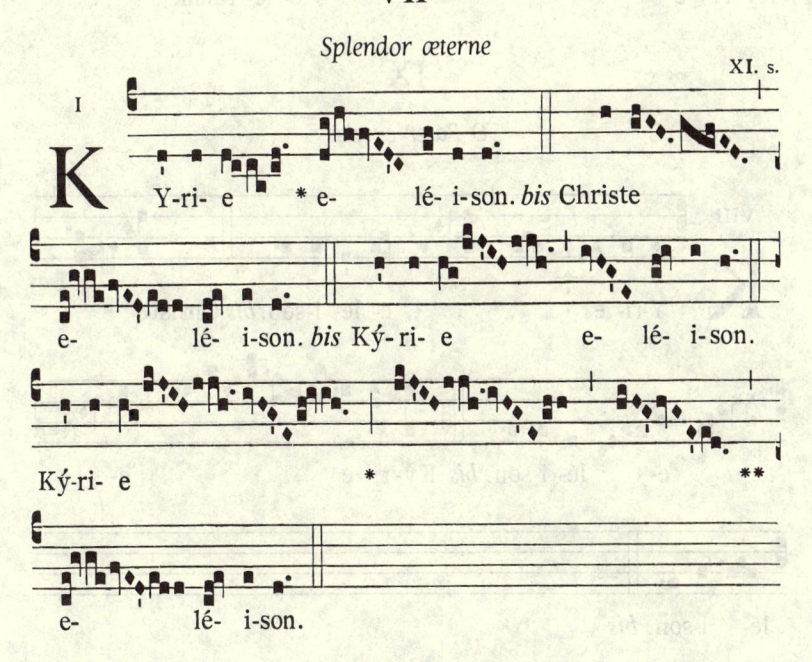

Splendor æterne

XI. s.

I

Ký-ri- e　　* e- lé- i-son. *bis* Christe

e- lé- i-son. *bis* Ký-ri- e　　e- lé- i-son.

Ký-ri- e　　　　*　　　　　　**

e- lé- i-son.

VIII

Firmator sancte

XIII. s.

VI

Ký-ri- e　　* e-lé- i- son. *bis* Chri-ste

Chants of the Mass Ordinary

e- lé- i- son. *bis* Ký-ri- e   e- lé- i- son.

Ký-ri- e   e- lé- i- son.

IX

O Pater excelse

XI. s.

VIII

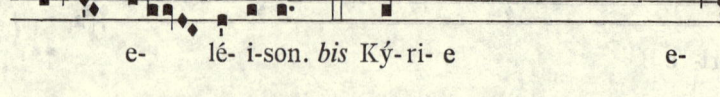

K Y-ri- e * e- lé- i- son. *bis* Christe

e- lé- i- son. *bis* Ký-ri- e   e-

lé- i-son. *bis*

X. *Cf.* XI A, p. *113*.
XI. *Cf.* XVII A, p. *129*.

GLORIA

I

VIII. Glória in excélsis Deo. Et in terra pax homínibus bonae voluntátis. Laudámus te. Benedícimus te. Adorámus te. Glorificámus te. Grátias ágimus tibi propter magnam glóriam tuam. Dómine Deus, Rex caeléstis, Deus Pater omnípotens. Dómine Fili unigénite Iesu Christe. Dómine Deus, Agnus Dei, Fílius Patris. Qui tollis peccáta mundi, miserére nobis. Qui tollis peccáta mundi, súscipe deprecatiónem nostram. Qui sedes ad déxteram Patris, miserére nobis. Quóniam tu solus sanctus. Tu solus Dóminus. Tu solus Altíssimus, Iesu Christe. Cum Sancto Spíritu, in glória Dei Patris. Amen.

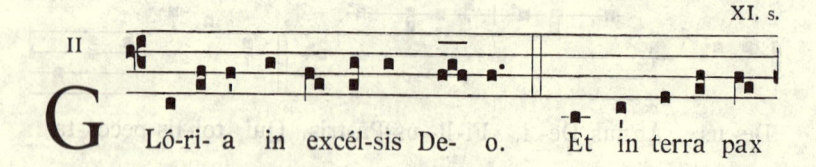

II

XI. s.

G Lória in excélsis Deo. Et in terra pax

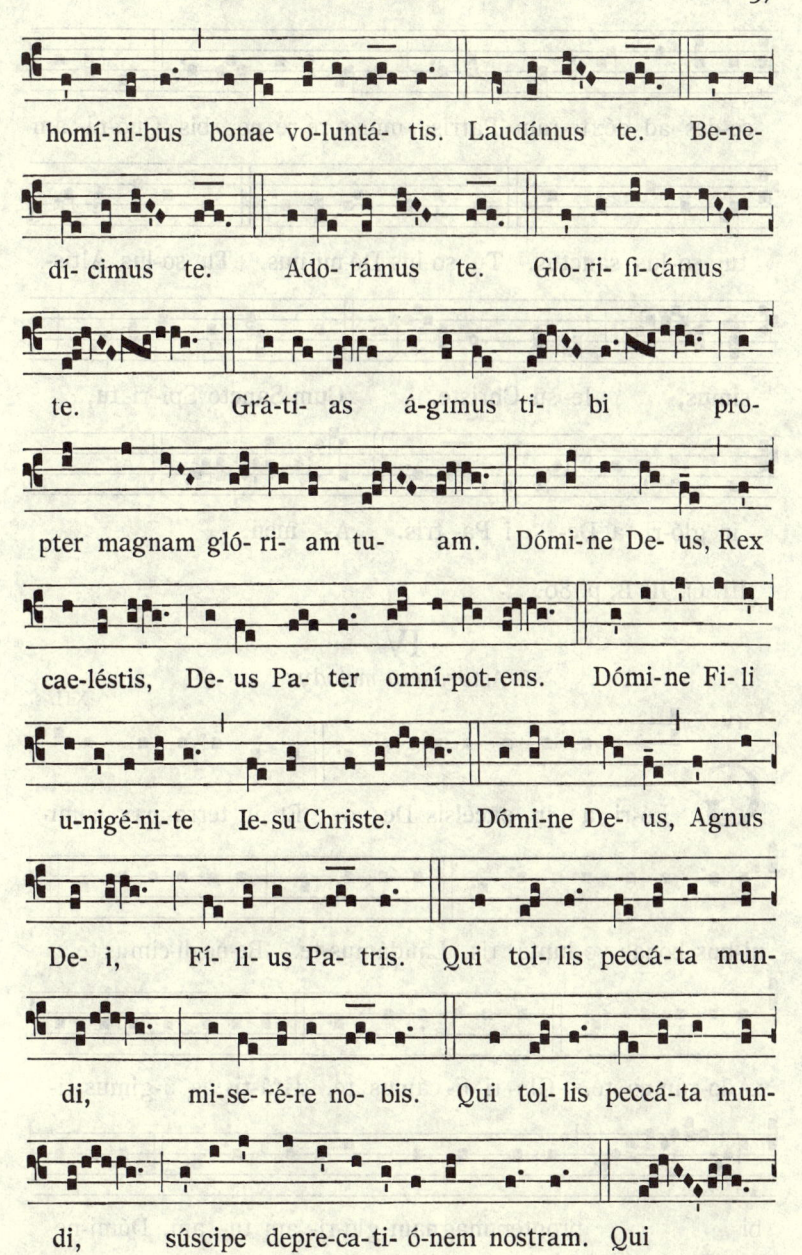

Additional Chants – Gloria

homí-ni-bus bonae vo-luntá- tis. Laudámus te. Bene-

dí- cimus te. Ado- rámus te. Glo- ri- fi-cámus

te. Grá-ti- as á-gimus ti- bi pro-

pter magnam gló- ri- am tu- am. Dómi-ne De- us, Rex

cae-léstis, De- us Pa- ter omní-pot-ens. Dómi-ne Fi- li

u-nigé-ni-te Ie- su Christe. Dómi-ne De- us, Agnus

De- i, Fí- li- us Pa- tris. Qui tol- lis peccá-ta mun-

di, mi-se-ré-re no- bis. Qui tol- lis peccá-ta mun-

di, súscipe depre-ca-ti- ó-nem nostram. Qui

Chants of the Mass Ordinary

se-des ad déxte-ram Patris, mi-se- ré-re no- bis. Quó-ni- am

tu so-lus sanctus. Tu so-lus Dó-mi-nus. Tu so-lus Altís-

simus, Ie- su Christe. Cum Sancto Spí-ri- tu,

in gló-ri- a De- i Pa- tris. A- men.

III. *Cf.* III B, *p. 86.*

IV
Ambrosian melody

XII. s.

G Ló-ri- a in excélsis De- o. Et in terra pax homí-

ni-bus bonae vo-luntá- tis. Laudámus te. Be-ne-dí-cimus te.

Ado-rámus te. Glo-ri- fi- cámus te. Grá-ti- as á-gimus ti-

bi propter magnam gló-ri- am tu- am. Dómi-ne

Additional Chants – Gloria

De-us, Rex caeléstis, De-us Pa-ter omní-pot-ens. Dómi-ne Fí-li u-ni-géni-te, Ie-su Christe. Dómi-ne De-us, Agnus De-i, Fí-li-us Pa-tris. Qui tol-lis peccá-ta mundi, mi-se-ré-re no-bis. Qui tol-lis peccá-ta mundi, súsci-pe depre-ca-ti-ó-nem nostram. Qui sedes ad déxte-ram Patris, mi-se-ré-re no-bis. Quó-ni-am tu so-lus sanctus. Tu so-lus Dómi-nus. Tu so-lus Altís-simus, Ie-su Christe. Cum Sancto Spí-ri-tu in gló-ri-a De-i Patris. ** Amen.

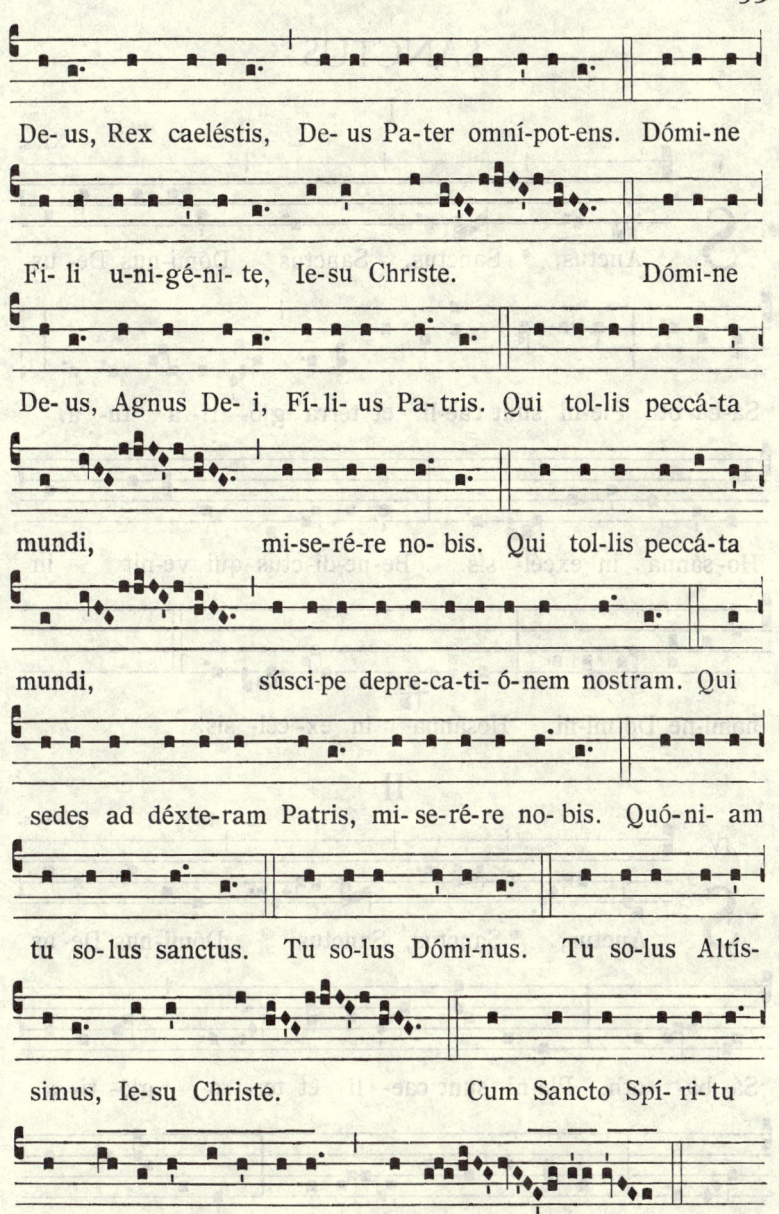

Chants of the Mass Ordinary

SANCTUS

I

XI. s.

Sanctus, *Sanctus, Sanctus Dóminus Deus Sábaoth. Pleni sunt caeli et terra glória tua. Hosánna in excélsis. Benedíctus qui venit in nómine Dómini. Hosánna in excélsis.

II

XI. s.

Sanctus, *Sanctus, Sanctus Dóminus Deus Sábaoth. Pleni sunt caeli et terra glória tua. Hosánna in excélsis. Benedíctus qui

Additional Chants – Agnus Dei

ve-nit in nó-mi-ne Dómi- ni. Ho-sánna in excél- sis.

III

SAnctus, * Sanctus, Sanctus Dómi- nus De- us Sá- ba- oth. Ple-ni sunt cae- li et ter- ra gló- ri- a tu- a. Ho-sánna in ex- cél- sis. Be- ne-dí- ctus qui ve- nit in nómi-ne Dómi- ni. Ho-sánna in ex-cél-sis.

AGNUS DEI

I

XII. s.

A- gnus De- i, * qui tol- lis peccá-ta

mundi : miserére nobis. Agnus Dei, * qui tollis peccáta mundi : miserére nobis. Agnus Dei, * qui tollis peccáta mundi : dona nobis pacem.

II

VI
Agnus Dei, * qui tollis peccáta mundi : miserére nobis. Agnus Dei, * qui tollis peccáta mundi : miserére nobis. Agnus Dei, * qui tollis peccáta mundi : dona nobis pacem.

THE LITURGICAL YEAR

ADVENT SEASON

FIRST SUNDAY OF ADVENT

Introit   Ps 24 : 1-4

VIII

AD te levávi * ánimam meam : Deus meus in te confído, non erubéscam : neque irrídeant me inimíci mei : étenim univérsi qui te exspéctant, non confundéntur. *Ps.* Vias tuas, Dómine, demónstra mihi : et sémitas tuas édoce me.

Unto you have I lifted up my soul. O my God, I trust in you, let me not be put to shame; do not allow my enemies to laugh at me; for none of those who are awaiting you will be disappointed. ℣. Make your ways known unto me, O Lord, and teach me your paths.

In Advent, the Gloria is not sung.

1st Sunday of Advent

Opening Prayer

Da, quǽsumus, omnípotens Deus, hanc tuis fidélibus voluntátem, ut, Christo tuo veniénti iustis opéribus occurréntes, eius déxteræ sociáti, regnum mereántur possidére cæléste.

All-powerful God, increase our strength of will for doing good that Christ may find an eager welcome at his coming and call us to his side in the kingdom of heaven.

First reading
A. Is 2: 1-5: *The gathering of the nations.*
B. Is 63: 16b-17, 19b; 64: 2b-7: *Rend the heavens and come down.*
C. Jer 33: 14-16: *The Lord is our justice.*

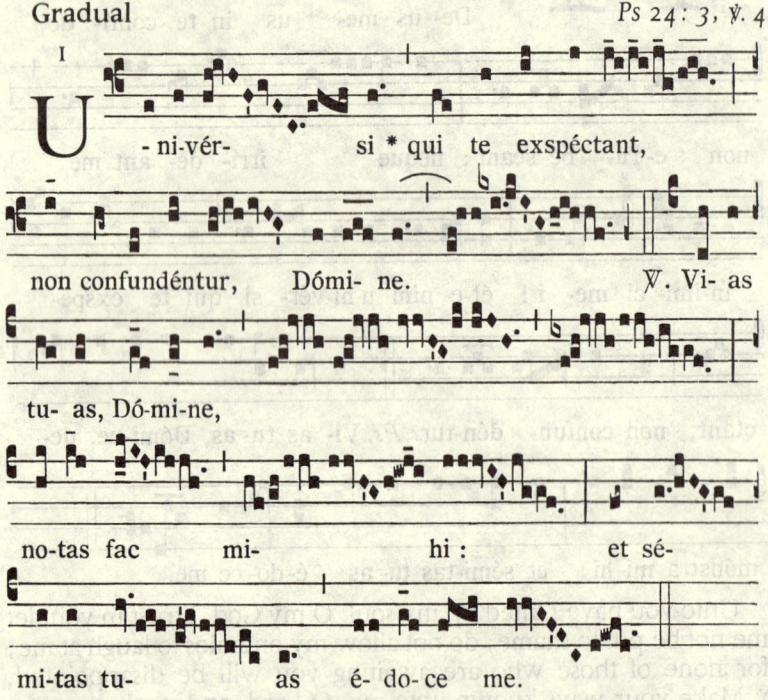

Gradual
Ps 24: 3, ℣. 4

Univérsi * qui te exspéctant, non confundéntur, Dómine. ℣. Vias tuas, Dómine, notas fac mihi : et sémitas tuas é-do-ce me.

They will not be disappointed, O Lord, all those who are awaiting you. ℣. Make your ways known unto me, O Lord, and teach me your paths.

1st Sunday of Advent

Second reading

A. Rom 13: 11-14: *Salvation is at hand.*
B. 1 Cor 1: 3-9: *Awaiting the revelation of the Lord.*
C. 1 Thess 3: 12-4: 2: *How to please God.*

Alleluia   Ps 84: 8

VIII

A-le-lú-ia. ℣. Osténde nobis Dómine misericórdiam tuam: et salutáre tuum da nobis.

Show us your mercy, O Lord, and grant us your salvation.

Gospel

A. Mt 24: 37-44: *Watch in order to be ready.*
B. Mk 13: 33-37: *Be watchful, for he will come!*
C. Lk 21: 25-28, 34-36: *Your redemption is drawing near.*

Credo

Offertory   Ps 24: 1-3

II

AD te Dómine *levávi á-

1st Sunday of Advent

nimam meam: Deus meus, in te confído, non erubéscam: neque irrídeant me inimíci mei: étenim univérsi qui te exspéctant, non confundéntur.

Unto you, O Lord, have I lifted up my soul; O my God, I trust in you, let me not be put to shame; do not allow my enemies to laugh at me; for none of those who are awaiting you will be disappointed.

Prayer over the Gifts

Suscipe, quæsumus, Dómine, múnera quæ de tuis offérimus colláta benefíciis, et, quod nostræ devotióni concédis éffici temporáli, tuæ nobis fiat præmium redemptiónis ætérnæ.

Father, from all you give us we present this bread and wine. As we serve you now, accept our offering and sustain us with your promise of eternal life.

Advent Preface I, p. 49.

Communion Ps 84: 13

Dóminus *dabit benignitátem: et

2nd Sunday of Advent

ter- ra no-stra da- bit fructum su- um.

The Lord will bestow his loving kindness, and our land will yield its fruit.

Prayer after Communion

Prosint nobis, quæsumus, Dómine, frequentáta mystéria, quibus nos, inter prætereúntia ambulántes, iam nunc instítuis amáre cæléstia et inhærére mansúris.

Father, may our communion teach us to love heaven. May its promise and hope guide our way on earth.

SECOND SUNDAY OF ADVENT

Introit — Cf. Is 30: 19, 30; Ps 79

VII

*Po-pulus Si- on, * ec- ce Dó- mi-nus vé-ni- et ad salván-das gen-tes: et audí- tam fá- ci- et Dómi- nus gló- ri- am vo- cis su- ae, in laetí- ti- a cor-*

... dis ve-stri. *Ps.* Qui re-gis Isra- el, inténde: qui dedú-cis vel-ut ovem Io- seph.

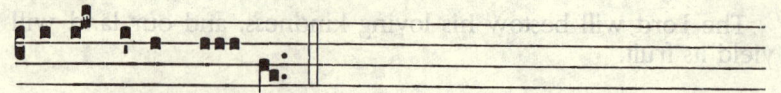

People of Zion behold, the Lord is coming to save all nations; and the Lord shall cause you to hear his majestic voice for the joy of your heart. ℣. O Shepherd of Israel hear us, you who lead Joseph like a flock!

Opening Prayer

OMNIPOTENS et miséricors Deus, in tui occúrsum Fílii festinántes nulla ópera terréni actus impédiant, sed sapiéntiæ cæléstis erudítio nos fáciat eius esse consórtes.

GOD of power and mercy, open our hearts in welcome. Remove the things that hinder us from receiving Christ with joy, so that we may share his wisdom and become one with him when he comes in glory.

A. Is 11: 1-10: *A shoot comes forth from Jesse.*
B. Is 40: 1-5, 9-11: *Prepare the way of the Lord.*
C. Bar 5: 1-9: *Behold, O Jerusalem!*

Gradual

Ps 49: 2, 3, ℣. 5

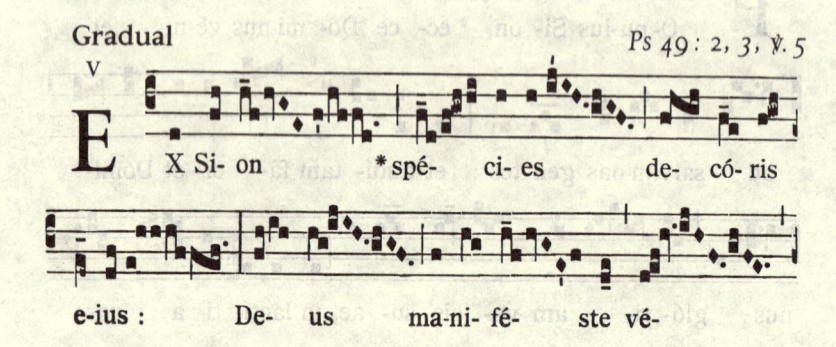

EX Si- on *spé- ci- es de- có- ris e-ius: De- us ma-ni-fé- ste vé-

2nd Sunday of Advent

... ni- et. ℣. Congregá- te il-li sanctos e- ius, qui ordina-vé- runt testaméntum e- ius super sacri- fí- ci- a.

Out of Zion his perfect beauty shines forth. God is coming in broad daylight. ℣. Summon before him the consecrated nation who made a covenant with him by sacrifice.

Second reading

A. Rom 15: 4-9: *Scripture, the source of our hope.*
B. 2 Pet 3: 8-14: *A new heaven and a new earth.*
C. Phil 1: 4-6, 8-11: *Advance towards the day of Christ.*

Alleluia

Ps 121: 1

Al-le- lú- ia.

2nd Sunday of Advent

℣. Laetátus sum in his quae dicta sunt mihi : in domum Dómini íbimus.

I rejoiced when it was said unto me: "Let us go to the house of the Lord!"

Gospel

A. Mt 3: 1-12: *Repent!*
B. Mk 1: 1-8: *Prepare the way of the Lord.*
C. Lk 3: 1-6: *All flesh shall see God's salvation.*

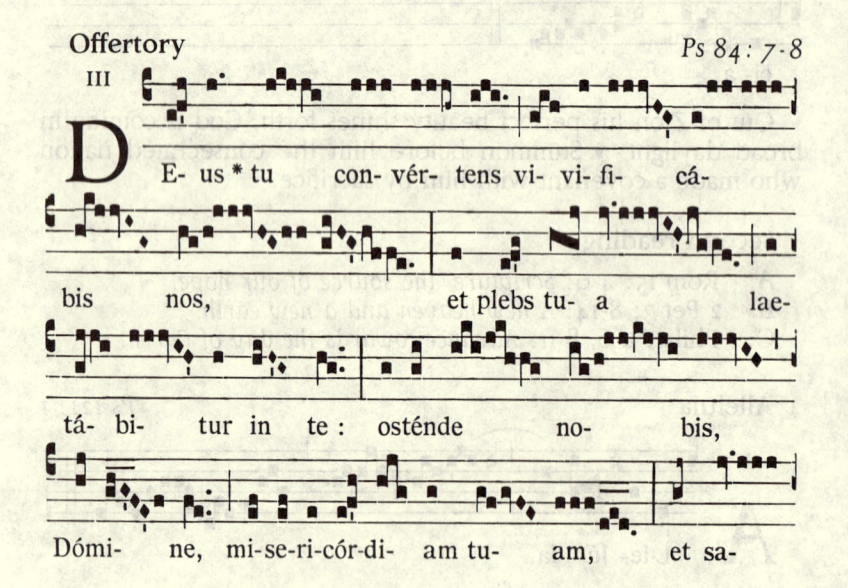

Offertory   Ps 84: 7-8

III

Deus * tu convértens vivificábis nos, et plebs tua laetábitur in te: osténde nobis, Dómine, misericórdiam tuam, et sa-

2nd Sunday of Advent

lu-tá-re tu- um da no- bis.

You will turn toward us, O God, and restore our life again, and your people will rejoice in you. Show us, Lord, your mercy and grant us your salvation.

Prayer over the Gifts

PLACARE, Dómine, quǽsumus, nostræ précibus humilitátis et hóstiis, et, ubi nulla súppetunt suffrágia meritórum, tuæ nobis indulgéntiæ succúrre præsídiis.

LORD, we are nothing without you. As you sustain us with your mercy, receive our prayers and offerings.

Advent Preface I, p. 49.

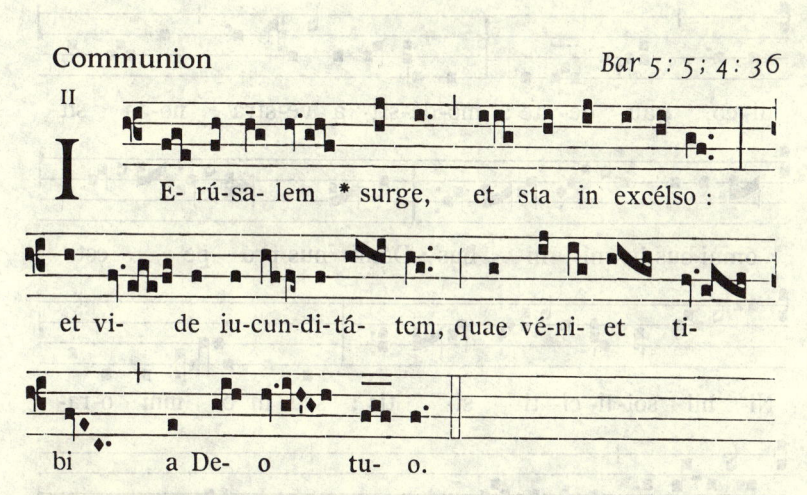

Communion

Bar 5: 5; 4: 36

IE-rú-sa-lem * surge, et sta in excélso: et vi- de iu-cun-di-tá- tem, quae vé-ni- et ti- bi a De- o tu- o.

Arise, O Jerusalem, and stand on high; and behold the joy that shall come to you from your God.

3rd Sunday of Advent

Prayer after Communion

REPLETI cibo spiritális alimóniæ, súpplices te, Dómine, deprecámur, ut, huius participatióne mystérii, dóceas nos terréna sapiénter perpéndere, et cæléstibus inhærére.

FATHER, you give us food from heaven. By our sharing in this mystery, teach us to judge wisely the things of earth and to love the things of heaven.

THIRD SUNDAY OF ADVENT

Introit *Phil 4 : 4, 5 ; Ps 84*

Gaudéte * in Dómino semper : íterum dico, gaudéte : modéstia vestra nota sit ómnibus homínibus : Dóminus prope est. Nihil sollíciti sitis : sed in omni oratióne petitiónes vestræ innotéscant apud

3rd Sunday of Advent

De- um. *Ps.* Be-ne-di-xísti, Dómi-ne, terram tu- am : a-vertísti capti-vi-tá-tem Ia- cob.

Rejoice in the Lord always; again I say, rejoice. Let your forbearance be known to all men. The Lord is at hand. Do not be anxious over anything; but in all manner of prayer, let your requests be made known unto God. ℣. Lord, you have blessed your land; you have put an end to Jacob's captivity.

Opening Prayer

DEUS, qui cónspicis pópulum tuum nativitátis domínicæ festivitátem fidéliter exspectáre, præsta, quæsumus, ut valeámus ad tantæ salútis gáudia perveníre, et ea votis sollémnibus álacri semper lætítia celebráre.

LORD GOD, may we, your people, who look forward to the birthday of Christ experience the joy of salvation and celebrate that feast with love and thanksgiving.

First reading

A. Is 35: 1-6a, 10: *Behold your God.*
B. Is 61: 1-2a; 10-11: *The Spirit of the Lord is upon me.*
C. Zeph 3: 14-18a *The Lord will rejoice in you.*

Gradual A & C

Ps 79: 2, 3, ℣. 2

VII

QUI se-des, Dómi- ne, * su- per Ché-rubim, éxci-ta pot-énti-am tu- am, et

3rd Sunday of Advent

ve- ni. ℣. Qui re-

gis Isra- el, inténde:

qui de-dú- cis vel-ut o- vem Io- seph.

O Lord, who are enthroned upon the Cherubim, stir up your might and come forth. ℣. O Shepherd of Israel, hear us, you who lead Joseph like a flock.

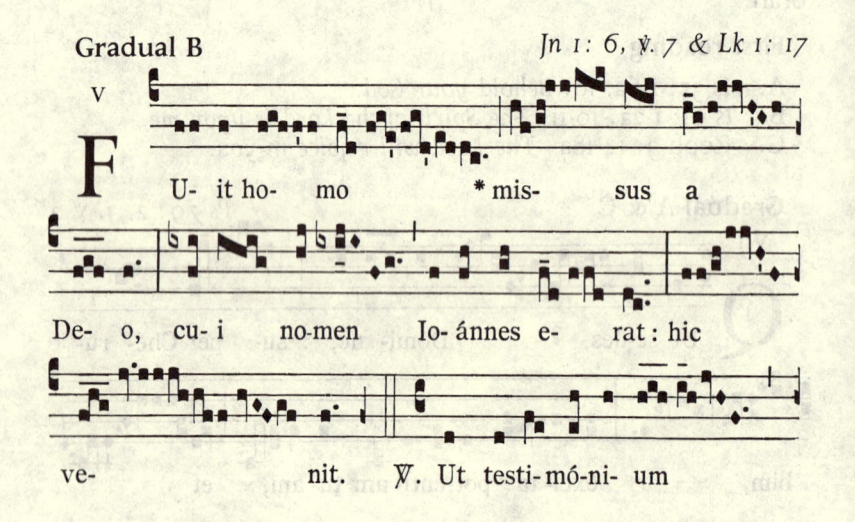

Gradual B *Jn 1: 6, ℣. 7 & Lk 1: 17*

FU- it ho- mo *mis- sus a

De- o, cu- i no-men Io-ánnes e- rat: hic

ve- nit. ℣. Ut testi-mó-ni- um

3rd Sunday of Advent

... perhi-bé-ret de lú- mi- ne, et pa-rá-re Dó-mi-no ple- bem perfé- ctam.

There was a man sent from God whose name was John; he came. ℣. To bear witness to the light, to prepare an upright people for the Lord.

Second reading

- A. Jas 5: 7-10: *Brothers, be patient.*
- B. 1 Thess 5: 16-24: *Joyful expectation.*
- C. Phil 4: 4-7: *The Lord is at hand.*

Alleluia Ps 79:3

IV

A L-le- lú- ia. ℣. Exci- ta, Dó- mi-ne, pot-énti- am tu- am, et ve- ni, ut salvos fá-

3rd Sunday of Advent

ci- as nos.

Stir up your might, O Lord, and come to save us.

Gospel

A. Mt 11: 2-11: *Are you the one who is to come?*
B. Jn 1: 6-8, 19-28: *John came to bear witness.*
C. Lk 3: 10-18: *What must we do?*

Offertory   Ps 84: 2

IV

B Ene-di-xí- sti, * Dó-mi- ne, ter- ram tu- am: aver-tí- sti capti-vi-tá-tem Ia- cob: remi-sí- sti in-iqui- tá- tem ple- bis tu- ae.

O Lord, you have blessed your land, you have put an end to Jacob's captivity; you have forgiven the guilt of your people.

Prayer over the Gifts

Devotionis nostræ tibi, Dómine, quæsumus, hostia iúgiter immolétur, quæ et sacri péragat institúta mystérii, et salutáre tuum nobis poténter operétur.

Lord, may the gift we offer in faith and love be a continual sacrifice in your honour and truly become our eucharist and our salvation.

3rd Sunday of Advent

Advent Preface I or II, p. 49.

Communion *Cf. Is 35: 4*

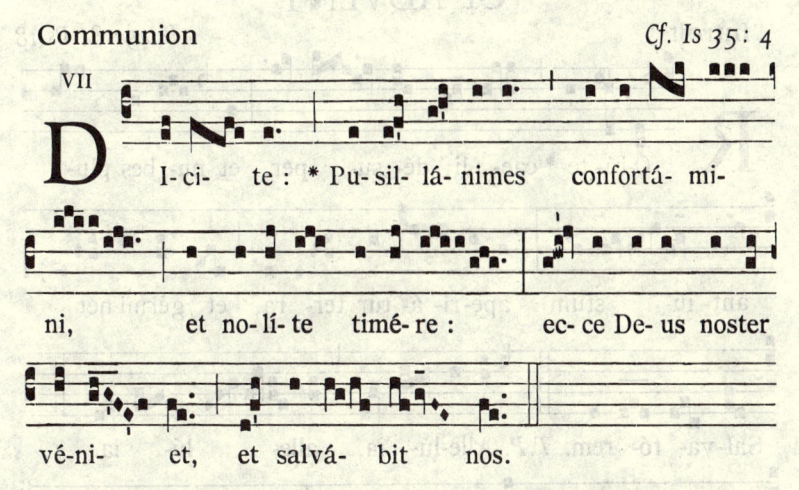

Dícite: * Pusillánimes confortámini, et nolíte timére: ecce Deus noster véniet, et salvábit nos.

Say: "Take courage, you who are fainthearted, and do not fear; behold, our God will come and he will save us."

Prayer after Communion

Tuam, Dómine, cleméntiam implorámus, ut hæc divína subsídia, a vítiis expiátos, ad festa ventúra nos præparent.

God of mercy, may this eucharist bring us your divine help, free us from our sins, and prepare us for the birthday of our Savior.

FOURTH SUNDAY OF ADVENT

Introit   Is 45 : 8; Ps 18

R Oráte *caeli désuper, et nubes pluant iustum: aperiátur terra, et gérminet Salvatórem. *T.P.* Allelúia, allelúia.

Ps. Cæli enárrant glóriam Dei: et ópera mánuum eius annúntiat firmaméntum.

Skies, let the Just One come forth like the dew, let him descend from the clouds like the rain. The earth will open up and give birth to our Saviour. ℣. The heavens declare the glory of God, and the firmament proclaims the work of his hands.

Opening Prayer

GRATIAM TUAM, quæsumus, Dómine, méntibus nostris infúnde, ut qui, Angelo nuntiánte, Christi Fílii tui incarnatiónem cognóvimus, per passiónem eius et crucem ad resurrectiónis glóriam perducámur.

LORD, fill our hearts with your love, and as you revealed to us by an angel the coming of your Son as man, so lead us through his suffering and death to the glory of his resurrection.

4th Sunday of Advent

First reading
A. Is 7: 10-14: *Behold, a Virgin shall conceive.*
B. 2 Sam 7: 1-5, 8b-12, 14a, 16: *David's royalty will endure.*
C. Mic 5: 1-4a: *You, O Bethlehem of Judah!*

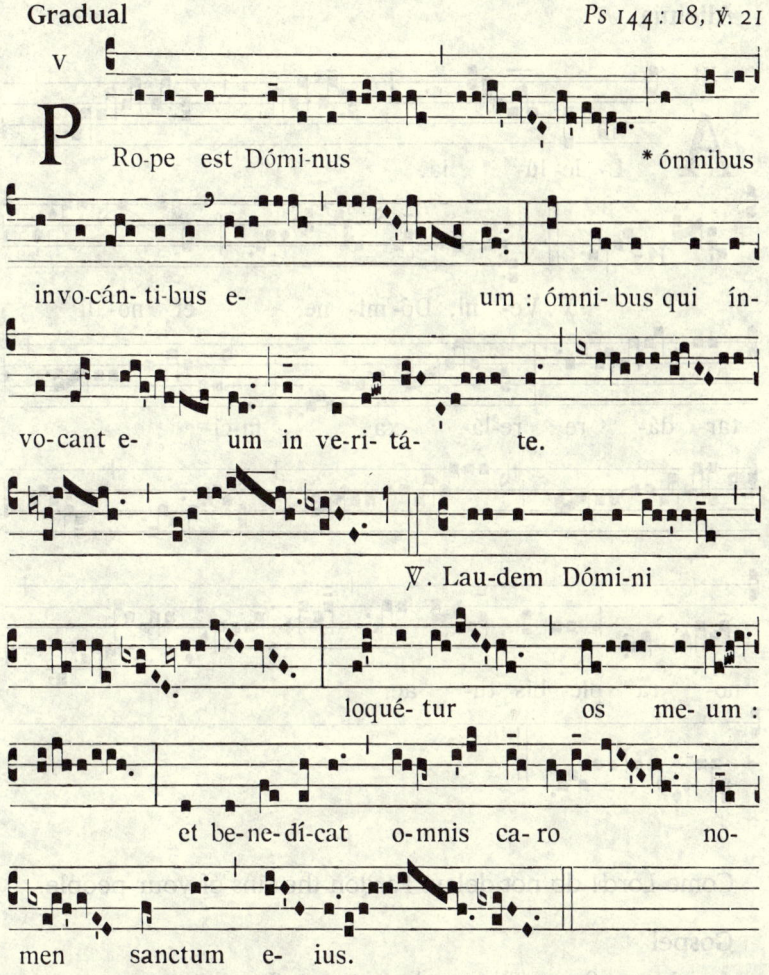

Gradual Ps 144: 18, ℣. 21

Prope est Dóminus *ómnibus invocántibus eum: ómnibus qui ínvocant eum in veritáte. ℣. Laudem Dómini loquétur os meum: et benedícat omnis caro nomen sanctum eius.

The Lord is close to all who call him, who call on him in the sincerity of their hearts. ℣. My mouth shall speak the praises of the Lord; let all flesh bless his holy name.

4th Sunday of Advent

Second reading

A. Rom 1: 1-7: *This good news concerns Jesus.*
B. Rom 16: 25-27: *This mystery has been revealed.*
C. Heb 10: 5-10: *Here I am to do your will.*

Alleluia

Alleluia. ℣. Veni, Dómine, et noli tardáre: reláxa facínora plebis tuae.

Come Lord! do not delay. Pardon the sins of your people.

Gospel

A. Mt 1: 18-24: *The angel appears to Joseph.*
B. Lk 1: 26-38: *The Annunciation.*
C. Lk 1: 39-45: *The Visitation.*

4th Sunday of Advent

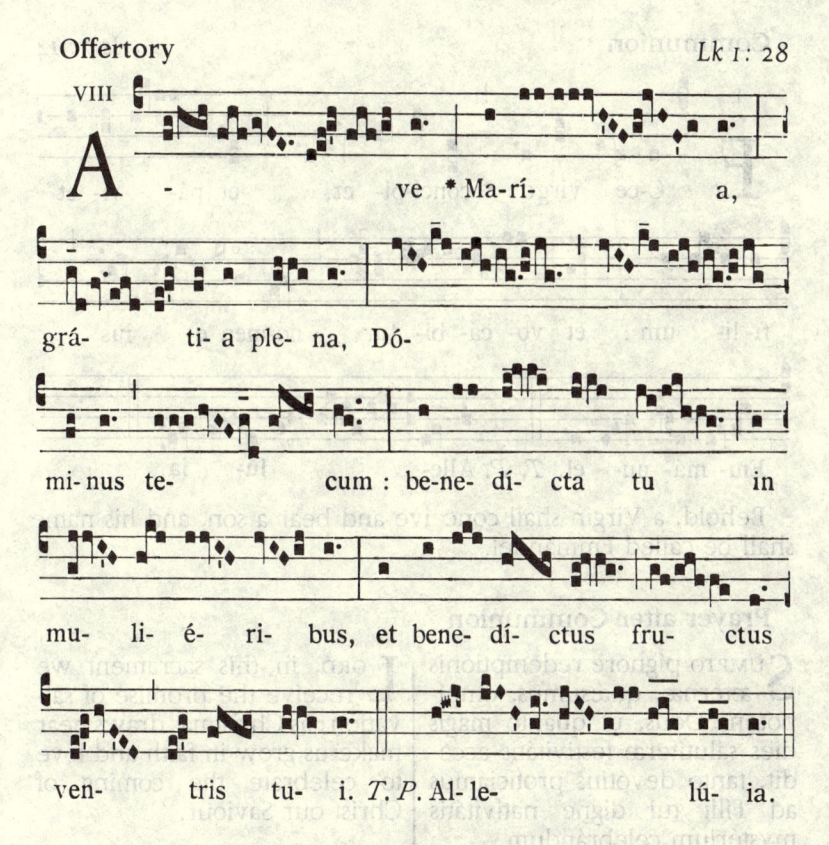

Offertory — Lk 1: 28

A- ve * Ma-rí- a, grá- ti- a ple- na, Dó- mi- nus te- cum: be-ne- dí- cta tu in mu- li- é- ri- bus, et bene- dí- ctus fru- ctus ven- tris tu- i. T. P. Al- le- lú- ia.

Hail Mary, full of grace, the Lord is with thee. Blessed art thou amongst women, and blessed is the fruit of thy womb.

Prayer over the Gifts

Altari tuo, Dómine, superpósita múnera Spíritus ille sanctíficet, qui beátæ Maríæ víscera sua virtúte replévit.

Lord, may the power of the Spirit, which sanctified Mary the mother of your Son, make holy the gifts we place upon this altar.

Advent Preface II, p. 49.

4th Sunday of Advent

Communion   Is 7: 14

E C-ce virgo * concí-pi-et, et pá-ri-et fí-li-um: et vo-cá-bi-tur no-men e-ius Em-má-nu-el. *T. P.* Alle-lú-ia.

Behold, a Virgin shall conceive and bear a son, and his name shall be called Emmanuel.

Prayer after Communion

SUMPTO pígnore redemptiónis ætérnæ, quæsumus, omnípotens Deus, ut quanto magis dies salutíferæ festivitátis accédit, tanto devótius proficiámus ad Fílii tui digne nativitátis mystérium celebrándum.

LORD, in this sacrament we receive the promise of salvation; as Christmas draws near make us grow in faith and love to celebrate the coming of Christ our Saviour.

December 25
CHRISTMAS
Solemnity

VIGIL MASS

Introit   *Cf. Ex* 16: 6, 7; *Is* 35: 4; *Ps* 23

Hódie sciétis, * quia véniet Dóminus, et salvábit nos: et mane vidébitis glóriam eius. *Ps.* Dómini est terra, et plenitúdo eius: orbis terrárum, et univérsi qui hábitant in eo.

Today you will know that the Lord is coming to save us; and tomorrow you will see his glory. ℣. The earth is the Lord's and the fulness thereof; the world, and all those who dwell therein.

Opening Prayer

DEUS, qui nos redemptiónis nostræ ánnua exspectatióne lætíficas, præsta, ut Unigénitum tuum, quem læti suscípimus Redemptórem, veniéntem quoque Iúdicem secúri vidére mereámur.

GOD our Father, every year we rejoice as we look forward to this feast of our salvation. May we welcome Christ as our Redeemer, and meet him with confidence when he comes to be our judge.

First reading

Is 62: 1-5: *The Lord delights in you.*

Christmas – Vigil Mass

Gradual *Cf. Ex 16: 6, 7; Is 35: 4, ℣. Ps 79: 2, 3*

Hódie * sciétis, quia véniet Dóminus, et salvábit nos: et mane vidébitis glóriam eius. ℣. Qui regis Israel, inténde: qui dedúcis velut ovem Ioseph: qui sedes super Chérubim, appáre coram Ephraim,

Christmas – Vigil Mass

Béniamin, et Manásse.

Today you will know that the Lord is coming to save us; and tomorrow you will see his glory. ℣. O Shepherd of Israel, hear us; you who lead Joseph like a flock, and who are enthroned upon the Cherubim; we beseech you to appear before Ephraim, Benjamin and Manasseh.

Second reading

Acts 13: 16-17; 22-25: *Paul bears witness to Christ, son of David.*

Alleluia

VIII

A Lleluia.

℣. Crástina die delébitur iníquitas terrae: et regnábit super nos Salvátor mundi.

Tomorrow the sin of the land will be destroyed, and the Saviour of the world will establish over us his kingdom.

Gospel

Mt 1: 1-25: *The origins of Jesus Christ, son of David.*

Christmas – Vigil Mass

Offertory   Ps 23:7

Tol- li-te * por- tas, prín- ci-pes, ve-stras: et e-le-vá- mi-ni, por- tae ae-ter-ná- les, et intro- í- bit Rex gló- ri- ae.

O Princes, lift up your gates; be lifted high, o eternal gates, and the King of Glory shall make his entry.

Prayer over the Gifts

Tanto nos, Dómine, quǽsumus, promptióre servítio hæc præcúrrere concéde sollémnia, quanto in his constáre princípium nostræ redemptiónis osténdis.

Lord, as we keep tonight the vigil of Christmas, may we celebrate this eucharist with greater joy than ever since it marks the beginning of our redemption.

Christmas Preface, p. 50 or 51. With the First Eucharistic Prayer, proper Communicantes, p. 23.

Communion   Cf. Is 40:5

Reve- lá- bi- tur * gló- ri- a Dó- mi- ni: et vi- dé- bit o- mnis ca- ro sa- lu- tá- re

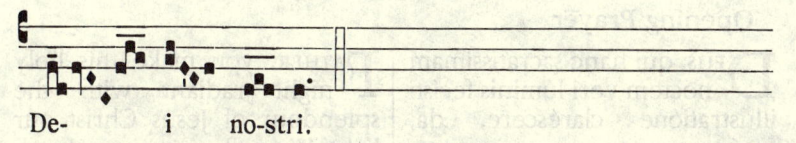

Christmas – Midnight Mass

De- i no-stri.

The glory of the Lord shall be revealed, and all flesh shall see the salvation which comes from our God.

Prayer after Communion

DA nobis, quæsumus, Dómine, unigéniti Fílii tui recénsita nativitáte vegetári, cuius cælésti mystério páscimur et potámur.

FATHER, we ask you to give us a new birth as we celebrate the beginning of your Son's life on earth. Strengthen us in spirit as we take your food and drink.

MIDNIGHT MASS

Introit — *Ps 2: 7, ℣. 1, 2, 8*

DO-MI-NUS * dí- xit ad me: Fí- li- us me- us es tu, e- go hó- di- e gé- nu- i te. *Ps.* Qua-re fremu- é- runt gentes: et pópu-li me-di-tá-ti sunt in-á-ni- a?

The Lord said unto me: You are my Son, today I have begotten you. ℣. Why do the nations conspire and the peoples plot in vain?

Christmas – Midnight Mass

Opening Prayer

Deus, qui hanc sacratíssimam noctem veri lúminis fecísti illustratióne claréscere, da, quǽsumus, ut, cuius in terra mystéria lucis agnóvimus, eius quoque gáudiis perfruámur in cælo.

Father, you make this holy night radiant with the splendour of Jesus Christ our light. We welcome him as Lord, the true light of the world. Bring us to eternal joy in the kingdom of heaven.

First reading

Is 9: 1-3, 5-6: *Unto us a son is given.*

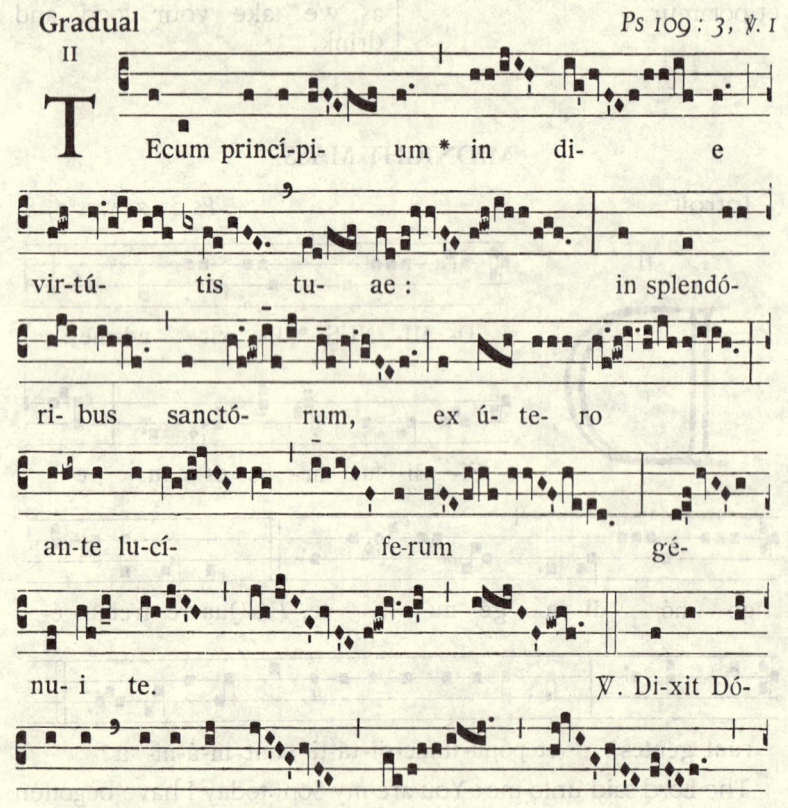

Gradual

Ps 109: 3, ℣. 1

Tecum princípium * in die virtútis tuae: in splendóribus sanctórum, ex útero ante lucíferum génui te. ℣. Dixit Dóminus Dómino me-

Christmas – Midnight Mass

o : Se- de a dextris me- is : do- nec po- nam in-imí- cos tu- os sca- bél- lum pe- dum tu- ó- rum.

Sovereign strength is yours on the day of your great might. Amidst the splendours of the heavenly sanctuary, from the womb, before the morning star, I have begotten you. ℣. The Lord said unto my Lord: "Sit at my right hand, until I make your enemies a stool for your feet".

Second reading

Tit 2: 11-14: *The grace of God has been manifested.*

Alleluia Ps 2: 7

VIII

A- L- le- lú- ia. ℣. *Dó- mi-nus di- xit ad me: Fí- li- us me- us es tu, e- go hó-*

Christmas – Midnight Mass

di- e gé- nu- i te.

The Lord said unto me: "You are my Son, today I have begotten you".

Gospel
Lk 2: 1-14: *Today a Saviour is born for you.*

Offertory
Ps 95, 11

Laeténtur * cae- li, et exsúl- tet ter- ra an- te fá- ci- em Dó- mi- ni: quó-ni- am ve- nit.

Let the heavens rejoice and let the earth be glad before the face of the Lord for he cometh.

Prayer over the Gifts

GRATA tibi sit, Dómine, quǽsumus, hodiérnæ festivitátis oblátio, ut, per hæc sacrosáncta commércia, in illíus inveniámur forma, in quo tecum est nostra substántia.

LORD, accept our gifts on this joyful feast of our salvation. By our communion with God made man, may we become more like him who joins our lives to yours.

Christmas – Mass at Dawn

Christmas Preface, p. 50 or 51. With the First Eucharistic Prayer, proper Communicantes, p. 23.

Communion
Ps 109 : 3

VI

IN splendóribus sanctórum,* ex útero ante lucíferum génui te.

Amidst the splendours of the heavenly sanctuary, from the womb, before the morning star, I have begotten you.

Prayer after Communion

DA NOBIS, quǽsumus, Dómine Deus noster, ut, qui nativitátem Redemptóris nostri frequentáre gaudémus, dignis conversatiónibus ad eius mereámur perveníre consórtium.

GOD our Father, we rejoice in the birth of our Saviour. May we share his life completely by living as he has taught.

MASS AT DAWN

Introit
Cf. Is 9 : 2, 6; Lk 1 : 33; Ps 92

VIII

LUX fulgébit *hódie super nos : quia natus est nobis Dóminus : et vocábitur Admi-

Christmas – Mass at Dawn

...rábilis, Deus, Princeps pacis, Pater futúri saéculi: cuius regni non erit finis.

Ps. Dóminus regnávit, decórem indútus est: indútus est Dóminus fortitúdinem, et praecínxit se.

Radiant light will shine upon us today, for the Lord is born unto us. He shall be called Wonderful God, Prince of Peace, Father of the world to come. His reign shall have no end. ℣. The Lord reigns, he is enrobed with majesty; the Lord is clothed with strength, he has girded himself.

Opening Prayer

Da, quæsumus, omnípotens Deus, ut dum nova incarnáti Verbi tui luce perfúndimur, hoc in nostro respléndeat ópere, quod per fidem fulget in mente.

Father, we are filled with the new light by the coming of your Word among us. May the light of faith shine in our words and actions.

First reading

Is 62: 11-12: *Behold, your Saviour comes.*

Gradual

Ps 117: 26, 27, ℣. 23

Benedíctus *qui venit in nómine

Christmas – Mass at Dawn

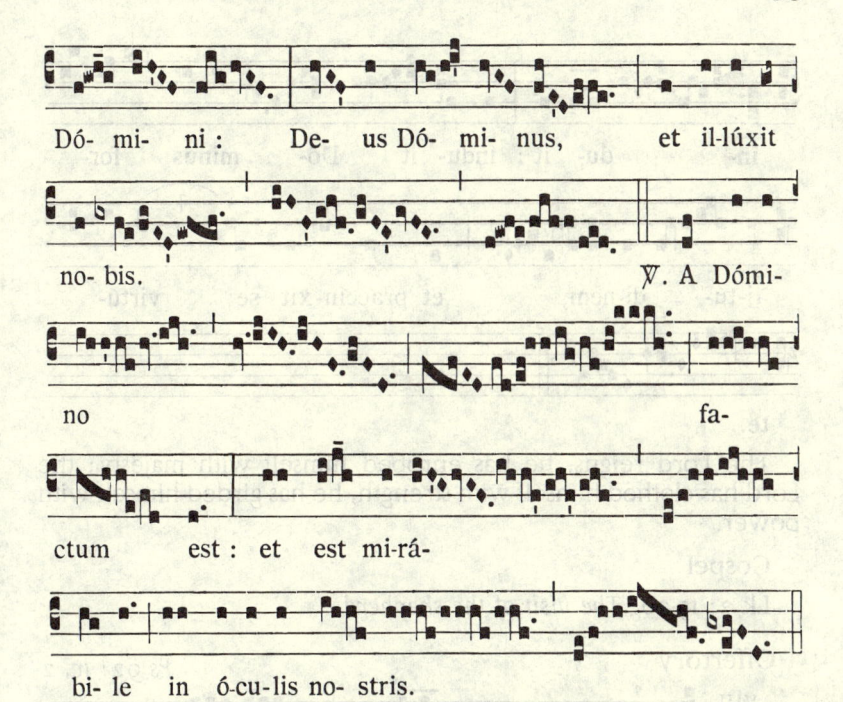

Dó- mi- ni: De- us Dó- mi- nus, et il-lúxit no- bis. ℣. A Dómi- no fa- ctum est: et est mi-rá- bi- le in ó-cu-lis no- stris.

Blessed is he who comes in the name of the Lord. The Lord God is our light. ℣. This is the Lord's doing; it is marvellous in our eyes.

Second reading

Tit 3: 4-7: *God has delivered us in his love.*

Alleluia
Ps 92: 1ab

A L-le-lú- ia. ℣. Dó- mi- nus re-gná- vit, de-có- rem

Christmas – Mass at Dawn

ín- du- it : índu- it Dóminus fortitú- di-nem, et praecín-xit se virtú- te.

The Lord reigns, he has enrobed himself with majesty; the Lord has clothed himself with strength, he has girded himself with power.

Gospel

Lk 2: 15-20: *The visit of the shepherds.*

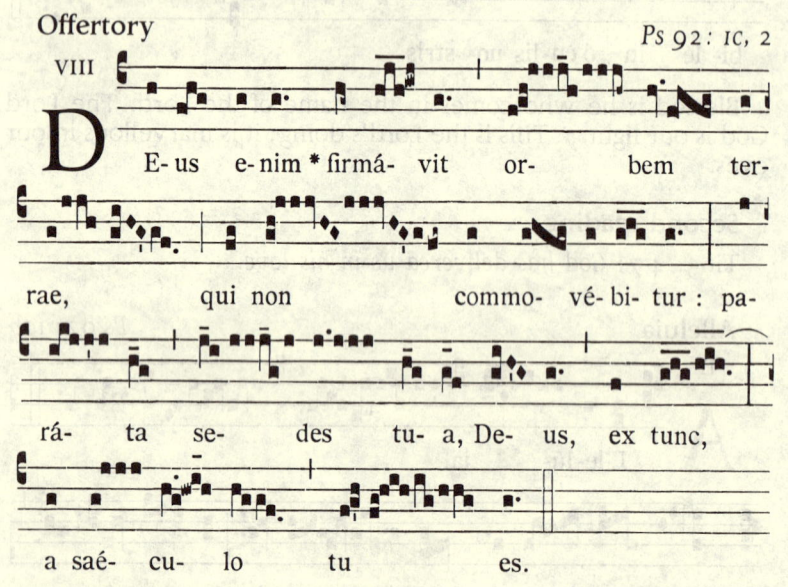

Offertory

Ps 92: 1C, 2

DE-us e-nim * firmá- vit or- bem terrae, qui non commo- vé- bi- tur : pa- rá- ta se- des tu- a, De- us, ex tunc, a saé- cu- lo tu es.

For it is God who has established the world, it shall never be

Christmas – Mass at Dawn

moved; your throne is established from of old; you are from all eternity.

Prayer over the Gifts

MUNERA nostra, quæsumus, Dómine, nativitátis hodiérnæ mystériis apta provéniant, ut sicut homo génitus idem præfúlsit et Deus, sic nobis hæc terréna substántia cónferat quod divínum est.

FATHER, may we follow the example of your Son who became man and lived among us. May we receive the gift of divine life through these offerings here on earth.

Christmas Preface, p. 50 or 51. With the First Eucharistic Prayer, proper Communicantes, p. 23.

Communion — Zech 9:9

EX-súlta * fí-li-a Si-on, lauda fí-li-a Ie-rú-sa-lem: ecce Rex tu-us ve-nit sanctus, et Salvá-tor mun-di.

Exult, O daughter of Zion, sing praises, O daughter of Jerusalem; behold, your King is coming, the Holy One, the Saviour of the world.

Prayer after Communion

DA NOBIS, Dómine, Fílii tui nativitátem læta devotióne coléntibus, huius arcána mystérii et plena fide cognóscere, et plenióre caritátis ardóre dilígere.

LORD, with faith and joy we celebrate the birthday of your Son. Increase our understanding and our love of the riches you have revealed in him.

Christmas – Mass of the Day

MASS OF THE DAY

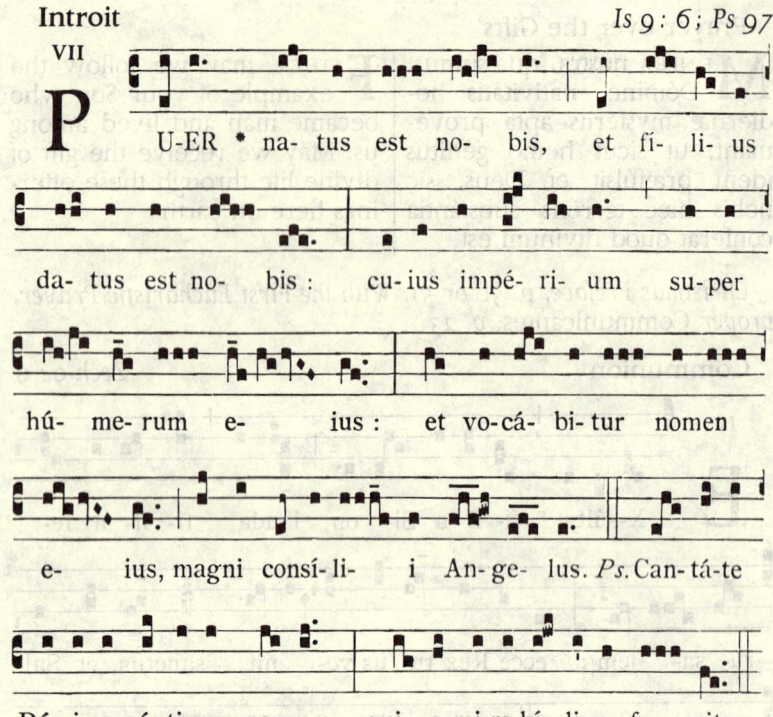

Introit *Is 9 : 6; Ps 97*

VII

PU-ER * na-tus est no- bis, et fí-li-us da-tus est no- bis : cu-ius impé-ri- um su-per hú- me-rum e- ius : et vo-cá- bi-tur nomen e- ius, magni consí-li- i An-ge- lus. *Ps.* Can-tá-te Dómi-no cánti-cum no-vum : qui- a mi-ra-bí- li- a fe- cit.

Unto us a child is born, unto us a son is given. Dominion is on his shoulder and his name shall be called the Angel of Great Counsel. ℣. Sing unto the Lord a new song, for he has accomplished wondrous deeds.

Opening Prayer

Deus, qui humánæ substántiæ dignitátem et mirabíliter condidísti, et mirabílius reformásti, da, quǽsumus, nobis eius divinitátis esse consórtes, qui humanitátis nostræ fíeri dignátus est párticeps.

Lord God, we praise you for creating man, and still more for restoring him in Christ. Your Son shared our weakness: may we share his glory.

Christmas – Mass of the Day

First reading

Is 52: 7-10: *The Lord has comforted his people.*

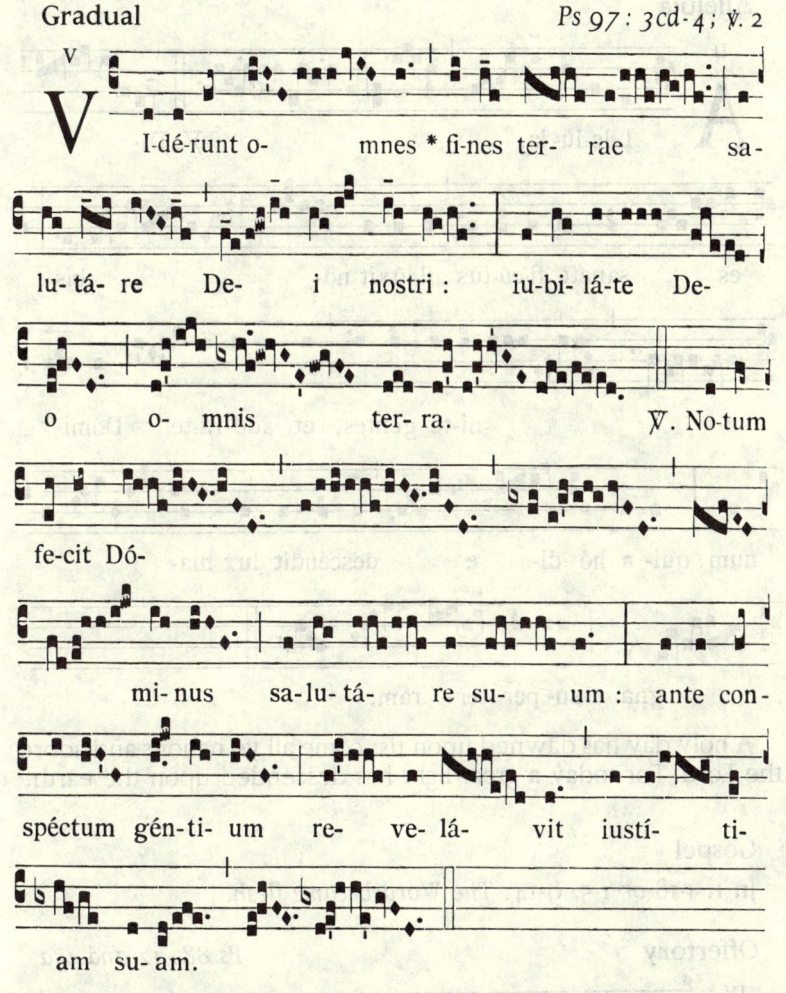

Gradual Ps 97: 3cd-4; ℣. 2

Vidérunt omnes * fines terrae salutáre Dei nostri: iubiláte Deo omnis terra. ℣. Notum fecit Dóminus salutáre suum: ante conspéctum géntium revelávit iustítiam suam.

All the ends of the earth have seen the salvation which comes from our God; sing joyfully to God all the earth. ℣. The Lord has made known his salvation; he has revealed his righteousness in the sight of the nations.

Christmas – Mass of the Day

Second reading
Heb 1: 1-6: *God has spoken to us through his Son.*

Alleluia

Alle-lú-ia. ℣. Dies sancti-fi-cá-tus il-lúxit nobis: veníte gentes, et adoráte Dóminum: qui-a hó-di-e descéndit lux magna super terram.

A holy day has dawned upon us; come all ye nations and adore the Lord. For today a great light has descended upon the earth.

Gospel
Jn 1: 1-18 *or* 1-5, 9-14: *The Word became flesh.*

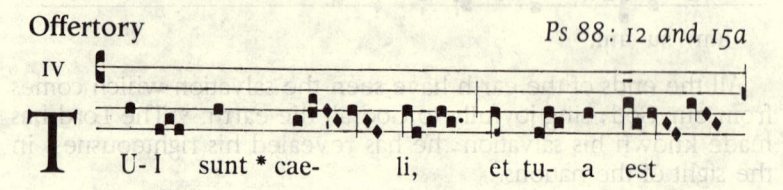

Offertory
Ps 88: 12 and 15a

TU-I sunt * caeli, et tu-a est

Christmas – Mass of the Day

ter- ra : orbem ter- rá- rum, et ple- ni- tú- di- nem e- ius tu fundá- sti : iu- stí- ti- a et iu- dí- ci- um praepa- rá- ti- o se- dis tu- ae.

Yours are the heavens, yours is the earth, the world and the fullness thereof have been founded by you. Righteousness and justice are the foundation of your throne.

Prayer over the Gifts

OBLATIO tibi sit, Dómine, hodiérnæ sollemnitátis accépta, qua et nostræ reconciliatiónis procéssit perfécta placátio, et divíni cultus nobis est índita plenitúdo.

ALMIGHTY God, the saving work of Christ made our peace with you. May our offering today renew that peace within us and give you perfect praise.

Christmas Preface, p. 50 or 51. With the First Eucharistic Prayer, proper Communicantes, *p. 23.*

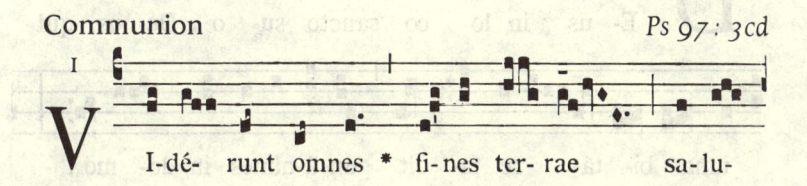

Communion   Ps 97 : 3cd

*VI- dé- runt omnes * fi- nes ter- rae sa- lu-*

tá- re De- i no-stri.

All the ends of the earth have seen the salvation which comes from our God.

Prayer after Communion

PRÆSTA, miséricors Deus, ut natus hódie Salvátor mundi, sicut divínæ nobis generatiónis est auctor, ita et immortalitátis sit ipse largítor.

FATHER, the child born today is the Saviour of the world. He made us your children. May he welcome us into your kingdom.

Sunday in the Octave of Christmas
HOLY FAMILY OF JESUS, MARY & JOSEPH
Feast

If there is no Sunday in the Octave, this feast is celebrated on December 30, with only one of the two readings before the Gospel.

Introit   *Ps 67: 6, 7, 36 and 2*

DE- us * in lo- co sancto su- o : De- us, qui

inha- bi- tá- re fa- cit un-á-nimes in do- mo :

Holy Family

ipse dabit virtútem et fortitúdinem plebi suæ. Ps. Exsúrgat Deus, et dissipéntur inimíci ejus: et fúgiant, qui odérunt eum, a fácie ejus.

God is in his holy dwelling place; the God who causes us to dwell together, one at heart, in his house; he himself will give power and strength to his people. ℣. Let God arise, and let his enemies be scattered; and let those who hate him flee before his face.

Opening Prayer

DEUS, qui præclára nobis sanctæ Famíliæ dignátus es exémpla præbére, concéde propítius, ut, domésticis virtútibus caritatísque vínculis illam sectántes, in lætítia domus tuæ præmiis fruámur ætérnis.

FATHER, help us to live as the holy family, united in respect and love. Bring us to the joy and peace of your eternal home.

First reading

Sir 3: 2-6, 12-14: *Authentic family ties.*
Or:
B. Gen 15: 1-6; 21: 1-3: *The posterity of Abraham.*
C. 1 Sam 1: 20-22, 24-28: *The young Samuel is offered by his mother.*

Holy Family

Gradual   Ps 26: 4

U-nam pétii * a Dómino, hanc requíram, ut inhábitem in domo Dómini. ℣. Ut vídeam voluptátem Dómini: et prótegar a templo sancto eius.

One thing have I asked of the Lord, this will I seek after; that I may dwell in the house of the Lord. ℣. To gaze in delight upon the Lord's beauty and to be sheltered in his holy temple.

Second reading

Col 3: 12-21: *Family life in the Lord.*
Or:
B.   Heb 11: 8, 11-12, 17-19: *The faith of Abraham.*
C.   1 Jn 3: 1-2, 21-24: *We are the children of God.*

Holy Family

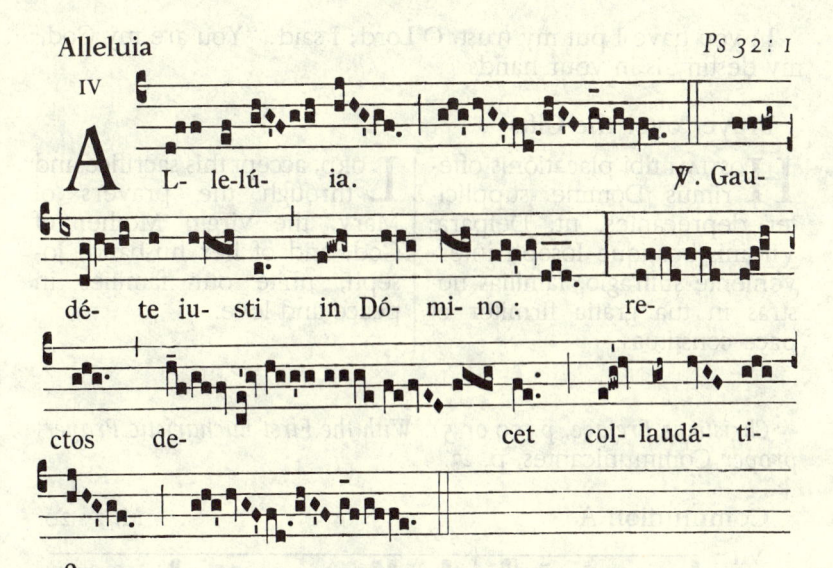

Alleluia — Ps 32:1

Alleluia. ℣. Gaudete iusti in Domino: rectos decet collaudatio.

Rejoice in the Lord, O you just. It is fitting that loyal hearts should praise him.

Gospel
Mt 2: 13-15, 19-23: *The flight into Egypt.*
Or:
B. Lk 2: 22-40 or 22, 39-40: *The presentation in the Temple.*
C. Lk 2: 41-52: *Jesus in the midst of the teachers.*

Offertory — Ps 30: 15, 16

In te speravi, Domine: * dixi: Tu es Deus meus, in manibus tuis tempora mea.

Holy Family

In you have I put my trust, O Lord; I said: "You are my God, my destiny is in your hands."

Prayer over the Gifts

Hostiam tibi placatiónis offérimus, Dómine, supplíciter deprecántes, ut, Deíparæ Virginis beatíque Ioseph interveniénte suffrágio, famílias nostras in tua grátia fírmiter et pace constítuas.

Lord, accept this sacrifice and through the prayers of Mary, the virgin Mother of God, and of her husband, Joseph, unite our families in peace and love.

Christmas Preface, p. 50 or 51. With the First Eucharistic Prayer, proper Communicantes, *p. 23.*

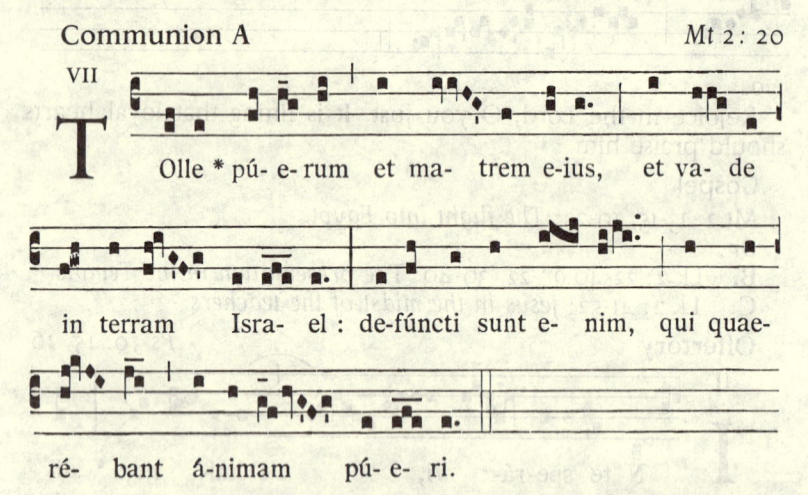

Communion A   Mt 2: 20

VII

Tolle * pú-e-rum et ma-trem e-ius, et vade in terram Isra-el: de-fúncti sunt e-nim, qui quaerébant á-nimam pú-e-ri.

Take the child and his mother, and go into the land of Israel; for those who sought the child's life are dead.

Communion B & C   Lk 2: 48, 49

I

Fi-li, * quid fe-císti no-bis sic? e-go et

Mary, Mother of God

pa-ter tu- us do-lén- tes quaere-bá-mus te. Et quid est quod me quaere-bá- tis? nesci- e-bá- tis qui- a in his quae Patris me- i sunt, o-pórtet me es- se?

My son, why have you treated us so? Your father and I have been anxiously looking for you. How is it that you were seeking me? Did you not know that I must be about my Father's business?

Prayer after Communion

Quos cæléstibus réficis sacraméntis, fac, clementíssime Pater, sanctæ Famíliæ exémpla iúgiter imitári, ut, post ærúmnas sǽculi, eius consórtium consequámur ætérnum.

Eternal Father, we want to live as Jesus, Mary, and Joseph, in peace with you and one another. May this communion strengthen us to face the troubles of life.

January 1. Octave of Christmas
MARY, MOTHER OF GOD
Solemnity

Introit Sedulius; Ps 44: 2, 11, 12

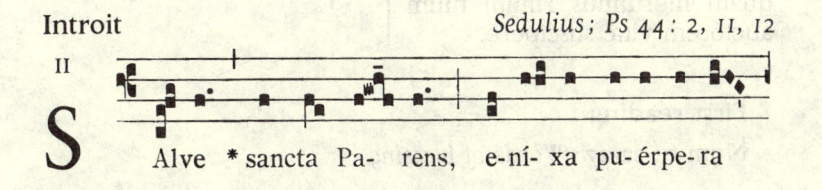

S Alve * sancta Pa- rens, e-ní- xa pu-érpe-ra

Mary, Mother of God

Re- gem, qui caelum terrám- que re- git in saé-cu-la sae-cu- ló- rum. *T. P.* Al-le- lú- ia, al-le- lú-ia. *Ps.* E-ructávit cor me- um verbum bonum: di- co ego ópe-ra me- a re- gi.

Hail holy Mother, the Child-Bearer who has brought forth the King, the ruler of heaven and earth for ever. ℣. My heart overflows with a goodly theme; I address my works to the King.

Or:

Lux fulgébit, *p. 193.*

Opening Prayer

DEUS, qui salútis ætérnæ, beátæ Maríæ virginitáte fecúnda, humáno géneri præmia præstitísti, tríbue, quæsumus, ut ipsam pro nobis intercédere sentiámus, per quam merúimus Fílium tuum auctórem vitæ suscípere.

GOD OUR FATHER, may we always profit by the prayers of the Virgin Mother Mary, for you bring us life and salvation through Jesus Christ her Son.

First reading

Num 6: 22-27: *Words of blessing.*

Mary, Mother of God

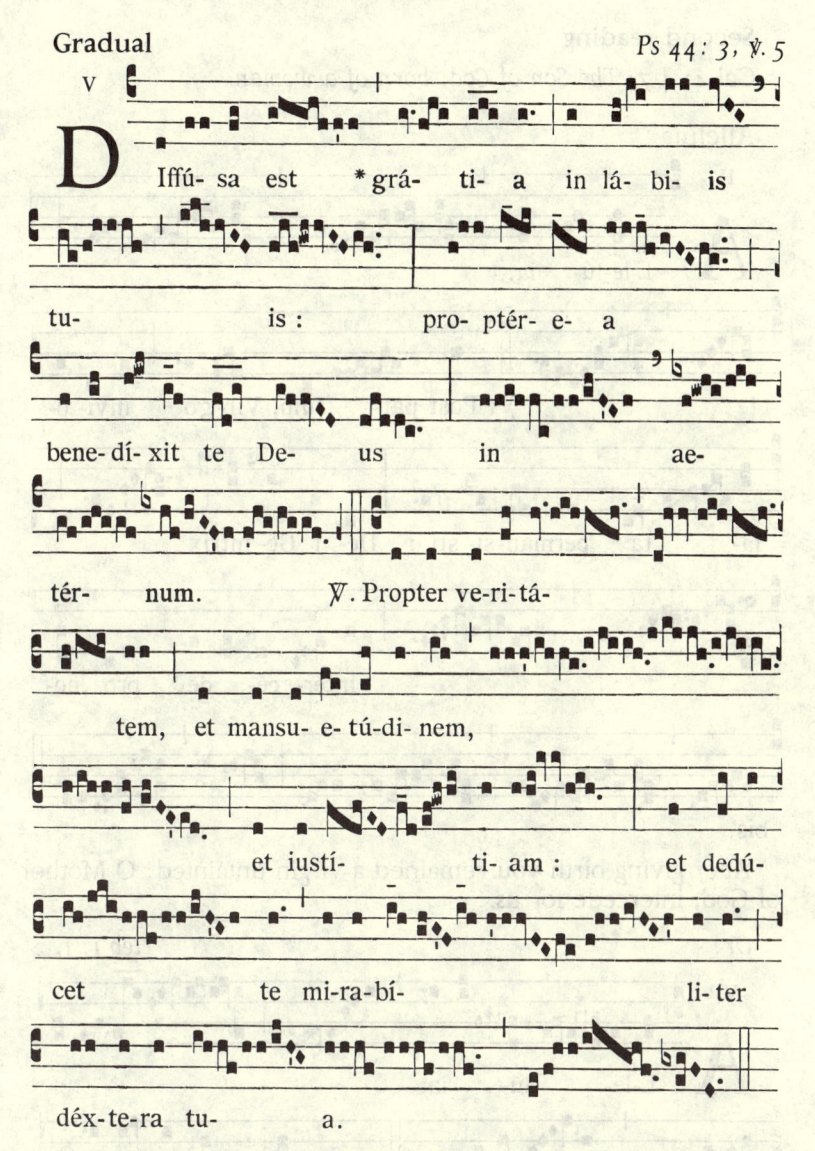

Gradual — Ps 44: 3, ℣. 5

Diffúsa est *grátia in lábiis tuis: proptérea benedíxit te Deus in aetérnum. ℣. Propter veritátem, et mansuetúdinem, et iustítiam: et dedúcet te mirabíliter déxtera tua.

Grace is poured out upon your lips; therefore has God blessed you for ever. ℣. For the cause of truth and goodness and righteousness, your right hand shall lead you wonderfully.

Second reading

Gal 4: 4-7: *The Son of God, born of a woman.*

Alleluia

*A*Lle-lú- ia.

℣. Post par- tum, Vir-go invi-o-lá- ta perman-sí-sti: De- i Gé-nitrix inter- cé- de pro no-bis.

After giving birth you remained a virgin untainted; O Mother of God, intercede for us.

Or: *Heb 1: 1, 2*

*A*Lle- lú- ia.

℣. Multi- fá- ri- e

Mary, Mother of God

...o- lim De- us loquens in prophé- tis, no-vís-si-me di-é-bus i- stis lo-cú-tus est no- bis in Fí- li- o su- o.

On many occasions in the past, God spoke through the prophets; at long last, in these present days, he has spoken to us through his Son.

Gospel

Lk 2: 16-21: *The shepherds visit Bethlehem.*

Offertory

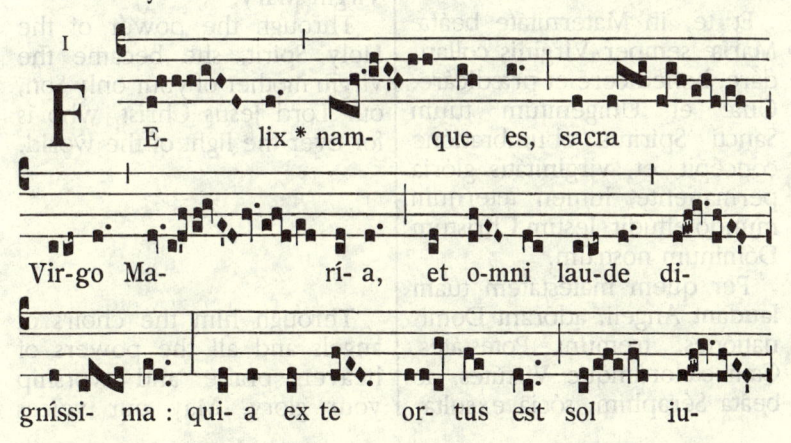

*FE- lix * nam- que es, sacra Vir-go Ma- rí- a, et o-mni lau-de di-gníssi- ma: qui- a ex te or- tus est sol iu-*

...stí-ti-ae, Chri-stus De-us no-ster.

Blessed are you, O holy Virgin Mary, and worthy of all praise; for from you has come forth the sun of justice, Christ our God.

Prayer over the Gifts

DEUS, qui bona cuncta ínchoas benígnus et pérficis, da nobis, de sollemnitáte sanctæ Dei Genetrícis lætántibus, sicut de inítiis tuæ grátiæ gloriámur, ita de perfectióne gaudére.

GOD OUR FATHER, we celebrate at this season the beginning of our salvation. On this feast of Mary, the Mother of God, we ask that our salvation will be brought to its fulfilment.

Preface

VERE dignum et iustum est, æquum et salutáre, nos tibi semper et ubíque grátias ágere : Dómine, sancte Pater, omnípotens ætérne Deus :

Et te, in Maternitáte beátæ Maríæ semper Vírginis collaudáre, benedícere et prædicáre. Quæ et Unigénitum tuum Sancti Spíritus obumbratióne concépit, et, virginitátis glória permanénte, lumen ætérnum mundo effúdit, Iesum Christum Dóminum nostrum.

Per quem maiestátem tuam laudant Angeli, adórant Dominatiónes, tremunt Potestátes. Cæli cælorúmque Virtútes, ac beáta Séraphim, sócia exsulta-

FATHER, all-powerful and ever-living God, we do well always and everywhere to give you thanks as we celebrate the motherhood of the Blessed Virgin Mary.

Through the power of the Holy Spirit, she became the virgin mother of your only Son, our Lord Jesus Christ, who is for ever the light of the world.

Through him the choirs of angels and all the powers of heaven praise and worship your glory. May our voices

tióne concélebrant. Cum quibus et nostras voces ut admítti iúbeas, deprecámur, súpplici confessióne dicéntes:

blend with theirs as we join in their unending hymn: Holy...

With the First Eucharistic Prayer, proper Communicantes, *p. 23.*

Communion
Exsúlta, *p. 197.*

Prayer after Communion

SUMPSIMUS, Dómine, læti sacraménta cæléstia: præsta, quǽsumus, ut ad vitam nobis profíciant sempitérnam, qui beátam semper Vírginem Maríam Fílii tui Genetrícem et Ecclésiæ Matrem profitéri gloriámur.

FATHER, as we proclaim the Virgin Mary to be the mother of Christ and the mother of the Church, may our communion with her Son bring us to salvation.

SECOND SUNDAY AFTER CHRISTMAS

In certain regions, the solemnity of the Epiphany is celebrated today, p. 217.

Introit
Wis 18: 14-15; Ps 92

VIII

DUM médium siléntium * tenérent ómnia, et nox in suo cursu médium iter

2nd Sunday after Christmas

habéret, omnípotens sermo tuus, Dómine, de caelis a regálibus sédibus venit.

Ps. Dóminus regnávit, decórem indútus est: indútus est Dóminus fortitúdinem, et praecínxit se.

While a profound silence enveloped all things, and night was in the midst of her course, your all-powerful Word, O Lord, leaped down from your royal throne. ℣. The Lord reigns, he is enrobed with majesty; the Lord is clothed with strength, he has girded himself.

Opening Prayer

OMNIPOTENS sempitérne Deus, fidélium splendor animárum, dignáre mundum glória tua implére benígnus, et cunctis pópulis appáre per tui lúminis claritátem.

GOD of power and life, glory of all who believe in you, fill the world with your splendour and show the nations the light of your truth.

First reading

Sir 24: 1-2, 12-16: *Wisdom praises herself.*

Gradual
Ps 44: 3 and 2

*Speciósus * forma*

prae fí- li- is hó- mi- num : dif-fú-sa est grá-ti- a in lá- bi- is tu- is. ℣. E-ructá-vit cor me- um ver- bum bo- num : di-co e- go ó- pe-ra me- a re- gi : lingua me- a cá- la- mus scribae ve- ló- ci- ter scri- bén- tis.

Your beauty surpasses that of all the children of men; grace is poured out upon your lips. ℣. My heart overflows with a goodly theme; I address my works to the King; my tongue is like the pen of an agile scribe.

2nd Sunday after Christmas

Second reading
Eph 1: 3-6, 15-18: *Blessed be God the Father.*

Alleluia
Dóminus regnávit, decórem, *p. 195.*

Gospel
Jn 1: 1-18 *or* 1-5,9-14: *The Word became flesh.*

Offertory
Bénedic, ánima mea, *p. 584.*

Prayer over the Gifts

OBLATA, Dómine, múnera Unigéniti tui nativitáte sanctífica, qua nobis et via osténditur veritátis, et regni cæléstis vita promíttitur.

LORD, make holy these gifts through the coming of your Son, who shows us the way of truth and promises the life of your kingdom.

Christmas Preface, p. 50 or 51.

Communion
Dómine Dóminus noster, *p. 575.*

Prayer after Communion

DOMINE Deus noster, supplíciter te rogámus, ut, huius operatióne mystérii, vítia nostra purgéntur, et iusta desidéria compleántur.

LORD, hear our prayers. By this eucharist free us from sin and keep us faithful to your word.

January 6
THE EPIPHANY OF THE LORD
Solemnity

In certain regions, the Epiphany is celebrated on the Second Sunday after Christmas.

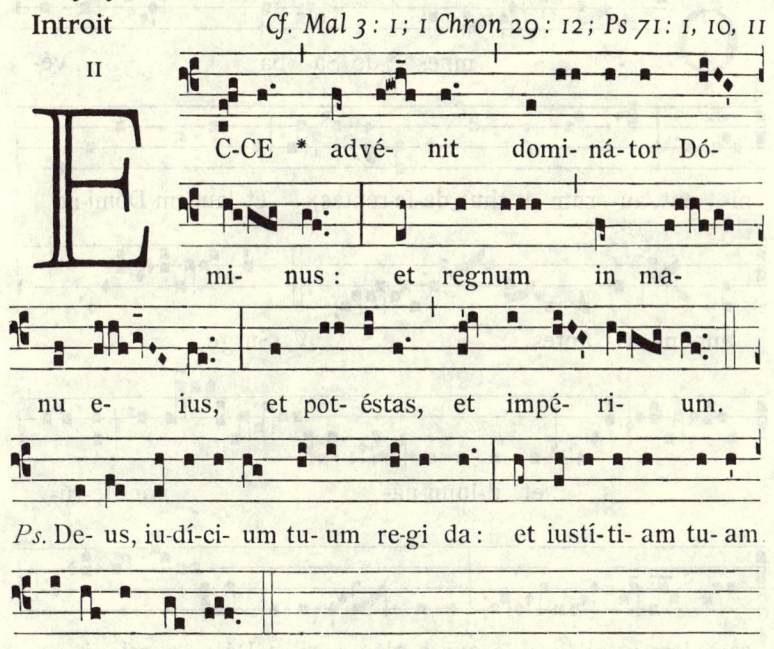

Introit *Cf. Mal 3: 1; 1 Chron 29: 12; Ps 71: 1, 10, 11*

E C-CE * advénit dominátor Dóminus: et regnum in manu eius, et potéstas, et impérium.

Ps. Deus, iudícium tuum regi da: et iustítiam tuam fílio regis.

Behold, the Sovereign Lord is coming; kingship, government and power are in his hands. ℣. Endow the King with your judgment, O God, and the King's son with your righteousness.

Opening Prayer

DEUS, qui hodiérna die Unigénitum tuum géntibus stella duce revelásti, concéde propítius, ut qui iam te ex fide cognóvimus, usque ad contemplándam spéciem tuæ celsitúdinis perducámur.

FATHER, you revealed your Son to the nations by the guidance of a star. Lead us to your glory in heaven by the light of faith.

First reading

Is 60: 1-6: *Jerusalem, behold!*

Gradual

Is 60: 6, ℣. 1

O-mnes *de Saba vénient, aurum et thus deferéntes, et laudem Dómino annuntiántes. ℣. Surge, et illumináre Ierúsalem: quia glória Dómini super te orta est.

All those from Sheba shall come, bringing gold and frankincense; and showing forth praise to the Lord. ℣. Arise and shine out, O Jerusalem, for the glory of the Lord is rising upon you.

Second reading

Eph 3: 2-3a, 5-6: *The mystery now revealed.*

Epiphany

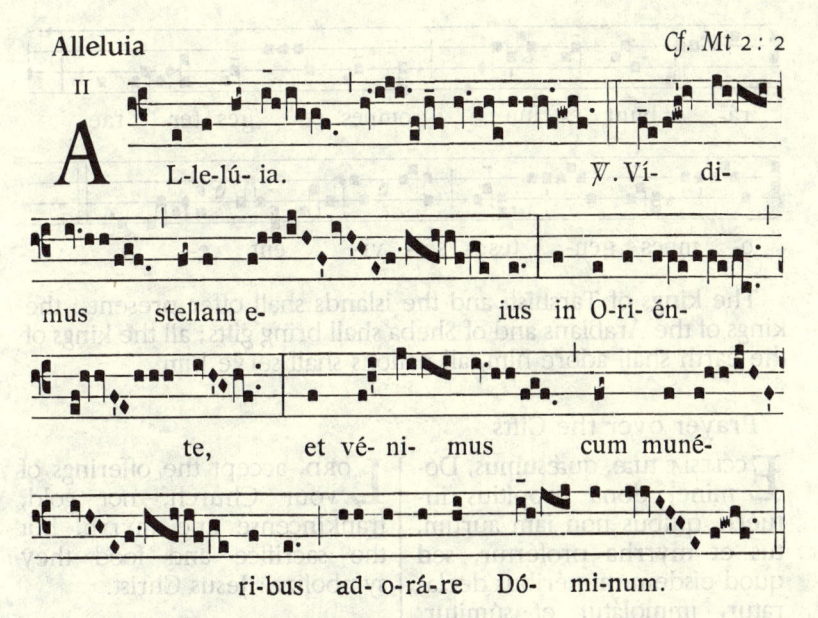

Alleluia *Cf. Mt 2 : 2*

Alleluia. ℣. Vídimus stellam eius in Oriénte, et vénimus cum munéribus adoráre Dóminum.

We have seen his star in the East, and we have come with our gifts, to worship the Lord.

Gospel

Mt 2 : 1-12: *Adoration of the wise men.*

Offertory *Ps 71 : 10, 11*

Reges Tharsis * et ínsulae múnera ófferent : reges Arabum et Saba dona addúcent : et ado-

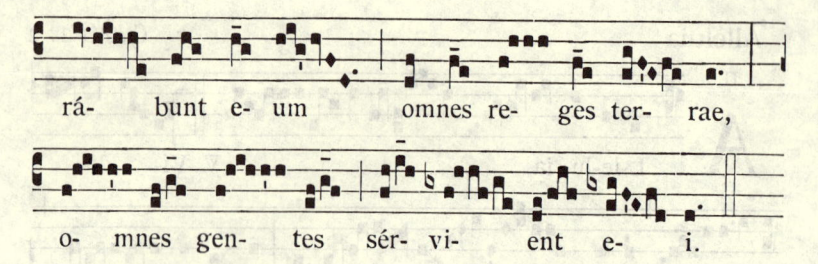

rá- bunt e- um omnes re- ges ter- rae, o- mnes gen- tes sér- vi- ent e- i.

The kings of Tarshish and the islands shall offer presents; the kings of the Arabians and of Sheba shall bring gifts; all the kings of the earth shall adore him, all nations shall serve him.

Prayer over the Gifts

ECCLESIÆ tuæ, quæsumus, Dómine, dona propítius intuére, quibus non iam aurum, tus et myrrha profértur, sed quod eísdem munéribus declarátur, immolátur et súmitur, Iesus Christus.

LORD, accept the offerings of your Church, not gold, frankincense and myrrh, but the sacrifice and food they symbolize: Jesus Christ.

Preface

VERE dignum et iustum est, æquum et salutáre, nos tibi semper et ubíque grátias ágere: Dómine, sancte Pater, omnípotens ætérne Deus:

Quia ipsum in Christo salútis nostræ mystérium hódie ad lumen géntium revelásti, et, cum in substántia nostræ mortalitátis appáruit, nova nos immortalitátis eius glória reparásti.

Et ídeo cum Angelis et Archángelis, cum Thronis et Dominatiónibus, cumque omni milítia cæléstis exércitus, hymnum glóriæ tuæ cánimus, sine fine dicéntes:

FATHER, all-powerful and ever-living God, we do well always and everywhere to give you thanks.

Today you revealed in Christ your eternal plan of salvation and showed him as the light of all peoples. Now that his glory has shone among us you have renewed humanity in his immortal image.

Now, with angels and archangels, and the whole company of heaven, we sing the unending hymn of your praise: Holy...

With the First Eucharistic Prayer, proper Communicantes, p. 23.

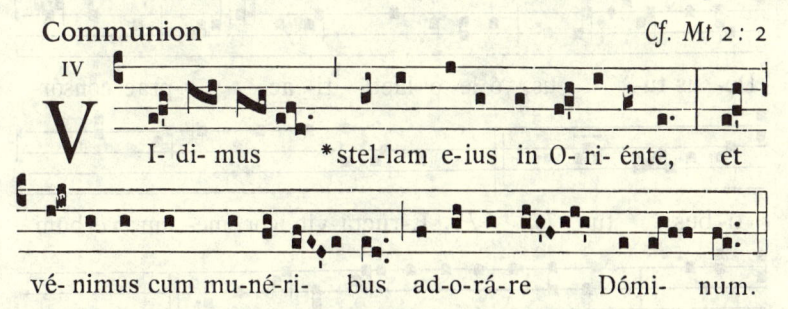

Communion   *Cf. Mt* 2 : 2

VIdimus *stellam eius in Oriénte, et vénimus cum munéribus adoráre Dóminum.

We have seen his star in the East, and we have come with our gifts, to worship the Lord.

Prayer after Communion

CÆLESTI lúmine, quǽsumus, Dómine, semper et ubíque nos prǽveni, ut mystérium, cuius nos partícipes esse voluísti, et puro cernámus intúitu, et digno percipiámus afféctu.

FATHER, guide us with your light. Help us to recognize Christ in this eucharist and welcome him with love.

Sunday after January 6

THE BAPTISM OF THE LORD

Feast

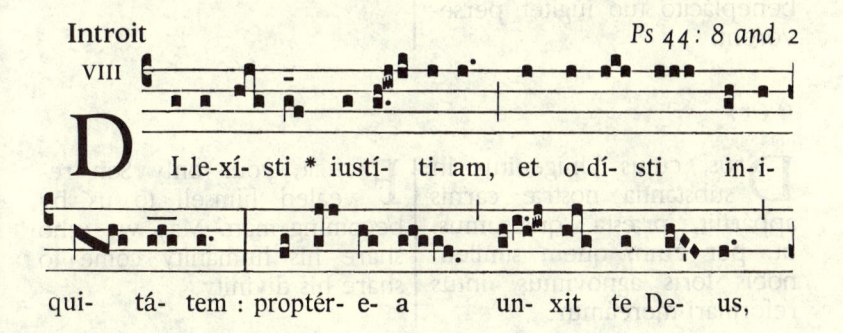

Introit   *Ps* 44 : 8 and 2

DIlexísti * iustítiam, et odísti iniquitátem : proptérea unxit te Deus,

Baptism of the Lord

De- us tu- us, ó-le- o laetí- ti- ae prae consór-ti-bus tu- is. Ps. E-ructá-vit cor me- um verbum bonum : di- co e-go ó-pe-ra me- a re-gi.

You have loved justice and hated iniquity; therefore God, your God, has anointed you with the oil of gladness above your companions. ℣. My heart overflows with a goodly theme; I address my works to the King.

Opening Prayer

Omnipotens sempitérne Deus, qui Christum, in Iordáne flúmine baptizátum, Spíritu Sancto super eum descendénte, diléctum Fílium tuum sollémniter declarásti, concéde fíliis adoptiónis tuæ, ex aqua et Spíritu Sancto renátis, ut in beneplácito tuo iúgiter persevérent.

Almighty, eternal God, when the Spirit descended upon Jesus at his baptism in the Jordan, you revealed him as your own beloved Son. Keep us, your children born of water and the Spirit, faithful to our calling.

Or:

Deus, cuius Unigénitus in substántia nostræ carnis appáruit, præsta, quæsumus, ut, per eum, quem símilem nobis foris agnóvimus, intus reformári mereámur.

Father, your only Son revealed himself to us by becoming man. May we who share his humanity come to share his divinity.

Baptism of the Lord

First reading
Is 42: 1-4, 6-7: *Behold my servant.*
Or:
B. Is 55: 1-11: *Come to the waters.*
C. Is 40: 1-5, 9-11: *Behold your God*

Gradual   Ps 71: 18, ℣. 3

Benedíctus * Dóminus Deus Israel, qui facit mirabília magna solus a saéculo. ℣. Suscípiant montes pacem pópulo tuo, et colles iustítiam.

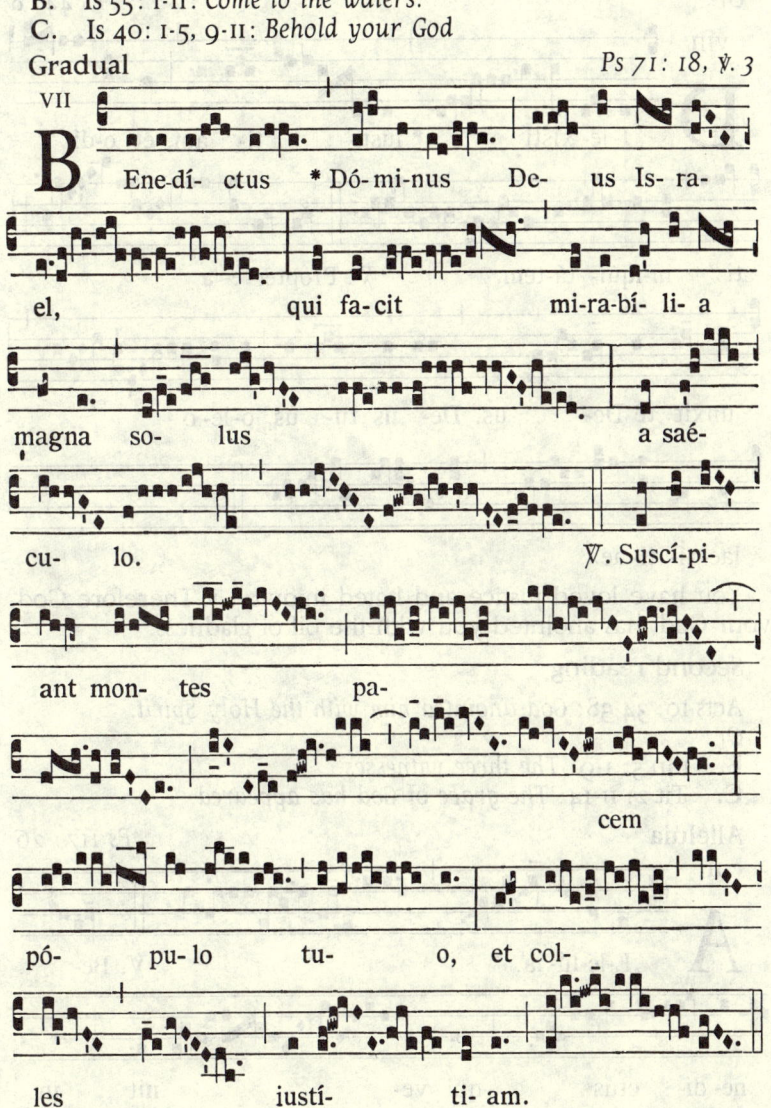

Blessed be the Lord, the God of Israel, who alone accomplishes great wonders from all eternity. ℣. Let the mountains receive peace for the people, and the hills justice.

Or: Ps 44: 8

DI-lexísti * iustítiam, et odísti iniquitátem. ℣. Proptérea unxit te Deus, Deus tuus, óleo laetítiae.

You have loved justice and hated iniquity. ℣. Therefore God, your God, has anointed you with the oil of gladness.

Second reading

Acts 10: 34-38: *God anointed him with the Holy Spirit.*
Or:
B.   1 Jn 5: 1-9: *The three witnesses.*
C.   Tit 2: 11-14: *The grace of God has appeared.*

Alleluia

Ps 117: 26

ALlelúia. ℣. Benedíctus qui venit in

Baptism of the Lord

... nómine Dómini: Deus Dóminus et illúxit nobis.

Blessed is he who comes in the name of the Lord. The Lord God is our light.

Or: Ps 88: 21

ALlelúia. ℣. Invéni David servum meum: óleo sancto meo unxi eum.

I have found David my servant; with my holy oil have I anointed him.

Gospel

A. Mt 3: 13-17: *The baptism of Jesus.*
B. Mk 1: 6b-11: *The baptism of Jesus.*
C. Lk 3: 15-16, 21-22: *The baptism of Jesus.*

Offertory
Ps 117 : 26, 27

VIII

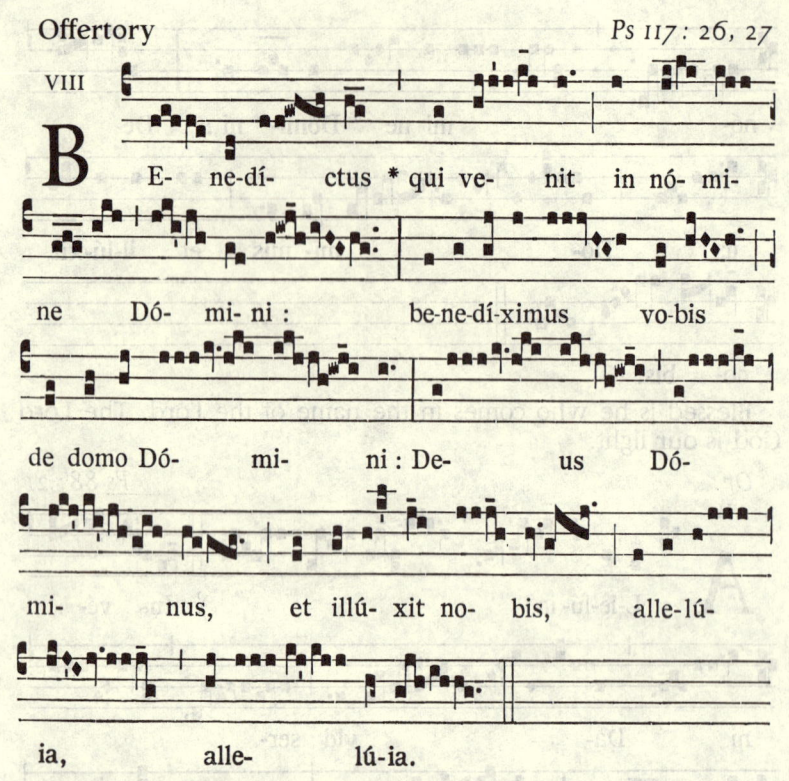

Be-ne-dí-ctus * qui ve-nit in nó-mi-ne Dó-mi-ni : be-ne-dí-ximus vo-bis de domo Dó-mi-ni : De-us Dó-mi-nus, et illú-xit no-bis, alle-lú-ia, alle-lú-ia.

Blessed is he who comes in the name of the Lord. We bless you from the house of the Lord; the Lord God is our light, alleluia, alleluia.

Prayer over the Gifts

Súscipe múnera, Dómine, in dilécti Fílii tui revelatióne deláta, ut fidélium tuórum oblátio in eius sacrifícium tránseat, qui mundi vóluit peccáta miserátus ablúere.

Lord, we celebrate the revelation of Christ your Son who takes away the sins of the world. Accept our gifts and let them become one with his sacrifice.

Preface

Vere dignum et iustum est, æquum et salutáre, nos

Father, all-powerful and ever-living God, we do

Baptism of the Lord

tibi semper et ubíque grátias ágere : Dómine, sancte Pater, omnípotens ætérne Deus :

Qui miris signásti mystériis novum in Iordáne lavácrum, ut, per vocem de cælo delápsam, habitáre Verbum tuum inter hómines crederétur ; et, per Spíritum in colúmbæ spécie descendéntem, Chistus Servus tuus óleo perúngi lætítiæ ac mitti ad evangelizándum paupéribus noscerétur.

Et ídeo cum cælórum virtútibus in terris te iúgiter celebrámus, maiestáti tuæ sine fine clamántes :

well always and everywhere to give you thanks.

You celebrated your new gift of baptism by signs and wonders at the Jordan. Your voice was heard from heaven to awaken faith in the presence among us of the Word made man. Your Spirit was seen as a dove, revealing Jesus as your servant, and anointing him with joy as the Christ, sent to bring to the poor the good news of salvation.

In our unending joy we echo on earth the song of the angels in heaven as they praise your glory for ever: Holy...

Communion *Gal 3 : 27*

O-mnes * qui in Christo baptizáti estis, Christum induístis, alle-lúia.

As for all of you who have been baptised in Christ, you have put on Christ, alleluia.

Prayer after Communion

SACRO múnere satiáti, cleméntiam tuam, Dómine, supplíciter exorámus, ut, Unigénitum tuum fidéliter audiéntes, fílii tui vere nominémur et simus.

LORD, you feed us with bread from heaven. May we hear your Son with faith and become your children in name and in fact.

Baptism of the Lord

After the Baptism of the Lord, Ordinary Time begins. The following Sunday is therefore the Second Sunday in Ordinary Time, p. 431.

If, as in some regions, Epiphany is transferred to Sunday, and this Sunday falls on January 7 or 8, the feast of the Baptism of the Lord is celebrated on the following Monday, with only one reading before the Gospel. The following Sunday is the Second Sunday in Ordinary Time.

The series of Sundays in Ordinary Time is interrupted by Lent and resumed after Pentecost.

THE LENTEN SEASON

ASH WEDNESDAY

Introit   Wis 11: 24-25, 27; Ps 56

MIseréris * ómnium, Dómine, et nihil odísti eórum quae fecísti, dissímulans peccáta hóminum propter paeniténtiam, et parcens illis: quia tu es Dóminus Deus noster. *Ps.* Miserére mei Deus, miserére mei: quóniam in te confídit ánima mea.

Your mercy extends to all things, O Lord, and you despise none of the things you have made. You overlook the sins of men for the sake of repentance. You grant them your pardon, because you are the Lord our God. ℣. Be merciful to me, O God, be merciful to me, for my soul confides in you.

The Glória is not sung during Lent.

Opening Prayer

CONCEDE NOBIS, Dómine, præsídia milítiæ christiánæ sanctis inchoáre ieiúniis, ut, contra spiritáles nequítias pugnatúri, continéntiæ muniámur auxíliis.

LORD, protect us in our struggle against evil. As we begin the discipline of Lent, make this season holy by our self-denial.

First reading

Joel 2: 12-18: *Rend your hearts and not your garments.*

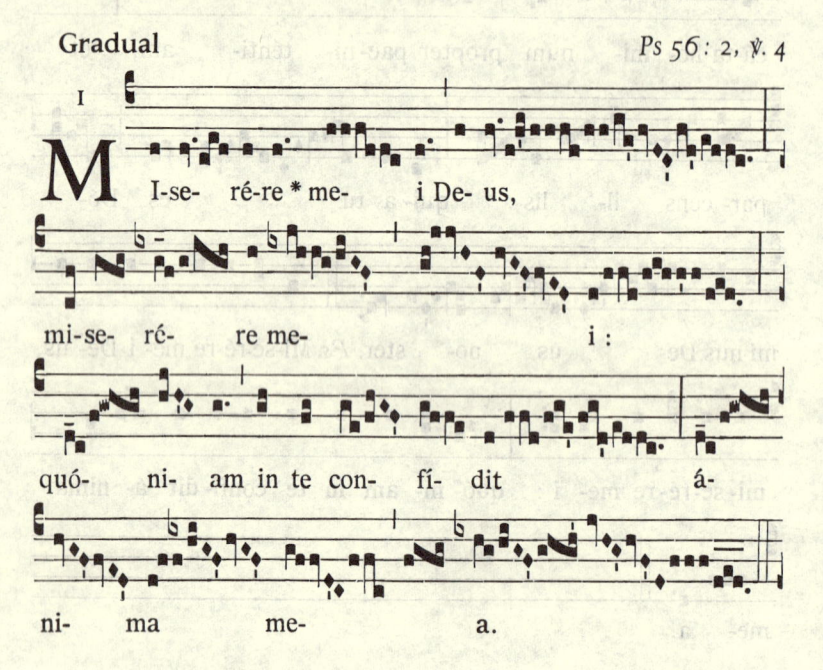

Gradual   Ps 56: 2, ℣. 4

Mi-se-ré-re * me-i De-us, mi-se-ré-re me-i: quó-ni-am in te con-fí-dit á-ni-ma me-a.

Ash Wednesday

℣. Mi-sit de cae- lo, et li- be-rá- vit me: dedit in oppró- bri- um con- cul-cán- tes me.

Be merciful to me, O God, be merciful to me, for my soul confides in you. ℣. He has sent from heaven and saved me; he has put to shame those who trampled upon me.

Second reading
2 Cor 5: 20-6: 2: *Be reconciled to God.*

Tract   *Ps 102: 10 and 78: 8 and 9*

Dómine, *non secúndum pec- cá-ta nostra, quae fé-cimus nos: neque se-cúndum in-iqui-tá-tes no- stras re-trí- bu- as no- bis.

℣. Dó- mi-ne, ne memí-ne-

...ris iniquitátum nostrárum antiquárum: cito antícipent nos misericórdiae tuae, quia páuperes facti sumus nimis. ℣. Ad-iuva nos, Deus salutáris noster: et propter glóriam nóminis tui, Dómine, líbera nos: et propítius esto peccátis nostris, propter nomen tuum.

Lord, do not requite us according to the sins we have committed or according to our iniquity. ℣. Lord, remember not our sins of old; let your compassion come speedily to meet us, for we are brought very low. ℣. Help us, O God, our Saviour, and for the glory of your name, deliver us, O Lord; and forgive us our sins, for your name's sake.

Ash Wednesday

Gospel

Mt 6: 1-6, 16-18: *Your Father who sees in secret will reward you.*

Blessing of the Ashes

After the homily, the priest says:

Deum Patrem, fratres caríssimi, supplíciter deprecémur, ut hos cíneres, quos pæniténtiæ causa capítibus nostris impónimus, ubertáte grátiæ suæ benedícere dignétur.

Dear friends in Christ, let us ask our Father to bless these ashes which we will use as the mark of our repentance.

After a brief moment of silence, he says one of the following prayers:

Deus, qui humiliatióne flécteris et satisfactióne placáris, aurem tuæ pietátis précibus nostris inclína, et super fámulos tuos, horum cínerum aspersióne contáctos, grátiam tuæ benedictiónis effúnde propítius, ut, quadragesimálem observántiam prosequéntes, ad Fílii tui paschále mystérium celebrándum purificátis méntibus pervenire mereántur.

Lord, bless the sinner who asks for your forgiveness and bless all those who receive these ashes. May they keep this lenten season in preparation for the joy of Easter.

Or:

Deus, qui non mortem sed conversiónem desíderas peccatórum, preces nostras cleménter exáudi, et hos cíneres, quos capítibus nostris impóni decérnimus, benedícere pro tua pietáte dignáre, ut qui nos cínerem esse et in púlverem reversúros cognóscimus, quadragesimális exercitatiónis studio, peccatórum véniam et novitátem vitæ, ad imáginem Fílii tui resurgéntis cónsequi valeámus.

Lord, bless these ashes by which we show that we are dust. Pardon our sins and keep us faithful to the discipline of Lent, for you do not want sinners to die but to live with the risen Christ.

Ash Wednesday

Giving of the ashes. *The priest says to each person:*

Pænitémini, et crédite Evan-gélio. | Turn away from sin and be faithful to the Gospel.

Or:

Meménto, homo, quia pulvis es, et in púlverem revertéris. | Remember, man, you are dust and to dust you will return.

Meanwhile, the following chants are sung:
Antiphons *Cf. Joel 2 : 13*

I

Mmutémur * hábitu, in cínere et cilício : ieiunémus, et plorémus ante Dóminum : quia a multum miséricors est dimíttere peccáta nostra Deus noster.

Let us change the appearance of our garments with ashes and sackcloth; let us come before the Lord with fasting and tears. For in his great mercy, our God will forgive us our sins.

Joel 2 : 17 ; Esther 13 : 17

IV

Uxta vestíbulum * et altáre plorábunt sacerdótes et levítae minístri Dómi-

♭ ni, et dicent : Parce Dómine, parce pópulo tuo : et ne díssipes ora clamántium ad te, Dómine.

Between the vestibule and the altar, the priests and the Levites, the ministers of the Lord, will weep and say: "Spare your people, spare them O Lord, and do not destroy the mouth of those who call upon you."

Responsory *Cf. Bar 3: 2, ℣. Ps 78: 9*

II

E-mendémus * in mélius, quae ignoránter peccávimus : ne súbito praeoccupáti die mortis, quaerámus spátium paeniténtiae, et inveníre non possímus. * Atténde Dómine, et miserére : quia peccávimus tibi. ℣. Ad- iuva

Ash Wednesday

nos, De- us sa-lu-tá-ris no- ster : et propter honó-rem nó-mi-nis tu- i, Dómi-ne, lí-be- ra nos. * Atténde.

Let us make amends for the sins we have committed in ignorance, lest death's day come upon us suddenly, when we might seek more time for repentance and find none. * Hearken, O Lord, and have mercy, for we have sinned against you. ℣. Help us, O God, our Saviour, and for the glory of your name, deliver us, O Lord. * Hearken, O Lord...

The Credo is not said.

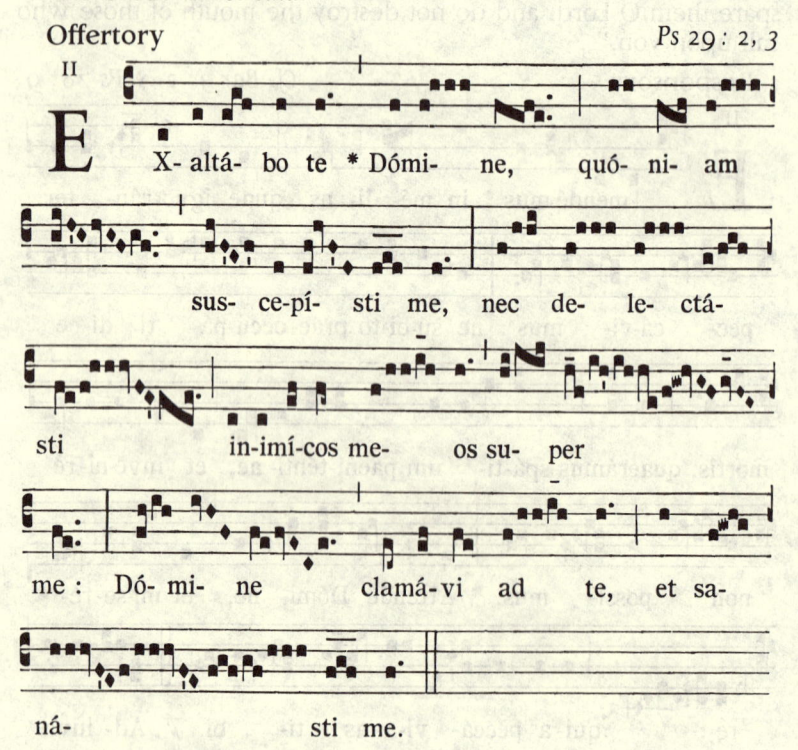

Offertory *Ps 29 : 2, 3*

EX- altá- bo te * Dómi- ne, quó- ni- am sus- ce-pí- sti me, nec de- le- ctá- sti in-imí-cos me- os su- per me : Dó- mi- ne clamá-vi ad te, et sa-ná- sti me.

Ash Wednesday

I will extol you, O Lord, for you have drawn me up, and have not let my foes rejoice over me. O Lord, I cried unto you and you healed me.

Prayer over the Gifts

SACRIFICIUM quadragesimális inítii sollémniter immolámus, te, Dómine, deprecántes, ut per pæniténtiæ caritatísque labóres a nóxiis voluptátibus temperémus, et, a peccátis mundáti, ad celebrándam Fílii tui passiónem mereámur esse devóti.

LORD, help us to resist temptation by our lenten works of charity and penance. By this sacrifice may we be prepared to celebrate the death and resurrection of Christ our Saviour and be cleansed from sin and renewed in spirit.

Lenten Preface, p. 52 or 53.

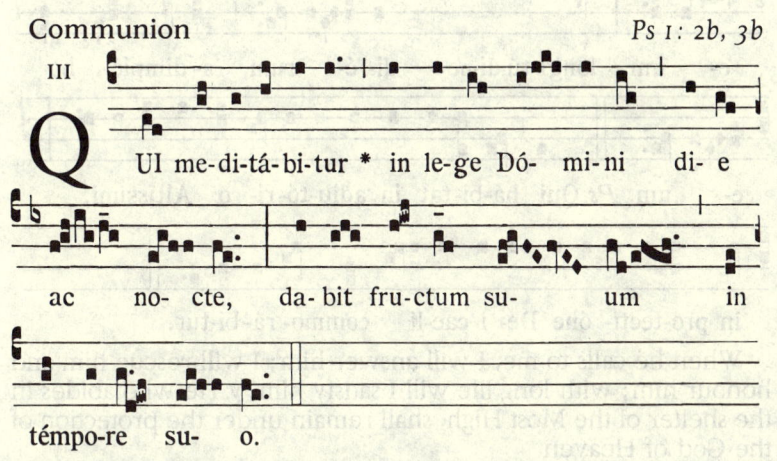

Communion   Ps 1: 2b, 3b

Qui meditábitur in lege Dómini die ac nocte, dabit fructum suum in témpore suo.

He who meditates day and night on the law of the Lord, shall bear fruit in due season.

Prayer after Communion

PERCEPTA nobis, Dómine, præbeant sacraménta subsídium, ut tibi grata sint nostra ieiúnia, et nobis profíciant ad medélam.

LORD, through this communion may our lenten penance give you glory and bring us your protection.

FIRST SUNDAY OF LENT

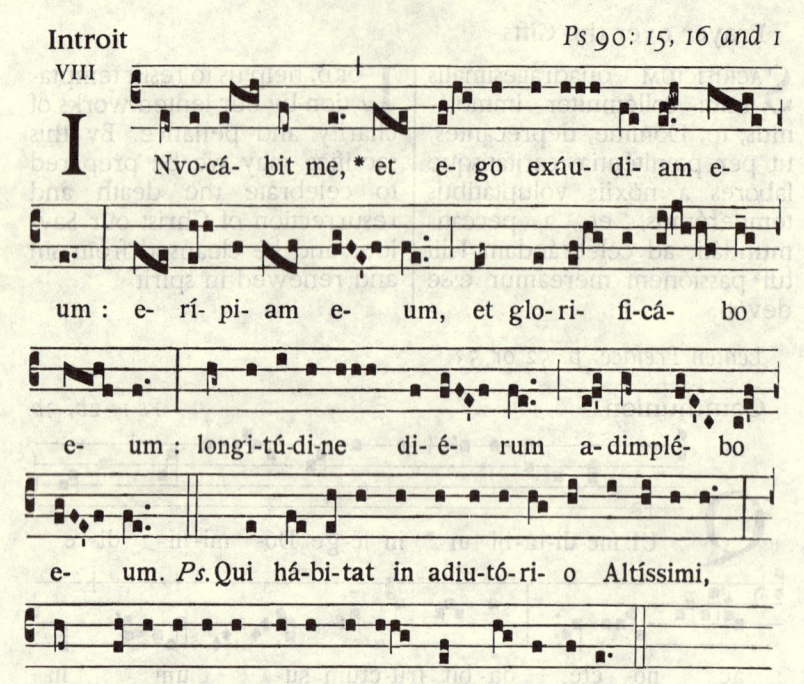

Introit   Ps 90: 15, 16 and 1

VIII

Invocábit me, * et ego exáudiam eum: erípiam eum, et glorificábo eum: longitúdine diérum adimplébo eum. *Ps.* Qui hábitat in adiutório Altíssimi, in protectióne Dei caeli commorábitur.

When he calls to me, I will answer him; I will rescue him and honour him; with long life will I satisfy him. ℣. He who abides in the shelter of the Most High, shall remain under the protection of the God of Heaven.

Opening Prayer

Concede nobis, omnípotens Deus, ut, per ánnua quadragesimális exercítia sacraménti, et ad intellegéndum Christi proficiámus arcánum, et efféctus eius digna conversatióne sectémur.

Father through our observance of Lent, help us to understand the meaning of your Son's death and resurrection, and teach us to reflect it in our lives.

1st Sunday of Lent

First reading
A. Gen 2: 7-9; 3: 1-7: *Creation and sin of our first parents.*
B. Gen 9: 8-15: *The covenant with Noah and his sons.*
C. Deut 26: 4-10: *Profession of faith of the Chosen People.*

Gradual Ps 90: 11-12

ANgelis * suis mandávit de te, ut custódiant te in ómnibus viis tuis. ℣. In mánibus portábunt te, ne unquam offéndas ad lápidem pedem tuum.

To his Angels he has given a commandment concerning you, to keep you in all your ways. ℣. On their hands they will bear you up, lest you dash your foot against a stone.

1st Sunday of Lent

Second reading
A. Rom 5: 12-19 *or* 5: 12, 17-19: *Adam and Christ.*
B. 1 Pet 3: 18-22: *The baptism which now saves.*
C. Rom 10: 8-13: *The message of faith, received and proclaimed.*

Tract   Ps 90: 1-7 and 11-16

Qui hábitat * in adiutório Altíssimi, in protectióne Dei caeli commorábitur. ℣. Dicet Dómino: Suscéptor meus es, et refúgium meum, Deus meus: sperábo in eum. ℣. Quóniam ipse liberávit me de láqueo

He who abides in the shelter of the Most High, shall remain under the protection of the Lord of Heaven. ℣. He shall say to the Lord: "You are my protector and my refuge;" my God, in whom I trust. ℣. For he has set me free from the snare of the fowler, and

1st Sunday of Lent

ve- nán- ti- um, et a ver-bo á- spe-ro.

℣. Scápu- lis su- is ob-umbrá- bit ti- bi, et sub pennis e- ius spe- rá- bis. ℣. Scu-to circúmda- bit te vé-ri- tas e- ius : non timé- bis a timó-re noctúr- no. ℣. A sa- gít- ta vo-lán- te per di- em, a negó- ti- o per-ambu-lán- te in té- nebris, a ru- í-na et daemó- ni- o me-ri-di- á-

from cutting words. ℣. He will conceal you with his pinions, and under his wings you will find refuge. ℣. His faithfulness will shield you as with a buckler, you will not suffer the terrors of the night: ℣. You shall fear neither the arrow that flies by day, nor the conspiracy that stalks in the darkness, nor destruction, nor the

no. ℣. Ca- dent a lá-te-re tu-o mil- le, et decem míl- li- a a dextris tu- is: ti-bi au- tem non appro-pinquá- bit. ℣. Quó-ni- am Ange- lis su- is mandá- vit de te, ut custó-di- ant te in ómni-bus vi- is tu- is. ℣. In má-ni- bus por- tá- bunt te, ne unquam of-fén-das ad lá- pi-dem pe-dem tu- um.

demon of noonday. ℣. A thousand will fall at your side, and ten thousand at your right, but you shall remain unharmed. ℣. For to his Angels he has given a commandment concerning you, to keep you in all your ways. ℣. In their hands they will bear you up, lest

1st Sunday of Lent

℣. Super áspidem et basilíscum ambulábis, et conculcábis leónem et dracónem.

℣. Quóniam in me sperávit, liberábo eum: prótegam eum, quóniam cognóvit nomen meum. ℣. Invocábit me, et ego exáudiam eum: cum ipso sum in tribulatióne. ℣. Erípiam

you dash your foot against a stone. ℣. On the asp and the basilisk you will tread and trample the lion and the dragon. ℣. Because he has put his hope in me I will deliver him; I will protect him, because he knows my name. ℣. He shall call out to me, and I shall

e- um, et glo-ri- fi- cábo e- um : longi-tú- di-ne di- é-rum ad-implébo e- um, et osténdam il- li sa- lu-tá- re me- um.

answer him: I am with him in tribulation. ℣. I will rescue him and honour him; with long days will I satisfy him; and I shall let him see my saving power.

Gospel
A. Mt 4: 1-11: *The temptation of Jesus in the desert.*
B. Mk 1: 12-15: *Jesus in the desert and in Galilee.*
C. Lk 4: 1-13: *The temptation of Jesus in the desert.*

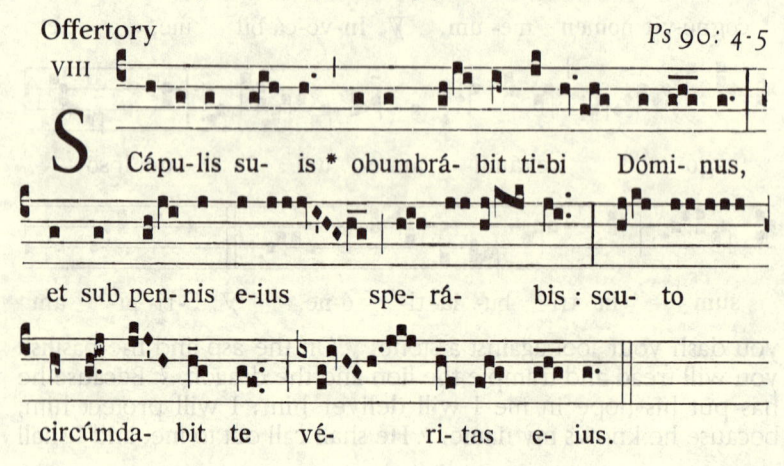

Offertory Ps 90: 4-5

S Cápu-lis su- is * obumbrá- bit ti-bi Dómi- nus, et sub pen- nis e-ius spe- rá- bis : scu- to circúmda- bit te vé- ri- tas e- ius.

The Lord will overshadow you with his pinions, and you will find refuge under his wings. His faithfulness will encompass you with a shield.

Prayer over the Gifts

Fac nos, quæsumus, Dómine, his munéribus offeréndis conveniénter aptári, quibus ipsíus venerábilis sacraménti celebrámus exórdium.

Lord, make us worthy to bring you these gifts. May this sacrifice help to change our lives.

Preface

Vere dignum et iustum est, æquum et salutáre, nos tibi semper et ubíque grátias ágere, Dómine, sancte Pater, omnípotens ætérne Deus, per Christum Dóminum nostrum.

Qui quadragínta diébus, terrénis ábstinens aliméntis, formam huius observántiæ ieiúnio dedicávit, et, omnes evértens antíqui serpéntis insídias,ферméntum malítiæ nos dócuit superáre, ut, paschále mystérium dignis méntibus celebrántes, ad pascha demum perpétuum transeámus.

Et ídeo cum Angelórum atque Sanctórum turba hymnum laudis tibi cánimus, sine fine dicéntes:

Father, all-powerful and ever-living God, we do well always and everywhere to give you thanks through Jesus Christ our Lord.

His fast of forty days makes this a holy season of self-denial. By rejecting the devil's temptations he has taught us to rid ourselves of the hidden corruption of evil, and so to share his paschal meal in purity of heart, until we come to its fulfilment in the promised land of heaven.

Now we join the angels and the saints as they sing their unending hymn of praise: Holy...

Communion Ps 90: 4-5

S Cá- pu-lis su- is * obumbrá- bit ti- bi, et

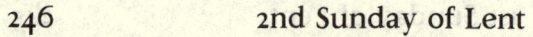

sub pen- nis e-ius spe- rá- bis : scu- to cir- cúmda- bit te vé-ri-tas e- ius.

He will overshadow you with his pinions, and you will find refuge under his wings. His faithfulness will encompass you with a shield.

Prayer after Communion

Cælesti pane refécti, quo fides álitur, spes provéhitur et cáritas roborátur, quæsumus, Dómine, ut ipsum, qui est panis vivus et verus, esuríre discámus, et in omni verbo, quod procédit de ore tuo, vívere valeámus.

Father, you increase our faith and hope, you deepen our love in this communion. Help us to live by your words and to seek Christ, our bread of life.

SECOND SUNDAY OF LENT

Introit — Ps 26: 8, 9 and 1

TI-bi di-xit cor me- um, quaesí-vi vul- tum tu- um, vultum tu- um Dómi-ne requí-ram : ne*

2nd Sunday of Lent

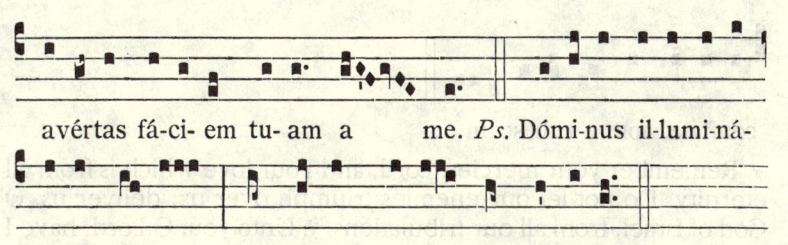

avértas fá-ci- em tu- am a me. *Ps.* Dómi-nus il-lumi-ná-ti- o me- a, et sa-lus me- a : quem timé-bo?

My heart declared to you: "Your countenance have I sought; I shall ever seek your countenance, O Lord; do not turn your face from me." ℣. The Lord is my light and my salvation; whom shall I fear?

Or: *Ps* 24: 6, 3, 22 *and* 1-2

IV

R Emi- nísce-re * mi- se-ra-ti- ó- num tu- á-rum, Dómi- ne, et mi- se-ri-cór-di- ae tu- ae, quae a saécu-lo sunt : ne unquam domi- néntur nobis in-imí- ci no- stri : lí-be-ra nos De- us Is- ra- el ex ómnibus angú- sti- is no- stris. *Ps.* Ad te Dómi-ne levá-vi á-nimam me- am : De- us me-us in te

2nd Sunday of Lent

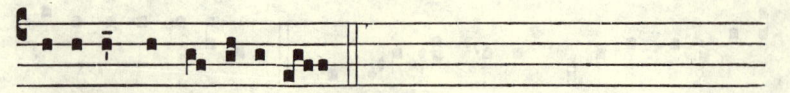

confí-do, non e-rubéscam.

Remember your mercies, Lord, and your love which is from all eternity. Do not let our enemies triumph over us; deliver us, O God of Israel, from all our tribulations. ℣. Unto you, O Lord, have I lifted up my soul; O my God, I trust in you, let me not be put to shame.

Opening Prayer

DEUS, qui nobis diléctum Fílium tuum audíre præcepísti, verbo tuo intérius nos páscere dignéris, ut, spiritáli purificáto intúitu, glóriæ tuæ lætémur aspéctu.

GOD OUR FATHER, help us to hear your Son. Enlighten us with your word, that we may find the way to your glory.

First reading

A. Gen 12: 1-4a: *The vocation of Abraham.*
B. Gen 22: 1-2, 9a, 10-13, 15-18: *The sacrifice of Isaac.*
C. Gen 15: 5-12, 17-18: *The covenant with Abraham.*

Gradual
Ps 82: 19, ℣. 14

Sci-ant gen-tes * quó-ni-am no-men ti-bi De-us: tu so-lus Al-tís-simus super o-mnem ter-ram. ℣. De-us me-us, pone il-

2nd Sunday of Lent

los ut ro- tam, et sic- ut stí- pu- lam an- te fá- ci- em ven- ti.

Let the nations know that God is your name; you alone are the Most High over all the earth. ℣. O my God, sweep them away like whirling dust, like chaff before the wind.

Second reading

A. 2 Tim 1: 8b-10: *God has saved us.*
B. Rom 8: 31b-34: *God did not spare his own Son.*
C. Phil 3: 17-4: 1 *or* 3: 20-4: 1: *We have our citizenship in heaven.*

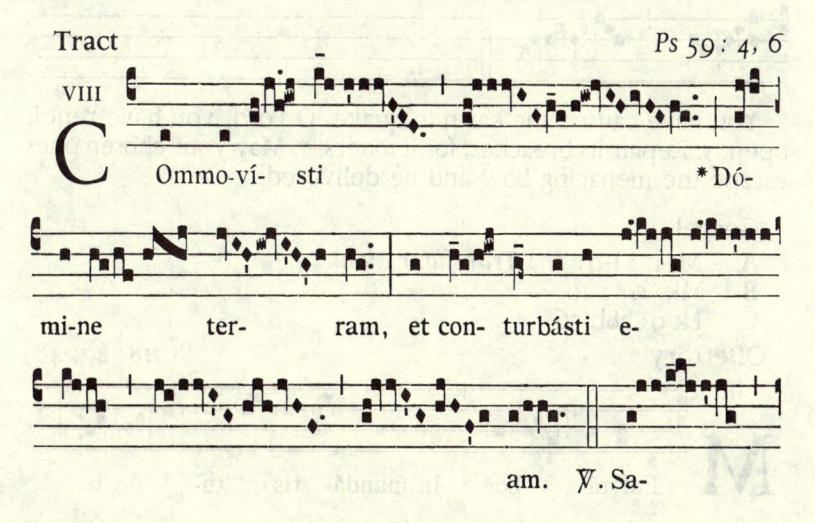

Tract

Ps 59: 4, 6

VIII C

Ommo-ví- sti *Dó- mi-ne ter- ram, et con- turbásti e- am.* ℣. Sa-

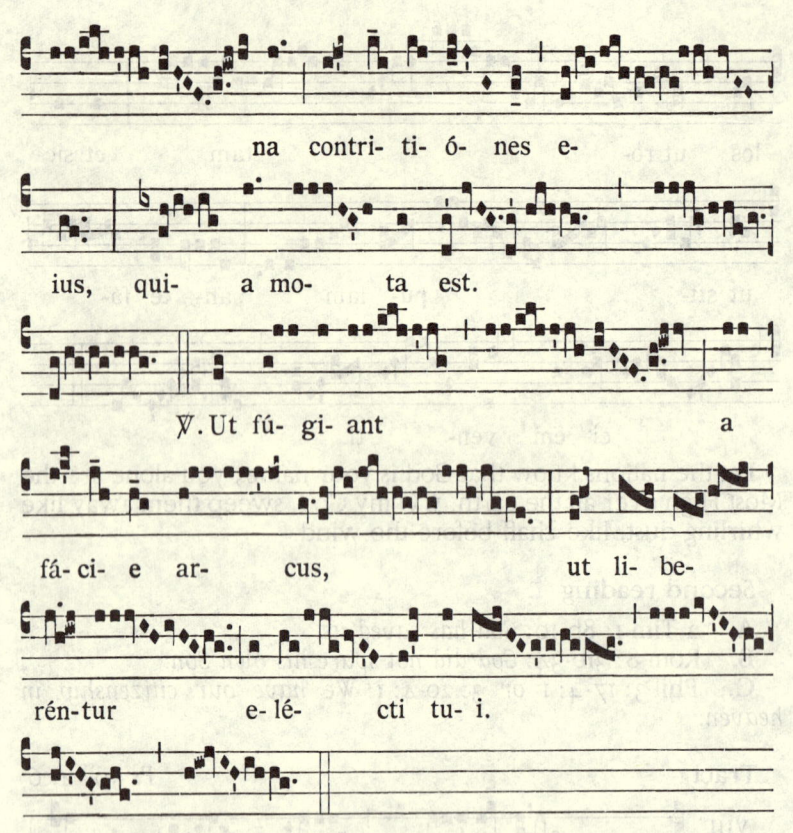

... na contritiónes eius, quia mota est. ℣. Ut fúgiant a fácie arcus, ut liberéntur elécti tui.

You have caused the earth to quake, O Lord, you have rent it open. ℣. Repair its breaches, for it totters. ℣. May your chosen ones escape the menacing bow and be delivered.

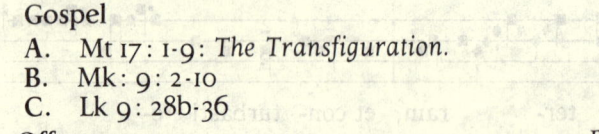

Gospel
A. Mt 17: 1-9: *The Transfiguration.*
B. Mk: 9: 2-10
C. Lk 9: 28b-36

Offertory   Ps 118: 47, 48

MEditábor * in mandátis tuis,

2nd Sunday of Lent

quae di-léxi valde: et levábo manus meas ad mandáta tua, quae diléxi.

I will meditate on your commandments which I love exceedingly; I will lift up my hands towards your commandments which I love.

Prayer over the Gifts

Hæc hóstia, Dómine, quæsumus, emúndet nostra delícta et ad celebránda festa paschália fidélium tuórum córpora mentésque sanctíficet.

Lord, make us holy. May this eucharist take away our sins that we may be prepared to celebrate the resurrection.

Preface

Vere dignum et iustum est, æquum et salutáre, nos tibi semper et ubíque grátias ágere: Dómine, sancte Pater, omnípotens ætérne Deus: per Christum Dóminum nostrum.

Qui, própria morte prænuntiáta discípulis, in monte sancto suam eis apéruit claritátem, ut per passiónem, étiam lege prophetísque testántibus, ad glóriam resurrectiónis perveníri constáret.

Father, all-powerful and ever-living God, we do well always and everywhere to give you thanks through Jesus Christ our Lord.

On your holy mountain he revealed himself in glory in the presence of his disciples. He had already prepared them for his approaching death. He wanted to teach them through the Law and the Prophets that the promised Christ had first to suffer and so come to the glory of his resurrection.

Et ídeo cum cælórum virtútibus in terris te iúgiter celebrámus, maiestáti tuæ sine fine clamántes :

In our unending joy we echo on earth the song of the angels in heaven as they praise your glory for ever : Holy...

Communion Mt 17 : 9

*VI-si-ó-nem * quam vi- dístis, némi-ni dí-xé- ri- tis, do-nec a mórtu- is re-súrgat Fí- li- us hómi-nis.*

Tell no one about the vision you have seen until the Son of Man has risen from the dead.

Prayer after Communion

PERCIPIENTES, Dómine, gloriósa mystéria, grátias tibi reférre satágimus, quod, in terra pósitos, iam cæléstium præstas esse partícipes.

LORD, we give thanks for these holy mysteries which bring to us here on earth a share in the life to come.

THIRD SUNDAY OF LENT

Introit Ps 24 : 15, 16 and 1-2

*O- cu-li me- i * sem- per ad Dó- mi- num, qui- a ipse evél- let de lá-que- o pedes me- os :*

3rd Sunday of Lent

réspice in me, et miserére mei, quóniam únicus et pauper sum ego.

Ps. Ad te Dómine levávi ánimam meam: Deus meus, in te confído, non erubéscam.

My eyes are forever turned towards the Lord; for he shall release my feet from the snare; look upon me and have mercy on me, for I am abandoned and destitute. ℣. Unto you, O Lord, have I lifted up my soul; O my God, I trust in you, let me not be put to shame.

Or:

Dum sanctificátus, *p. 391.*

Opening Prayer

Deus, ómnium misericordiárum et totíus bonitátis auctor, qui peccatórum remédia in ieiúniis, oratiónibus et eleemósynis demonstrásti, hanc humilitátis nostræ confessiónem propítius intuére, ut, qui inclinámur consciéntia nostra, tua semper misericórdia sublevémur.

Father, you have taught us to overcome our sins by prayer, fasting and works of mercy. When we are discouraged by our weakness, give us confidence in your love.

First reading

A. Ex 17: 3-7: *Thirst in the desert.*
B. Ex 20: 1-17 or 20: 1-3; 7-8; 12-17: *The Law is given to Moses.*
C. Ex 3: 1-8a, 13-15: *The burning bush.*

3rd Sunday of Lent

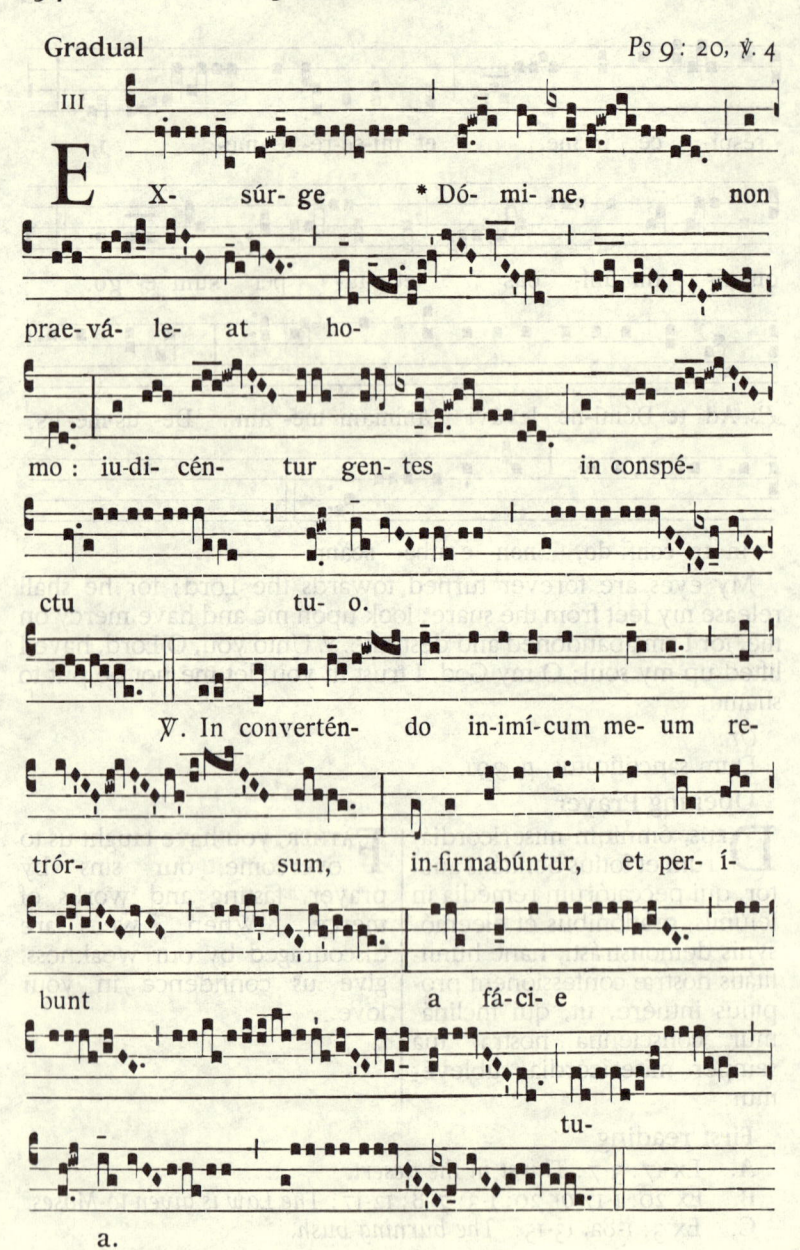

Gradual — Ps 9 : 20, ℣. 4

Exsúrge * Dómine, non praeváleat homo: iudicéntur gentes in conspéctu tuo.

℣. In converténdo inimícum meum retrórsum, infirmabúntur, et períbunt a fácie tua.

3rd Sunday of Lent

Arise, O Lord, let not man prevail; let the gentiles be judged in your presence. ℣. When my enemies are turned back in defeat, they shall lose strength and perish before your face.

Second reading
A. Rom 5: 1-2, 5-8: *Christ has died for us all.*
B. 1 Cor 1: 22-25: *We preach Christ crucified.*
C. 1 Cor 10: 1-6, 10-12: *The rock was Christ.*

Tract
Ps 122: 1-3

VIII

AD te levávi * óculos meos, qui hábitas in caelis. ℣. Ecce sicut óculi servórum in mánibus dominórum suórum: ℣. Et sicut óculi ancíllae in mánibus dóminae suae: ℣. Ita óculi no-

3rd Sunday of Lent

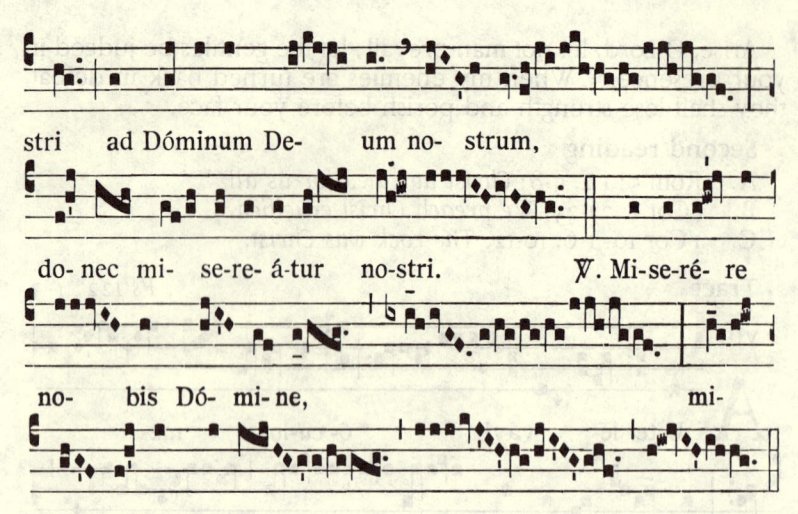

...stri ad Dóminum Deum nostrum, donec misereátur nostri. ℣. Miserére nobis Dómine, miserére nobis.

I have lifted my eyes up unto you, who dwell in the heavens. ℣. Behold, as the eyes of servants look to the hands of their masters; ℣. And as the eyes of a maidservant to the hands of her mistress; ℣. So do our eyes look unto the Lord our God until he have mercy on us. ℣. Have mercy on us, O Lord, have mercy on us.

Gospel

A. Jn 4: 5-42 *or* 4: 5-15, 19b-26, 39a, 40-42: *The Samaritan woman.*
B. Jn 2: 13-25: *The sellers expelled from the Temple.*
C. Lk 13: 1-9: *The sterile fig tree.*
(The readings from Year A can be used for the other years.)

Offertory — Ps 18: 9, 10, 11, 12

Iustítiae Dómini * rectae, laetificántes corda, et dulcióra su-

per mel et favum : nam et servus tuus custodiet e- a.

The ordinances of the Lord are right, bringing joy to all hearts, sweeter than honey or the honeycomb. Therefore your servant will observe them.

Prayer over the Gifts

His sacrifíciis, Dómine, concéde placátus, ut, qui própriis orámus absólvi delíctis, fratérna dimíttere studeámus.

Lord, by the grace of this sacrifice may we who ask forgiveness be ready to forgive one another.

Preface *when the Gospel of the Samaritan woman is read:*

Vere dignum et iustum est, æquum et salutáre, nos tibi semper et ubíque grátias ágere : Dómine, sancte Pater, omnípotens ætérne Deus : per Christum Dóminum nostrum.

Qui, dum aquæ sibi pétiit potum a Samaritána præbéri, iam in ea fídei donum ipse creáverat, et ita eius fidem sitíre dignátus est, ut ignem in illa divíni amóris accénderet.

Unde et nos tibi grátias ágimus, et tuas virtútes cum Angelis prædicámus, dicéntes :

Father, all-powerful and ever-living God, we do well always and everywhere to give you thanks through Jesus Christ our Lord.

When he asked the woman of Samaria for water to drink, Christ had already prepared for her the gift of faith. In his thirst to receive her faith he awakened in her heart the fire of your love.

With thankful praise, in company with the angels, we glorify the wonders of your power: Holy...

Otherwise, one of the Lenten Prefaces is used, p. 52 or 53.

3rd Sunday of Lent

Communion Passer invénit, p. 502. Or, when the Gospel of the Samaritan woman is read:

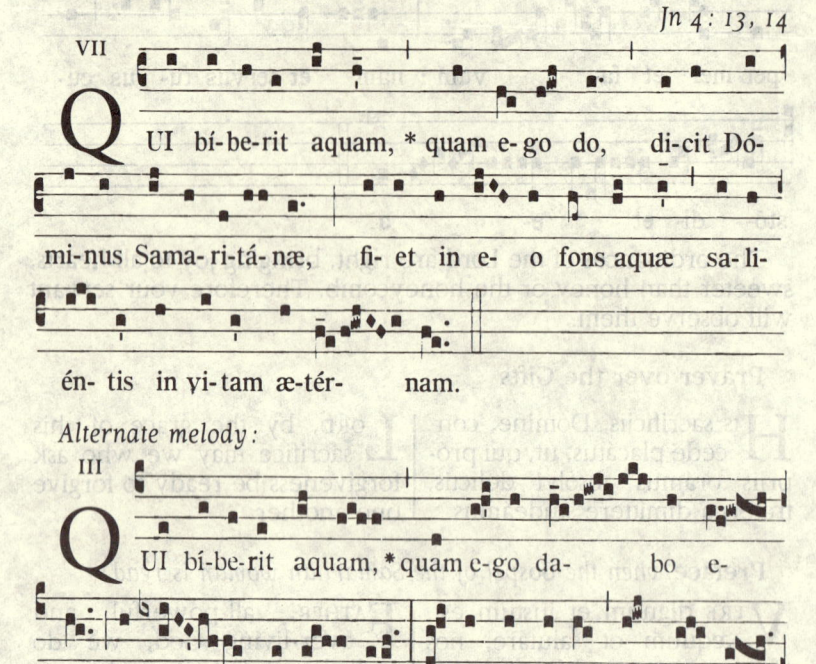

Jn 4: 13, 14

VII

QUI bí-be-rit aquam, * quam e-go do, di-cit Dó-mi-nus Sama-ri-tá-næ, fi-et in e-o fons aquæ sa-li-én-tis in vi-tam æ-tér-nam.

Alternate melody:

III

QUI bí-be-rit aquam, * quam e-go da-bo e-i, di-cit Dómi-nus, fi-et in e-o fons aquae sa-li-én-tis in vi-tam ae-tér-nam.

"Whosoever drinks the water that I shall offer", said the Lord (to the Samaritan woman), "shall have within him a spring of water welling up unto eternal life."

Prayer after Communion

SUMENTES pignus cæléstis arcáni, et in terra pósiti iam supérno pane satiáti, te, Dómine, súpplices deprecámur, ut, quod in nobis mystério géritur, ópere impleátur.

LORD, in sharing this sacrament may we receive your forgiveness and be brought together in unity and peace.

FOURTH SUNDAY OF LENT

Introit *Cf. Is 66: 10, 11; Ps 121*

Lae-tá- re * Ie-rú-sa-lem : et convén- tum fá- ci- te omnes qui di- lí-gi- tis e- am : gau- dé-te cum lae-tí- ti- a, qui in tristí- ti- a fu- í- stis : ut exsulté- tis, et sa-ti- é- mi- ni ab u-bé- ri-bus conso-la-ti- ó- nis ve- strae.

Ps. Laetá-tus sum in his quae dicta sunt mi-hi : in domum Dómi-ni í-bimus.

Rejoice, O Jerusalem; and gather round, all you who love her; rejoice in gladness, after having been in sorrow; exult and be replenished with the consolation flowing from her motherly bosom. ℣. I rejoiced when it was said unto me: "Let us go to the house of the Lord."

4th Sunday of Lent

Opening Prayer

DEUS, qui per Verbum tuum humáni géneris reconciliatiónem mirabíliter operáris, præsta quæsumus, ut pópulus christiánus prompta devotióne et álacri fide ad ventúra sollémnia váleat festináre.

FATHER of peace, we are joyful in your Word, your Son Jesus Christ, who reconciles us to you. Let us hasten toward Easter with the eagerness of faith and love.

First reading

A. 1 Sam 16: 1b, 6-7, 10-13a: *David is anointed King.*
B. 2 Chron 36: 14-16, 19-23: *The exile and liberation of the Chosen People.*
C. Josh 5: 9a, 10-12: *The celebration of the Passover.*

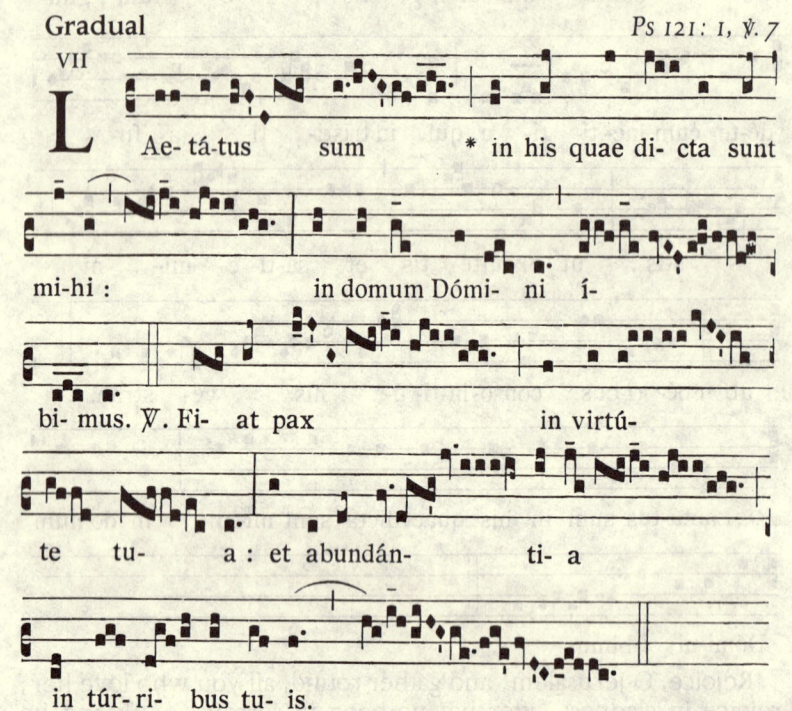

Gradual
Ps 121: 1, ℣. 7

VII

L Ae-tá-tus sum * in his quae di-cta sunt mi-hi: in domum Dómi- ni í-bi- mus. ℣. Fi- at pax in virtú- te tu- a: et abundán- ti- a in túr-ri- bus tu- is.

I rejoiced when it was said unto me: "Let us go to the house of the Lord." ℣. Let peace reign within your walls, and abundance in your towers.

4th Sunday of Lent

Second reading
A. Eph 5: 8-14: *Live as sons of light.*
B. Eph 2: 4-10: *God is rich in mercy.*
C. 2 Cor 5: 17-21: *God has reconciled us to himself.*

Tract Ps 124: 1, 2

VIII

QUI confí- dunt * in Dó- mi- no, sic- ut mons Si- on: non commové- bi- tur in aetér- num, qui há- bi- tat in Ie-rú- sa- lem. ℣. Mon- tes in circú- i-tu e- ius: et Dómi- nus in circú- i-tu pópu- li su- i, ex hoc nunc et us-que in saé-cu-lum.

4th Sunday of Lent

Those who trust in the Lord are like Mount Zion; the inhabitants of Jerusalem shall never be shaken. ℣. As the mountains are round about Jerusalem, so the Lord is round about his people, from this time forth and for evermore.

Gospel

A. Jn 9: 1-41 *or* 9: 1, 6-9, 13-17, 34-38: *Healing of the man born blind.*
B. Jn 3, 14-21: *The Son has come to save the world.*
C. Lk 15: 1-3, 11-32: *The Prodigal Son.*

(The readings for Year A may be used for the two other years.)

Offertory
Ps 134: 3, 6

Laudáte *Dóminum, quia benígnus est: psállite nómini eius, quóniam suávis est: ómnia quaecúmque vóluit, fecit in caelo et in terra.

Praise the Lord, for he is loving; sing in honour of his name, for he is gracious. He has accomplished whatever he resolved to do in heaven and on earth.

When the Gospel of the Prodigal Son has been read:
Illúmina óculos meos, *p. 475.*

4th Sunday of Lent

Prayer over the Gifts

REMEDII sempitérni múnera, Dómine, lætántes offérimus, supplíciter exorántes, ut éadem nos et fidéliter venerári, et pro salúte mundi congruénter exhibére perfícias.

LORD, we offer you these gifts which bring us peace and joy. Increase our reverence by this eucharist, and bring salvation to the world.

Preface *when the Gospel of the Man Born Blind has been read:*

VERE dignum et iustum est, æquum et salutáre, nos tibi semper et ubíque grátias ágere : Dómine, sancte Pater, omnípotens ætérne Deus : per Christum Dóminum nostrum.

Qui genus humánum, in ténebris ámbulans, ad fídei claritátem per mystérium incarnatiónis addúxit, et, qui servi peccáti véteris nascebántur, per lavácrum regeneratiónis in fílios adoptiónis assúmpsit.

Propter quod cæléstia tibi atque terréstria cánticum novum cóncinunt adorándo, et nos, cum omni exércitu Angelórum, proclamámus, sine fine dicéntes :

FATHER, all-powerful and ever-living God, we do well always and everywhere to give you thanks, through Jesus Christ our Lord.

He came among us as a man, to lead mankind from darkness into the light of faith. Through Adam's fall we were born as slaves of sin, but now through baptism in Christ we are reborn as your adopted children.

Earth unites with heaven to sing the new song of creation, as we adore and praise you for ever: Holy...

Otherwise, one of the Lenten Prefaces is used, p. 52 or 53.

Communion
Ps 121: 3, 4

IE-rú-sa-lem, * quae ae-di- fi-cá-tur ut cí-vi-tas, cu-ius parti- ci-pá-ti-o e-ius in id-ípsum : illuc e- nim

4th Sunday of Lent

ascendérunt tribus, tribus Dómini, ad confiténdum nómini tuo, Dómine.

Jerusalem, built as a city whose parts are bound firmly together! It is there that the tribes go up, the tribes of the Lord, to give thanks unto your name, O Lord.

Or, when the Gospel of the Man Born Blind has been read:

Jn 9: 6, 11, 38

VI

Lutum fecit * ex sputo Dóminus, et linívit óculos meos: et ábii, et lavi, et vidi, et crédidi Deo.

The Lord made some clay with his spittle, and he spread it over my eyes; and I went forth, I washed myself, I began to see, and I put my faith in God..

Or, when the Gospel of the Prodigal Son has been read:

Lk 15: 32

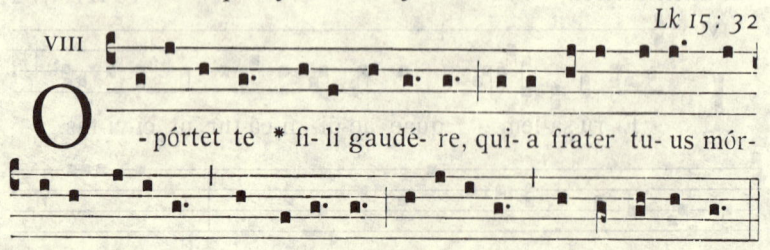

VIII

Opórtet te * fili gaudére, quia frater tuus mórtuus fúerat, et revíxit; períerat, et invéntus est.

My son, you should rejoice; for your brother who was dead has come back to life; he was lost and he has been found.

Prayer after Communion

Deus, qui illúminas omnem hóminem veniéntem in hunc mundum, illúmina, quǽsumus, corda nostra grátiæ tuæ splendóre, ut digna ac plácita maiestáti tuæ cogitáre semper, et te sincére dilígere valeámus.

Father, you enlighten all who come into the world. Fill our hearts with the light of your gospel, that our thoughts may please you, and our love be sincere.

FIFTH SUNDAY OF LENT

Introit *Ps 42: 1, 2, 3*

IUdica me Deus,* et discérne causam meam de gente non sancta: ab hómine iníquo et dolóso éripe me: quia tu es Deus meus, et fortitúdo mea. *Ps.* Emítte lucem tuam, et veritátem tuam: ipsa me dedu-xérunt, et adduxérunt in montem sanctum tu- um, et in taberná- cu- la tu- a.

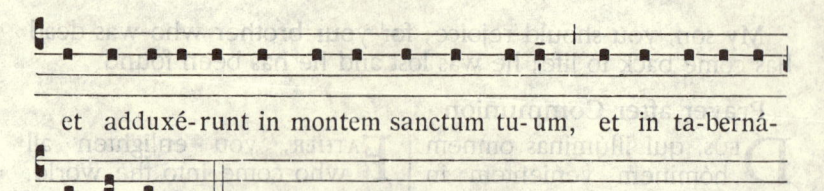

Vindicate me, O God, and defend my cause against an ungodly nation; from wicked and deceitful men deliver me, for you are my God and my strength. ℣. Send forth your light and your truth; these have led me and brought me to your holy mountain and to your dwelling place.

Opening Prayer

QUÆSUMUS, Dómine Deus noster, ut in illa caritáte, qua Fílius tuus díligens mundum morti se trádidit, inveniámur ipsi, te opitulánte, alácriter ambulántes.

FATHER, help us to be like Christ your Son, who loved the world and died for our salvation. Inspire us by his love, guide us by his example.

First reading
A. Ezek 37: 12-14: *I shall put my Spirit in you.*
B. Jer 31: 31-34: *The New Covenant.*
C. Is 43: 16-21: *I am creating a new world.*

Gradual   Ps 142: 9, 10, ℣. Ps 17: 48, 49

E- ri- pe me, * Dó- mi- ne, de in-imí- cis me- is: do- ce me fá- ce- re vo- luntá-

5th Sunday of Lent

tem tu- am.

℣. Li-be-rá-tor me- us, Dó- mi- ne, de gén- ti- bus i-racún- dis : ab insurgénti- bus in me ex- altá- bis me : a vi- ro in- íquo e- rí- pi- es me.

Rescue me, Lord, from my enemies; teach me to do your will. ℣. O Lord, you who save me from the wrath of the nations, you shall cause me to triumph over my assailants; you will save me from the man of evil.

Second reading
A. Rom 8: 8-11: *The Spirit of Jesus dwells in you.*
B. Heb 5: 7-9: *He learned obedience.*
C. Phil 3: 8-14: *Apprehended by Christ.*

5th Sunday of Lent

Tract VIII — *Ps 128: 1-4*

Saepe * expugnavérunt me a iuventúte mea.

℣. Dicat nunc Israel: saepe expugnavérunt me a iuventúte mea. ℣. Etenim non potuérunt mihi: supra dorsum meum fabricavérunt peccatóres. ℣. Prolongavérunt iniquitátem sibi: Dóminus iustus con-

5th Sunday of Lent

... cí- det cerví- ces peccató- rum.

Often have they fought against me from my youth. ℣. Let Israel now say: Often have they fought against me from my youth. ℣. Yet, they have not prevailed against me: my back has become an anvil for the hammering of sinners. ℣. They have long oppressed me with their iniquities. But the Lord of justice will break the neck of sinners.

Gospel
A. Jn 11: 1-45 *or* 11: 3-7, 20-27, 33b-45: *The resurrection of Lazarus.*
B. Jn 12: 20-33: *The grain of wheat which falls into the ground.*
C. Jn 8: 1-11: *The woman taken in adultery.*
(*The readings for Year A may be used for the two other years.*)

Offertory
Ps 118: 7, 10, 17, 25

Confitébor * tibi, Dómine, in toto corde meo: retríbue servo tuo: vivam, et custódiam sermónes tuos: vivífica me secúndum verbum tu-um, Dómi- ne.

I will praise you, O Lord, with my whole heart; deal bountifully with your servant, that I may live and observe your word; revive me according to your word, O Lord.

Prayer over the Gifts

Exaudi nos, omnípotens Deus, et fámulos tuos, quos fídei christiánæ eruditiónibus imbuísti, huius sacrifícii tríbuas operatióne mundári.

Almighty God, may the sacrifice we offer take away the sins of those whom you enlighten with the Christian faith.

Preface *when the Gospel of Lazarus has been read:*

Vere dignum et iustum est, æquum et salutáre, nos tibi semper et ubíque grátias ágere : Dómine, sancte Pater, omnípotens ætérne Deus : per Christum Dóminum nostrum.

Ipse enim verus homo Lázarum flevit amícum, et Deus ætérnus e túmulo suscitávit, qui, humáni géneris miserátus, ad novam vitam sacris mystériis nos addúcit.

Per quem maiestátem tuam adórat exércitus Angelórum, ante conspéctum tuum in æternitáte lætántium. Cum quibus et nostras voces ut admítti iúbeas, deprecámur, sócia exsultatióne dicéntes:

Father, all-powerful and ever-living God, we do well always and everywhere to give you thanks through Jesus Christ our Lord.

As a man like us, Jesus wept for Lazarus his friend. As the eternal God, he raised Lazarus from the dead. In his love for us all, Christ gives us the sacraments to lift us up to everlasting life.

Through him the angels of heaven offer their prayer of adoration as they rejoice in your presence for ever. May our voices be one with theirs in their triumphant hymn of praise: Holy...

Otherwise, one of the Lenten Prefaces is used, p. 52 or 53.

Communion   Jn 12: 26

QUI mi- hi mi- ní-strat, * me sequá- tur : et u-bi

5th Sunday of Lent

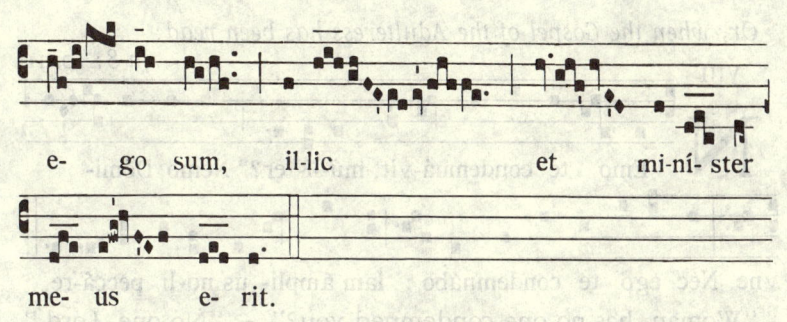

e- go sum, il-lic et mi-ní- ster me- us e- rit.

If a man would serve me, let him follow me; wherever I am, my servant will be there too.

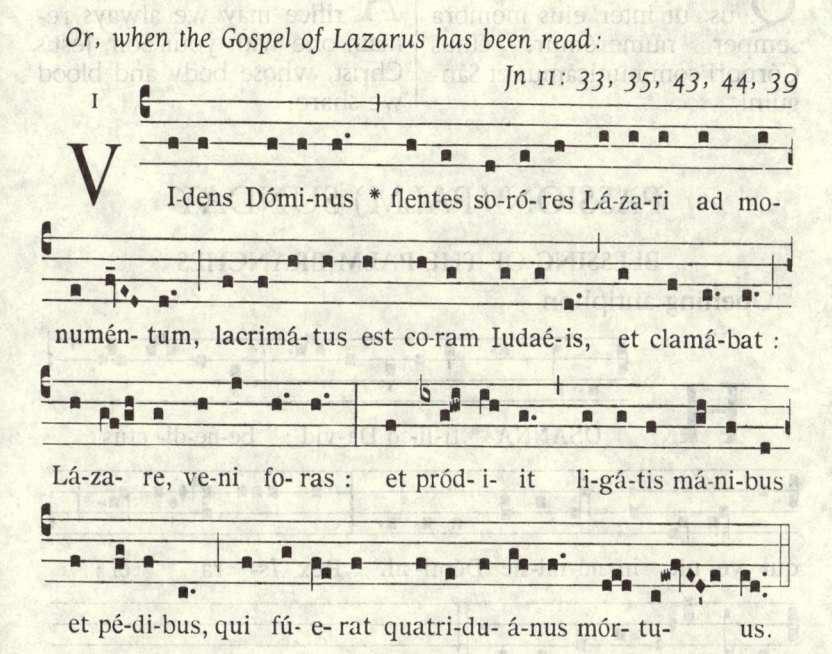

Or, when the Gospel of Lazarus has been read:

Jn 11: 33, 35, 43, 44, 39

VI-dens Dómi-nus * flentes so-ró- res Lá-za-ri ad mo- numén- tum, lacrimá-tus est co-ram Iudaé-is, et clamá-bat: Lá-za- re, ve-ni fo- ras: et pród- i- it li-gá-tis má-ni-bus et pé-di-bus, qui fú- e- rat quatri-du- á-nus mór- tu- us.

When the Lord saw the sisters of Lazarus in tears near the tomb, he wept in the presence of the Jews and cried: "Lazarus, come forth." And out he came, hands and feet bound, the man who had been dead for four days.

Or, when the Gospel of the Adulteress has been read:

VIII — *Jn 8: 10, 11*

NEmo te condemná-vit, mú-li- er?* Nemo, Dómine. Nec ego te condemnábo : iam ámpli- us no-li peccá-re.

"Woman, has no one condemned you?" – "No one, Lord." – "Neither do I condemn you; go and do not sin again."

Prayer after Communion

QUÆSUMUS, omnípotens Deus, ut inter eius membra semper numerémur, cuius Córpori communicámus et Sánguini.

ALMIGHTY FATHER, by this sacrifice may we always remain one with your Son, Jesus Christ, whose body and blood we share.

PASSION (PALM) SUNDAY

BLESSING OF THE PALM BRANCHES

Opening antiphon

VII

HOSANNA * fí-li- o Da-vid : be-ne-dí- ctus qui ve- nit in nó-mi-ne Dómi- ni. Rex Is- ra- ël : Ho-sánna in excél- sis.

Hosanna to the Son of David, the King of Israel. Blessed is he who comes in the name of the Lord. Hosanna in the highest.

Passion (Palm) Sunday

Blessing

OMNIPOTENS sempitérne Deus, hos pálmites tua benedictióne sanctífica, ut nos, qui Christum Regem exsultándo proséquimur, per ipsum valeámus ad ætérnam Ierúsalem pervenίre

ALMIGHTY God, we pray you bless these branches and make them holy. Today we joyfully acclaim Jesus our Messiah and King. May we reach one day the happiness of the new and everlasting Jerusalem by faithfully following him.

Or:

AUGE fidem in te sperántium, Deus, et súpplicum preces cleménter exáudi, ut, qui hódie Christo triumphánti pálmites exhibémus, in ipso fructus tibi bonórum óperum afferámus.

LORD, increase the faith of your people and listen to our prayers. Today we honour Christ our triumphant King by carrying these branches. May we honour you every day by living always in him.

Gospel

A. Mt 21: 1-11: *The solemn entry into Jerusalem.*
B. Mk 11: 1-10 *or* Jn 12: 12-16.
C. Lk 19: 28-40.

After the Gospel, the priest may give a brief homily. Then the deacon, or, in his absence, the priest, announces the beginning of the procession:

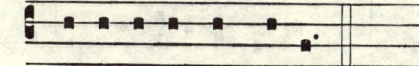

Pro-ce-dámus in pa-ce.
Let us go forth in peace.

All respond:

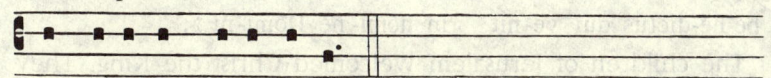

In nómi-ne Christi. Amen.
In the name of Christ. Amen.

Passion (Palm) Sunday

PROCESSION

Antiphon *Cf. Mt 21: 9*

PUeri Hebraeórum, * portántes ramos olivárum, obviavérunt Dómino, clamántes et dicéntes: « Hosánna in excélsis ».

The children of Jerusalem welcomed Christ the King. They carried olive branches and loudly praised the Lord: "Hosanna in the highest."

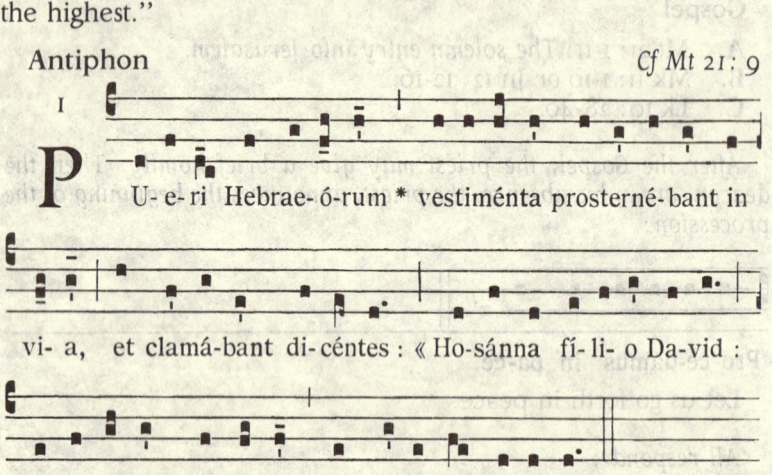

Antiphon *Cf Mt 21: 9*

PUeri Hebraeórum * vestiménta prosternébant in via, et clamábant dicéntes: « Hosánna fílio David: benedíctus qui venit in nómine Dómini ».

The children of Jerusalem welcomed Christ the King. They spread their cloaks before him and loudly praised the Lord: "Hosanna to the Son of David! Blessed is he who comes in the name of the Lord!"

Passion (Palm) Sunday

Hymn to Christ the King

Glóri-a, laus et honor ti-bi sit, Rex Christe Redémptor : Cu-i pu-e-rí-le de-cus prompsit Ho-sánna pi-um.

All glory, laud, and honour to thee, Redeemer, King, to whom the lips of children made sweet hosannas ring.

The cantors sing this refrain, which the choir repeats immediately, and again, after each verse.

1. Isra-ël es tu Rex, Da-ví-dis et ínclita pro-les 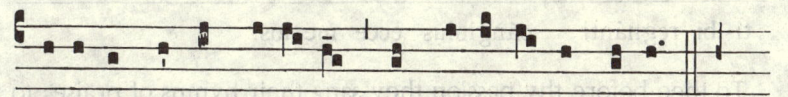 : Nómi-ne qui in Dómi-ni, Rex bene-dí-cte, ve-nis.

Thou art the King of Israel, Thou David's royal Son, who in the Lord's name comest, the King and Blessed One.

2. Cœtus in excél-sis te laudat caé-li-cus omnis, Et mortá-lis ho-mo, et cuncta cre-á-ta simul.

The company of angels are praising thee on high, and mortal men and all things created make reply.

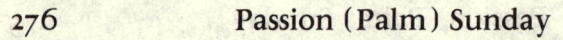

3. Plebs Hebraé-a tibi cum palmis óbvia venit:
Cum prece, voto, hymnis, ádsumus ecce tibi.

The people of the Hebrews with palms before thee went; our praise and prayers and anthems before thee we present.

4. Hi tibi passú-ro solvébant múnia laudis: Nos
tibi regnánti pángimus ecce melos.

To thee before thy passion they sang their hymns of praise; to thee now high exalted, our melody we raise.

5. Hi placuére tibi, pláceat devótio nostra:
Rex bone, Rex clemens, cui bona cuncta placent.

Thou didst accept their praises, accept the prayers we bring, who in all good delightest, Thou good and gracious King.

Passion (Palm) Sunday

Responsory *sung during the entry into the church.*

Ingrediénte Dómino * in sanctam civitátem, Hebraeórum púeri resurrectiónem vitae pronuntiántes, * Cum ramis palmárum: « Hosánna, clamábant, in excélsis ». ℣. Cumque audísset pópulus, quod Iesus veníret Ierosólymam, exiérunt óbviam ei.

* Cum ramis.

As the Lord entered the Holy City, the children of the Hebrews proclaimed the resurrection of life, * and, waving olive branches, they loudly praised the Lord: "Hosanna in the highest." ℣. When the people heard that Jesus was entering Jerusalem, they went to meet him * and, waving...

When the priest reaches the altar, he venerates it and then goes to his chair. When all have reached their places, the celebrant says the opening collect of Mass. Today, the penitential rite and the Kýrie are omitted.

Passion (Palm) Sunday

Opening Prayer

OMNIPOTENS sempitérne Deus, qui humáno géneri, ad imitándum humilitátis exémplum, Salvatórem nostrum carnem súmere, et crucem subíre fecísti, concéde propítius, ut et patiéntiæ ipsíus habére documénta et resurrectiónis consórtia mereámur.

ALMIGHTY, ever-living God, you have given the human race Jesus Christ our Saviour as a model of humility. He fulfilled your will by becoming man and giving his life on the cross. Help us to bear witness to you by following his example of suffering and make us worthy to share in his resurrection.

First reading

Is 50: 4-7: *The suffering Servant of the Lord.*

Tract   *Ps 21: 2-9, 18, 19, 22, 24, 32*

DE- us, *De- us me- us, réspi-ce in me: qua-re me de-re-li-quí-sti? ℣. Lon- ge a sa-lú-te me- a ver-ba de-li-ctó- rum me-ó- rum. ℣. De- us me- us cla-

My God, my God, look upon me, why have you forsaken me? ℣. My words of sin have drawn me far from salvation. ℣. O my God, I call by day and you give no reply; I call by night and not

má- bo per di- em, nec exáu- di- es: in nocte, et non ad insi-pi- én- ti- am mi- hi. ℣. Tu au- tem in sancto há- bi- tas, laus Is- ra- el. ℣. In te spe- ravé- runt patres no- stri: spe-ravé- runt, et li- be-rásti e- os. ℣. Ad te cla-mavé- runt, et sal-vi fa- cti sunt: in te spe-ravé- runt, et non sunt confú- si.

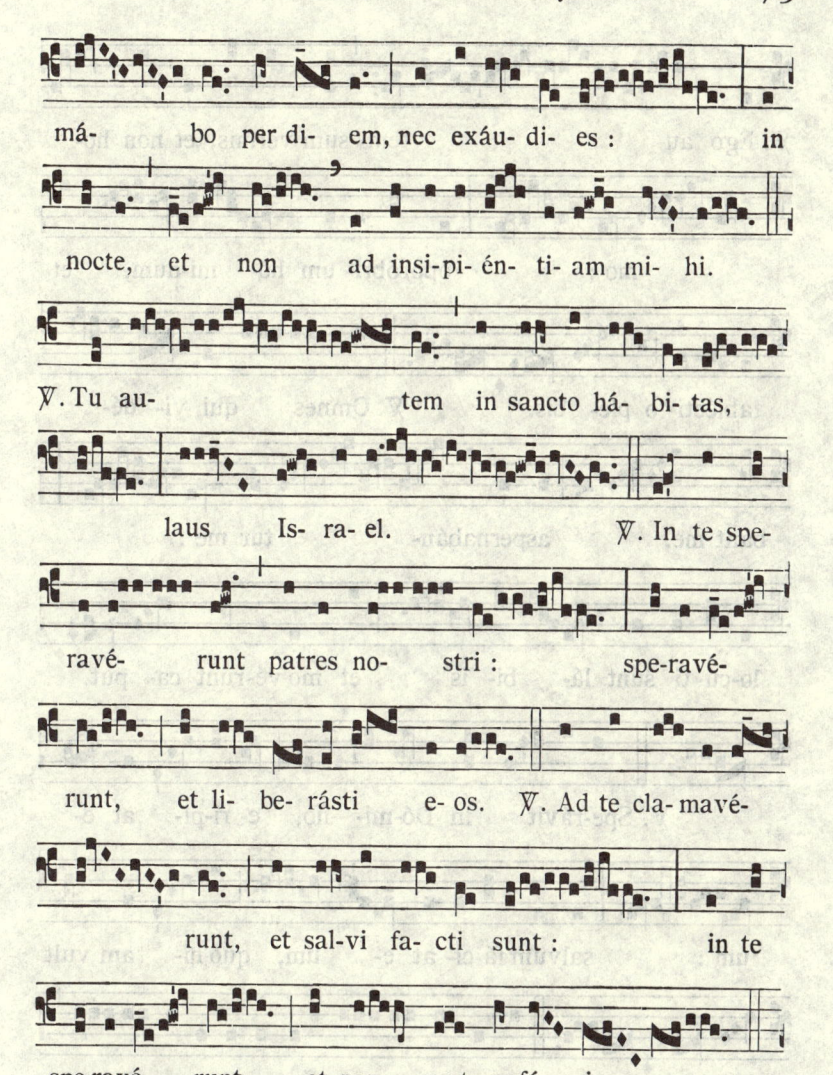

without reason. ℣. Yet, you dwell in the sanctuary; you are the praise of Israel. ℣. Our fathers placed their hope in you; they trusted and you delivered them. ℣. They cried out to you and they were saved; they put their hope in you and they were not confounded. ℣. But I am a worm and no man; scorned by men

℣. Ego autem sum vermis, et non homo: oppróbrium hóminum, et abiéctio plebis. ℣. Omnes qui vidébant me, aspernabántur me: locúti sunt lábiis et movérunt caput. ℣. Sperávit in Dómino, erípiat eum: salvum fáciat eum, quóniam vult eum. ℣. Ipsi vero considerávérunt,

and despised by the people. ℣. All who see me mock at me, they make mouths at me, they wag their heads. ℣. "He trusted in the Lord; let him deliver him, let him rescue him, for he delights in him." ℣. And so they looked and gazed upon me; they divided

Passion (Palm) Sunday

et conspexérunt me: divisérunt sibi vestiménta me- a, et super vestem me- am mi- sérunt sortem. ℣. Líbera me de o- re le- ónis: et a córnibus unicornuórum humilitátem meam. ℣. Qui timétis Dóminum, laudáte e- um: univérsum semen Iacob, magnificáte e- um. ℣. Annun-

my garments among themselves, and for my raiment they have cast lots. ℣. Save me from the mouth of the lion; my afflicted soul from the horns of the unicorn. ℣. You who fear the Lord, praise him! All you sons of Jacob, glorify him. ℣. A future generation shall

ti- á-bi- tur Dómi- no ge-ne-rá-ti- o ventú-ra: et annunti- ábunt cae- li iu- stí- ti- am e- ius. ℣. Pó-pu-lo qui nascé- tur, quem fe- cit Dó- mi- nus.

be announced on behalf of the Lord, and the heavens will declare his justice; ℣. Unto a nation yet to be born, and whom the Lord has prepared.

Second reading

Phil 2: 6-11: *The mystery of Christ, humbled and exalted.*

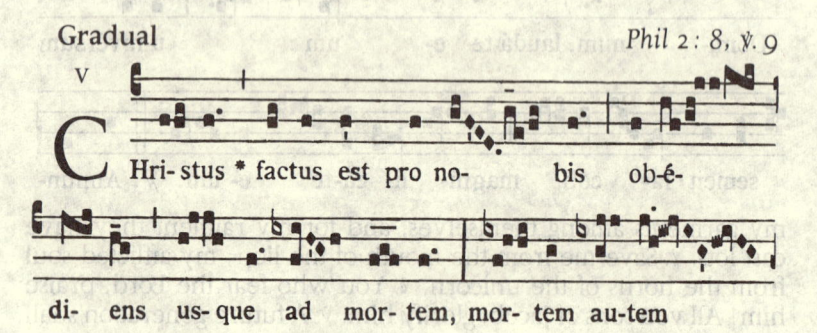

Gradual

Phil 2: 8, ℣. 9

CHri- stus * factus est pro no- bis ob-é- di- ens us-que ad mor- tem, mor- tem au-tem

Passion (Palm) Sunday

cru- cis. ℣. Propter quod et De- us exaltá- vit il-lum, et de- dit il-li no- men, quod est super o-mne no- men.

Christ became obedient for us unto death, even death on a Cross. ℣. Therefore God has highly exalted him, and bestowed on him the name which is above every name.

Gospel

A. Mt 26: 14-27: 66 or 27: 11-54: *The Passion.*
B. Mk 14: 1-15: 47 or 15: 1-39.
C. Lk 22: 14-23: 56 or 23: 1-49.

Offertory
Ps 68: 21, 22

VIII

IM- propé- ri- um * exspectá- vit cor me- um, et mi- sé- ri- am: et sustí-

Passion (Palm) Sunday

nu- i qui si- mul contrista-ré- tur, et non fu- it: con- so-lán- tem me quae- sí- vi, et non invé- ni: et de-dé- runt in e-scam me- am fel, et in si- ti me- a po-ta- vé- runt me acé- to.

My heart awaited reproach and misery; and I hoped for one that would grieve together with me, but there was none; I looked for one who would comfort me, and found no one. For food they gave me gall; in my thirst they gave me vinegar to drink.

Prayer over the Gifts

PER UNIGENITI TUI passiónem placátio tua nobis, Dómine, sit propínqua, quam, etsi nostris opéribus non merémur, interveniénte sacrifício singulári, tua percipiámus miseratióne prævénti.

LORD, may the suffering and death of Jesus, your only Son, make us pleasing to you. Alone we can do nothing, but may this perfect sacrifice win us your mercy and love.

Passion (Palm) Sunday

Preface

VERE dignum et iustum est, æquum et salutáre, nos tibi semper et ubíque grátias ágere : Dómine, sancte Pater, omnípotens ætérne Deus : per Christum Dóminum nostrum.

Qui pati pro ímpiis dignátus est ínnocens, et pro scelerátis indébite condemnári. Cuius mors delícta nostra detérsit, et iustificatiónem nobis resurréctio comparávit.

Unde et nos cum ómnibus Angelis te laudámus, iucúnda celebratióne clamántes:

FATHER, all-powerful and ever-living God, we do well always and everywhere to give you thanks through Jesus Christ our Lord.

Though he was sinless, he suffered willingly for sinners. Though innocent, he accepted death to save the guilty. By his dying he has destroyed our sins. By his rising he has raised us up to holiness of life.

We praise you, Lord, with all the angels in their song of joy: Holy...

Communion — Mt 26: 42

PA-ter, * si non pot-est hic ca-lix transí-re, ni-si bi-bam il-lum : fi-at vo-lúntas tu-a.

Father, if this cup cannot pass away unless I drink it, thy will be done.

Prayer after Communion

SACRO múnere satiáti, súpplices te, Dómine, deprecámur, ut, qui fecísti nos morte Fílii tui speráre quod crédimus, fácias nos, eódem resurgénte, perveníre quo téndimus.

LORD, you have satisfied our hunger with this eucharistic food. The death of your Son gives us hope and strengthens our faith. May his resurrection give us perseverance and lead us to salvation.

HOLY THURSDAY

EVENING MASS OF THE LORD'S SUPPER

Introit *Cf. Gal 6: 14; Ps 66*

IV

NOS autem * gloriári opórtet, in cruce Dómini nostri Iesu Christi: in quo est salus, vita, et resurréctio nostra: per quem salváti, et liberáti sumus. *Ps.* Deus misereátur nostri, et benedícat nobis: illúminet vultum suum super nos, et misereátur nostri.

Let our glory be in the cross of our Lord Jesus Christ; in him we have salvation, life and resurrection; through him we are rescued and set free. ℣. May God have mercy on us and bless us; may he cause his face to shine upon us and may he have mercy on us.

Glória in excélsis.

Holy Thursday

Opening Prayer

SACRATISSIMAM, Deus, frequentántibus Cenam, in qua Unigénitus tuus, morti se traditúrus, novum in sǽcula sacrifícium dilectionísque suæ convívium Ecclésiæ commendávit, da nobis, quǽsumus, ut ex tanto mystério plenitúdinem caritátis hauriámus et vitæ.

GOD OUR FATHER, we are gathered here to share in the supper which your only Son left to his Church to reveal his love. He gave it to us when he was about to die and commanded us to celebrate it as the new and eternal sacrifice. We pray that in this eucharist we may find the fullness of love and life.

First reading

Ex 12: 1-8, 11-14: *Commandments concerning the Passover meal.*

Gradual

Ps 144: 15, ℣. 16

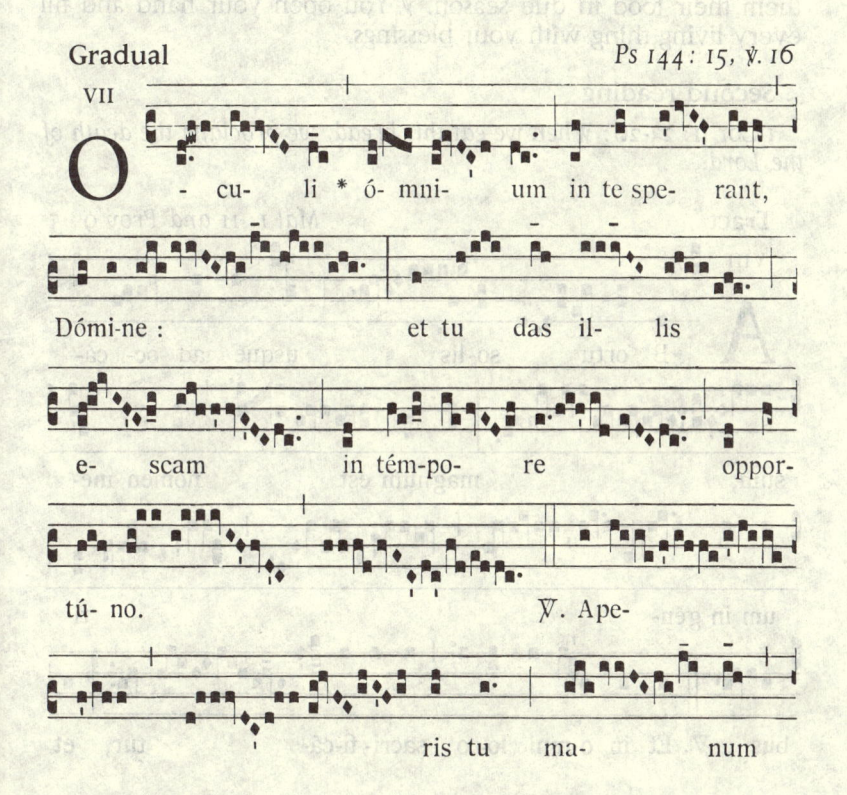

VII

O- cu- li * ó- mni- um in te spe- rant, Dómi-ne : et tu das il- lis e- scam in témpo- re oppor- tú- no. ℣. Ape- ris tu ma- num

Holy Thursday

tu- am : et imples omne á-ni- mal be-ne-di-cti-ó-ne.

The eyes of all creatures look to you, O Lord, and you give them their food in due season. ℣. You open your hand and fill every living thing with your blessings.

Second reading

1 Cor 11: 23-26: *When we eat this bread, we proclaim the death of the Lord.*

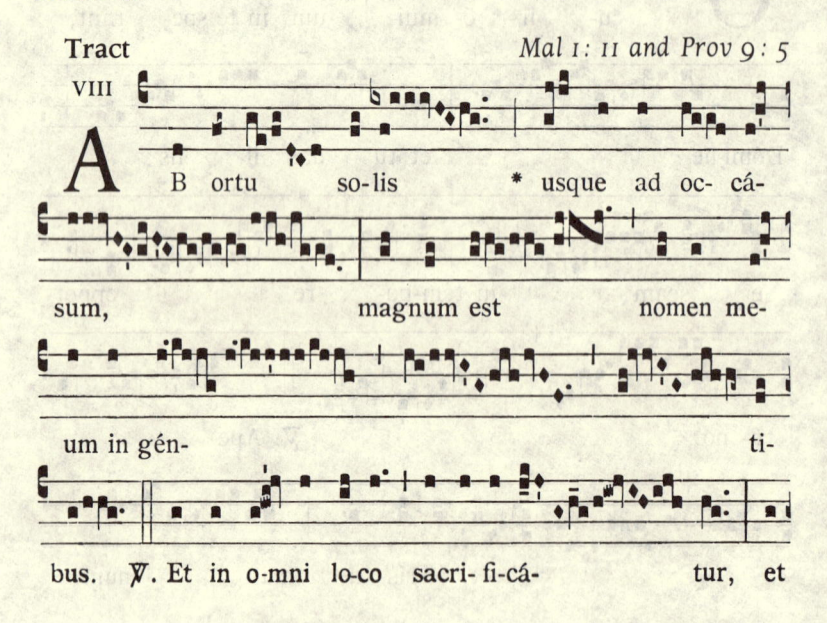

Tract   Mal 1: 11 and Prov 9: 5

VIII

A B ortu so-lis * usque ad oc-cá-sum, magnum est nomen me-um in gén- ti-bus. ℣. Et in o-mni lo-co sacri-fi-cá- tur, et

Holy Thursday

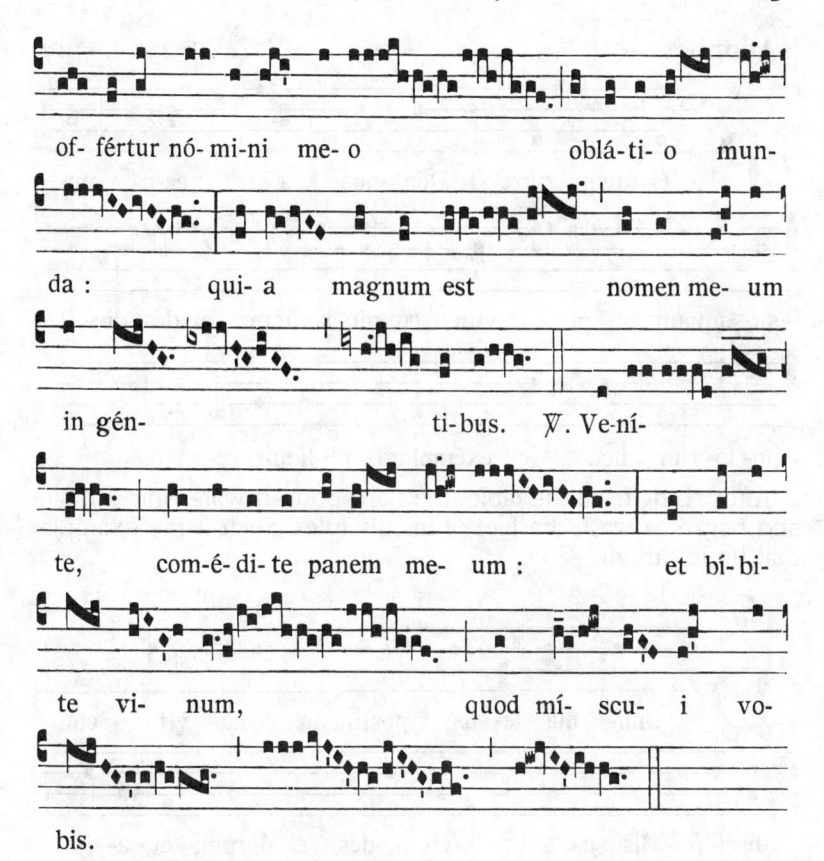

of- fértur nómini meo oblátio munda: quia magnum est nomen meum in géntibus. ℣. Veníte, comédite panem meum: et bíbite vinum, quod míscui vobis.

From the place where the sun rises to the place of its setting, my name is great among the nations. ℣. And in every place, a sacrifice is offered to my name, a pure offering, for my name is truly great among the nations. ℣. Come, eat of my bread, and drink of the wine I have prepared for you.

Gospel

Jn 13: 1-15: *He loved them to the end.*

After the homily, the washing of feet takes place, during which time, some of the following antiphons are sung:

Holy Thursday

Antiphons *Cf. Jn 13 : 4, 5, 15*

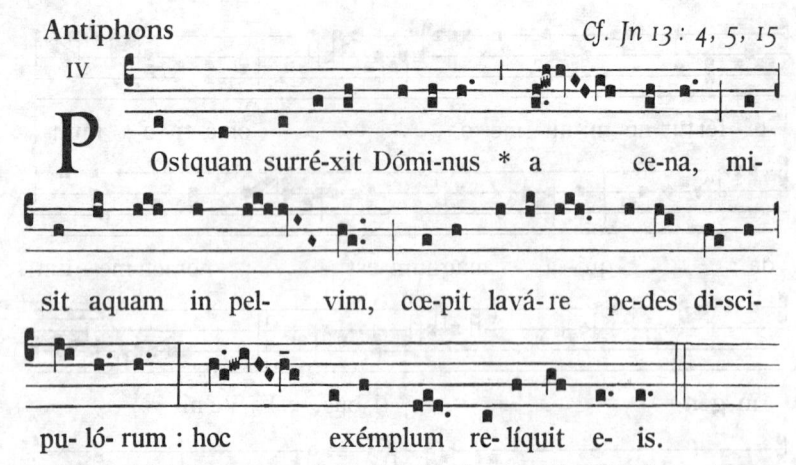

POstquam surré-xit Dómi-nus * a ce-na, mi-sit aquam in pel- vim, cœ-pit lavá-re pe-des di-sci-pu-ló-rum : hoc exémplum re-líquit e- is.

After rising from the table, the Lord poured water into a basin and began to wash the feet of his disciples. Such is the example that he left them.

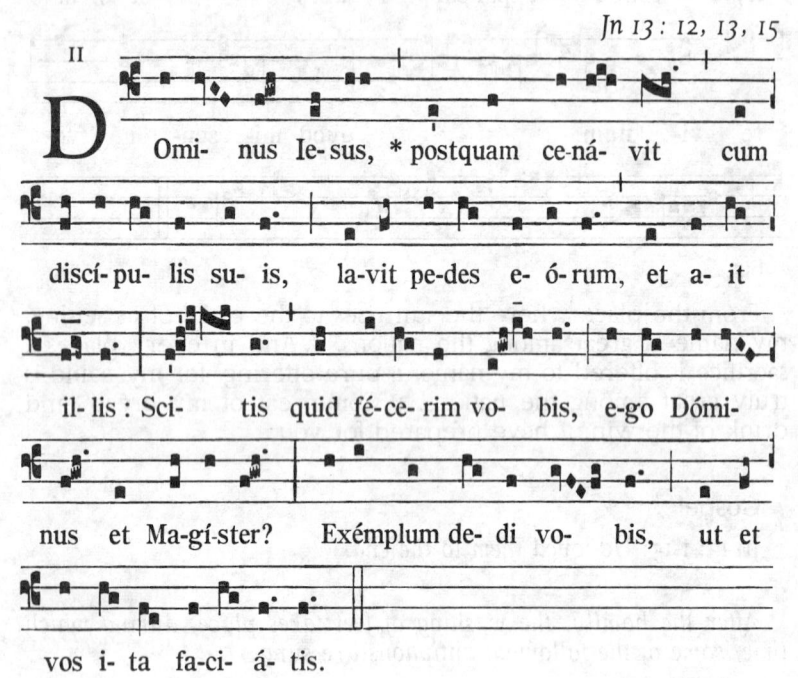

Jn 13 : 12, 13, 15

DOmi- nus Ie-sus, * postquam ce-ná-vit cum discí-pu-lis su- is, la-vit pe-des e- ó-rum, et a- it il- lis : Sci- tis quid fé-ce-rim vo- bis, e-go Dómi-nus et Ma-gí-ster? Exémplum de- di vo- bis, ut et vos i- ta fa-ci- á- tis.

Holy Thursday

The Lord Jesus, after eating supper with his disciples, washed their feet and said to them: "Do you realize what I have done for you, I who am your Lord and your Master? I have given you an example so that you may do likewise."

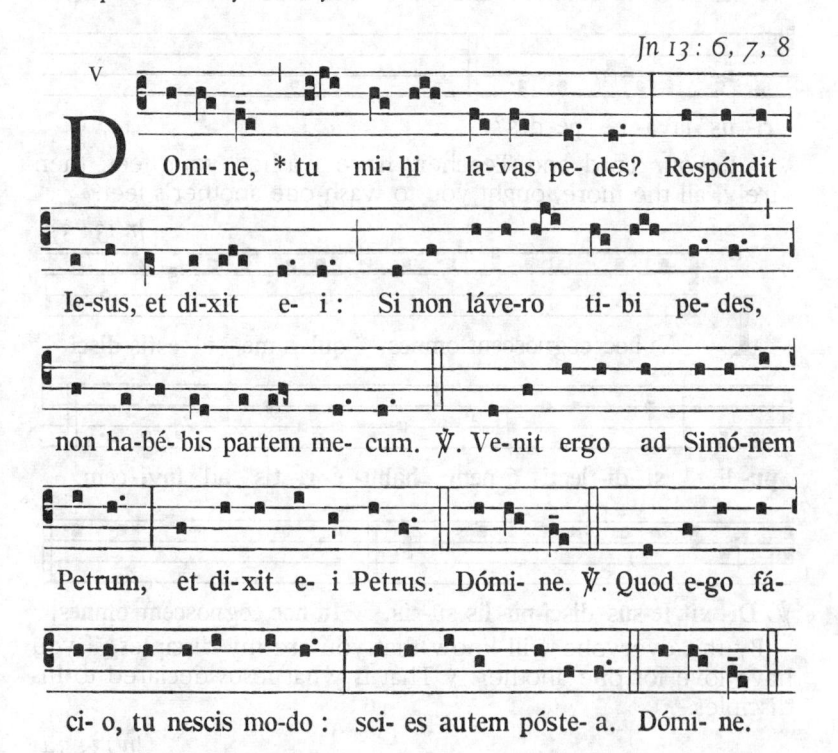

Jn 13: 6, 7, 8

DOmi- ne, * tu mi- hi la- vas pe- des? Respóndit Ie-sus, et di- xit e- i : Si non láve- ro ti- bi pe- des, non ha-bé- bis partem me- cum. ℣. Ve- nit ergo ad Simó- nem Petrum, et di- xit e- i Petrus. Dómi- ne. ℣. Quod e- go fá- ci- o, tu nescis mo- do : sci- es autem póste- a. Dómi- ne.

"Lord, are you going to wash my feet?" Jesus answered, "If I do not wash your feet, you will have no portion with me." ℣. Jesus came to Simon Peter, and Peter said to him: ℟. "Lord,..." ℣. "At the moment you do not know what I am doing, but later you will understand." ℟. "Lord,...".

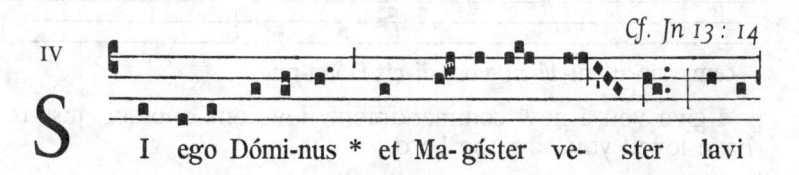

Cf. Jn 13: 14

SI ego Dómi-nus * et Ma- gíster ve- ster lavi

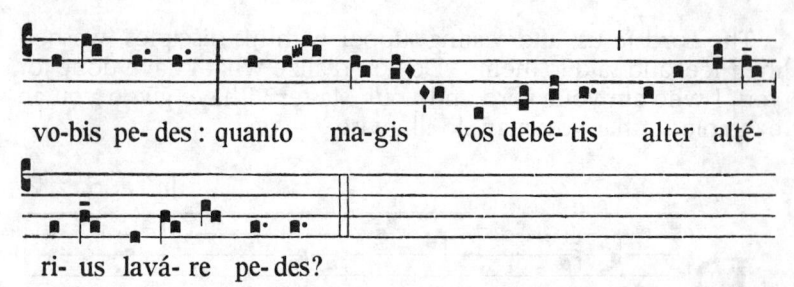

vo-bis pe- des : quanto ma-gis vos debé- tis alter alté-ri- us lavá- re pe- des?

If I, your Lord and Teacher, have washed your feet, then surely, all the more, ought you to wash one another's feet.

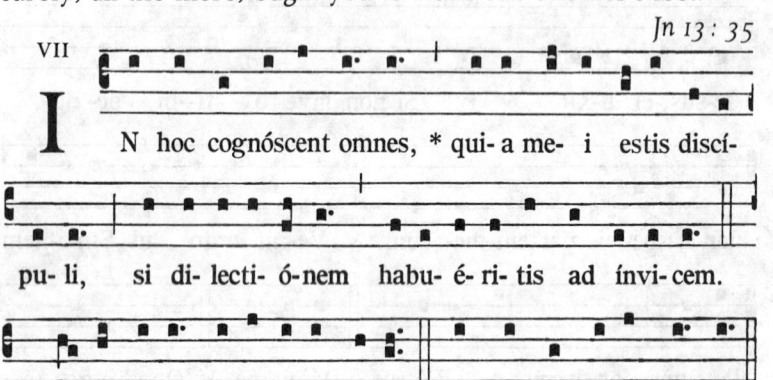

Jn 13 : 35

VII

IN hoc cognóscent omnes, * qui- a me- i estis discí-pu- li, si di- lecti- ó-nem habu- é- ri- tis ad ínvi- cem.

℣. Di- xit Iesus discí-pu- lis su- is. In hoc cognóscent omnes.

By this everyone will know that you are my disciples, if you have love for one another. ℣. That is what Iesus declared to his disciples.

Jn 13 : 34

III

MAndá-tum novum do vo-bis : * ut di- li-gá-tis ínvi-cem, sic- ut di- lé-xi vos, di-cit Dómi-nus.

I give you a new commandment: love one another, just as I have loved you, says the Lord.

Holy Thursday

I Cor 13 : 13

MAne- ant in vo- bis * fi-des, spes, cá-ri-tas, tri- a haec : ma-ior autem ho- rum est cá-ri-tas. ℣. Nunc autem manent fi-des, spes, cá-ri-tas, tri- a haec : ma- ior autem ho-rum est cá-ri- tas. Má-ne- ant in vo- bis.

Let these three abide in you: faith, hope and love; but the greatest of these is love. ℣. Now faith, hope and love remain, these three; but the greatest of these is love.

Offertory

All sing the refrain, while the verses are alternated between the cantors and the choir.

U- bi cá-ri- tas est ve-ra, De- us i-bi est.

Where love is found to be authentic, God is there.

℣. Congregá-vit nos in u-num Christi amor.

℣. Exsultémus et in i-pso iu-cundémur.

Holy Thursday

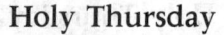

℣. Time-ámus et amé-mus De-um vi-vum.

℣. Et ex corde di-li-gá-mus nos sin-cé- ro.

The love of Christ has gathered us together into one. Let us rejoice and be glad in Him. Let us fear and love the living God, and love each other from the depths of our heart.

U - bi cá-ri- tas est ve-ra, De-us i-bi est.

Where love is found to be authentic, God is there.

℣. Simul ergo cum in u-num congregámur :

℣. Ne nos mente di- vi-dámur, cave- ámus.

℣. Cessent iúrgi- a ma-lígna, cessent li-tes.

℣. Et in mé-di- o nostri sit Christus De- us.

Therefore when we are together, let us take heed not to be divided in mind. Let there be an end to bitterness and quarrels, an end to strife, and in our midst be Christ our God.

Holy Thursday

U - bi cá-ri-tas est ve-ra, De-us i-bi est.
Where love is found to be authentic, God is there.

℣. *Simul quoque cum be-á-tis vi-de-ámus*

℣. *Glo-ri-ánter vul-tum tu-um, Christe De-us :*

℣. *Gáudi-um, quod est imménsum, atque probum,*

℣. *Saécu-la per infi-ní-ta saecu-ló-rum.*

And, in company with the blessed, may we see your face in glory, Christ our God: pure and unbounded joy for ever and for ever.

Prayer over the Gifts

CONCEDE nobis, quæsumus, Dómine, hæc digne frequentáre mystéria, quia, quóties huius hóstiæ commemorátio celebrátur, opus nostræ redemptiónis exercétur.

LORD, make us worthy to celebrate these mysteries. Each time we offer this memorial sacrifice the work of our redemption is accomplished.

Preface of the Holy Eucharist I, p. 63. With the First Eucharistic Prayer, the following proper Communicántes, Hanc ígitur *and* Qui prídie *are used.*

Communicántes, et diem sacratíssimum celebrántes, quo Dóminus noster Iesus Christus pro nobis est tráditus, sed et memóriam venerántes, in primis gloriósæ semper Vírginis Maríæ, Genetrícis eiúsdem Dei et Dómini nostri Iesu Christi: sed et beáti Ioseph, eiúsdem Vírginis Sponsi, et beatórum Apostolórum ac Mártyrum tuórum, Petri et Pauli, Andréæ, (Iacóbi, Ioánnis, Thomæ, Iacóbi, Philíppi, Bartholomǽi, Matthǽi, Simónis et Thaddǽi: Lini, Cleti, Cleméntis, Xysti, Cornélii, Cypriáni, Lauréntii, Chrysógoni, Ioánnis et Pauli, Cosmæ et Damiáni) et ómnium Sanctórum tuórum; quorum méritis precibúsque concédas, ut in ómnibus protectiónis tuæ muniámur auxilio. (Per Christum Dóminum nostrum. Amen.)

In union with the whole Church we celebrate that day when Jesus Christ, our Lord, was betrayed for us. We honour Mary, the ever-virgin mother of Jesus Christ our Lord and God. We honour Joseph, her husband, the apostles and martyrs Peter and Paul, Andrew, (James, John, Thomas, James, Philip, Bartholomew, Matthew, Simon and Jude; we honour Linus, Cletus, Clement, Sixtus, Cornelius, Cyprian, Lawrence, Chrysogonus, John and Paul, Cosmas and Damian) and all the saints. May their merits and prayers gain us your constant help and protection. (Through Christ our Lord. Amen.)

Hanc ígitur oblatiónem servitútis nostræ, sed et cunctæ famíliæ tuæ, quam tibi offérimus ob diem, in qua Dóminus noster Iesus Christus trádidit discípulis suis Córporis et Sánguinis sui mystéria celebránda, quǽsumus, Dómine, ut placátus accípias: diésque nostros in tua pace dispónas, atque ab ætérna damnatióne nos éripi et in electórum tuórum iúbeas grege numerári. (Per Christum Dóminum nostrum. Amen.)

Father, accept this offering from your whole family in memory of the day when Jesus Christ, our Lord, gave the mysteries of his body and blood for his disciples to celebrate. Grant us your peace in this life, save us from final damnation, and count us among those you have chosen. (Through Christ our Lord. Amen.)

Quam oblatiónem tu, Deus, in ómnibus, quǽsumus, benedíctam, adscríptam, ratam, rationábilem, acceptabilémque fácere dignéris: ut nobis Corpus et Sanguis fiat dilectíssimi Fílii tui, Dómini nostri Iesu Christi.

Qui, prídie quam pro nostra omniúmque salúte paterétur, hoc est hódie, accépit panem in sanctas ac venerábiles manus suas, et elevátis óculis in cælum ad te Deum Patrem suum omnipoténtem, tibi grátias agens benedíxit, fregit, dedítque discípulis suis, dicens:

«ACCÍPITE ET MANDUCÁTE EX HOC OMNES: HOC EST ENIM CORPUS MEUM, QUOD PRO VOBIS TRADÉTUR.»

Bless and approve our offering; make it acceptable to you, an offering in spirit and in truth. Let it become for us the body and blood of Jesus Christ, your only Son, our Lord.

The day before he suffered to save us and all men, that is today, he took bread in his sacred hands and looking up to heaven, to you, his almighty Father, he gave you thanks and praise. He broke the bread, gave it to his disciples, and said:

"TAKE THIS, ALL OF YOU, AND EAT IT: THIS IS MY BODY WHICH WILL BE GIVEN UP FOR YOU."

Continuation, p. 26.

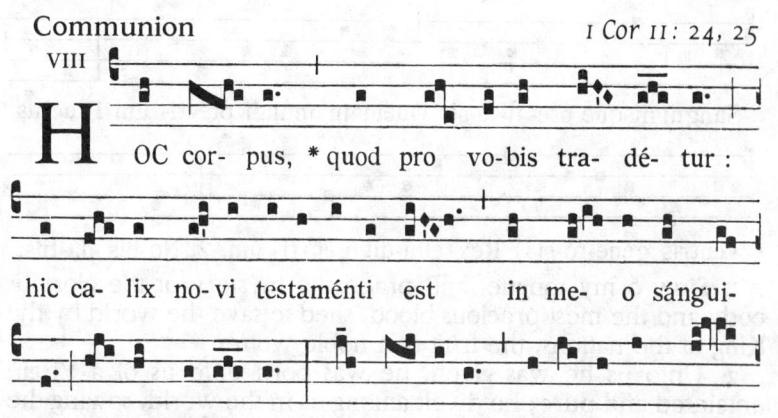

Communion   1 Cor 11: 24, 25

VIII

HOC cor-pus, *quod pro vo-bis tra- dé- tur: hic ca- lix no-vi testaménti est in me- o sángui- ne, di- cit Dómi- nus: hoc fá- ci- te, quo-ti- escúmque súmi- tis, in me- am commemo- ra- ti- ó- nem.

"This is my body which is given up for you; this is the cup of the new covenant in my blood", says the Lord. "Each time that you partake thereof, do it in memory of me."

Prayer after Communion

CONCEDE nobis, omnípotens Deus, ut sicut Cena Fílii tui refícimur temporáli, ita satiári mereámur ætérna.

ALMIGHTY God, we receive new life from the supper your Son gave us in this world. May we find full contentment in the meal we hope to share in your eternal kingdom.

When the Prayer after Communion has been said, the priest, accompanied by the ministers, carries the Blessed Sacrament through the church in procession, to the place of reposition where it is to remain until the following day.

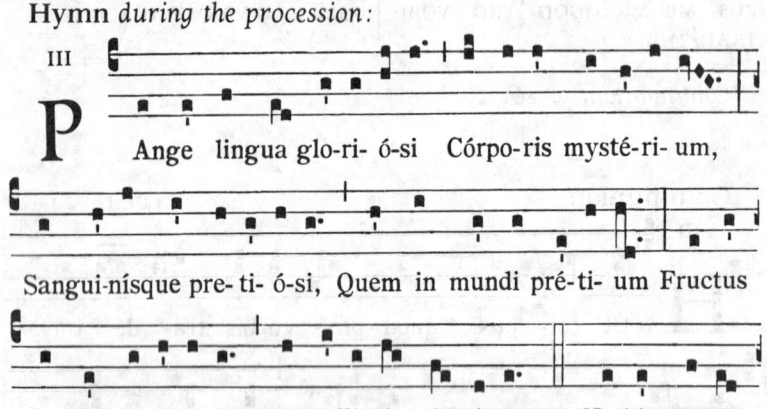

Hymn *during the procession:*

PAnge lingua glo-ri- ó-si Córpo-ris mysté-ri- um,

Sangui-nísque pre- ti- ó-si, Quem in mundi pré- ti- um Fructus

ventris gene-ró-si Rex effú-dit gén- ti- um. 2. No-bis da-tus,

1. Sing, o my tongue, and praise the mystery of the glorious body and the most precious blood, shed to save the world by the King of the nations, the fruit of a noble womb.

2. Unto us he was given, he was born unto us of a Virgin untainted and pure; he dwelt among us in the world, sowing the seeds of God's word; and he ended the time of his stay on earth in

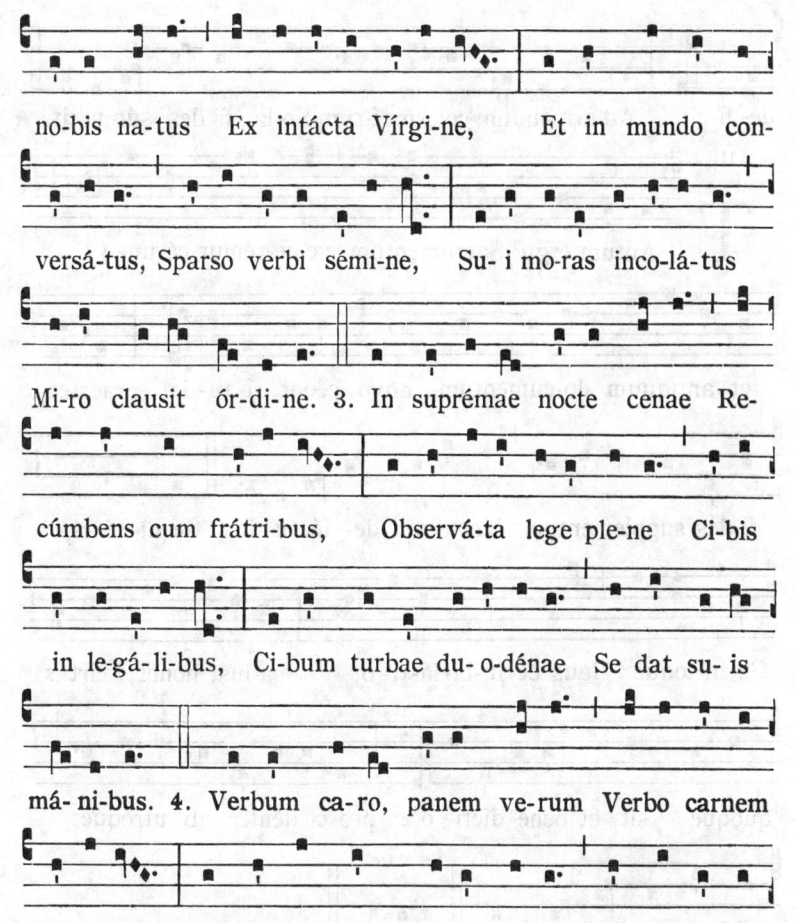

nobis natus Ex intácta Vírgine, Et in mundo conversátus, Sparso verbi sémine, Sui moras incolátus Miro clausit órdine. 3. In suprémae nocte cenae Recúmbens cum frátribus, Observáta lege plene Cibis in legálibus, Cibum turbae duodénae Se dat suis mánibus. 4. Verbum caro, panem verum Verbo carnem éfficit: Fitque sanguis Christi merum, Et si sensus

the most wondrous of fashions.

3. On his last night at supper, reclining at table in the midst of his brethren disciples, He fully observed the Ancient Law and partook of the Passover meal; and then, with his own hands, he gave himself up as food for the group of the Twelve.

4. The Word made flesh, by a simple word, makes of his flesh the true bread; the blood of Christ becomes our drink; and though senses cannot perceive, for confirming pure hearts in true belief, faith alone suffices.

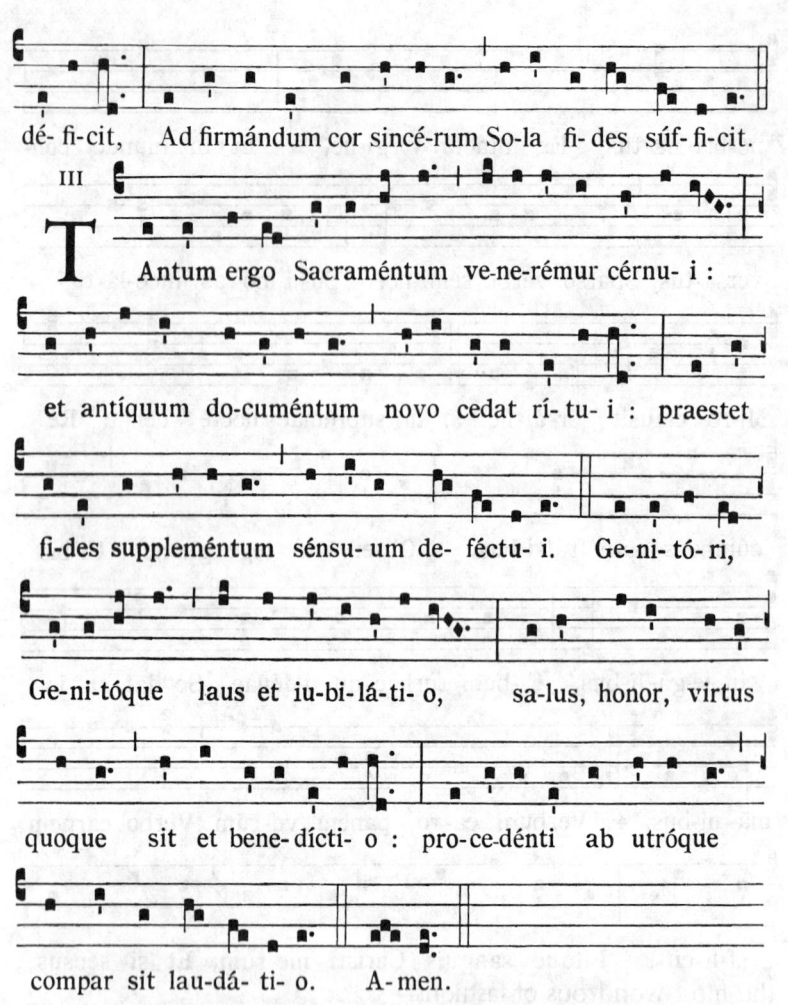

déficit, Ad firmándum cor sincérum Sola fides súfficit.

TAntum ergo Sacraméntum venerémur cérnui : et antíquum documéntum novo cedat rítui : praestet fides suppleméntum sénsuum deféctui. Genitóri, Genitóque laus et iubilátio, salus, honor, virtus quoque sit et benedíctio : procedénti ab utróque compar sit laudátio. Amen.

5. In face of so great a mystery, therefore, let us bow down and worship; let precepts of the Ancient Law give way to the new Gospel rite; and let faith assist us and help us make up for what senses fail to perceive.

6. Unto the Father and the Son, our praise and our joyful singing; unto whom saving power, honour and might, and every holy blessing; and to the Spirit who proceeds from both, an equal tribute of glory.

GOOD FRIDAY

CELEBRATION OF THE LORD'S PASSION

The priest, clothed in red Mass vestments, approaches the altar together with the ministers. There, they prostrate themselves or kneel. All pray silently for a while.

Then, the priest goes to his chair and immediately says one of the two following prayers.

Prayer

REMINISCERE miseratiónum tuárum, Dómine, et fámulos tuos ætérna protectióne sanctífica, pro quibus Christus, Fílius tuus, per suum cruórem instítuit paschále mystérium.

LORD, by shedding his blood for us, your Son, Jesus Christ, established the paschal mystery. In your goodness, make us holy and watch over us always.

Or:

DEUS, qui peccáti véteris hereditáriam mortem, in qua posteritátis genus omne succésserat, Christi Fílii tui, Dómini nostri, passióne solvísti, da, ut confórmes eídem facti, sicut imáginem terréni hóminis natúræ necessitáte portávimus, ita imáginem cæléstis grátiæ sanctificatióne portémus.

LORD, by the suffering of Christ your Son you have saved us all from the death we inherited from sinful Adam. By the law of nature we have borne the likeness of his manhood. May the sanctifying power of grace help us to put on the likeness of our Lord in heaven.

LITURGY OF THE WORD

First reading

Is 52 : 13 - 53 : 12 : *He was pierced for our offenses.*

Good Friday

Tract — Ps 101: 2-5 and 14

II

DOmine, *exáudi orationem meam, et clamor meus ad te véniat. ℣. Ne avértas fáciem tuam a me: in quacúmque die tríbulor, inclína ad me aurem tuam. ℣. In quacúmque die invocávero te, velóciter exáudi

Lord, hear my prayer, and let my cry come unto you. ℣. Do not turn your face away from me; in the day of my distress, lend me your ear. ℣. On each day that I call upon you, please make haste

Good Friday

me. ℣. Qui- a de- fe-cé-runt sic-ut fu- mus di- es me- i : et ossa me- a sic-ut in fri-xó- ri- o con- frí- xa sunt.

℣. Percússus sum sic-ut fe- num, et á-ru- it cor me- um : qui- a oblí- tus sum man- du- cá- re panem me- um.

℣. Tu exsúrgens, Dómi- ne, mi-se- ré- be- ris

to hear me. ℣. For my days pass away like smoke, and my bones burn as if in a furnace. ℣. I am smitten like grass, and my heart is withered; I have forgotten even to eat my bread. ℣. O Lord, you

Si-on: qui-a ve-nit tempus mi- se-rén-di e- ius.

will arise and have pity on Zion; for the time has come to have mercy on her.

Second reading
Heb 4: 14-16; 5: 7-9: *He learned obedience.*

Gradual
Christus factus est, *p.* 282.

Gospel
Jn 18: 1-19: 42: *The Passion.*

General Intercessions
The priest states each intention in the introduction. All kneel and pray silently, and then the priest says the prayer. All respond: Amen, and then rise.

I. *For the Church*

Orémus, dilectíssimi nobis, pro Ecclésia sancta Dei, ut eam Deus et Dóminus noster pacificáre, adunáre et custodíre dignétur toto orbe terrárum, detque nobis, quiétam et tranquíllam vitam degéntibus, glorificáre Deum Patrem omnipoténtem.

Let us pray, dear friends, for the holy Church of God throughout the world, that God the almighty Father guide it and gather it together so that we may worship him in peace and tranquility.

Good Friday

Omnípotens sempitérne Deus, qui glóriam tuam ómnibus in Christo géntibus revelásti: custódi ópera misericórdiæ tuæ, ut Ecclésia tua, toto orbe diffúsa, stábili fide in confessióne tui nóminis persevéret.

Almighty and eternal God, you have shown your glory to all nations in Christ, your Son. Guide the work of your Church. Help it to persevere in faith, proclaim your name, and bring your salvation to people everywhere.

2. *For the pope*

Orémus et pro beatíssimo Papa nostro N., ut Deus et Dóminus noster, qui elégit eum in órdine episcopátus, salvum atque incólumen custódiat Ecclésiæ suæ sanctæ, ad regéndum pópulum sanctum Dei.

Let us pray for our Holy Father, Pope N., that God who chose him to be bishop may give him health and strength to guide and govern God's holy people.

Omnípotens sempitérne Deus, cuius iudício univérsa fundántur, réspice propítius ad preces nostras, et eléctum nobis Antístitem tua pietáte consérva, ut christiána plebs, quæ te gubernátur auctóre, sub ipso Pontífice, fídei suæ méritis augeátur.

Almighty and eternal God, you guide all things by your word, you govern all Christian people. In your love protect the Pope you have chosen for us. Under his leadership deepen our faith and make us better Christians.

3. *For the clergy and laity of the Church*

Orémus et pro epíscopo nostro N., pro ómnibus epíscopis, presbýteris, diáconis Ecclésiæ, et univérsa plebe fidélium.

Let us pray for N., our bishop, for all bishops, priests, and deacons; for all who have a special ministry in the Church and for all God's people.

Omnípotens sempitérne Deus, cuius Spíritu totum corpus Ecclésiæ sanctificátur et régitur, exáudi nos pro minístris tuis supplicántes, ut, grátiæ tuæ múnere, ab ómnibus tibi fidéliter serviátur.

Almighty and eternal God, your Spirit guides the Church and makes it holy. Listen to our prayers and help each of us in his own vocation to do your work more faithfully.

4. For those preparing for baptism

Orémus et pro catechúmenis (nostris), ut Deus et Dóminus noster adapériat aures præcordiórum ipsórum ianuámque misericórdiæ, ut, per lavácrum regeneratiónis accépta remissióne ómnium peccatórum, et ipsi inveniántur in Christo Iesu Dómino nostro.

Let us pray for those (among us) preparing for baptism, that God in his mercy make them responsive to his love, forgive their sins through the waters of new birth, and give them life in Jesus Christ our Lord.

Omnípotens sempitérne Deus, qui Ecclésiam tuam nova semper prole fecúndas, auge fidem et intelléctum catechúmenis (nostris), ut, renáti fonte baptísmatis, adoptiónis tuæ fíliis aggregéntur.

Almighty and eternal God, you continually bless your Church with new members. Increase the faith and understanding of those (among us) preparing for baptism. Give them a new birth in these living waters and make them members of your chosen family.

5. For the unity of Christians

Orémus et pro univérsis frátribus in Christum credéntibus, ut Deus et Dóminus noster eos, veritátem faciéntes, in una Ecclésia sua congregáre et custodíre dignétur.

Let us pray for all our brothers and sisters who share our faith in Jesus Christ, that God may gather and keep together in one Church all those who seek the truth with sincerity.

Omnípotens sempitérne Deus, qui dispérsa cóngregas et congregáta consérvas, ad gregem Fílii tui placátus inténde, ut, quos unum baptísma sacrávit, eos et fídei iungat intégritas et vínculum sóciet caritátis.

Almighty and eternal God, you keep together those you have united. Look kindly on all who follow Jesus your Son. We are all consecrated to you by our common baptism. Make us one in the fullness of faith, and keep us one in the fellowship of love.

6. For the Jewish people

Orémus et pro Iudǽis, ut, ad quos prius locútus est Dóminus Deus noster, eis tríbuat in sui nóminis amóre et in sui fœderis fidelitáte profícere.

Let us pray for the Jewish people, the first to hear the word of God, that they may continue to grow in the love of his name and in faithfulness to his covenant.

Omnípotens sempitérne Deus, qui promissiónes tuas Abrahæ eiúsque sémini contulísti, Ecclésiæ tuæ preces cleménter exáudi, ut pópulus acquisitiónis prióris ad redemptiónis mereátur plenitúdinem perveníre.

Almighty and eternal God, long ago you gave your promise to Abraham and his posterity. Listen to your Church as we pray that the people you first made your own may arrive at the fullness of redemption.

7. For those who do not believe in Christ

Orémus et pro iis qui in Christum non credunt, ut, luce Sancti Spíritus illustráti, viam salútis et ipsi váleant introíre.

Let us pray for those who do not believe in Christ, that the light of the Holy Spirit may show them the way to salvation.

Omnípotens sempitérne Deus, fac ut qui Christum non confiténtur, coram et sincéro corde ambulántes, invéniant veritátem, nosque, mútuo proficiéntes semper amóre et ad tuæ vitæ mystérium plénius percipiéndum sollícitos, perfectióres éffice tuæ testes caritátis in mundo.

Almighty and eternal God, enable those who do not acknowledge Christ to find the truth as they walk before you in sincerity of heart. Help us to grow in love for one another, to grasp more fully the mystery of your godhead, and to become more perfect witnesses of your love in the sight of men.

8. For those who do not believe in God

Orémus et pro iis qui Deum non agnóscunt, ut, quæ recta

Let us pray for those who do not believe in God, that they

sunt sincéro corde sectántes, ad ipsum Deum perveníre mereántur.

Omnípotens sempitérne Deus, qui cunctos hómines condidísti, ut te semper desiderándo quǽrerent et inveniéndo quiéscerent, præsta, quǽsumus, ut inter nóxia quæque obstácula, omnes tuæ signa pietátis et in te credéntium testimónium bonórum óperum percipiéntes, te solum verum Deum nostríque géneris Patrem gáudeant confitéri.

may find him by sincerely following all that is right.

Almighty and eternal God, you created mankind so that all might long to find you and have peace when you are found. Grant that, in spite of the hurtful things that stand in their way, they may all recognize in the lives of Christians the tokens of your love and mercy, and gladly acknowledge you as the one true God and Father of us all.

9. *For all in public office*

Orémus et pro ómnibus rempúblicam moderántibus, ut Deus et Dóminus noster mentes et corda eórum secúndum voluntátem suam dírigat ad veram ómnium pacem et libertátem.

Let us pray for those who serve us in public office, that God may guide their minds and hearts, so that all men may live in true peace and freedom.

Omnípotens sempitérne Deus, in cuius manu sunt hóminum corda et iura populórum, réspice benígnus ad eos, qui nos in potestáte moderántur, ut ubíque terrárum populórum prospéritas, pacis secúritas, et religiónis libértas, te largiénte, consístant.

Almighty and eternal God, you know the longings of men's hearts and you protect their rights. In your goodness watch over those in authority, so that people everywhere may enjoy religious freedom, security, and peace.

10. *For those in special need*

Orémus, dilectíssimi nobis, Deum Patrem omnipoténtem, ut cunctis mundum purget erróribus, morbos áuferat, famem

Let us pray, dear friends, that God the almighty Father may heal the sick, comfort the dying, give safety to travellers,

Good Friday

depéllat, apériat cárceres, víncula solvat, viatóribus securitátem, peregrinántibus réditum, infirmántibus sanitátem atque moriéntibus salútem indúlgeat.

free those unjustly deprived of liberty, and rid the world of falsehood, hunger, and disease.

Omnípotens sempitérne Deus, mæstórum consolátio, laborántium fortitúdo, pervéniant ad te preces de quacúmque tribulatióne clamántium, ut omnes sibi in necessitátibus suis misericórdiam tuam gáudeant affuísse.

Almighty, ever-living God, you give strength to the weary and new courage to those who have lost heart. Hear the prayers of all who call on you in any trouble that they may have the joy of receiving your help in their need.

VENERATION OF THE CROSS

The priest and ministers carry the cross in procession through the church. At the start of the procession, in the middle of the church, and finally, before the sanctuary, the celebrant raises up the cross and sings:

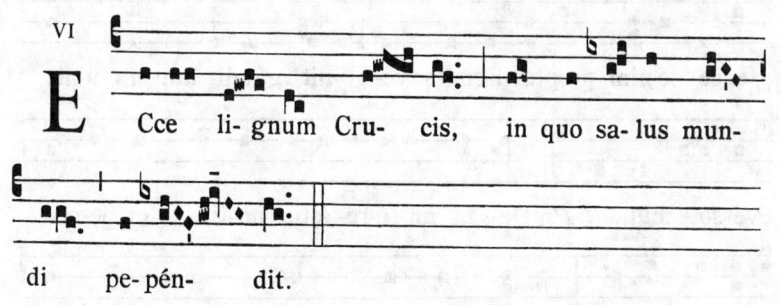

Ecce li-gnum Cru-cis, in quo sa-lus mundi pe-péndit.

This is the wood of the cross, on which hung the Saviour of the world.

Good Friday

Ve- ní- te, ad- o-ré- mus.

℟. Come, let us worship.

After each response, all kneel silently for a few moments. The cross is then set up in the place where it is to be venerated. All approach, in order, after the priest and his ministers, to venerate the cross. During this time, the antiphon of the cross is sung, together with the Improperia (Reproaches) or with the hymn of the Cross.

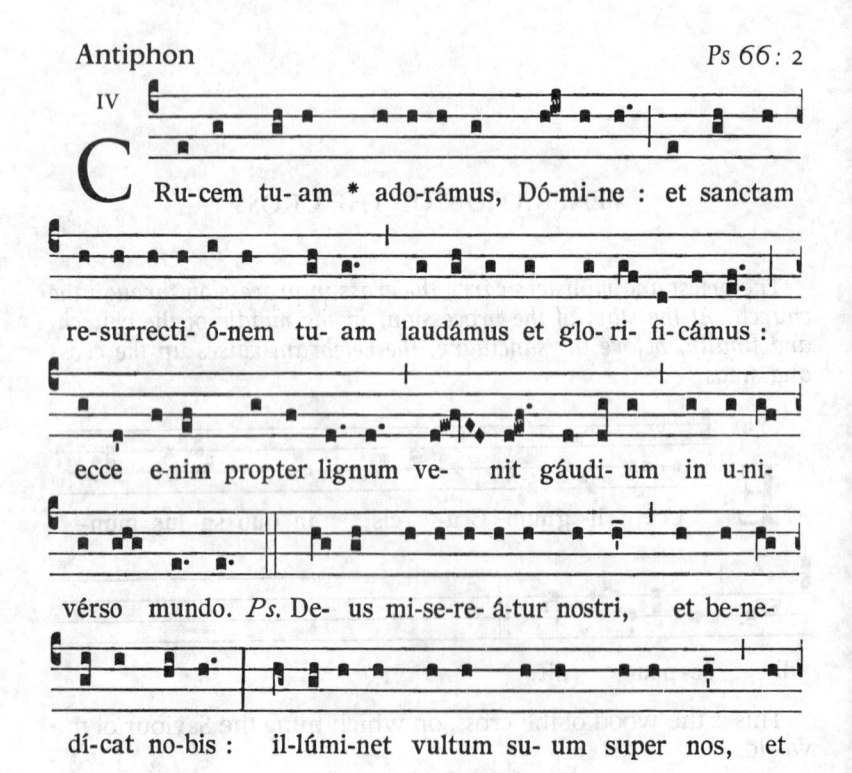

Antiphon   Ps 66 : 2

IV

CRu-cem tu- am * ado-rámus, Dó-mi-ne : et sanctam re-surrecti- ó-nem tu- am laudámus et glo- ri- fi- cámus : ecce e-nim propter lignum ve- nit gáudi- um in u-ni- vérso mundo. *Ps.* De- us mi-se-re- á-tur nostri, et be-ne-dí-cat no-bis : il-lúmi-net vultum su- um super nos, et

Good Friday

mi-se-re- á- tur nostri.

We worship you, Lord, we venerate your cross, we praise your resurrection. Through the cross you brought joy to the world. ℣. May God be gracious and bless us; and let his face shed its light upon us. *The antiphon is repeated from the beginning.*

Improperia *Mic 6: 3*

Popule me- us, quid fe- ci ti- bi? Aut in quo contristávi te? Respón- de mi-hi. ℣. Qui- a e-dú- xi te de ter-ra Ægýpti: pa- rá- sti Cru-cem Sal- va-tó- ri tu- o.

My people, what have I done to you? How have I offended you? Answer me!

I led you out of Egypt, from slavery to freedom, but you led your Saviour to the cross.

The cantors on each side of the choir alternate in singing the couplets, whereas the Greek and Latin portions of the refrain are alternated between the two sides of the choir.

Good Friday

H Agi- os o The- ós. **S** Anctus De- us.

H Agi- os Ischy-rós. **S** Anctus Fortis.

H Agi- os Athána-tos, e- lé- i- son hy-más.

S Anctus Immortá-lis, mi-se- ré-re no- bis.

Holy is God!
Holy and strong!
Holy immortal One, have mercy on us!

Q Ui- a e-dú- xi te per de-sér- tum quadra-gínta an-nis, et manna ci- bávi te, et intro- dú-xi in ter- ram sa- tis óptimam : pa- rá- sti Crucem Salva-tó- ri tu- o.

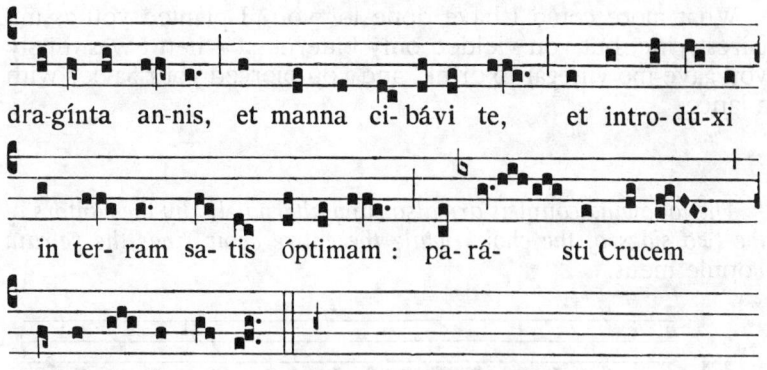

For forty years I led you safely through the desert. I fed you with manna from heaven and brought you to a land of plenty; but you led your Saviour to the cross.

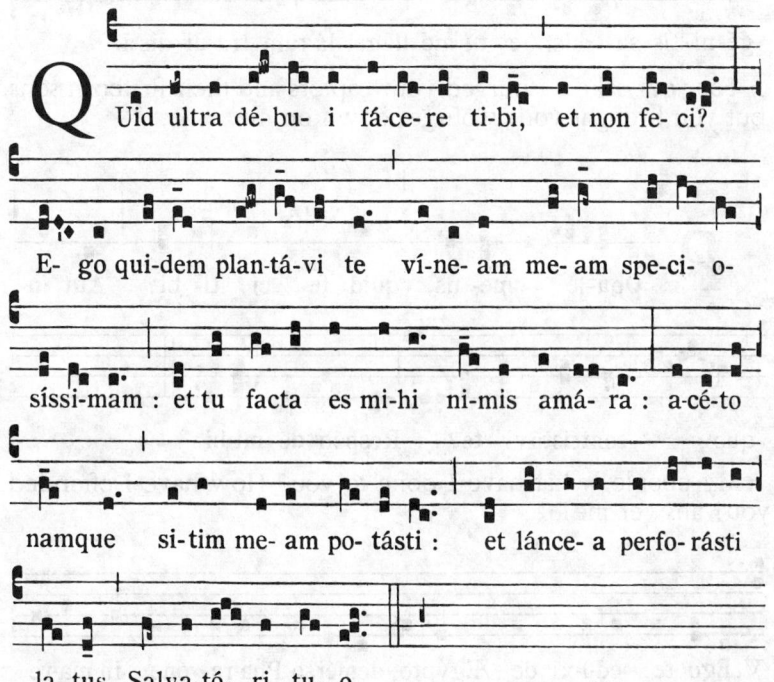

Quid ultra dé- bu- i fá-ce- re ti-bi, et non fe- ci? E- go qui-dem plan-tá-vi te ví-ne- am me- am spe-ci- o- síssi-mam : et tu facta es mi-hi ni-mis amá- ra : a-cé-to namque si-tim me- am po- tásti : et lánce- a perfo- rásti la- tus Salva-tó- ri tu- o.

Good Friday

What more could I have done for you? I planted you as my fairest vine, but you yielded only bitterness: when I was thirsty you gave me vinegar to drink, and you pierced your Savior with a lance.

The following couplets are also sung alternately, by the cantors of the two sides of the choir, while the entire choir sings the refrain Popule meus.

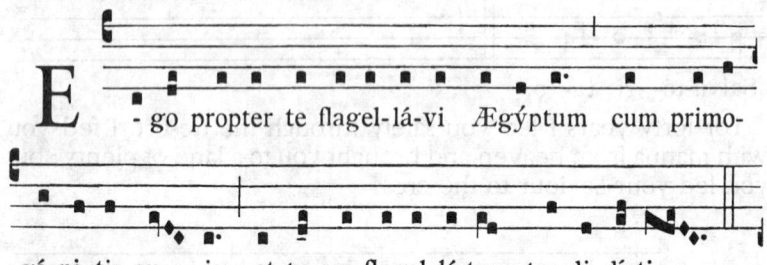

E- go propter te flagel-lá-vi Ægýptum cum primo-gé-ni-tis su- is: et tu me flagel-lá-tum tra-di-dísti.

For your sake I scourged your captors and their firstborn sons, but you brought your scourges down on me.

Opu-le me-us, quid fe- ci ti-bi? Aut in quo contristávi te? Respón-de mi-hi.

My people, what have I done to you? How have I offended you? answer me!

℣. Ego te edú-xi de Ægýpto, demérso Pha-ra- óne in ma-re

Good Friday

Ru-brum : et tu me tra-di-dísti princí-pi-bus sa-cerdó-tum.

I led you from slavery to freedom and drowned your captors in the sea, but you handed me over to your high priests. ℟. My people...

℣. Ego ante te apé-ru-i ma- re : et tu ape-ru-ísti lán-ce-a la-tus me-um. Pópule meus.

I opened the sea before you, but you opened my side with a spear. ℟. My people...

℣. Ego ante te prae-í-vi in co-lúmna nu- bis : et tu me du-xísti ad praetó-ri- um Pi-lá-ti. Pópule meus.

I led you on your way in a pillar of cloud, but you led me to Pilate's court. ℟. My people...

℣. Ego te pavi manna per de-sér- tum : et tu me ce-ci-dísti

á-la-pis et flagél-lis. Pópule meus.

I bore you up with manna in the desert, but you struck me down and scourged me. ℟. My people...

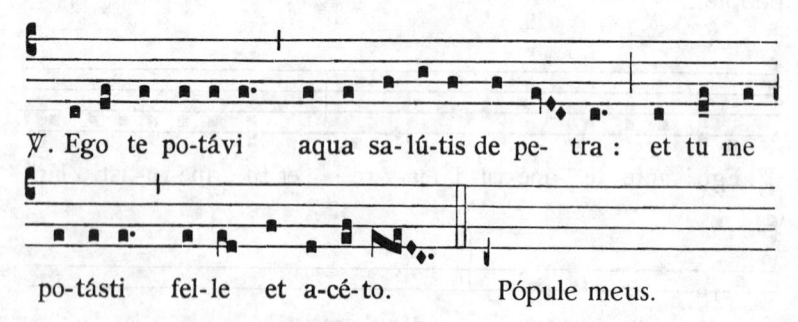

℣. Ego te potávi aqua salútis de petra : et tu me potásti felle et acéto. Pópule meus.

I gave you saving water from the rock, but you gave me gall and vinegar to drink. ℟. My people...

℣. Ego propter te Chananaeórum reges percússi : et tu percussísti arúndine caput meum. Pópule meus.

For you I struck down the kings of Canaan, but you struck my head with a reed. ℟. My people...

℣. Ego dedi tibi sceptrum regále : et tu dedísti cápiti

Good Friday

me- o spí-ne- am co-ró-nam. Pópule meus.

I gave you a royal sceptre, but you gave me a crown of thorns. ℟. My people...

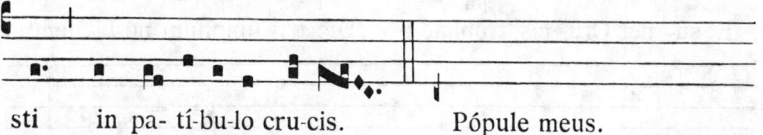

℣. Ego te exaltá-vi magna virtú- te : et tu me suspendí-sti in pa- tí-bu-lo cru-cis. Pópule meus.

I raised you to the height of majesty, but you have raised me high on a cross. ℟. My people...

Hymn

CRux fi-dé- lis, inter omnes Arbor una nó-bi- lis : Nulla ta-lem silva pro- fert, Fronde, flo- re, gérmi- ne.

* Dulce lignum, dulci clavo, Dulce pondus sústi- nens.

O faithful Cross, incomparable Tree, the noblest of all; no forest hath ere put forth the likes of thine own leaves, thy flowers, thy fruits; * Gentle wood with a gentle nail, to support so gentle a burden!

This stanza serves as the refrain. The choir takes it up one time all the way through, and the next time with the last line only, in between the other stanzas which are given by the cantors.

PAnge, lingua, glori- ó- si Praé-li- um certámi- nis,

Et su- per Cru- cis trophaé-o Dic tri- úmphum nó-bi- lem :

Quá-li- ter Red-émptor orbis Immo-lá- tus ví-ce- rit.
Crux fidélis.

1. Sing, O my tongue, of the battle, of the glorious struggle; and over the trophy of the Cross, proclaim the noble triumph; tell how the redeemer of the world won victory through his sacrifice.

De pa-réntis pro-toplá-sti Fraude Factor cóndo- lens, Quan-

do pomi no-xi- á-lis Mor- te morsu córru- it : Ipse

lignum tunc no- tá-vit, Damna lign*i* ut sólve- ret. * Dulce.

2. The Creator looked on sadly as the first man, our forefather, was deceived, and as he fell into the snare of death, taking a bite of a lethal fruit; it was then that God chose this blessed piece of wood to destroy the other tree's curse.

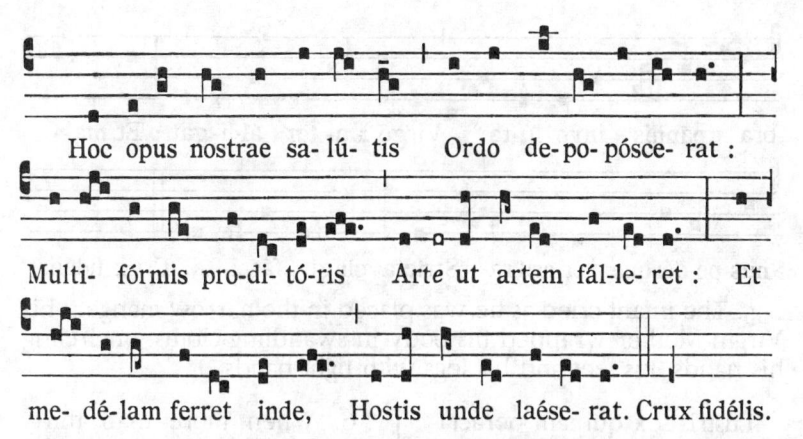

Hoc opus nostrae sa-lú-tis Ordo de-po-pósce-rat: Multi-fórmis pro-di-tó-ris Arte ut artem fál-le-ret: Et me-dé-lam ferret inde, Hostis unde laése-rat. Crux fidélis.

3. Such was the act called for by the economy of our salvation: to outwit the resourceful craftiness of the Traitor and to obtain our remedy from the very weapon with which our enemy struck.

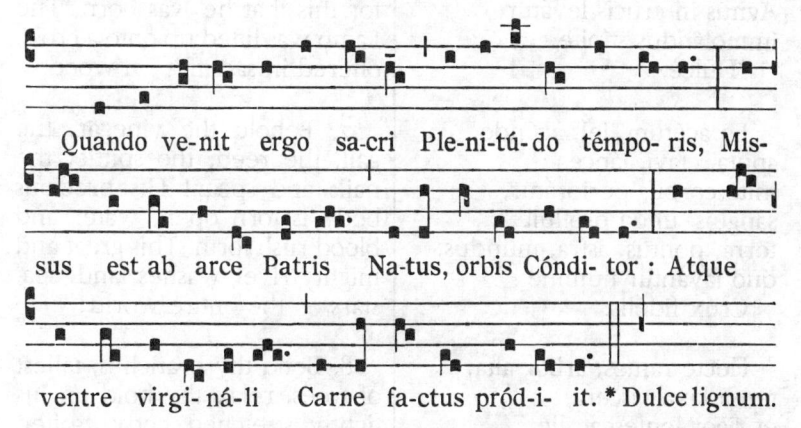

Quando ve-nit ergo sa-cri Ple-ni-tú-do témpo-ris, Missus est ab arce Patris Na-tus, orbis Cóndi-tor: Atque ventre virgi-ná-li Carne fa-ctus pród-i-it. * Dulce lignum.

4. And so, when the fulness of that blessed time had come, the Son, the Creator of the world, was sent from the throne of the Father, and having become flesh, he came forth from the womb of a Virgin.

Va-git infans inter arcta Cóndi-tus prae-sé-pi-a: Membra pannis invo-lú-ta Virgo Ma-ter ál-li-gat : Et ma-nus pe-désque et cru-ra Stricta cingit fásci- a. Crux fidélis.

5. The infant cried as he was placed in the narrow manger; his Virgin Mother wrapped his body in swaddling cloths, encircling his hands, his feet and his legs with tight bands.

Lustris sex qui iam perácta tempus implens córporis,
se volénte, natus ad hoc, passióni déditus,
Agnus in crucis levátur immolándus stípite.
*Dulce.

6. When more than thirty years had past, at the end of his earthly life, he willingly gave himself up to the Passion; it was for this that he was born. The Lamb was lifted up onto a cross, offered in sacrifice on wood.

En acétum, fel, arúndo, sputa, clavi, láncea :
mite corpus perforátur, sanguis, unda prófluit
terra, pontus, astra, mundus, quo lavántur flúmine !
Crux fidélis.

7. Behold the vinegar, the gall, the reed, the spittle, the nails and spear! His precious body is torn open, water and blood rush forth. This great and mighty river washes land, sea, stars — the entire world!

Flecte ramos, arbor alta, tensa laxa víscera,
et rigor lentéscat ille, quem dedit nativítas,
ut supérni membra regis miti tendas stípite.
* Dulce.

8. Bend thy branches, tallest of trees, relax thy hold on his tightly stretched body; soften up the hardness which nature hath given thee, and present to the body of the Heavenly King a more bearable support.

Sola digna tu fuísti ferre sæcli prétium,
atque portum præparáre nauta mundo náufrago,

9. Thou alone hast been worthy to carry the ransom of the world; mankind's ship had gone down beneath the waves,

quem sacer cruor perúnxit,
fusus Agni córpore.
   Crux fidélis.

but thou openest the way to our port of rescue. For thou art anointed with the sacred blood which sprung forth from the body of the Lamb.

This hymn always concludes with the following stanza:

Æqua Patri Fi- li- óque, Incli- to Pa- rácli- to, Sempi- térna sit be- á-tæ Tri-ni- tá- ti gló-ri- a; Cu-ius alma nos red-émit Atque servat grá-ti- a. A- men. * Dulce.

10. Equal and eternal glory to the Father and to the Son and to the Illustrious Paraclete, the Blessed Trinity whose divine grace redeems and conserves us always. Amen.

COMMUNION

The deacon or the priest goes to bring the Blessed Sacrament from the place of reposition to the altar. Upon the invitation of the priest, all say the Pater noster *which the priest concludes with the* Líbera, *p. 41. Holy Communion is then distributed in the ordinary manner.*

Prayer after Communion

OMNIPOTENS sempitérne Deus, qui nos Christi tui beáta morte et resurrectióne reparásti, consérva in nobis opus misericórdiæ tuæ, ut huius mystérii participatióne perpétua devotióne vivámus.

ALMIGHTY and eternal God, you have restored us to life by the triumphant death and resurrection of Christ. Continue this healing work within us. May we who participate in this mystery never cease to serve you.

Then the priest says the following prayer, extending his hands towards the people in sign of blessing.

Conclusion

SUPER pópulum tuum, quǽsumus, Dómine, qui mortem Fílii tui in spe suæ resurrectiónis recóluit, benedíctio copiósa descéndat, indulgéntia véniat, consolátio tribuátur, fides sancta succréscat, redémptio sempitérna firmétur.

LORD, send down your abundant blessing upon your people who have devoutly recalled the death of your Son in the sure hope of the resurrection. Grant them pardon; bring them comfort. May their faith grow stronger and their eternal salvation be assured.

EASTER SUNDAY

THE EASTER VIGIL

BLESSING OF THE FIRE
LIGHTING OF THE EASTER CANDLE

The people, all supplied with candles, assemble outside the church, at the place where the fire has been prepared. If the gathering cannot be held outdoors, the faithful should enter the church directly, remaining all together, if possible, near the entrance, so that they can later move up in procession behind the Easter candle, towards the place where the Liturgy of the Word is to be celebrated.

When the people have assembled, the priest approaches the fire, with the ministers, one of whom is carrying the Easter candle. He greets the assembly, and explains briefly the meaning of this night's vigil.

He then blesses the fire:

DEUS, qui per Fílium tuum claritátis tuæ ignem fidélibus contulísti, novum hunc ignem sanctífica, et concéde nobis, ita per hæc festa paschália cæléstibus desidériis inflammári, ut ad perpétuæ claritátis puris méntibus valeámus festa pertíngere.

FATHER, we share in the light of your glory through your Son, the light of the world. Make this new fire holy, and inflame us with new hope. Purify our minds by this Easter celebration and bring us one day to the feast of eternal light.

The priest then lights the Easter candle with a flame taken from the new fire. He says:

Lumen Christi gloriósæ resurgéntis díssipet ténebras cordis et mentis.

May the light of Christ, rising in glory, dispel the darkness of our hearts and minds.

PROCESSION

The deacon, or, if there is no deacon, the priest, takes the Easter candle, lifts it high, and sings: Lumen Christi! (Christ our light!) *All answer:* Deo grátias. (Thanks be to God).

All advance towards the church, led by the deacon carrying the Easter candle, and by the priest.

At the door of the church, the deacon stops and sings again: Lumen Christi! *The candles of the faithful are lit with a flame taken from the Easter candle and then, all enter into the church.*

When the deacon reaches the altar, he sings for the third time: Lumen Christi! *Then, the lights in the church are put on.*

EASTER PROCLAMATION

The Easter candle is set up on its stand. All take their places and remain standing with lighted candles during the solemn Easter Proclamation which is sung by the deacon, or, if there is no deacon, by a cantor, or even by the priest.

E XSULTET iam angélica turba cælórum: exsúltent divína mystéria: et pro tanti Regis victória tuba ínsonet salutáris. Gáudeat et tellus tantis irradiáta fulgóribus: et, ætérni Regis splendóre illustráta, totíus orbis se séntiat amisísse calíginem. Lætétur et mater Ecclésia, tanti lúminis adornáta fulgóribus: et magnis populórum vócibus hæc aula resúltet.

R EJOICE, heavenly powers! Sing, choirs of angels! Exult, all creation around God's throne! Jesus Christ, our King, is risen! Sound the trumpet of salvation! Rejoice, O earth, in shining splendour, radiant in the brightness of your King! Christ has conquered! Glory fills you! Darkness vanishes for ever! Rejoice, O Mother Church! Exult in glory! The risen Saviour shines upon you! Let this place resound with joy, echoing the mighty song of all God's people!

This paragraph is only used when a deacon is singing.

(Quaprópter astántes vos, fratres caríssimi, ad tam miram

(My dearest friends, standing with me in this holy light, join

The Easter Vigil

huius sancti lúminis claritátem, una mecum, quæso, Dei omnipoténtis misericórdiam invocáte. Ut, qui me non meis méritis intra Levitárum númerum dignátus est aggregáre, lúminis sui claritátem infúndens, cérei huius laudem implére perfíciat.)

℣. Dóminus vobíscum.
℟. Et cum spíritu tuo.
℣. Sursum corda.
℟. Habémus ad Dóminum.

℣. Grátias agámus Dómino Deo nostro.
℟. Dignum et iustum est.

Vere dignum et iustum est, invisíbilem Deum Patrem omnipoténtem Filiúmque eius unigénitum, Dóminum nostrum Iesum Christum, toto cordis ac mentis afféctu et vocis ministério personáre. Qui pro nobis ætérno Patri Adæ débitum solvit, et véteris piáculi cautiónem pio cruóre detérsit.

Hæc sunt enim festa paschália, in quibus verus ille Agnus occíditur, cuius sánguine postes fidélium consecrántur.

Hæc nox est, in qua primum patres nostros, fílios Israel edúctos de Ægýpto, Mare Rubrum sicco vestígio transíre fecísti. Hæc ígitur nox est, quæ peccatórum ténebras colúmnæ illuminatióne purgávit.

me in asking God for mercy, that he may give his unworthy minister grace to sing his Easter praises).

℣. The Lord be with you.
℟. And also with you.
℣. Lift up your hearts.
℟. We lift them up to the Lord.
℣. Let us give thanks to the Lord our God.
℟. It is right to give him thanks and praise.

It is truly right that with full hearts and minds and voices we should praise the unseen God, the all-powerful Father, and his only Son, our Lord Jesus Christ. For Christ has ransomed us with his blood, and paid for us the price of Adam's sin to our eternal Father!

This is our passover feast, when Christ, the true Lamb, is slain, whose blood consecrates the homes of all believers.

This is the night when first you saved our fathers: you freed the people of Israel from their slavery and led them dryshod through the sea.

This is the night when the pillar of fire destroyed the darkness of sin!

The Easter Vigil

Hæc nox est, quæ hódie per univérsum mundum in Christo credéntes, a vítiis sǽculi et calígine peccatórum segregátos, reddit grátiæ, sóciat sanctitáti.

Hæc nox est, in qua, destrúctis vínculis mortis, Christus ab ínferis victor ascéndit.

Nihil enim nobis nasci prófuit, nisi rédimi profuísset.

O mira circa nos tuæ pietátis dignátio! O inæstimábilis diléctio caritátis: ut servum redímeres, Fílium tradidísti!

O certe necessárium Adæ peccátum, quod Christi morte delétum est!

O felix culpa, quæ talem ac tantum méruit habére Redemptórem!

O vere beáta nox, quæ sola méruit scire tempus et horam, in qua Christus ab ínferis resurréxit!

Hæc nox est, de qua scriptum est: «Et nox sicut dies illuminábitur: et nox illuminátio mea in delíciis meis.»

Huius ígitur sanctificátio noctis fugat scélera, culpas lavat: et reddit innocéntiam lapsis et mæstis lætítiam. Fugat ódia, concórdiam parat et curvat impéria.

This is the night when Christians everywhere, washed clean of sin and freed from all defilement, are restored to grace and grow together in holiness.

This is the night when Jesus Christ broke the chains of death and rose triumphant from the grave.

What good would life have been to us, had Christ not come as our Redeemer?

Father, how wonderful your care for us! How boundless your merciful love! To ransom a slave you gave away your Son.

O happy fault, O necessary sin of Adam, which gained for us so great a Redeemer!

Most blessed of all nights, chosen by God to see Christ rising from the dead!

Of this night scripture says: "The night will be as clear as day: it will become my light, my joy."

The power of this holy night dispels all evil, washes guilt away, restores lost innocence, brings mourners joy; it casts out hatred, brings us peace, and humbles earthly pride. Night truly blessed when heaven is wedded to earth and man is reconciled with God!

The Easter Vigil

In huius ígitur noctis grátia, súscipe, sancte Pater, laudis huius sacrifícium vespertínum, quod tibi in hac cérei oblatióne sollémni, per ministrórum manus de opéribus apum, sacrosáncta reddit Ecclésia.

Sed iam colúmnæ huius præcónia nóvimus, quam in honórem Dei rútilans ignis accéndit. Qui, licet sit divísus in partes, mutuáti tamen lúminis detriménta non novit. Alitur enim liquántibus ceris, quas in substántiam pretiósæ huius lámpadis apis mater edúxit.

O vere beáta nox, in qua terrénis cæléstia, humánis divína iungúntur!

Orámus ergo te, Dómine, ut céreus iste in honórem tui nóminis consecrátus, ad noctis huius calíginem destruéndam, indefíciens persevéret. Et in odórem suavitátis accéptus, supérnis lumináribus misceátur. Flammas eius lúcifer matutínus invéniat: Ille, inquam, lúcifer, qui nescit occásum: Christus Fílius tuus, qui, regréssus ab ínferis, humáno géneri serénus illúxit, et vivit et regnat in sǽcula sæculórum. ℟. Amen.

Therefore, heavenly Father, in the joy of this night, receive our evening sacrifice of praise, your Church's solemn offering.

Accept this Easter Candle, a flame divided but undimmed, a pillar of fire that glows to the honour of God!

Let it mingle with the lights of heaven and continue bravely burning to dispel the darkness of this night! May the Morning Star which never sets find this flame still burning: Christ, that Morning Star, who came back from the dead, and shed his peaceful light on all mankind, your Son who lives and reigns for ever and ever.
℟. Amen.

LITURGY OF THE WORD

First reading
Gen 1: 1 - 2: 2 *or* 1: 26-31a: *Creation.*

Canticle *Ps 99 : 2,3*

VIII

JUBILATE * Dómino omnis terra: servíte Dómino in laetítia. ℣. Intráte in conspéctu eius, in exsultatióne. ℣. Scitóte quod Dóminus ipse est Deus. ℣. Ipse fecit nos, et non ipsi nos: nos autem pópulus eius, et oves páscuae eius.

The Easter Vigil

Make a joyful noise to the Lord all the earth; serve the Lord with gladness. ℣. Come into his presence in exultation. ℣. Know that the Lord is God. ℣. It is he that made us and not we ourselves; we are his people and the sheep of his pasture.

Prayer

OMNIPOTENS sempitérne Deus, qui es in ómnium óperum tuórum dispensatióne mirábilis, intéllegant redémpti tui, non fuísse excelléntius, quod inítio factus est mundus, quam quod in fine sæculórum Pascha nostrum immolátus est Christus.

ALMIGHTY and eternal God, you created all things in wonderful beauty and order. Help us now to perceive how still more wonderful is the new creation by which in the fullness of time you redeemed your people through the sacrifice of our passover, Jesus Christ.

Or:

DEUS, qui mirabíliter creásti hóminem et mirabílius redemísti, da nobis, quæsumus, contra oblectaménta peccáti mentis ratióne persístere, ut mereámur ad ætérna gáudia perveníre.

LORD GOD, the creation of man was a wonderful work, his redemption still more wonderful. May we persevere in right reason against all that entices to sin and so attain to everlasting joy.

Second reading

Gen 22: 1-13, 15-18 *or* 1-2, 10-13, 15-18: *The sacrifice and deliverance of Isaac.*

Canticle

Qui confídunt, p. 261.

Prayer

Deus, Pater summe fidélium, qui promissiónis tuæ fílios diffúsa adoptiónis grátia in toto terrárum orbe multíplicas, et per paschále sacraméntum Abraham púerum tuum universárum, sicut iurásti, géntium éfficis patrem, da pópulis tuis digne ad grátiam tuæ vocatiónis intráre.

God and Father of all who believe in you, you promised Abraham that he would become the father of all nations, and through the death and resurrection of Christ you fulfill that promise: everywhere throughout the world you increase your chosen people. May we respond to your call by joyfully accepting your invitation to the new life of grace.

Third reading

Ex 14: 15-15: 1a: *The passage through the Red Sea.*

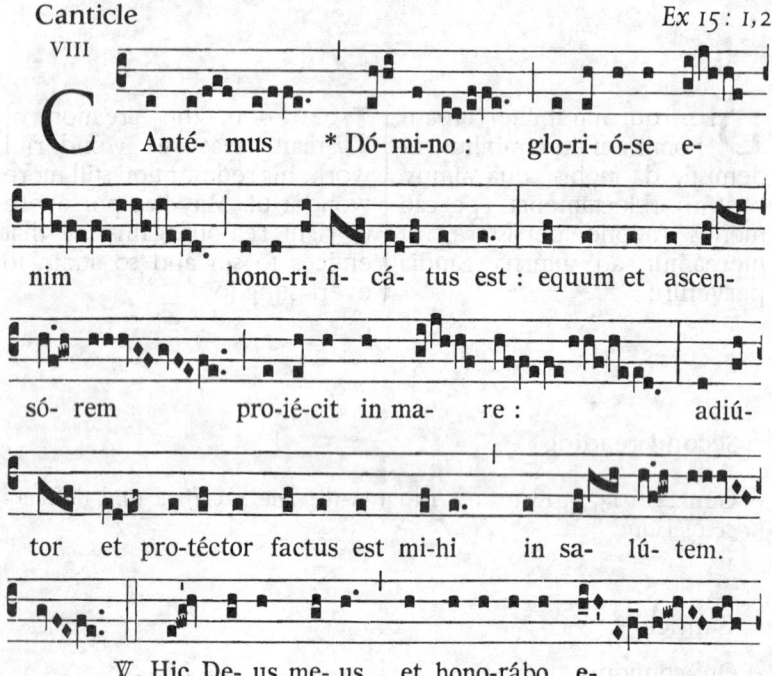

Canticle

Ex 15: 1, 2

C Antémus * Dómino: glorióse enim honorificátus est: equum et ascensórem proiécit in mare: adiútor et protéctor factus est mihi in salútem.

℣. Hic Deus meus, et honorábo e-

The Easter Vigil

[Chant notation]

um : De- us patris me- i, et ex-al- tá-bo e- um. ℣. Dó- mi-nus cónte-rens bel-la : Dó- mi-nus no-men est il-li.

Let us sing to the Lord, for he has triumphed gloriously; the horse and his rider he has thrown into the sea; he has become my strength and my protection unto my salvation. ℣. This is my God and I will praise him, my father's God and I will exalt him. ℣. The Lord shatters the forces of war; the Lord is his name.

Prayer

DEUS, cuius antíqua mirácula étiam nostris tempóribus coruscáre sentímus, dum, quod uni pópulo a persecutióne Pharaónis liberándo déxteræ tuæ poténtia contulísti, id in salútem géntium per aquam regeneratiónis operáris, præsta, ut in Abrahæ fílios et in Israelíticam dignitátem totíus mundi tránseat plenitúdo.

FATHER, even today we see the wonders of the miracles you worked long ago. You once saved a single nation from slavery, and now you offer that salvation to all through baptism. May the peoples of the world become true sons of Abraham and prove worthy of the heritage of Israel.

Or:

DEUS, qui primis tempóribus impléta mirácula novi testaménti luce reserásti, ut et

LORD GOD, in the new covenant you shed light on the miracles you worked in ancient

Mare Rubrum forma sacri fontis exsísteret, et plebs a servitúte liberáta christiáni pópuli sacraménta præférret, da, ut omnes gentes, Israélis privilégium mérito fídei consecútæ, Spíritus tui participatióne regeneréntur.

times: the Red Sea is a symbol of our baptism, and the nation you freed from slavery is a sign of your Christian people. May every nation share the faith and privilege of Israel and come to new birth in the Holy Spirit.

Fourth reading

Is 54: 5-14: *God's love for Jerusalem, his Spouse.*

Canticle   Ps 116

VIII

L Audáte * Dóminum, omnes gentes: et collaudáte eum, omnes pópuli. ℣. Quóniam confirmáta est super nos misericórdia eius: et véritas Dómini manet in aetérnum.

Praise the Lord, all nations; praise him in unison, all peoples. ℣. For his mercy is confirmed upon us and the faithfulness of the Lord endures for ever.

Prayer

OMNIPOTENS sempitérne Deus, multíplica in honórem nóminis tui quod patrum fídei spopondísti, et promissiónis fílios sacra adoptióne diláta, ut, quod prióres sancti non dubitavérunt futúrum, Ecclésia tua magna ex parte iam cognóscat implétum.

ALMIGHTY and eternal God, glorify your name by increasing your chosen people as you promised long ago. In reward for their trust, may we see in the Church the fulfillment of your promise.

Fifth reading

Is 55: 1-11: *The mystery of water and the word.*

Canticle

Is 5: 1, 2

VIII

VI-ne- a * fa-cta est di- lé- cto in cornu, in lo-co ú- be- ri.

℣. Et ma-cé- ri- am circúmde-dit, et circumfó-dit: et plantá-vit ví-ne- am So- rec, et aedi- fi- cá- vit turrim in mé-di- o e- ius.

℣. Et tórcu-lar fo-dit in e- a: ví-ne- a e- nim Dómi-ni Sá- ba- oth, do- mus Is- ra- el est.

My beloved had a vineyard on a hill, in a fruitful place. ℣. And he fenced it in and made a ditch around it, and planted it with the vine of Sorec and built a watchtower in the midst of it. ℣. He hewed out a wine vat in it. Now, the vineyard of the Lord of hosts is the house of Israel.

Prayer

OMNIPOTENS sempitérne Deus, spes única mundi, qui prophetárum tuórum præcónio præséntium témporum declarásti mystéria, auge pópuli tui vota placátus, quia in nullo fidélium nisi ex tua inspiratióne provéniunt quarúmlibet increménta virtútum.

ALMIGHTY, ever-living God, only hope of the world, by the preaching of the prophets you proclaimed the mysteries we are celebrating tonight. Help us to be your faithful people, for it is by your inspiration alone that we can grow in goodness.

Sixth reading

Bar 3: 9-15, 32 - 4: 4 *God offers men true wisdom.*

Canticle

Deut 32: 1-4

VIII

A T-tén- de * cae- lum, et lo- quar :

et áudi- at terra verba ex o-re me-

o. ℣. Exspecté- tur sic-ut plúvi- a e-lóqui- um

me- um : et descéndant sic-ut ros verba me-

a, sic-ut imber su- per grámi- na.

℣. Et sic-ut nix su-per fe- num : qui- a nomen

Dó- mi-ni invo- cá- bo. ℣. Da- te magni-tú-di-

nem De- o no- stro : De- us, ve-ra ó-pe-ra e-

ius, et omnes vi- ae e-ius iu-dí- ci-

a. ℣. De- us fi-dé-lis, in quo non est in-íqui-

[music notation]

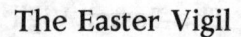

tas : iu- stus et sanctus Dómi-nus.

[music notation]

Give ear, O heavens, and I will speak; let the earth hearken to the words of my mouth. ℣. Let my speech be longed for as the rain; let my words come down like the dew, like showers upon the grass. ℣. Yes, and like snow upon the dry herb; for I will invoke the name of the Lord. ℣. Ascribe greatness to our God; the works of God are true and all his ways are justice. ℣. God is faithful, there is no iniquity in him; the Lord is just and holy.

Prayer

Deus, qui Ecclésiam tuam semper géntium vocatióne multíplicas, concéde propítius, ut, quos aqua baptísmatis ábluis, contínua protectióne tueáris.

Father, you increase your Church by continuing to call all people to salvation. Listen to our prayers and always watch over those you cleanse in baptism.

Seventh reading

Ezek 36: 16-17a, 18-28: *A new heart and a new spirit.*

Canticle

Ps 41: 2, 3, 4

[music notation]

Sic- ut cer- vus * de-sí- de- rat ad fontes aquá- rum : i- ta de- sí-de-rat á-nima

The Easter Vigil

me- a ad te, De- us. ℣. Si- tí- vit á-nima me- a ad De- um vi- vum: quando vé- ni- am, et appa- ré- bo ante fá- ci- em De- i me- i? ℣. Fu- é- runt mi-hi lácrimae me- ae panes di- e ac no- cte, dum dí-ci- tur mi-hi per síngu-los di- es: U- bi est De- us tu- us?

As a hart longs for flowing streams, so longs my soul for you, O God. ℣. My soul thirsts for the living God; when shall I come and appear before the face of my God? ℣. My tears have been my food day and night, while men say to me daily: "Where is your God?"

Prayer

Dᴇᴜs, incommutábilis virtus et lumen ætérnum, réspice propítius ad totíus Ecclésiæ sacraméntum, et opus salútis humánæ perpétuæ dispositiónis efféctu tranquíllius operáre; totúsque mundus experiátur et vídeat deiécta érigi, inveteráta renovári et per ipsum Christum redíre ómnia in íntegrum, a quo sumpsére princípium.

God of unchanging power and light, look with mercy and favour on your entire Church. Bring lasting salvation to mankind, so that the world may see the fallen lifted up, the old made new, and all things brought to perfection, through him who is their origin, our Lord Jesus Christ, who lives and reigns for ever and ever.

Or:

Dᴇᴜs, qui nos ad celebrándum paschále sacraméntum utriúsque Testaménti páginis ínstruis, da nobis intellégere misericórdiam tuam, ut ex perceptióne præséntium múnerum firma sit exspectátio futurórum.

Father, you teach us in both the Old and the New Testament to celebrate this passover mystery. Help us to understand your great love for us. May the goodness you now show us confirm our hope in your future mercy.

Glória in excélsis.

Prayer

Dᴇᴜs, qui hanc sacratíssimam noctem glória domínicæ resurrectiónis illústras, éxcita in Ecclésia tua adoptiónis spíritum, ut, córpore et mente renováti, puram tibi exhibeámus servitútem.

Lord god, you have brightened this night with the radiance of the risen Christ. Quicken the spirit of sonship in your Church; renew us in mind and body to give you whole-hearted service.

The Easter Vigil

Epistle

Rom 6: 3-11: *Christ, having risen from the dead, will never die again.*

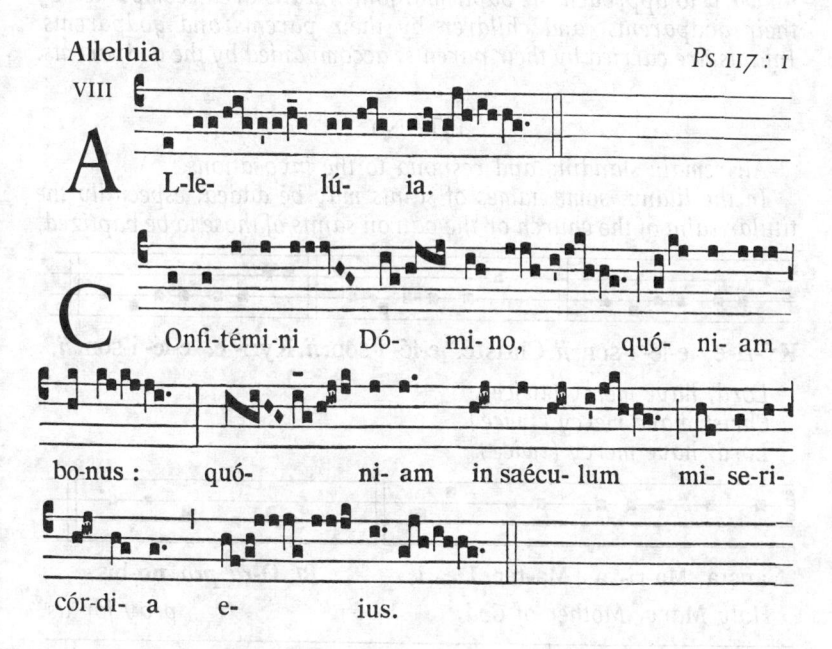

Alleluia *Ps 117: 1*

VIII

A-llelúia.

Confitémini Dómino, quóniam bonus: quóniam in saéculum misericórdia eius.

Give thanks to the Lord, for he is good; his mercy endures forever.

Gospel

A. Mt 28: 1-10: *Christ has risen.*
B. Mk 16: 1-8.
C. Lk 24: 1-12.

If no one is to be baptized and the font is not to be blessed, the blessing of water takes place at once, p. 344 bottom.

LITURGY OF BAPTISM

If there are candidates to be baptized, they are called and come forward to approach the baptismal font. Adults are accompanied by their godparents, and children by their parents and godparents. Infants are carried by their parents, accompanied by the godparents.

LITANY

All remain standing and respond to the invocations.
In the litany, some names of saints may be added, especially the titular saint of the church or the patron saints of those to be baptized.

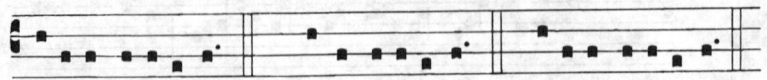

Ký-ri-e, e-lé-i-son. *ii.* Christe, e-lé-i-son. *ii.* Kýri-e, e-lé-i-son. *ii.*

Lord, have mercy *(twice)*.
Christ, have mercy *(twice)*.
Lord, have mercy *(twice)*.

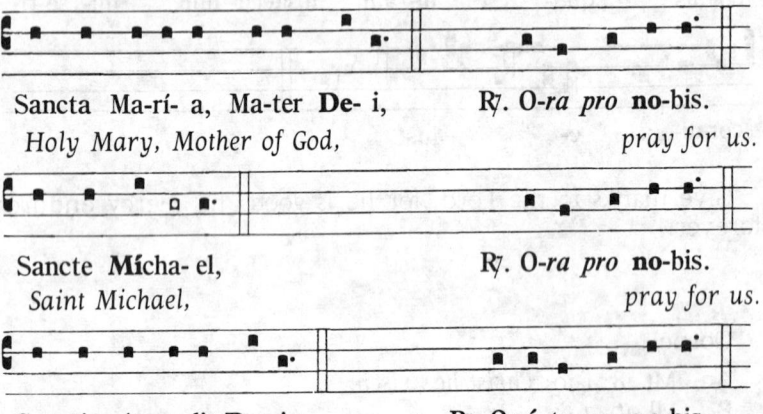

Sancta Ma-rí-a, Ma-ter **De**-i,   ℟. **O**-*ra pro* **no**-bis.
  Holy Mary, Mother of God,   pray for us.

Sancte **Mí**cha-el,   ℟. **O**-*ra pro* **no**-bis.
  Saint Michael,   pray for us.

Sancti Ange-li **De**-i,   ℟. **O**-rá-*te pro* **no**-bis.
  Holy angels of God,   pray for us.

Sancte Ioánnes Baptísta,   ora pro nobis.
  Saint John the Baptist,   pray for us.
Sancte Ioseph,   ora pro nobis.
  Saint Joseph   pray for us.

The Easter Vigil

Sancti Petre et **Paule**,	oráte pro nobis.
Saint Peter and Saint Paul,	pray for us.
Sancte Andréa,	ora pro nobis.
Saint Andrew,	
Sancte Ioánnes,	ora pro nobis.
Saint John,	
Sancta María Magdaléna,	ora pro nobis.
Saint Mary Magdalene,	
Sancte Stéphane,	ora pro nobis.
Saint Stephen,	
Sancte Ignáti Antiochéne,	ora pro nobis.
Saint Ignatius of Antioch,	
Sancte Laurénti,	ora pro nobis.
Saint Lawrence,	
Sanctæ Perpétua et Felícitas,	oráte pro nobis.
Saint Perpetua and Saint Felicity,	
Sancta Agnes,	ora pro nobis.
Saint Agnes,	
Sancte Gregóri,	ora pro nobis.
Saint Gregory,	
Sancte Augustíne,	ora pro nobis.
Saint Augustine,	
Sancte Athanási,	ora pro nobis.
Saint Athanasius,	
Sancte Basíli,	ora pro nobis.
Saint Basil,	
Sancte Martíne,	ora pro nobis.
Saint Martin,	
Sancte Benedícte,	ora pro nobis.
Saint Benedict,	
Sancte Francísce et Domínice,	oráte pro nobis.
Saint Francis and Saint Dominic,	
Sancte Francísce (Xavier),	ora pro nobis.
Saint Francis Xavier,	
Sancte Ioánnes María (Vianney),	ora pro nobis.
Saint John Vianney	
Sancta Catharína (Senénsis),	ora pro nobis.
Saint Catherine of Siena,	
Sancta Terésia a Iesu,	ora pro nobis.
Saint Teresa of Avila,	
Omnes Sancti et Sanctæ **Dei**,	oráte pro nobis.
All holy men and women	

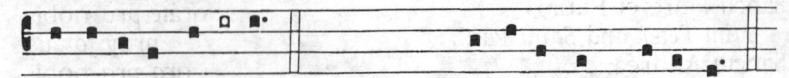

Pro-pí-*ti*-*us* **e**-sto, ℟. Lí-be-ra nos, Dómi-ne.
  Lord, be merciful, *Lord, save your people.*
Ab *omni* **malo**, líbera nos, Dómine.
  From all evil,
Ab omni peccáto, líbera nos, Dómine.
  From every sin,
A morte perpétua, líbera nos, Dómine.
  From everlasting death,
Per incarnatiónem tuam, líbera nos, Dómine.
  By your coming as man,
Per mortem et resurrectiónem tuam líbera nos, Dómine.
  By your death and rising to new life,
Per effusiónem Spíritus Sancti, líbera nos, Dómine.
  By your gift of the Holy Spirit,

Pec*ca*-tó-res, ℟. Te ro-gámus, audi nos.
  Be merciful to us sinners, *Lord, hear our prayer.*
Ut hos eléctos per grátiam Baptísmi
  regeneráre dignéris, te rogámus, audi nos.
  Give new life to these chosen ones by the grace of baptism,
(*In place of the last invocation, if no one is to be baptized:* Ut hunc fontem, regenerándis tibi fíliis, grátia tua sanctificáre dignéris,
  te rogámus, audi nos.)
(*By your grace bless this font where your children will be reborn.*)
Iesu, Fili Dei vivi, te rogámus, audi nos.
  Jesus, Son of the living God,

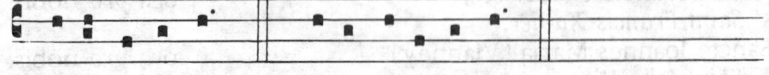

Christe, audi nos. *ii*. Christe, exáudi nos. *ii*.
  Christ, hear us (twice).
  Lord Jesus, hear our prayer (twice).

OMNIPOTENS sempitérne Deus, adésto magnæ pietátis | ALMIGHTY and eternal God, be present in this sacra-

The Easter Vigil

tuæ sacraméntis, et ad recreándos novos pópulos, quos tibi fons baptísmatis párturit, spíritum adoptiónis emítte, ut, quod nostræ humilitátis geréndum est ministério, virtútis tuæ impleátur efféctu.

ment of your love. Send your Spirit of adoption on those to be born again in baptism. And may the work of our humble ministry be brought to perfection by your mighty power.

Blessing of Water

Deus, qui invisíbili poténtia per sacramentórum signa mirábilem operáris efféctum, et creatúram aquæ multis modis præparásti, ut baptísmi grátiam demonstráret;

Father, you give us grace through sacramental signs, which tell us of the wonders of your unseen power. In baptism we use your gift of water, which you have made a rich symbol of the grace you give us in this sacrament.

Deus, cuius Spíritus super aquas inter ipsa mundi primórdia ferebátur, ut iam tunc virtútem sanctificándi aquárum natúra concíperet;

At the very dawn of creation your Spirit breathed on the waters, making them the wellspring of all holiness.

Deus, qui regeneratiónis spéciem in ipsa dilúvii effusióne signásti, ut uníus eiusdémque eleménti mystério et finis esset vítiis et orígo virtútum;

The waters of the great flood you made a sign of the waters of baptism, that make an end of sin and a new beginning of goodness.

Deus, qui Abrahæ fílios per Mare Rubrum sicco vestígio transíre fecísti, ut plebs, a Pharaónis servitúte liberáta, pópulum baptizatórum præfiguráret;

Through the waters of the Red Sea you led Israel out of slavery, to be an image of God's holy people, set free from sin by baptism.

Deus, cuius Fílius, in aqua Iordánis à Ioánne baptizátus, Sancto Spíritu est inúnctus, et, in cruce pendens, una cum sánguine aquam de látere suo prodúxit, ac post resurrectiónem suam, discípulis iussit:

In the waters of the Jordan your Son was baptized by John and anointed with the Spirit. Your Son willed that water and blood should flow from his side as he hung upon the cross. After his resurrection he told

«Ite, docéte omnes gentes, baptizántes eos in nómine Patris, et Fílii, et Spíritus Sancti»:

Réspice in fáciem Ecclésiæ tuæ, eique dignáre fontem baptísmatis aperíre. Sumat hæc aqua Unigéniti tui grátiam de Spíritu Sancto, ut homo, ad imáginem tuam cónditus, sacraménto baptísmatis a cunctis squalóribus vetustátis ablútus, in novam infántiam ex aqua et Spíritu Sancto resúrgere mereátur.

his disciples: "Go out and teach all nations, baptizing them in the name of the Father and of the Son and of the Holy Spirit."

Father, look now with love upon your Church, and unseal for her the fountain of baptism. By the power of the Spirit give to the water of this font the grace of your Son. You created man in your own likeness: cleanse him from sin in a new birth of innocence by water and the Spirit.

The priest may lower the Easter candle into the water as he says:

Descéndat, quæsumus, Dómine, in hanc plenitúdinem fontis per Fílium tuum virtus Spíritus Sancti, ut omnes, cum Christo consepúlti per baptísmum in mortem, ad vitam cum ipso resúrgant. Per Christum Dóminum nostrum. ℟. Amen.

We ask you, Father, with your Son to send the Holy Spirit upon the waters of this font. May all who are buried with Christ in the death of baptism rise also with him to newness of life. We ask this through Christ our Lord.
℟. Amen.

After the blessing of the water, the catechumens are baptized individually. Newly baptized adults are confirmed immediately afterwards, either by the bishop, or by the priest who baptized them.

Blessing of Water *when baptism is not celebrated*

Dóminum Deum nostrum, fratres caríssimi, supplíciter exorémus, ut hanc creatúram aquæ benedícere dignétur, super nos aspergéndam in nostri memóriam baptísmi. Ipse autem nos renováre dignétur, ut fidéles Spirítui, quem accépimus, maneámus.

My brothers and sisters, let us ask the Lord our God to bless this water he has created, which we shall use to recall our baptism. May he renew us and keep us faithful to the Spirit we have all received.

The Easter Vigil

All pray silently for a short while. With hands joined, the priest continues:

Dómine Deus noster, pópulo tuo hac nocte sacratíssima vigilánti adésto propítius; et nobis, mirábile nostræ creatiónis opus, sed et redemptiónis nostræ mirabílius, memorántibus, hanc aquam benedícere tu dignáre. Ipsam enim tu fecísti, ut et arva fecunditáte donáret, et levámen corpóribus nostris munditiámque præbéret. Aquam étiam tuæ minístram misericórdiæ condidísti: nam per ipsam solvísti tui pópuli servitútem illiúsque sitim in desérto sedásti; per ipsam novum fœdus nuntiavérunt prophétæ, quod eras cum homínibus initúrus; per ipsam dénique, quam Christus in Iordáne sacrávit, corrúptam natúræ nostræ substántiam in regeneratiónis lavácro renovásti. Sit ígitur hæc aqua nobis suscépti baptísmatis memória, et cum frátribus nostris, qui sunt in Páschate baptizáti, gáudia nos tríbuas sociáre. Per Christum Dóminum nostrum. ℟. Amen.

Lord our God, this night your people keep prayerful vigil. Be with us as we recall the wonder of our creation and the greater wonder of our redemption. Bless this water: it makes the seed to grow, it refreshes us and makes us clean. You have made of it a servant of your loving kindness: through water you set your people free, and quenched their thirst in the desert. With water the prophets announced a new covenant that you would make with man. By water, made holy by Christ in the Jordan, you made our sinful nature new in the bath that gives rebirth. Let this water remind us of our baptism; let us share the joys of our brothers who are baptized this Easter. We ask this through Christ our Lord. ℟. Amen.

Renewal of Baptismal Promises

All present stand with lighted candles. The priest speaks to the people in these or similar words:

Dear friends, through the paschal mystery we have been buried with Christ in baptism, so that we may rise with him to a new life. Now that we have completed our lenten observance, let us renew the promises we made in baptism when we rejected Satan and his works, and promised to serve God faithfully in his holy Catholic Church. And so:

>Do you reject Satan? ℟. I do.
>And all his works? ℟. I do.
>And all his empty promises? ℟. I do.

Or:

Do your reject sin, so as to live in the freedom of God's children? ℟. I do.

Do you reject the glamour of evil, and refuse to be mastered by sin? ℟. I do.

Do you reject Satan, father of sin and prince of darkness? ℟. I do.

Then the priest continues:

Do you believe in God, the Father almighty, creator of heaven and earth? ℟. I do.

Do you believe in Jesus Christ, his only Son, our Lord, who was born of the Virgin Mary, was crucified, died, and was buried, rose from the dead, and is now seated at the right hand of the Father? ℟. I do.

Do you believe in the Holy Spirit, the holy Catholic Church, the communion of saints, the forgiveness of sins, the resurrection of the body, and life everlasting? ℟. I do.

The priest concludes:

God, the all-powerful Father of our Lord Jesus Christ, has given us a new birth by water and the Holy Spirit, and forgiven all our sins. May he also keep us faithful to our Lord Jesus Christ for ever and ever. ℟. Amen.

Then, the priest sprinkles the assembly while the Vidi aquam, *p. 71, is sung.*

The Credo *is omitted.*

The Easter Vigil

LITURGY OF THE EUCHARIST

Offertory *Ps 117 : 16, 17*

Dextera Dómini * fecit virtútem, déxtera Dómini exaltávit me: non móriar, sed vivam, et narrábo ópera Dómini, allelúia.

The right hand of the Lord has done valiantly, the right hand of the Lord has exalted me; I shall not die, but I shall live, and recount the deeds of the Lord, alleluia.

Suscipe, quæsumus, Dómine, preces pópuli tui cum oblatiónibus hostiárum, ut, paschálibus initiáta mystériis, ad æternitátis nobis medélam, te operánte, profíciant.

Lord, accept the prayers and offerings of your people. With your help may this Easter mystery of our redemption bring to perfection the saving work you have begun in us.

Easter Preface I, p. 55. With the First Eucharistic Prayer, proper Communicántes *and* Hanc ígitur, *p. 24.*

Communion

Pascha nostrum, *p. 354.*

The Easter Vigil

Or:

VI

A-lle-lú-ia, * alle-lú-ia, alle-lú-ia.

Prayer after Communion

SPIRITUM nobis, Dómine, tuæ caritátis infúnde, ut, quos sacraméntis paschálibus satiásti, tua fácias pietáte concórdes.

LORD, you have nourished us with your Easter sacraments. Fill us with your Spirit, and make us one in peace and love.

From the Easter Vigil to the Second Sunday of Easter inclusive and on the day of Pentecost, the dimissal is sung as follows:

I - te, missa est, alle-lú-ia, alle- lú- ia.

℣. The Mass is ended, go in peace, alleluia, alleluia.

All respond:

℟. De-o grá-ti-as, alle-lú-ia, alle- lú- ia.

℟. Thanks be to God, alleluia, alleluia.

SUNDAY OF THE RESURRECTION

Introit — Ps 138: 18, 5, 6 and 1-2

IV

RE-SURRE-XI, * et adhuc tecum sum, alle-lú-ia: po-su-í-sti super me manum tu-am, alle-lú-ia: mi-rá-bi-lis fa-cta est sci-én-ti-a tu-a, alle-lú-ia, alle-lú-ia. *Ps.* Dó-mi-ne probásti me, et cognoví-sti me: tu cognoví-sti sessi-ó-nem me-am, et re-surrecti-ó-nem me-am.

I am risen, and I am always with you, alleluia; you have placed your hand upon me, alleluia; your wisdom has been shown to be most wonderful, alleluia, alleluia. ℣. O Lord, you have searched me and known me; you know when I sit down and when I rise up.

Easter Sunday

Opening Prayer

Deus, qui hodiérna die, per Unigénitum tuum, æternitátis nobis áditum, devícta morte, reserásti, da nobis, quæsumus, ut, qui resurrectiónis domínicæ sollémnia cólimus, per innovatiónem tui Spíritus in lúmine vitæ resurgámus.

God our Father, by raising Christ your Son you conquered the power of death and opened for us the way to eternal life. Let our celebration today raise us up and renew our lives by the Spirit that is within us.

First reading
Acts 10: 34a, 37-43: *God rose him up on the third day.*

Gradual *Ps 117 : 24 and 1*

Haec di- es, * quam fe- cit Dó- mi- nus: exsulté- mus, et lae- té- mur in e- a. ℣. Confi- témi- ni Dó- mi- no, quó- ni- am bo- nus: quó- ni- am in saé- cu- lum

Easter Sunday

mi-se- ri-cór- di- a e- ius.

This is the day that the Lord has made; let us rejoice and be glad in it. ℣. Praise the Lord, for he is good, for his mercy endures forever.

Second reading

Col 3: 1-4: *Aspire towards things above.*
Or: 1 Cor 5: 6b-8: *Christ, our paschal sacrifice.*

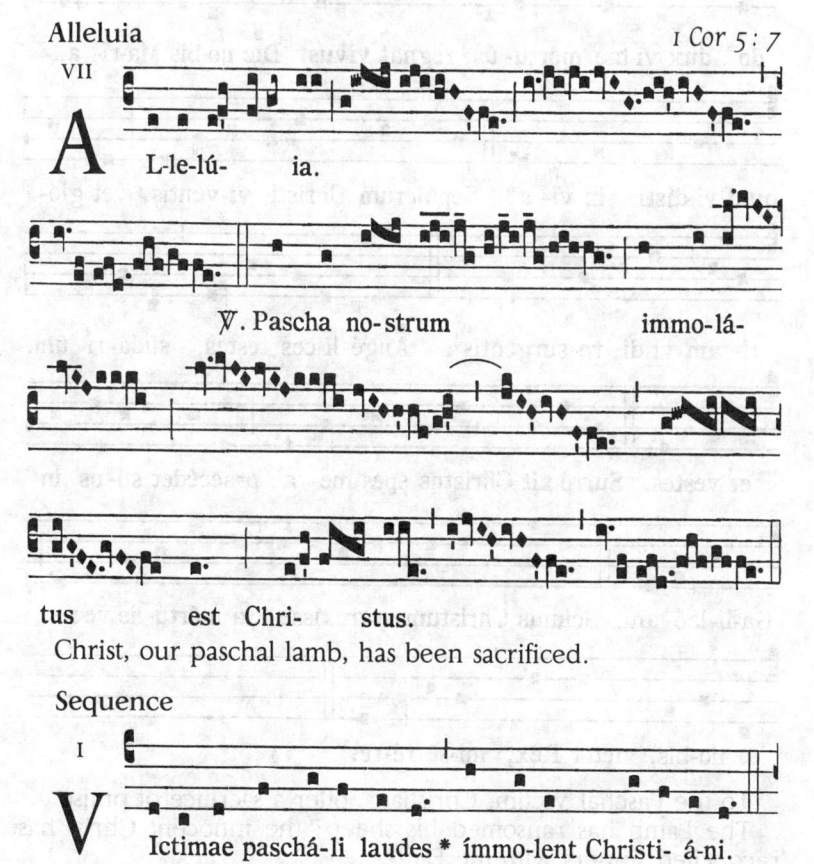

Alleluia

1 Cor 5: 7

VII

A L-le-lú- ia.

℣. Pascha no-strum immo-lá-tus est Chri- stus.

Christ, our paschal lamb, has been sacrificed.

Sequence

I

Victimae paschá-li laudes * ímmo-lent Christi- á-ni.

Agnus redémit oves : Christus ínnocens Patri reconciliávit peccatóres. Mors et vita duéllo conflixére mirándo : dux vitae mórtuus, regnat vivus. Dic nobis María, quid vidísti in via? Sepúlcrum Christi vivéntis, et glóriam vidi resurgéntis : Angélicos testes, sudárium, et vestes. Surréxit Christus spes mea : praecédet suos in Galilaéam. Scimus Christum surrexísse a mórtuis vere : tu nobis, victor Rex, miserére.

To the Paschal Victim, Christians, offer a sacrifice of praise.
 The Lamb has ransomed his sheep; the innocent Christ has reconciled sinners with the Father.

Easter Sunday

Death and life confronted each other in a prodigious battle; the Prince of life who died, now lives and reigns.

"Tell us, Mary, what did you see upon the way?"

"I saw the sepulchre of the living Christ; I saw the glory of the Risen One. I saw the angels, his witnesses, the shroud and the garments. Christ, my Hope, is risen; he will go before his own into Galilee."

We know that Christ is truly risen from the dead; O Victorious King, have mercy on us.

Gospel

Jn 20: 1-9: *He saw and he believed.*

Offertory
Ps 75: 9, 10

Terra *trémuit, et quiévit, dum resúrgeret in iudício Deus, allelúia.

The earth trembled and was still, when God arose in judgment, alleluia.

Prayer over the Gifts

SACRIFICIA, Dómine, pascháli- bus gáudiis exsultántes offérimus, quibus Ecclésia tua mirabíliter renáscitur et nutrítur.

LORD, with Easter joy we offer you the sacrifice by which your Church is reborn and nourished.

Easter Preface I, p. 55. With the First Eucharistic Prayer, proper Communicantes *and* Hanc igitur, *p. 24.*

Easter Sunday

Communion   1 Cor 5: 7, 8

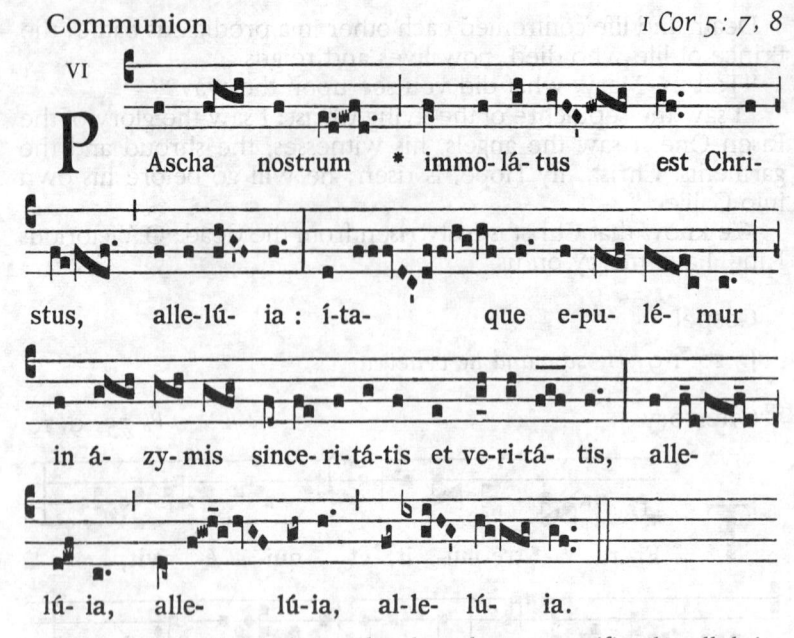

*Pascha nostrum * immolátus est Christus, allelúia: ítaque epulémur in ázymis sinceritátis et veritátis, allelúia, allelúia, allelúia.*

Christ, our Paschal Lamb, has been sacrificed, alleluia; therefore, let us keep the feast by sharing the unleavened bread of uprightness and truth, alleluia, alleluia, alleluia.

Prayer after Communion

Perpetuo, Deus Ecclésiam tuam pio favóre tuére, ut, paschálibus renováta mystériis, ad resurrectiónis pervéniat claritátem.

Father of love, watch over your Church and bring us to the glory of the resurrection promised by this Easter sacrament.

MASS FOR EASTER SUNDAY EVENING

Gospel

Lk 24: 13-35: *The disciples of Emmaus.*

SECOND SUNDAY OF EASTER

Introit — *1 Pet 2 : 2*

QUasi modo * géniti infántes, alle-lúia : ratio-nábiles, sine dolo lac concu-píscite, alle-lúia, alle-lúia, alle-lúia.

Ps. Exsultáte De-o adiu-tóri nostro : iu-bi-láte De-o Ia-cob.

As newborn babes, alleluia, long for pure spiritual milk, alleluia, alleluia, alleluia. ℣. Rejoice in honour of God our helper; shout for joy to the God of Jacob.

Opening Prayer

Deus misericórdiæ sempitérnæ, qui in ipso paschális festi recúrsu fidem sacrátæ tibi plebis accéndis, auge grátiam quam dedísti, ut digna

God of mercy, you wash away our sins in water, you give us new birth in the Spirit, and redeem us in the blood of Christ. As we cele-

2nd Sunday of Easter

omnes intellegéntia comprehéndant, quo lavácro ablúti, quo spíritu regeneráti, quo sánguine sunt redémpti.

brate Christ's resurrection increase our awareness of these blessings, and renew your gift of life within us.

First reading

A. Acts 2: 42-47: *They lived in brotherly fellowship.*
B. Acts 4: 32-35: *They were of one heart and one soul.*
C. Acts 5: 12-16: *Their number increased continually.*

Alleluia
Mt 28: 7

A-Lle-lú- ia.

℣. In di- e re-sur-re-cti- ó-nis me- ae, di- cit Dómi- nus, prae- cé- dam vos in Ga-li-laé- am.

On the day of my resurrection, says the Lord, I will go before you into Galilee.

Second reading

A. 1 Pet 1: 3-9: *An inheritance stored up in heaven.*
B. 1 Jn 5: 1-6: *To overcome the world.*
C. Rev 1: 9-11a, 12-13, 17-19: *Behold, I am alive for evermore.*

2nd Sunday of Easter

Alleluia   Jn 20: 26

VII

A-lle-lú-ia.

℣. Post di- es o- cto, iá- nu- is clau- sis, ste-tit Ie- sus in mé- di- o disci-pu- ló- rum su- ó- rum, et di-xit: Pax vo- bis.

Eight days later, while all the doors were shut, Jesus came and stood in the midst of his disciples and said: "Peace be with you."
After the Alleluia, *the* Sequence *of Easter Sunday may be sung.*
Víctimæ pascháli, p. 351.

Gospel
Jn 20: 19-31: *Apparition of the Lord to Thomas.*

Offertory   Mt 28: 2, 5, 6

VIII

A-Nge- lus * Dó- mi- ni descén- dit de cae- lo, et di-

2nd Sunday of Easter

xit mu-li-é- ri-bus : Quem quaé- ri-tis, surré- xit, sic-ut di- xit, al-le- lú- ia.

The Angel of the Lord came down from heaven and said to the women: "The One whom you seek has risen, as he said he would", alleluia.

Prayer over the Gifts

SUSCIPE, quæsumus, Dómine, plebis tuæ (et tuórum renatórum) oblatiónes, ut, confessióne tui nóminis et baptísmate renováti, sempitérnam beatitúdinem consequántur.

LORD, through faith and baptism we have become a new creation. Accept the offerings of your people (and of those born again in baptism) and bring us to eternal happiness.

Easter Preface I, p. 55 . With the First Eucharistic Prayer, proper Communicántes *and* Hanc ígitur, *p. 24.*

Communion   Jn 20: 27

MItte * manum tu-am, et cognósce lo-ca clavórum, alle-lú- ia : et no-li esse incré-du-lus, sed fi-dé- lis, alle-lú- ia, alle- lú- ia.

Stretch forth your hand, and feel the place where the nails were, alleluia; and be not doubtful but believing, alleluia, alleluia.

Prayer after Communion

CONCEDE, quæsumus, omnípotens Deus, ut paschális percéptio sacraménti contínua in nostris méntibus persevéret.

ALMIGHTY GOD, may the Easter sacraments we have received live for ever in our minds and hearts.

THIRD SUNDAY OF EASTER

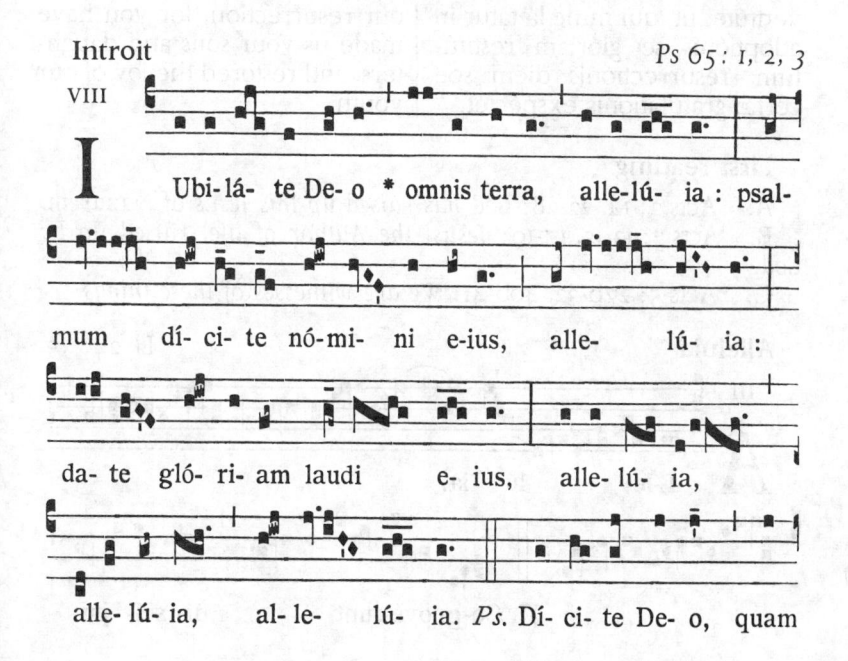

Introit — Ps 65: 1, 2, 3

VIII

Iubi-lá- te De-o * omnis terra, alle-lú- ia : psalmum dí-ci- te nó-mi- ni e-ius, alle- lú- ia : da- te gló- ri- am laudi e-ius, alle-lú- ia, alle-lú- ia, al- le- lú- ia. Ps. Dí- ci- te De- o, quam

3rd Sunday of Easter

terri- bí- li- a sunt ó-pe-ra tu- a, Dómi-ne! in multi-tú-di-ne virtú- tis tu- ae menti- éntur ti- bi in- i- mí- ci tu- i.

Shout joyfully to God, all the earth, alleluia; sing a psalm to his name, alleluia; praise him with magnificence, alleluia, alleluia, alleluia. ℣. Say to God: "How awesome are your deeds, O Lord! In the greatness of your power, your enemies will be convicted of lying to you".

Opening Prayer

SEMPER exsúltet pópulus tuus, Deus, renováta ánimæ iuventúte, ut, qui nunc lætátur in adoptiónis se glóriam restitútum, resurrectiónis diem spe certæ gratulatiónis exspéctet.

GOD OUR FATHER, may we look forward with hope to our resurrection, for you have made us your sons and daughters, and restored the joy of our youth.

First reading

A. Acts 2: 14, 22-28: *God has raised up this Jesus of Nazareth.*
B. Acts 3: 13-15, 17-19: *Jesus, the Author of life, raised up by God.*
C. Acts 5: 27b-32, 40b-41: *We are witnesses of these things.*

Alleluia   Lk 24: 35

III

A*L-le- lú- ia.*

℣. *Co-gnové-runt   di- scí- pu-*

3rd Sunday of Easter

li Dóminum Iesum in fractióne panis.

The disciples recognized the Lord Jesus at the breaking of the bread.

Second reading

A. 1 Pet 1: 17-21: *Made free by the precious blood of Christ.*
B. 1 Jn 2: 1-5a: *Jesus, sacrificial victim offered for our sins.*
C. Rev 5: 11-14: *Glory and praise to the Lamb who was slain.*

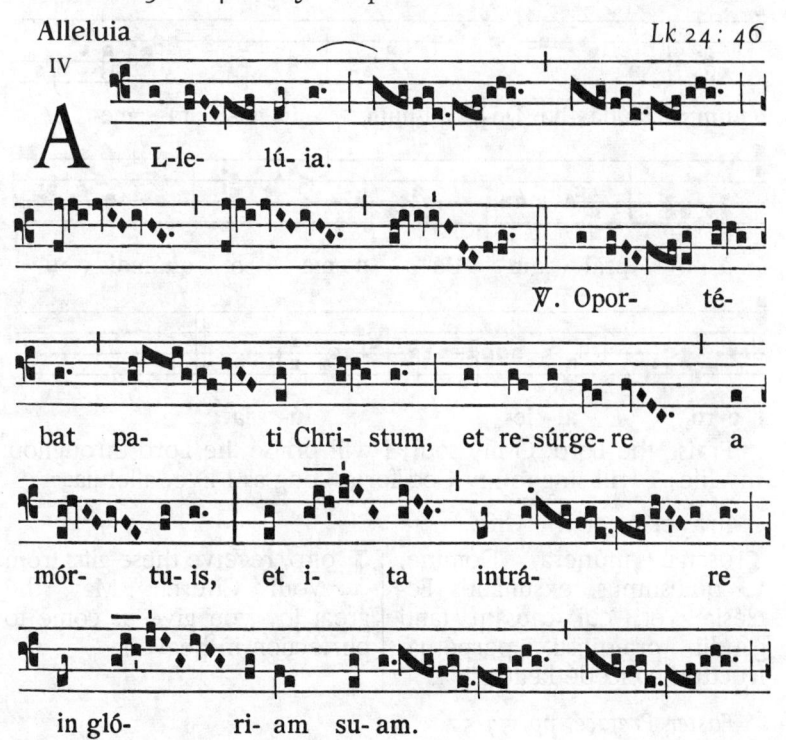

Alleluia   Lk 24: 46

Allelúia.

℣. Oportébat pati Christum, et resúrgere a mórtuis, et ita intráre in glóriam suam.

3rd Sunday of Easter

It was necessary that Christ should suffer and rise from the dead, and so enter into his glory.

Gospel
A. Lk 24: 13-35: *The disciples of Emmaus.*
B. Lk 24: 35-48: *Look, it is really I myself!*
C. Jn 21: 1-19 *or* 1-14: *Peter, do you love me?*

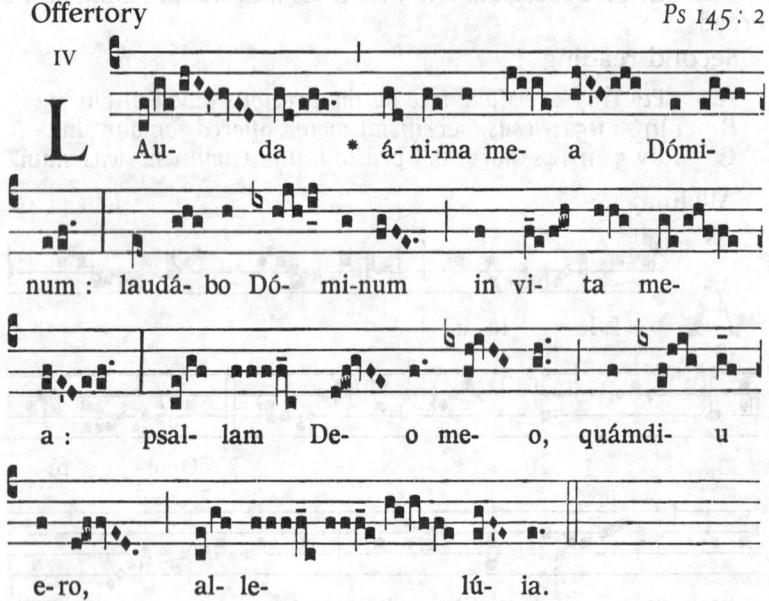

Offertory
Ps 145: 2

Lauda * ánima mea Dóminum: laudábo Dóminum in vita mea: psallam Deo meo, quámdiu ero, allelúia.

Praise the Lord, O my soul; I will praise the Lord throughout my life; I will sing to my God for as long as I live, alleluia.

Prayer over the Gifts

Suscipe múnera, Dómine, quæsumus, exsultántis Ecclésiæ, et, cui causam tanti gáudii præstitísti, perpétuæ fructum concéde lætítiæ.

Lord, receive these gifts from your Church. May the great joy you give us come to perfection in heaven.

Easter Preface, pp. 55-57.

3rd Sunday of Easter

Communion A — Lk 24: 34

VI

Surréxit * Dóminus, et appáruit Petro, allelúia.

The Lord has risen and has appeared to Peter, alleluia.

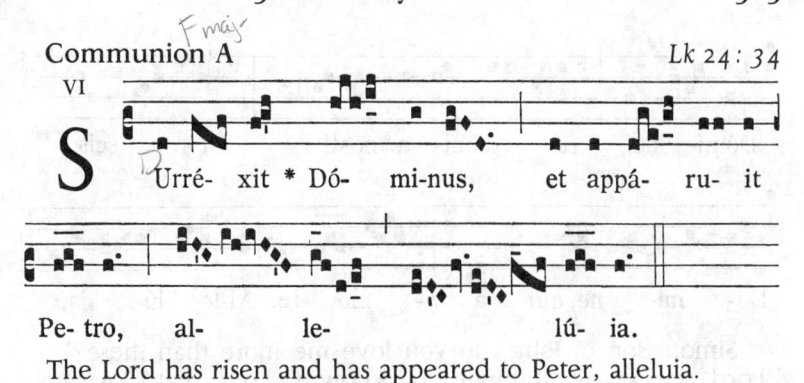

Communion B — Ps 95: 2

II

Cantáte Dómino, * allelúia : cantáte Dómino, benedícite nomen eius : benenuntiáte de die in diem salutáre eius, allelúia, allelúia.

Sing unto the Lord, alleluia; sing to the Lord, bless his name; proclaim his salvation day after day, alleluia, alleluia.

Communion C — Jn 21: 15, 17

VI

Simon Ioánnis, * díligis me plus his?

4th Sunday of Easter

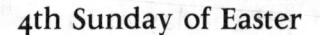

Dómine, tu ómnia nosti: tu scis,
Dómine, quia amo te. Allelúia.

"Simon, son of John, do you love me more than these?" – "Lord, you know all things, you know, O Lord, that I love you, alleluia."

Prayer after Communion

POPULUM tuum, quæsumus, Dómine, intuére benígnus, et, quem ætérnis dignátus es renováre mystériis, ad incorruptíbilem glorificándæ carnis resurrectiónem perveníre concéde.

LORD, look on your people with kindness and by these Easter mysteries bring us to the glory of the resurrection.

FOURTH SUNDAY OF EASTER

Introit *Ps 32: 5, 6 and 1*

MIsericórdia Dómini * plena est terra, allelúia: verbo Dei caeli firmáti sunt,

4th Sunday of Easter

alle- lú- ia, al-le- lú- ia. *Ps.* Exsultá-te iu-sti in Dómi-no : re-ctos de-cet collaudá-ti- o.

The earth is full of the mercy of the Lord, alleluia; by the word of the Lord, the heavens were established, alleluia, alleluia. ℣. Rejoice in the Lord, O you righteous! Praising befits those who are upright.

Opening Prayer

OMNIPOTENS sempitérne Deus, deduc nos ad societátem cæléstium gaudiórum, ut eo pervéniat humílitas gregis, quo procéssit fortitúdo pastóris.

ALMIGHTY and ever-living God, give us new strength from the courage of Christ our shepherd, and lead us to join the saints in heaven.

First reading
A. Atcs 2: 14a, 36-41: *God has made him Lord.*
B. Acts 4: 8-12: *Outside of him, there is no salvation.*
C. Acts 13: 14, 43-52: *We are now turning to the Gentiles.*

Alleluia   Ps 110: 9

AL-le-lú- ia. ℣. Red-em- pti- ó- nem mi- sit Dó- mi- nus in pópu-lo su- o.

The Lord has sent deliverance to his people.

4th Sunday of Easter

Second reading

A. 1 Pet 2: 20b-25: *Christ has left you an example.*
B. 1 Jn 3: 1-2: *We shall see him as he is.*
C. Rev 9: 14b-17: *The Lamb shall be their shepherd.*

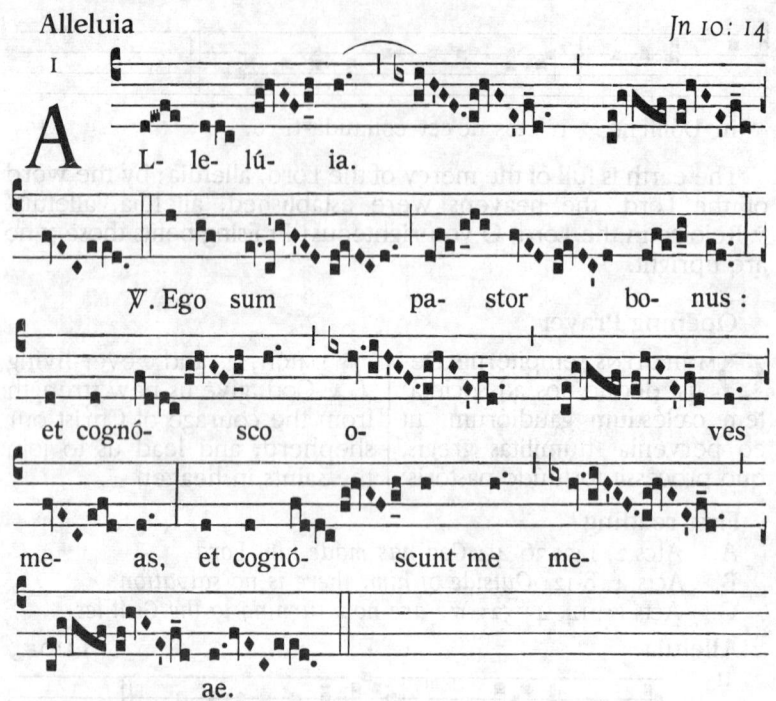

Alleluia Jn 10: 14

A-lle-lú-ia. ℣. Ego sum pastor bonus: et cognósco oves meas, et cognóscunt me meae.

I am the good shepherd; I know my sheep and my own know me.

Gospel

A. Jn 10: 1-10: *I am the door of the sheep.*
B. Jn 10: 11-18: *I am the good shepherd.*
C. Jn 10: 27-30: *My sheep hear my voice.*

Offertory Ps 62: 2, 5

De-us, *De-us me-us, ad te de lu-

4th Sunday of Easter

...ce ví- gi- lo : et in nómi-ne tu- o le- vá- bo ma- nus me- as, alle- lú- ia.

O God, my God, from daybreak do I watch for you; and in invocation of your name will I lift up my hands.

Prayer over the Gifts

CONCEDE, quǽsumus, Dómine, semper nos per hæc mystéria paschália gratulári, ut contínua nostræ reparatiónis operátio perpétuæ nobis fiat causa lætítiæ.

LORD, restore us by these Easter mysteries. May the continuing work of our redeemer bring us eternal joy.

Easter Preface, pp. 55-57.

Communion
Jn 10: 14

E- go sum * pa-stor bo- nus, alle-lú- ia : et cognósco oves me- as, et cognóscunt me me- ae, alle- lú- ia, alle-lú- ia.

I am the good shepherd, alleluia; I know my sheep and my own know me, alleluia, alleluia.

Prayer after Communion

GREGEM tuum, Pastor bone, placátus inténde, et oves, quas pretióso Fílii tui sánguine redemísti, in ætérnis páscuis collocáre dignéris.

FATHER, eternal shepherd, watch over the flock redeemed by the blood of Christ and lead us to the promised land.

FIFTH SUNDAY OF EASTER

Introit — Ps 97: 1,2

VI

C Antáte Dómino * cánticum novum, allelúia: quia mirabília fecit Dóminus, allelúia: ante conspéctum géntium revelávit iustítiam suam, allelúia, allelúia.

Ps. Salvávit sibi déxtera eius: et bráchium sanctum

5th Sunday of Easter

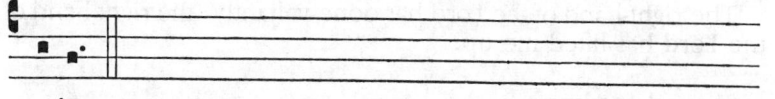

e-ius.

Sing to the Lord a new song, alleluia; for the Lord has accomplished wondrous deeds, alleluia; he has revealed his justice in the sight of the Gentiles, alleluia, alleluia. ℣. His right hand and his holy arm have given him victory.

Opening Prayer

DEUS, per quem nobis et redémptio venit et præstátur adóptio, fílios dilectiónis tuæ benígnus inténde, ut in Christo credéntibus et vera tribuátur libértas et heréditas ætérna.

GOD OUR FATHER, look upon us with love. You redeem us and make us your children in Christ. Give us true freedom and bring us to the inheritance you promised.

First reading

A. Acts 6: 1-7: *The appointment of the seven deacons.*
B. Acts 9: 26-31: *Paul in Jerusalem, with the Apostles.*
C. Acts 14: 21-27: *First missionary journey of Paul.*

Alleluia

Ps 117: 16

AL-le-lú-ia. ℣. Déxtera Dei fecit virtútem: déxtera Dómini exaltávit me.

5th Sunday of Easter

The right hand of the Lord has done valiantly; the right hand of the Lord has lifted me up.

Second reading
A. 1 Pet 2: 4-9: *You are a chosen race.*
B. 1 Jn 3: 18-24: *To love in deed and in truth.*
C. Rev 21: 1-5a: *Behold, I am making all things new.*

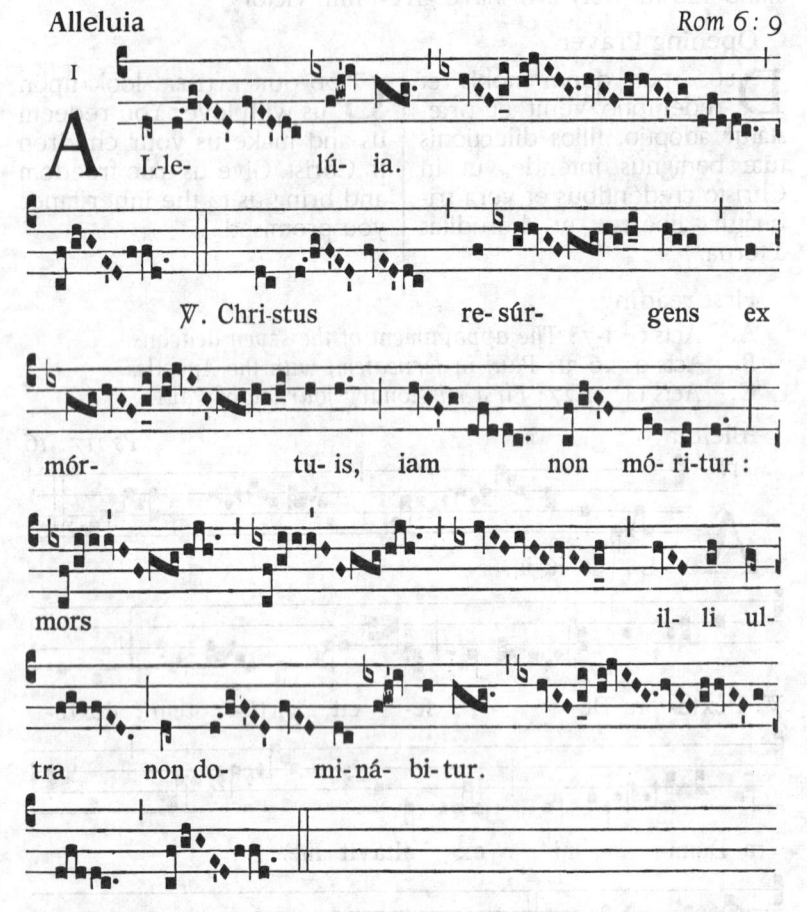

Alleluia — Rom 6: 9

Alleluia. ℣. Christus resúrgens ex mórtuis, iam non móritur: mors illi ultra non dominábitur.

Christ has been raised from the dead and will never die again; death no longer has dominion over him.

5th Sunday of Easter

Gospel
A. Jn 14: 1-12: *I am the way, the truth and the life.*
B. Jn 15: 1-8: *I am the true vine.*
C. Jn 13: 31-33a, 34-35: *Love one another.*

Offertory   Ps 65: 1, 2, 16

Iubiláte * Deo univérsa terra: iubiláte Deo univérsa terra: psalmum dícite nómini eius: veníte, et audíte, et narrábo vobis, omnes qui timétis Deum, quanta fecit Dóminus ánimae meae, allelúia.

5th Sunday of Easter

Shout joyfully to God, all the earth; shout with joy to God, all the earth; sing a psalm in honour of his name; come and hear, all you who fear God, and I will tell you what great things the Lord has done for my soul, alleluia.

Prayer over the Gifts

DEUS, qui nos, per huius sacrifícii veneránda commércia, uníus summǽque divinitátis partícipes effecísti, præsta, quǽsumus, ut, sicut tuam cognóvimus veritátem, sic eam dignis móribus assequámur.

LORD GOD, by this holy exchange of gifts you share with us your divine life. Grant that everything we do may be directed by the knowledge of your truth.

Easter Preface, pp. 55-57.

Communion A

Jn 14: 9

Tanto témpore * vobíscum sum, et non cognovístis me? Philíppe, qui videt me, videt et Patrem, allelúia: non credis quia ego in Patre, et Pater in me est? allelúia, allelúia.

Have I been with you so long, and yet you do not know me? Philip, he who sees me, sees the Father. Do you not believe that I am in the Father, and the Father in me? Alleluia, alleluia.

Communion B & C

Jn 15:5

VIII

E-go sum * vi- tis ve- ra et vos pálmi- tes, qui ma-net in me, et ego in e- o, hic fert fructum mul- tum, alle- lú- ia, alle- lú- ia.

I am the true vine, and you are the branches; he who abides in me and I in him, he it is who bears much fruit, alleluia, alleluia.

Prayer after Communion

POPULO tuo, quæsumus, Dómine, adésto propítius, et, quem mystériis cæléstibus imbuísti, fac ad novitátem vitæ de vetustáte transíre.

MERCIFUL FATHER, may these mysteries give us new purpose and bring us to a new life in you.

SIXTH SUNDAY OF EASTER

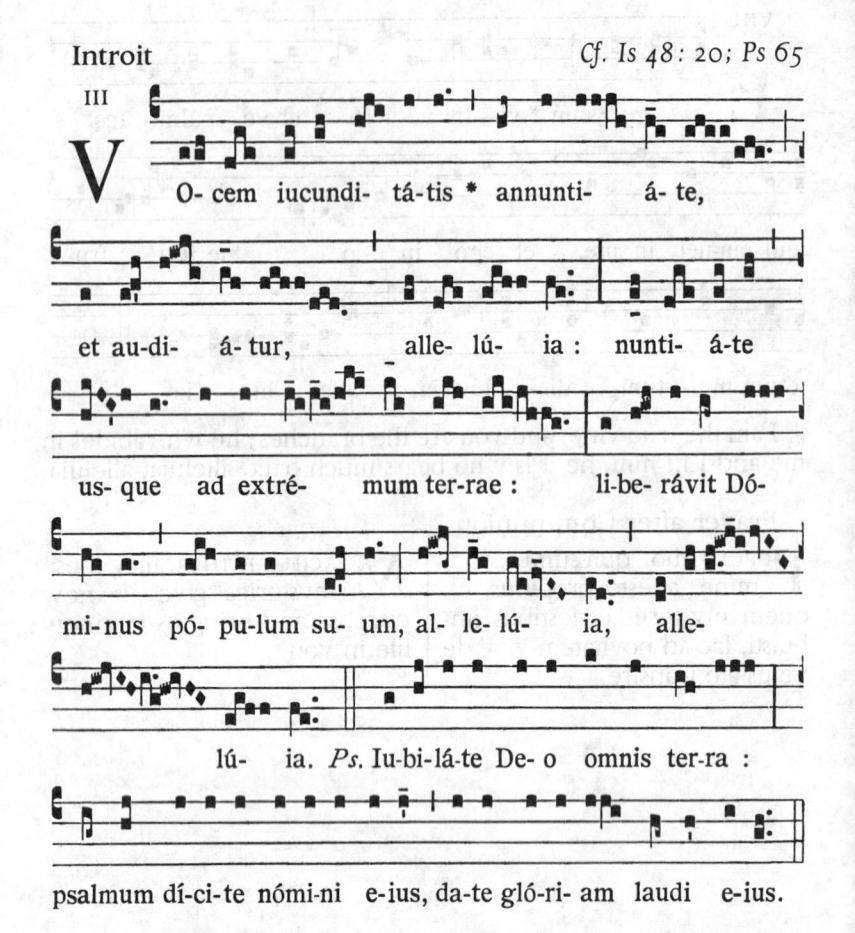

Introit *Cf. Is 48 : 20; Ps 65*

Vocem iucunditátis * annuntiáte, et audiátur, allelúia : nuntiáte usque ad extrémum terrae : liberávit Dóminus pópulum suum, allelúia, allelúia. *Ps.* Iubiláte Deo omnis terra : psalmum dícite nómini eius, date glóriam laudi eius.

Spread the news with a voice of joy; let it be heard, alleluia; speak it out to the very ends of the earth; the Lord has liberated his people, alleluia, alleluia. ℣. Shout joyfully to God all the earth; sing a psalm to his name; praise him with magnificence.

6th Sunday of Easter

Opening Prayer

FAC NOS, omnípotens Deus, hos lætítiæ dies, quos in honórem Dómini resurgéntis exséquimur, afféctu sédulo celebráre, ut quod recordatióne percúrrimus semper in ópere teneámus.

EVER-LIVING GOD, help us to celebrate our joy in the resurrection of the Lord and to express in our lives the love we celebrate.

First reading

A. Acts 8: 5-8, 14-17: *Conversions in Samaria.*
B. Acts 10: 25-26, 34-35, 44-48: *Peter at Cæsarea.*
C. Acts 15: 1-2, 22-29: *The Council of Jerusalem.*

Alleluia A

A-L-le- lú- ia. ℣. Surré- xit Chri- stus, et il-lú-xit no- bis, quos redé- mit sán- gui- ne su- o.

Christ has risen and he has shone upon us whom he has ransomed with his own blood.

6th Sunday of Easter

Alleluia B — Jn 16: 28

A-lle-lú-ia. ℣. Exí-vi a Pa-tre, et ve-ni in mun-dum : í-te-rum re-línquo mun-dum, et va-do ad Pa-trem.

I came forth from the Father and have come into the world; now I am leaving the world and going to the Father.

Alleluia C
Choice of one of the two alleluias given above.

Second reading
A. 1 Pet 3: 15-18: *Be ready to give an account of your hope.*
B. 1 Jn 4: 7-10: *God is love.*
C. Rev 21: 10-14, 22-23: *The holy city.*

6th Sunday of Easter

Alleluia A
Non vos relínquam, *p. 389.*

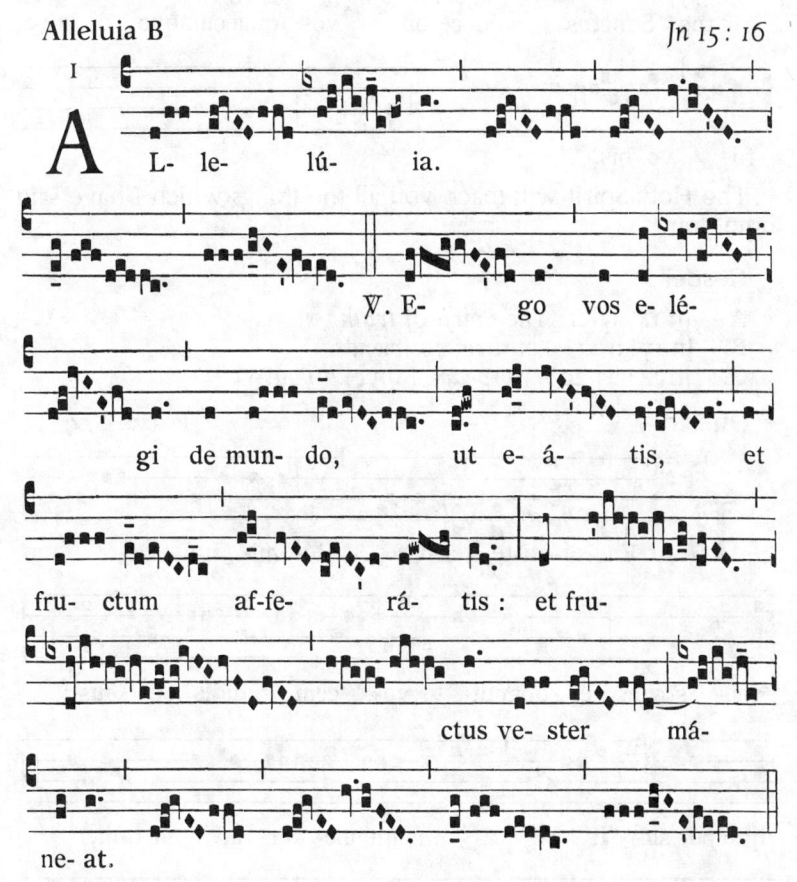

Alleluia B *Jn 15 : 16*

A L- le- lú- ia. ℣. E- go vos e- lé- gi de mun- do, ut e- á- tis, et fru- ctum af-fe- rá- tis : et fru- ctus ve- ster má- ne- at.

I have chosen you from the world, in order that you might go, and bear fruit, and that your fruit should last.

Alleluia C *Jn 14 : 26*

A L-le- lú- ia. ℣. Spí-

...ri- tus Sanctus do- cé- bit vos quaecúmque dí- xe-ro vo- bis.

The Holy Spirit will teach you all the things which I have said unto you.

Gospel

A. Jn 14: 15-21: *The Spirit of truth.*
B. Jn 15: 9-17: *You are my friends.*
C. Jn 14: 23-29: *My peace I give to you.*

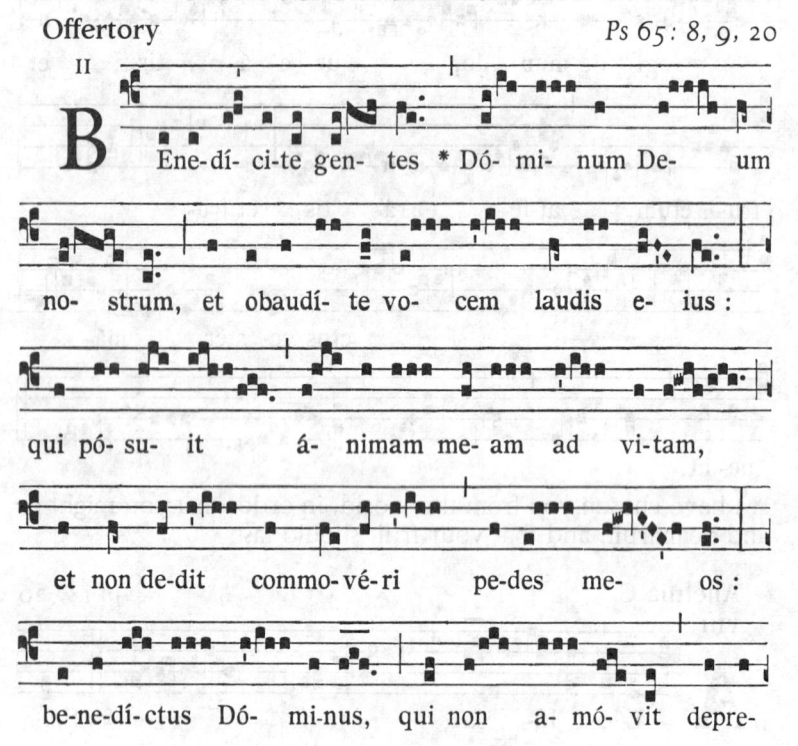

Offertory
Ps 65: 8, 9, 20

BEne- dí- ci- te gen- tes * Dó- mi- num De- um no- strum, et obaudí- te vo- cem laudis e- ius: qui pó- su- it á- nimam me- am ad vi- tam, et non dedit commo- vé- ri pe- des me- os: be-ne-dí-ctus Dó- mi-nus, qui non a- mó- vit depre-

6th Sunday of Easter

...ca- ti- ó- nem me- am, et mi- se- ri- cór- di- am su- am a me, alle- lú- ia.

O nations, bless the Lord our God, let the voice of his praises resound; he has restored my soul to life and he has not suffered my feet to stumble; blessed be the Lord who has neither rejected my prayer nor turned his mercy away from me, alleluia.

Prayer over the Gifts

Ascendant ad te, Dómine, preces nostræ cum oblatiónibus hostiárum, ut, tua dignatióne mundáti, sacraméntis magnæ pietátis aptémur.

Lord, accept our prayers and offerings. Make us worthy of your sacraments of love by granting us your forgiveness.

Easter Preface, pp. 55-57.

Communion A

Jn 14 : 18

NON vos re-línquam órpha- nos : * vé-ni- am ad vos í- te-rum, alle- lú- ia : et gaudé-bit cor ve- strum, alle- lú- ia, alle- lú- ia.

I will not leave you orphans, I will come to you again, alleluia; and your heart will rejoice, alleluia, alleluia.

6th Sunday of Easter

Communion B *Jn 15 : 16*

E- go *vos e- lé-gi de mun- do, ut e- á- tis, et fru-ctum af-fe-rá- tis : et fru- ctus ve-ster máne- at. Alle- lú- ia.

I have chosen you from the world, in order that you might go and bring forth fruit, and that your fruit should last, alleluia.

Communion C *Jn 14 : 26*

S Pi- ri-tus Sanctus * do-cé-bit vos, alle-lú- ia : quae- cúmque dí-xe-ro vo- bis, alle-lú- ia, alle- lú- ia.

The Holy Spirit will teach you, alleluia; all the things that I have said unto you, alleluia, alleluia.

Prayer after Communion

OMNIPOTENS sempitérne Deus, qui ad ætérnam vitam in Christi resurrectióne nos réparas, fructus in nobis paschális multíplica sacraménti, et fortitúdinem cibi salutáris nostris infúnde pectóribus.

ALMIGHTY and ever-living Lord, you restored us to life by raising Christ from death. Strengthen us by this Easter sacrament; may we feel its saving power in our daily life.

Thursday of the Sixth Week
(or the Seventh Sunday of Easter)

THE ASCENSION OF THE LORD
Solemnity

Introit Acts 1: 11; Ps 46

VII

VI-RI Ga- li- laé- i, * quid admi- rá- mi- ni aspi- ci- én- tes in cae- lum? alle- lú- ia : quemádmodum vi-dístis e- um ascendéntem in cae- lum, i-ta vé- ni- et, alle- lú- ia, alle- lú- ia, alle- lú- ia. *Ps.* Omnes gentes pláudi- te má- ni- bus : iu- bi- lá-te De- o in vo-ce exsulta- ti- ó- nis.

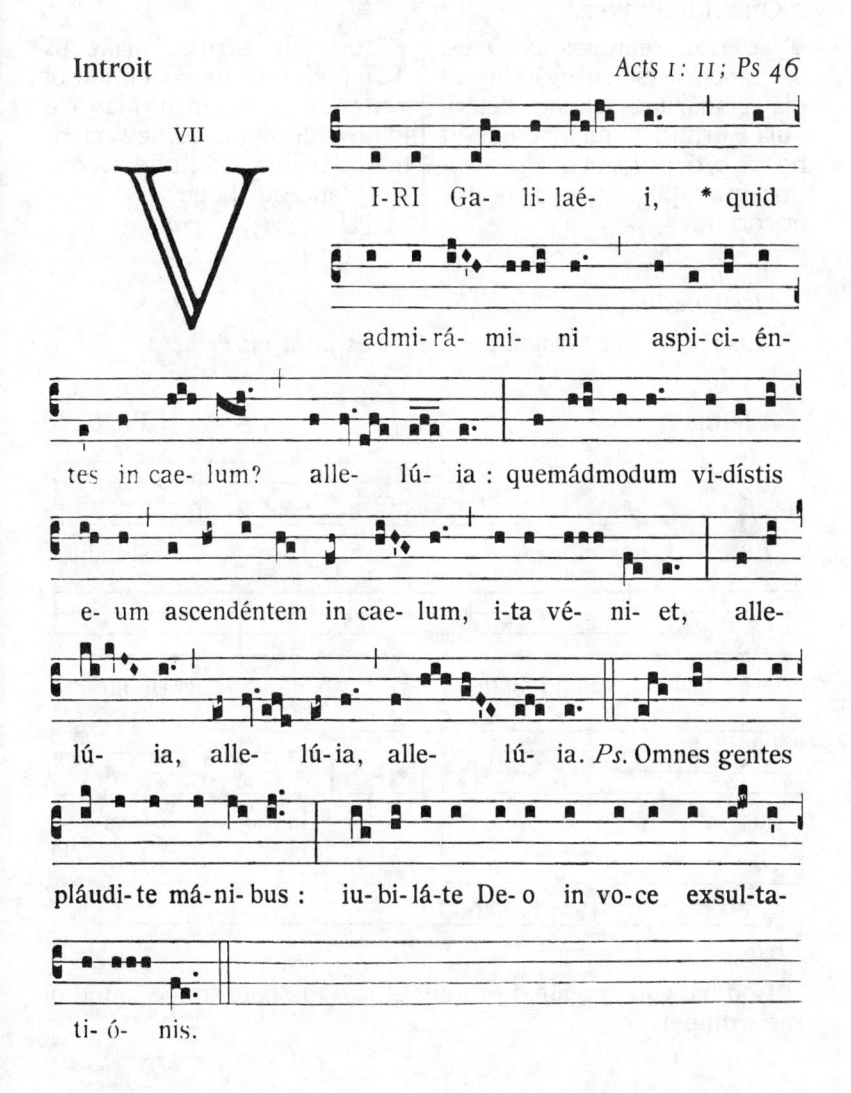

Ascension

Men of Galilee, why are you gazing in astonishment at the sky? alleluia; just as you have seen him ascend into heaven, so, in like manner, shall he return, alleluia, alleluia, alleluia. ℣. All nations, clap your hands; shout unto God with a voice of joy.

Opening Prayer

FAC NOS, omnípotens Deus, sanctis exsultáre gáudiis, et pia gratiárum actióne lætári, quia Christi Fílii tui ascénsio est nostra provéctio, et quo procéssit glória cápitis, eo spes vocátur et córporis.

GOD OUR FATHER, make us joyful in the ascension of your Son Jesus Christ. May we follow him into the new creation, for his ascension is our glory and our hope.

First reading

Acts 1: 1-11: *They looked on as he was lifted up.*

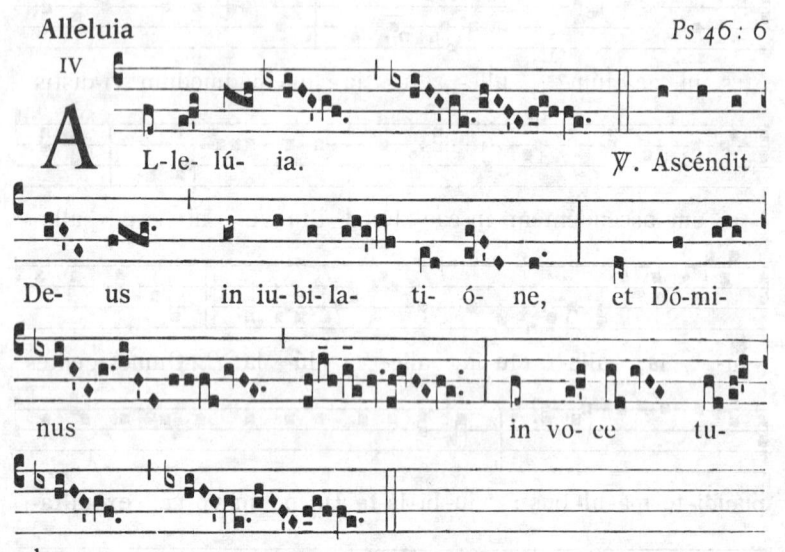

Alleluia   Ps 46: 6

A-lle- lú- ia.   ℣. Ascéndit Deus in iu- bi- la- ti- ó- ne, et Dómi- nus in vo- ce tu- bae.

God has gone up amidst shouts of joy, the Lord to the sound of the trumpet.

Ascension

Second reading
Eph 1: 17-23: *Christ, seated at the Father's right hand.*
Or: B. Eph 4: 1-13 or 1-7, 11-13: *The fulness of Christ.*
  C. Heb 9: 24-28; 10: 19-23: *Christ has gone up to heaven.*

Alleluia Ps 67: 18, 19

A- L- le- lú- ia. ℣. Dó-mi-nus in Si-na in san- cto, ascén-dens in al-tum, capti- vam du-xit capti-vi-tá- tem.

The Lord is in Sinai, in the holy place; ascending on high, he has led captivity captive.

Gospel
A. Mt 28: 16-20: *All power has been given unto me.*
B. Mk 16: 15-20: *These are the signs.*
C. Lk 24: 46-53: *You are my witnesses.*

Offertory
Ascéndit Deus, p. 389, or:

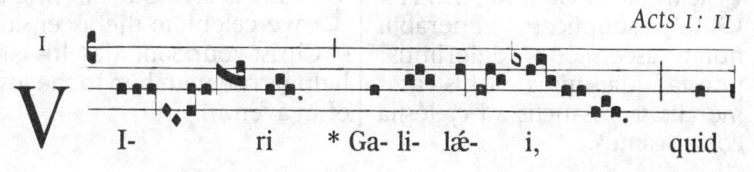

Acts 1: 11

V- I- ri *Ga-li-læ- i, quid

Ascension

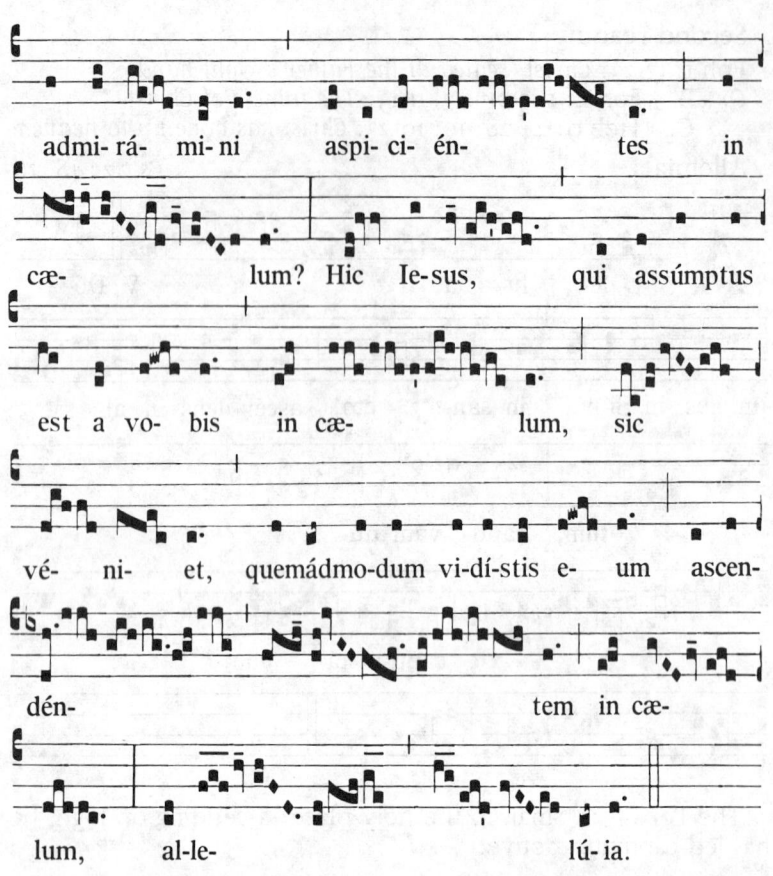

...admirámini aspiciéntes in cælum? Hic Iesus, qui assúmptus est a vobis in cælum, sic véniet, quemádmodum vidístis eum ascendéntem in cælum, allelúia.

Men of Galilee, why do you gaze at the sky in astonishment? This same Jesus who was taken up from you into heaven, will come by the very way in which you saw him go into heaven, alleluia.

Prayer over the Gifts

SACRIFICIUM, Dómine, pro Fílii tui súpplices venerábili nunc ascensióne deférimus: præsta, quæsumus, ut his commérciis sacrosánctis ad cæléstia consurgámus.

LORD, receive our offering as we celebrate the ascension of Christ your Son. May his gifts help us rise with him to the joys of heaven.

Ascension

Preface of the Ascension, p. 57 or 58. With the First Eucharistic Prayer, proper Communicántes, *p. 24.*

Communion A   Mt 28: 18, 19

Data est mihi * omnis potéstas in caelo et in terra, allelúia : eúntes, docéte omnes gentes, baptizántes eos in nómine Patris, et Fílii, et Spíritus Sancti, allelúia, allelúia.

All power has been given to me in heaven and on earth, alleluia; go therefore and teach all the nations, baptizing them in the name of the Father and of the Son and of the Holy Spirit, alleluia, alleluia.

Commmunion B   Mk 16: 17,18

Signa eos * qui in me credunt, haec sequéntur : daemónia eícient : super aegros manus impónent, et bene habébunt.

Al-le- lú- ia.

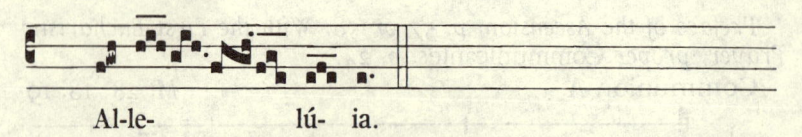

These signs will accompany those who believe: they will cast out demons, and when they lay their hands upon the sick, these will recover, alleluia.

Communion C Ps 67: 33, 34

PSállite Dómino, *qui ascéndit super caelos caelórum ad Oriéntem, allelúia.

Sing to the Lord who has ascended the highest heavens, towards the East, alleluia.

Prayer after Communion

OMNIPOTENS sempitérne Deus, qui in terra constitútos divína tractáre concédis, præsta, quǽsumus, ut illuc tendat christiánæ devotiónis afféctus, quo tecum est nostra substántia.

FATHER, in this eucharist we touch the divine life you give to the world. Help us to follow Christ with love to eternal life.

SEVENTH SUNDAY OF EASTER

Introit *Ps 26: 7, 8, 9 and 1*

E X- áudi, Dómine, * vocem meam, qua clamávi ad te, allelúia: tibi dixit cor meum, quaesívi vultum tuum, vultum tuum Dómine requíram: ne avértas fáciem tuam a me, allelúia, allelúia. *Ps.* Dóminus illuminátio mea, et salus mea: quem timébo?

Hearken, O Lord, unto my voice which has called out to you, alleluia; my heart declared to you: "Your countenance have I sought; I shall ever seek your countenance, O Lord; do not turn your face from me, alleluia, alleluia." ℣. The Lord is my light and my salvation; whom shall I fear?

7th Sunday of Easter

Opening Prayer

SUPPLICATIONIBUS NOSTRIS, Dómine, adésto propítius, ut, sicut humáni géneris Salvatórem tecum in tua crédimus maiestáte, ita eum usque ad consummatiónem sǽculi manére nobíscum, sicut ipse promísit, sentiámus.

FATHER, help us keep in mind that Christ our Saviour lives with you in glory and promised to remain with us until the end of time.

First reading

A. Acts 1: 12-14: *Prayers in the upper room.*
B. Acts 1: 15-17, 20a, 20c-26: *The election of Matthias.*
C. Acts 7: 55-60: *The martyrdom of Stephen.*

Alleluia   Ps 46: 9

Alleluia. ℣. Regnávit Dóminus super omnes gentes: Deus sedet super sedem sanctam suam.

The Lord is King over all the nations; God sits on his holy throne.

Second reading

A. 1 Pet 4: 13-16: *A share in Christ's sufferings.*
B. 1 Jn 4: 11-16: *God is love.*
C. Rev 22: 12-14, 16-17, 20: *Come, Lord Jesus.*

Alleluia A

Exívi a Patre, *p. 376.*

7th Sunday of Easter

Alleluia B & C *Jn 14 : 18*

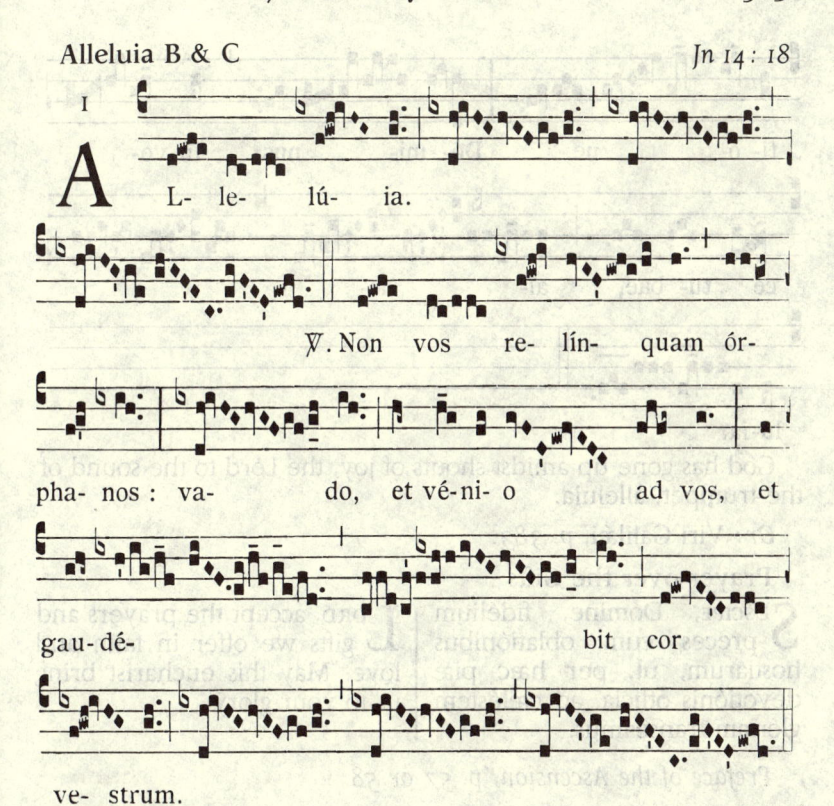

Alleluia. ℣. Non vos relinquam orphanos: vado, et vénio ad vos, et gaudébit cor vestrum.

I will not leave you orphans; I am going, but I will come back to you, and your hearts will be full of joy.

Gospel
- A. Jn 17 : 1-11a: *Father, glorify your Son.*
- B. Jn 17 : 11b-19: *Sanctify them in truth.*
- C. Jn 17 : 20-26: *That they may be one.*

Offertory *Ps 46 : 6*

Ascéndit * Deus in iubila-

7th Sunday of Easter

...ti-ó-ne, Dóminus in voce tubae, allelúia.

God has gone up amidst shouts of joy, the Lord to the sound of the trumpet, alleluia.

Or: Viri Galilǽi, *p. 383.*

Prayer over the Gifts

SUSCIPE, Dómine, fidélium preces cum oblatiónibus hostiárum, ut, per hæc piæ devotiónis offícia, ad cæléstem glóriam transeámus.

LORD, accept the prayers and gifts we offer in faith and love. May this eucharist bring us to your glory.

Preface of the Ascension, p. 57 or 58.

Communion   *Jn 17 : 12, 13, 15*

PATER, * cum essem cum eis, ego servábam eos, quos dedísti mihi, allelúia: nunc autem ad te vénio: non rogo ut tollas eos de

Pentecost – Vigil Mass

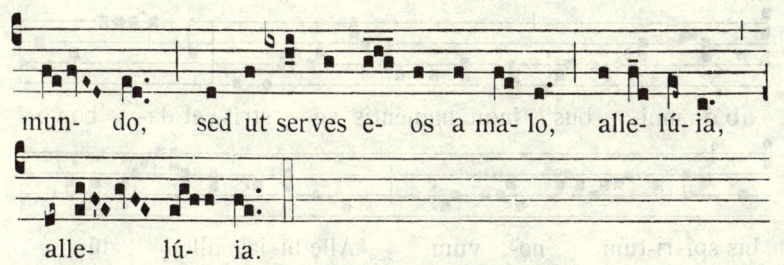

mun- do, sed ut serves e- os a ma- lo, alle- lú- ia, alle- lú- ia.

Father, when I was amongst them, I kept those whom you had given me, alleluia; but now I am coming to you; I do not ask you to take them out of the world, but to keep them from evil, alleluia, alleluia.

Prayer after Communion

Exaudi nos, Deus, salutáris noster, ut per hæc sacrosáncta mystéria in totíus Ecclésiæ confidámus córpore faciéndum, quod eius præcéssit in cápite.

God our saviour, hear us, and through this holy mystery give us hope that the glory you have given Christ will be given to the Church, his body.

PENTECOST SUNDAY

SATURDAY EVENING VIGIL MASS

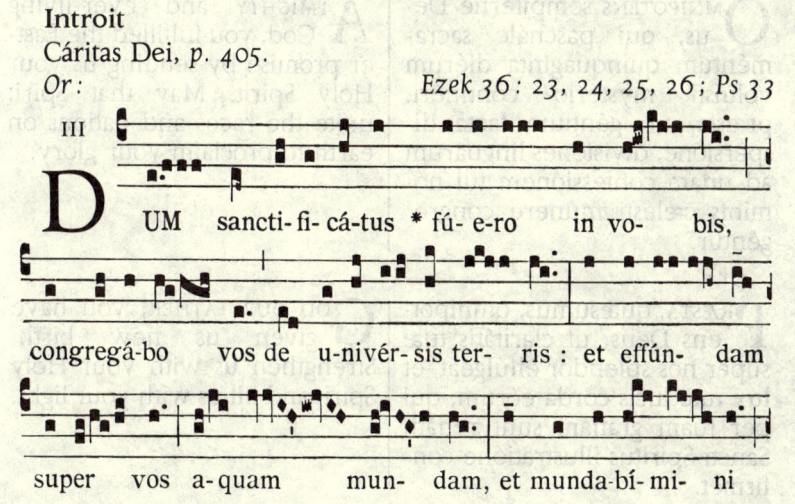

Introit

Cáritas Dei, p. 405.

Or: *Ezek 36: 23, 24, 25, 26; Ps 33*

III

Dum sancti- fi- cá- tus * fú- e- ro in vo- bis, congregá- bo vos de u- nivér- sis ter- ris: et effún- dam super vos a- quam mun- dam, et munda-bí- mi- ni

Pentecost – Vigil Mass

ab ó- mni- bus inqui-naméntis ve- stris: et da- bo vo-bis spí- ri-tum no- vum. Alle-lú- ia, alle- lú-ia. *Ps.* Be-ne-dí-cam Dóminum in omni tempó- re: semper laus e-ius in o- re me- o.

When I vindicate my holiness through you, I will gather you from all lands, and I will sprinkle clean water upon you, and you shall be cleansed from all your filthiness; and I will give you a new Spirit; alleluia, alleluia. ℣. I will bless the Lord at all times; his praise shall continually be in my mouth.

Opening Prayer

OMNIPOTENS sempitérne Deus, qui paschále sacraméntum quinquagínta diérum voluísti mystério continéri, præsta, ut, géntium facta dispersióne, divisiónes linguárum ad unam confessiónem tui nóminis cælésti múnere congregéntur.

ALMIGHTY and ever-living God, you fulfilled the Easter promise by sending us your Holy Spirit. May that Spirit unite the races and nations on earth to proclaim your glory.

Or:

PRÆSTA, quǽsumus, omnípotens Deus, ut claritátis tuæ super nos splendor effúlgeat, et lux tuæ lucis corda eórum, qui per tuam grátiam sunt renáti, Sancti Spíritus illustratióne confírmet.

GOD OUR FATHER, you have given us new birth. Strengthen us with your Holy Spirit and fill us with your light.

Pentecost – Vigil Mass

First reading

Gen 11: 1-9: *The Tower of Babel.*
Or: Ex 19: 3-8a, 16-20b: *The manifestation of God on Mount Sinai.*
Or: Ezek 37: 1-14: *The dry bones.*
Or: Joel 3: 1-5: *I will pour out my Spirit.*

Alleluia — Ps 103: 30

A-L-le- lú- ia. ℣. Emítte Spí- ri- tum tu- um, et cre- a- bún- tur: et reno- vá- bis fá- ci- em ter- ræ.

Send forth your Spirit and all things shall be created anew; and you shall renew the face of the earth.

Second reading

Rom 8: 22-27: *The sighs of all creation.*

Alleluia — Cf. Acts 2: 1

A-L-le- lú- ia. ℣. Dum comple-réntur di- es Pen- te- có- stes, e- rant o-

Pentecost – Vigil Mass

... mnes páriter sedéntes.

When the day of Pentecost had come, they were all seated together.

Gospel

Jn 7: 37-39: *Rivers of living water.*

Offertory   Ps 103: 30, 31

VIII

E-mítte *Spíritum tuum, et creabúntur, et renovábis fáciem terrae: sit glória Dómini in saécula, allelúia.

Send forth your Spirit and all things shall be created anew, and you shall renew the face of the earth; glory be unto the Lord for ever, alleluia.

Pentecost – Vigil Mass

Prayer over the Gifts

PRÆSENTIA munera, quæsumus, Dómine, Spíritus tui benedictióne perfúnde, ut per ipsa Ecclésiæ tuæ ea diléctio tribuátur, per quam salutáris mystérii toto mundo véritas enitéscat.

LORD, send your Spirit on these gifts and through them help the Church you love to show your salvation to all the world.

Preface p. 402. With the First Eucharistic Prayer, proper Communicántes, p. 24.

Communion Jn 7: 37-39

ULtimo * festivitátis die dicébat Iesus: Qui in me credit, flúmina de ventre eius fluent aquae vivae. Hoc autem dixit de Spíritu, quem acceptúri erant credéntes in eum, allelúia, allelúia.

On the last day of the feast, Jesus said: "He who believes in me, out of his heart shall flow rivers of living water". Now, this he said about the Spirit, which those who believed in him were to receive, alleluia, alleluia.

Prayer after Communion

Hæc nobis, Dómine, múnera sumpta profíciant, ut illo iúgiter Spíritu ferveámus, quem Apóstolis tuis ineffabíliter infudísti.

Lord, through this eucharist, send the Holy Spirit of Pentecost into our hearts to keep us always in your love.

MASS OF THE DAY

Introit *Wis 1: 7; Ps 67*

VIII

SPI-RI-TUS Dó-mi- ni * replé- vit or- bem ter- rá-rum, al-le- lú- ia : et hoc quod cón- ti- net ómni- a, sci- énti- am habet vo- cis, alle- lú- ia, al-le-lú- ia, alle- lú- ia.

Ps. Exsúrgat De- us, et dissi-péntur in-i-mí-ci e-ius : et fú-gi- ant, qui o-dé-runt e- um, a fá- ci- e e-ius.

The Spirit of the Lord has filled the whole world, alleluia; and that which contains all things, knows every language spoken by men, alleluia, alleluia, alleluia. ℣. Let God arise, and let his enemies be scattered; and let those who hate him flee before his face.

Pentecost Sunday

Opening Prayer

Deus, qui sacraménto festivitátis hodiérnæ univérsam Ecclésiam tuam in omni gente et natióne sanctíficas, in totam mundi latitúdinem Spíritus Sancti dona defúnde, et, quod inter ipsa evangélicæ prædicatiónis exórdia operáta est divína dignátio, nunc quoque per credéntium corda perfúnde.

God our Father, let the Spirit you sent on your Church to begin the teaching of the gospel continue to work in the world through the hearts of all who believe.

First reading
Acts 2: 1-11: *Pentecost in Jerusalem*

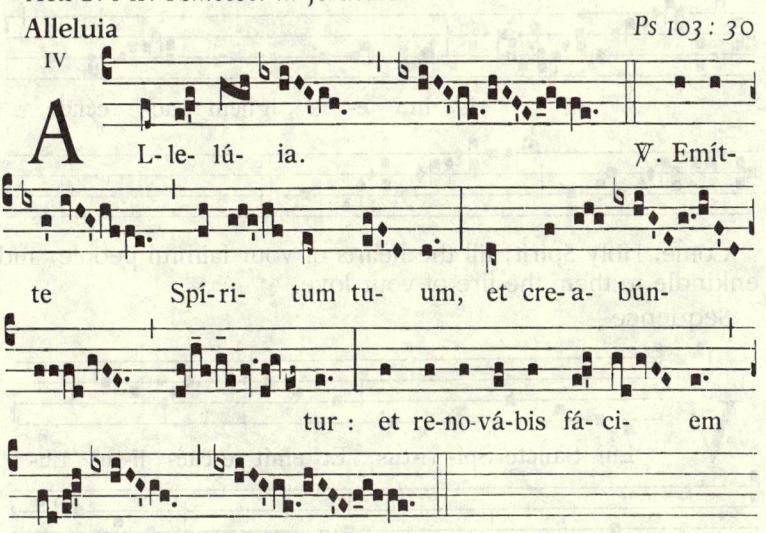

Alleluia
Ps 103: 30

A-lle-lú-ia. ℣. Emítte Spíritum tuum, et creabúntur: et renovábis fáciem terrae.

Send forth your Spirit and all things shall be created anew; and you shall renew the face of the earth.

Second reading
1 Cor 12: 3b-7, 12-13: *The same Spirit.*
Or:
B. Gal 5: 16-25: *The fruits of the Spirit.*
C. Rom 8: 8-17: *Children of God.*

Pentecost Sunday

Alleluia II

Alleluia.

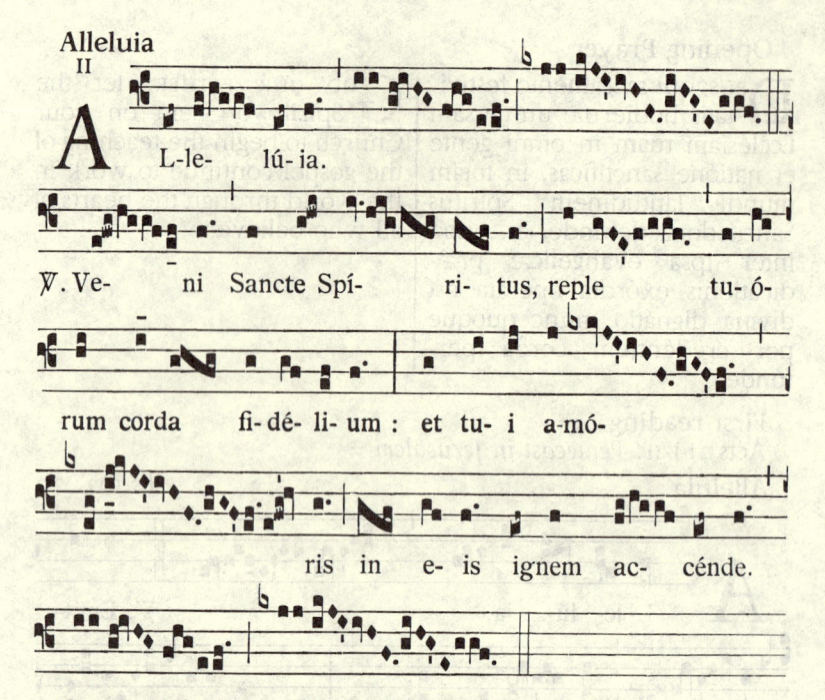

℣. Veni Sancte Spiritus, reple tuorum corda fidelium: et tui amoris in eis ignem accende.

Come, Holy Spirit; fill the hearts of your faithful people, and enkindle in them the fire of your love.

Sequence

I

Veni Sancte Spiritus, Et emitte caelitus Lucis tuae radium. Veni pater pauperum, Veni dator

> Come, Holy Spirit,
> Send forth from on high
> The radiance of thy light.
>
> Come, thou, father of the poor,
> Come, dispenser of all good gifts,
> Come thou, light of our hearts.

mú- ne-rum, Ve-ni lumen cór- di- um. Conso-lá-tor ó-pti- me, Dulcis ho-spes á- nimae, Dulce refri-gé- ri- um. In labó- re réqui- es, In aestu tempé- ri- es, In fle-tu so-lá- ti- um. O lux be- a-tís- sima, Reple cordis íntima Tu- ó-rum fi-dé- li- um. Si-ne tu- o nú-mi-ne, Ni-hil est in hómi-ne, Ni- hil est innó- xi- um. Lava quod est sór-di-dum, Ri-ga

   Supreme Comforter,
Beloved guest of our soul,
Its most desirable nourishment.

   In the midst of labour, rest,
A cool breeze to temper the heat,
Solace in the midst of woe.

   O most blessed light,
Fill the innermost being,
The very hearts of thy faithful.

   Without thy divine strength
No good dwells in man,
Nothing but what turns to ill.

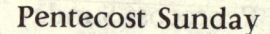

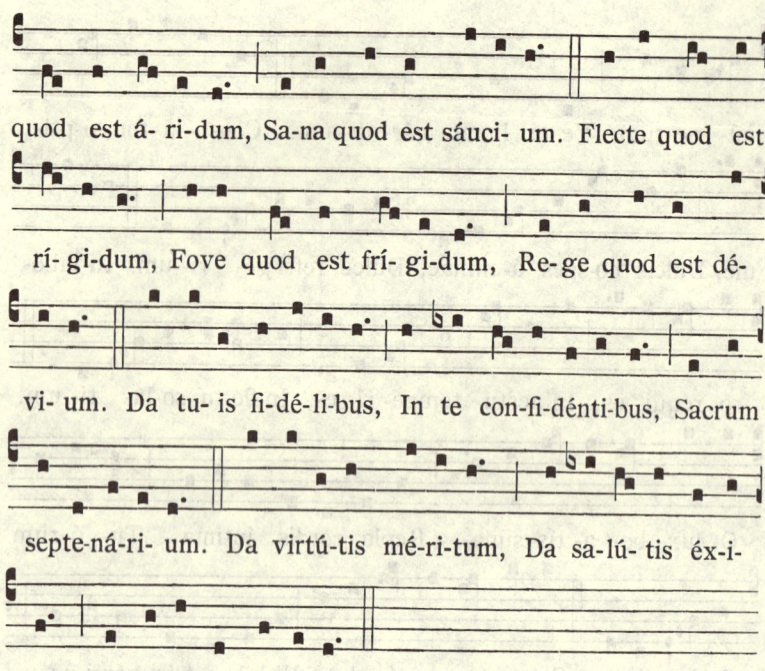

quod est á-ri-dum, Sa-na quod est sáuci-um. Flecte quod est rí-gi-dum, Fove quod est frí-gi-dum, Re-ge quod est dé-vi-um. Da tu-is fi-dé-li-bus, In te con-fi-dénti-bus, Sacrum septe-ná-ri-um. Da virtú-tis mé-ri-tum, Da sa-lú-tis éx-i-tum, Da per-énne gáudi-um.

> Wash away every stain,
> Irrigate all dryness,
> Heal every wound.
>
> Make supple all that is rigid,
> Give ardour to things grown cold,
> Straighten every crooked path.
>
> Grant to thy faithful
> Who put their trust in thee,
> The blessing of thy sevenfold gifts.
>
> Grant us the reward of a virtuous life,
> A death which leads to salvation,
> To the gift of eternal joy.

Gospel

Jn 20: 19-23: *Receive the Holy Spirit.*

Pentecost Sunday

Or:
B. Jn 15: 26-27; 16: 12-15: *The Spirit will make the entire truth known unto you.*
C. Jn 14: 15-16, 23b-26: *The Spirit will teach you all things.*

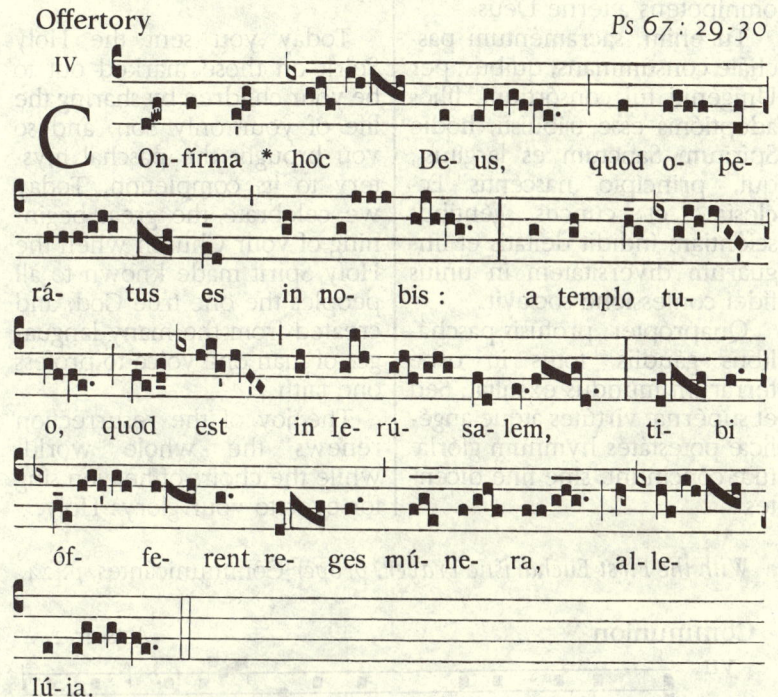

Offertory — Ps 67: 29-30

Confírma * hoc Deus, quod operátus es in nobis: a templo tuo, quod est in Ierúsalem, tibi ófferent reges múnera, allelúia.

Confirm, O God, that which you have accomplished in our midst; from your holy temple which is in Jerusalem, kings shall offer presents to you, alleluia.

Prayer over the Gifts

PRÆSTA, quǽsumus, Dómine, ut, secúndum promissiónem Fílii tui, Spíritus Sanctus huius nobis sacrifícii copiósius revélet arcánum, et omnem propítius réseret veritátem.

LORD, may the Spirit you promised lead us into all truth and reveal to us the full meaning of this sacrifice.

Pentecost Sunday

Preface

VERE dignum et iustum est, æquum et salutáre, nos tibi semper et ubíque grátias ágere : Dómine, sancte Pater, omnípotens ætérne Deus.

Tu enim, sacraméntum paschále consúmmans, quibus, per Unigéniti tui consórtium, fílios adoptiónis esse tribuísti, hódie Spíritum Sanctum es largítus ; qui, princípio nascéntis Ecclésiæ, et cunctis géntibus sciéntiam índidit deitátis et linguárum diversitátem in uníus fídei confessióne sociávit.

Quaprópter, profúsis paschálibus gáudiis, totus in orbe terrárum mundus exsúltat. Sed et supérnæ virtútes atque angélicæ potestátes hymnum glóriæ tuæ cóncinunt, sine fine dicéntes :

FATHER, all-powerful and ever-living God, we do well always and everywhere to give you thanks.

Today you sent the Holy Spirit on those marked out to be your children by sharing the life of your only Son, and so you brought the paschal mystery to its completion. Today we celebrate the great beginning of your Church when the Holy Spirit made known to all peoples the one true God, and created from the many languages of man one voice to profess one faith.

The joy of the resurrection renews the whole world, while the choirs of heaven sing for ever to your glory: Holy...

With the First Eucharistic Prayer, proper Communicántes, p. 24.

Communion
Acts 2: 2, 4

VII

F Actus est re-pénte * de cae-lo so- nus adveni- éntis spí-ri-tus ve-he-méntis, u-bi e- rant se-dén- tes, alle- lú- ia : et replé- ti sunt omnes Spí-ri-tu Sancto,

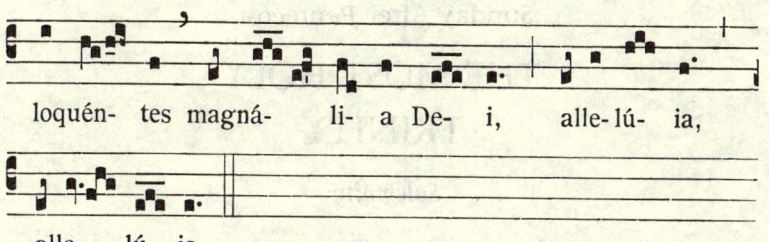

Pentecost Sunday

loquéntes magnália Dei, allelúia, alle- lúia.

Suddenly, a sound came from heaven like the rush of a mighty wind, in the place where they were sitting, alleluia; and they were all filled with the Holy Spirit, and announced the great things God had done, alleluia, alleluia.

Prayer after Communion

Deus, qui Ecclésiæ tuæ cæléstia dona largíris, custódi grátiam quam dedísti, ut Spíritus Sancti vígeat semper munus infúsum, et ad ætérnæ redemptiónis augméntum spiritális esca profíciat.

Father, may the food we receive in the eucharist help our eternal redemption. Keep within us the vigour of your Spirit and protect the gifts you have given to your Church.

Ordinary Time is resumed after Pentecost. The Most Holy Trinity is, however, celebrated on the following Sunday.

Sunday After Pentecost

THE MOST HOLY TRINITY

Solemnity

Introit A & B *Tob* 12 : 6; *Ps* 8

VIII

BENEDICTA sit * sancta Trínitas, atque indivísa Unitas: confitébimur ei, quia fecit nobíscum misericórdiam suam. *Ps.* Dómine Dóminus noster: quam admirábile est nomen tuum in univérsa terra!

Blessed be the Holy Trinity and its undivided Unity; we shall ever give him thanks, for he has dealt with us according to his mercy. ℣. O Lord, our Governor, how admirable is your name in all the earth!

Trinity Sunday

Introit C — *Rom 5: 5; 10: 11; Ps 102*

CAritas Dei * diffusa est in córdibus nostris, allelúia: per inhabitántem Spíritum eius in nobis, allelúia, allelúia. *Ps.* Bénedic ánima mea Dómino : et ómnia quae intra me sunt, nómini sancto eius.

The love of God has been poured into our hearts, alleluia; by his Spirit which dwells in us, alleluia, alleluia. ℣. Bless the Lord, O my soul; and all that is within me, bless his holy name.

Opening Prayer

DEUS PATER, qui, Verbum veritátis et Spíritum sanctificatiónis mittens in mundum, admirábile mystérium tuum homínibus declarásti, da nobis, in confessióne veræ fídei, æ-

FATHER, you sent your Word to bring us truth and your Spirit to make us holy. Through them we come to know the mystery of your life. Help us to worship you, one God in three

térnæ glóriam Trinitátis agnóscere, et Unitátem adoráre in poténtia maiestátis.

Persons, by proclaiming and living our faith in you.

First reading
A. Ex 34: 4b-6, 8-9: *God proclaims his name.*
B. Deut 4: 32-34, 39-40: *The Lord is God.*
C. Prov 8: 22-31: *Eternal Wisdom.*

Gradual *Dan 3 : 55, ℣. 56*

Bene-dí-ctus es, * Dó-mi-ne, qui in-tu-é-ris a-býs-sos, et se-des su-per Ché-ru-bim. ℣. Be-ne-dí-ctus es Dó-mi-ne, in firmamén-to cae-li, et laudá-bi-lis in saé-cu-la.

Blessed are you, O Lord, who gaze into the depths and who are enthroned upon the Cherubim. ℣. Blessed are you, O Lord, in the firmament of heaven, and worthy of praise for ever.

Trinity Sunday

Or: **Hymn** Dan 3: 52-56

BEnedíctus es Dómine Deus patrum nostrórum.* Et laudábilis et gloriósus in saécula. Et benedíctum nomen glóriae tuae, quod est sanctum,* Et laudábile et gloriósum in saécula. Benedíctus es in templo sancto glóriae tuae.* Et laudábilis et gloriósus in saécula. Benedíctus es super thronum sanctum regni tui.* Et laudábilis et gloriósus

Blessed are you, O Lord, the God of our fathers. * And worthy to be praised and glorified for ever.

And blessed is your glorious, holy name. * And worthy to be praised and glorified for ever.

Blessed are you in the holy temple of your glory. * And worthy to be praised and glorified for ever.

Blessed are you upon the sacred throne of your kingdom. * And worthy to be praised and glorified for ever.

Trinity Sunday

in saécula. Benedíctus es super sceptrum divinitátis tuae. * Et laudábilis et gloriósus in saécula. Benedíctus es qui sedes super Chérubim, íntuens abýssos. * Et laudábilis et gloriósus in saécula. Benedíctus es qui ámbulas super pennas ventórum, et super undas maris. * Et laudábilis et gloriósus in saécula. Benedícant te omnes Angeli et Sancti

Blessed are you through the mighty sceptre of your divinity. * And worthy to be praised and glorified for ever.

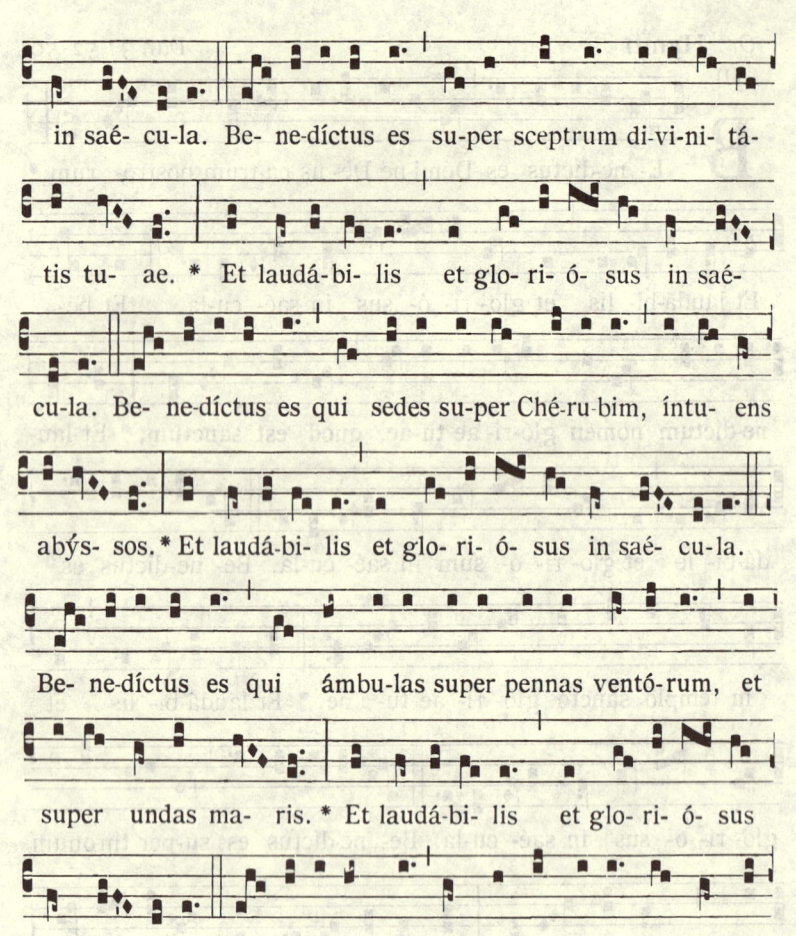

Blessed are you as you gaze into the depths, enthroned upon the Cherubim. * And worthy to be praised and glorified for ever.

Blessed are you as you tread upon the wings of the wind, and on the waves of the sea. * And worthy to be praised and glorified for ever.

Let all your Angels and Saints bless you. * And praise you and glorify you for ever.

Trinity Sunday

tu- i. * Et laudent te, et glo-rí-fi-cent in saé-cu-la.

Be-ne-dí-cant te cae-li, terra, ma-re, et ómni-a quae in

e- is sunt. * Et laudent te, et glo-rí-fi-cent in saé-

cu-la. Gló-ri-a Pa-tri, et Fí-li-o, et Spi-rí-tu-i San-cto.

* Et laudá-bi-li et glo-ri-ó-so in saé-cu-la. Sic-ut

e-rat in princí-pi-o, et nunc, et semper, et in saécu-la

saecu-ló-rum. A-men. * Et laudá-bi-li et glo-ri-ó-so

Let the heavens, the earth, the sea, and all the things that dwell therein, bless you. * And praise you and glorify you for ever.

Glory be to the Father, and to the Son, and to the Holy Spirit. * Who is worthy to be praised and glorified for ever.

As it was in the beginning, is now, and ever shall be, world without end. Amen. * And worthy to be praised and glorified for ever.

Trinity Sunday

in saé-cu-la. Be- ne-díctus es, Dó-mi-ne De- us patrum no-stró- rum,* Et laudá-bi- lis et glo- ri- ó- sus in saé- cu-la.

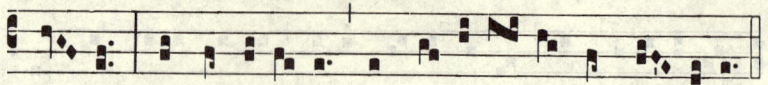

Blessed are you, O Lord, the God of our fathers. * And worthy to be praised and glorified for ever.

Second reading

A. 2 Cor 13: 11-13: *A doxology.*
B. Rom 8: 14-17: *Abba, Father.*
C. Rom 5: 1-5: *The love of God in our hearts.*

Alleluia
Dan 3: 52

VIII

Al-le-lú-ia.

℣. Be- ne-díctus es, Dómi-ne De- us patrum no-stró- rum, et laudá-bi- lis in saécu- la.

Blessed are you, O Lord, the God of our fathers; and worthy to be praised for ever.

Gospel

A. Jn 3: 16-18: *God so loved the world.*
B. Mt 28: 16-20: *Go forth and baptize!*
C. Jn 16: 12-15: *The Spirit of truth.*

Trinity Sunday

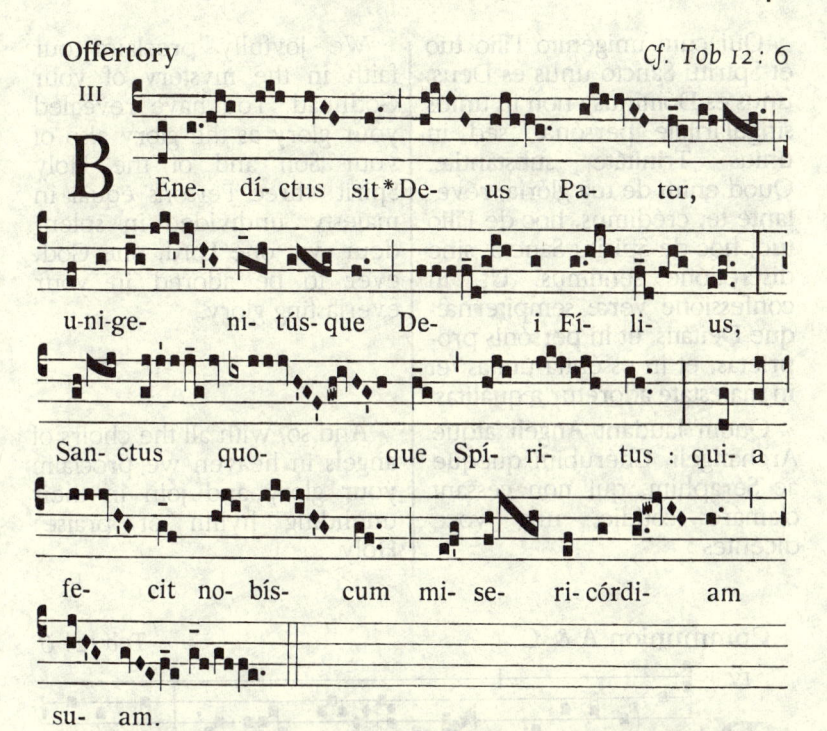

Offertory *Cf. Tob* 12: 6

Bene-dí-ctus sit * De- us Pa- ter, u-ni-ge- ni- tús- que De- i Fí- li- us, San- ctus quo- que Spí- ri- tus : qui- a fe- cit no- bís- cum mi- se- ri- córdi- am su- am.

Blessed be God the Father, and the only begotten Son of God, and the Holy Spirit; for he has dealt with us according to his mercy.

Prayer over the Gifts

Sanctifica, quæsumus, Dómine Deus noster, per tui nóminis invocatiónem, hæc múnera nostræ servitútis, et per ea nosmetípsos tibi pérfice munus ætérnum.

Lord our God, make these gifts holy, and through them make us a perfect offering to you.

Preface

Vere dignum et iustum est, æquum et salutáre, nos tibi semper et ubíque grátias ágere : Dómine, sancte Pater, omnípotens ætérne Deus :

Father, all-powerful and ever-living God, we do well always and everywhere to give you thanks.

Qui cum unigénito Fílio tuo et Spíritu Sancto unus es Deus, unus es Dóminus : non in uníus singularitáte persónæ, sed in uníus Trinitáte substántiæ. Quod enim de tua glória, revelánte te, crédimus, hoc de Fílio tuo, hoc de Spíritu Sancto, sine discretióne sentímus. Ut, in confessióne veræ sempiternǽque Deitátis, et in persónis propríetas, et in esséntia únitas, et in maiestáte adorétur æquálitas.

Quem laudant Angeli atque Archángeli, Chérubim quoque ac Séraphim, qui non cessant clamáre cotídie, una voce dicéntes :

We joyfully proclaim our faith in the mystery of your Godhead. You have revealed your glory as the glory also of your Son and of the Holy Spirit: three Persons equal in majesty, undivided in splendour, yet one Lord, one God, ever to be adored in your everlasting glory.

And so, with all the choirs of angels in heaven we proclaim your glory and join in their unending hymn of praise: Holy...

Communion A & C *Tob 12 : 6*

Benedícimus * Deum caeli, et coram ómnibus vivéntibus confitébimur ei : quia fecit nobíscum misericórdiam suam.

Let us bless the God of heaven and utter his praises before all who live; for he has dealt with us according to his mercy.

Communion B: Data est mihi, *p. 385.*

Prayer after Communion

PROFICIAT nobis ad salútem córporis et ánimæ, Dómine Deus noster, huius sacraménti suscéptio, et sempitérnæ sanctæ Trinitátis eiusdémque indivíduæ unitátis conféssio.

LORD GOD, we worship you, a Trinity of Persons, one eternal God. May our faith and the sacrament we receive bring us health of mind and body.

Thursday or Sunday After Holy Trinity

THE BODY & BLOOD OF CHRIST
(CORPUS CHRISTI)
Solemnity

Introit   Ps 80: *17 and* 2, 3, 11

CIBAVIT e- os * ex á-di- pe fruménti, alle- lú- ia : et de petra, mel-le sa-tu-rá-vit e- os, alle-lú- ia, al-le- lú- ia, al-le- lú- ia. *Ps.* Exsul-tá-te De- o adiu-tó- ri nostro : iu- bi- lá-te De- o Ia-cob. **Ant.**

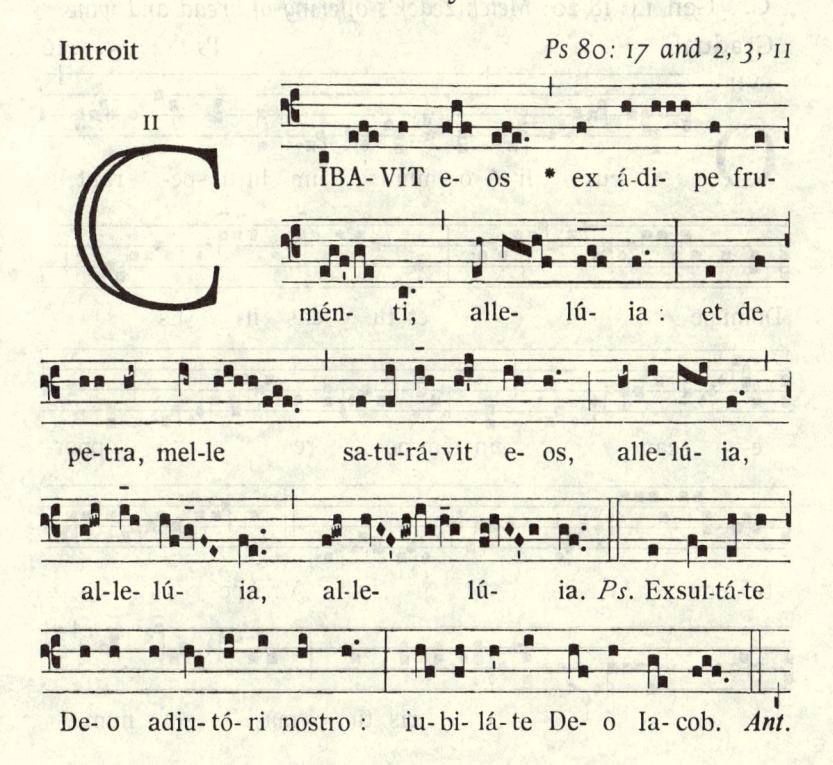

The Body and Blood of Christ

He fed them with the finest of wheat, alleluia; and with honey from the rock he satisfied them, alleluia, alleluia. ℣. Rejoice in honour of God our helper; shout for joy to the God of Jacob.

Opening Prayer

DEUS, qui nobis sub sacraménto mirábili passiónis tuæ memóriam reliquísti, tríbue, quǽsumus, ita nos Córporis et Sánguinis tui sacra mystéria venerári, ut redemptiónis tuæ fructum in nobis iúgiter sentiámus.

LORD JESUS CHRIST, you gave us the eucharist as the memorial of your suffering and death. May our worship of this sacrament of your body and blood help us to experience the salvation you won for us and the peace of the kingdom.

First reading
A. Deut: 8: 2-3, 14b-16a: *The Lord gave you manna.*
B. Ex 24: 3-8: *This is the blood of the Covenant.*
C. Gen 14: 18-20: *Melchizedek's offering of bread and wine.*

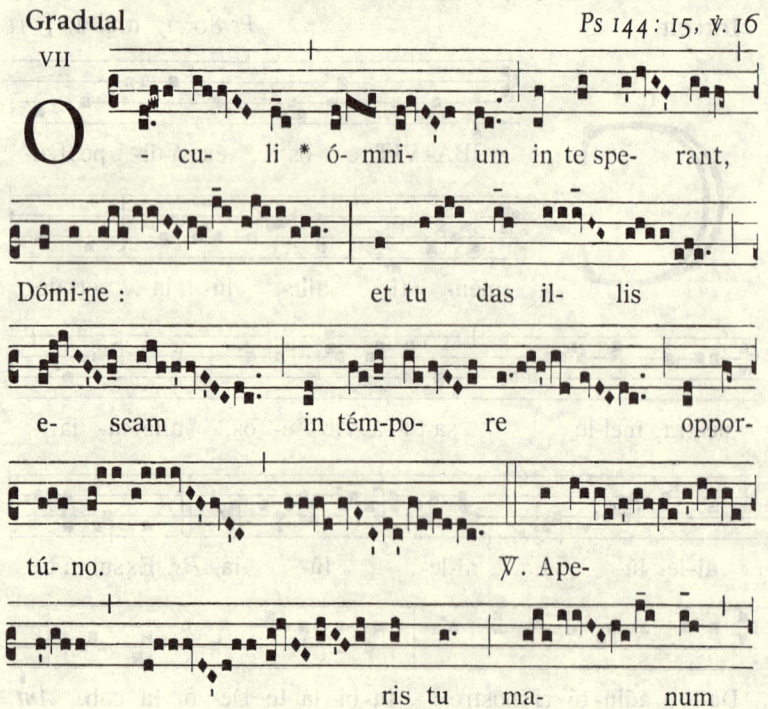

Gradual   Ps 144: 15, ℣. 16

O-cu-li * ó-mni- um in te spe- rant, Dómi-ne: et tu das il- lis e- scam in témpo- re opportú- no. ℣. Ape- ris tu ma- num

The Body and Blood of Christ

tu- am : et imples omne á-ni- mal be-ne-di-cti-ó-ne.

The eyes of all look towards you in hope, O Lord; and you give them their food in due season. ℣. You open your hand and fill every living thing with your blessings.

Second reading
A. 1 Cor 10: 16-17: *One bread and one body.*
B. Heb 9: 11-15: *The blood of Christ will purify our conscience.*
C. 1 Cor 11: 23-26: *You proclaim the death of the Lord.*

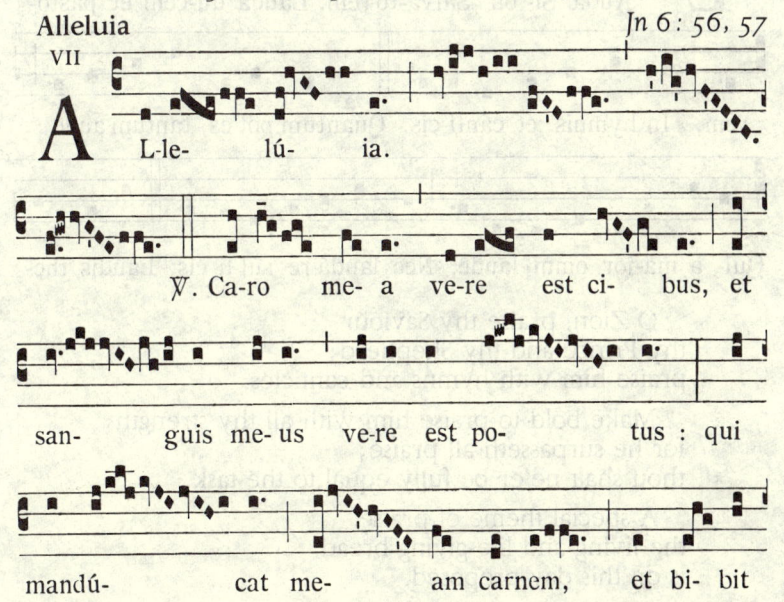

Alleluia Jn 6: 56, 57

VII

A L-le- lú- ia. ℣. Ca-ro me- a ve-re est ci- bus, et san- guis me- us ve-re est po- tus : qui mandú- cat me- am carnem, et bi- bit

me- um sán- gui- nem, in me ma- net,

et e- go in e- o.

My flesh is the true food, my blood is the true drink; he who eats my flesh and drinks my blood abides in me, and I in him.

After the Alleluia, the Sequence may be sung, either in its entirety or starting at the asterisk.

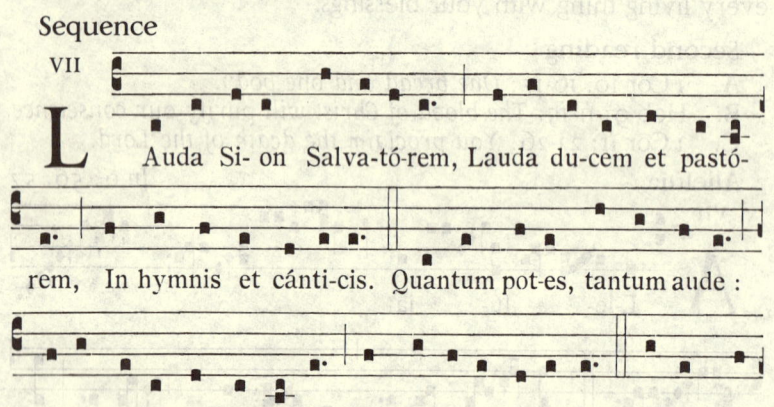

Sequence

VII

L Auda Si- on Salva-tó-rem, Lauda du-cem et pastó-rem, In hymnis et cánti-cis. Quantum pot-es, tantum aude : Qui- a ma-ior omni laude, Nec laudá-re súf-fi-cis. Laudis the-

  O Zion, praise thy Saviour
thy Prince and thy Shepherd;
praise him with hymns and canticles.

  Make bold to praise him with all thy strength;
for he surpasseth all praise;
thou shalt ne'er be fully equal to the task.

  A special theme of praise,
the living and life-giving bread,
is on this day proposed.

The Body and Blood of Christ

ma spe-ci-á-lis, Panis vi-vus et vi-tá-lis Hó-di-e pro-pó-ni-tur. Quem in sacrae mensa ce-nae, Turbae fratrum du-odénae Da-tum non ambí-gi-tur. Sit laus plena, sit so-nó-ra, Sit iucúnda, sit de-có-ra Mentis iu-bi-lá-ti-o. Di-es e-nim sol-émnis á-gi-tur, In qua mensae prima recó-li-tur Hu-ius insti-tú-ti-o. In hac mensa no-vi Re-gis, Novum

Upon the table of the Last Supper,
to the group of the brethren Twelve,
this bread was truly given.

Let our praise ring out full and resonant,
a song of the heart,
joyful and radiant.

For today is a most solemn festival,
recalling how this sacred banquet
first was instituted.

At this banquet of our newly crowned King,
the Paschal mystery of the New Law
bringeth to its end the ancient Passover rite.

The Body and Blood of Christ

Pascha novae legis, Phase vetus términat. Vetustátem nóvitas, Umbram fugat véritas, Noctem lux elíminat.

Quod in cena Christus gessit, Faciéndum hoc exprèssit In sui memóriam. Docti sacris institútis, Panem, vinum in salútis Consecrámus hóstiam. Dogma datur christiánis, Quod in carnem transit panis, Et vinum in sán-

    Novelty replaceth that which is old,
reality chaseth away the shadows,
radiance doth eliminate the night.

    That which Christ accomplished at this supper
he ordered to be done again,
in memory of him.

    Taught by his divine precepts,
We consecrate the bread and wine,
a sacrificial victim for salvation.

    This sacred doctrine do Christians receive:
the bread into his body
and the wine into his blood is changed.

The Body and Blood of Christ

gui-nem. Quod non ca-pis, quod non vi-des, Animó-sa firmat

fi-des, Praeter re-rum órdi-nem. Sub di-vérsis spe-ci- ébus,

Signis tantum, et non rebus, La- tent res ex-ími- ae. Ca-ro

ci-bus, sanguis po-tus : Manet tamen Christus to-tus Sub utrá-

que spé-ci- e. A suménte non concí-sus, Non confráctus, non

di-ví-sus : Integer accí-pi-tur. Sumit unus, sumunt mil-le :

 What thou can neither grasp nor perceive
is affirmed by ardent faith,
beyond the natural order of things.

 Beneath these double appearances –
mere signs, and not the realities themselves –
is hidden the most sublime of mysteries.

 His body is food, his blood, a beverage
but Christ remains entirely present
under each.

 His flesh, when eaten, is not torn apart,
broken asunder or divided;
intact he is received.

The Body and Blood of Christ

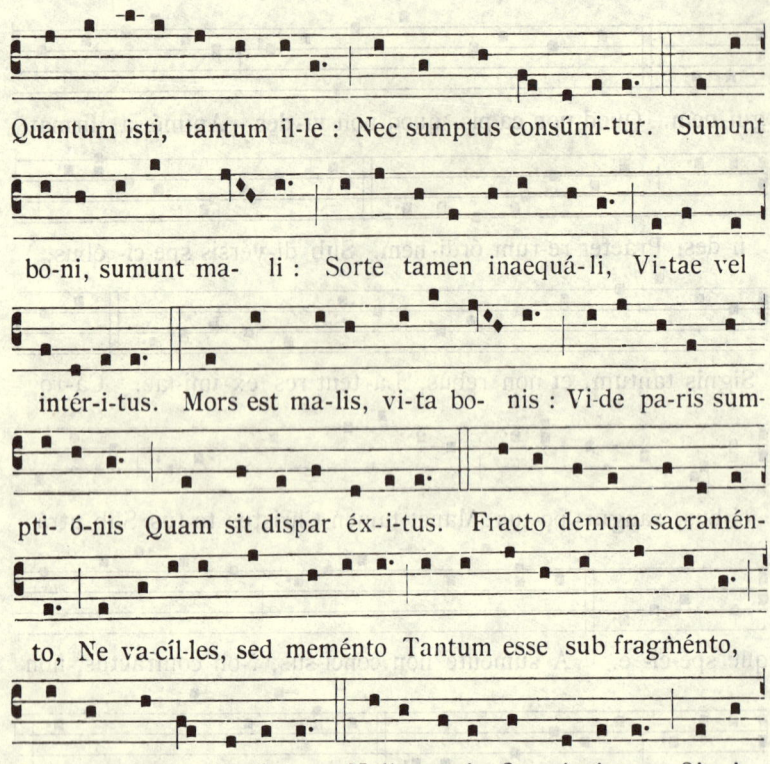

Quantum isti, tantum il-le : Nec sumpsit consúmi-tur. Sumunt bo-ni, sumunt ma- li : Sorte tamen inaequá-li, Vi-tae vel intér-i-tus. Mors est ma-lis, vi-ta bo- nis : Vi-de pa-ris sumpti- ó-nis Quam sit dispar éx-i-tus. Fracto demum sacraménto, Ne va-cíl-les, sed meménto Tantum esse sub fragménto, Quantum to-to té-gi-tur. Nulla re- i fit scissú- ra : Signi

> Though one alone be fed, though thousands be fed,
> all receive the same reality,
> which perisheth not at meal's end.
>
> The good and the guilty may all have part therein,
> but with different results:
> life or death.
>
> Death for sinners, life everlasting for the just;
> mark well the varied effects
> of this single food.
>
> And when the bread is fragmented,
> be thou not troubled, but remenber:
> he is present in each fragment
> just as much as in the whole.

The Body and Blood of Christ

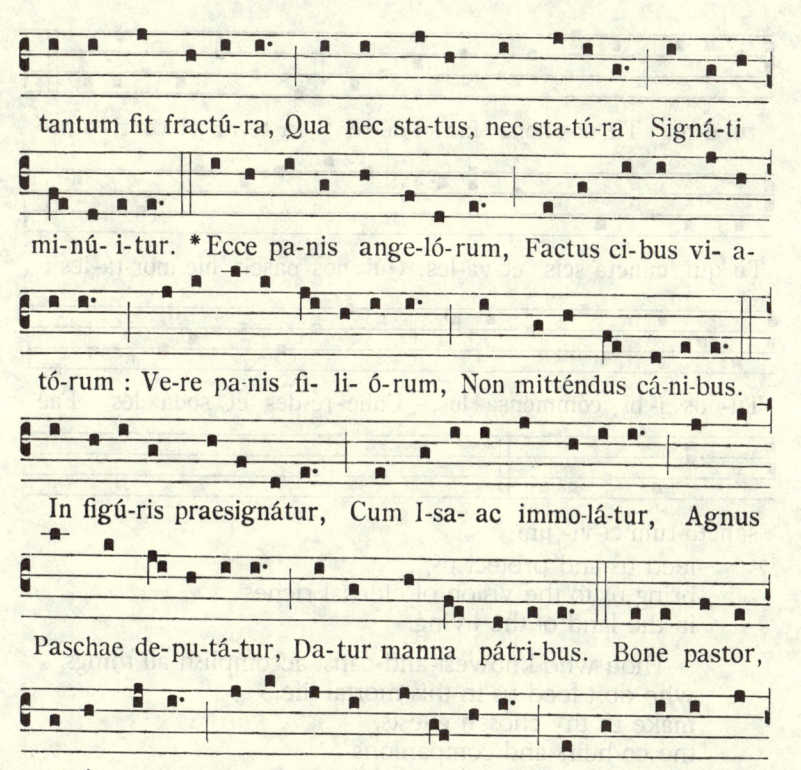

tantum fit fractú-ra, Qua nec sta-tus, nec sta-tú-ra Signá-ti mi-nú- i-tur. *Ecce pa-nis ange-ló-rum, Factus ci-bus vi- a- tó-rum : Ve-re pa-nis fi- li- ó-rum, Non mitténdus cá-ni-bus. In figú-ris praesignátur, Cum I-sa- ac immo-lá-tur, Agnus Paschae de-pu-tá-tur, Da-tur manna pátri-bus. Bone pastor, pa-nis ve- re, Ie-su, nostri mi-se-ré-re : Tu nos pasce, nos

 The hidden reality is not divided,
the sign only is fragmented;
He whose presence is signified,
suffereth no diminution in stature or in strength.

 * Behold this bread of Angels
which hath become food for us on our pilgrimage;
it is truly the bread of God's children,
let it ne'er be thrown to dogs.

 Scripture announced it figuratively
by Isaac's sacrifice,
by the paschal lamb
and by the manna given to our forefathers.

 O Good Shepherd and most true bread of life,
Lord Jesus, have mercy on us;

tu- é-re, Tu nos bona fac vi-dé-re In terra vi-vénti- um.

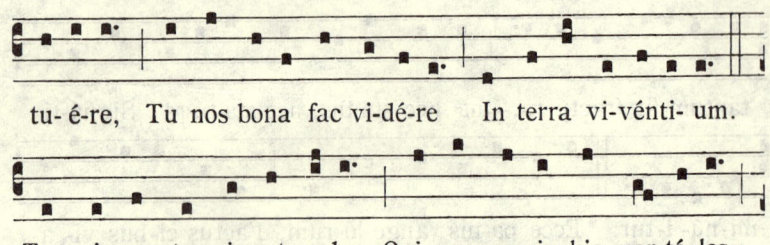

Tu qui cuncta scis et va-les, Qui nos pascis hic mor-tá-les :

Tu- os i- bi commensá- les, Cohe-ré-des et sodá- les Fac

sanctó-rum cí-vi- um.

> feed us and protect us,
> bring us to the vision of eternal riches
> in the land of the living.
>
> Thou who knowest and canst accomplish all things,
> who dost feed us in this mortal life,
> make us thy chosen guests,
> the co-heirs and companions
> of thy saints in the heavenly city.

Gospel

A. Jn 6: 51-59: *I am the bread of life.*
B. Mk 14: 12-16, 22-26: *Institution of the Eucharist.*
C. Lk 9: 11b-17: *Multiplication of the loaves.*

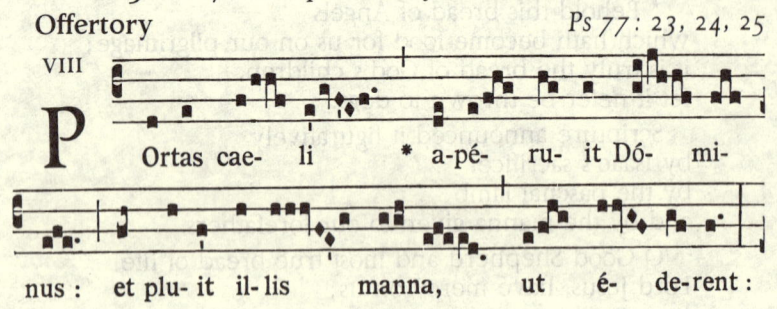

Offertory
Ps 77: 23, 24, 25

VIII

Portas cae- li * a-pé- ru- it Dó- mi-

nus : et plu- it il- lis manna, ut é- de-rent :

The Body and Blood of Christ

pa-nem cae- li de- dit il- lis: pa-nem ange-ló- rum mandu-cá- vit ho- mo, alle- lú- ia.

The Lord opened the doors of heaven and rained down manna upon them to eat; he gave them bread from heaven; man ate the bread of angels, alleluia.

Or:
Sanctificávit Moýses, p. 549.

Prayer over the Gifts

ECCLESIÆ tuæ, quǽsumus, Dómine, unitátis et pacis propítius dona concéde, quæ sub oblátis munéribus mýstice designántur.

LORD, may the bread and cup we offer bring your Church the unity and peace they signify.

Preface of the Holy Eucharist, p. 63 or 64.

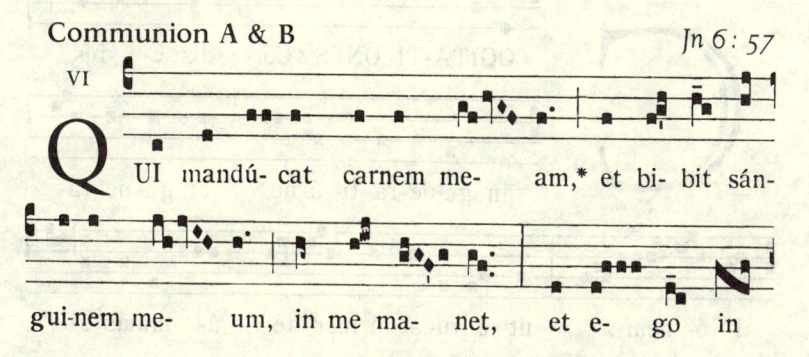

Communion A & B
Jn 6: 57

VI

QUI mandú- cat carnem me- am,* et bi- bit sán- gui-nem me- um, in me ma- net, et e- go in e- o, di- cit Dómi- nus.

He who eats my flesh and drinks my blood, abides in me, and I in him, says the Lord.

Communion C: Hoc corpus, p. 297.

Prayer after Communion

Fac nos, quæsumus, Dómine, divinitátis tuæ sempitérna fruitióne repléri, quam pretiósi Córporis et Sánguinis tui temporális percéptio præfigúrat.

Lord Jesus Christ, you give us your body and blood in the eucharist as a sign that even now we share your life. May we come to possess it completely in the kingdom, where you live for ever and ever.

The Friday following the Second Sunday After Pentecost

THE SACRED HEART OF JESUS

Solemnity

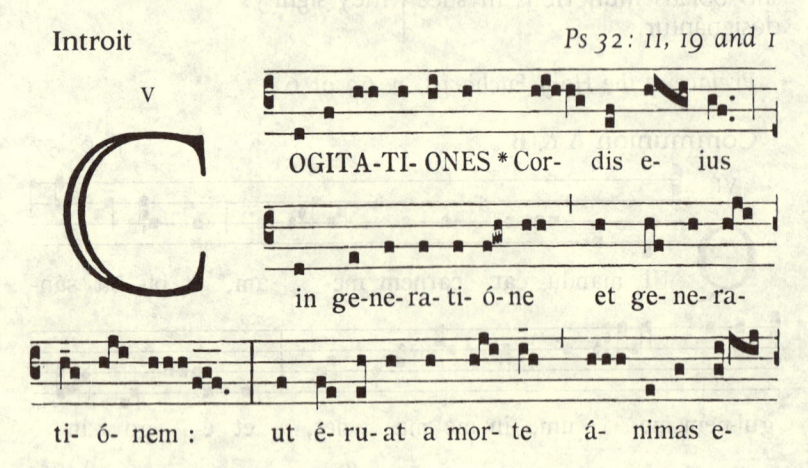

Introit   Ps 32: 11, 19 and 1

V

COGITA-TI- ONES * Cor- dis e- ius in ge- ne- ra- ti- ó- ne et ge- ne- ra- ti- ó- nem: ut é- ru- at a mor- te á- nimas e-

The Sacred Heart

ó- rum et a-lat e- os in fa- me.

T. P. Alle- lú- ia, al- le- lú- ia. *Ps.* Exsul-

tá-te, iusti, in Dómi-no, rectos de-cet collaudá-ti- o.

The thoughts of his heart stand from generation to generation: that he might deliver their souls from death, and nourish them in times of famine. ℣. Rejoice in the Lord, O you righteous; praising befits those who are upright.

Opening Prayer

Concede, quæsumus, omnípotens Deus, ut qui, dilécti Fílii tui Corde gloriántes, eius præcípua in nos benefícia recólimus caritátis, de illo donórum fonte cælésti supereffluéntem grátiam mereámur accípere.

Father, we rejoice in the gifts of love we have received from the heart of Jesus your Son. Open our hearts to share his life and continue to bless us with his love.

Or:

Deus, qui nobis in Corde Fílii tui, nostris vulneráto peccátis, infinítos dilectiónis thesáuros misericórditer largíri dignáris, concéde, quæsumus, ut, illi devótum pietátis nostræ præstántes obséquium, dignæ quoque satisfactiónis exhibeámus offícium.

Father, we have wounded the heart of Jesus your Son, but he brings us forgiveness and grace. Help us to prove our grateful love and make amends for our sins.

First reading
A. Deut 7: 6-11: *The people chosen through love.*
B. Hos 11: 1, 3-4, 8c-9: *Israel, the beloved nation.*
C. Ezek 34: 11-16: *The Lord, shepherd of Israel.*

The Sacred Heart

Gradual — Ps 24: 8, ℣. 9

Dulcis * et rectus Dóminus, propter hoc legem dabit delinquéntibus in via. ℣. Díriget mansuétos in iudício, docébit mites vias suas.

Good and upright is the Lord, therefore will he impart his law to sinners lost in the way. ℣. He will guide the humble in what is right, and teach the meek his ways.

Second reading

A. 1 Jn 4: 7-16: *It was God who first loved us.*
B. Eph 3: 8-12, 14-19: *To know the love of Christ.*
C. Rom 5: 5-11: *The proof that God loves us.*

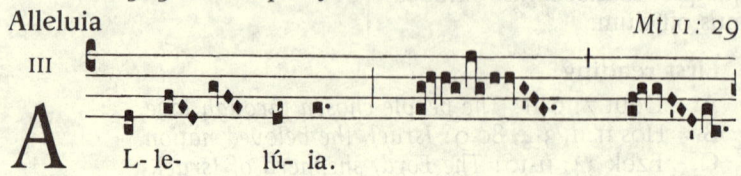

Alleluia — Mt 11: 29

Alleluia.

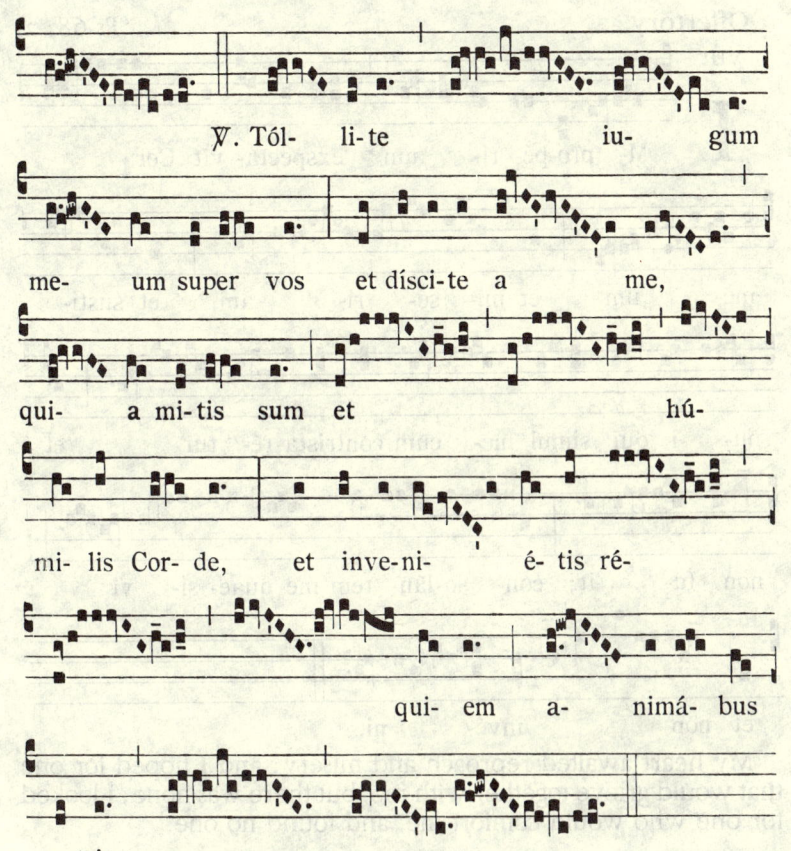

℣. Tóllite iugum meum super vos et díscite a me, qui a mitis sum et húmilis Corde, et inveniétis réquiem animábus vestris.

Take my yoke upon you and learn from me; for I am meek and lowly in heart, and you will find rest for your souls.

Or:

Veníte ad me, p. 666.

Gospel

A. Mt 11: 25-30: *Meek and lowly in heart.*
B. Jn 19: 31-37: *A soldier pierced his side.*
C. Lk 15: 3-7: *The sheep which was lost and found.*

The Sacred Heart

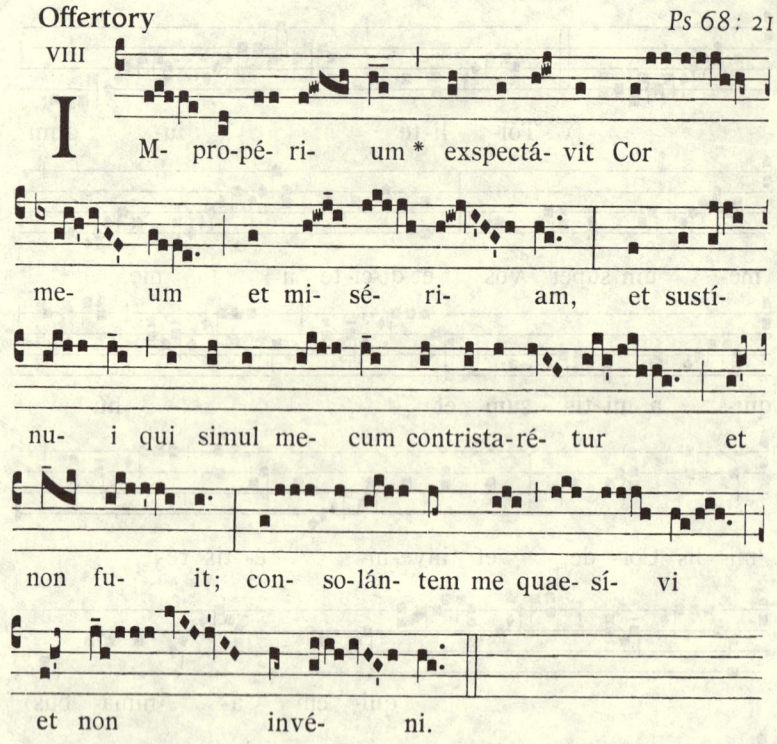

Offertory *Ps 68: 21*

IM- pro-pé- ri- um * exspectá- vit Cor me- um et mi- sé- ri- am, et sustí- nu- i qui simul me- cum contrista-ré- tur et non fu- it; con- so-lán- tem me quae- sí- vi et non invé- ni.

My heart awaited reproach and misery; and I hoped for one that would grieve together with me, but there was none; I looked for one who would comfort me, and found no one.

Prayer over the Gifts

Respice, quæsumus, Dómine, ad ineffábilem Cordis dilécti Fílii tui caritátem, ut quod offérimus sit tibi munus accéptum et nostrórum expiátio delictórum.

Lord, look on the heart of Christ your Son filled with love for us. Because of his love accept our eucharist and forgive our sins.

Preface

Vere dignum et iustum est, æquum et salutáre, nos tibi semper et ubíque grátias

Father, all-powerful and ever-living God, we do well always and everywhere to

ágere: Dómine, sancte Pater, omnípotens ætérne Deus: per Christum Dóminum nostrum.

Qui, mira caritáte, exaltátus in cruce, pro nobis trádidit semetípsum, atque de transfíxo látere sánguinem fudit et aquam, ex quo manárent Ecclésiæ sacraménta, ut omnes, ad Cor apértum Salvatóris attrácti, iúgiter haurírent e fóntibus salútis in gáudio.

Et ídeo, cum Sanctis et Angelis univérsis, te collaudámus, sine fine dicéntes:

give you thanks through Jesus Christ our Lord.

Lifted high on the cross, Christ gave his life for us, so much did he love us. From his wounded side flowed blood and water, the fountain of sacramental life in the Church. To his open heart the Saviour invites all men, to draw water in joy from the springs of salvation.

Now, with all the saints and angels, we praise you for ever: Holy...

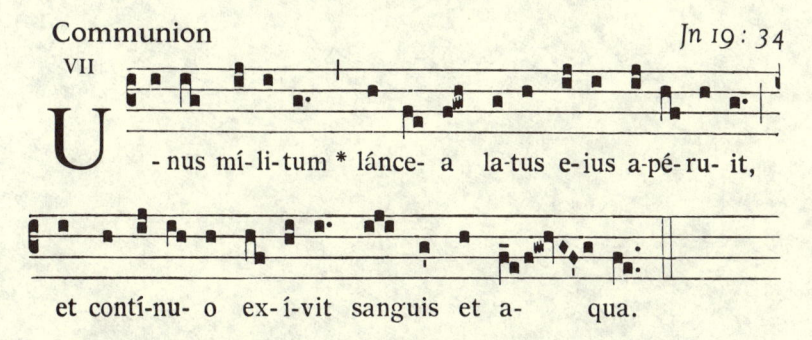

Communion *Jn 19 : 34*

VII

U-nus mí-li-tum * lánce-a la-tus e-ius a-pé-ru-it, et contí-nu-o ex-í-vit sanguis et a- qua.

One of the soldiers opened his side with a spear, and at once there came forth blood and water.

Or:

Gustáte et vidéte, p. 495.

Or: *Lk 15 : 10*

V

DI-co vo-bis, * gáudi-um est ánge-lis De- i super

uno pecca-tó-re   paeni-ténti- am   agén-te.

I say unto you: there is joy among the Angels of God for one single sinner who repents.

Prayer after Communion

SACRAMENTUM caritátis, Dómine, sancta nos fáciat dilectióne fervére, qua, ad Fílium tuum semper attrácti, ipsum in frátribus agnóscere discámus.

FATHER, may this sacrament fill us with love. Draw us closer to Christ your Son and help us to recognize him in others.

ORDINARY TIME

The Sunday of the Baptism of the Lord, p. 221, opens the first week of Ordinary Time.

SECOND SUNDAY

Introit *Ps 65: 4 and 1-2*

O-mnis ter-ra * adó-ret te, De- us, et psal-lat ti- bi: psal- mum di- cat nó- mi- ni tu- o, Al- tís- si- me. *Ps.* Iu-bi-lá-te De-o omnis terra, psalmum dí-ci-te nómi-ni e-ius: da-te gló-ri- am laudi e-ius.

Let all the earth worship you and praise you, O God; may it sing in praise of your name, O Most High. ℣. Shout joyfully to God all the earth; sing a psalm in honour of his name; praise him with magnificence.

Opening Prayer

Omnipotens sempitérne Deus, qui cæléstia simul et terréna moderáris, supplicatiónes pópuli tui cleménter exáudi, et pacem tuam nostris concéde tempóribus.

Father of heaven and earth, hear our prayers, and show us the way to peace in the world.

First reading
A. Is 49 : 3, 5-6 : *The light of the nations.*
B. 1 Sam 3 : 3b-10, 19 : *Speak, O Lord.*
C. Is 62 : 1-5 : *God shall rejoice over you.*

Gradual
Ps 106 : 20, ℣. 21

MIsit Dóminus * verbum suum, et sanávit eos : et erípuit eos de intéritu eórum. ℣. Confiteántur Dómino misericórdiae e-

2nd Sunday

ius : et mirabília eius fíliis hóminum.

The Lord sent forth his word, and healed them, and delivered them from destruction. ℣. Let them thank the Lord for his mercy, for his wondrous works on behalf of the sons of men!

Second reading

- **A.** 1 Cor 1: 1-3: *To you, God's holy people.*
- **B.** 1 Cor 6: 13c-15a, 17-20: *Your bodies are members of Christ.*
- **C.** 1 Cor 12: 4-11: *Your body is the temple of the Holy Spirit.*

Alleluia

Ps 148: 2

Allelúia. ℣. Laudáte Deum omnes ángeli eius : laudáte eum omnes virtútes eius.

Praise God, all his Angels; praise him, all his host.

Ordinary Time

Gospel
A. Jn 1: 29-34: *Behold the Lamb of God.*
B. Jn 1: 35-42: *Come and see.*
C. Jn 2: 1-12: *The marriage feast at Cana.*

Offertory *Ps 65: 1, 2, 16*

Iubiláte * Deo univérsa terra: iubiláte Deo univérsa terra: psalmum dícite nómini eius: veníte, et audíte, et narrábo vobis, omnes qui timétis Deum, quanta fecit Dóminus ánimae meae, allelúia.

2nd Sunday

Sing joyfully to God all the earth; let the entire earth cry out with joy to God; sing a psalm in honour of his name. Come and hear, all you who fear God, and I will tell you what the Lord has done for my soul, alleluia.

Prayer over the Gifts

CONCEDE nobis, quæsumus, Dómine, hæc digne frequentáre mystéria, quia, quóties huius hóstiæ commemorátio celebrátur, opus nostræ redemptiónis exercétur.

FATHER, may we celebrate the eucharist with reverence and love, for when we proclaim the death of the Lord you continue the work of his redemption.

For this and all masses of Sundays in Ordinary Time, the prefaces to be used are found starting on page 59.

Communion A

Lætábimur in salutári tuo, p. 580.

Communion B

Jn 1: 41, 42

VIII

DI- cit André- as * Simó- ni fratri su- o: Invé-nimus Messí- am, qui dí- ci- tur Chri- stus: et addúxit e- um ad Ie-sum.

Andrew said to his brother Simon: "We have found the Messiah" (which means Christ); and he led him to Jesus.

Ordinary Time

Communion C *Jn 2: 7, 8, 9 and 10-11*

DIcit Dóminus : * Impléte hýdrias aqua et ferte architriclíno. Cum gustásset architriclínus aquam vinum factam, dicit sponso : Servásti vinum bonum usque adhuc. Hoc signum fecit Iesus primum coram discípulis suis.

The Lord said : "Fill the jars with water and bring some to the master of the feast." When the master of the feast tasted the water, which had now become wine, he declared to the bridegroom : "You have kept the good wine until now". This was the first sign which Jesus accomplished before his disciples.

Prayer after Communion

SPIRITUM nobis, Dómine, tuæ caritátis infúnde, ut, quos uno cælésti pane satiásti, una fácias pietáte concórdes.

LORD, you have nourished us with bread from heaven. Fill us with your Spirit, and make us one in peace and love.

THIRD SUNDAY

Introit A & B *Mt 4: 18, 19; Ps 18*

DOminus * secus mare Galilææ vidit duos fratres, Petrum et Andréam, et vocávit eos: Veníte post me: fáciam vos fíeri piscatóres hóminum. *Ps.* Cæli enárrant glóriam Dei: et ópera mánuum eius annúntiat firmaméntum.

The Lord, walking by the sea of Galilee, saw two brothers, Peter and Andrew, and he called out to them: "Follow me, and I will make you fishers of men." ℣. The heavens declare the glory of God, and the firmament proclaims the work of his hands.

Ordinary Time

Introrit C *Ps 96: 7, 8 and 1*

Adoráte Deum * omnes ángeli eius: audívit, et laetáta est Sion: et exsultavérunt fíliae Iudae. *Ps.* Dóminus regnávit, exsúltet terra: laeténtur ínsulae multae.

Bow down before God, all you Angels of his. Zion has heard and is glad; and the daughters of Juda have rejoiced. ℣. The Lord reigns, let the earth rejoice; let all the isles be glad.

Opening Prayer

OMNIPOTENS sempitérne Deus, dírige actus nostros in beneplácito tuo, ut in nómine dilécti Fílii tui mereámur bonis opéribus abundáre.

ALL-POWERFUL and ever-living God, direct your love that is within us, that our efforts in the name of your Son may bring mankind to unity and peace.

First reading
A. Is 8: 23-9: 3: *The people have seen a great light.*
B. Jon 3: 1-5, 10: *The people of Nineveh believed God.*
C. Neh 8: 1-4a, 5-6, 8-10: *The reading of the Law of God.*

Gradual *Ps 101: 16, ℣. 17*

Timébunt gentes *nomen tuum,

3rd Sunday

Dómine, et omnes reges terrae glóriam tuam. ℣. Quóniam aedificávit Dóminus Sion, et vidébitur in maiestáte sua.

The nations shall fear your name, O Lord, and all the kings of the earth your glory. ℣. For the Lord has built up Zion, and he shall appear in his majesty.

Second reading

A. 1 Cor 1: 10-13, 17: *Is Christ divided?*
B. 1 Cor 7: 29-31: *This world is passing away.*
C. 1 Cor 12: 12-30 or 12: 12-14, 27: *You are the body of Christ.*

Alleluia   Ps 96: 1

Alleluia. ℣. Dóminus regnávit, exsúltet ter-

Ordinary Time

ra : lae-tén-tur ínsulae mul-tae.

The Lord reigns, let the earth rejoice; let all the isles be glad!

Gospel
- A. Mt 4: 12-23 *or* 4: 12-17: *Repent!*
- B. Mk 1: 14-20: *The kingdom of God is at hand.*
- C. Lk 1: 1-4; 4: 14-21: *Jesus in the synagogue of Nazareth.*

Offertory   Ps 117: 16, 17

D Exte- ra Dómi- ni * fe- cit vir- tú- tem, déx-te-ra Dó- mi-ni exaltá- vit me : non mó-ri- ar, sed vi- vam, et narrábo ó- pe- ra Dómi-ni.

The Lord's right hand has shown strength, the Lord's right hand has exalted me. I shall not die, but live; and I shall declare the works of the Lord.

3rd Sunday

Prayer over the Gifts

Munera nostra, Dómine, súscipe placátus, quæ sanctificándo nobis, quǽsumus, salutária fore concéde.

Lord, receive our gifts. Let our offerings make us holy and bring us salvation.

Communion A & B   *Mt 4: 19, 20*

Veníte post me: * fáciam vos piscatóres hóminum: at illi, relíctis rétibus et navi, secúti sunt Dóminum.

"Follow me; I will make you fishers of men." Whereupon they, leaving their nets and their boat, followed the Lord.

Communion C   *2 Esd 8: 10*

Comédite pínguia, * et bíbite mulsum, et míttite partes eis qui non præparavérunt sibi: sanctus enim dies Dómini est, nolíte contristári: gáudium étenim Dómini est fortitúdo nostra.

Go, eat rich meat, and drink sweet wine, and send portions to those who have prepared nothing for themselves; this is a holy day in honour of the Lord; do not be sad; for the joy of the Lord is our strength.

Prayer after Communion

PRÆSTA nobis, quæsumus, omnípotens Deus, ut, vivificatiónis tuæ grátiam consequéntes, in tuo semper múnere gloriémur.

GOD, all-powerful Father, may the new life you give us increase our love and keep us in the joy of your kingdom.

FOURTH SUNDAY

Introit — Ps 104: 3, 4 and 1

Laetétur cor * quaeréntium Dóminum: quaérite Dóminum, et confirmámini: quaérite fáciem eius semper. *Ps.* Confitémini Dómino, et invocáte nomen eius: annuntiáte inter gentes ópera eius.

4th Sunday

Let the hearts of those who seek the Lord rejoice; seek the Lord and be strengthened; seek his face for evermore. ℣. Give thanks to the Lord and call upon his name; declare his deeds among the gentiles.

Opening Prayer

CONCEDE NOBIS, Dómine Deus noster, ut te tota mente venerémur, et omnes hómines rationábili diligámus afféctu.

LORD our God, help us to love you with all our hearts and to love all men as you love them.

First reading
A. Zeph 2: 3; 3: 12-13: *Seek the Lord.*
B. Deut 18: 15-20: *The prophet of the Lord.*
C. Jer 1: 4-5, 17-19: *The vocation of Jeremiah.*

Gradual — Ps 112: 5, 6, ℣. 7

Quis sic-ut Dó-minus * De-us nos-ter, qui in altis há-bi-tat: humí-li-a réspi-cit in cae-lo et in terra? ℣. Súsci-tans a ter-ra ín-o-pem, et de stérco-re *é- ri-gens páu- pe-rem.*

Who is like the Lord our God who dwells on high and looks down on that which is humble in heaven and on earth? ℣. He raises the needy from the earth and lifts up the poor out of the mire.

Second reading

A. 1 Cor 1: 26-31: *The Lord's choice.*
B. 1 Cor 7: 32-35: *To please the Lord.*
C. 1 Cor 12: 31-13: 13 or 13: 4-13: *In praise of charity.*

Alleluia Ps 137: 2

VII

A L-le- lú- ia.

℣. Ado- rá- bo ad templum san- ctum tu- um : et confi- té- bor nómi- ni tu- o.

I will bow down toward your holy temple and give thanks to your name.

4th Sunday

Gospel
A. Mt 5: 1-12a: *The Beatitudes.*
B. Mk 1: 21-28: *He teaches with authority.*
C. Lk 4: 21-30: *Jesus persecuted in Nazareth.*

Offertory
Ps 91: 2

VIII

BOnum est * confi-té-ri Dómi-no, et psál-le-re nó-mi-ni tu- o, Al-tís-sime.

It is good to give thanks unto the Lord, and to sing in honour of your name, O Most High.

Prayer over the Gifts

ALTARIBUS tuis, Dómine, múnera nostræ servitútis inférimus, quæ, placátus assúmens, sacraméntum nostræ redemptiónis effícias.

LORD, be pleased with the gifts we bring to your altar, and make them the sacrament of our salvation.

Communion A

Beáti mundo corde, *p. 669.*

Communion B & C
Ps 30: 17, 18

I

Ill-lú-mi-na * fá-ci-em tu-am super servum tu- um,

et salvum me fac in tu- a mi- se-ri- córdi- a:

Dó- mi-ne, non confúndar, quó- ni- am invo- cá- vi te.

Let your face shine down upon your servant, deliver me in your mercy. Lord, let me not be confounded, for I have called upon you.

REDEMPTIONIS nostræ múnere vegetáti, quǽsumus, Dómine, ut hoc perpétuæ salútis auxílio fides semper vera profíciat.

LORD, you invigorate us with this help to our salvation. By this eucharist give the true faith continued growth throughout the world.

FIFTH SUNDAY

Introit — Ps 94: 6, 7 and 1

VENÍ-te, * adorémus Deum, et procidámus ante Dóminum: plorémus ante eum, qui fecit nos: qui a ipse est Dóminus

5th Sunday

De- us no- ster. *Ps.* Ve-ní- te, exsul-témus Dómi-no : iu- bi-lémus De- o sa-lu-tá- ri nostro.

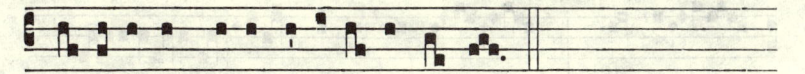

Come, let us worship God and bow down before the Lord; let us shed tears before the Lord who made us, for he is the Lord our God. ℣. Come, let us sing to the Lord; let us make a joyful noise unto God our Saviour.

Opening Prayer

FAMILIAM tuam, quæsumus, Dómine, contínua pietáte custódi, ut, quæ in sola spe grátiæ cæléstis innítitur, tua semper protectióne muniátur.

FATHER, watch over your family and keep us safe in your care, for all our hope is in you.

First reading

A. Is 58: 7-10: *Sharing with the poor.*
B. Job 7: 1-4; 6-7: *The suffering of man on earth.*
C. Is 6: 1-2a; 3-8: *The vocation of Isaiah.*

Gradual A   Ps 111: 9, ℣. 2

DIspérsit, * de- dit paupé- ri- bus : iustí- ti- a e- ius ma- net in saé- cu-lum saé- cu- li.

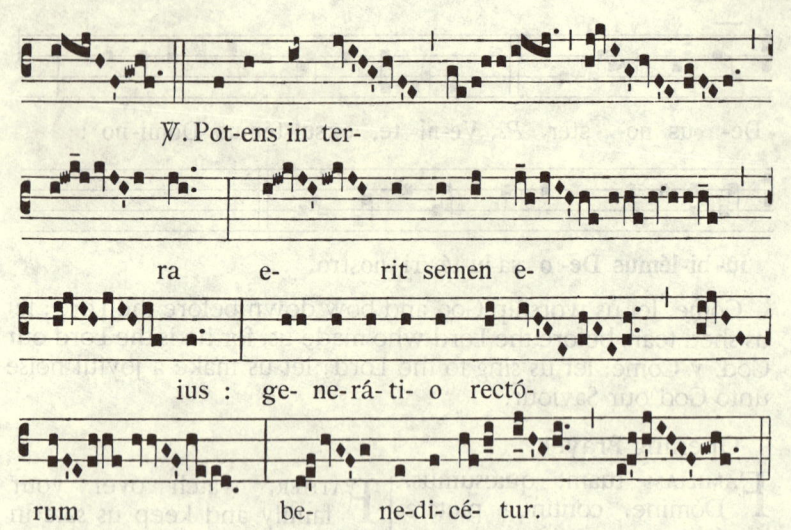

℣. Pot-ens in ter- ra e- rit semen e- ius: ge- ne-rá- ti- o rectó- rum be- ne-di- cé- tur.

He has distributed freely, he has given to the poor; his justice endures for ever and ever. ℣. His seed shall be mighty upon earth; the descendants of the righteous will be blessed.

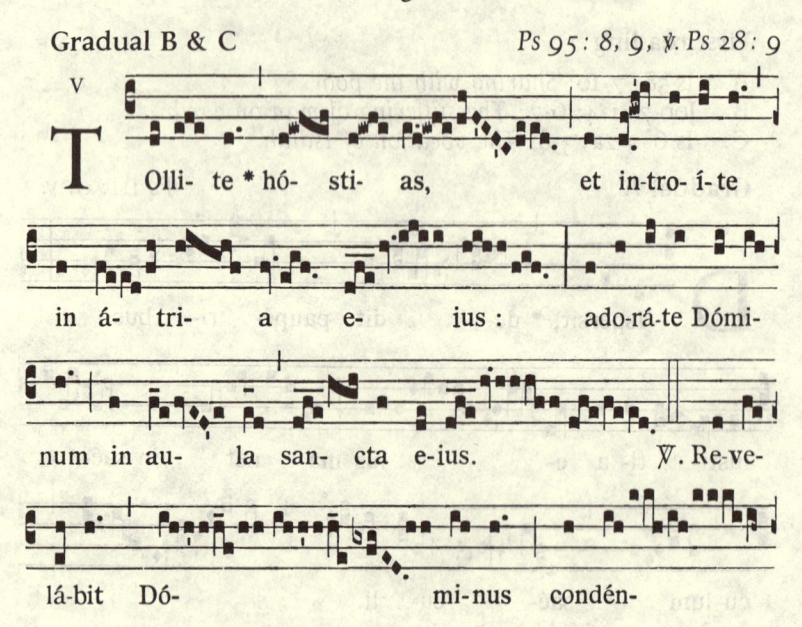

Gradual B & C Ps 95: 8, 9, ℣. Ps 28: 9

Tolli- te * hó- sti- as, et in-tro- í- te in á- tri- a e- ius: ado-rá-te Dómi-num in au- la san-cta e-ius. ℣. Re-ve- lá-bit Dó- mi-nus condén-

...sa: et in templo eius omnes dicent gloriam.

Bring your offerings and come into his courts; worship the Lord in his holy dwelling place. ℣. The Lord shall strip bare the thick forests and in his temple all shall proclaim his glory.

Second reading

A. 1 Cor 2: 1-5: *Preaching Christ crucified.*
B. 1 Cor 9: 16-19, 22-23: *St. Paul, servant to all.*
C. 1 Cor 15: 1-11 or 3-8, 11: *The message of the faith.*

Alleluia — Ps 116: 1

II

Alleluia. ℣. Laudáte Dóminum, omnes gentes: et collaudáte eum, omnes pópuli.

Praise the Lord all nations; praise him in unison, all peoples.

Gospel

A. Mt 5: 13-16: *The salt of the earth and the light of the world.*
B. Mk 1: 29-39: *Jesus' preaching.*
C. Lk 5: 1-11: *The miraculous catch of fish.*

Ordinary Time

Offertory   Ps 16 : 5, 6, 7

Perfice * gressus meos in sémitis tuis, ut non moveántur vestígia mea: inclína aurem tuam, et exáudi verba mea: mirífica misericórdias tuas, qui salvos facis sperántes in te, Dómine.

Render secure my footsteps in your paths so that my feet do not slip; incline your ear and hear my words; display your wonderful mercies, O Lord, Saviour of those who place their hope in you.

Prayer over the Gifts

Dómine Deus noster, qui has pótius creatúras ad fragilitátis nostræ subsídium condidísti, tríbue, quæsumus, ut étiam æternitátis nobis fiant sacraméntum.

Lord our God, may the bread and wine you give us for our nourishment on earth become the sacrament of our eternal life.

5th Sunday

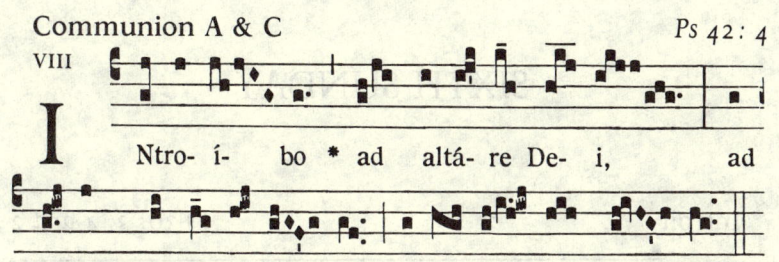

Communion A & C — Ps 42:4

INtroíbo * ad altáre Dei, ad Deum qui laetíficat iuventútem meam.

I will go in to the altar of God, to the God who gives joy to my youth.

Communion B — Lk 6:17, 18, 19

MUltitúdo * languéntium, et qui vexabántur a spirítibus immúndis, veniébant ad eum: quia virtus de illo exíbat, et sanábat omnes.

A multitude with diseases, and those who were troubled by unclean spirits, came unto him, because a power emanated from him which healed them all.

Prayer after Communion

DEUS, qui nos de uno pane et de uno cálice partícipes esse voluísti, da nobis, quaésumus, ita vívere, ut, unum in Christo effécti, fructum afferámus pro mundi salúte gaudéntes.

GOD OUR FATHER, you give us a share in the one bread and the one cup and make us one in Christ. Help us to bring your salvation and joy to all the world.

SIXTH SUNDAY

Introit *Ps 30: 3, 4 and 2*

IV

E-sto mi-hi * in De- um pro- te-ctó- rem, et

in lo-cum re- fú-gi- i, ut salvum me fá-ci- as :

quó-ni- am firmaméntum me- um, et re-fú-gi- um me- um

es tu : et pro-pter nomen tu- um dux mi- hi e- ris,

et e-nú- tri- es me. *Ps.* In te Dómi-ne spe-rávi, non confún

dar in aetérnum : in iustí- ti- a tu-a lí- be-ra me.

Be unto me a protecting God and a house of refuge, to save me; for you are my support and my refuge; and for the sake of your name you will lead me and nourish me. ℣. In you O Lord, do I trust; let me never be put to shame; deliver me in your righteousness.

6th Sunday

Opening Prayer

DEUS, qui te in rectis et sínceris manére pectóribus ásseris, da nobis tua grátia tales exsístere, in quibus habitáre dignéris.

GOD OUR FATHER, you have promised to remain for ever with those who do what is just and right. Help us to live in your presence.

First reading

A. Sir 15: 15-20: *The proposed choice.*
B. Lev 13: 1-2, 44-46: *The rejection of lepers.*
C. Jer 17: 5-8: *An invitation to trust in the Lord.*

Gradual
Ps 76: 15, ℣. 16

Tū es * Deus, qui facis mirabília solus: notam fecísti in géntibus virtútem tuam. ℣. Liberásti in bráchio tuo pópulum tuum, fí-li-os Isra-el et Io-seph.

You alone are the God who works wonders; you manifested your strength among the nations. ℣. With your arm you delivered your people, the sons of Israel and Joseph.

Second reading

A. 1 Cor 2: 6-10: *The wisdom of the mystery of God.*
B. 1 Cor 10: 31-11: 1: *Do everything for the glory of God.*
C. 1 Cor 15: 12, 16-20: *Christ, the first of the risen.*

Alleluia Ps 97: 1

A-lle- lú- ia. ℣. Cantá- te Dó- mi-no cán- ti-cum nó- vum: qui- a mi-ra- bí- li-a fe- cit Dó- mi-nus.

Sing to the Lord a new song; for the Lord has accomplished wondrous deeds.

6th Sunday

Gospel
A. Mt 5: 17-37: *As for me, I say to you...*
B. Mk 1: 40-45: *The healing of a leper.*
C. Lk 6: 17, 20-26: *The Beatitudes.*

Offertory — Ps 118: 12, 13

III

Bene-dí-ctus es Dómi-ne, * do-ce me iusti-fi-ca-ti-ó-nes tu-as : be-ne-dí-ctus es Dómi-ne, do-ce me iusti-fi-ca-ti-ó-nes tu-as : in lábi-is me-is pronunti-á-vi ómni-a iudí-ci-a o-ris tu-i.

Blessed are you, O Lord, teach me your commandments. O Lord, you are blessed, teach me your commandments. With my lips have I declared all the judgments spoken by your mouth.

Prayer over the Gifts

Hæc nos oblátio, quæsumus, Dómine, mundet et rénovet, atque tuam exsequéntibus voluntátem fiat causa remuneratiónis ætérnæ.

Lord, we make this offering in obedience to your word. May it cleanse and renew us, and lead us to our eternal reward.

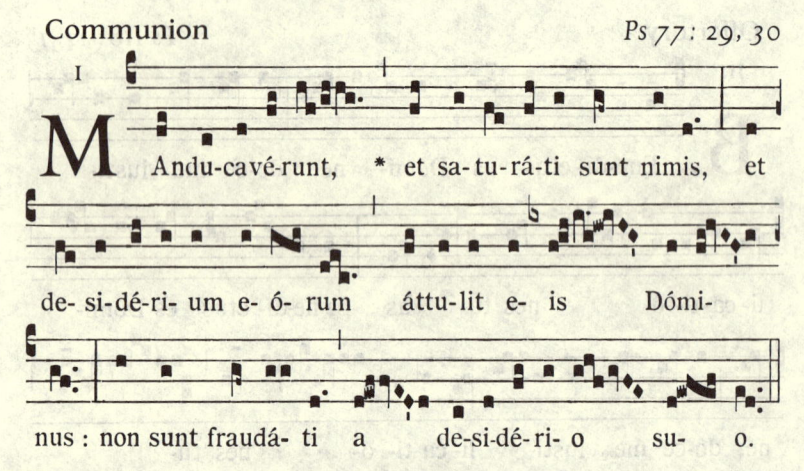

Communion
Ps 77: 29, 30

Mandu-cavé-runt, * et sa-tu-rá-ti sunt nimis, et de-si-dé-ri- um e- ó- rum áttu-lit e- is Dómi-nus: non sunt fraudá- ti a de-si-dé-ri- o su- o.

They ate and were fully satisfied; the Lord gave them all that they desired; they were not deprived of their wants.

Prayer after Communion

Cæléstibus, Dómine, pasti delíciis, quæsumus, ut semper éadem, per quæ veráciter vívimus, appetámus.

Lord, you give us food from heaven. May we always hunger for the bread of life.

SEVENTH SUNDAY

Introit   *Ps 12: 6 and 1*

Dómine, * in tua misericórdia sperávi: exsultávit cor meum in salutári tuo: cantábo Dómino, qui bona tríbuit mihi. *Ps.* Usquequo Dómine obliviscéris me in finem? úsquequo avértis fáciem tuam a me?

O Lord, I have placed my trust in your merciful love; my heart has rejoiced in your salvation. I will sing unto the Lord who has dealt bountifully with me. ℣. How long will you forget me, O Lord? For ever? How long will you hide your countenance from me?

Opening Prayer

PRÆSTA, quæsumus, omnípotens Deus, ut, semper rationabília meditántes, quæ tibi sunt plácita, et dictis exsequámur et factis.

FATHER, keep before us the wisdom and love you have revealed in your Son. Help us to be like him in word and deed.

Ordinary Time

First reading
A. Lev 19: 1-2, 17-18: *You shall be holy, because I am holy.*
B. Is 43: 18-19, 21-22, 24b-25: *Behold, I am creating a new world.*
C. 1 Sam 26: 2, 7-9, 12-13, 22-23: *David refuses to avenge himself.*

Gradual   Ps 40: 5, ℣. 2

Ego * dixi: Dómine, miserére mei: sana ánimam meam, quóniam peccávi tibi. ℣. Beátus qui intélligit super egénum et páuperem: in die mala liberábit eum Dóminus.

7th Sunday

I said: "Lord, have mercy on me; heal my soul because I have sinned against you." ℣. Blessed is he who considers the needy and the poor; the Lord will deliver him on the day of evil.

Second reading

A. 1 Cor 3: 16-23: *You are the temple of God.*
B. 2 Cor 1: 18-22: *The seal of God upon us.*
C. 1 Cor 15: 45-49: *Christ, the leader of a renewed humanity.*

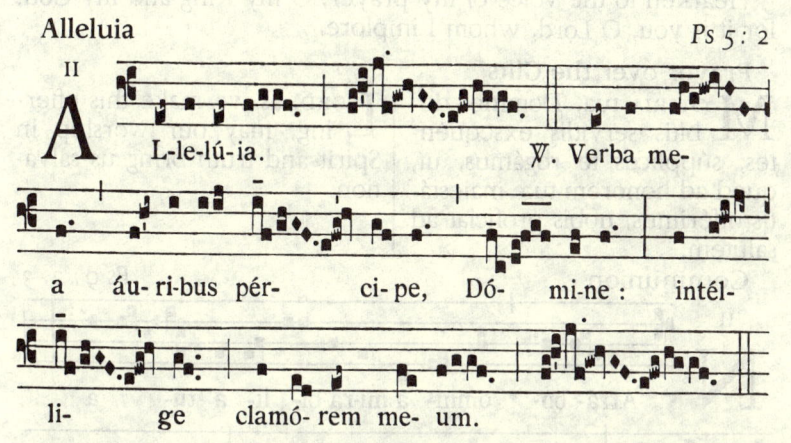

Alleluia   Ps 5: 2

A-lle-lú-ia. ℣. Verba me-a áu-ri-bus pér-ci-pe, Dómine: intél-li-ge clamórem me-um.

Lend ear to my words, O Lord; consider my cry.

Gospel

A. Mt 5: 38-48: *Be perfect.*
B. Mk 2: 1-12: *The paralytic of Capernaum.*
C. Lk 6: 27-38: *Be merciful.*

Offertory   Ps 5: 3, 4

INténde * voci orati-ónis meae, Rex meus, et De-us me-

Ordinary Time

... us: quó- ni- am ad te o-rá-bo, Dó- mi- ne.

Hearken to the voice of my prayer, O my King and my God, for it is you, O Lord, whom I implore.

Prayer over the Gifts

Mystéria tua, Dómine, débitis servítiis exsequéntes, súpplices te rogámus, ut, quod ad honórem tuæ maiestátis offérimus, nobis profíciat ad salútem.

Lord, as we make this offering, may our worship in Spirit and truth bring us salvation.

Communion
Ps 9 : 2, 3

Narrá- bo * ómni- a mi-ra-bí- li- a tu- a: laetá- bor, et exsultá- bo in te: psal- lam nómi-ni tu- o, Al- tíssi- me.

I will relate all your wondrous deeds. I will be glad and rejoice in you; I will sing to the honour of your name, O Most High.

Prayer after communion

Præsta, quæsumus, omnípotens Deus, ut illíus salútis capiámus efféctum, cuius per hæc mystéria pignus accépimus.

Almighty God, help us to live the example of love we celebrate in this eucharist, that we may come to its fulfilment in your presence.

EIGHTH SUNDAY

Introit   *Ps 17: 19, 20 and 2-3*

F Actus est Dómi-nus * pro- té- ctor me- us, et e- dú-xit me in la- ti- tú-di- nem : salvum me fe- cit, quó-ni- am vó- lu- it me. *Ps.* Dí- li-gam te Dómi-ne forti-túdo me- a : Dó-mi-nus firmaméntum me- um, et re-fúgi- um me- um, et li-be- rá-tor me- us.

The Lord has become my protector; he has brought me forth into free and open spaces; he delivered me because he was well pleased with me. ℣. I will love you always, O Lord my strength; the Lord is my support, my refuge and my deliverer.

Opening Prayer

DA NOBIS, quæsumus, Dómine, ut et mundi cursus pacífico nobis tuo órdine dirigátur, et Ecclésia tua tranquílla devotióne lætétur.

LORD, guide the course of world events and give your Church the joy and peace of serving you in freedom.

Ordinary Time

First reading
A. Is 49: 14-15: *The Lord is more loving than a mother.*
B. Hos 2: 16b, 17b, 21-22: *The word of the Lord to his betrothed.*
C. Sir 27: 4-7: *A man's authentic worth.*

Gradual A & B *Ps 119: 1, ℣. 2*

AD Dóminum, *dum tribulárer, clamávi, et exaudívit me. ℣. Dómine, líbera ánimam meam a lábiis iníquis, et a lingua dolósa.

In my distress I cried to the Lord and he heard me. ℣. O Lord, deliver my soul from wicked lips and from a deceitful tongue.

Gradual C: Bonum est confitéri, p. 533.

8th Sunday

Second reading
A. 1 Cor 4: 1-5: *The Lord is my judge.*
B. 2 Cor 3: 1b-6: *Christians are God's message to the world.*
C. 1 Cor 15: 54-58: *God's victory over death.*

Alleluia   Ps 7: 2

Al-le-lú-ia.

℣. Dómine Deus meus, in te sperávi: salvum me fac ex ómnibus persequéntibus me, et líbera me.

O Lord my God, I have put my trust in you; save me from all those who persecute me, and deliver me.

Gospel
A. Mt 6: 24-34: *The Father's concern for his children.*
B. Mk 2: 18-22: *The presence of Christ, the bridegroom.*
C. Lk 6: 39-45: *The blind guide.*

Ordinary Time

Offertory   Ps 6 : 5

VI

DOmine *convértere, et éripe ánimam meam: salvum me fac propter misericórdiam tuam.

Turn to me, O Lord, and deliver my soul; save me for the sake of your love.

Prayer over the Gifts

DEUS, qui offerénda tuo nómini tríbuis, et obláta devotióni nostræ servitútis ascríbis, quǽsumus cleméntiam tuam, ut, quod præstas unde sit méritum, profícere nobis largiáris ad præmium.

GOD OUR CREATOR, may this bread and wine we offer as a sign of our love and worship lead us to salvation.

Communion A

Primum quǽrite, *p. 531.*

Communion B & C   Ps 12 : 6

II

CAntábo Dómino, *qui bona tríbuit mihi: et psallam nómini Dómini al- tíssi- mi.

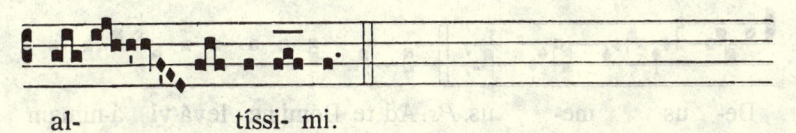

I will sing unto the Lord who has dealt bountifully with me; I will praise the name of the Lord, the Most High.

Prayer after Communion

Satiati múnere salutári, tuam, Dómine, misericórdiam deprecámur, ut, hoc eódem quo nos temporáliter végetas sacraménto, perpétuæ vitæ partícipes benígnus effícias.

God of salvation, may this sacrament which strengthens us here on earth bring us to eternal life.

NINTH SUNDAY

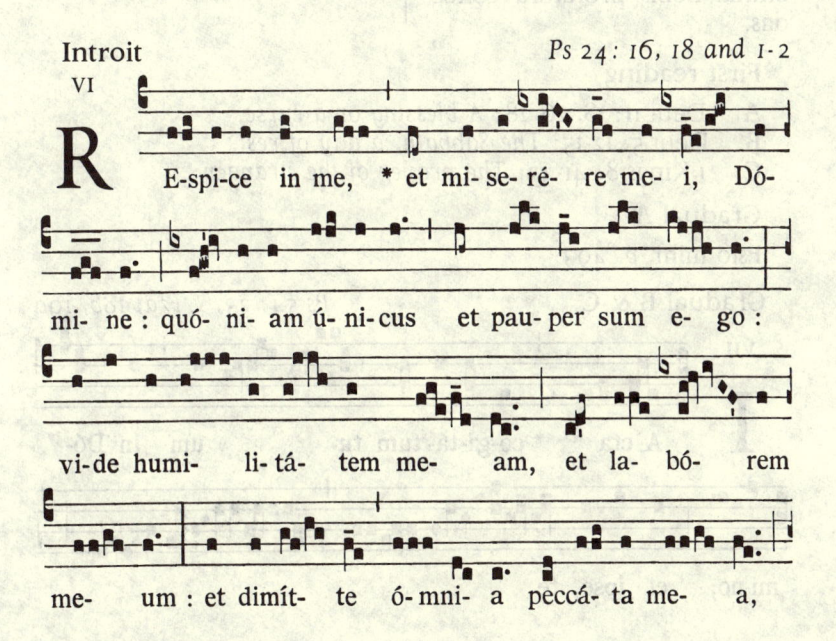

Introit — Ps 24: 16, 18 and 1-2

Respice in me, * et miserére mei, Dómine: quóniam únicus et pauper sum ego: vide humilitátem meam, et labórem meum: et dimítte ómnia peccáta mea,

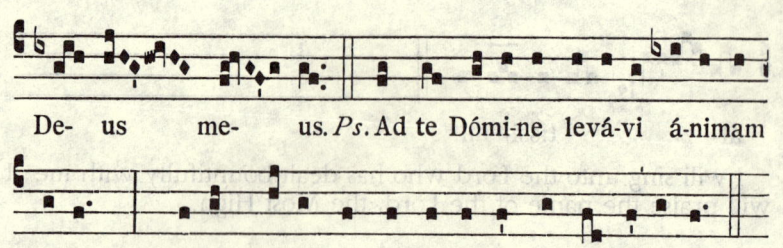

Ordinary Time

De- us me- us. Ps. Ad te Dómine levávi ánimam meam : Deus meus, in te confído, non erubéscam.

Look upon me and have mercy on me, O Lord; for I am abandoned and destitute; consider my abjection and my labour, and forgive me all my sins, my dear God. ℣. Unto you, O Lord, have I lifted up my soul; O my God, I trust in you; let me not be put to shame.

Opening Prayer

DEUS, cuius providéntia in sui dispositióne non fállitur, te súpplices exorámus, ut nóxia cuncta submóveas, et ómnia nobis profutúra concédas.

FATHER, your love never fails. Hear our call. Keep us from danger and provide for all our needs.

First reading

A. Deut 11: 18, 26-28: *A blessing or a curse.*
B. Deut 5: 12-15: *The Sabbath, a day of rest.*
C. 1 Kings 8: 41-43: *The prayer of the stranger.*

Gradual A

Esto mihi, p. 493.

Gradual B & C

Ps 54: 23, ℣. 17a, 18b, 19a

*I Acta * cogitátum tuum in Dómino, et ipse te*

9th Sunday

e- nútri- et. ℣. Dum cla-má-rem ad Dómi-num, exau-dí-vit vo- cem me- am ab his qui appro-pínquant mi- hi.

Cast your cares upon the Lord, and he shall sustain you.
℣. When I cried out to the Lord, he heeded my call against my assailants.

Second reading

A. Rom 3: 21-25a, 28: *Salvation through faith.*
B. 2 Cor 4: 6-11: *The life of Jesus manifested in us.*
C. Gal 1: 1-2, 6-10: *The unique Gospel.*

Alleluia

Ps 7 : 12

VIII

A L-le-lú- ia. ℣. De- us iu- dex iustus, for- tis et pá-ti- ens : numquid i- ra- scé-tur per síngu- los di- es?

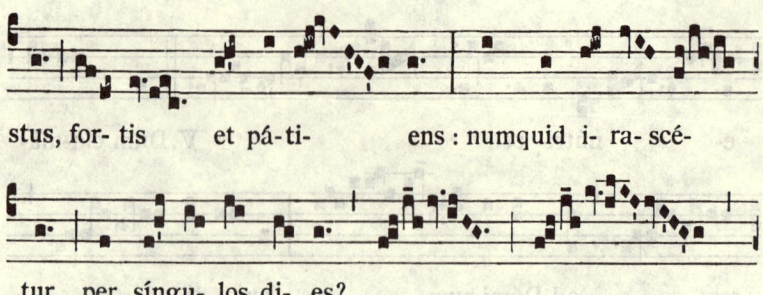

God is a just judge, strong and patient. Could he remain in anger continually?

Gospel
A. Mt 7: 21-27: *To accomplish the will of the Father.*
B. Mk 2: 23-3: 6 *or* 2: 23-28: *Jesus is Lord of the Sabbath.*
C. Lk 7: 1-10: *The centurion's faith.*

Offertory Ps 9: 11, 12, 13

S Pe- rent in te * omnes, qui no- vé- runt no- men tu- um, Dómi- ne : quó- ni- am non de- re- línquis quaerén- tes te : psál- li- te

9th Sunday

Dómino, qui hábitat in Sion: quóniam non est oblítus oratiónem páuperum.

Let those who know your name trust in you, O Lord; for you do not abandon those who seek you. Sing psalms to the Lord who dwells in Zion; for he does not forget the cry of the poor.

Prayer over the Gifts

IN TUA PIETATE confidéntes, Dómine, cum munéribus ad altária veneránda concúrrimus, ut, tua purificánte nos grátia, iísdem quibus famulámur mystériis emundémur.

LORD, as we gather to offer our gifts confident in your love, make us holy by sharing your life with us and by this eucharist forgive our sins.

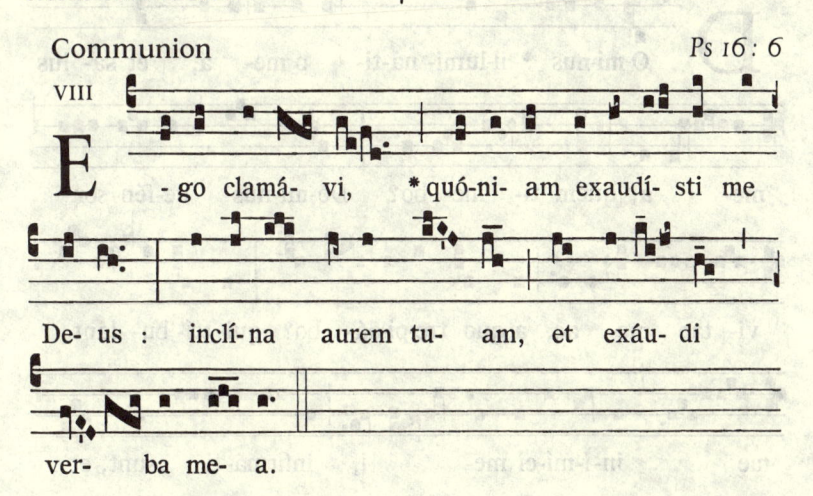

Communion
Ps 16: 6

*Ego clamávi, *quóniam exaudísti me Deus: inclína aurem tuam, et exáudi verba mea.*

I have called out because you hear me, O God; incline your ear and hear my words.

Or: Amen dico vobis: Quidquid, p. 596.

Prayer after Communion

R<small>EGE</small> <small>NOS</small> Spíritu tuo, quǽsumus, Dómine, quos pascis Fílii tui Córpore et Sánguine, ut te, non solum verbo neque lingua, sed ópere et veritáte confiténtes, intráre mereámur in regnum cælórum.

L<small>ORD</small>, as you give us the body and blood of your Son, guide us with your Spirit that we may honour you not only with our lips, but also with the lives we lead, and so enter your kingdom.

TENTH SUNDAY

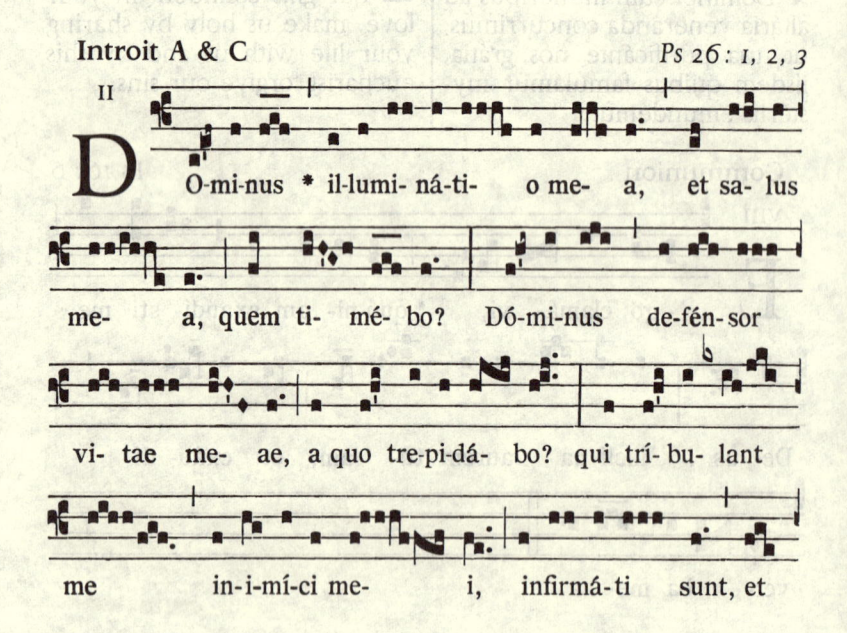

Introit A & C *Ps 26: 1, 2, 3*

DOminus * illumi- náti- o me- a, et sa- lus me- a, quem ti- mé- bo? Dóminus de- fén- sor vi- tae me- ae, a quo trepi-dá- bo? qui tríbu- lant me in-i-míci me- i, infirmá- ti sunt, et

10th Sunday

ce-ci-dé-runt. Ps. Si consístant advérsum me castra: non timébit cor me-um.

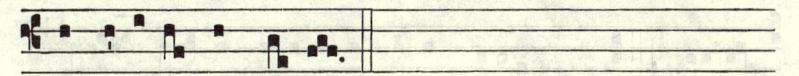

The Lord is my light and my salvation, whom shall I fear? The Lord is the protector of my life, of whom shall I be afraid? My enemies who trouble me have themselves grown weak and have fallen. ℣. Though a host encamp against me, my heart shall not fear.

Introit B

Si iniquitátes, p. 566.

Opening Prayer

Deus, a quo bona cuncta procédunt, tuis largíre supplícibus, ut cogitémus, te inspiránte, quæ recta sunt, et, te gubernánte, éadem faciámus.

God of wisdom and love, source of all good, send your Spirit to teach us your truth and guide our actions in your way of peace.

First reading

A. Hos 6: 3-6: *God's desire.*
B. Gen 3: 9-15: *After the fall.*
C. 1 Kings 17: 17-24: *The widow of Zarephath.*

Gradual A & B   Ps 78: 9c, 10a, ℣. 9ab

*Propítius esto * Dómine peccátis nostris: ne quando dicant gentes:*

U- bi est De- us e- ó- rum?

℣. Adiuva nos, De- us sa-lu-tá-ris noster:

et propter honó-rem nómi-nis tu- i Dómi-ne, lí- be-ra nos.

Lord, forgive us our sins, lest they should say among the Gentiles: "Where is their God?" ℣. Help us, O God, our Saviour, and for the sake of your name deliver us, O Lord.

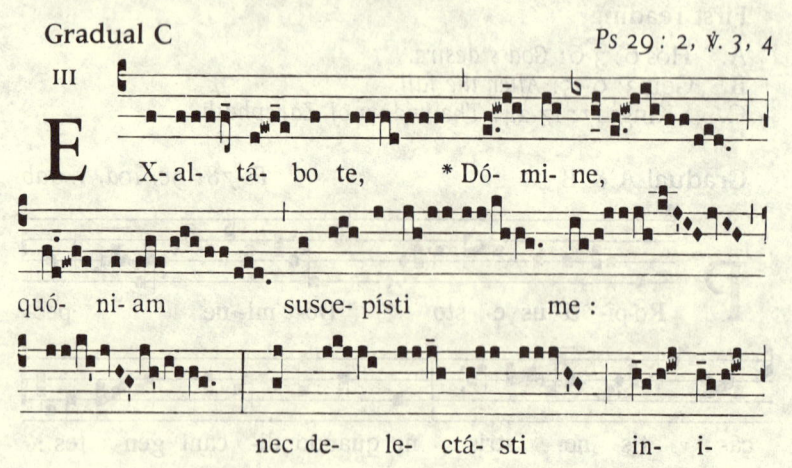

Gradual C Ps 29 : 2, ℣. 3, 4

III

E X- al- tá- bo te, * Dó- mi- ne,

quó- ni- am susce- písti me:

nec de- le- ctá- sti in- i-

10th Sunday

mí- cos me- os su-per me. ℣. Dómine Deus meus, clamávi ad te, et sanásti me: Dómine, abstraxísti ab ínferis ánimam meam, salvásti me a descendénti- bus in la- cum.

I will extol you, O Lord, for you have drawn me up and have not allowed my enemies to rejoice over me. ℣. O Lord, my God, I called out unto you and you have healed me; O Lord, you have brought back my soul from hell; you have delivered me from among those who go down into the pit.

Second reading
A. Rom 4: 18-25: *The example of Abraham.*
B. 2 Cor 4: 13-5: 1: *The power of faith.*
C. Gal 1: 11-19: *The conversion of St. Paul.*

Alleluia Ps 9: 5, 10

A-lle-lú-ia.

℣. De- us, qui se- des super thro- num, et iú-di-cas aequi-tá-tem: e-sto re-fúgi- um páu- pe- rum in tri-bu-la-ti-ó- ne.

10th Sunday

O God, you sit on your throne and judge with righteousness; deign to be a refuge for the poor in their distress.

Gospel
A. Mt 9: 9-13: *Jesus has come to call sinners.*
B. Mk 3: 20-35: *Satan is expelled.*
C. Lk: 7: 11-17: *The son of the widow of Naïm.*

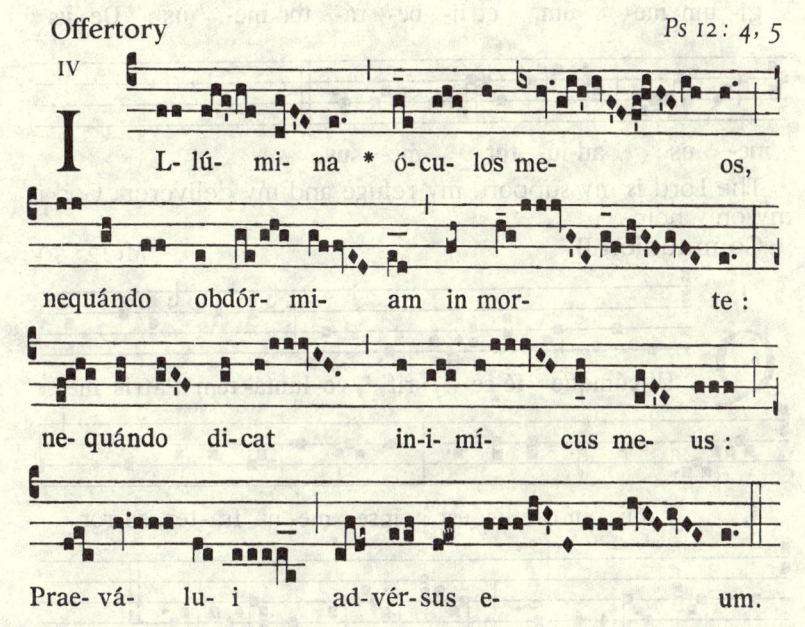

Offertory
Ps 12: 4, 5

IV

ILlúmina * óculos meos, nequándo obdórmiam in morte: ne quándo dicat inimícus meus: Praeválui advérsus eum.

Enlighten my eyes lest I fall into the sleep of death; lest my enemy say: "I have prevailed against him."

Prayer over the Gifts

Respice, Dómine, quæsumus, nostram propítius servitútem, ut quod offérimus sit tibi munus accéptum, et nostræ caritátis augméntum.

Lord, look with love on our service. Accept the gifts we bring and help us grow in Christian love.

Ordinary Time

Communion A & C — Ps 17 : 3

DOminus * firmaméntum meum, et refúgium meum, et liberátor meus: Deus meus adiútor meus.

The Lord is my support, my refuge and my deliverer; God is my only help.

Communion B — Mt 12 : 50

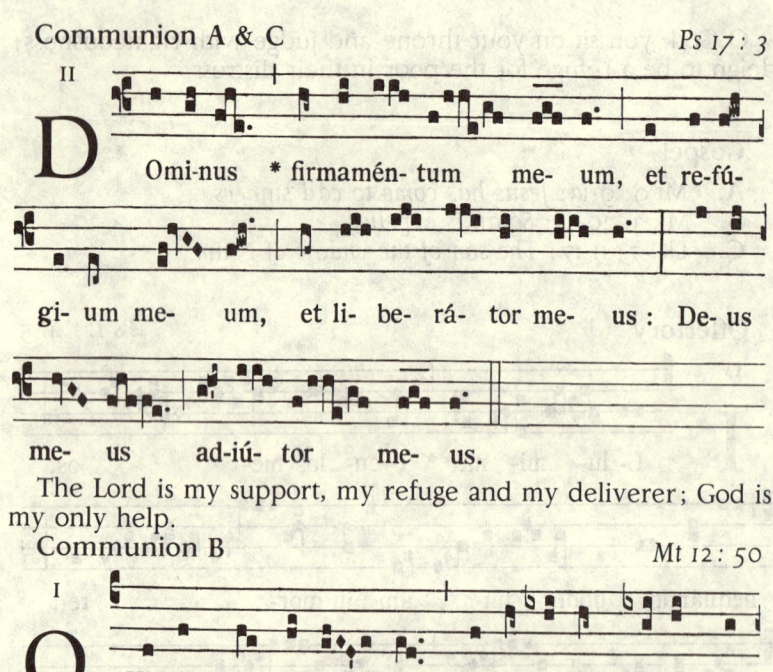

QUicúmque fécerit * voluntátem Patris mei, qui in caelis est: ipse meus frater, soror, et mater est, dicit Dóminus.

Whosoever does the will of my Father in heaven is my brother, my sister and my mother, says the Lord.

Prayer after communion

Tua nos, Dómine, medicinális operátio, et a nostris perversitátibus cleménter expédiat, et ad ea quæ sunt recta perdúcat.

Lord, may your healing love turn us from sin and keep us on the way that leads to you.

ELEVENTH SUNDAY

Introit Ps 26: 7, 9 and 1

IV

EX-áudi Dómine * vocem meam, qua clamávi ad te: adiútor meus esto, ne derelínquas me neque despícias me, Deus salutáris meus. *Ps.* Dóminus illuminátio mea, et salus mea: quem timébo?

Hearken, O Lord, unto my voice which has called out to you; deign to be my help, forsake me not, do not despise me, O God my Saviour. ℣. The Lord is my light and my salvation; whom shall I fear?

Opening Prayer

Deus, in te sperántium fortitúdo, invocatiónibus nostris adésto propítius, et, quia sine te nihil potest mortális infírmitas, grátiæ tuæ præsta semper auxílium, ut, in exsequéndis mandátis tuis, et voluntáte tibi et actióne placeámus.

Almighty god, our hope and our strength, without you we falter. Help us to follow Christ and to live according to your will.

Ordinary Time

First reading
A. Ex 19: 2-6a: *God chose Israel.*
B. Ezek 17: 22-24: *The chosen branch.*
C. 2 Sam: 12: 7-10, 13: *God forgives David.*

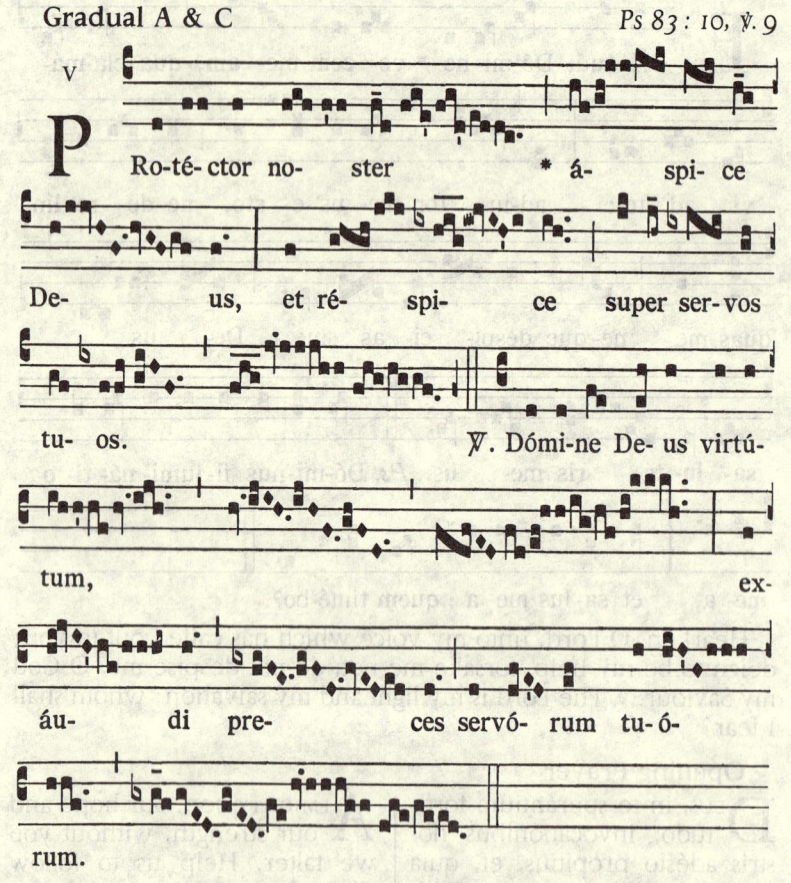

Gradual A & C Ps 83: 10, ℣. 9

Protéctor noster * áspice Deus, et réspice super servos tuos. ℣. Dómine Deus virtútum, exáudi preces servórum tuórum.

Behold, O God our protector, and look down upon your servants. ℣. O Lord God of hosts, hear the prayers of your servants.

Gradual B: Bonum est confitéri, p. 533.

11th Sunday

Second reading
A. Rom 5: 6-11: *Christ died for us.*
B. 2 Cor 5: 6-10: *To please the Lord.*
C. Gal 2: 16, 19-21: *Christ lives in me.*

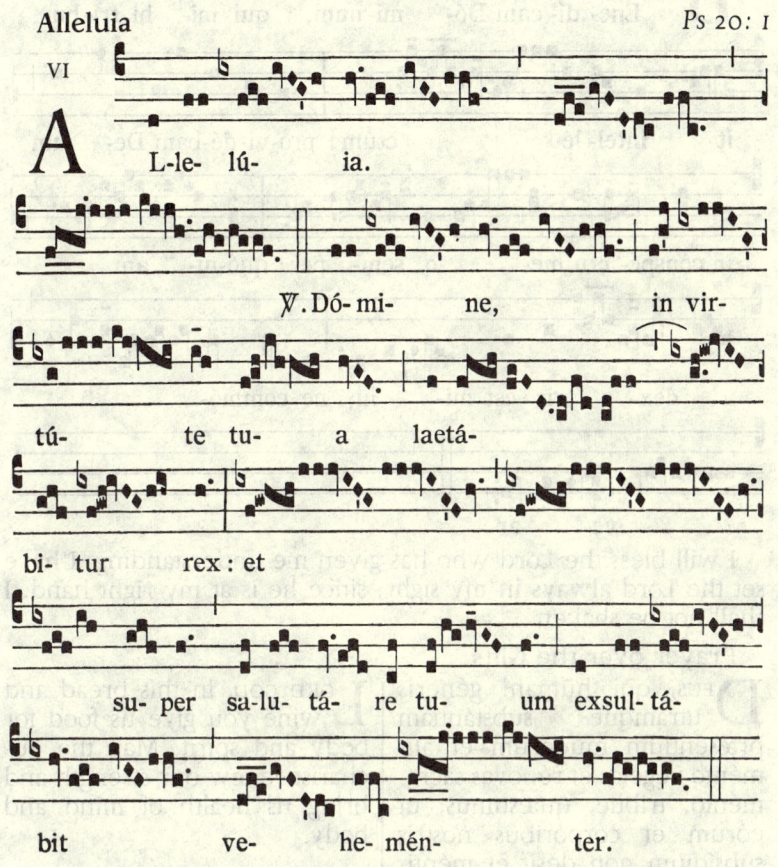

Alleluia Ps 20: 1

A-lle-lú-ia. ℣. Dómine, in virtúte tua laetábitur rex: et super salutáre tuum exsultábit veheménter.

The King shall rejoice in your strength, O Lord, and in your salvation shall he be exceedingly joyful.

Gospel
A. Mt 9: 36 - 10: 8: *The Apostles sent on a mission.*
B. Mk 4: 26-34: *Two parables of the kingdom.*
C. Lk 7: 36 - 8: 3 or 7: 36-50: *A woman's sins are forgiven.*

Offertory — Ps 15: 7, 8

*Benedícam Dóminum, * qui mihi tríbuit intelléctum: providébam Deum in conspéctu meo semper: quóniam a dextris est mihi, ne commovéar.*

I will bless the Lord who has given me understanding. I have set the Lord always in my sight; since he is at my right hand, I shall not be shaken.

Prayer over the Gifts

DEUS, qui humáni géneris utrámque substántiam præséntium múnerum et aliménto végetas et rénovas sacraménto, tríbue, quæsumus, ut eórum et corpóribus nostris subsídium non desit et méntibus.

LORD GOD, in this bread and wine you give us food for body and spirit. May the eucharist renew our strength and bring us health of mind and body.

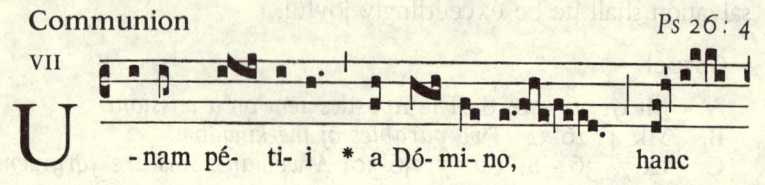

Communion — Ps 26: 4

*Unam pétii * a Dómino, hanc*

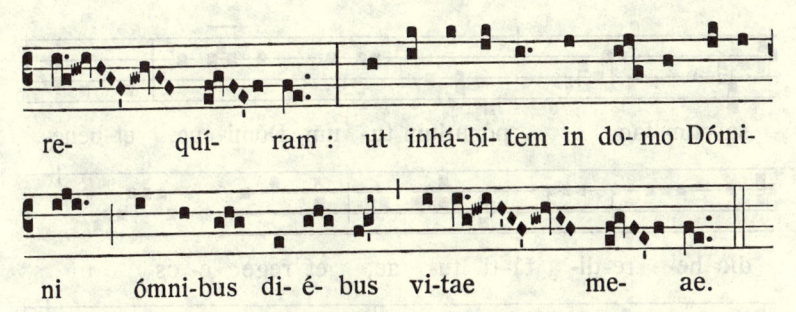

...re- quí- ram: ut inhá-bi-tem in do-mo Dómi-ni ómni-bus di-é-bus vi-tae me- ae.

One thing have I asked of the Lord, this will I seek after: that I may dwell in the house of the Lord all the days of my life.

Prayer after Communion

Hæc tua, Dómine, sumpta sacra commúnio, sicut fidélium in te uniónem præsígnat, sic in Ecclésia tua unitátis operétur efféctum.

Lord, may this eucharist accomplish in your Church the unity and peace it signifies.

TWELFTH SUNDAY

Introit
Ps 27: 8, 9 and 1

DOmi-nus * for-ti-túdo ple-bis su- ae, et protéctor sa- lu-tá- ri- um Chri-sti su- i est:

salvum fac pópulum tuum, Dómine, et benedic hereditáti tuae, et rege eos usque in saéculum. Ps. *Ad te Dómine clamábo, Deus meus ne síleas a me: nequándo táceas a me, et assimilábor descendéntibus in lacum.*

The Lord is the strength of his people, and the guardian of salvation for his Anointed. Save your people, O Lord, and bless your inheritance; be their guide for ever. ℣. Unto you, O Lord, will I cry; O my God, be not silent with me; if you remain silent, I will become like those who go down into the grave.

Opening Prayer

SANCTI nóminis tui, Dómine, timórem páriter et amórem fac nos habére perpétuum, quia numquam tua gubernatióne destítuis, quos in soliditáte tuæ dilectiónis institúis.

FATHER, guide and protector of your people, grant us an unfailing respect for your name, and keep us always in your love.

First reading

A. Jer 20: 10-13: *The Lord who rescues.*
B. Job 38: 1, 8-11: *God, the Lord of Creation.*
C. Zech 12: 10-11: *To gaze on the one who has been pierced.*

12th Sunday

Gradual — Ps 89: 13, ℣. 1

Convértere *Dómine aliquántulum, et deprecáre super servos tuos. ℣. Dómine refúgium factus es nobis, a generatióne et progénie.

Turn back, O Lord, ever so slightly, we beseech you, and consent to be entreated by your servants. ℣. O Lord, you have been unto us a refuge, from age to age.

Second reading
A. Rom 5: 12-15: *Solidarity in sin and grace.*
B. 2 Cor 5: 14-17: *The new world.*
C. Gal 3: 26-29: *Union through baptism.*

Alleluia — Ps 30: 2, 3

Allelúia.

℣. In te Dómine sperávi, non confúndar in aetérnum: in tua iustítia líbera me, et éripe me: inclína ad me aurem tuam, accélera ut erípias me.

In you, Lord, do I trust, let me never be put to shame; in your righteousness deliver me and rescue me; lend me your ear and make haste to save me.

Gospel
A. Mt 10: 26-33: *Fear not.*
B. Mk 4: 35-41: *The calming of a tempest.*
C. Lk 9: 18-24: *Carry the Cross each day.*

Offertory
Ps 16: 5, 6, 7

IV

PErfice * gressus meos in sémitis tuis, ut non moveántur vestígia

12th Sunday

...me- a: incli- na au- rem tu- am, et exáudi verba me- a: mi-rí- fi-ca mi- se-ri-córdi- as tu- as, qui salvos fa-cis spe- rántes in te, Dómi- ne.

Render secure my footsteps in your paths so that my feet do not slip; incline your ear and hear my words; display your wonderful mercies O Lord, Saviour of those who place their hope in you.

Prayer over the Gifts

SUSCIPE, Dómine, sacrifícium placatiónis et laudis, et præsta, ut, huius operatióne mundáti, beneplácitum tibi nostræ mentis offerámus afféctum.

LORD, receive our offering, and may this sacrifice of praise purify us in mind and heart and make us always eager to serve you.

Communion A
Mt 10: 27

*Quod di-co vo-bis * in ténebris, dí-ci-te in lúmi-ne, di-cit Dómi-nus: et quod in aure audí-tis, praedi-cá-te super te- cta.*

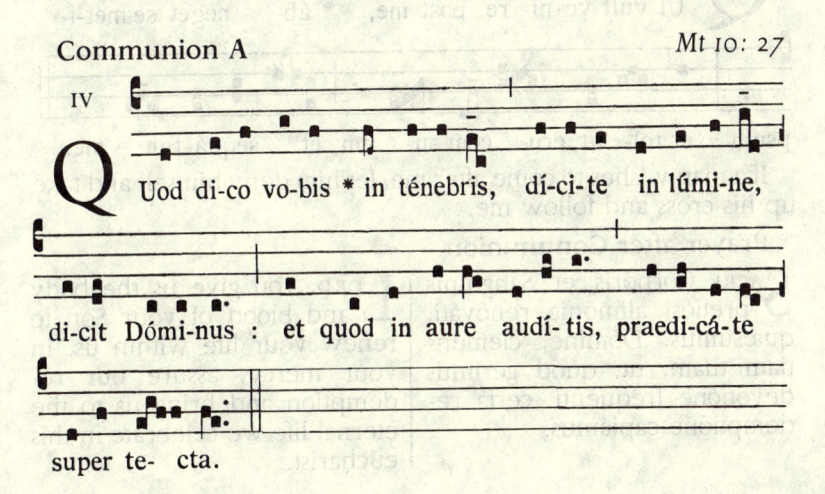

"That which I tell you in the dark, utter in the light", says the Lord; "and that which you hear whispered into your ear, proclaim upon the housetops".

Communion B — Ps 26 : 6

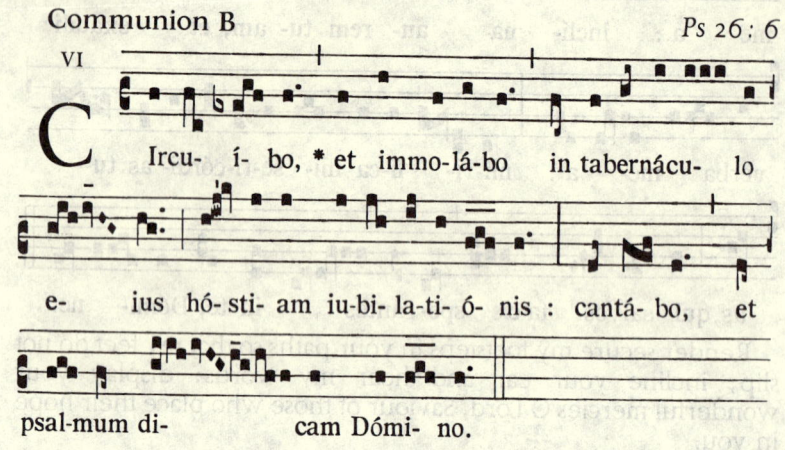

Circuíbo, * et immolábo in tabernáculo eius hóstiam iubilatiónis : cantábo, et psalmum dicam Dómino.

I shall walk round about his sanctuary, offering a sacrifice of jubilation; I will sing and recite a psalm to the Lord.

Communion C — Mt 16 : 24

Qui vult veníre post me, * ábneget semetípsum : et tollat crucem suam, et sequátur me.

If a man wishes to come after me, let him deny himself and take up his cross and follow me.

Prayer after Communion

Sacri Córporis et Sánguinis pretiósi alimónia renováti, quǽsumus, Dómine, cleméntiam tuam, ut, quod gérimus devotióne frequénti, certa redemptióne capiámus.

Lord, you give us the body and blood of your Son to renew your life within us. In your mercy, assure our redemption and bring us to the eternal life we celebrate in this eucharist.

THIRTEENTH SUNDAY

Introit   Ps 46: 2, 3

Omnes gentes *pláudite mánibus: iubiláte Deo in voce exsultatiónis. *Ps.* Quóniam Dóminus excélsus, terríbilis: Rex magnus super omnem terram.

All nations, clap your hands; shout unto God with a voice of joy. ℣. For the Lord is high and awesome; a great king over all the earth.

Opening Prayer

DEUS, qui, per adoptiónem grátiæ, lucis nos esse fílios voluísti, præsta, quǽsumus, ut errórum non involvámur ténebris, sed in splendóre veritátis semper maneámus conspícui.

FATHER, you call your children to walk in the light of Christ. Free us from darkness and keep us in the radiance of your truth.

First reading

A. 2 Kings 4: 8-11, 14-16a: *Elisha in the house of the Shunammite.*

B. Wis 1: 13-15; 2: 23-24: *Death entered the world through the devil.*

C. 1 Kings 19: 16b, 19-21: *The calling of Elisha.*

Ordinary Time

Gradual A & C Ps 33: 12, ℣. 6

Venite filii, * audite me: timorem Domini docebo vos. ℣. Accedite ad eum, et illuminamini: et facies vestrae non confundentur.

Come, children, hearken unto me; I will teach you the fear of the Lord. ℣. Go forth unto him and receive enlightenment, and your faces shall not be put to shame.

Gradual B: Exaltabo te, *p. 472.*

Second reading
A. Rom 6: 3-4, 8-11: *A new life.*
B. 2 Cor 8: 7, 9, 13-15: *Assistance to the poor.*
C. Gal 5: 1, 13-18: *True liberty.*

Alleluia A
Christus resúrgens, *p. 370.*

Alleluia B & C Ps 46: 2

Alleluia.

13th Sunday

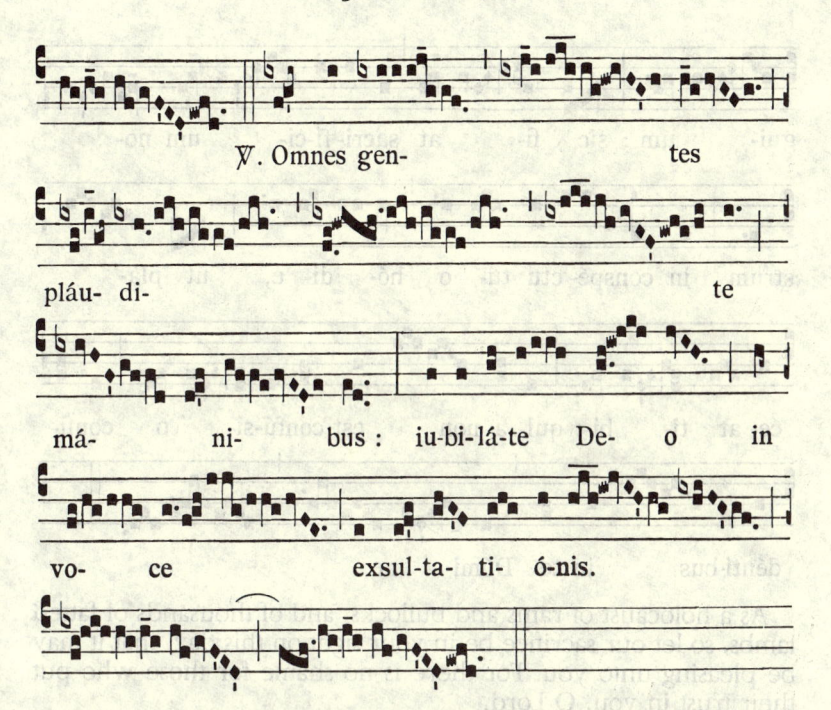

℣. Omnes gentes pláudite mánibus: iubiláte Deo in voce exsultatiónis.

All nations, clap your hands; shout unto God with a voice of joy.

Gospel
A. Mt 10: 37-42: *To receive Christ.*
B. Mk 5: 21-43 or 21-24, 35b-43: *The daughter of Jaïrus.*
C. Lk 9: 51-62: *To follow Christ.*

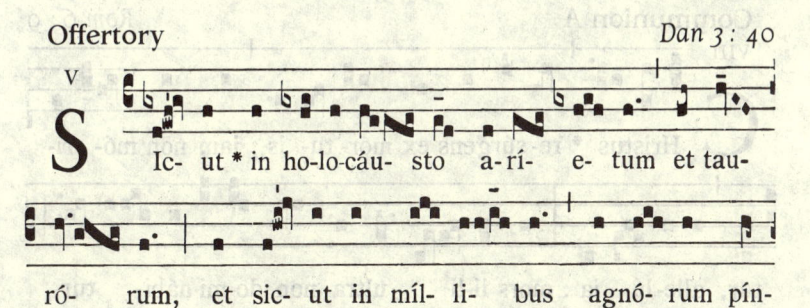

Offertory
Dan 3: 40

Sicut * in holocáusto aríetum et taurórum, et sic- ut in míllibus agnórum píngui- um : sic fi- at sacri- fí-ci- um no-

strum in conspé- ctu tu- o hó- di- e, ut plá-

ce- at ti- bi : qui- a non est confú-si- o confi-

dénti-bus in te Dómi- ne.

As a holocaust of rams and bullocks, and of thousands of fatted lambs, so let our sacrifice be in your sight on this day, that it may be pleasing unto you. For there is no shame for those who put their trust in you, O Lord.

Prayer over the Gifts

Deus, qui mysteriórum tuórum dignánter operáris efféctus, præsta, quæsumus, ut sacris apta munéribus fiant nostra servítia.

Lord God, through your sacraments you give us the power of your grace. May this eucharist help us to serve you faithfully.

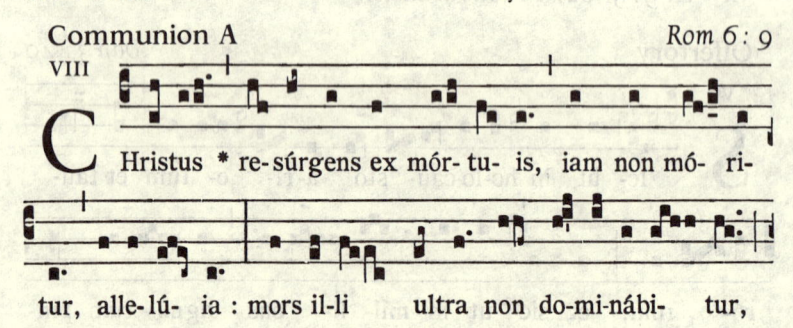

Communion A   Rom 6 : 9

VIII

Christus * re-súrgens ex mór- tu- is, iam non mó- ri-

tur, alle-lú- ia : mors il-li ultra non do-mi-nábi- tur,

13th Sunday

alle-lú-ia, alle-lú-ia.

Christ, rising from the dead, dies now no more, alleluia; death shall no longer have any dominion over him, alleluia, alleluia.

Communion B & C *Ps 30: 3ab*

Inclína * aurem tu- am, accéle-ra, ut é-ru-as nos.

Lend your ear and make haste to rescue us.

Prayer after Communion

Vivíficet nos, quæsumus, Dómine, divína quam obtúlimus et súmpsimus hóstia, ut, perpétua tibi caritáte coniúncti, fructum qui semper máneat afferámus.

Lord, may this sacrifice and communion give us a share in your life and help us bring your love to the world.

Ordinary Time

FOURTEENTH SUNDAY

Introit *Ps 47: 10, 11 and 2*

Suscépimus, * Deus, misericórdiam tuam in médio templi tui: secúndum nomen tuum Deus, ita et laus tua in fines terrae: justítia plena est déxtera tua.

Ps. Magnus Dóminus et laudábilis nimis: in civitáte Dei nostri, in monte sancto ejus.

We have received your mercy, O God, in the midst of your temple; even as your name, so also does your praise extend to the ends of the earth; your right hand is filled with righteousness. ℣. Great is the Lord and worthy of all praise, in the city of our God, on his holy mountain.

14th Sunday

Opening Prayer

Deus, qui in Fílii tui humilitáte iacéntem mundum erexísti, fidélibus tuis sanctam concéde lætítiam, ut, quos eripuísti a servitúte peccáti, gáudiis fácias pérfrui sempitérnis.

Father, through the obedience of Jesus, your servant and your Son, you raised a fallen world. Free us from sin and bring us the joy that lasts for ever.

First reading
A. Zech 9: 9-10: *The humble king.*
B. Ezek 2: 2-5: *Rebellious sons.*
C. Is 66: 10-14c: *The joy of the Messianic Age.*

Gradual   Ps 70: 3, ℣. 1

E-sto mi-hi * in De-um pro- tectórem, et in lo- cum re- fú-gi-i, ut sal- vum me fá- ci-as. ℣. De-us, in te sperá-vi : Dó-mi-ne, non confún- dar in aetér- num.

Be unto me a protecting God, and a house of refuge, to save me.
℣. My God, in you do I trust; O Lord, let me never be put to shame.

Second reading
A. Rom 8: 9, 11-13: *Live by the Spirit of Christ.*
B. 2 Cor 12: 7-10: *Strength in weakness.*
C. Gal 6: 14-18: *The marks of Jesus' suffering.*

Alleluia A
Venite ad me, p. 666.

Alleluia B & C
Ps 47: 2

Alleluia. ℣. Magnus Dóminus, et laudábilis valde, in civitáte Dei, in monte sancto eius.

Great is the Lord and worthy of all praise; in the city of God, on his holy mountain.

Gospel
A. Mt 11: 25-30: *Meek and humble of heart.*
B. Mk 6: 1-6: *Jesus, prophet without honour.*
C. Lk 10: 1-12, 17-20: *The demands of the apostolate.*

14th Sunday

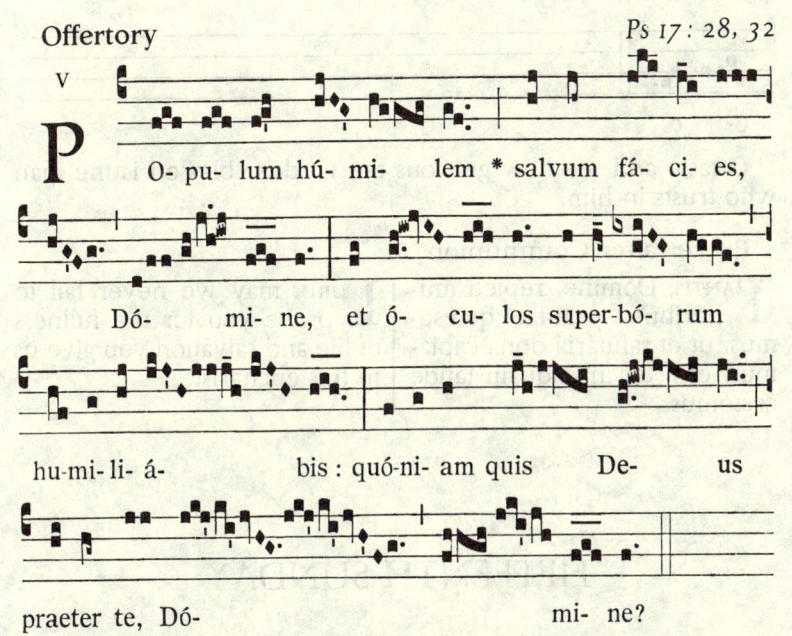

Offertory — Ps 17 : 28, 32

Populum humilem * salvum facies, Domine, et oculos superborum humiliabis : quoniam quis Deus praeter te, Domine?

You will save the humble nation, O Lord, and bring down the eyes of the proud. For who is God, other than you, O Lord?

Prayer over the Gifts

Oblatio nos, Domine, tuo nomini dicata purificet, et de die in diem ad cælestis vitæ transferat actionem.

Lord, let this offering to the glory of your name purify us and bring us closer to eternal life.

Communion — Ps 33 : 9

Gustate et videte,* quoniam suavis est Dominus : beatus vir, qui sperat in e- o.

O taste and see how gracious the Lord is; blessed is the man who trusts in him.

Prayer after Communion

TANTIS, Dómine, repléti munéribus, præsta, quæsumus, ut et salutária dona capiámus, et a tua numquam laude cessémus.

LORD, may we never fail to praise you for the fullness of life and salvation you give us in this eucharist.

FIFTEENTH SUNDAY

Introit *Ps 54: 17, 18, 19, 20, 23 and 2*

III

DUM clamárem ad Dóminum,* exaudívit vocem meam, ab his qui appropínquant mihi: et humiliávit eos, qui est ante saécula, et manet in ætérnum: iacta cogi-

15th Sunday

tá-tum tu-um in Dómi- no, et ipse te e-nútri- et. *Ps.* Exáudi De- us o-ra-ti- ó-nem me- am, et ne despé-xe-ris depre-ca-ti- ó-nem me- am : inténde mi-hi, et ex-áudi me.

When I cried out to the Lord, he heeded my call against my assailants; he who is before the beginning of the world and who endures forever has humbled them. Cast your cares upon the Lord, and he will sustain you. ℣. Hear my prayer, O God, and despise not my supplication; be attentive to me and hear me.

Or: *Ps 16 : 15 and 1*

Ego autem * cum iustí- ti- a ap-pa-ré- bo in conspé- ctu tu- o: sa-ti- á- bor, dum mani-fe-stá-bi-tur gló-ri- a tu- a. *Ps.* Exáudi Dómi-ne iustí-ti- am me- am : inténde depre-ca-ti- ó-nem me- am.

As for me, I will appear before you in righteousness; I will be satisfied when your glory is made manifest. ℣. Give heed, O Lord, to my righteousness; be attentive to my supplication.

Opening Prayer

Deus, qui erràntibus, ut in viam possint redíre, veritátis tuæ lumen osténdis, da cunctis qui christiána professióne censéntur, et illa respúere, quæ huic inimíca sunt nómini, et ea quæ sunt apta sectári.

God our father, your light of truth guides us to the way of Christ. May all who follow him reject what is contrary to the gospel.

First reading

A. Is 55 : 10-11 : *The efficacy of God's Word.*
B. Amos 7 : 12-15 : *The vocation of Amos.*
C. Deut 30 : 10-14 : *The Word is in your heart.*

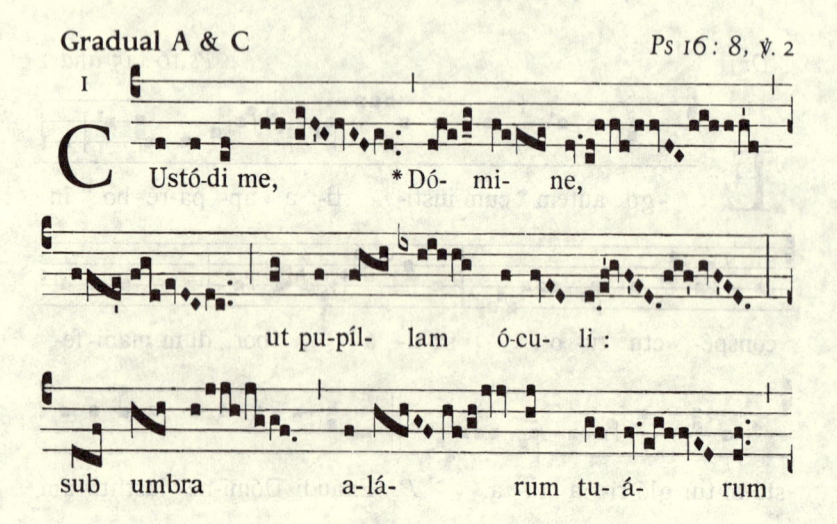

Gradual A & C   Ps 16 : 8, ℣. 2

Custódi me, *Dómine, ut pupíllam óculi : sub umbra alárum tuárum

15th Sunday

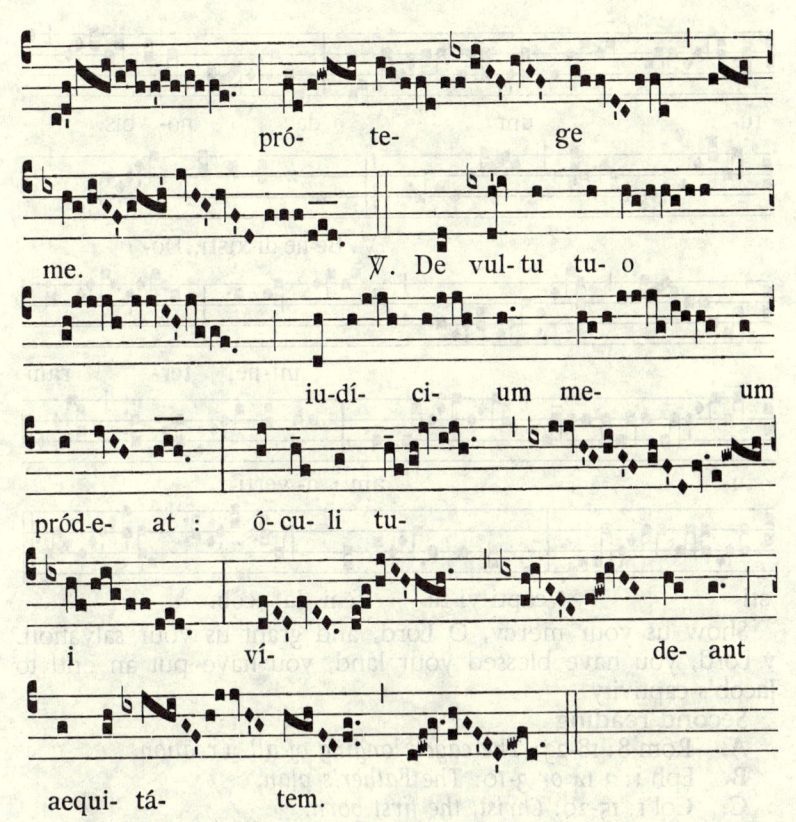

pró- te- ge me. ℣. De vultu tuo iudícium meum pródeat : óculi tui vídeant aequitátem.

Keep me, O Lord, as the apple of your eye; shield me under the shadow of your wings. ℣. Let judgment in my favour come forth from your presence; may your eyes discern what is right.

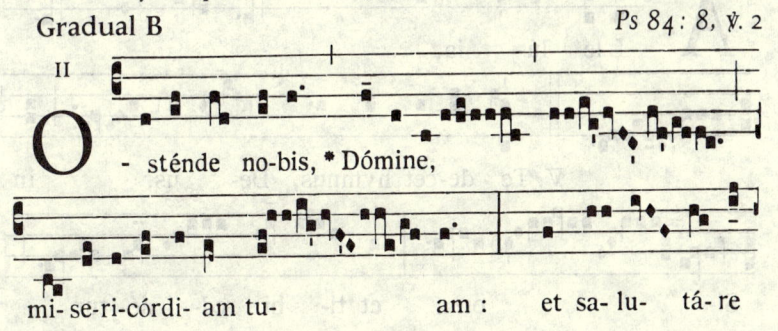

Gradual B
Ps 84 : 8, ℣. 2

O- sténde nobis, * Dómine, misericórdiam tuam : et salutáre

tu- um   da   no- bis.

℣. Be-ne-di-xísti, Dó-mi-ne, ter- ram tu- am : a- vertí- sti   capti-vi-tá- tem Ia- cob.

Show us your mercy, O Lord, and grant us your salvation.
℣. Lord, you have blessed your land, you have put an end to Jacob's captivity.

Second reading
A. Rom 8: 18-23: *The eager longing of all Creation.*
B. Eph 1: 3-14 *or* 3-10: *The Father's plan.*
C. Col 1: 15-20: *Christ, the first born.*

Alleluia *Ps* 64: 2

VII

A L-le- lú- ia.

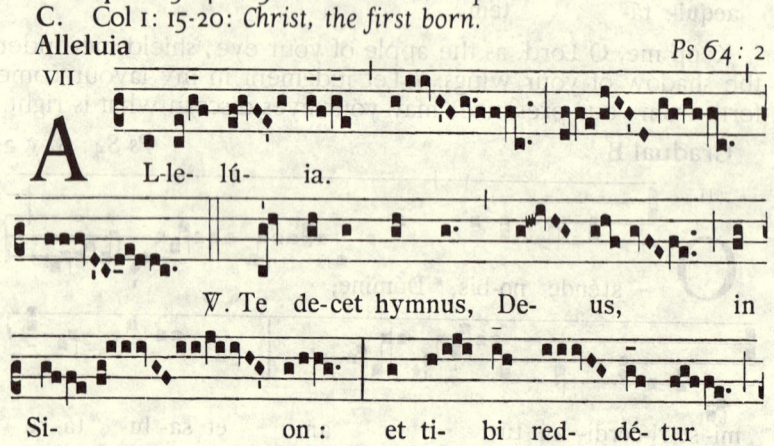

℣. Te de-cet hymnus, De- us, in Si- on : et ti- bi red- dé- tur

15th Sunday

vo- tum in Ie-rú-sa-lem.

It is fitting, O God, to sing a hymn unto you on Mount Zion, and our vows shall be carried out for you in Jerusalem.

Gospel
A. Mt 13: 1-23 or 1-9: *The parable of the sower.*
B. Mk 6: 7-13: *Sent on mission.*
C. Lk 10: 25-37: *The good Samaritan.*

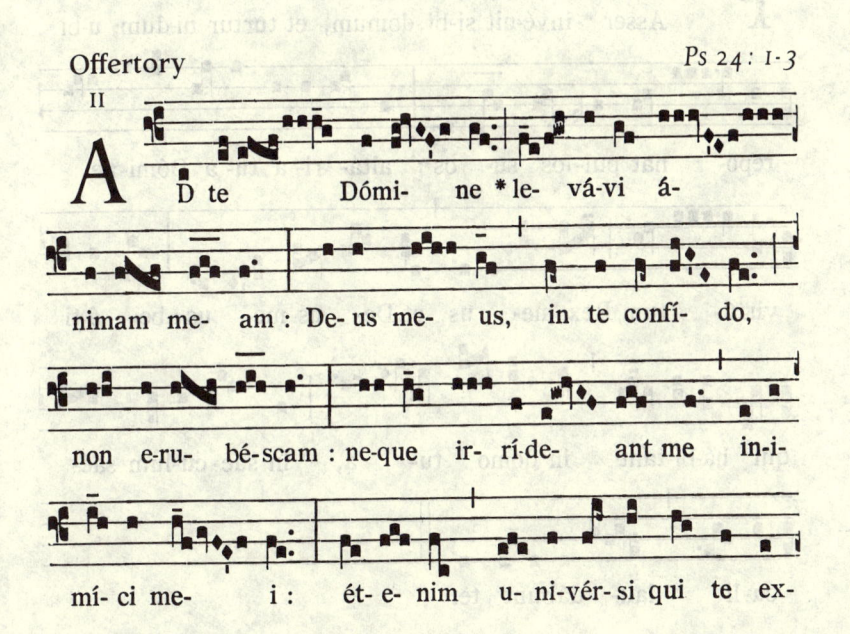

Offertory
Ps 24: 1-3

AD te Dómine *le-vá-vi á-nimam me-am: Deus me-us, in te confí-do, non e-ru-bé-scam: neque ir-rí-de-ant me in-i-mí-ci me-i: ét-e-nim u-ni-vér-si qui te exspé- ctant, non confun- dén- tur.

Unto you, O Lord, have I lifted up my soul; O my God, I trust in you, let me not be put to shame; do not allow my enemies to laugh at me; for none of those who are awaiting you will be disappointed.

Prayer over the Gifts

RESPICE, Dómine, múnera supplicántis Ecclésiæ, et pro credéntium sanctificatiónis increménto suménda concéde.

LORD, accept the gifts of your Church. May this eucharist help us grow in holiness and faith.

Communion Ps 83 : 4, 5

PAsser * invé-nit si-bi domum, et turtur ni-dum, u-bi repó- nat pul-los su- os: altá- ri- a tu- a Dómi-ne virtú- tum, Rex me- us, et De- us me- us: be- á-ti qui há-bi-tant in domo tu- a, in saé-cu-lum saé- cu-li lau- dábunt te.

The sparrow has found herself a home, and the turtle dove a nest in which to lay her young: at your altars, O Lord of hosts, my King and my God! Blessed are they who dwell in your house, they shall praise you for ever and ever.

Or:

Qui mandúcat, *p. 423.*

Prayer after Communion

Sumptis munéribus, quæsumus, Dómine, ut, cum frequentióne mystérii, crescat nostræ salútis efféctus.

Lord, by our sharing in the mystery of this eucharist, let your saving love grow within us.

SIXTEENTH SUNDAY

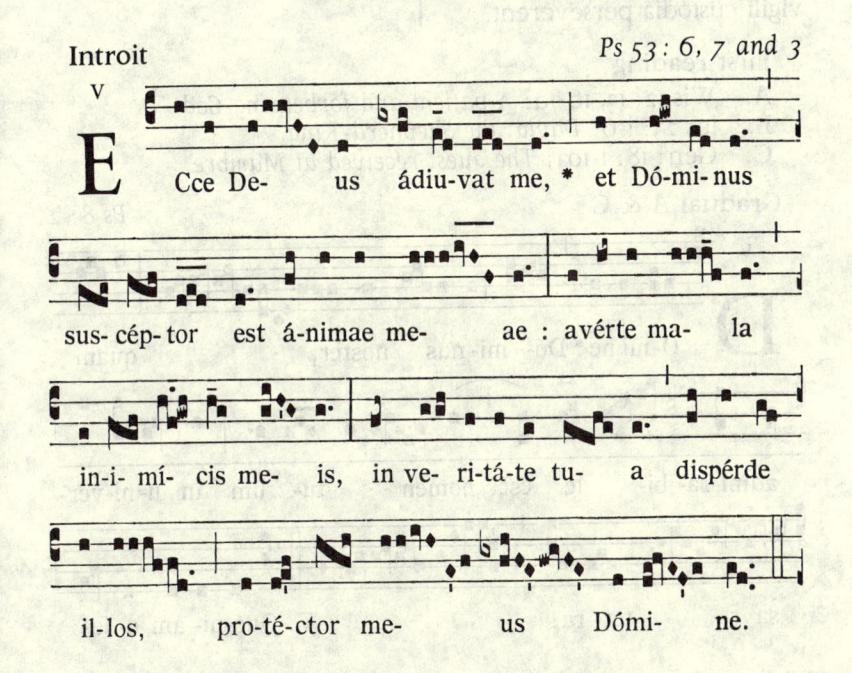

Introit   Ps 53 : 6, 7 and 3

Ecce Deus ádiuvat me, * et Dóminus suscéptor est ánimae meae : avérte mala inimícis meis, in veritáte tua dispérde illos, protéctor meus Dómine.

Ordinary Time

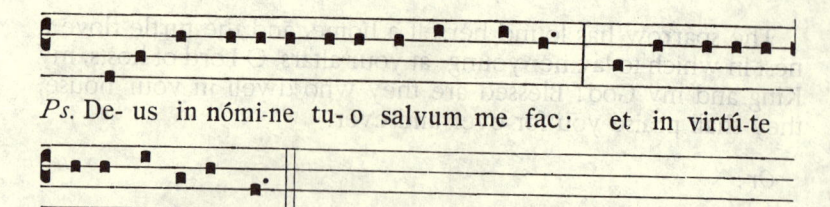

Ps. De-us in nómi-ne tu-o salvum me fac: et in virtú-te tu-a iú-di-ca me.

Behold, God is my helper, and the Lord is the upholder of my soul; turn back all the evil against my enemies, destroy them in your fidelity, O Lord, the Protector of my life. ℣. Save me, O God, by your name, and render justice unto me in your strength.

Opening Prayer

PROPITIARE, Dómine, fámulis tuis, et cleménter grátiæ tuæ super eos dona multíplica, ut, spe, fide et caritáte fervéntes, semper in mandátis tuis vígili custódia persevérent.

LORD, be merciful to your people. Fill us with your gifts and make us always eager to serve you in faith, hope, and love.

First reading

A. Wis 12: 13, 16-19: *A patient and forbearing God.*
B. Jer 23: 1-6: *David, the Shepherd-King.*
C. Gen: 18: 1-10a: *The guest received at Mambre.*

Gradual A & C

Ps 8: 2

DOmine * Dóminus noster, quam admi-rá-bi-le est nomen tu-um in u-ni-vér-sa ter-ra! ℣. Quó-ni-am e-le-

16th Sunday

... váta est magnifi-céntia tua super caelos.

O Lord, our governor, how admirable is your name in all the earth! ℣. For your magnificence is elevated above the heavens.

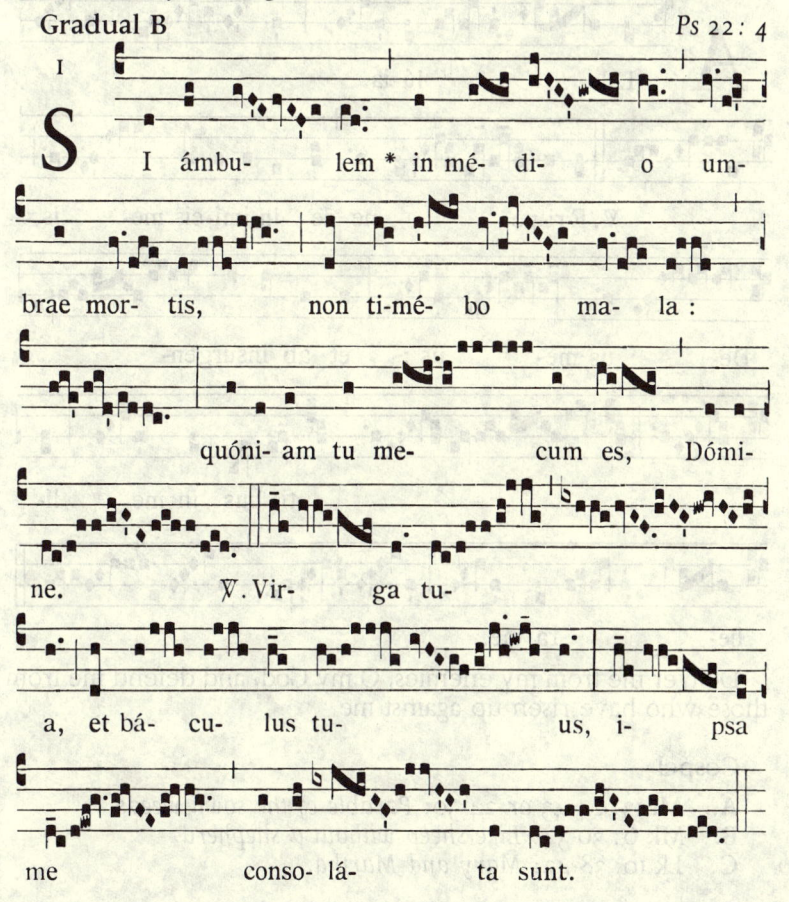

Gradual B *Ps 22 : 4*

SI ámbulem * in médio umbrae mortis, non timébo mala: quóniam tu mecum es, Dómine. ℣. Virga tua, et báculus tuus, ipsa me consoláta sunt.

Though I should walk in the midst of the shadow of death, I will fear no evil, for you are with me, O Lord. ℣. Your rod and your staff have comforted me.

Second reading
A. Rom 8: 26-27: *The prayer of the Spirit within us.*
B. Eph 2: 13-18: *Christ, our peace.*
C. Col 1: 24-28: *The mystery now made manifest.*

Alleluia — Ps 58: 2

A-lle- lú-ia. ℣. E-ri-pe me de in-imí-cis me- is, De- us me- us: et ab insurgén- ti- bus in me lí- be- ra me.

Deliver me from my enemies, O my God, and defend me from those who have risen up against me.

Gospel
A. Mt 13: 24-43 or 24-30: *Parable of the sown weeds.*
B. Mk 6: 30-34: *Like sheep without a shepherd.*
C. Lk 10: 38-42: *Mary and Martha.*

16th Sunday

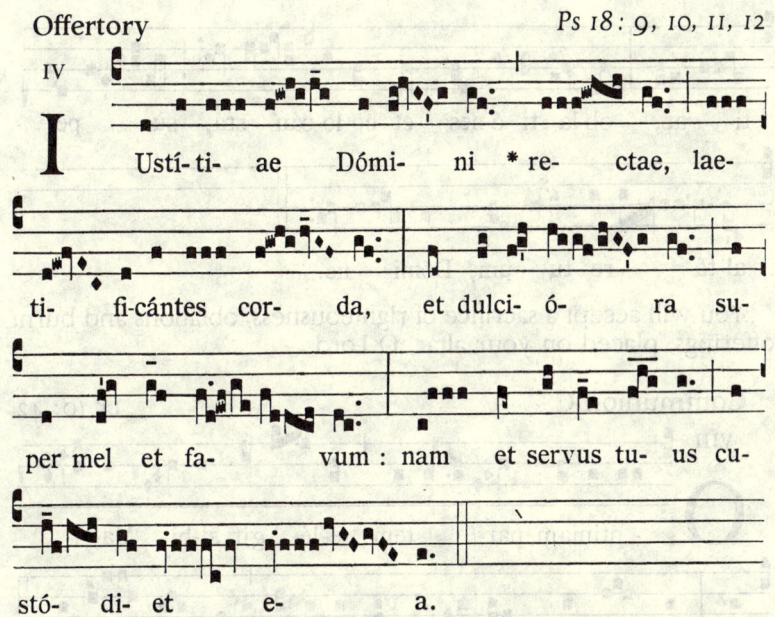

Offertory — *Ps 18: 9, 10, 11, 12*

IUstítiae Dómini * rectae, laetificántes corda, et dulcióra super mel et favum : nam et servus tuus custódiet ea.

The ordinances of the Lord are right, bringing joy to all hearts, sweeter than honey or the honeycomb. Therefore your servant will observe them.

Prayer over the Gifts

DEUS, qui legálium differéntiam hostiárum uníus sacrifícii perfectióne sanxísti, áccipe sacrifícium a devótis tibi fámulis, et pari benedictióne, sicut múnera Abel, sanctífica, ut, quod sínguli obtulérunt ad maiestátis tuæ honórem, cunctis profíciat ad salútem.

LORD, bring us closer to salvation through these gifts which we bring in your honour. Accept the perfect sacrifice you have given us, bless it as you blessed the gifts of Abel.

Communion A & B — *Ps 50: 21*

ACceptábis * sacrifícium iustí-

Ordinary Time

...tiae, oblatiónes et holocáusta, super altáre tuum, Dómine.

You will accept a sacrifice of righteousness, oblations and burnt offerings, placed on your altar, O Lord.

Communion C
Lk 10: 42

VIII

*Optimam partem * elégit sibi María, quae non auferétur ab ea in aetérnum.*

Mary has chosen for herself the best portion, which shall never be taken away from her.

Prayer after Communion

Populo tuo, quæsumus, Dómine, adésto propítius, et, quem mystériis cæléstibus imbuísti, fac ad novitátem vitæ de vetustáte transíre.

Merciful Father, may these mysteries give us new purpose and bring us to a new life in you.

SEVENTEENTH SUNDAY

Introit   *Ps 67: 6, 7, 36 and 2*

Deus * in loco sancto suo: Deus, qui inhabitáre facit unánimes in domo: ipse dabit virtútem et fortitúdinem plebi suae. *Ps.* Exsúrgat Deus, et dissipéntur inimíci eius: et fúgiant, qui odérunt eum, a fácie eius.

God is in his holy dwelling place; the God who causes us to dwell together, one at heart, in his house; he himself will give power and strength to his people. ℣. Let God arise, and let his enemies be scattered; and let those who hate him flee before his face.

Ordinary Time

Opening Prayer

Protector in te sperántium, Deus, sine quo nihil est válidum, nihil sanctum, multíplica super nos misericórdiam tuam, ut, te rectóre, te duce, sic bonis transeúntibus nunc utámur, ut iam possímus inhærére mansúris.

God our Father and protector, without you nothing is holy, nothing has value. Guide us to everlasting life by helping us to use wisely the blessings you have given to the world.

First reading

A. 1 Kings 3: 5, 7-12: *Solomon's request.*
B. 2 Kings 4: 42-44: *Elisha's miracle.*
C. Gen 18: 20-32: *Abraham's intercession on behalf of Sodom.*

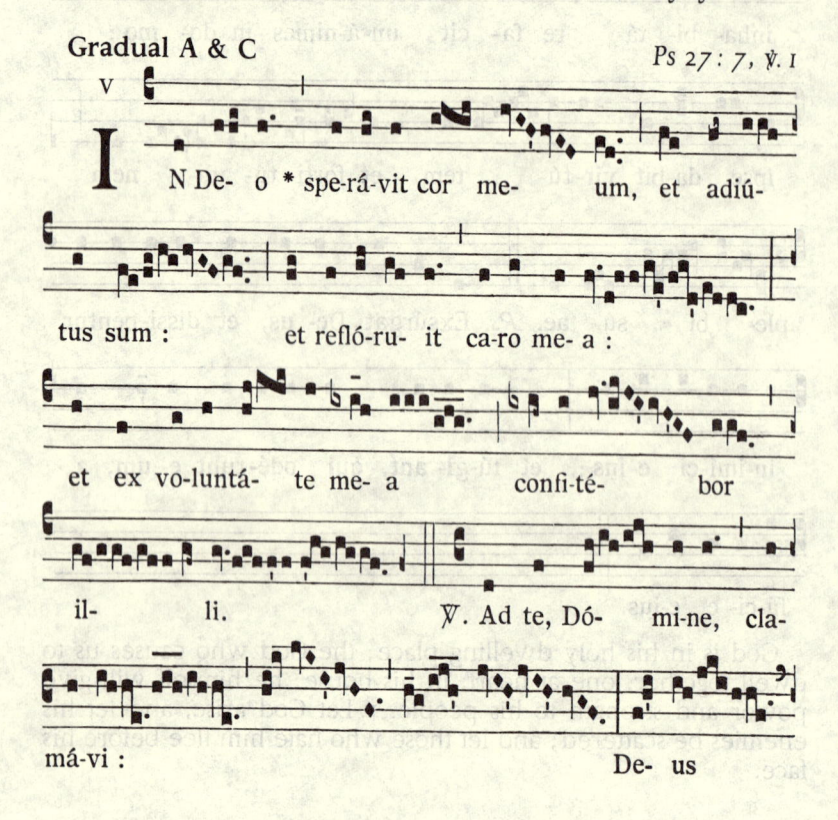

Gradual A & C

Ps 27: 7, ℣. 1

IN Deo * sperávit cor meum, et adiútus sum: et reflóruit caro mea: et ex voluntáte mea confitébor illi. ℣. Ad te, Dómine, clamávi: Deus

17th Sunday

... me- us, ne sí- le- as : ne discé- das a me.

In God has my heart placed its trust and I have been helped; and my flesh has flowered anew, and with all my desire I will give thanks unto him. ℣. Unto you, O Lord, do I cry; O my God, do not remain silent, depart not from me.

B: Oculi ómnium, p. 414.

Second reading
A. Rom 8: 28-30: *To be the image of the Son.*
B. Eph 4: 1-6: *Unity in the Spirit.*
C. Col 2: 12-14: *God has forgiven us our sins.*

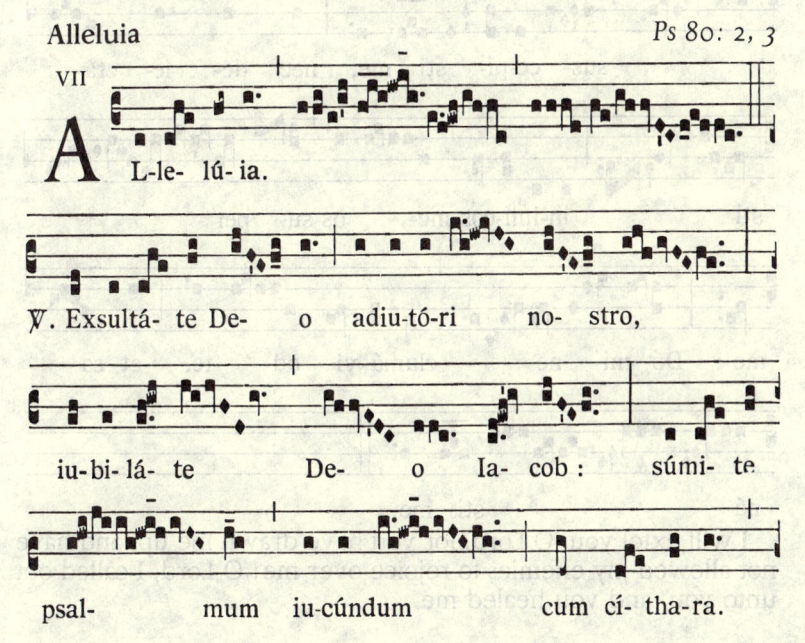

Alleluia   Ps 80: 2, 3

VII

Al-le- lú- ia.

℣. *Exsultá- te De- o adiu-tó-ri no- stro, iu-bi-lá- te De- o Ia- cob: súmi- te psal- mum iu-cúndum cum cí- tha-ra.*

Ordinary Time

Rejoice in honour of God our helper; shout for joy to the God of Jacob; intone a most beautiful psalm with the harp.

Gospel

A. Mt 13: 44-52 or 44-46: *The parables of the kingdom.*
B. Jn 6: 1-15: *The multiplying of the loaves.*
C. Lk 11: 1-13: *Perseverance in prayer.*

Offertory Ps 29: 2, 3

EX- altá- bo te * Dómi- ne, quó- ni- am sus- ce- pí- sti me, nec de- le- ctá- sti in- imí- cos me- os su- per me: Dó- mi- ne clamá- vi ad te, et sa- ná- sti me.

I will extol you, O Lord, for you have drawn me up, and have not allowed my enemies to rejoice over me; O Lord, I called out unto you, and you healed me.

17th Sunday

Prayer over the Gifts

SUSCIPE, quæsumus, Dómine, múnera, quæ tibi de tua largitáte deférimus, ut hæc sacrosáncta mystéria, grátiæ tuæ operánte virtúte, et præséntis vitæ nos conversatióne sanctíficent, et ad gáudia sempitérna perdúcant.

LORD, receive these offerings chosen from your many gifts. May these mysteries make us holy and lead us to eternal joy.

Communion A

Mt 13 : 45, 46

SImile est * regnum caelórum hómini negotiatóri, quaerénti bonas margarítas: invénta una pretiósa margaríta, dedit ómnia sua, et comparávit eam.

The kingdom of heaven is like unto a merchant seeking fine pearls; having found one of great worth, he went and sold all that he had, and he bought it.

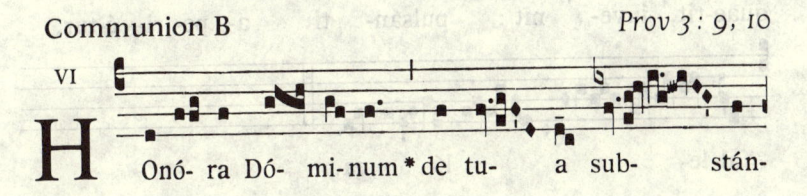

Communion B

Prov 3 : 9, 10

HOnóra Dóminum * de tua substán-

...ti- a, et de primí- ti- is fru- gum tu- á- rum: ut imple- án- tur hórre- a tu- a sa- tu- ri- tá- te, et vi- no torcu- lá- ri- a red- un- dá- bunt.

Honour the Lord with your substance and with the first fruits of all your produce; then shall your barns be filled with abundance, and your presses shall run over with wine.

Communion C   Lk 11: 9, 10; cf. Mt 7: 7, 8 and 10: 1

I

PEtite, * et ac-ci-pi- é- tis: quaéri- te, et inve- ni- é- tis: pulsá- te, et ape- ri- é-tur vo- bis: omnis e-nim qui pe- tit, ácci- pit: et qui quae-rit, ínve- nit: pulsán- ti a- pe- ri- é-tur, al- le- lú- ia.

18th Sunday

Ask, and you will receive; seek, and you shall find; knock, and it shall be opened to you; for all who ask, receive, he who seeks, finds, and to him who knocks it shall be opened, alleluia.

Prayer after Communion

SUMPSIMUS, Dómine, divínum sacraméntum, passiónis Fílii tui memoriále perpétuum; tríbue, quæsumus, ut ad nostram salútem hoc munus profíciat, quod ineffábili nobis caritáte ipse donávit.

LORD, we receive the sacrament which celebrates the memory of the death and resurrection of Christ your Son. May this gift bring us closer to our eternal salvation.

EIGHTEENTH SUNDAY

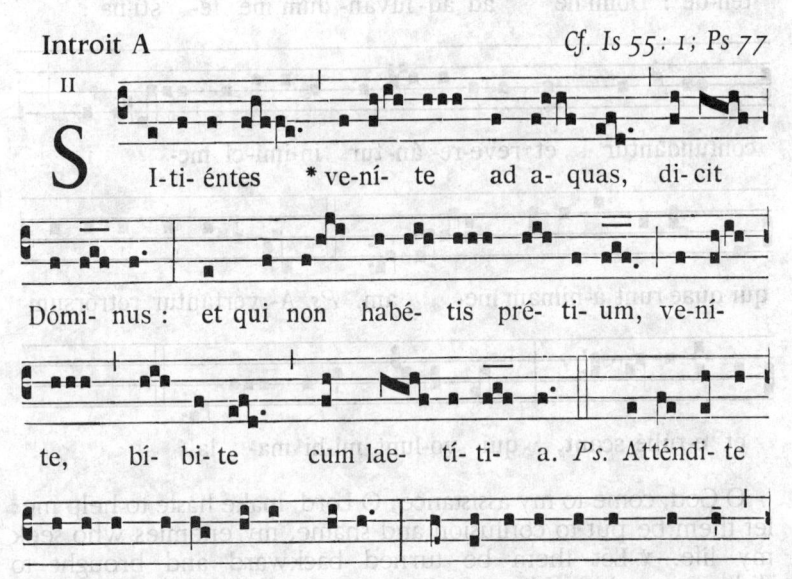

Introit A *Cf. Is 55: 1; Ps 77*

SItiéntes * veníte ad aquas, dicit Dóminus: et qui non habétis prétium, veníte, bíbite cum laetítia. *Ps.* Atténdite pópule meus legem meam: inclináte aurem vestram in verba o- ris me- i.

All you who are thirsty, come to the waters, says the Lord, and you who have no money, come, drink in gladness. ℣. Attend, O my people, to my law; incline your ears to the words of my mouth.

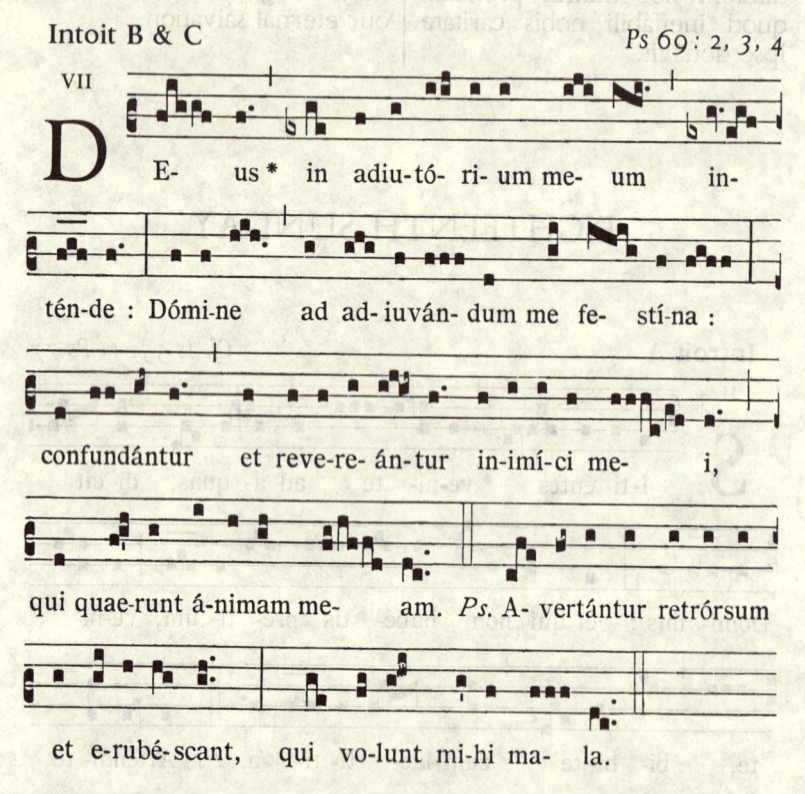

Intoit B & C *Ps 69: 2, 3, 4*

VII

De- us * in adiu-tó- ri- um me- um in- tén-de : Dómi-ne ad ad-iuván- dum me fe- stí-na : confundántur et reve-re- án-tur in-imí-ci me- i, qui quae-runt á-nimam me- am. *Ps.* A- vertántur retrórsum et e-rubé-scant, qui vo-lunt mi-hi ma- la.

O God, come to my assistance; O Lord, make haste to help me; let them be put to confusion and shame, my enemies who seek my life. ℣. Let them be turned backward and brought to dishonour, who wish me evil.

Opening Prayer

A DESTO, Dómine, fámulis tuis, et perpétuam benignitátem largíre poscéntibus, ut his, qui te auctórem et gubernatórem gloriántur habére, et grata restáures, et restauráta consérves.

F ATHER of everlasting goodness, our origin and guide, be close to us and hear the prayers of all who praise you. Forgive our sins and restore us to life. Keep us safe in your love.

First reading

A. Is 55: 1-3: *Come ye.*
B. Ex 16: 2-4, 12-15: *Manna.*
C. Eccles 1: 2; 2: 21-23: *All is vanity.*

Gradual A

Oculi ómnium, p. 414.

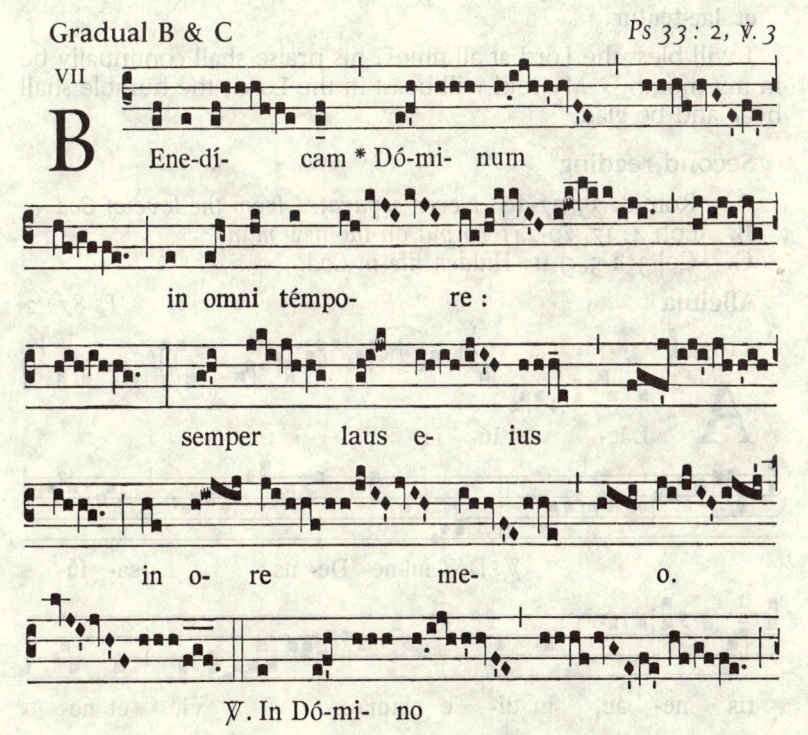

Gradual B & C

Ps 33: 2, ℣. 3

VII

B Ene-dí- cam * Dó- mi- num in omni témpo- re: semper laus e- ius in o- re me- o.

℣. In Dó- mi- no

laudá-bi-tur á- ni- ma me- a:

áudi- ant mansu- é-

ti,

et lae-téntur.

I will bless the Lord at all times; his praise shall continually be in my mouth. ℣. My soul will boast in the Lord; the humble shall hear and be glad.

Second reading

A. Rom 8: 35, 37-39: *Never separated from the love of God.*
B. Eph 4: 17, 20-24: *To put on the new man.*
C. Col 3: 1-5, 9-11: *Hidden life in God.*

Alleluia

Ps 87: 2

III

A L-le- lú- ia.

℣. Dó- mi-ne De- us sa- lú-

tis me- ae, in di- e clamá- vi, et no-

18th Sunday

cte co- ram te.

O Lord God of my salvation, day and night have I called out unto you.

Gospel
A. Mt 14: 13-21: *The multiplying of the loaves.*
B. Jn 6: 24-35: *The bread of God.*
C. Lk 12: 13-21: *The foolish rich man.*

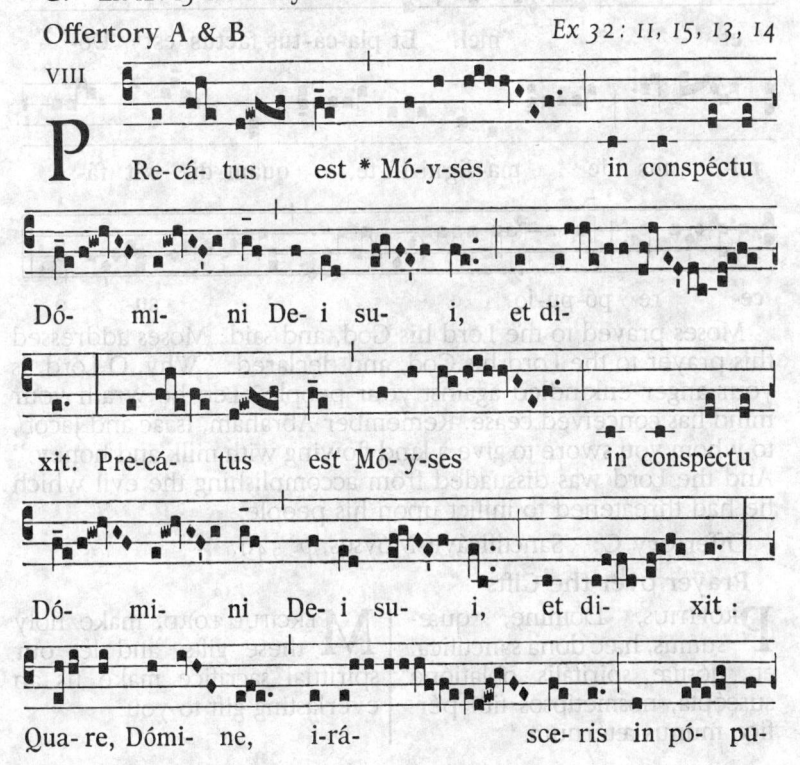

Offertory A & B   Ex 32: 11, 15, 13, 14

VIII

Pre-cá- tus est * Mó-y-ses in conspéctu Dó- mi- ni De- i su- i, et di- xit. Pre-cá- tus est Mó-y-ses in conspéctu Dó- mi- ni De- i su- i, et di- xit: Qua- re, Dómi- ne, i-rá- sce- ris in pó- pu-

lo tu- o? Par- ce irae á- nimae tu- ae: memén-to Abraham, I-sa- ac et Ia-cob, qui-bus iu-rásti da- re terram flu- éntem lac et mel. Et pla-cá- tus factus est Dó- mi- nus de ma-ligni-tá-te, quam di- xit fá- ce- re pó-pu-lo su- o.

Moses prayed to the Lord his God, and said; Moses addressed this prayer to the Lord his God, and declared: "Why, O Lord, is your anger enkindled against your people? Let the wrath your mind has conceived cease. Remember Abraham, Isaac and Jacob, to whom you swore to give a land flowing with milk and honey." And the Lord was dissuaded from accomplishing the evil which he had threatened to inflict upon his people.

Offertory C: Sanctificávit Móyses, p. 549.

Prayer over the Gifts

PROPITIUS, Dómine, quæsumus, hæc dona sanctífica, et, hóstiæ spirituális oblatióne suscépta, nosmetípsos tibi pérfice munus ætérnum.

MERCIFUL LORD, make holy these gifts, and let our spiritual sacrifice make us an everlasting gift to you.

18th Sunday

Communion — Wis 16: 20

Pa-nem de cae-lo * de-dísti no-bis, Dómine, habéntem omne delectaméntum, et omnem sapórem suavitátis.

You gave us bread from heaven, O Lord, having in it all that is delicious, and the sweetness of every taste.

Prayer after Communion

Quos cælésti récreas múnere, perpétuo, Dómine, comitáre præsídio, et, quos fovére non désinis, dignos fíeri sempitérna redemptióne concéde.

Lord, you give us the strength of new life by the gift of the eucharist. Protect us with your love and prepare us for eternal redemption.

NINETEENTH SUNDAY

Introit *Ps 73 : 20, 19, 22, 23 and 1*

VII

Respice, Dómine,* in testaméntum tuum, et ánimas páuperum tuórum ne derelínquas in finem: exsúrge Dómine, et iúdica causam tuam: et ne obliviscáris voces quaeréntium te. *Ps.* Ut quid Deus repulísti in finem: irátus est furor tuus super oves páscuae tuae?

Remember, O Lord, your covenant, and do not abandon for ever the souls of your poor; arise, O Lord, and judge your own cause; forget not the cries of those who seek you. ℣. O God, why have you cast us off unto the end; why is your wrath enkindled against the sheep of your pasture?

19th Sunday

Opening Prayer

OMNIPOTENS sempitérne Deus, quem patérno nómine invocáre præsúmimus, pérfice in córdibus nostris spíritum adoptiónis filiórum, ut promíssam hereditátem íngredi mereámur.

ALMIGHTY and ever-living God, your Spirit made us your children, confident to call you Father. Increase your Spirit within us and bring us to our promised inheritance.

First reading

A. 1 Kings 19: 9a, 11-13a: *Elijah encounters God.*
B. 1 Kings 19: 4-8: *Elijah, restored on the road to Horeb.*
C. Wis 18: 6-9: *The night of deliverance.*

Gradual A

Osténde, p. 499.

Gradual B

Ps 73: 20, 19, ℣. 22, 23

R E-spi-ce, Dómi-ne, * in testaméntum tu- um: et á-ni-mas páupe- rum tu-ó- rum ne obli-viscá- ris in fi- nem. ℣. Exsúrge Dómi-ne, et iú- di-ca

cau- sam tu- am : me-

mor e- sto oppróbri- i servó- rum

tu- ó- rum.

Remember, O Lord, your covenant and do not forget for ever the souls of your poor. ℣. Arise, O Lord, and judge your own cause; remember the scorn to which your servants have been subjected.

Gradual C

Beáta gens, p. 543.

Second reading

A. Rom 9: 1-5: *Israel, the nation of the promises.*
B. Eph 4: 30 - 5: 2: *To live in love.*
C. Heb 11: 1-2, 8-19 or 1-2, 8-12: *The strength of faith.*

Alleluia
Ps 89: 1

VII

A L-le-lú- ia.

℣. Dó- mi- ne, re-fú-

gi- um fa- ctus es nobis a ge-ne-ra-ti- ó- ne et progé- ni- e.

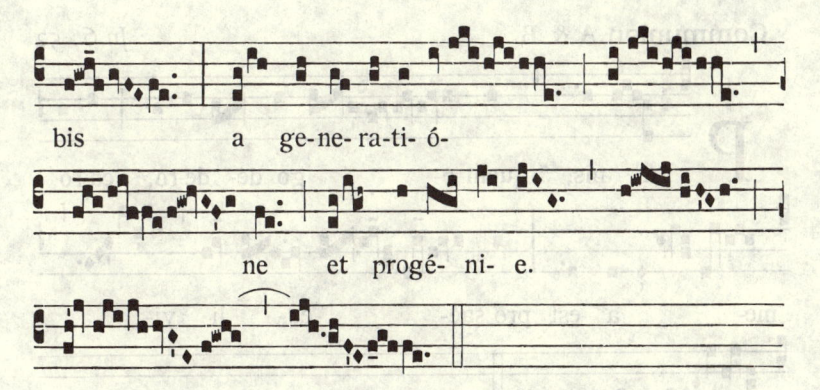

O Lord, you have been unto us a refuge from age to age.

Gospel
A. Mt 14: 22-33: *Peter walks on the waters.*
B. Jn 6: 41-51: *I am the bread of life.*
C. Lk 12: 32-48 or 35-40: *Be ready!*

Offertory Ps 30: 15, 16

IN te sperá- vi, Dómi- ne : * di- xi : Tu es De- us me- us, in má- ni-bus tu- is tém- po- ra me- a.

In you have I put my trust, O Lord; I said: "You are my God, my destiny is in your hands."

Prayer over the Gifts

ECCLESIÆ tuæ, Dómine, múnera placátus assúme, quæ et miséricors offerénda tribuísti, et in nostræ salútis poténter éfficis transíre mystérium.

GOD of power, giver of the gifts we bring, accept the offering of your Church and make it the sacrament of our salvation.

Ordinary Time

Communion A & B *Jn 6 : 52*

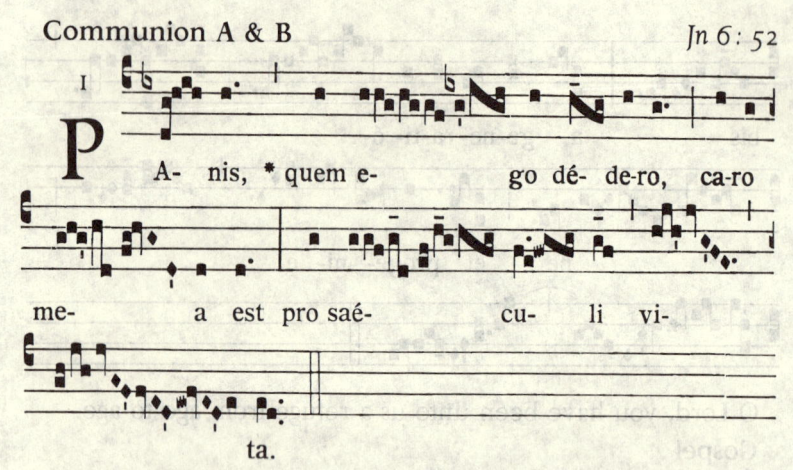

Panis, * quem ego dédero, caro mea est pro saéculi vita.

The bread which I will give is my flesh for the life of the world.

Communion C *Mt 24 : 46, 47*

Beátus servus, * quem, cum vénerit Dóminus, invénerit vigilántem : amen dico vobis, super ómnia bona sua constítuet eum.

Blessed is the servant whom the Lord, when he comes, will find to be vigilant. Truly, I say to you, he will establish him over all his possessions.

Prayer after Communion

Sacramentorum tuórum, Dómine, commúnio sumpta nos salvet, et in tuæ veritátis luce confírmet.

Lord, may the eucharist you give us bring us to salvation and keep us faithful to the light of your truth.

TWENTIETH SUNDAY

Introit *Ps 83 : 10, 11 and 2, 3*

PRotéctor noster * áspice, Deus, et réspice in fáciem Christi tui: quia mélior est dies una in átriis tuis super míllia. *Ps.* Quam dilécta tabernácula tua, Dómine virtútum! concupíscit, et déficit ánima mea in átria Dómini.

Behold, O God our protector, and consider the face of your Anointed; for one day in your house is better than a thousand elsewhere. ℣. How lovely is your tabernacle, O Lord of hosts! My soul longs and pines after the courts of the Lord.

Ordinary Time

Opening Prayer

Deus, qui diligéntibus te bona invisibília præparásti, infúnde córdibus nostris tui amóris afféctum, ut, te in ómnibus et super ómnia diligéntes, promissiónes tuas, quæ omne desidérium súperant, consequámur.

God our Father, may we love you in all things and above all things and reach the joy you have prepared for us beyond all our imagining.

First reading

A. Is 56: 1, 6-7: *My house will be called a house of prayer.*
B. Prov 9: 1-6: *Wisdom invites to a banquet.*
C. Jer 38: 4-6, 8-10: *Jeremiah accused and mistreated.*

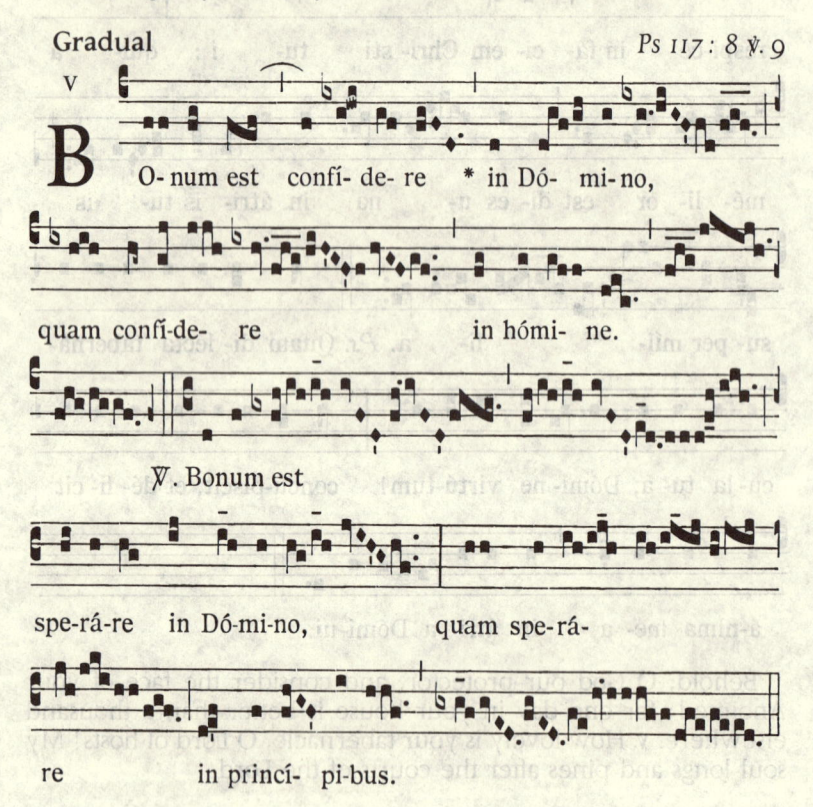

Gradual Ps 117: 8 ℣. 9

Bonum est confídere * in Dómino, quam confídere in hómine.

℣. Bonum est speráre in Dómino, quam speráre in princípibus.

20th Sunday

It is better to confide in the Lord than to have confidence in man. ℣. Better is it to trust in the Lord than to trust in princes.

Second reading
- A. Rom 11: 13-15, 29-32: *The gifts of God are irrevocable.*
- B. Eph 5: 15-20: *Praise the Lord with all your heart.*
- C. Heb 12: 1-4: *The combat of faith.*

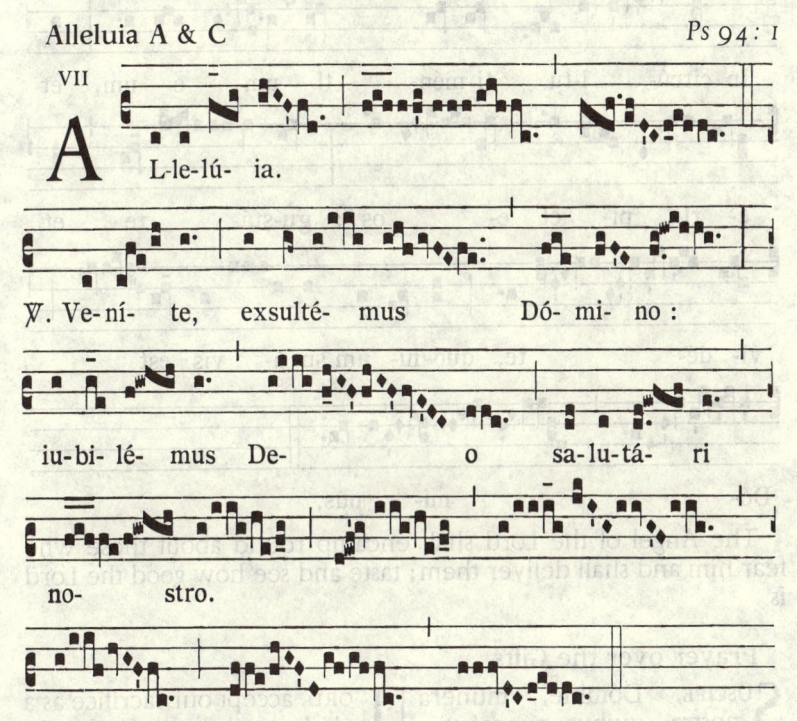

Alleluia A & C — Ps 94: 1

VII

A-lle-lú- ia.

℣. Ve-ní- te, exsulté- mus Dó- mi- no: iu-bi- lé- mus De- o sa-lu-tá- ri no- stro.

Come, let us sing to the Lord; let us make a joyful noise unto God our Saviour.

Alleluia B: Caro mea, p. 415.

Gospel
- A. Mt 15: 21-28: *The healing of a foreign woman's daughter.*
- B. Jn 6: 51-58: *To eat my flesh and drink my blood.*
- C. Lk 12: 49-53: *Jesus, a sign of contradiction.*

Ordinary Time

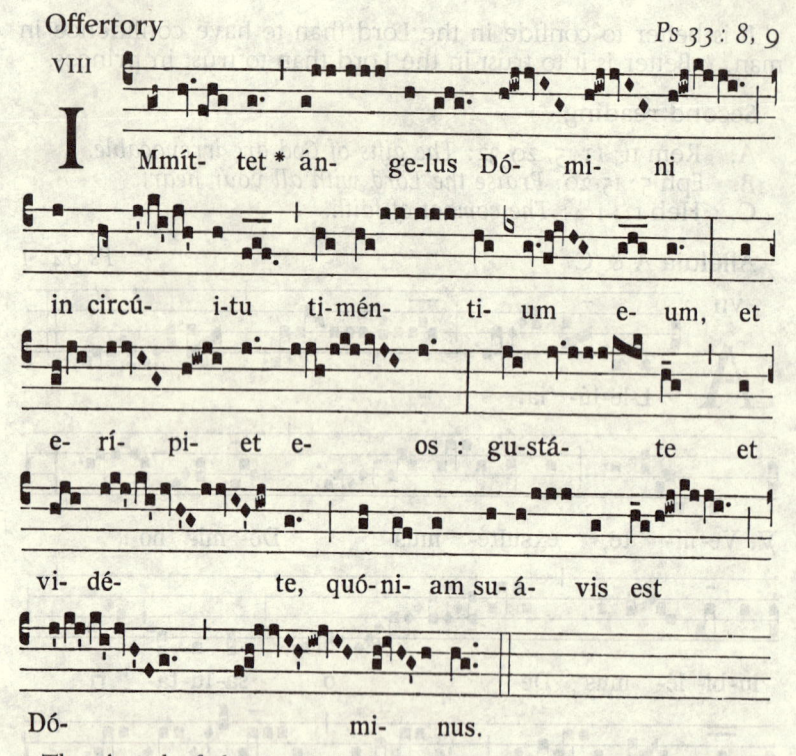

Offertory   *Ps 33 : 8, 9*

Immíttet * ángelus Dómini in circúitu timéntium eum, et erípiet eos : gustáte et vidéte, quóniam suávis est Dóminus.

The Angel of the Lord shall encamp round about those who fear him and shall deliver them; taste and see how good the Lord is.

Prayer over the Gifts

SUSCIPE, Dómine, múnera nostra, quibus exercéntur commércia gloriósa, ut, offeréntes quæ dedísti, teípsum vereámur accípere.

LORD, accept our sacrifice as a holy exchange of gifts. By offering what you have given us may we receive the gift of yourself.

Communion A

Domus mea, *p. 686.*

Communion B: Qui manducat, *p. 423.*

21st Sunday

Communion C — Mt 6 : 33

*Primum quaerite * regnum Dei, et omnia adicientur vobis, dicit Dóminus.*

Seek first the kingdom of God, and all the rest will be given to you in addition, says the Lord.

Prayer after Communion

Per hæc sacraménta, Dómine, Christi partícipes effécti, cleméntiam tuam humíliter implorámus, ut, eius imáginis confórmes in terris, et eius consórtes in cælis fíeri mereámur.

God of mercy, by this sacrament you make us one with Christ. By becoming more like him on earth, may we come to share his glory in heaven.

TWENTY-FIRST SUNDAY

Introit — Ps 85 : 1, 2, 3, 4

*Inclína, * Dómine, aurem tuam ad me, et exáudi me: salvum fac servum tuum, Deus*

...meus, sperántem in te: miserére mihi, Dómine, quóniam ad te clamávi tota die. Ps. Laetífica ánimam servi tui: quóniam ad te, Dómine, ánimam meam levávi.

Incline your ear to me, O Lord, and hear me; O God, save your servant who trusts in you; have mercy on me, O Lord, for unto you do I cry all the day. ℣. Gladden the soul of your servant, for unto you, O Lord, have I lifted up my soul.

Opening Prayer

Deus, qui fidélium mentes uníus éfficis voluntátis, da pópulis tuis id amáre quod præcipis, id desideráre quod promíttis, ut, inter mundánas varietátes, ibi nostra fixa sint corda, ubi vera sunt gáudia.

Father, help us to seek the values that will bring us lasting joy in this changing world. In our desire for what you promise make us one in mind and heart.

First reading

A. Is 22: 19-23: *He will bear the key of the house of David.*
B. Josh 24: 1-2a, 15-17, 18b: *The assembly of Shechem.*
C. Is 66: 18-21: *Jerusalem, center of all the nations.*

21st Sunday

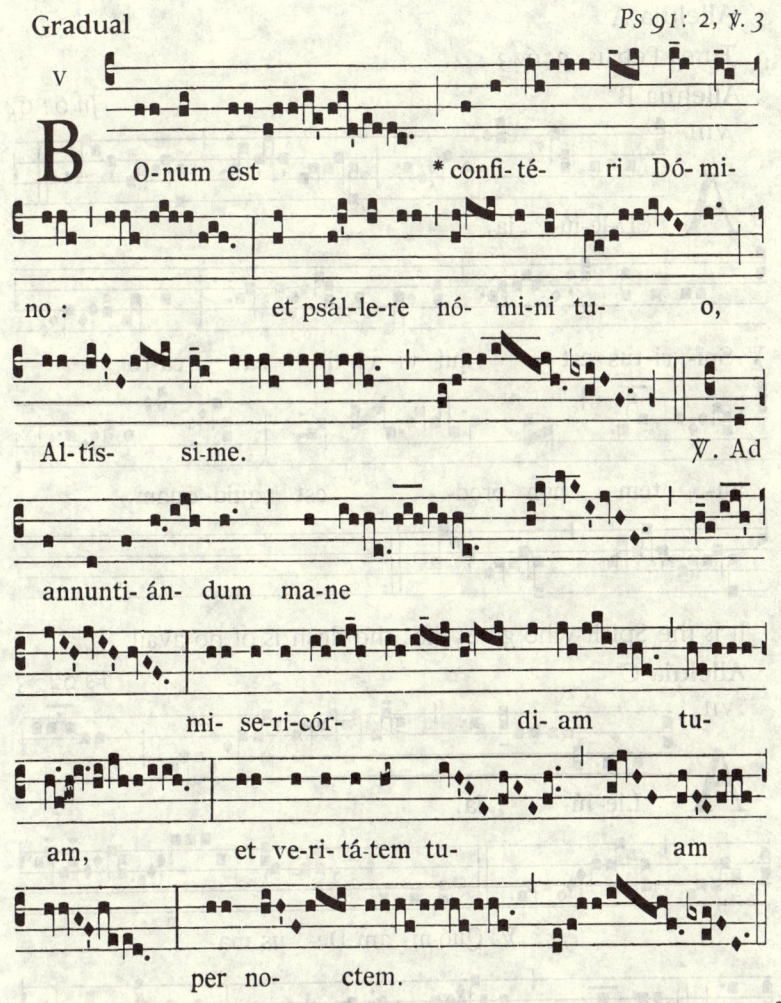

Gradual — Ps 91: 2, ℣. 3

Bonum est *confitéri Dómino: et psállere nómini tuo, Altíssime. ℣. Ad annuntiándum mane misericórdiam tuam, et veritátem tuam per noctem.

It is good to give thanks unto the Lord, and to sing in honour of your name, O Most High. ℣. To show forth your mercy in the morning, and your fidelity in the night.

Second reading
A. Rom 11: 33-36: *A hymn to the wisdom of God.*
B. Eph 5: 21-32: *Christ loved the Church.*
C. Heb 12: 5-7, 11-13: *The Lord chastises in love.*

Alleluia A
Tu es Petrus, p. 643.

Alleluia B
Jn 6 : 64

VIII

A L-le-lú- ia.

℣. Spí- ri-tus est qui vi- ví- fi- cat : ca-ro au- tem non prod- est quid- quam.

It is the Spirit who gives life; the flesh is of no avail.

Alleluia C
Ps 94 : 3

VII

A Lle-lú- ia.

℣. Quó-ni- am De- us ma- gnus Dó- mi- nus, et Rex ma- gnus super o- mnem ter-ram.

For the Lord is a great God; a great king over all the earth.

Gospel
A. Mt 16: 13-20: *Peter's confession at Cæsarea.*
B. Jn 6: 60-69: *Peter's fidelity to Christ.*
C. Lk 13: 22-30: *How to enter the Kingdom.*

Offertory   Ps 39: 2, 3, 4

E Xspé- ctans * exspectá- vi Dómi- num, et re- spé- xit me: et ex-au-dí- vit depreca- ti- ó- nem me- am, et immí- sit in os me- um cán-ti- cum novum, hymnum De- o no- stro.

With expectation I have waited for the Lord, and he has cast his look upon me; he has heard my supplication and he has put a new canticle into my mouth, a song to our God.

Ordinary Time

Prayer over the Gifts

Qui una semel hóstia, Dómine, adoptiónis tibi pópulum acquisísti, unitátis et pacis in Ecclésia tua propítius nobis dona concédas.

Merciful God, the perfect sacrifice of Jesus Christ made us your people. In your love, grant peace and unity to your Church.

Communion

Ps 103 : 13, 14, 15

VI

De fructu * óperum tuórum, Dómine, satiábitur terra: ut edúcas panem de terra, et vinum laetíficet cor hóminis: ut exhílaret fáciem in óleo, et panis cor hóminis confírmet.

The earth will be satisfied by the work of your hands, O Lord, as you bring forth bread from the land and wine to gladden the heart of man; oil to make his face shine, and bread to strengthen man's heart.

Or: Qui mandúcat, p. 423.

Prayer after Communion

Plenum, quæsumus, Dómine, in nobis remédium tuæ miseratiónis operáre, ac tales nos esse pérfice propítius et sic fovéri, ut tibi in ómnibus placére valeámus.

Lord, may this eucharist increase within us the healing power of your love. May it guide and direct our efforts to please you in all things.

TWENTY-SECOND SUNDAY

Introit   Ps 85: 3, 5 and 1

VIII

MIserére mihi Dómine, * quóniam ad te clamávi tota die: quia tu Dómine suávis ac mitis es, et copiósus in misericórdia ómnibus invocántibus te. *Ps.* Inclína Dómine aurem tuam et exáudi me: quóniam inops et pauper sum ego.

Have mercy on me, O Lord, for I have called out to you all the day; for you, O Lord, are good and forgiving and plenteous in mercy to all who call upon you. ℣. Incline your ear, O Lord, and hear me, for I am needy and poor.

Ordinary Time

Opening Prayer

DEUS virtútum, cuius est totum quod est óptimum, ínsere pectóribus nostris tui nóminis amórem, et præsta, ut in nobis, religiónis augménto, quæ sunt bona nútrias, ac, vigilánti stúdio, quæ sunt nutríta custódias.

ALMIGHTY GOD, every good thing comes from you. Fill our hearts with love for you, increase our faith, and by your constant care protect the good you have given us.

First reading

A. Jer 20: 7-9: *The prophet Jeremiah held in derision.*
B. Deut 4: 1-2, 6-8: *Fidelity to the law.*
C. Sir 3: 17-18, 20, 28-29: *The benefits of humility.*

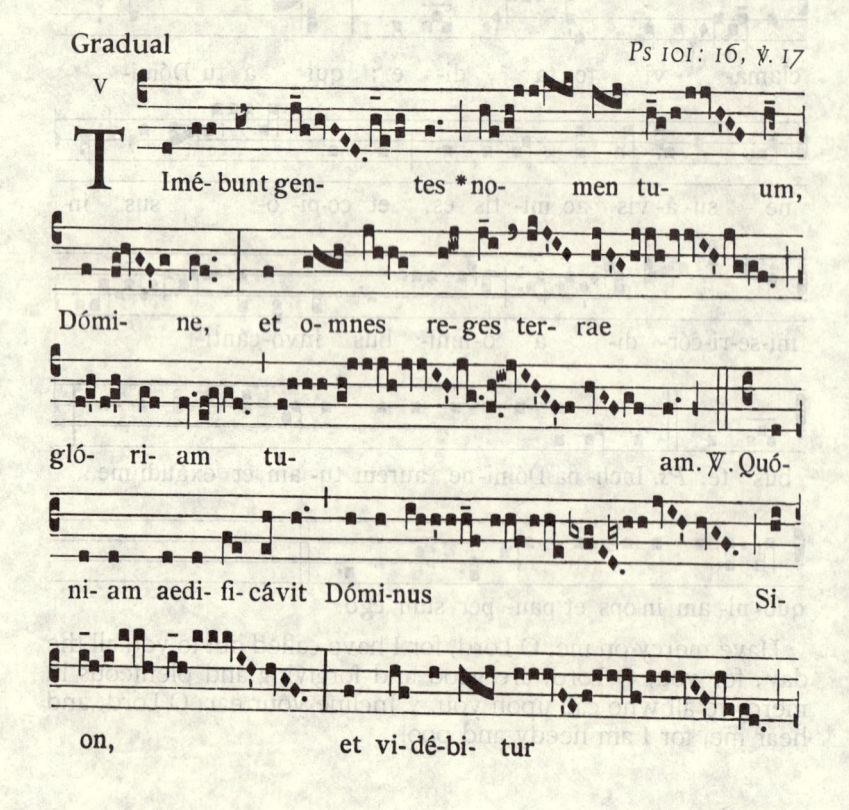

Gradual

Ps 101: 16, ℣. 17

Timébunt gentes *nomen tuum, Dómine, et omnes reges terrae glóriam tuam. ℣. Quóniam aedificávit Dóminus Sion, et vidébitur

22nd Sunday

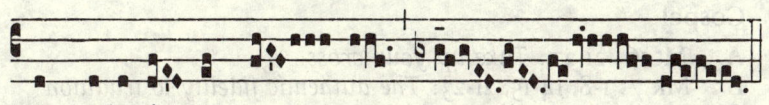

in ma-iestá- te su-   a.

The nations shall fear your name, O Lord, and all the kings of the earth your glory. ℣. For the Lord has built up Zion, and he shall appear in his majesty.

Second reading

A. Rom 12: 1-2: *Offer yourselves as a sacrifice.*
B. Jas 1: 17-18, 21b-22, 27: *Put the Word into practice.*
C. Heb 12: 18-19, 22-24a: *You have come to God.*

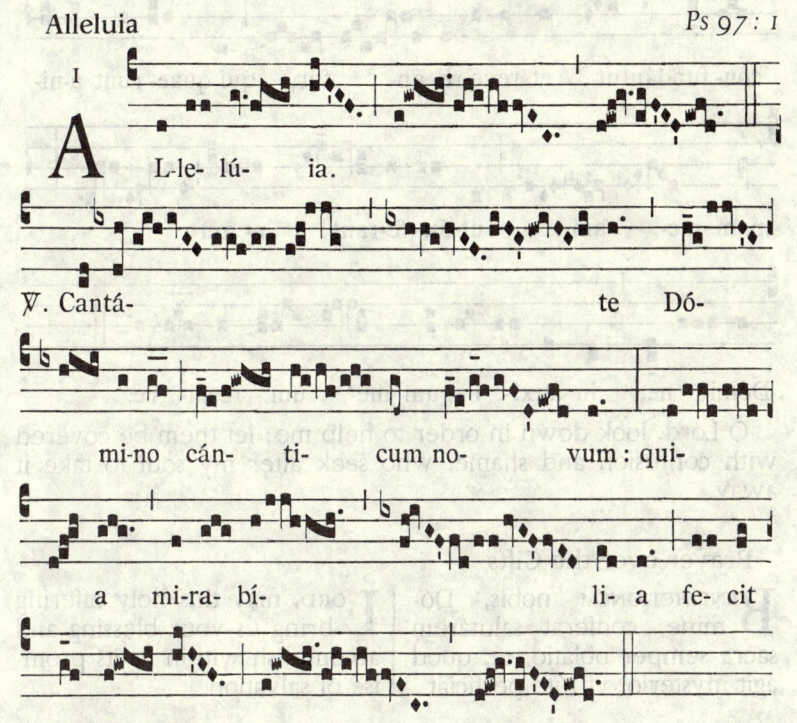

Alleluia   Ps 97: 1

A L-le- lú-   ia.

℣. Cantá-   te   Dó-

mi-no cán- ti-   cum no-   vum: qui-

a mi-ra-bí-   li- a fe- cit

Dó-mi- nus.

Sing to the Lord a new song; for the Lord has accomplished wondrous deeds.

Ordinary Time

Gospel
A. Mt 16: 21-27: *Take up your cross.*
B. Mk 7: 1-8, 14-15, 21-23: *The authentic fidelity to tradition.*
C. Lk 14: 1, 7-14: *Choose the last place.*

Offertory
Ps 39: 14, 15

VI

Dómine, * in auxílium meum réspice: confundántur et revereántur, qui quaerunt ánimam meam, ut áuferant eam: Dómine, in auxílium meum réspice.

O Lord, look down in order to help me; let them be covered with confusion and shame, who seek after my soul to take it away.

Prayer over the Gifts

Benedictionem nobis, Dómine, cónferat salutárem sacra semper oblátio, ut, quod agit mystério, virtúte perfíciat.

Lord, may this holy offering bring us your blessing and accomplish within us its promise of salvation.

Communion A
Qui vult veníre, p. 486.

22nd Sunday

Communion B & C *Ps 70: 16, 17, 18*

VIII

DOmine,* memorábor iustítiae tuae solíus: Deus, docuísti me a iuventúte mea, et usque in senéctam et sénium, Deus, ne derelínquas me.

O Lord, I will be mindful of your justice alone; you have taught me, O God, from my youth; and so, unto old age and grey hairs, O God, forsake me not.

Prayer after Communion

PANE mensæ cæléstis refécti, te, Dómine, deprecámur, ut hoc nutriméntum caritátis corda nostra confírmet, quátenus ad tibi ministrándum in frátribus excitémur.

LORD, you renew us at your table with the bread of life. May this food strengthen us in love and help us to serve you in each other.

TWENTY-THIRD SUNDAY

Introit   *Ps 118: 137, 124 and 1*

IUstus es Dómine, * et rectum iudícium tuum : fac cum servo tuo secúndum misericórdiam tuam. *Ps.* Beáti immaculáti in via : qui ámbulant in lege Dómini.

You are righteous, O Lord, and right is your judgement; deal with this servant of yours according to your mercy. ℣. Blessed are those whose way is blameless, who walk in the law of the Lord.

Opening prayer

DEUS, per quem nobis et redémptio venit et præstátur adóptio, fílios dilectiónis tuæ benígnus inténde, ut in Christo credéntibus et vera tribuátur líbertas, et heréditas ætérna.

GOD OUR FATHER, you redeem us and make us your children in Christ. Look upon us, give us true freedom and bring us to the inheritance you promised.

23rd Sunday

First reading
A. Ezek 33: 7-9: *Be a watchman for your neighbor.*
B. Is 35: 4-7a: *Announcement of salvation.*
C. Wis 9: 13-18b: *To seek the will of God.*

Gradual A & B *Ps 32: 12, ℣. 6*

Be-á-ta gens, * cu-ius est Dó-mi-nus De-us e-ó-rum : pó-pu-lus, quem e-lé-git Dó-mi-nus in he-re-di-tá-tem si-bi. ℣. Verbo Dó-mi-ni cae-li firmá-ti sunt : et spí-ri-tu o-ris e-ius o-mnis virtus e-ó-rum.

Blessed is the nation whose God is the Lord; the people whom he has chosen as his inheritance. ℣. By the Word of the Lord, the heavens were established, and all the power therein by the Spirit of his mouth.

Gradual C
Dómine, refúgium, p. 562.

Second reading
- A. Rom 13: 8-10: *Love which accomplishes the law.*
- B. Jas 2: 1-5: *Assistance to the poor.*
- C. Philem 9b-10, 12-17: *Paul pleads on behalf of a slave.*

Alleluia
Ps 101: 2

Al-le-lú-ia. ℣. Dómine, ex-áudi oratiónem meam, et clamor meus ad te véniat.

O Lord, hear my prayer; and let my cry come unto you.

Gospel
- A. Mt 18: 15-20: *Fraternal correction and prayer.*
- B. Mk 7: 31-37: *The healing of a man deaf and dumb.*
- C. Lk 14: 25-33: *Abnegation for Christ.*

23rd Sunday

Offertory — *Dan 9: 4, (2,) 17, 19*

Orávi *Deum meum ego Dániel, dicens: Exáudi, Dómine, preces servi tui: illúmina fáciem tuam super sanctuárium tuum: et propítius inténde pópulum istum, super quem invocátum est nomen tuum, Deus.

I prayed to my God, I, Daniel, and I said: "Hearken, O Lord, unto the prayers of your servant, and cause your face to shine upon your sanctuary; look with forgiveness upon this nation over whom your name has been invoked, O God."

Prayer over the Gifts

DEUS, auctor sincéræ devotiónis et pacis, da, quǽsumus, ut et maiestátem tuam conveniénter hoc múnere venerémur, et sacri participatióne mystérii fidéliter sénsibus uniámur.

GOD of peace and love, may our offering bring you true worship and make us one with you.

Communion

Ps 75: 12, 13

VO-vé-te, * et réd-di-te Dómino Deo vestro, omnes qui in circú-i-tu eius affér-tis múne-ra : terrí-bi-li, et e-i qui aufert spí-ri-tum príncipum : terrí-bi-li a-pud omnes re-ges ter-rae.

Make vows unto the Lord your God, and accomplish them, all you who gather around him to present offerings; to the awesome God who takes away the life of princes; he is greatly feared by all the kings of the earth.

Prayer after Communion

DA fidélibus tuis, Dómine, quos et verbi tui et cælésti sacraménti pábulo nutris et vivíficas, ita dilécti Fílii tui tantis munéribus profícere, ut eius vitæ semper consórtes éffici mereámur.

LORD, your word and your sacrament give us food and life. May this gift of your Son lead us to share his life for ever.

TWENTY-FOURTH SUNDAY

Introit *Sir 36 : 18; Ps 121*

DA pacem, * Dómine, sustinéntibus te, ut prophétae tui fidéles inveniántur : exáudi preces servi tui, et plebis tuae Israel. *Ps.* Laetátus sum in his quae dicta sunt mihi : in domum Dómini íbimus.

Grant peace to those who are waiting for you, O Lord, so that your prophets may be proved trustworthy; hear the prayers of your servant and of your people Israel. ℣. I rejoiced when it was said unto me: "Let us go to the house of the Lord."

Opening Prayer

RESPICE nos, rerum ómnium Deus creátor et rector, et, ut tuæ propitiatiónis sentiámus efféctum, toto nos tríbue tibi corde servíre.

ALMIGHTY GOD, our creator and guide, may we serve you with all our heart and know your forgiveness in our lives.

Ordinary Time

First reading
A. Sir 27: 30 - 28: 9: *Forgive your fellow man.*
B. Is 50: 5-9a: *The suffering servant.*
C. Ex 32: 7-11, 13-14: *The golden calf.*

Gradual
VII   Ps 121: 1, ℣. 7

Laetátus sum * in his quae dicta sunt mihi : in domum Dómini íbimus. ℣. Fiat pax in virtúte tua : et abundántia in túrribus tuis.

I rejoiced when it was said unto me: "Let us go to the house of the Lord!" ℣. Let peace reign within your walls, and abundance in your towers.

Second reading
A. Rom 14: 7-9: *To live for Christ.*
B. Jas 2: 14-18: *Faith which is active.*
C. 1 Tim 1: 12-17: *Christ has come for salvation.*

24th Sunday

Alleluia *Ps 101: 16*

A- L- le- lú- ia.
℣. Ti- mé- bunt gen- tes no- men tu- um, Dó-mi- ne: et o- mnes re- ges ter- rae gló- ri- am tu- am.

The nations will fear your name, O Lord, and all the kings of the earth your glory.

Gospel
A. Mt 18: 21-35: *The merciless debtor.*
B. Mk 8: 27-35: *The confession of Peter at Cæsarea.*
C. Lk 15: 1-32 or 1-10: *The merciful Father.*

Offertory A & B *Cf. Ex 24: 4, 5*

S Ancti- fi- cá- vit * Mó- y- ses altá- re

Ordinary Time

Dómino, ófferens super illud holocáusta, et immolans víctimas: fecit sacrifícium vespertínum in odórem suavitátis Dómino Deo, in conspéctu filiórum Israel.

Moses consecrated an altar to the Lord, and presented thereupon burnt offerings and sacrificial victims; he made an evening sacrifice as a fragrant offering to the Lord, in the presence of the sons of Israel.

Offertory C
Precátus est, p. 519.

Prayer over the Gifts

PROPITIARE, Dómine, supplicatiónibus nostris, et has oblatiónes famulórum tuórum benígnus assúme, ut, quod sínguli ad honórem tui nóminis obtulérunt, cunctis profíciat ad salútem.

LORD, hear the prayers of your people and receive our gifts. May the worship of each one here bring salvation to all.

24th Sunday

Communion A — Ps 95: 8, 9

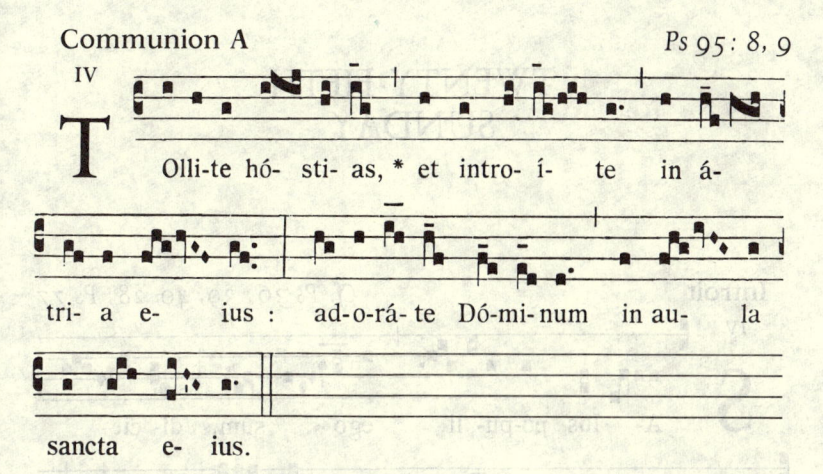

Tollite hóstias, * *et introíte in átria ejus: adoráte Dóminum in aula sancta ejus.*

Bring up your sacrifices and come into his courts; adore the Lord in his holy temple.

Communion B

Qui vult veníre, p. 486.

Communion C

Dico vobis: gáudium, p. 429.

Prayer after Communion

MENTES nostras et córpora possídeat, quǽsumus, Dómine, doni cæléstis operátio, ut non noster sensus in nobis, sed eius prævéniat semper efféctus.

LORD, may the eucharist you have given us influence our thoughts and actions. May your Spirit guide and direct us in your way.

TWENTY-FIFTH SUNDAY

Introit *Cf. Ps 36: 39, 40, 28; Ps 77*

Salus pópuli * ego sum, dicit Dóminus : de quacumque tribulatióne clamáverint ad me, exáudiam eos : et ero illórum Dóminus in perpétuum. *Ps.* Atténdite pópule meus legem meam : inclináte aurem vestram in verba oris mei.

I am the salvation of the people, says the Lord; from whatever tribulations they cry out to me, I will give heed to them; and I will be their Lord for ever. ℣. Attend, O my people, to my law; incline your ear to the words of my mouth.

25th Sunday

Opening Prayer

DEUS, qui sacræ legis ómnia constitúta in tua et próximi dilectióne posuísti, da nobis, ut, tua præcépta servántes, ad vitam mereámur perveníre perpétuam.

FATHER, guide us, as you guide creation according to your law of love. May we love one another and come to perfection in the eternal life prepared for us.

First reading
A. Is 55: 6-9: *Seek the Lord!*
B. Wis 2: 17-20: *The righteous man condemned.*
C. Amos 8: 4-7: *Perverse selling practices.*

Gradual A: Prope est Dóminus, p. *181.*

Gradual B: Dirigátur, p. *587.*

Gradual C: Quis sicut Dóminus, p. *443.*

Second reading
A. Phil 1: 20c-24, 27a: *To live, is Christ.*
B. Jas 3: 16 - 4: 3: *The wisdom of God and human passions.*
C. 1 Tim 2: 1-8: *God desires the salvation of all.*

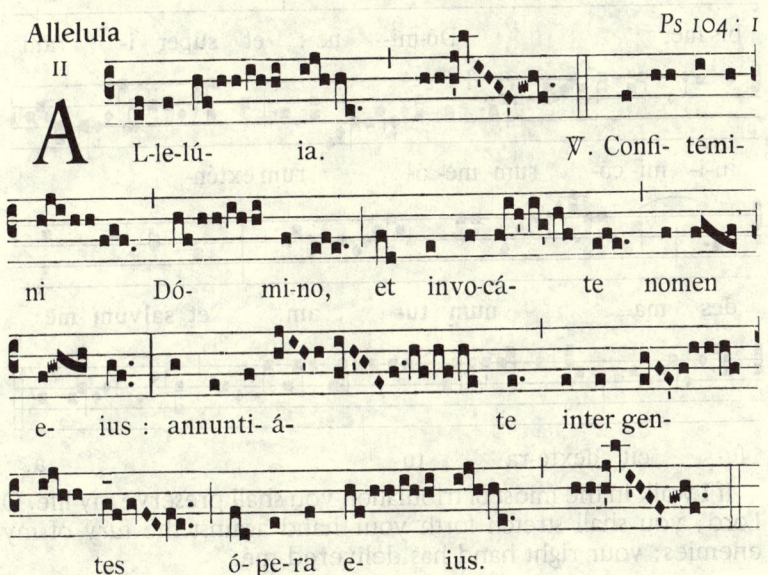

Alleluia Ps 104: 1

Al-le-lú- ia. ℣. Confitémini Dómino, et invocáte nomen eius: annuntiáte inter gentes ópera eius.

Ordinary Time

Give thanks unto the Lord, and call upon his name; declare his deeds among the nations.

Gospel

A. Mt: 20: 1-16a: *The labourers in the vineyard.*
B. Mk 9: 30-37: *Humility and service.*
C. Lk 16: 1-13 or 10-13: *The dishonest steward.*

Offertory

Ps 137: 7

VIII

SI ambulávero * in médio tribulatiónis, vivificábis me, Dómine: et super iram inimicórum meórum exténdes manum tuam, et salvum me fecit déxtera tua.

If I walk in the midst of tribulation you shall preserve my life, O Lord; you shall stretch forth your hand against the fury of my enemies; your right hand has delivered me.

25th Sunday

Prayer over the Gifts

MUNERA, quæsumus, Dómine, tuæ plebis propitiátus assúme, ut, quæ fídei pietáte profiténtur, sacraméntis cæléstibus apprehéndant.

LORD, may these gifts which we now offer to show our belief and our love be pleasing to you. May they become for us the eucharist of Jesus Christ your Son.

Communion Ps 118: 4, 5

TU mandásti * mandáta tua custodíri nimis: útinam dirigántur viae meae, ad custodiéndas iustificatiónes tuas.

You have ordered that your commandments be kept diligently; O that my ways may be guided towards the keeping of your statutes.

Prayer after Communion

QUOS tuis, Dómine, réficis sacraméntis, contínuis attólle benígnus auxíliis, ut redemptiónis efféctum et mystériis capiámus et móribus.

LORD, help us with your kindness. Make us strong through the eucharist. May we put into action the saving mystery we celebrate.

Ordinary Time

TWENTY-SIXTH SUNDAY

Introit A — *Phil 2: 10, 8, 11; Ps 101: 2*

IN nómine Dómini * omne genu flectátur, caeléstium, terréstrium et infernórum: quia Dóminus factus obédiens usque ad mortem, mortem autem crucis: ídeo Dóminus Iesus Christus in glória est Dei Patris.

Ps. Dómine exáudi oratiónem meam: et clamor meus ad te véniat.

At the name of the Lord let every knee bend, in heaven, on earth and under the earth; for the Lord became obedient unto death, even death on the Cross; that is why Jesus Christ is the Lord, to the glory of God the Father. ℣. O Lord, hear my prayer, and let my cry come unto you.

26th Sunday

Introit B & C *Dan 3: 31, 29, 30, 43, 42, Ps 118: 1*

O-mnia * quae fe-císti no- bis, Dó-mi- ne, in ve- ro iu-dí-ci-o fe- cí-sti, qui- a peccá-vi-mus ti- bi, et mandá-tis tu- is non obe-dí-vi- mus: sed da gló-ri- am nó-mi-ni tu- o, et fac no-bís- cum se-cún- dum multi-tú- di- nem mi- se- ri-cór-di- ae tu- ae. *Ps.* Be- á-ti imma-cu-lá-ti in vi- a: qui ámbu-lant in le- ge Dómi-ni.

All that you have inflicted upon us, O Lord, has been dealt out in true justice, for we have sinned against you and we have failed to obey your commandments; but give glory to your name and deal with us according to the abundance of your mercy. ℣. Blessed are those whose way is blameless, who walk in the law of the Lord.

Opening Prayer

DEUS, qui omnipoténtiam tuam parcéndo máxime et miserándo maniféstas, grátiam tuam super nos indesinénter infúnde, ut, ad tua promíssa curréntes, cæléstium bonórum fácias esse consórtes.

FATHER, you show your almighty power in your mercy and forgiveness. Continue to fill us with your gifts of love. Help us to hurry toward the eternal life you promise and come to share in the joys of your kingdom.

First reading

A. Ezek 18: 25-28: *Save your life by conversion.*
B. Num 11: 25-29: *The Lord gives his Spirit to whomever he chooses.*
C. Amos 6: 1a, 4-7: *The false security of the rich.*

Gradual A

Christus factus est, *p. 282.*

Gradual B & C : Oculi ómnium, *p. 414.*

Second reading

A. Phil 2: 1-11 *or* 1-5: *Imitate Christ's example.*
B. Jas 5: 1-6: *The injustices of the rich.*
C. 1 Tim 6: 11-16: *Be faithful to God.*

Alleluia

Ps 107: 2

Al- le- lú- ia. ℣. Pa- rá-tum cor me- um, De- us, pa- rá- tum cor me- um : cantá- bo, et psal- lam

26th Sunday

ti- bi gló- ri- a me- a.

My heart is ready, O God, my heart is ready; I will sing to you and praise you, my glory.

Gospel
A. Mt 21: 28-32: *Parable of the two sons.*
B. Mk 9: 38-43, 45, 47-48: *Requirements for entry into the Kingdom.*
C. Lk 16: 19-31: *The rich man and Lazarus the pauper.*

Offertory   *Ps 136: 1*

SU-per flúmi- na *Baby-lónis, il- lic sé- di- mus, et flé- vi-mus, dum re-corda-ré- mur tu- i, Si- on.

Upon the rivers of Babylon, there we sat down and we wept, as we remembered you, O Zion.

Prayer over the Gifts

CONCEDE nobis, miséricors Deus, ut hæc nostra tibi oblátio sit accépta, et per eam nobis fons omnis benedictiónis aperiátur.

GOD of mercy, accept our offering and make it a source of blessing for us.

Communion

Ps 118: 49, 50

M Eménto * verbi tui servo tuo, Dómine in quo mihi spem dedísti : haec me consoláta est in humilitáte mea.

Be mindful of your word to your servant, O Lord, in which you caused me to hope; this has been my comfort in my affliction.

Prayer after Communion

SIT nobis, Dómine, reparátio mentis et córporis cæléste mystérium, ut simus eius in glória coherédes, cui, mortem ipsíus annuntiándo, compátimur.

LORD, may this eucharist in which we proclaim the death of Christ bring us salvation and make us one with him in glory.

TWENTY-SEVENTH SUNDAY

Introit *Esther 13 : 9, 10, 11, Ps 118 : 1*

IN voluntáte tua, Dómine, * univérsa sunt pósita, et non est qui possit resístere voluntáti tuae: tu enim fecísti ómnia, caelum et terram, et univérsa quae caeli ámbitu continéntur: Dóminus universórum tu es. *Ps.* Beáti immaculáti in via: qui ámbulant in lege Dómini.

All things are submitted to your will, O Lord, and no one can resist your decisions; you have made all things, heaven and earth, and all that is contained under the vault of the sky; you are the master of the universe. ℣. Blessed are those whose way is blameless, who walk in the law of the Lord.

Opening Prayer

OMNIPOTENS sempitérne Deus, qui abundántia pietátis tuæ et mérita súpplicum excédis et vota, effúnde super nos misericórdiam tuam, ut dimíttas quæ consciéntia métuit, et adícias quod orátio non præsúmit.

FATHER, your love for us surpasses all our hopes and desires. Forgive our failings, keep us in your peace and lead us in the way of salvation.

First reading

A. Is 5: 1-7: *The song of the beloved to his vineyard.*
B. Gen 2: 18-24: *Creation of woman.*
C. Hab 1: 2-3; 2: 2-4: *The righteous will live by his fidelity.*

Gradual
Ps 89: 1, ℣. 2

DOmine, *refúgium factus es nobis, a generatióne et progénie.

℣. Priúsquam montes fí-

27th Sunday

... e-rent, aut forma-ré-tur terra et or- bis: a sǽ- cu- lo et in sǽ-cu-lum tu es De- us.

O Lord, you have been for us a refuge from age to age. ℣. Before the mountains were created, and before the land and the world were formed, from everlasting to everlasting, you are God.

Second reading

A. Phil 4: 6-9: *The God of peace will be with you.*
B. Heb 2: 9-11: *Jesus, son of God and our brother.*
C. 2 Tim 1: 6-8, 13-14: *A witness of fidelity.*

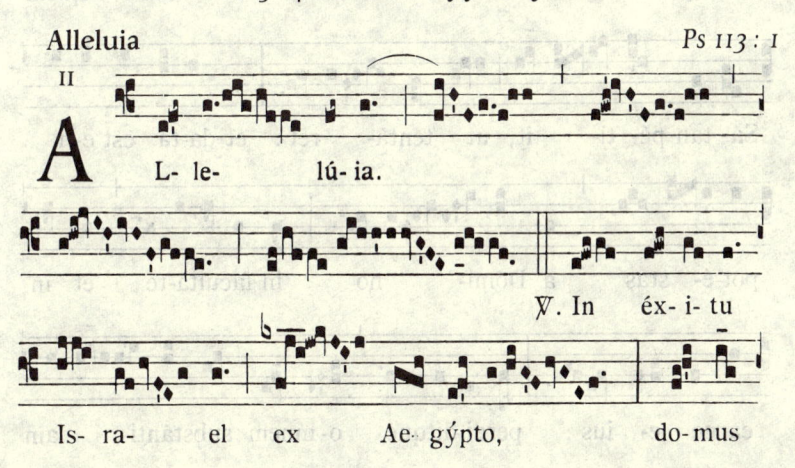

Alleluia   Ps 113 : 1

II

A L- le- lú- ia. ℣. In éx- i- tu Is- ra- el ex Ae- gýpto, do- mus

Ia- cob de pó- pu-lo bárba-ro.

When Israel went out of Egypt; the house of Jacob from a barbarous nation...

Gospel

A. Mt 21: 33-43: *The murderous vineyard tenants.*
B. Mk 10: 2-16 or 2-12: *Condemnation of divorce.*
C. Lk 17: 5-10: *The useless servants.*

Offertory *Job 1 and 2. 7*

VIR e-rat * in ter- ra nómi- ne Iob, simplex et re- ctus, ac ti-mens De- um: quem Satan pé- ti- it, ut tentá- ret: et data est e-i pot-é- stas a Dómi- no in facultá-te et in carne e- ius: perdi-dítque o-mnem substánti- am

27th Sunday

ipsíus, et fílios : carnem quoque eius gravi úlcere vulnerávit.

There was a man in the land of Hus whose name was Job, a blameless, upright and God-fearing man; Satan asked to be allowed to tempt him, and the Lord gave him power over his possessions and his body; and so, he destroyed his possessions and his children, and he ravaged his flesh with horrible sores.

Prayer over the Gifts

Súscipe, quǽsumus, Dómine, sacrifícia tuis institúta præcéptis, et sacris mystériis, quæ débitæ servitútis celebrámus offício, sanctificatiónem tuæ nobis redemptiónis dignánter adímple.

Father, receive these gifts which our Lord Jesus Christ has asked us to offer in his memory. May our obedient service bring us to the fullness of your redemption.

Communion — Ps 118: 81, 84, 86

In salutári tuo ánima mea, et in verbum tuum sperávi : quando fácies de persequéntibus me iudícium? iníqui persecúti sunt me, ádiuva* *me, Dómi- ne   De- us me- us.*

My soul aspires after your salvation; I hope in your word; when will you judge those who persecute me? The wicked are persecuting me; come to my assistance, O Lord my God.

Prayer after Communion

Concede nobis, omnípotens Deus, ut de percéptis sacraméntis inebriémur atque pascámur, quátenus in id quod súmimus transeámus.

Almighty God, let the eucharist we share fill us with your life. May the love of Christ which we celebrate here touch our lives and lead us to you.

TWENTY-EIGHTH SUNDAY

Introit *Ps 129: 3, 4 and 1, 2*

III

*SI in- iqui-tá-tes * observá- ve- ris Dó- mi- ne, Dómi-ne quis sus- ti-né- bit? qui- a apud te pro-pi-ti- á- ti- o est,   De- us   Isra- el. Ps. De*

28th Sunday

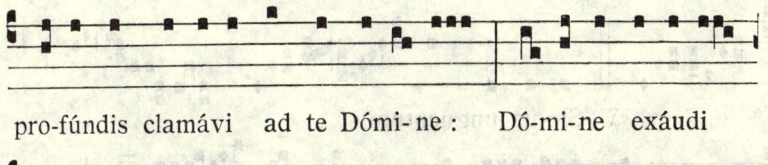

[chant: pro-fúndis clamávi ad te Dómi-ne: Dómi-ne exáudi vocem me-am.]

O Lord, if you were to take into account our iniquitites, who would withstand the test? But forgiveness abides with you, O God of Israel. ℣. Out of the depths have I cried to you, O Lord; Lord, hear my voice.

Opening Prayer

TUA NOS, quæsumus, Dómine, grátia semper et prævéniat et sequátur, ac bonis opéribus iúgiter præstet esse inténtos.

LORD, our help and guide, make your love the foundation of our lives. May our love for you express itself in our eagerness to do good for others.

First reading

A. Is 25: 6-10a: *A banquet which the Lord has prepared.*
B. Wis 7: 7-11: *Desire for Wisdom.*
C. 2 Kings 5: 14-17: *The healing of Naaman.*

Gradual A

Si ámbulem, p. 505.

Gradual B & C   Ps 132: 1, ℣. 2

*[chant: E-ce * quam bonum, et quam iucúndum habitáre fratres in unum!]*

℣. Sic-ut unguéntum in cá-pi-te, quod de-scén-dit in bar-bam, bar-bam A- a- ron.

Behold how good and how pleasant it is for brethren to dwell in unity. ℣. Like the precious ointment on the head, that ran down upon the beard, the beard of Aaron.

Second reading
A. Phil 4: 12-14, 19-20: *To endure all things.*
B. Heb 4: 12-13: *The power of God's Word.*
C. 2 Tim 2: 8-13: *I suffer for Him.*

Alleluia   Ps 113: 11

I
A L-le- lú- ia.
℣. Qui ti- ment Dó- mi-num, spe- rent in e- o: ad-

28th Sunday

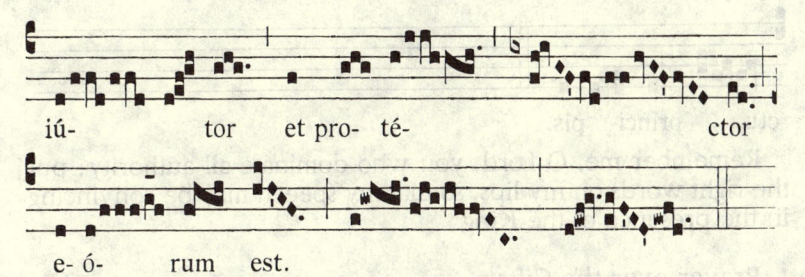

(music) iú- tor et pro- té- ctor e- ó- rum est.

Let those who fear the Lord put their trust in him; he is their help and their protection.

Gospel
A. Mt 22: 1-14 *or* 1-10: *The parable of the banquet.*
B. Mk 10: 17-30 *or* 17-27: *The rich young man.*
C. Lk 17: 11-19: *The curing of the ten lepers.*

Offertory
Esther 14: 12, 13

(music) R. E- cordá- re me- i, * Dó- mi- ne, omni pot-entá- tu- i dó- mi- nans: da sermó-nem re- ctum in os me- um, ut plá- ce- ant ver- ba me- a in conspé-

ctu   prínci- pis.

Remember me, O Lord, you who dominate all authority; put the right words on my lips, so that my speech may be convincing in the presence of the King.

Prayer over the Gifts

S USCIPE, Dómine, fidélium preces cum oblatiónibus hostiárum, ut, per hæc piæ devotiónis offícia, ad cæléstem glóriam transeámus.

L ORD, accept the prayers and gifts we offer in faith and love. May this eucharist bring us to your glory.

Communion

Ps 118: 22, 24

A U-fer a me * oppróbri- um et contémptum, qui- a man-dá-ta tu- a exqui- sí-vi, Dómi-ne : nam et te- stimó-ni- a tu- a me-di-tá- ti- o me- a est.

Remove from me all scorn and contempt, for I have kept your commandments; for your law is the object of my meditations.

Prayer after Communion

M AIESTATEM tuam, Dómine, supplíciter deprecámur, ut, sicut nos Córporis et Sánguinis sacrosáncti pascis aliménto, ita divínæ natúræ fácias esse consórtes.

A LMIGHTY Father, may the body and blood of your Son give us a share in his life.

TWENTY-NINTH SUNDAY

Introit *Ps 16: 6, 8 and 1*

E-go clamá- vi, * quó-ni- am exaudí-sti me, De- us: inclí-na aurem tu- am, et ex-áu- di verba me- a: cu-stó-di me, Dómi- ne, ut pu-píl-lam ó- cu- li: sub umbra a- lá- rum tu-á- rum pró- te-ge me. *Ps.* Exáudi Dómi-ne iustí-ti- am me- am: inténde depre-ca-ti- ó-nem me- am.

I have called out because you answer me, O God; incline your ear and hear my words; keep me, O Lord, like the apple of your eye; protect me under the shadow of your wings. ℣. Hear my just cause, O Lord; attend to my supplication.

Ordinary Time

Opening Prayer

OMNIPOTENS sempitérne Deus, fac nos tibi semper et devótam gérere voluntátem, et maiestáti tuæ sincéro corde servíre.

ALMIGHTY and ever-living God, our source of power and inspiration, give us strength and joy in serving you as followers of Christ.

First reading
A. Is 45: 1, 4-6: *The free choice of the Lord.*
B. Is 53: 10-11: *Redemptive suffering.*
C. Ex 17: 8-13: *Perseverance in prayer.*

Gradual

Ps 27: 9, ℣. 1

VII

S Al- vum fac * pó- pu- lum tu- um, Dó- mi- ne: et bé- ne- dic he-re-di-tá- ti tu- ae. ℣. Ad te Dó- mi- ne clamá- vi: De- us me- us, ne sí- le- as a me, et e- ro sí-mi-

29th Sunday

... lis de- scendén- ti-bus in la- cum.

Save your people, O Lord, and bless your inheritance. ℣. Unto you have I cried, O Lord; O my God, be not silent with me, lest I become like those who go down into the grave.

Second reading
A. 1 Thess 1: 1-5b: *Thanksgiving.*
B. Heb 4: 14-16: *Jesus, the Hig Priest.*
C. 2 Tim 3: 14 - 4: 2: *The strength of God's Word.*

Alleluia *Ps 145 : 2*

VIII

A L- le- lú- ia.

℣. Lauda, ánima mea, Dóminum : laudábo Dóminum in vita mea : psallam Deo meo, quámdiu ero.

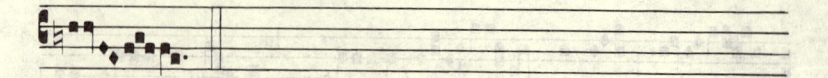

Praise the Lord, O my soul; I will praise the Lord throughout my life; I will sing in honour of my God as long as I have being.

Gospel

A. Mt 22: 15-21: *Cæsar's tax.*
B. Mk 10: 35-45 or 42-45: *The request of the sons of Zebedee.*
C. Lk 18: 1-8: *The widow and the unjust judge.*

Offertory
Ps 118: 47, 48

M Edi-tá- bor * in mandá- tis tu- is, quae di- lé- xi valde : et levá- bo ma- nus me- as ad mandá- ta tu- a, quae di- lé- xi.

I shall meditate upon your commandments which I greatly love; I will extend my hands towards your commandments which I love.

Prayer over the Gifts

TRIBUE nos, Dómine, quæsumus, donis tuis líbera mente servíre, ut, tua purificánte nos grátia, iísdem quibus famulámur mystériis emundémur.

LORD God, may the gifts we offer bring us your love and forgiveness and give us freedom to serve you with our lives.

30th Sunday

Communion — Ps 8: 2ab

*DOmine * Dóminus noster, quam admirábile est nomen tuum in univérsa terra!*

O Lord our governor, how admirable is your name in all the earth!

Prayer after Communion

FAC NOS, quæsumus, Dómine, cæléstium rerum frequentatióne profícere, ut et temporálibus benefíciis adiuvémur, et erudiámur ætérnis.

LORD, may this eucharist help us to remain faithful. May it teach us the way to eternal life.

THIRTIETH SUNDAY

Introit — Ps 104: 3, 4 and 1

*LAetétur cor * quaeréntium Dóminum: quaérite Dóminum, et confirmámini:*

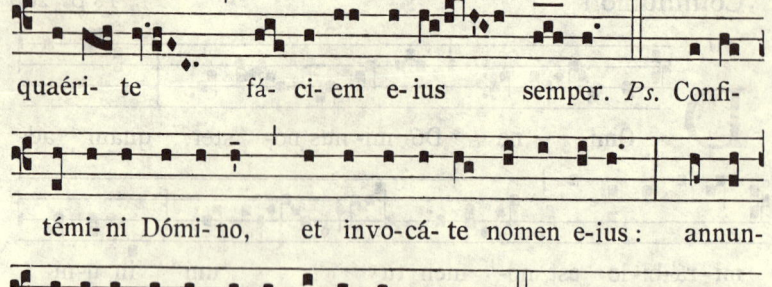

quaéri- te   fá- ci- em e- ius   semper. *Ps.* Confi-
témi- ni Dómi- no,   et invo-cá- te nomen e-ius :   annun-
ti- á-te   inter gentes ó- pe-ra   e- ius.

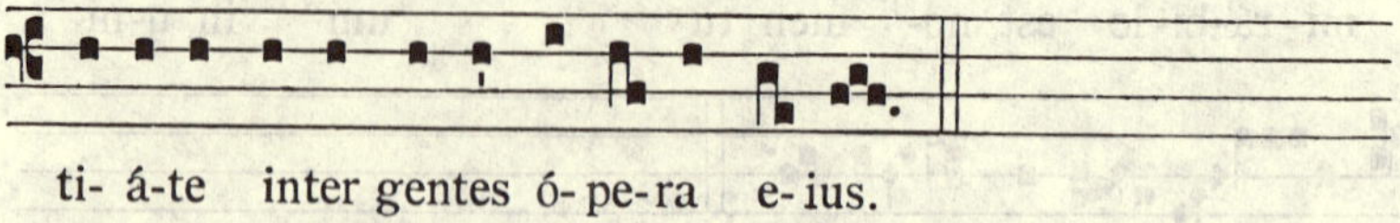

Let the hearts of those who seek the Lord rejoice; seek the Lord and be strengthened; seek his face for evermore. ℣. Give thanks to the Lord and call upon his name; declare his deeds among the gentiles.

Opening Prayer

OMNIPOTENS sempitérne Deus, da nobis fídei, spei et caritátis augméntum, et, ut mereámur ásseque quod promíttis, fac nos amáre quod præcipis.

ALMIGHTY and ever-living God, strengthen our faith, hope, and love. May we do with loving hearts what you ask of us and come to share the life you promise.

First reading

A. Ex 22: 20-26: *Responsibilities towards the weak.*
B. Jer 31: 7-9: *The joy of the return.*
C. Sir 35: 12-14, 16-18: *The Lord is merciful to all.*

Gradual A & B   Ps 26: 4

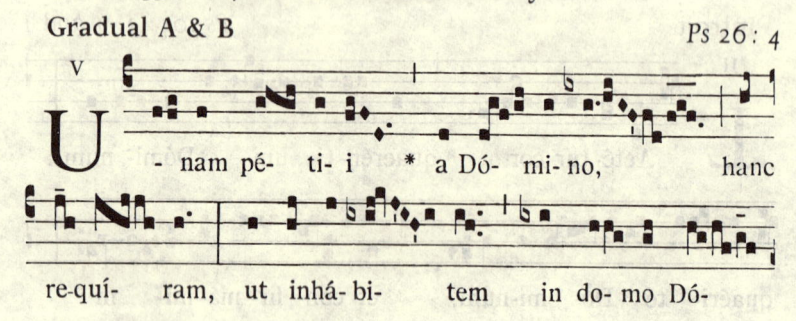

U- nam pé- ti- i * a Dó- mi- no,   hanc
re-quí- ram, ut inhá-bi-   tem   in do- mo Dó-

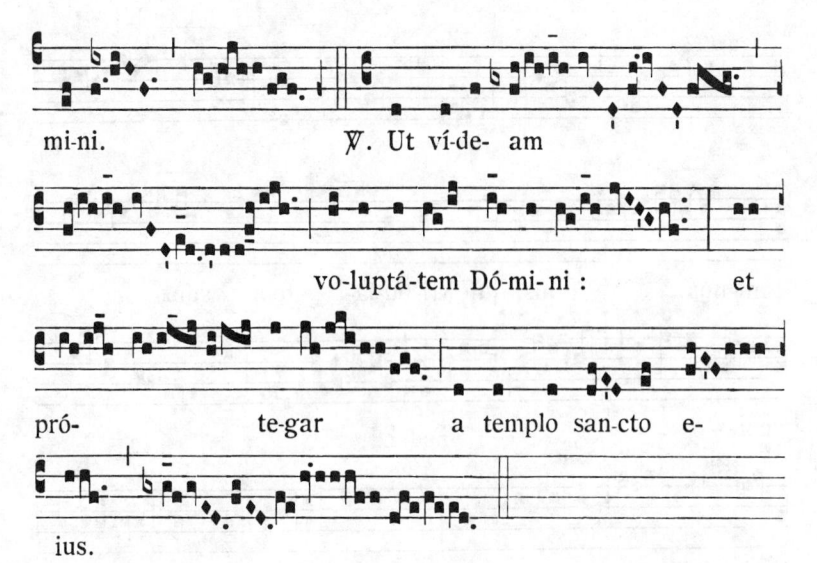

mi-ni. ℣. Ut ví-de- am vo-luptá-tem Dó-mi- ni : et pró- te-gar a templo san-cto e- ius.

One thing have I asked of the Lord, this will I seek after; that I may dwell in the house of the Lord. ℣. To gaze in delight upon the Lord's beauty, and to be sheltered in his holy temple.

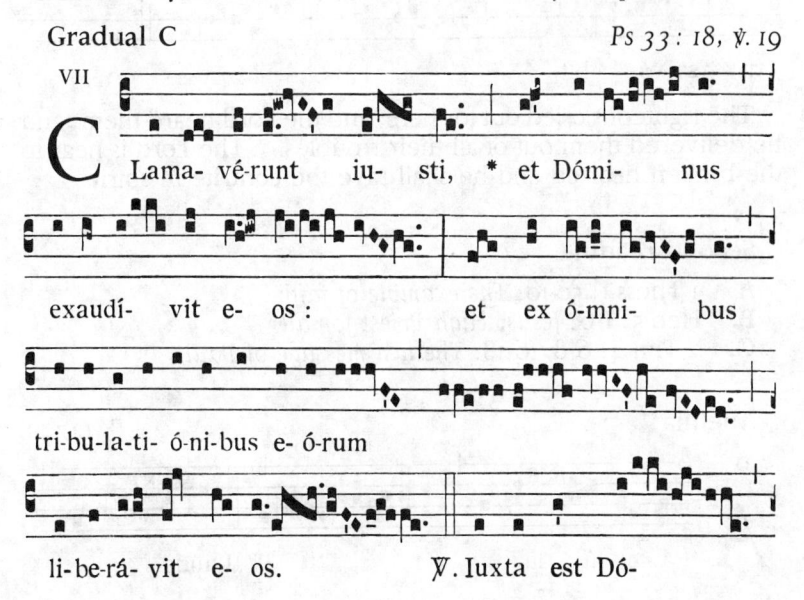

Gradual C *Ps 33 : 18, ℣. 19*

VII

Clama- vé-runt iu- sti, * et Dómi- nus exaudí- vit e- os : et ex ó-mni- bus tri-bu-la-ti- ó-ni-bus e- ó-rum li-be-rá- vit e- os. ℣. Iuxta est Dó-

... Dó- mi-nus his, qui tribu-lá- to sunt cor- de: et hú- mi- les spí-ri-tu salvá- bit.

The righteous cried out for help, and the Lord heard them; and he delivered them out of all their troubles. ℣. The Lord is near to the broken-hearted and he shall save the contrite in spirit.

Second reading

A. 1 Thess 1: 5c-10: *The example of faith.*
B. Heb 5: 1-6: *Jesus, High Priest for all.*
C. 2 Tim 4: 6-8, 16-18: *The last message of Paul.*

Alleluia Ps 147: 1

IV

A L-le- lú- ia. ℣. Lauda,

30th Sunday

Ierúsalem, Dóminum : lauda Deum tuum, Sion.

Praise the Lord, O Jerusalem; praise your God, O Zion.

Gospel
A. Mt 22: 34-40: *The greatest commandment.*
B. Mk 10: 46-52: *The blind man of Jericho.*
C. Lk 18: 9-14: *The Pharisee and the publican.*

Offertory
Ps 118: 107, 125

III

Dómine, * vivífica me secúndum elóquium tuum : ut sciam testimónia tua.

O Lord, grant me life according to your word, so that I may learn your commandments.

Prayer over the Gifts

RESPICE, quǽsumus, Dómine, múnera quæ tuæ offérimus maiestáti, ut, quod nostro servítio géritur, ad tuam glóriam pótius dirigátur.

LORD God of power and might, receive the gifts we offer and let our service give you glory.

Communion

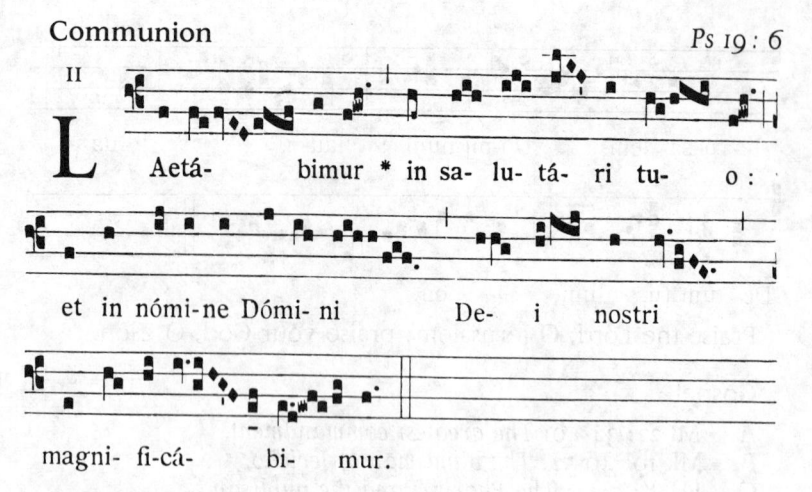

Ps 19 : 6

Lætábimur * in salutári tuo: et in nómine Dómini Dei nostri magnificábimur.

We shall rejoice in your salvation; and in the name of the Lord our God shall we place our pride.

Prayer after Communion

Perficiant in nobis, Dómine, quæsumus, tua sacraménta quod cóntinent, ut, quæ nunc spécie gérimus, rerum veritáte capiámus.

Lord, bring to perfection within us the communion we share in this sacrament. May our celebration have an effect in our lives.

THIRTY-FIRST SUNDAY

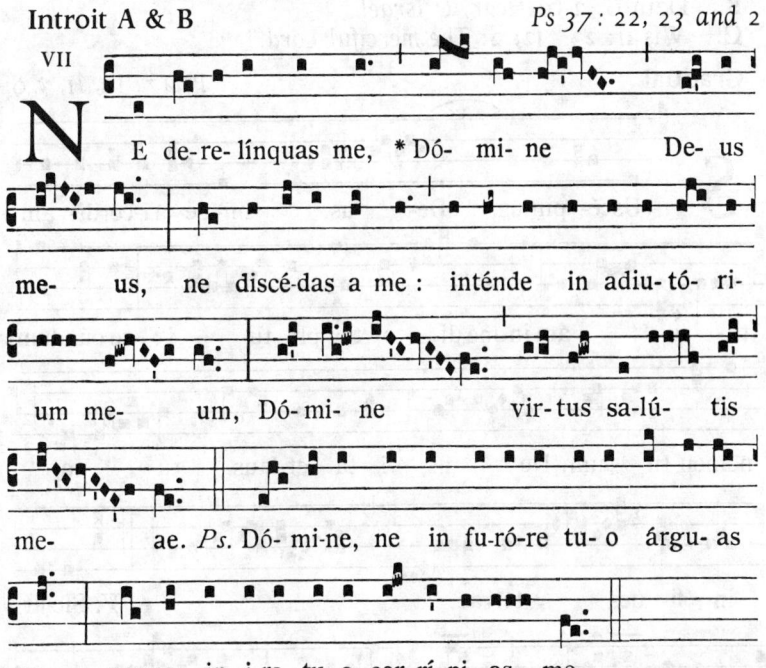

Introit A & B *Ps 37 : 22, 23 and 2*

NE de-re-línquas me, * Dómine Deus meus, ne discédas a me : inténde in adiutórium meum, Dómine virtus salútis meae. *Ps.* Dómine, ne in furóre tuo árguas me : neque in i-ra tua corrípias me.

Abandon me not, O Lord my God, do not depart from me; come to my assistance, O Lord, mainstay of my deliverance. ℣. O Lord, do not rebuke me in your anger; chastise me not in your wrath.

Introit C: Miseréris ómnium, p. 229.

Opening Prayer

OMNIPOTENS et miséricors Deus, de cuius múnere venit, ut tibi a fidélibus tuis digne et laudabíliter serviátur, tríbue, quǽsumus, nobis, ut ad promissiónes tuas sine offensióne currámus.

GOD of power and mercy, only with your help can we offer you fitting service and praise. May we live the faith we profess and trust your promise of eternal life.

Ordinary Time

First reading
A. Mal 1: 14b - 2: 2b, 8-10: *The Lord's warning.*
B. Deut 6: 2-6: *Hear, O Israel.*
C. Wis 11: 23 - 12: 2: *The merciful Lord.*

Gradual *Ps 47: 10, 11, ℣. 9*

Suscépimus, Deus, * misericórdiam tuam in médio templi tui: secúndum nomen tuum, Deus, ita et laus tua in fines terrae. ℣. Sicut audívimus, ita et vídimus in civitáte Dei nostri, in monte sancto eius.

We have received your mercy, O God, in the midst of your temple; even as your name, so does your praise extend to the ends of the earth. ℣. All that we have heard, we have now seen, in the city of our God, on his holy mountain.

31st Sunday

Second reading
A. 1 Thess 2: 7b-9, 13: *The Apostle's total gift of self.*
B. Heb 7: 23-28: *Jesus, High Priest for an eternal priesthood.*
C. 2 Thess 1: 11 - 2: 2: *Remain in the true faith.*

Alleluia A & B — Ps 32: 6

Al-le-lú-ia. ℣. Verbo Dómini caeli firmáti sunt, et Spíritu oris eius omnis virtus eórum.

By the Word of the Lord, the heavens were established, and all the power therein by the Spirit of his mouth.

Alleluia C — Wis 12: 1

Al-le-lú-ia. ℣. O quam bonus et suávis est, Dómine, Spíritus tu-

us in no- bis!

O Lord, how good and delightful your Spirit is in us!

Gospel

A. Mt 23: 1-12: *They preach but do not practice.*
B. Mk 12: 28b-34: *The two greatest commandments.*
C. Lk 19: 1-10: *Jesus at the house of Zacchæus.*

Offertory Ps 102: 2, 5

Benedic * ánima mea Dómino, et noli oblivísci omnes retributiónes eius: et renovábitur, sicut áquilae, iuvéntus tua.

31st Sunday

Bless the Lord, O my soul, and forget not all his benefits; and your youth shall be renewed like the eagle's.

Prayer over the Gifts

Fiat hoc sacrificium, Dómine, oblátio tibi munda, et nobis misericórdiæ tuæ sancta largítio.

God of mercy, may we offer a pure sacrifice for the forgiveness of our sins.

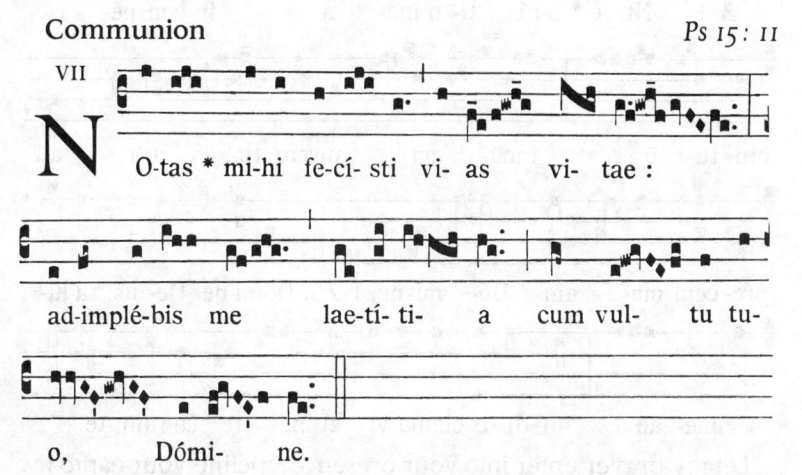

Communion
Ps 15: 11

Notas * mi-hi fe-cí-sti vi-as vi- tae: ad-implé-bis me lae-tí-ti- a cum vul-tu tu- o, Dómi- ne.

You have made known unto me the ways of life; you will fill me with joy at the sight of your countenance, O Lord.

Prayer after Communion

Augeatur in nobis, quæsumus, Dómine, tuæ virtútis operátio, ut, refécti cæléstibus sacraméntis, ad eórum promíssa capiénda tuo múnere præparémur.

Lord, you give us new hope in this eucharist. May the power of your love continue its saving work among us and bring us to the joy you promise.

THIRTY-SECOND SUNDAY

Introit — *Ps 87 : 3 and 2*

Intret * orátio mea in conspéctu tuo : inclína aurem tuam ad precem meam Dómine. *Ps.* Dómine Deus salútis meæ : in die clamávi, et nocte coram te.

Let my prayer enter into your presence; incline your ear to my supplication, O Lord. ℣. O Lord, God of my salvation, day and night have I cried before you.

Opening Prayer

OMNIPOTENS et miséricors Deus, univérsa nobis adversántia propitiátus exclúde, ut, mente et córpore páriter expedíti, quæ tua sunt líberis méntibus exsequámur.

GOD of power and mercy, protect us from all harm. Give us freedom of spirit and health in mind and body to do your work on earth.

First reading

A. Wis 6: 12-16: *To seek Wisdom.*
B. 1 Kings 17: 10-16: *Elijah and the widow of Zarephath.*
C. 2 Macc 7: 2, 9-14: *Faith in immortality.*

32nd Sunday

Gradual — Ps 140: 2

VII

Dirigátur * orátio mea sicut incénsum in conspéctu tuo, Dómine. ℣. Eleváthio mánuum meárum sacrifícium vespertínum.

Let my prayer ascend like incense in your presence, O Lord.
℣. May the lifting up of my hands be an evening sacrifice.

Second reading

A. 1 Thess 4: 13-18 or 13-14: *Hope in the resurrection.*
B. Heb 9: 24-28: *Christ offered himself once and for all.*
C. 2 Thess 2: 16 - 3: 5: *Paul's confidence in the Lord.*

Alleluia A — Mt 25: 4, 6

VII

Allelúia.

℣. Quinque pru- déntes vír-gi-nes acce- pé-runt ó-le-um in va-sis su- is cum lampá- di-bus: mé-di-a au-tem no- cte cla-mor factus est: Ecce sponsus ve- nit: ex- í- te ób- vi- am Christo Dó- mi-no.

The five wise virgins took oil in flasks with their lamps; at midnight there was a cry; "Behold, the bridegroom is here; come out to meet Christ the Lord."

Alleluia B & C *Ps 147 : 3*

A L-le- lú- ia. ℣. Qui pó-su- it fí- nes tu- os pa- cem, et á-di-pe fru-mén- ti sá- ti- at te.

32nd Sunday

He has established peace in your boundaries, and he fills you with the finest wheat.

Gospel

A. Mt 25: 1-13: *Parable of the ten virgins.*
B. Mk 12: 38-44 or 41-44: *The widow's penny.*
C. Lk 20: 27-38 or 27, 34-38: *A lesson concerning the resurrection.*

Offertory   Ps 118: 133

VIII

Gressus me-os * dí- ri- ge Dó- mi- ne secúndum e- ló- qui- um tu- um: ut non domi- né-tur omnis iniustí- ti- a, Dó-mi- ne.

Guide my footsteps, O Lord, according to your word, so that no iniquity may ever gain the upper hand, O Lord.

Prayer over the Gifts

SACRIFICIIS præséntibus, Dómine, quǽsumus, inténde placátus, ut, quod passiónis Fílii tui mystério gérimus, pio consequámur afféctu.

GOD of mercy, in this eucharist we proclaim the death of the Lord. Accept the gifts we present and help us follow him with love.

Ordinary Time

Communion A — *Mt 25: 4, 6*

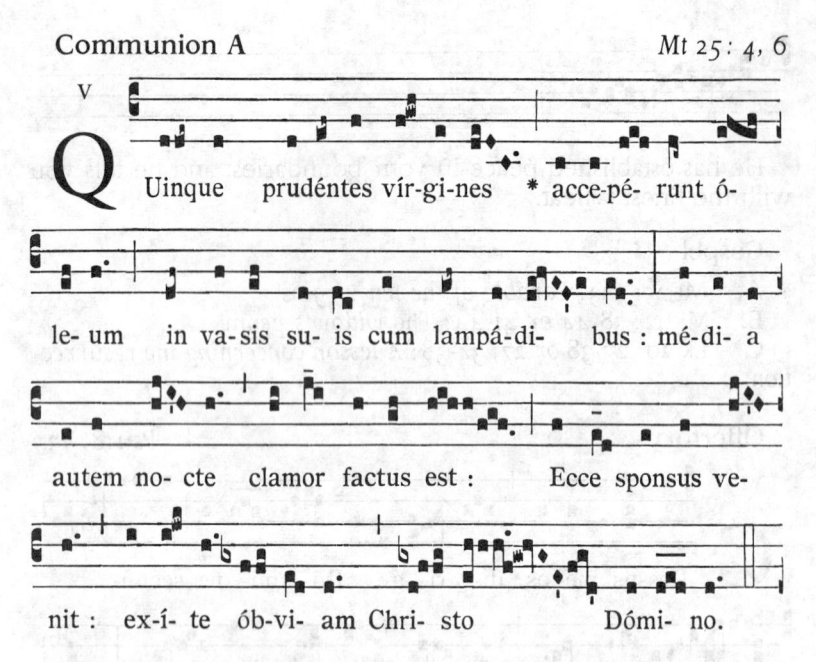

♪ QUinque prudéntes vírgines * accepérunt óleum in vasis suis cum lampádibus : média autem nocte clamor factus est : Ecce sponsus venit : exíte óbviam Christo Dómino.

The five wise virgins took oil in flasks with their lamps; at midnight there was a cry: "Behold, the bridegroom is here; come out to meet Christ the Lord."

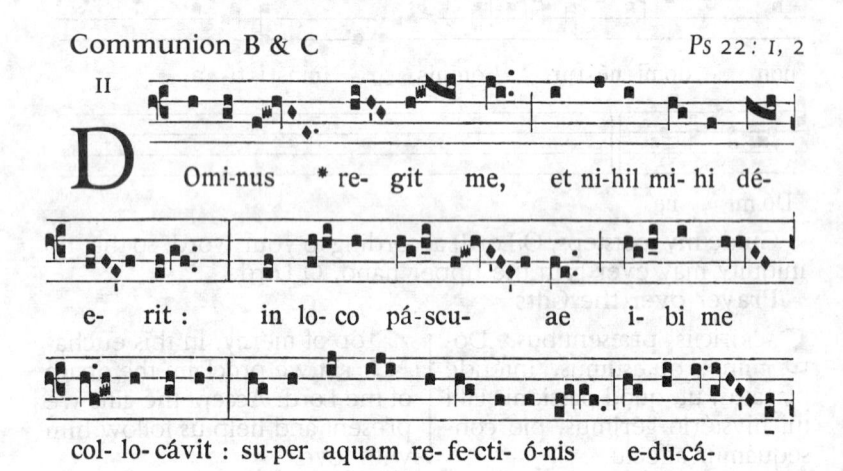

Communion B & C — *Ps 22: 1, 2*

♪ DOminus * regit me, et nihil mihi déerit : in loco páscuae ibi me collocávit : super aquam refectiónis educávit me.

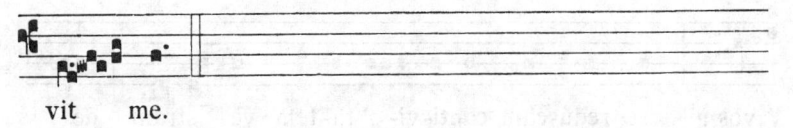

The Lord is my shepherd and I shall want nothing; he has set me in a land of abundant pastures; he has led me to life-renewing waters.

Prayer after Communion

GRATIAS tibi, Dómine, reféri-mus sacro múnere vegetáti, tuam cleméntiam implorántes, ut, per infusiónem Spíritus tui, in quibus cæléstis virtus introívit, sinceritátis grátia persevéret.

LORD, we thank you for the nourishment you give us through your holy gift. Pour out your Spirit upon us and in the strength of this food from heaven keep us single-minded in your service.

THIRTY-THIRD SUNDAY

Introit *Jer 29: 11, 12, 14; Ps 84*

VI

Dicit Dóminus : * Ego cógito cogitatiónes pacis, et non afflictiónis : invocábitis me, et ego exáudiam vos : et redú-cam capti-vi- tá-tem ve- stram de cunctis lo- cis. *Ps.* Be-ne-di-xísti Dómi-ne terram tu-am : avertísti capti-vi-tá-tem Ia-cob.

The Lord says: "I am pondering thoughts of peace and not of affliction; you shall call upon me, and I will hear you; and I will bring you back from all the lands where you are held captive."
℣. O Lord, you have blessed your land; you have put an end to Jacob's captivity.

Opening Prayer

DA NOBIS, quæsumus, Dómine, Deus noster, in tua semper devotióne gaudére, quia perpétua est et plena felícitas, si bonórum ómnium iúgiter serviámus auctóri.

FATHER of all that is good, keep us faithful in serving you, for to serve you is our lasting joy.

First reading
A. Prov 31: 10-13, 19-20, 30-31: *The valiant woman.*
B. Dan 12: 1-3: *The end of time.*
C. Mal 3: 19-20a: *The Lord's day.*

Gradual
Ps 43 : 8, ℣. 9

LI-be- rásti nos, *Dó- mi-ne, ex af-fli- génti-bus nos : et e-os qui nos odé-

33rd Sunday

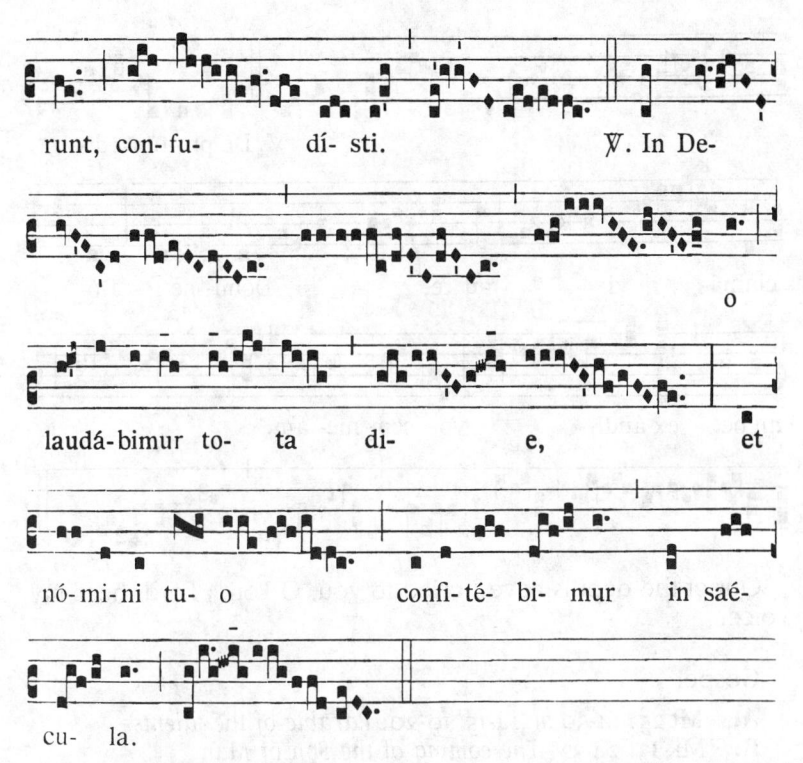

...runt, confudísti. ℣. In Deo laudábimur tota die, et nómini tuo confitébimur in saécula.

You have delivered us, Lord, from those who afflict us; and you have put to shame those who hate us. ℣. In God we shall take pride all day long; and we shall celebrate your name forever.

Second reading

A. 1 Thess 5: 1-6: *The coming of the Lord.*
B. Heb 10: 11-14, 18: *Jesus has offered the unique sacrifice.*
C. 2 Thess 3: 7-12: *We are bound to work.*

Alleluia Ps 129: 1, 2

VII

Al-le-lú- ia.

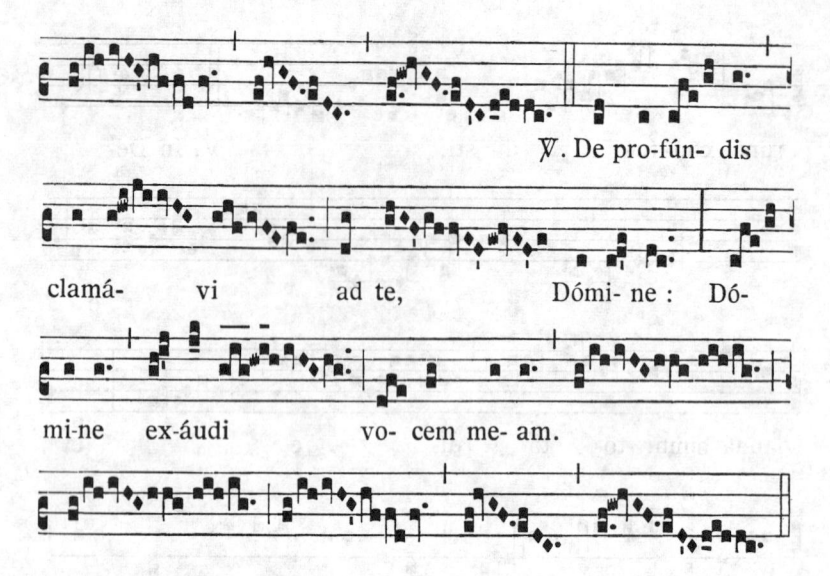

Ordinary Time

℣. De profúndis clamávi ad te, Dómine: Dómine exáudi vocem meam.

Out of the depths have I cried to you, O Lord; Lord, hear my voice.

Gospel

A. Mt 25: 14-30 or 14-15, 19-20: *Parable of the talents.*
B. Mk 13: 24-32: *The coming of the Son of Man.*
C. Lk 21: 5-19: *The trials of the last days.*

Offertory

Ps 129: 1,2

DE profúndis *clamávi ad te, Dómine: Dómine exáudi oratiónem meam:

33rd Sunday

de profún- dis clamá- vi ad te, Dómi- ne.

Out of the depths have I cried to you O Lord, Lord hear my prayer; out of the depths have I cried to you, O Lord.

Prayer over the Gifts

CONCEDE, quǽsumus, Dómine, ut óculis tuæ maiestátis munus oblátum et grátiam nobis devotiónis obtíneat, et efféctum beátæ perennitátis acquírat.

LORD God, may the gifts we offer increase our love for you and bring us to eternal life.

Communion A

Mt 25: 20, 21

DOmine, *quinque talénta tradidísti mihi: ecce ália quinque super-lucrátus sum. Euge serve fidélis, quia in pauca fuísti fidélis, supra multa te constítuam, intra in gáudium Dómini tui.

"Lord, you delivered five talents unto me; behold, I have gained five more." – "Well done, good and faithful servant; because you have been faithful over a little, I will set you over much; enter into the joy of your Lord."

Communion B & C Mk 11: 24

A- men di-co vo- bis, * quidquid o-rántes pé- ti- tis, cré- di-te qui- a acci-pi- é- tis, et fi- et vo- bis.

Amen I say to you, whatever you ask in your prayers, believe that you shall receive it, and it shall be granted unto you.

Prayer after Communion

SUMPSIMUS, Dómine, sacri dona mystérii, humíliter deprecántes, ut, quæ in sui commemoratiónem nos Fílius tuus fácere præcépit, in nostræ profíciant caritatis augméntum.

FATHER, may we grow in love by the eucharist we have celebrated in memory of the Lord Jesus.

Last Sunday of Ordinary Time

CHRIST THE KING

Solemnity

Introit — Rev 5: 12 and 1: 6, Ps 71

III

DIGNUS est Agnus, *qui occísus est, accípere virtútem, et divinitátem, et sapiéntiam, et fortitúdinem, et honórem. Ipsi glória et impérium in saécula saeculórum. *Ps.* Deus, iudícium tuum Regi da: et iustítiam tuam Fílio Regis.

The Lamb who has been slain is worthy to receive power, and divinity, and wisdom, and strength, and honour; let glory and dominion be his for ever and ever. ℣. Endow the King with your judgment, O God, and the King's son with your righteousness.

Opening Prayer

OMNIPOTENS sempitérne Deus, qui in dilécto Fílio tuo, universórum Rege, ómnia instauráre voluísti, concéde propítius, ut tota creatúra, a servitúte liberáta, tuæ maiestáti desérviat ac te sine fine colláudet.

ALMIGHTY and merciful God, you break the power of evil and make all things new in your Son Jesus Christ, the King of the universe. May all in heaven and earth acclaim your glory and never cease to praise you.

First reading

A. Ezek 34: 11-12, 15-17: *The Lord, pastor of his flock.*
B. Dan 7: 13-14: *The vision of the Son of Man.*
C. 2 Sam 5: 1-3: *David becomes king of Israel.*

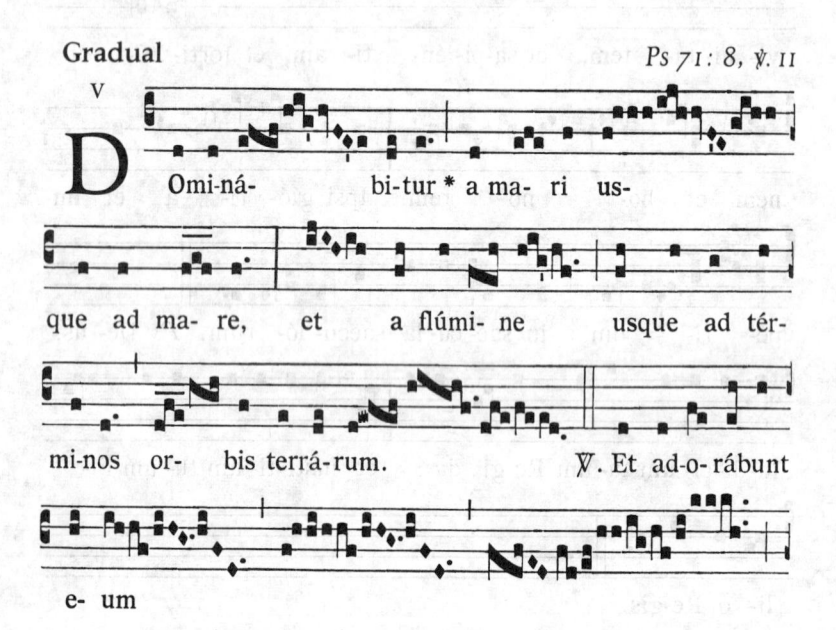

Gradual
Ps 71: 8, ℣. 11

Dominábitur * a mari usque ad mare, et a flúmine usque ad términos orbis terrárum. ℣. Et adorábunt eum

Christ The King

omnes re- ges ter- rae: o- mnes gen- tes sér- vi- ent e- i.

He shall rule from sea to sea, and from the river unto the ends of the earth. ℣. All the kings of the earth shall adore him; all nations shall serve him.

Second reading

A. 1 Cor 15: 20-26, 28: *God will be all in all.*
B. Rev 1: 5-8: *A kingdom of priests for God.*
C. Col 1: 12-20: *We have entered into the kingdom of the Son.*

Alleluia
Dan 7: 14

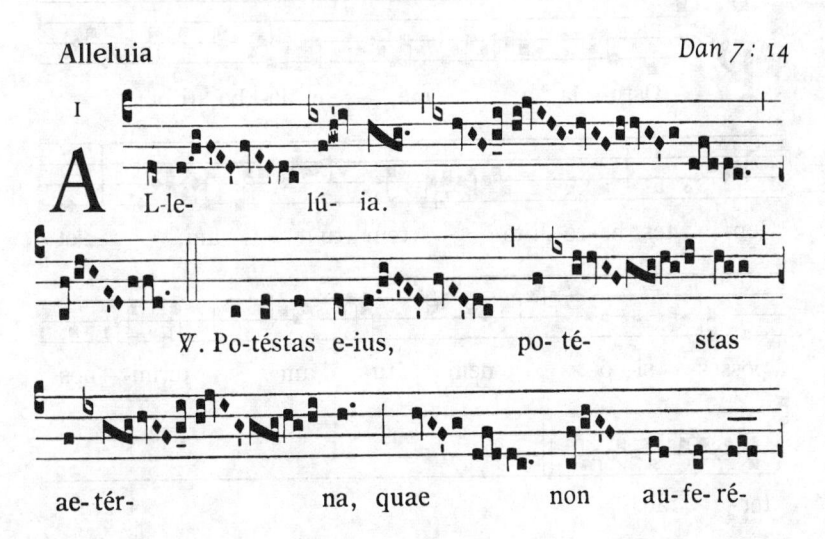

Al-le- lú- ia.

℣. Po-téstas e-ius, po- té- stas ae-tér- na, quae non au-fe-ré-

Christ The King

tur : et re- gnum e- ius, quod non cor- rumpé- tur.

His power is an everlasting power that shall not be taken away; and his kingdom shall not be destroyed.

Gospel

A. Mt 25: 31-46: *Judgment based on works of mercy.*
B. Jn 18: 33b-37: *Jesus before Pilate.*
C. Lk 23: 35-43: *The good thief.*

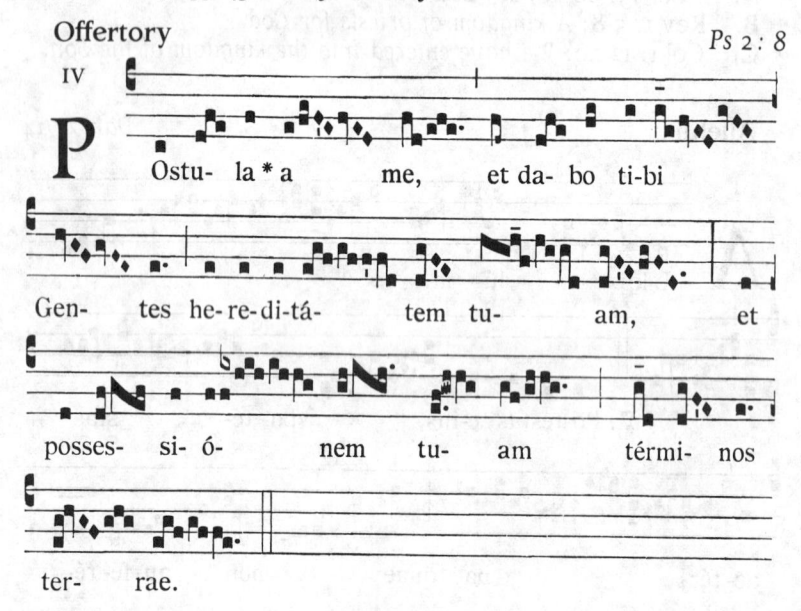

Offertory Ps 2: 8

POstu- la * a me, et da- bo ti-bi Gen- tes he- re- di- tá- tem tu- am, et posses- si- ó- nem tu- am térmi- nos ter- rae.

Christ The King

Ask of me, and I will give you the nations as your inheritance and the utmost parts of the earth as your possession.

Prayer over the Gifts

Hostiam tibi, Dómine, humánæ reconciliatiónis offeréntes, supplíciter deprecámur, ut ipse Fílius tuus cunctis géntibus unitátis et pacis dona concédat.

Lord, we offer you the sacrifice by which your Son reconciles mankind. May it bring unity and peace to the world.

Preface

Vere dignum et iustum est, æquum et salutáre, nos tibi semper et ubíque grátias ágere : Dómine, sancte Pater, omnípotens ætérne Deus :

Qui unigénitum Fílium tuum, Dóminum nostrum Iesum Christum, Sacerdótem ætérnum et universórum Regem, óleo exsultatiónis unxísti : ut, seípsum in ara crucis hóstiam immaculátam et pacíficam ófferens, redemptiónis humánæ sacraménta perágeret : et, suo subiéctis império ómnibus creatúris, ætérnum et universále regnum imménsæ tuæ tráderet maiestáti : regnum veritátis et vitæ ; regnum sanctitátis et grátiæ ; regnum iustítiæ, amóris et pacis.

Et ídeo cum Angelis et Archángelis, cum Thronis et Dominatiónibus, cumque omni milítia cæléstis exércitus, hymnum glóriæ tuæ cánimus, sine fine dicéntes :

Father, all-powerful and ever-living God, we do well always and everywhere to give you thanks.

You anointed Jesus Christ, your only Son, with the oil of gladness, as the eternal priest and universal King. As priest he offered his life on the altar of the cross and redeemed the human race by this one perfect sacrifice of peace. As king he claims dominion over all creation, that he may present to you, his almighty Father, an eternal and universal kingdom : a kingdom of truth and life, a kingdom of holiness and grace, a kingdom of justice, love, and peace.

And so, with all the choirs of angels in heaven we proclaim your glory and join in their unending hymn of praise: Holy...

Christ The King

Communion A *Mt 25: 40, 34*

A-men * di-co vo- bis: quod u- ni ex mí-ni-mis me- is fe- cístis, mi-hi fe- cístis: ve-ní- te bene-dícti Patris me- i, possi- dé-te praepa-rá-tum vo-bis regnum ab in- í- ti- o saécu- li.

Amen I say to you: in as much as you have done it to one of the least of these, my brethren, you have done it to me. Come, O blessed of my Father, inherit the kingdom prepared for you from the beginning of the world.

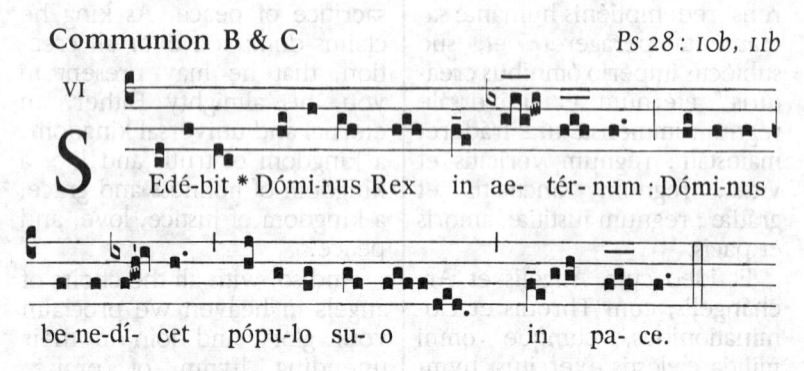

Communion B & C *Ps 28: 10b, 11b*

S Edé-bit * Dómi-nus Rex in ae- tér- num: Dómi-nus be-ne-dí- cet pópu-lo su- o in pa- ce.

The Lord will sit on his royal throne for ever; the Lord will bless his people in peace.

Christ The King

Prayer after Communion

IMMORTALITATIS alimóniam consecúti, quǽsumus, Dómine, ut, qui Christi Regis universórum gloriámur obœdíre mandátis, cum ipso in cælésti regno sine fine vívere valeámus.

LORD, you give us Christ, the King of all creation, as food for everlasting life. Help us to live by his gospel and bring us to the joy of his kingdom.

FEASTS OF THE LORD
&
SOLEMNITIES OF SAINTS

February 2

PRESENTATION OF THE LORD
Feast

BLESSING OF CANDLES

The people gather outside the church, carrying candles in their hands. While candles are being lit, the following antiphon is sung:

Antiphon   Is 35: 4, 5

III

EC-ce Dómi-nus noster * cum virtú-te vé-ni- et,

ut il-lúmi-net ó-cu-los servó-rum su- ó-rum, al-le-lú- ia.

Behold, Our Lord shall come with mighty power, to bring light to the eyes of those who serve him, alleluia.

The priest blesses the candles, using one of the two following prayers:

DEUS, omnis lúminis fons et orígo, qui iusto Simeóni Lumen ad revelatiónem géntium hódie demonstrásti, te súpplices deprecámur, ut hos céreos sanctificáre tua benedictióne dignéris, tuæ plebis vota suscípiens, quæ ad tui nóminis laudem eos gestatúra concúrrit, quátenus per virtútum sémitam ad lucem indeficiéntem perveníre mereátur.

GOD OUR FATHER, source of all light, today you revealed to Simeon your Light of revelation to the nations. Bless these candles and make them holy. May we who carry them to praise your glory walk in the path of goodness and come to the light that shines for ever.

February 2, Presentation

Or:

Deus, lumen verum, ætérnæ lucis propagátor et auctor, córdibus infúnde fidélium perpétui lúminis claritátem, ut, quicúmque in templo sancto tuo splendóre præséntium lúminum adornántur, ad lumen glóriæ tuæ felíciter váleant perveníre.

God our Father, source of eternal light, fill the hearts of all believers with the light of faith. May we who carry these candles in your church come with joy to the light of glory.

PROCESSION

The deacon or the priest says:

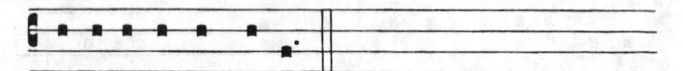

Pro-cedámus in pa-ce.
Let us go forth in peace.

All respond:

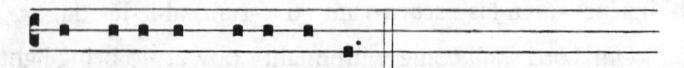

In nómi-ne Christi. Amen.
In the name of Christ. Amen.

Antiphons — Lk 2:32

VIII

LUMEN * ad re-ve-la-ti-ónem génti-um : et glóri-am ple-bis tu-ae Isra-el.

A Light for revelation to the gentiles, and for glory to your people Israel.

February 2, Presentation

VI

A-dór-na * thá-lamum tu- um, Si- on, et sús-cí-pe Regem Chri- stum: amplécte-re Ma- rí- am, quae est caelé- stis porta: i-psa e-nim por- tat Re-gem gló-ri- ae no-vi lúmi-nis: subsístit Virgo addú-cens má-ni-bus Fí- li- um ante lu-cí- fe- rum: quem accí-pi- ens Síme- on in ulnas su- as praedi-cá-vit pó-pu- lis Dó- mi-num e- um es-se vi- tae et mortis, et Salva-tó-rem mun- di.

Deck your bridal chamber, O Zion, and receive Christ the King. Embrace Mary, the gateway to heaven, for she bears the King of Glory and of new light; she remains a Virgin, holding within her hands a son begotten before the morning star; Simeon, taking him into his arms, declared to the nations that he is the Lord of life and of death, the Saviour of the world.

February 2, Presentation

Cf. Lk 2 : 26-29

℟. Espónsum * accépit Símeon a Spíritu Sancto, non visúrum se mortem, nisi vidéret Christum Dómini : et cum indúcerent púerum in templum, accépit eum in ulnas suas, et benedíxit Deum, et dixit : Nunc dimíttis, Dómine, servum tuum in pace.

Simeon had received a revelation from the Holy Spirit, that he should not see death before he had seen the Lord's Messiah. And when they brought the child into the Temple, he took him into his arms and blessed God, saying: "Lord, now you can let your servant go in peace."

February 2, Presentation

Responsory   Lk 2: 24, 23, ℣. 22

Obtulérunt * pro eo Dómino párturum, aut duos pullos columbárum : * Sicut scriptum est in lege Dómini. ℣. Postquam autem impléti sunt dies purgatiónis Maríae, secúndum legem Móysi, tulérunt Iesum in Ierúsalem, ut sísterent eum Dómino. * Sic-ut.

They offered for him unto the Lord "a pair of turtledoves or two young pigeons" as it is written in the law of the Lord. ℣. When the time of Mary's purification had been completed, according to the law of Moses, they brought Jesus to Jerusalem, to present him to the Lord.

THE MASS

As the procession enters the church, the Introit of the Mass is sung.

Introit: Suscépimus, p. 492, or Ecce, p. 217.

The Kýrie is omitted but the Glória is sung.

Opening Prayer

OMNIPOTENS sempitérne Deus, maiestátem tuam súpplices exorámus, ut, sicut unigénitus Fílius tuus hodiérna die cum nostræ carnis substántia in templo est præsentátus, ita nos fácias purificátis tibi méntibus præsentári.

ALL-POWERFUL Father, Christ your Son became man for us and was presented in the temple. May he free our hearts from sin and bring us into your presence.

First reading

Mal 3:1-4: *The manifestation of God in his temple.*

Gradual

Suscépimus, p. 582.

Second reading

Heb 2:14-18: *Jesus, like unto his brethren.*

Alleluia

Alle-lú-ia. ℣. Senex púerum portábat: puer au-

February 2, Presentation

... tem senem regébat.

The old man was carrying the infant child; but it was the child who was guiding the man.

Gospel
Lk 2: 22-40 or 22-32: *The presentation of Jesus in the Temple.*

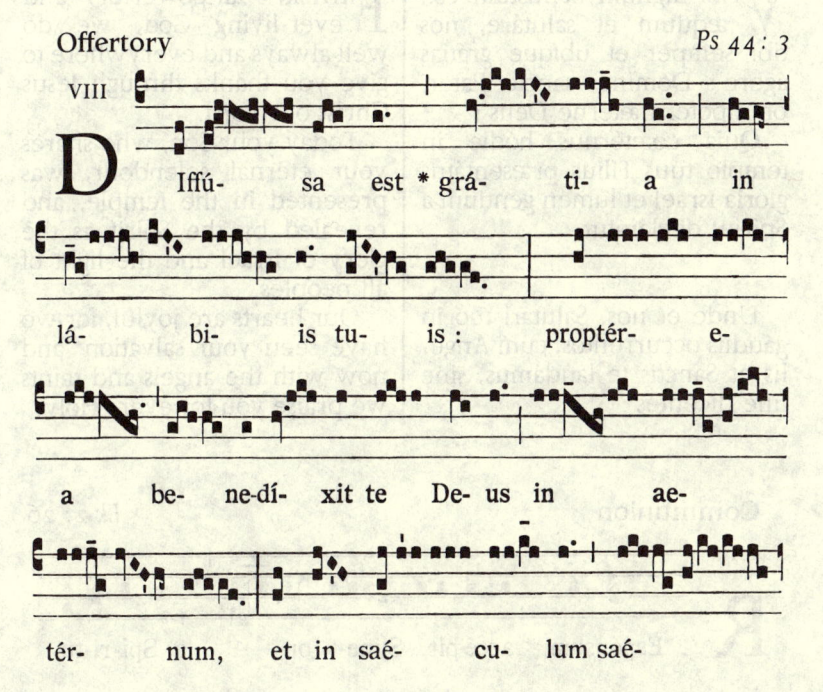

Offertory — Ps 44 : 3

VIII

Diffúsa est * grátia in lábiis tuis: proptérea benedíxit te Deus in aetérnum, et in saéculum saécu-li.

Grace has been poured out on your lips; therefore, God has blessed you for ever, world without end.

Prayer over the Gifts

Gratum tibi sit, Dómine, quǽsumus, exsultántis Ecclésiæ munus oblátum, qui unigénitum Fílium tuum voluísti Agnum immaculátum tibi offérri pro sǽculi vita.

Lord, accept the gifts your Church offers you with joy, since in fulfilment of your will your Son offered himself as a lamb without blemish for the life of the world.

Preface

Vere dignum et iustum est, æquum et salutáre, nos tibi semper et ubíque grátias ágere : Dómine, sancte Pater, omnípotens ætérne Deus :

Quia coætérnus hódie in templo tuus Fílius præsentátus glória Israel et lumen géntium a Spíritu declarátur.

Unde et nos, Salutári tuo in gáudiis occurréntes, cum Angelis et Sanctis te laudámus, sine fine dicéntes :

Father, all-powerful and ever-living God, we do well always and everywhere to give you thanks through Jesus Christ our Lord.

Today your Son, who shares your eternal splendour, was presented in the temple, and revealed by the Spirit as the glory of Israel and the light of all peoples.

Our hearts are joyful, for we have seen your salvation, and now with the angels and saints we praise you for ever: Holy...

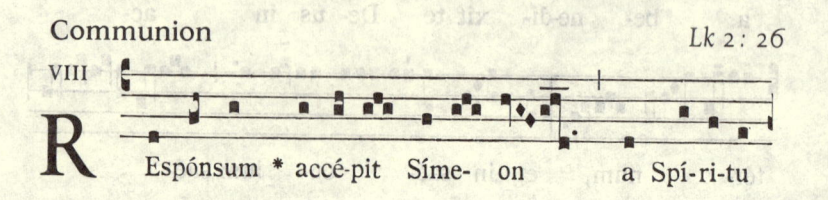

Communion

Lk 2 : 26

VIII

Respónsum * accépit Símeon a Spíritu

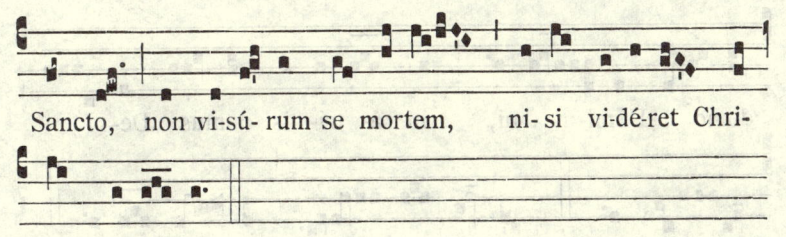

Sancto, non vi-sú-rum se mortem, ni-si vi-dé-ret Christum Dómi-ni.

Simeon had received a revelation from the Holy Spirit, that he would not see death before he had seen the Lord's Messiah.

Prayer after Communion

Per hæc sancta quæ súmpsimus, Dómine, pérfice in nobis grátiam tuam, qui exspectatiónem Simeónis implésti, ut, sicut ille mortem non vidit nisi prius Christum suscípere mererétur, ita et nos, in occúrsum Dómini procedéntes, vitam obtineámus ætérnam.

Lord, you fulfilled the hope of Simeon, who did not die until he had been privileged to welcome the Messiah. May this communion perfect your grace in us and prepare us to meet Christ when he comes to bring us into everlasting life.

March 19
SAINT JOSEPH
HUSBAND OF THE VIRGIN MARY
Solemnity

Introit — Ps 91: 13, 14 and 2

Iustus * ut palma floré-bit : sic-ut cedrus Lí-ba-ni multipli-cá-bi-tur : plantá-tus in

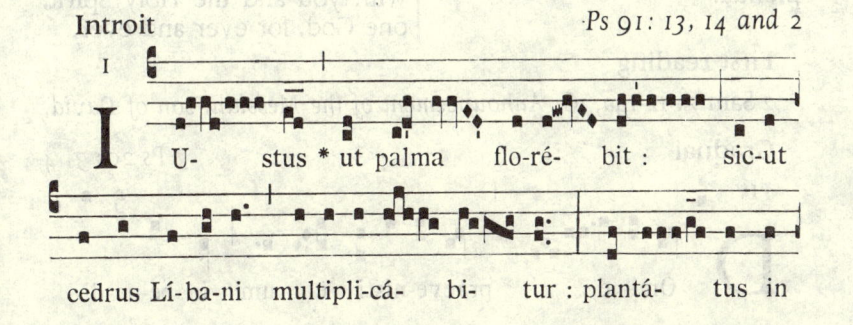

March 19, Saint Joseph

...domo Dómini, in átriis domus Dei nostri. T. P. Allelúia, allelúia.

Ps. Bonum est confitéri Dómino : et psállere nómini tuo, Altíssime.

The righteous man shall flourish like the palm tree; he shall grow up like the cedar of Lebanon; for he is planted in the house of the Lord, in the courts of our God. ℣. It is good to give praise to the Lord; and to sing in honour of your name, O Most High.

Opening Prayer

PRÆSTA, quǽsumus, omnípotens Deus, ut humánæ salútis mystéria, cuius primórdia beáti Ioseph fidéli custódiæ commisísti, Ecclésia tua, ipso intercedénte, iúgiter servet implénda.

FATHER, you entrusted our Saviour to the care of Saint Joseph. By the help of his prayers may your Church continue to serve its Lord, Jesus Christ, who lives and reigns with you and the Holy Spirit, one God, for ever and ever.

First reading

2 Sam 7: 12-14a, 16: *Announcement of the Messiah, son of David.*

Gradual

Ps 20: 3, 4

IV

Dómine, * praevenísti eum in benedi-

March 19, Saint Joseph

...ctiónibus dulcédinis: posuísti in cápite eius corónam de lápide pretióso. ℣. Vitam pétiit, et tribuísti ei longitúdinem diérum in saéculum saéculi.

O Lord, you have gone ahead to meet him with goodly blessings; you have placed a crown of precious stones on his head. ℣. He asked you for life, and you granted him length of days for ever and ever.

Second reading

Rom 4: 13, 16-18, 22: *A posterity received through faith.*

Tract *Ps 111: 1-3*

VIII

Beátus vir, * qui timet Dómi-

March 19, Saint Joseph

[musical notation]

num : in mandátis eius cupit nimis. ℣. Potens in terra erit semen eius : generátio rectórum benedicétur. ℣. Glória et divítiae in domo eius : et iustítia eius manet in saéculum saéculi.

Blessed is the man who fears the Lord; he shall delight exceedingly in his commandments. ℣. His seed shall be mighty upon earth; the descendants of the righteous will be blessed. ℣. Glory and wealth are in his house; and his righteousness endures for ever.

March 19, Saint Joseph

Gospel

Mt 1: 16-24: *Annunciation to Joseph.*
Or: Lk 2: 41-51: *The Finding in the Temple.*

Offertory   Ps 88: 25

VE- ri- tas me- a * et mi-se-ri-cór- di- a me- a cum i- pso: et in nómi- ne me- o exaltá-bi- tur cornu e- ius.

My fidelity and my mercy are with him; and in my name shall his horn be exalted.

Prayer over the Gifts

QUÆSUMUS, Dómine, ut, sicut beátus Ioseph Unigénito tuo, nato de María Vírgine, pia devotióne desérviit, ita et nos mundo corde tuis altáribus mereámur ministráre.

FATHER, with unselfish love Saint Joseph cared for your Son, born of the Virgin Mary. May we also serve you at your altar with pure hearts.

Preface

VERE dignum et iustum est, æquum et salutáre, nos tibi semper et ubíque grátias ágere: Dómine, sancte Pater, omnípotens ætérne Deus:
Et te in sollemnitáte beáti Ioseph débitis magnificáre præ-

FATHER, all-powerful and ever-living God, we do well always and everywhere to give you thanks as we honour Saint Joseph.
He is that just man, that wise and loyal servant, whom you

cóniis, benedícere et prædicáre. Qui et vir iustus, a te Deíparæ Vírgini Sponsus est datus, et fidélis servus ac prudens, super Famíliam tuam est constitútus, ut Unigénitum tuum, Sancti Spíritus obumbratióne concéptum, patérna vice custodíret, Iesum Christum Dóminum nostrum.

Per quem maiestátem tuam laudant Angeli, adórant Dominatiónes, tremunt Potestátes. Cæli cælorúmque Virtútes, ac beáta Séraphim, sócia exsultatióne concélebrant. Cum quibus et nostras voces ut admítti iúbeas, deprecámur, súpplici confessióne dicéntes :

placed at the head of your family. With a husband's love he cherished Mary, the Virgin Mother of God. With fatherly care he watched over Jesus Christ your Son, conceived by the power of the Holy Spirit.

Through Christ the choirs of angels and all the powers of heaven praise and worship your glory. May our voices blend with theirs as we join in their unending hymn: Holy...

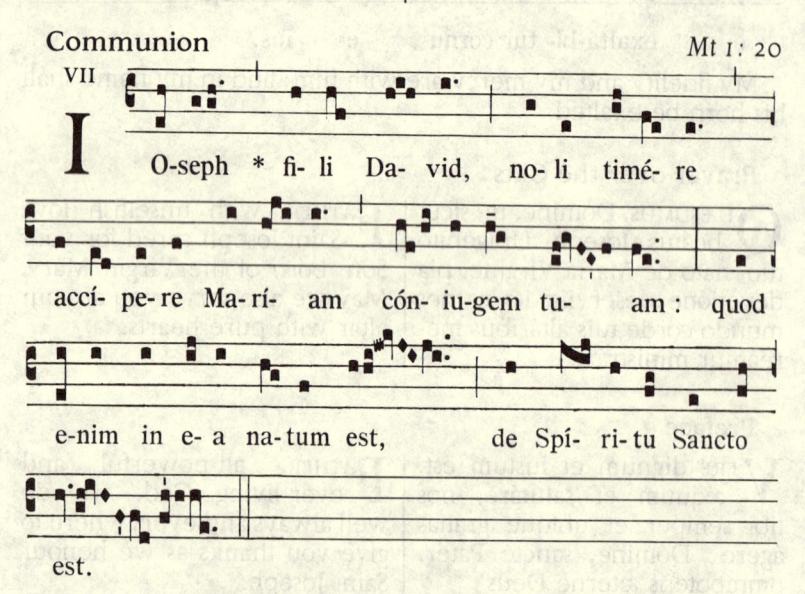

Communion — Mt 1: 20

IOseph * fi-li David, no-li timére accí-pe-re Marí-am cón-iu-gem tu-am : quod e-nim in e-a na-tum est, de Spí-ri-tu Sancto est.

Joseph, son of David, fear not to receive Mary as your wife; for that which is conceived in her comes from the Holy Spirit.

Or:

Fili, quid fecísti, *p. 206.*

Prayer after Communion

FAMILIAM tuam, quǽsumus, Dómine, quam de beáti Ioseph sollemnitáte lætántem ex huius altáris alimónia satiásti, perpétua protectióne defénde, et tua in ea propitiátus dona custódi.

LORD, today you nourish us at this altar as we celebrate the feast of Saint Joseph. Protect your Church always, and in your love watch over the gifts you have given us.

March 25
ANNUNCIATION OF THE LORD
Solemnity

Introit

Roráte, cæli, désuper, *p. 180*

Opening Prayer

DEUS, qui Verbum tuum in útero Vírginis Maríæ veritátem carnis humánæ suscípere voluísti, concéde, quǽsumus, ut, qui Redemptórem nostrum Deum et hóminem confitémur, ipsíus étiam divínæ natúræ mereámur esse consórtes.

GOD OUR FATHER, your Word became man and was born of the Virgin Mary. May we become more like Jesus Christ, whom we acknowledge as our redeemer, God and man.

First reading

Is 7: 10-14: *The announcement of the Messiah.*

March 25, Annunciation

Gradual — Ps 23 : 7, ℣. 3, 4

Tóllite * portas, príncipes, vestras: et elevámini portae aeternáles: et introíbit Rex glóriae.

℣. Quis ascéndet in montem Dómini? aut quis stabit in loco sancto eius? Ínnocens mánibus et mundo corde.

March 25, Annunciation

O princes, lift up your gates; be lifted high, O eternal gates, and the King of Glory shall make his entry. ℣. Who will go up to the mountain of the Lord, and who shall stand in his holy place? He who has innocent hands and a pure heart.

Or, during Eastertide:

Alleluia   Lk 1: 28

A-lle- lú- ia.

℣. Ave Ma- rí- a, grá-ti- a ple- na: Dó-mi- nus te- cum: be-ne- dí-cta tu in mu-li- é- ri-bus.

Hail Mary, full of grace, the Lord is with thee; blessed art thou amongst women.

Second reading
Heb 10: 4-10: *Christ enters into the world.*

Tract   Ps 44: 11, 12, 13, 10, 15, 16

A Udi fí- li- a, * et vi- de, et inclí-na aurem tu- am: qui- a concu-pí-vit

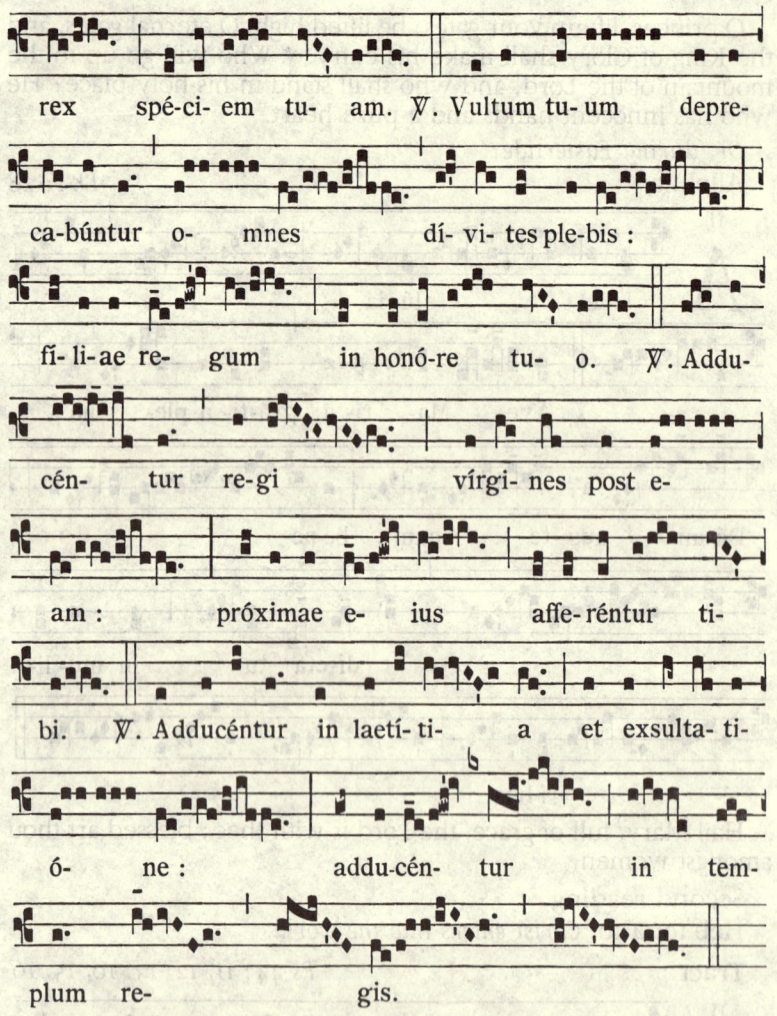

rex spé-ci-em tu- am. ℣. Vultum tu-um depre-
ca-búntur o- mnes dí-vi-tes ple-bis:
fí-li-ae re- gum in honó-re tu- o. ℣. Adducéntur re-gi vírgi-nes post e-
am: próximae e- ius affe-réntur ti-
bi. ℣. Adducéntur in laetí-ti- a et exsulta-ti-
ó- ne: addu-cén- tur in tem-
plum re- gis.

Hearken, O daughter, and behold, and incline your ear; for the king desires your beauty. ℣. All the rich among the people will implore your countenance; your maids of honour are the daughters of kings. ℣. Virgins will be brought to the king in her retinue; her companions will be taken to you. ℣. They will be brought with gladness and rejoicing; they shall be brought into the temple of the king.

March 25, Annunciation

Or, during Eastertide:

Alleluia   *Cf. Num 17 : 8*

ALleluia. ℣. Virga Iesse floruit : Virgo Deum et hominem genuit : pacem Deus reddidit, in se reconcilians ima summis.

The rod of Jesse has put forth buds, the Virgin has given birth to the God-Man; God has re-established peace; in himself, he has reconciled earth with heaven.

Gospel
Lk 1: 26-38: *The account of the Annunciation.*

Offertory
Ave, María, p. 183.

Prayer over the Gifts

ECCLESIÆ TUÆ munus, omnípotens Deus, dignáre suscípere, ut, quæ in Unigéniti tui incarnatióne primórdia sua constáre cognóscit, ipsíus gáudeat hac sollemnitáte celebráre mystéria.

ALMIGHTY Father, as we recall the beginning of the Church when your Son became man, may we celebrate with joy today this sacrament of your love.

March 25, Annunciation

Preface

Vere dignum et iustum est, æquum et salutáre, nos tibi semper et ubíque grátias ágere, Dómine, sancte Pater, omnípotens ætérne Deus, per Christum Dóminum nostrum.

Quem inter hómines et propter hómines nascitúrum, Spíritus Sancti obumbránte virtúte, a cælésti núntio Virgo fidénter audívit et immaculátis viscéribus amánter portávit, ut et promissiónes fíliis Israel perfíceret véritas, et géntium exspectátio patéret ineffabíliter adimplénda.

Per quem maiestátem tuam adórat exércitus Angelórum, ante conspéctum tuum in æternitáte lætántium. Cum quibus et nostras voces ut admítti iúbeas, deprecámur, sócia exsultatióne dicéntes:

Father, all-powerful and ever-living God, we do well always and everywhere to give you thanks through Jesus Christ our Lord.

He came to save mankind by becoming a man himself. The Virgin Mary, receiving the angel's message in faith, conceived by the power of the Spirit and bore your Son in purest love. In Christ, the eternal truth, your promise to Israel came true. In Christ, the hope of all peoples, man's hope was realized beyond all expectation.

Through Christ the angels of heaven offer their prayer of adoration as they rejoice in your presence for ever. May our voices be one with theirs in their triumphant hymn of praise: Holy...

Communion

Ecce Virgo concípiet, p. *184*.

Prayer after Communion

In méntibus nostris, quæsumus, Dómine, veræ fídei sacraménta confírma, ut, qui concéptum de Vírgine Deum verum et hóminem confitémur, per eius salutíferæ resurrectiónis poténtiam, ad ætérnam mereámur perveníre lætítiam.

Lord, may the sacrament we share strengthen our faith and hope in Jesus, born of a Virgin and truly God and man. By the power of his resurrection may we come to eternal joy.

June 24
BIRTH OF SAINT JOHN THE BAPTIST
Solemnity
VIGIL MASS

Introit — Lk 1: 13, 15, 14

VII

NE tímeas, * Zacharía, exaudíta est orátio tua : et Elísabeth uxor tua páriet tibi fílium, et vocábis nomen eius Ioánnem : et erit magnus coram Dómino : et Spíritu Sancto replébitur adhuc ex útero matris suae : et multi in nativitáte eius gaudébunt. *Ps.* Dómine, in virtúte tua laetábitur rex : et super salutáre tuum exsultábit veheménter.

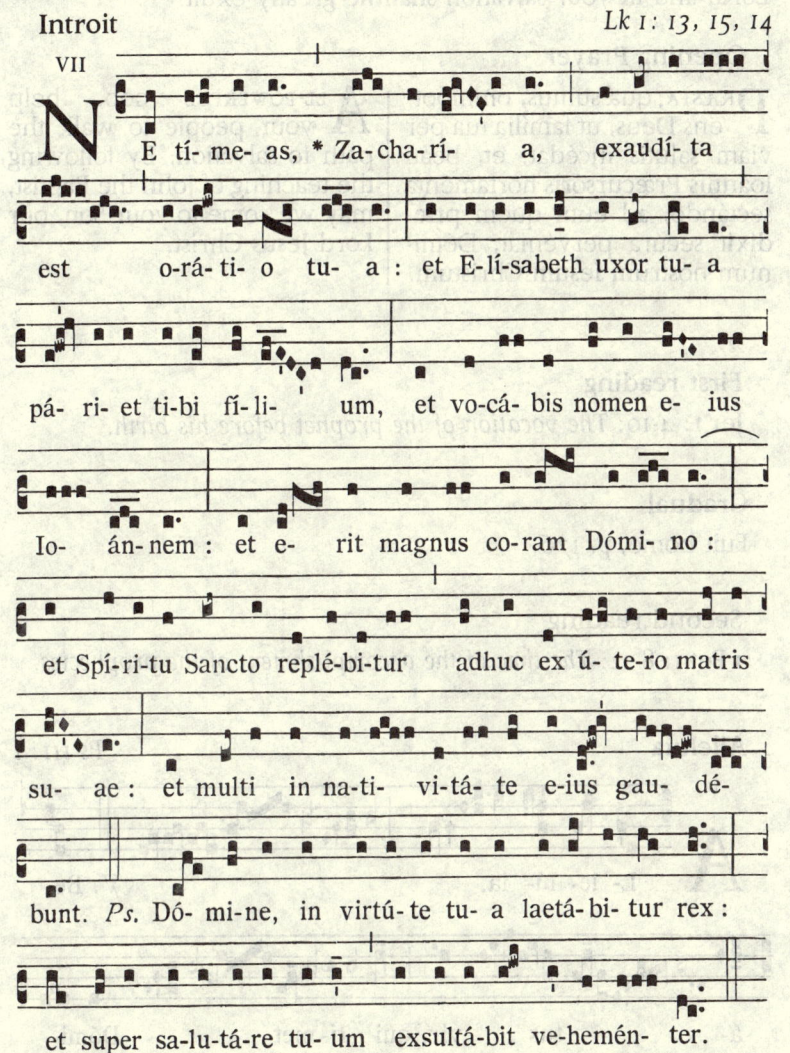

June 24, Saint John the Baptist

Fear not, Zechariah, your prayer has been answered; Elizabeth, your wife, will bear you a son, and you shall call his name John; he will be great before the Lord, and he will be filled with the Holy Spirit even from his mother's womb; and many will rejoice at his birth. ℣. In your strength shall the king rejoice, O Lord, and in your salvation shall he greatly exult.

Opening Prayer

PRÆSTA, quǽsumus, omnípotens Deus, ut família tua per viam salútis incédat, et, beáti Ioánnis Præcursóris hortaménta sectándo, ad eum quem prædíxit secúra pervéniat, Dóminum nostrum Iesum Christum.

ALL-POWERFUL GOD, help your people to walk the path to salvation. By following the teaching of John the Baptist, may we come to your Son, our Lord Jesus Christ.

First reading

Jer 1: 4-10: *The vocation of the prophet before his birth.*

Gradual

Fuit homo, p. 176.

Second reading

1 Pet 1: 8-12: *The time of the accomplishment of the prophecies.*

Alleluia

Ps 111: 1

Al- le- lú- ia. ℣. Be- á- tus vir, qui ti- met Dómi-

June 24, Saint John the Baptist

num : in mandá- tis e- ius
cu- pit nimis.

Blessed is the man who fears the Lord; he shall delight exceedingly in his commandments.

Gospel
Lk 1: 5-17: *Annunciation to Zechariah.*

Offertory
Ps 8: 6, 7

G Ló- ri- a * et ho- nó- re co-
ro- ná- sti e- um: et consti- tu- í- sti
e- um super ó- pe- ra má- nu- um
tu- á- rum, Dó- mi- ne.

You have crowned him with glory and honour; and you have established him over the work of your hands, O Lord.

June 24, Saint John the Baptist

Prayer over the Gifts

Munera pópuli tui, Dómine, propítius inténde, in beáti Ioánnis Baptístæ sollemnitáte deláta, et præsta, ut, quæ mystério gérimus, débitæ servitútis actióne sectémur.

Lord, look with favour on the gifts we bring on this feast of John the Baptist. Help us put into action the mystery we celebrate in this sacrament.

Preface p. 634

Communion Ps 20: 6

♪ Magna est glória eius * in salutári tuo: glóriam et magnum decórem impónes super eum, Dómine.

Great is his glory through your salvation; you have endowed him with glory and much splendour, O Lord.

Prayer after Communion

Sacris dápibus satiátos, beáti Ioánnis Baptístæ nos, Dómine, præclára comitétur orátio, et quem Agnum nostra ablatúrum crímina nuntiávit, ipsum Fílium tuum poscat nobis fore placátum.

Father, may the prayers of John the Baptist lead us to the Lamb of God. May this eucharist bring us the mercy of Christ.

June 24, Saint John the Baptist

MASS OF THE DAY

Introit *Is 49 : 1, 2; Ps 91*

De ventre matris meae * vocávit me Dóminus nómine meo: et pósuit os meum ut gládium acútum: sub teguménto manus suae protéxit me, pósuit me quasi sagíttam eléctam. *Ps.* Bonum est confitéri Dómino: et psállere nómini tuo, Altíssime.

    From my mother's womb the Lord called me by my name; and he made my mouth like unto a sharp sword; he protected me in the shadow of his hand, and he made me as his chosen arrow. ℣. It is good to give thanks to the Lord, and to praise your name, O Most High.

June 24, Saint John the Baptist

Opening Prayer

DEUS qui beátum Ioánnem Baptístam suscitásti, ut perféctam plebem Christo Dómino præparáret, da pópulis tuis spiritálium grátiam gaudiórum, et ómnium fidélium mentes dírige in viam salútis et pacis.

GOD our Father, you raised up John the Baptist to prepare a perfect people for Christ the Lord. Give your Church joy in spirit and guide those who believe in you into the way of salvation and peace.

First reading
Is 49: 1-6: *The vocation of Isaiah.*

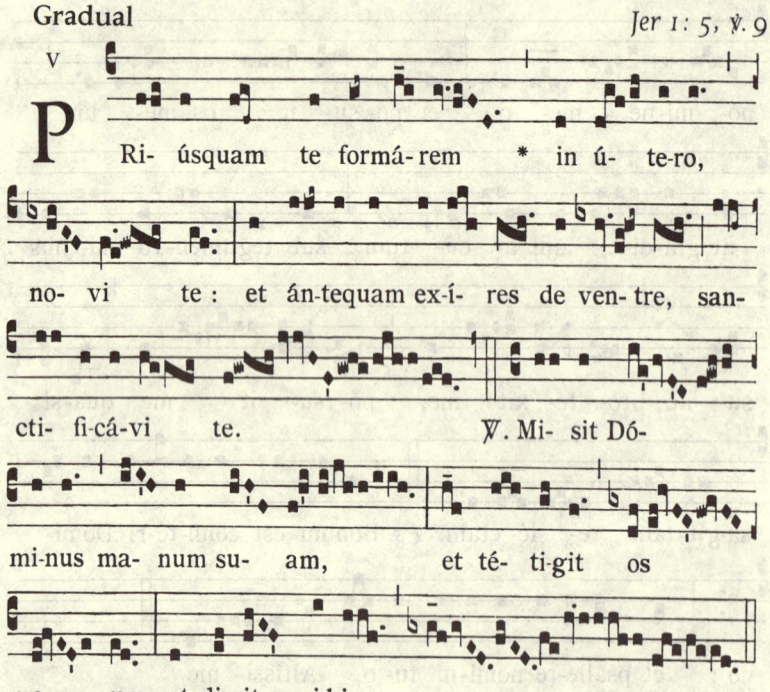

Gradual
Jer 1: 5, ℣. 9

Priusquam te formárem * in útero, novi te: et ántequam exíres de ventre, sanctificávi te. ℣. Misit Dóminus manum suam, et tétigit os meum, et dixit mihi.

Before I formed you in the womb, I knew you, and before you came out of the womb, I consecrated you. ℣. The Lord put forth his hand and touched my mouth, and he said unto me: Before I formed you etc.

June 24, Saint John the Baptist 633

Second reading

Acts 13: 22-26: *David, John the Baptist and Jesus.*

Alleluia   Lk 1: 76

A-lle-lú-ia. ℣. Tu, pu-er, prophé-ta Altíssimi vo-cábe-ris: prae-í-bis ante Dó-mi-num pa-rá-re vi-as e-ius.

And you, child, will be called the prophet of the Most High; you will go before the Lord to make ready his ways.

Gospel

Lk 1: 57-66, 80: *The birth of John the Baptist.*

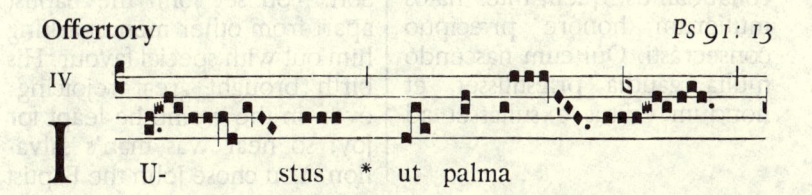

Offertory   Ps 91: 13

I-ustus * ut palma

floré- bit : sic-ut ce- drus, quae in Lí- ba- no est, mul- ti- pli- cá- bi- tur.

The righteous man shall flourish like the palm tree; he shall grow up like a cedar of Lebanon.

Prayer over the Gifs

Tua, Dómine, munéribus altária cumulámus, illíus nativitátem honóre débito celebrántes, qui Salvatórem mundi et cécinit affutúrum, et adésse monstrávit.

Father, accept the gifts we bring to your altar to celebrate the birth of John the Baptist, who foretold the coming of our Saviour and made him known when he came.

Preface

Vere dignum et iustum est, æquum et salutáre, nos tibi semper et ubíque grátias ágere : Dómine, sancte Pater, omnípotens ætérne Deus : per Christum Dóminum nostrum.

In cuius Præcursóre beáto Ioánne tuam magnificéntiam collaudámus, quem inter natos mulíerum honóre præcípuo consecrásti. Qui cum nascéndo multa gáudia præstitísset, et nondum éditus exsultásset ad

Father, all-powerful and ever-living God, we do well always and everywhere to give you thanks through Jesus Christ our Lord.

We praise your greatness as we honour the prophet who prepared the way before your Son. You set John the Baptist apart from other men, marking him out with special favour. His birth brought great rejoicing: even in the womb he leapt for joy, so near was man's salvation. You chose John the Baptist

humánæ salútis advéntum, ipse solus ómnium prophetárum Agnum redemptiónis osténdit. Sed et sanctificándis étiam aquæ fluéntis ipsum baptísmatis lavit auctórem, et méruit fuso sánguine suprémum illi testimónium exhibére.

Et ídeo, cum cælórum Virtútibus, in terris te iúgiter prædicámus, maiestáti tuæ sine fine clamántes :

from all the prophets to show the world its redeemer, the lamb of sacrifice. He baptized Christ, the giver of baptism, in waters made holy by the one who was baptized. You found John worthy of a martyr's death, his last and greatest act of witness to your Son.

In our unending joy we echo on earth the song of the angels in heaven as they praise your glory for ever: Holy...

Communion   Lk 1: 76

TU, pu- er, * pro-phé-ta Altíssi- mi vo-cá-be- ris : prae- í- bis e- nim an- te fá- ci- em Dó- mi-ni pa-rá- re vi- as e- ius.

You, child, will be called the prophet of the Most High; you will go before the Lord to prepare his ways.

Prayer after Communion

Cælestis Agni convívio refécti, quæsumus, Dómine, ut Ecclésia tua, sumens de beáti Ioánnis Baptístæ generatióne lætítiam, quem ille prænuntiávit ventúrum, suæ regeneratiónis cognóscat auctórem.

Lord, you have renewed us with this eucharist, as we celebrate the feast of John the Baptist, who foretold the coming of the Lamb of God. May we welcome your Son as our Saviour, for he gives us new life, and is Lord for ever and ever.

June 29
SAINT PETER & SAINT PAUL
Solemnity

VIGIL MASS

Introit *Jn 21: 18, 19; Ps 18*

IV

DIcit Dóminus Petro : * Cum esses iúnior, cingébas te, et ambulábas ubi volébas : cum autem senúeris, exténdes manus tuas, et álius te cinget, et ducet quo tu non vis : hoc autem dixit, signíficans qua morte clarificatúrus esset Deum. *Ps.* Caeli enárrant glóriam Dei : et ópera mánuum eius annúntiat firmaméntum.

The Lord said unto Peter: "When you were young, you girded yourself and walked where you would; but when you are old, you will stretch forth your hands, and another will gird you and lead you where you do not wish to go." This he said to signify by what death he was to glorify God. ℣. The heavens declare the glory of God; and the firmament proclaims the work of his hands.

Opening Prayer

Da nobis, quæsumus, Dómine Deus noster, beatórum apostolórum Petri et Pauli intercessiónibus subleári, ut per quos Ecclésiæ tuæ supérni múneris rudiménta donásti, per eos subsídia perpétuæ salútis impéndas.

Lord our God, encourage us through the prayers of Saints Peter and Paul. May the apostles who strengthened the faith of the infant Church help us on our way of salvation.

First reading

Acts 3: 1-10: *Peter and John heal a lame man.*

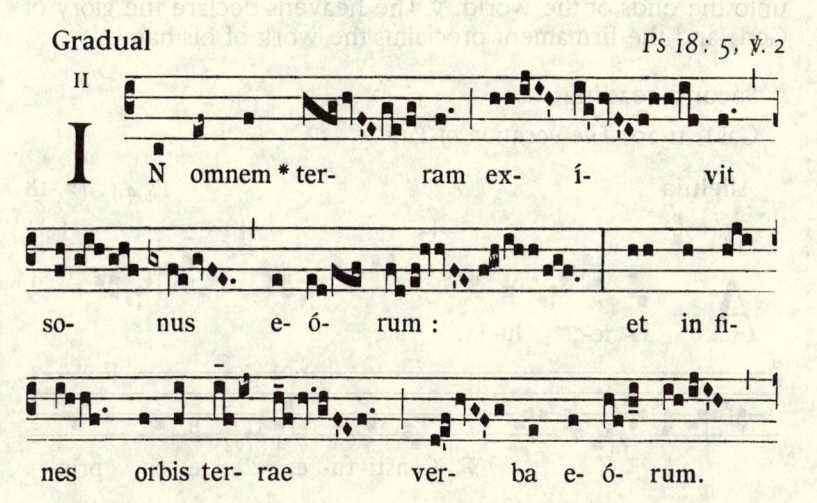

Gradual Ps 18: 5, ℣. 2

In omnem * terram exívit sonus eórum: et in fines orbis terrae verba eórum.

June 29, SS Peter and Paul

℣. Cae-li e-nár- rant gló- ri- am De- i : et ópe-ra mánu- um e- ius annún-ti- at firmamén- tum.

Their voice has gone forth into all the earth; and their words unto the ends of the world. ℣. The heavens declare the glory of God; and the firmament proclaims the work of his hands.

Second reading

Gal 1: 11-20: *The vocation of Paul.*

Alleluia *Ps 44: 17, 18*

A L- le- lú- ia.

℣. Constí- tu- es e- os prín-

June 29, SS Peter and Paul

ci- pes su- per omnem ter- ram : mé- mo-res e- runt nómi-nis tu- i, Dó- mi-ne.

You will make them princes over all the earth; they will keep the memorial of your name, O Lord.

Gospel

Jn 21: 15-19: *Jesus appoints Peter vicar of his Church.*

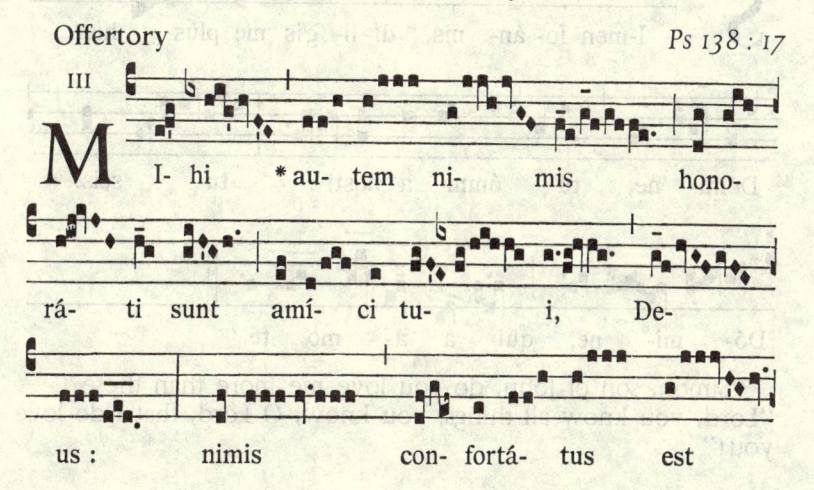

Offertory
Ps 138 : 17

MI-hi *au- tem ni- mis hono- rá- ti sunt amí- ci tu- i, De- us : nimis con- fortá- tus est

June 29, SS Peter and Paul

prin- ci- pá- tus e- ó- rum.

But in my eyes your friends are made exceedingly honorable, O God; their strength has been greatly reinforced.

Prayer over the Gifts

MUNERA, Dómine, tuis altáribus adhibémus, de beatórum apostolórum Petri et Pauli sollemnitátibus gloriántes, ut quantum sumus de nostro mérito formidántes, tantum de tua benignitáte gloriémur salvandi.

LORD, we present these gifts on this feast of the apostles Peter and Paul. Help us to know our own weakness and to rejoice in your saving power.

Preface, p. 645.

Communion
Jn 21: 15, 17

VI

*S I-mon Io- án- nis, * dí- li- gis me plus his? Dómi- ne, tu ómni- a nosti: tu scis, Dó- mi- ne, qui- a a- mo te.*

"Simon, son of John, do you love me more than these?" — "Lord, you know all things, you know, O Lord, that I do love you!"

June 29, SS Peter and Paul — 641

Prayer after Communion

CÆLESTIBUS sacraméntis, quǽsumus, Dómine, fidéles tuos corróbora, quos apostolórum doctrína illuminásti.

FATHER, you give us light by the teaching of your apostles. In this sacrament we have received fill us with your strength.

MASS OF THE DAY

Introit — Acts 12 : 11; Ps 138

III

NUNC sci- o ve- re, *qui- a mi- sit Dó- mi- nus Ange- lum su- um : et e-rí- pu- it me de manu He- ró- dis, et de omni exspecta-ti- ó- ne ple- bis Iu- dae- ó- rum. *Ps.* Dómi-ne probásti me, et cogno-ví-sti me :

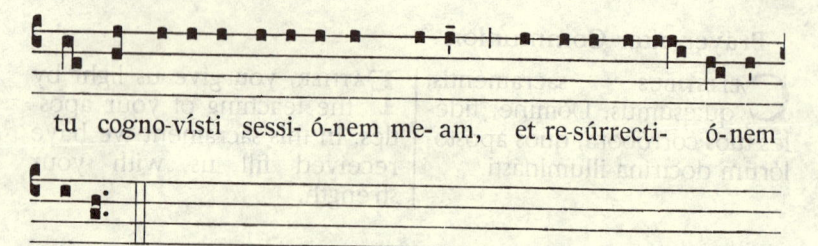

tu cogno-vísti sessi- ó-nem me- am, et re-súrrecti- ó-nem me- am.

Now I know that the Lord really has sent his Angel, and has delivered me out of the hands of Herod, and from all that the Jewish people were expecting. ℣. O Lord, you have searched me and known me; you know when I sit down and when I rise up.

Opening Prayer

DEUS, qui huius diéi venerándam sanctámque lætítiam in apostolórum Petri et Pauli sollemnitáte tribuísti, da Ecclésiæ tuæ eórum in ómnibus sequi præcéptum, per quos religiónis sumpsit exórdium.

GOD OUR FATHER, today you give us the joy of celebrating the feast of the apostles Peter and Paul. Through them your Church first received the faith. Keep us true to their teaching.

First reading

Acts 12: 1-11: *Peter delivered from prison.*

Gradual

Ps 44: 17, ℣. 18

*C Onstí- tu- es e- os * prín-ci-pes su- per omnem ter- ram: mé- mo- res*

June 29, SS Peter and Paul 643

e- runt nó- mi- nis tu- i, Dó- mi- ne.

℣. *Pro pá- tri-bus tu- is na- ti sunt ti- bi fí- i- i : pro- ptér- e- a pópu- li confi-tebúntur ti- bi.*

You will make them princes over all the earth; they shall conserve the memorial of your name, O Lord. ℣. In place of your fathers, sons have been born unto you; therefore, all people will give you thanks.

Second reading
2 Tim 4: 6-8, 17-18: *Paul's last message.*

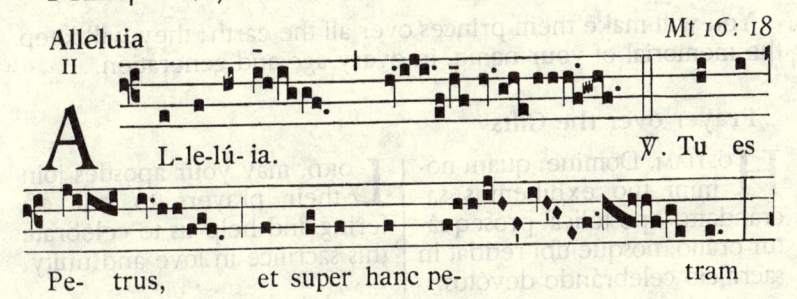

Alleluia   Mt 16: 18
II

A L-le-lú- ia. ℣. Tu es Pe- trus, et super hanc pe- tram

June 29, SS Peter and Paul

aedi-fi-cá- bo Eccé-si-am me-am.

You are Peter, and upon this rock I will build my Church.

Gospel
Mt 16: 13-19: *Profession of faith at Cæsarea.*

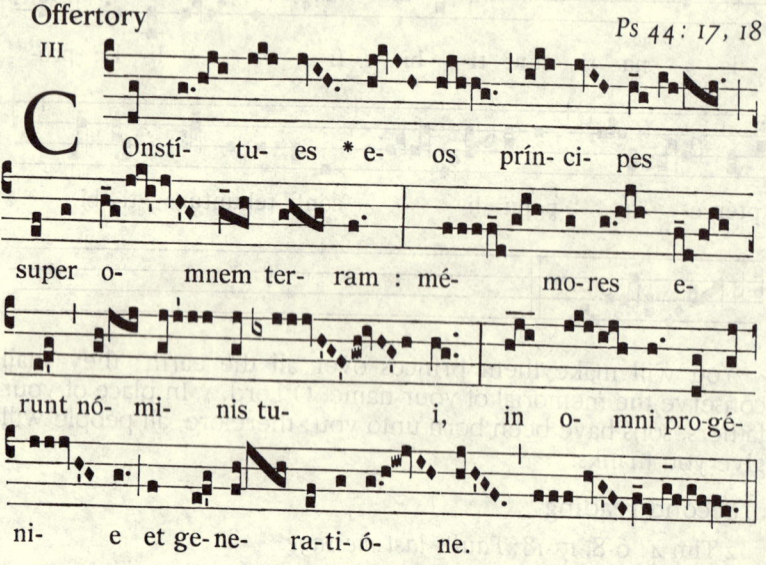

Offertory   Ps 44: 17, 18

COnstí-tu-es * e-os prín-ci-pes super o-mnem ter-ram : mé-mo-res e-runt nó-mi-nis tu-i, in o-mni pro-gé-ni-e et ge-ne-ra-ti-ó-ne.

You will make them princes over all the earth; they will keep the memorial of your name, in every age and generation.

Prayer over the Gifts

HOSTIAM, Dómine, quam nómini tuo exhibémus sacrándam, apostólica prosequátur orátio, nosque tibi reddat in sacrifício celebrándo devótos.

LORD, may your apostles join their prayers to our offering and help us to celebrate this sacrifice in love and unity.

June 29, SS Peter and Paul

Preface

Vere dignum et iustum est, æquum et salutáre, nos tibi semper et ubíque grátias ágere : Dómine, sancte Pater, omnípotens ætérne Deus.

Quia nos beáti apóstoli Petrus et Paulus tua dispositióne lætíficant: hic princeps fídei confiténdæ, ille intellegéndæ clarus assértor; hic relíquiis Israel instítuens Ecclésiam primitívam, ille magíster et doctor géntium vocandárum. Sic divérso consílio unam Christi famíliam congregántes, par mundo venerábile, una coróna sociávit.

Et ídeo cum Sanctis et Angelis univérsis te collaudámus, sine fine dicéntes :

Father, all-powerful and ever-living God, we do well always and everywhere to give you thanks.

You fill our hearts with joy as we honour your great apostles: Peter, our leader in the faith, and Paul, its fearless preacher. Peter raised up the Church from the faithful flock of Israel. Paul brought your call to the nations, and became the teacher of the world. Each in his chosen way gathered into unity the one family of Christ. Both shared a martyr's death and are praised throughout the world.

Now, with the apostles and all the angels and saints, we praise you for ever: Holy...

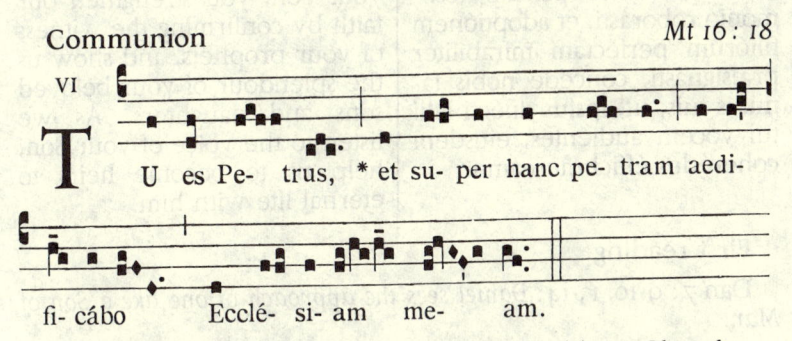

Communion
Mt 16 : 18

Tu es Petrus, * et super hanc petram aedificábo Ecclésiam meam.

You are Peter and upon this rock will I build my Church.

Prayer after Communion

Da nobis, Dómine, hoc sacraménto reféctis, ita in Ecclésia conversári, ut, perse-

Lord, renew the life of your Church with the power of this sacrament. May the break-

verántes in fractióne panis apostolorúmque doctrína, cor unum simus et ánima una, tua caritáte firmáti.

ing of bread and the teaching of the apostles keep us united in your love.

August 6
THE TRANSFIGURATION OF THE LORD
Feast

Introit
Tibi dixit cor meum, p. 246.

Opening Prayer

Deus, qui fídei sacraménta in Unigéniti tui gloriósa Transfiguratióne patrum testimónio roborásti, et adoptiónem filiórum perféctam mirabíliter præsignásti, concéde nobis fámulis tuis, ut, ipsíus dilécti Fílii tui vocem audiéntes, eiúsdem coherédes éffici mereámur.

God our Father, in the transfigured glory of Christ your Son, you strengthen our faith by confirming the witness of your prophets, and show us the splendour of your beloved sons and daughters. As we listen to the voice of your Son, help us to become heirs to eternal life with him.

First reading
Dan 7: 9-10, 13-14: *Daniel sees the approach of one like a Son of Man.*

Gradual
Speciósus forma, p. 214.

Second reading
2 Pet 1: 16-19: *Witnessing the Transfiguration.*

August 6, Transfiguration

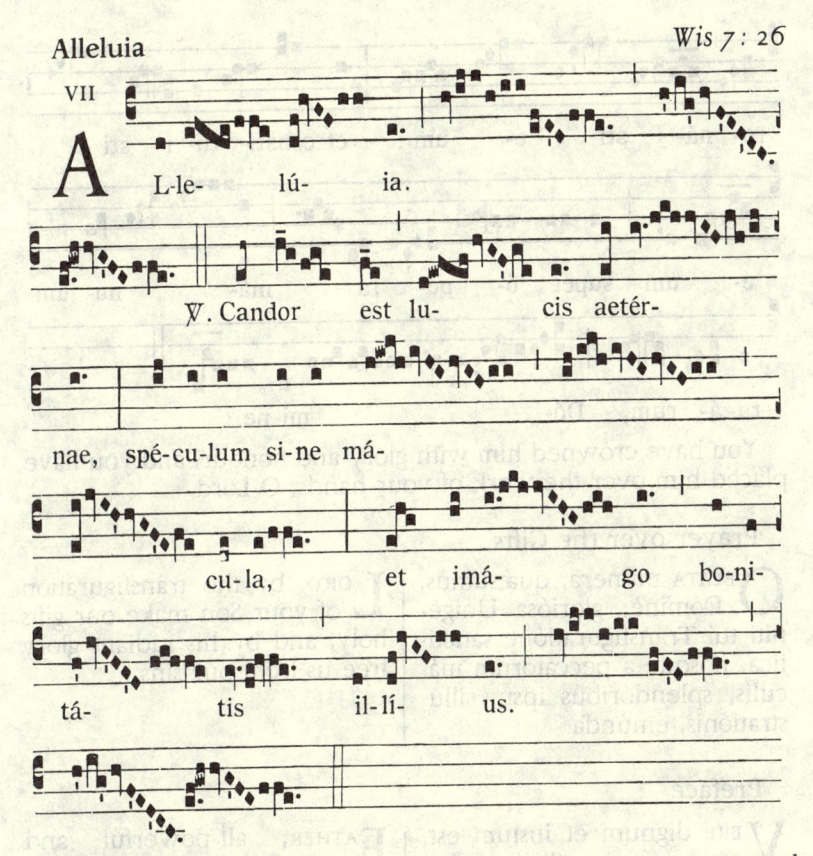

Alleluia *Wis 7: 26*

VII

Alleluia. ℣. Candor est lucis aeternae, spéculum sine mácula, et imágo bonitátis illíus.

He is the splendour of eternal light, an unspotted mirror and the image of His goodness.

Gospel
A. Mt 17: 1-9: *His face began to glow.*
B. Mk 9: 2-10: *His garments became glistening.*
C. Lk 9: 28b-36: *While Jesus was praying.*

Offertory *Ps 8: 6, 7*

I

Glória * et honóre co-

August 6, Transfiguration

ro-ná-sti e- um: et consti- tu- í- sti e- um super ó- pe- ra má- nu- um tu- á- rum, Dó- mi-ne.

You have crowned him with glory and honour, and you have placed him over the work of your hands, O Lord.

Prayer over the Gifts

OBLATA múnera, quæsumus, Dómine, gloriósa Unigéniti tui Transfiguratióne sanctífica, nosque a peccatórum máculis, splendóribus ipsíus illustratiónis, emúnda.

LORD, by the transfiguration of your Son make our gifts holy, and by his radiant glory free us from our sins.

Preface

VERE dignum et iustum est, æquum et salutáre, nos tibi semper et ubíque grátias ágere: Dómine, sancte Pater, omnípotens ætérne Deus: per Christum Dóminum nostrum.

Qui coram eléctis téstibus suam glóriam revelávit, et commúnem illam cum céteris córporis formam máximo splendóre perfúdit, ut de córdibus discipulórum crucis scándalum tollerétur, et in totíus Ecclésiæ córpore declaráret impléndum

FATHER, all-powerful and ever-living God, we do well always and everywhere to give you thanks through Jesus Christ our Lord.

He revealed his glory to the disciples to strengthen them for the scandal of the cross. His glory shone from a body like our own, to show that the Church, which is the body of Christ, would one day share his glory.

August 6, Transfiguration

quod eius mirabíliter præfúlsit in cápite.

Et ídeo cum cælórum Virtútibus in terris te iúgiter celebrámus, maiestáti tuæ sine fine clamántes :

In our unending joy we echo on earth the song of the angels in heaven as they praise your glory for ever: Holy...

Communion   Mt 17: 9

VI-si-ó-nem * quam vi-dístis, némi-ni di-xé-ri-tis, do-nec a mórtu-is re-súrgat Fí-li-us hómi-nis.

As for the vision you have seen, tell no one until the Son of Man has risen from the dead.

Prayer after Communion

Cælestia, quæsumus, Dómine, aliménta quæ súmpsimus in eius nos transfórment imáginem, cuius claritátem gloriósa Transfiguratióne manifestáre voluísti.

Lord, you revealed the true radiance of Christ in the glory of his transfiguration. May the food we receive from heaven change us into his image.

August 15
ASSUMPTION OF THE BLESSED VIRGIN MARY
Solemnity

VIGIL MASS

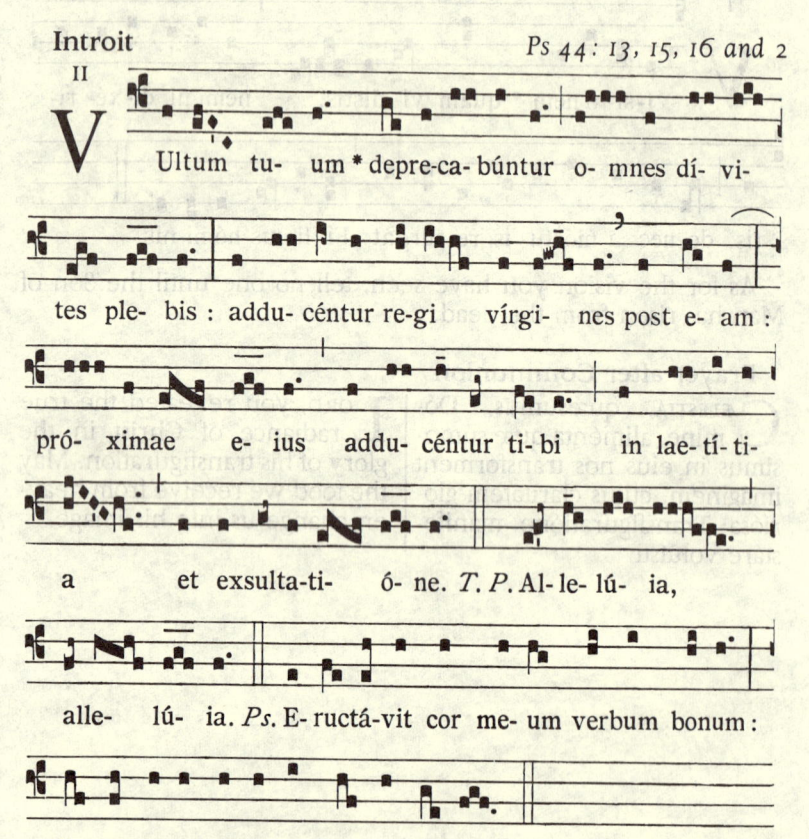

Introit — Ps 44: 13, 15, 16 and 2

Vultum tuum * deprecabúntur omnes dívites plebis: adducéntur regi vírgines post eam: próximae eius adducéntur tibi in laetítia et exsultatióne. *T. P.* Allelúia, allelúia. *Ps.* Eructávit cor meum verbum bonum: dico ego ópera mea regi.

All the rich among the people will implore your countenance. Virgins will be brought to the king in her retinue; her companions will be taken to you in gladness and rejoicing. ℣. My heart overflows with a goodly theme; I address my works to the king.

Opening Prayer

DEUS, qui beátam Vírginem Maríam, eius humilitátem respíciens, ad hanc grátiam evexísti, ut Unigénitus tuus ex ipsa secúndum carnem nascerétur, et hodiérna die superexcellénti glória coronásti, eius nobis précibus concéde, ut, redemptiónis tuæ mystério salváti, a te exaltári mereámur.

ALMIGHTY God, you gave a humble virgin the privilege of being the mother of your Son, and crowned her with the glory of heaven. May the prayers of the Virgin Mary bring us to the salvation of Christ and raise us up to eternal life.

First reading

1 Chron 15: 3-4, 15-16; 16: 1-2: *The ark of the covenant in Jerusalem.*

Gradual

IV

Benedícta * et venerábilis es, Virgo María: quae sine tactu pudóris invénta es mater Salvatóris. ℣. Virgo Dei

August 15, Assumpion

Gé-ni-trix, quem to-tus non ca-pit or-bis, in tu-a se clau-sit ví-sce-ra fa-ctus ho-mo.

You are blessed and worthy of veneration, O Virgin Mary; for without taint on your purity, you were found to be the Mother of our Saviour. ℣. O Virgin Mother of God, the One whom the entire universe cannot contain closed himself up in your womb and became man.

Second reading
1 Cor 15: 54-57: *Victory over death.*

Alleluia

VIII

A L-le-lú-ia.

℣. *Fe-lix es, sa-cra Virgo Ma-rí-a, et o-mni lau-de di-gnís-sima: qui-a ex te or-tus est sol iustí-ti-ae,*

August 15, Assumption

Christus De- us no- ster.

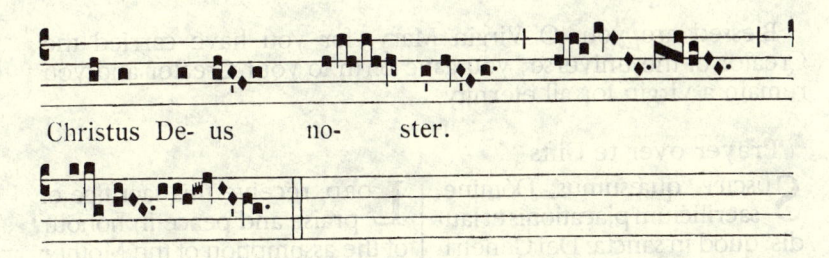

Blessed are you, O holy Virgin Mary, and worthy of all praise; for from you has come forth the sun of justice, Christ, our God.

Gospel

Lk 11: 27-28: *The true beatitude of the Mother of God.*

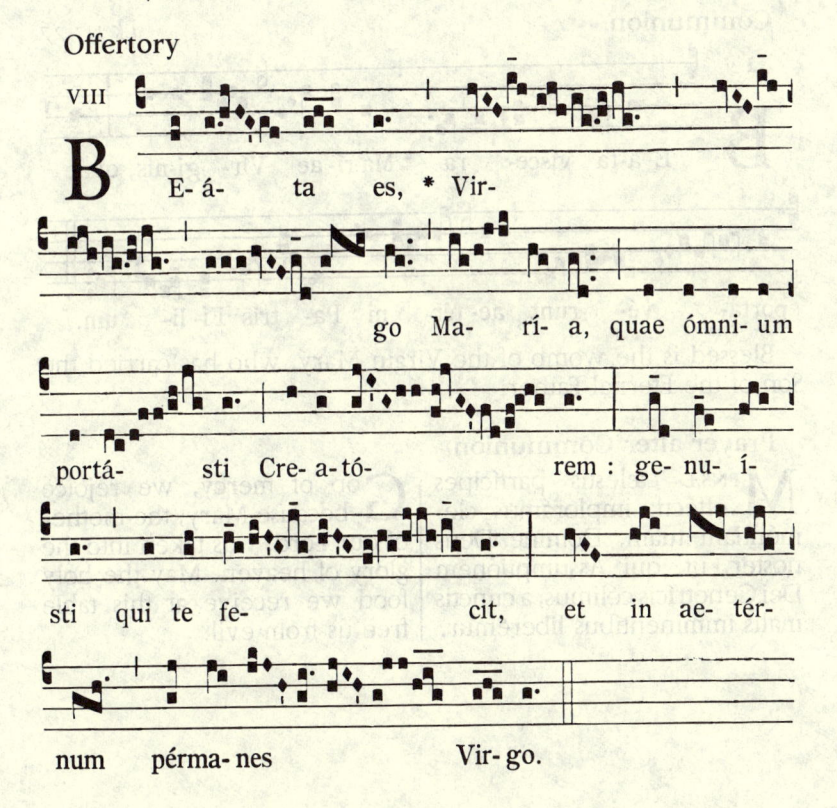

Offertory

VIII

Be- á- ta es, * Vir- go Ma- rí- a, quae ómni- um portá- sti Cre- a- tó- rem: ge- nu- í- sti qui te fe- cit, et in ae- tér- num pérma- nes Vir- go.

Blessed are you, O Virgin Mary, for you have carried the Creator of the universe; you gave birth to your Creator and you remain a virgin for all eternity.

Prayer over te Gifts

Suscipe, quæsumus, Dómine, sacrifícium placatiónis et laudis, quod in sanctæ Dei Genetrícis Assumptióne celebrámus, ut ad véniam nos obtinéndam perdúcat, et in perpétua gratiárum constítuat actióne.

Lord, receive this sacrifice of praise and peace in honour of the assumption of the Mother of God. May our offering bring us pardon and make our lives a thanksgiving to you.

Preface, p. 659.

Communion

Lk 11: 27

Be-á-ta víscera * Maríae Vírginis, quae portavérunt aetérni Patris Fílium.

Blessed is the womb of the Virgin Mary, who has carried the Son of the Eternal Father.

Prayer after Communion

Mensæ cæléstis partícipes effécti, implorámus cleméntiam tuam, Dómine Deus noster, ut, qui Assumptiónem Dei Genetrícis cólimus, a cunctis malis imminéntibus liberémur.

God of mercy, we rejoice because Mary, the mother of our Lord, was taken into the glory of heaven. May the holy food we receive at this table free us from evil.

August 15, Assumption

MASS OF THE DAY

Introit   Rev 12: 1; Ps 97

VII

SIGNUM ma- gnum * appá- ru- it in cae- lo : mú- li- er a-mí-cta so- le, et lu- na sub pé- di-bus e-ius, et in cá- pi- te e- ius co-ró-na stel-lá-rum du- ó-de- cim.

Ps. Can-tá- te Dómi-no cánti-cum no-vum : qui- a mi-ra-bí-li- a fe- cit.

A great sign appeared in heaven; a woman clothed with the sun, and the moon under her feet; and on her head, a crown of twelve stars. ℣. Sing unto the Lord a new song, for he has accomplished wondrous deeds.

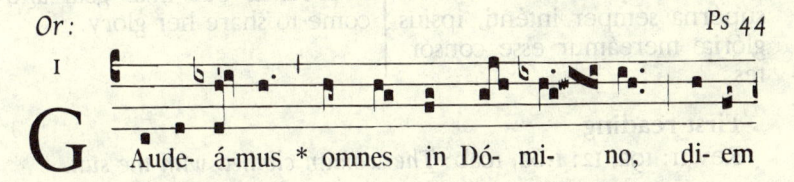

Or: Ps 44

I

Aude- á-mus * omnes in Dó- mi- no, di- em

August 15, Assumption

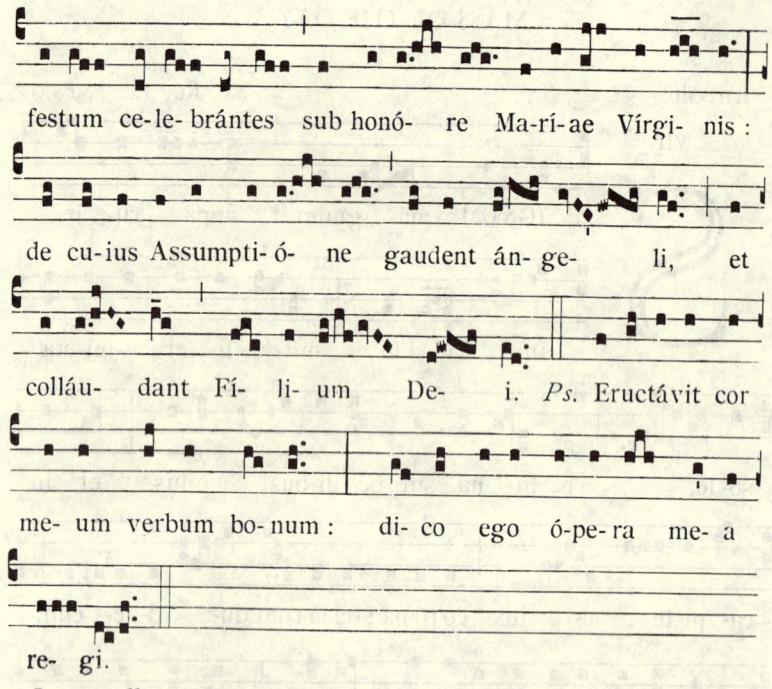

festum ce-le-brántes sub honóre Maríae Vírginis: de cuius Assumptióne gaudent ángeli, et colláudant Fílium Dei. Ps. Eructávit cor meum verbum bonum: dico ego ópera mea regi.

Let us all rejoice in the Lord, as we celebrate this feast day in honour of the Virgin Mary; her Assumption causes the Angels to rejoice and to praise together the Son of God. ℣. My heart overflows with a goodly theme; I address my works to the king.

Opening Prayer

OMNIPOTENS sempitérne Deus, qui immaculátam Vírginem Maríam, Fílii tui Genetrícem, córpore et anima ad cæléstem glóriam assumpsísti, concéde, quæsumus, ut, ad supérna semper inténti, ipsíus glóriæ mereámur esse consórtes.

ALL-POWERFUL and ever-living God, you raised the sinless virgin Mary, mother of your Son, body and soul to the glory of heaven. May we see heaven as our final goal and come to share her glory.

First reading
Rev 11: 19a, 12: 1-6a, 10ab: *The woman clothed with the sun.*

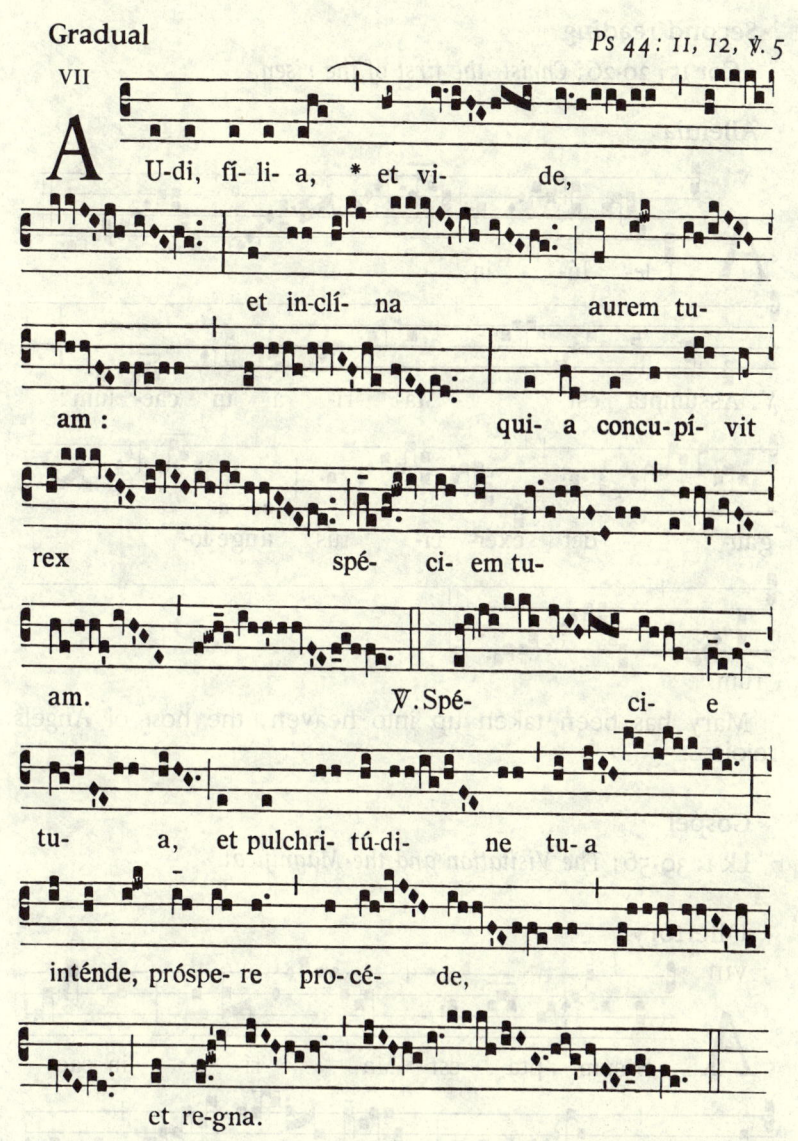

August 15, Assumption

Gradual — Ps 44: 11, 12, ℣. 5

VII

Audi, filia, * et vide, et inclina aurem tuam: quia concupivit rex speciem tuam. ℣. Specie tua, et pulchritudine tua intende, prospere procede, et regna.

Hearken, O daughter and see, incline your ear; for the king greatly desires your beauty. ℣. With your comeliness and your beauty, set out, proceed victoriously and reign.

Second reading
1 Cor 15: 20-26: *Christ, the first of the risen.*

Alleluia

AL·le- lú- ia.

℣. Assúmpta est María in caelum: gaudet exércitus angelórum.

Mary has been taken up into heaven; the host of Angels rejoices.

Gospel
Lk 1: 39-56: *The Visitation and the Magnificat.*

Offertory

AS-súmpta est * María in caelum : gaudent ánge-

August 15, Assumption

...li, collaudántes benedícunt Dóminum, allelúia.

Mary has been taken up into heaven; the Angels rejoice, praising the Lord together and blessing him, alleluia.

Prayer over the Gifts

Ascendat ad te, Dómine, nostræ devotiónis oblátio, et, beatíssima Vírgine María in cælum assúmpta intercedénte, corda nostra, caritátis igne succénsa, ad te iúgiter aspírent.

Lord, receive this offering of our service. You raised the Virgin Mary to the glory of heaven. By her prayers, help us to seek you and to live in your love.

Preface

Vere dignum et iustum est, æquum et salutáre, nos tibi semper et ubíque grátias ágere: Dómine, sancte Pater, omnípotens ætérne Deus: per Christum Dóminum nostrum.

Quóniam in cælos hódie Virgo Deípara est assúmpta, Ecclésiæ tuæ consummándæ inítium et imágo, ac pópulo peregrinánti certæ spei et solácii documéntum; corruptiónem enim sepúlcri eam vidére mérito noluísti, quæ Fílium tuum, vitæ omnis auctórem, ineffabíliter de se génuit incarnátum.

Et ídeo, choris angélicis sociáti, te laudámus, in gáudio confiténtes:

Father, all-powerful and ever-living God, we do well always and everywhere to give you thanks through Jesus Christ our Lord.

Today the virgin Mother of God was taken up into heaven to be the beginning and the pattern of the Church in its perfection, and a sign of hope and comfort for your people on their pilgrim way. You would not allow decay to touch her body, for she had given birth to your Son, the Lord of all life, in the glory of the incarnation.

In our joy we sing to your glory with all the choirs of angels: Holy...

September 14, Triumph of the Cross

Communion — Lk 1: 48, 49

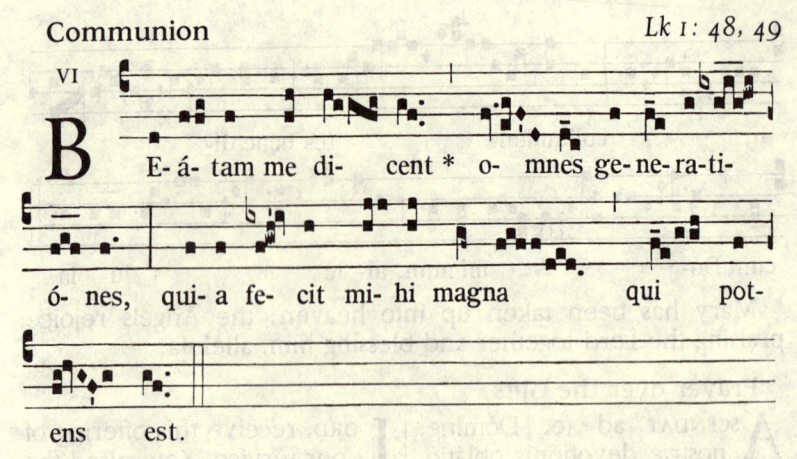

BE-á-tam me dicent * omnes generatiónes, quia fecit mihi magna qui potens est.

All generations shall call me blessed; for he who is mighty has accomplished great things on my behalf.

Prayer after Communion

SUMPTIS, Dómine, salutáribus sacraméntis, da, quǽsumus, ut, intercessióne beátæ Maríæ Vírginis in cælum assúmptæ, ad resurrectiónis glóriam perducámur.

LORD, may we who receive this sacrament of salvation be led to the glory of heaven by the prayers of the Virgin Mary.

September 14

THE TRIUMPH OF THE CROSS
Feast

Introit
Nos autem gloriári, p. 286.

September 14, Triumph of the Cross

Opening Prayer

Deus, qui Unigénitum tuum crucem subíre voluísti, ut salvum fáceret genus humánum, præsta, quǽsumus, ut, cuius mystérium in terra cognóvimus, eius redemptiónis prǽmia in cælo cónsequi mereámur.

God our Father, in obedience to you your only Son accepted death on the cross for the salvation of mankind. We acknowledge the mystery of the cross on earth. May we receive the gift of redemption in heaven.

First reading
Num 21: 4-9: *The bronze serpent.*

Gradual: Christus factus est, p. 282.

Second reading
Phil 2: 6-11: *Christ, humiliated and exalted.*

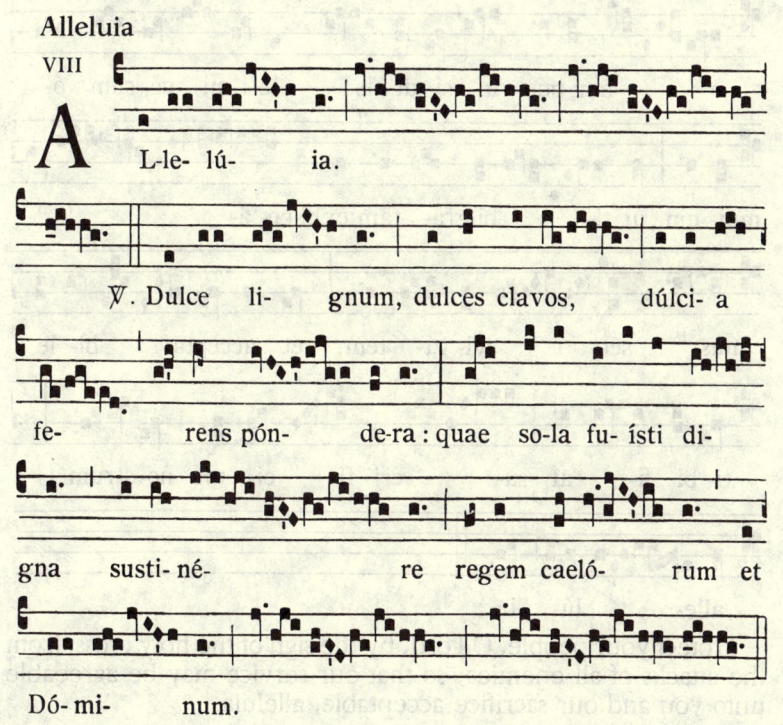

Alleluia

VIII

A-le- lú- ia.

℣. Dulce li- gnum, dulces clavos, dúlci- a fe- rens pón- de-ra : quae so-la fu- ísti digna susti- né- re regem caeló- rum et Dó- mi- num.

O precious wood, o precious nails, gently bearing so precious a burden; you alone were worthy to carry the King of heaven, the Lord.

Gospel

Jn 3: 13-17: *Christ raised up on the Cross.*

Offertory

PRótege, * Dómine, plebem tuam, per signum sanctae Crucis, ab ómnibus insídiis inimicórum ómnium: ut tibi gratam exhibeámus servitútem, et acceptábile tibi fiat sacrifícium nostrum allelúia.

Protect your people, O Lord, by the sign of the holy cross, from the attacks of all enemies; so that our service may be agreeable unto you and our sacrifice acceptable, alleluia.

September 14, Triumph of the Cross

Prayer over the Gifts

Hæc oblátio, Dómine, quæsumus, ab ómnibus nos purget offénsis, quæ in ara crucis totíus mundi tulit offénsam.

Lord, may this sacrifice once offered on the cross to take away the sins of the world now free us from our sins.

Preface

Vere dignum et iustum est, æquum et salutáre, nos tibi semper et ubíque grátias ágere: Dómine, sancte Pater, omnípotens, ætérne Deus:

Qui salútem humáni géneris in ligno crucis constituísti, ut unde mors oriebátur, inde vita resúrgeret; et, qui in ligno vincébat, in ligno quoque vincerétur: per Christum Dóminum nostrum.

Per quem maiestátem tuam laudant Angeli, adórant Dominatiónes, tremunt Potestátes. Cæli cælorúmque Virtútes, ac beáta Séraphim, sócia exsultatióne concélebrant. Cum quibus et nostras voces ut admítti iúbeas, deprecámur, súpplici confessióne dicéntes:

Father, all-powerful and ever-living God, we do well always and everywhere to give you thanks.

You decreed that man should be saved through the wood of the cross. The tree of man's defeat became his tree of victory; where life was lost, there life has been restored through Christ our Lord.

Through him the choirs of angels and all the powers of heaven praise and worship your glory. May our voices blend with theirs as we join in their unending hymn: Holy...

The Preface of the Passion of the Lord I, can also be used, p. 54.

Communion

IV

Per signum Crucis * de inimícis nostris líbera nos, Deus noster.

November 1, All Saints

By the sign of the cross, deliver us from our enemies, O Lord our God.

Prayer after Communion

REFECTIONE tua sancta enutríti, Dómine Iesu Christe, súpplices deprecámur, ut, quos per lignum crucis vivíficæ redemísti, ad resurrectiónis glóriam perdúcas.

LORD JESUS CHRIST, you are the holy bread of life. Bring to the glory of the resurrection the people you have redeemed by the wood of the cross.

November 1

ALL SAINTS
Solemnity

Introit *Ps 32*

GAUDEAMUS * omnes in Dómino, di- em festum ce-le-brántes sub honó-re Sanctó-rum ómni-um : de quo-rum sol-emni-tá- te gaudent án- ge- li, et colláu- dant

November 1, All Saints

Fílium Dei. Ps. Exsultáte iusti in Dómino : rectos decet collaudátio.

Let us all rejoice in the Lord as we celebrate this feast day in honour of all the saints; it is a solemnity which causes the Angels to rejoice, and to praise together the Son of God. ℣. Rejoice in the Lord, O you righteous; praising befits those who are upright.

Opening Prayer

OMNIPOTENS sempitérne Deus, qui nos ómnium Sanctórum tuórum mérita sub una tribuísti celebritáte venerári, quæsumus, ut desiderátam nobis tuæ propitiatiónis abundántiam, multiplicátis intercessóribus, largiáris.

FATHER, all-powerful and ever-living God, today we rejoice in the holy men and women of every time and place. May their prayers bring us your forgiveness and love.

First reading

Rev 7: 2-4, 9-14: *The great multitude of saints.*

Gradual

Ps 33: 10, ℣. 11b

*Timéte Dóminum * omnes sancti eius : quóniam nihil deest timén-*

ti-bus e- um. ℣. In- qui-rén- tes

au- tem

Dómi-num non de- fí- ci- ent o- mni bo-

no.

Revere the Lord, all you saints of his; for there is no want among those who fear him. ℣. Those who seek the Lord shall lack no good thing.

Second reading

I Jn 3: 1-3: *We shall see God as he is.*

Alleluia
Mt 11: 28

VIII

A L- le- lú- ia.

℣. Ve- ní- te ad

me, o- mnes qui la-bo-rá-

November 1, All Saints

... tis, et oneráti estis: et ego refíciam vos.

Come unto me, all you who labour and are heavily burdened, and I will comfort you.

Gospel
Mt 5: 1-12a: *The Beatitudes*.

Offertory Wis 3: 1, 2, 3

Iustórum * ánimae in manu Dei sunt, et non tanget illos torméntum malítiae: visi sunt óculis insipiéntium mori: illi autem sunt in pa- ce, alle- lú-ia.

The souls of the righteous are in the hand of God, and no malicious torment will ever touch them; in the eyes of the unwise, they seem to have died; but they are dwelling in peace, alleluia.

Prayer over the Gifts

GRATA tibi sint, Dómine, múnera, quæ pro cunctórum offérimus honóre Sanctórum, et concéde, ut, quos iam crédimus de sua immortalitáte secúros, sentiámus de nostra salúte sollícitos.

LORD, receive our gifts in honour of the holy men and women who live with you in glory. May we always be aware of their concern to help and save us.

Preface

VERE dignum et iustum est, æquum et salutáre, nos tibi semper et ubíque grátias ágere : Dómine, sancte Pater, omnípotens ætérne Deus :

Nobis enim hódie civitátem tuam tríbuis celebráre, quæ mater nostra est, cælestísque Ierúsalem, ubi fratrum nostrórum iam te in ætérnum coróna colláudat. Ad quam peregríni, per fidem accedéntes, alácriter festinámus, congaudéntes de Ecclésiæ sublímium glorificatióne membrórum, qua simul fragilitáti nostræ adiuménta et exémpla concédis.

Et ídeo, cum ipsórum Angelorúmque frequéntia, una te magnificámus, laudis voce clamántes :

FATHER, all-powerful and ever-living God, we do well always and everywhere to give you thanks.

Today we keep the festival of your holy city, the heavenly Jerusalem, our mother. Around your throne the saints, our brothers and sisters, sing your praise for ever. Their glory fills us with joy, and their communion with us in your Church gives us inspiration and strength as we hasten on our pilgrimage of faith, eager to meet them.

With their great company and all the angels we praise your glory as we cry out with one voice: Holy...

November 1, All Saints

Communion   Mt 5: 8, 9, 10

Be-á-ti mundo corde, * quóniam ipsi Deum vidébunt : beáti pacífici, quóniam fílii Dei vocabúntur : beáti qui persecutiónem patiúntur propter iustítiam, quóniam ipsórum est regnum caelórum.

Blessed are the pure in heart, for they shall see God; blessed are the peacemakers, for they shall be called sons of God; blessed are those who suffer persecution for the sake of justice, for theirs is the kingdom of heaven.

Prayer after Communion

Mirabilem te, Deus, et unum Sanctum in ómnibus Sanctis tuis adorántes, tuam grátiam implorámus, qua, sanctificatiónem in tui amóris plenitúdine consummántes, ex hac mensa peregrinántium ad cæléstis pátriæ convívium transeámus.

Father, holy one, we praise your glory reflected in the saints. May we who share at this table be filled with your love and prepared for the joy of your kingdom.

November 2

COMMEMORATION OF ALL THE FAITHFUL DEPARTED
(ALL SOULS)

The first mass formulary is the only sung mass on this day. The chants are to be selected from among those for Masses for the Dead, p. 688. The readings are indicated on p. 709.

Opening Prayer

PRECES nostras, quæsumus, Dómine, benígnus exáudi, ut, dum attóllitur nostra fides in Fílio tuo a mórtuis suscitáto, in famulórum tuórum præstolánda resurrectióne spes quoque nostra firmétur.

MERCIFUL FATHER, hear our prayers and console us. As we renew our faith in your Son, whom you raised from the dead, strengthen our hope that all our departed brothers and sisters will share in his resurrection.

Prayer over the Gifts

NOSTRIS, Dómine, propitiáre munéribus, ut fámuli tui defúncti assumántur in glóriam cum Fílio tuo, cuius magno pietátis iúngimur sacraménto.

LORD, we are united in this sacrament by the love of Jesus Christ. Accept these gifts and receive our brothers and sisters into the glory of your Son.

Prefaces for the Dead, p. 65-67.

Prayer after Communion

PRÆSTA, quæsumus, Dómine, ut fámuli tui defúncti in mansiónem lucis tránseant et pacis, pro quibus paschále celebrávimus sacraméntum.

LORD GOD, may the death and resurrection of Christ which we celebrate in this eucharist bring the departed faithful to the peace of your eternal home.

November 9
DEDICATION OF THE LATERAN BASILICA
Feast

See Mass for an Anniversary of Dedication, p. 679, except for the following:

Introit
Deus in loco sancto suo, p. 509

Gradual
Lætátus sum, p. 548.

Alleluia

A-L- le- lú- ia. ℣. Be-ne fundá- ta est do- mus Dó- mi- ni su- pra fir- mam pe- tram.

The house of the Lord is solidly built upon a firm rock.

November 9, Dedication of St. John Lateran

Offertory   1 Chron 29: 17, 18

DOmine Deus, * in simplicitáte cordis mei laetus óbtuli univérsa: et pópulum tuum, qui repértus est, vidi cum ingénti gáudio: Deus Israel, custódi hanc voluntátem, Dómine Deus.

T. P. Allelúia.

O Lord God, in the simplicity of my heart I have joyfully offered all things; and I have beheld with immense joy your people gathered here. God of Israel, preserve this good intention, O Lord God.

Communion

Ierúsalem quæ ædificátur, p. 263.

December 8
IMMACULATE CONCEPTION OF THE VIRGIN MARY
Solemnity

Introit   Is 61: 10; Ps 29

GAUDENS gaudébo * in Dómino et exsultábit ánima mea in Deo meo: quia índuit me vestiméntis salútis, et induménto iustítiae circúmdedit me, quasi sponsam ornátam monílibus suis. *Ps.* Exaltábo te, Dómine, quóniam suscepísti me: nec delectásti inimícos meos super

December 8, Immaculate Conception

me.

I will greatly rejoice in the Lord, and my soul shall be joyful in my God; for he has clothed me with the garments of salvation; and with the robe of righteousness he has covered me, as a bridegroom decked with a crown, and as a bride adorned with her jewels. ℣. I will extol you, O Lord, for you have lifted me up, and have not let my foes rejoice over me.

Opening Prayer

Deus, qui per immaculátam Vírginis Conceptiónem dignum Fílio tuo habitáculum præparásti, quǽsumus, ut, qui ex morte eiúsdem Fílii tui prævísa, eam ab omni labe præservásti, nos quoque mundos, eius intercessióne, ad te perveníre concédas.

Father, you prepared the Virgin Mary to be the worthy mother of your Son. You let her share beforehand in the salvation Christ would bring by his death, and kept her sinless from the first moment of her conception. Help us by her prayers to live in your presence without sin.

First reading

Gen 3: 9-15, 20: *The fall and the promise of victory over Satan.*

Gradual   Jdt 13: 23, ℣. 15: 10

Benedícta es tu, * Virgo María, a Dómino Deo excélso, prae ómnibus muliéribus super terram.

December 8, Immaculate Conception

℣. Tu glória Ierúsalem, tu laetítia Israel, tu honoríficéntia pópuli nostri.

Blessed are you, O Virgin Mary, by the Lord, the most high God, beyond all women upon the earth. ℣. You are the glory of Jerusalem, you are the joy of Israel, you are the honour of our people.

Second reading
Eph 1: 3-6, 11-12: *God's plan for salvation.*

Alleluia
Song 4: 7

ALlelúia.

℣. Tota pulchra es, María: et mácula originá-

December 8, Immaculate Conception

lis non est in te.

You are most fair, O Mary, and the taint of original sin dwells not within you.

Gospel
Lk 1: 26-38: *The Annunciation narrative.*

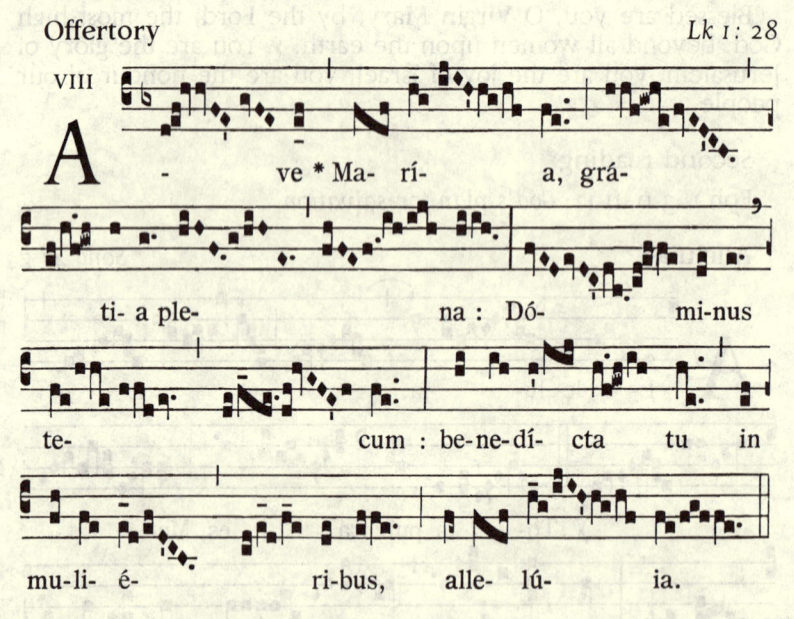

Offertory *Lk 1: 28*

VIII

A - ve * Ma- rí- a, grá- ti- a ple- na : Dó- mi-nus te- cum : be-ne-dí- cta tu in mu-li- é- ri-bus, alle- lú- ia.

Hail Mary, full of grace, the Lord is with thee; blessed art thou amongst women, alleluia.

December 8, Immaculate Conception

Prayer over the Gifts

Salutarem hóstiam, quam in sollemnitáte immaculátæ Conceptiónis beátæ Vírginis Maríæ tibi, Dómine, offérimus, súscipe dignánter, et præsta, ut, sicut illam tua grátia præveniénte ab omni labe profitémur immúnem, ita, eius intercessióne, a culpis ómnibus liberémur.

Lord, accept this sacrifice on the feast of the sinless Virgin Mary. You kept her free from sin from the first moment of her life. Help us by her prayers, and free us from our sins.

Preface

Vere dignum et iustum est, æquum et salutáre, nos tibi semper et ubíque grátias ágere : Dómine, sancte Pater, omnípotens ætérne Deus :

Qui beatíssimam Vírginem Maríam ab omni originális culpæ labe præservásti, ut in ea, grátiæ tuæ plenitúdine ditáta, dignam Fílio tuo Genetrícem præparáres, et Sponsæ eius Ecclésiæ sine ruga vel mácula formósæ signáres exórdium. Fílium enim erat puríssima Virgo datúra, qui crímina nostra Agnus ínnocens aboléret ; et ipsam præ ómnibus tuo pópulo disponébas advocátam grátiæ et sanctitátis exémplar.

Et ídeo, choris angélicis sociáti, te laudámus in gáudio confiténtes :

Father, all-powerful and ever-living God, we do well always and everywhere to give you thanks.

You allowed no stain of Adam's sin to touch the Virgin Mary. Full of grace, she was to be a worthy mother of your Son, your sign of favour to the Church at its beginning, and the promise of its perfection as the bride of Christ, radiant in beauty. Purest of virgins, she was to bring forth your Son, the innocent lamb who takes away our sins. You chose her from all women to be our advocate with you and our pattern of holiness.

In our joy we sing to your glory with all the choirs of angels : Holy...

Communion

Ps 86 : 3 ; Lk 1 : 49

VIII

Glo-ri-ó-sa * di-cta sunt de te, Ma-rí-a :

qui- a fe-cit ti- bi ma- gna qui pot- ens est.

Glorious things have been proclaimed concerning you, O Mary; for the Almighty has done marvelous things on your behalf.

Prayer after Communion

SACRAMENTA quæ súmpsimus, Dómine Deus noster, illíus in nobis culpæ vúlnera réparent, a qua immaculátam beátæ Maríæ Conceptiónem singuláriter præservásti.

LORD our God, in your love, you chose the Virgin Mary and kept her free from sin. May this sacrament of your love free us from our sins.

ANNIVERSARY OF THE DEDICATION OF A CHURCH

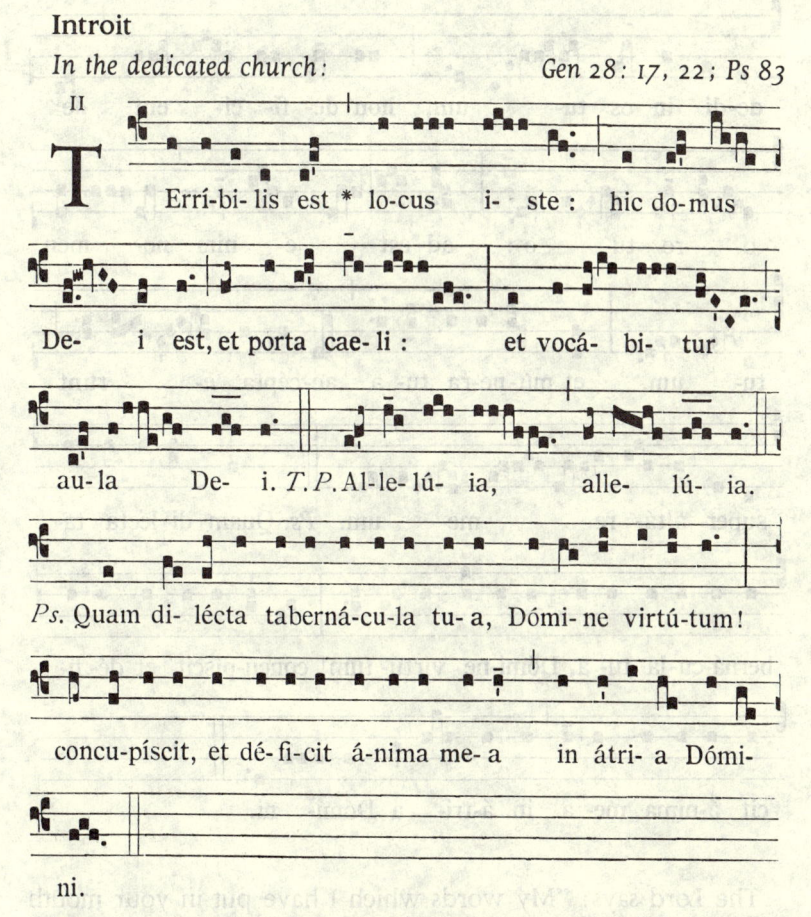

Introit

In the dedicated church: Gen 28: 17, 22; Ps 83

Errí-bi-lis est * lo-cus i-ste : hic do-mus De-i est, et porta cae-li : et vocá-bi-tur au-la De-i. T.P. Al-le-lú-ia, alle-lú-ia.

Ps. Quam di-lécta tabernácu-la tu-a, Dómi-ne virtú-tum! concu-píscit, et dé-fi-cit á-nima me-a in átri-a Dómi-ni.

How awesome this place is! This is the house of God and the gateway to heaven; and it will be called the courtyard of God. ℣. How lovely is your tabernacle, O Lord of hosts! My soul longs and pines after the courts of the Lord.

Dedication of a Church

Outside the dedicated church: Is 59: 21 and 56: 7; Ps 83

DIcit Dóminus : * Sermónes mei, quos dedi in os tuum, non defícient de ore tuo : adest enim nomen tuum, et múnera tua accépta erunt super altáre meum. *Ps.* Quam dilécta tabernácula tua, Dómine virtútum! concupíscit et déficit ánima mea in átria Dómini.

The Lord says: "My words which I have put in your mouth will not cease to be upon your lips; for your name is present to me, and your offerings will be accepted upon my altar. ℣. How lovely is your tabernacle, O Lord of hosts! My soul longs and pines after the courts of the Lord.

Dedication of a Church

Or:

Deus in loco sancto suo, *p. 202*.
Protéctor noster, *p. 527*.
Suscépimus, Deus, *p. 492*.

Opening Prayer

In the dedicated church:

Deus, qui nobis per síngulos annos huius sancti templi tui consecratiónis réparas diem, exáudi preces pópuli tui, et præsta, ut fiat hic tibi semper purum servítium et nobis plena redémptio.

Father, each year we recall the dedication of this church to your service. Let our worship always be sincere and help us to find your saving love in this church.

Outside the dedicated church:

Deus, qui de vivis et eléctis lapídibus ætérnum habitáculum tuæ præparas maiestáti, multíplica in Ecclésia tua spíritum grátiæ quem dedísti, ut fidélis tibi pópulus in cæléstis ædificatiónem Ierúsalem semper accréscat.

God our Father, from living stones, your chosen people, you built an eternal temple to your glory. Increase the spiritual gifts you have given to your Church, so that your faithful people may continue to grow into the new and eternal Jerusalem.

Or:

Deus, qui pópulum tuum Ecclésiam vocáre dignátus es, da, ut plebs in nómine tuo congregáta te tímeat, te díligat, te sequátur, et ad cæléstia promíssa, te ducénte, pervéniat.

Father, you called your people to be your Church. As we gather together in your name, may we love, honour, and follow you to eternal life in the kingdom you promise.

First reading

Ezek 47: 1-2, 8-9, 12: *The wellspring of the Temple.*

Or:

Rev 21: 1-5a: *The dwelling place of God with men.*

Dedication of a Church

Gradual

In the dedicated church:

LOcus iste * a Deo factus est, inaestimábile sacraméntum, irreprehensíbilis est. ℣. Deus, cui adstat angelórum chorus, áudi preces servórum tuórum.

This place is the work of God, a mystery surpassing all comprehension, above all reproach. ℣. O God, before whom a choir of Angels stands, answer the prayers of your servants.

Outside the dedicated church:
Lætátus sum, *p.548.*
Suscépimus, Deus, *p. 582.*
Tóllite hóstias, *p. 448.*
Unam pétii, *p. 576.*

Second reading

1 Cor 3: 9b-11, 16-17: *You are the temple of God.*

Alleluia

Adorábo ad templum, p. 444.
Bene fundáta est, p. 671.

Or: Ps 25: 8

A-L-le-lú-ia. ℣. Dó-mi-ne, di-lé-xi de-có-rem domus tu-æ et lo-cum taber-ná-cu-li gló-ri-æ tu-æ.

O Lord, I love the beauty of your house, and the tabernacle where your glory resides.

Or:

Lætátus sum, p. 171.
Te decet hymnus, p. 500.

Tract

Qui confídunt, p. 261.

Gospel

Jn 2: 13-22: *Jesus was speaking of the temple of his body.*

Offertory

Dómine Deus, p. 672.
Orávi Deum meum, p. 545.
Sanctificávit Móyses, p. 549.

Dedicace of a Church

Or, outside of lent: Rev 8: 3, 4

Stetit * ángelus iuxta aram templi, habens thuríbulum áureum in manu sua: et data sunt ei incénsa multa: et ascéndit fumus arómatum in conspéctu Dei, allelúia.

The Angel stood at the altar of the temple with a golden censer in his hand; and he was given much incense and the smoke of the incense ascended before the presence of God, alleluia.

Prayer over the Gifts

In the dedicated church:

MEMORES diéi quo domum tuam, Dómine, glória di-

LORD, as we recall the day you filled this church with

Dedication of a Church

gnátus es ac sanctitáte replére, nosmetípsos, quǽsumus, fac hóstias tibi semper accéptas.

Outside the dedicated church:

SUSCIPE, quǽsumus, Dómine, munus oblátum, et poscéntibus concéde, ut hic sacramentórum virtus et votórum obtineátur efféctus.

Preface

In the dedicated church:

VERE dignum et iustum est, ǽquum et salutáre, nos tibi semper et ubíque grátias ágere: Dómine, sancte Pater, omnípotens ætérne Deus: per Christum Dóminum nostrum.

Quia in domo visíbili quam nobis exstrúere concessísti, ubi famíliæ in hoc loco ad te peregrinánti favére non désinis, mystérium tuæ nobíscum communiónis mire figúras et operáris: hic enim tibi templum illud quod nos sumus ædíficas, et Ecclésiam per orbem diffúsam in domínici compágem córporis facis augéri, in pacis visióne compléndam, cælésti civitáte Ierúsalem.

Et ídeo, cum multitúdine órdinum beatórum, in templo glóriæ tuæ, te collaudámus, benedícimus et magnificámus, dicéntes:

your glory and holiness, may our lives also become an acceptable offering to you.

LORD, receive our gifts. May we who share this sacrament experience the life and power it promises, and hear the answer to our prayers.

FATHER, all-powerful and ever-living God, we do well always and everywhere to give you thanks.

We thank you now for this house of prayer in which you bless your family as we come to you on pilgrimage. Here you reveal your presence by sacramental signs, and make us one with you through the unseen bond of grace. Here you build your temple of living stones, and bring the Church to its full stature as the body of Christ throughout the world, to reach its perfection at last in the heavenly city of Jerusalem, which is the vision of your peace.

In communion with all the angels and saints we bless and praise your greatness in the temple of your glory: Holy...

Dedication of a Church

Outside the dedicated church:

VERE dignum et iustum est, æquum et salutáre, nos tibi semper et ubíque grátias ágere: Dómine, sancte Pater, omnípotens ætérne Deus:

Qui domum oratiónis munifícus inhabitáre dignáris, ut, grátia tua perpétuis fovénte subsídiis, templum Spíritus Sancti ipse nos perfícias, acceptábilis vitæ splendóre corúscans. Sed et visibílibus ædifíciis adumbrátam, Christi sponsam Ecclésiam perénni operatióne sanctíficas, ut, innumerábili prole mater exsúltans, in glóriam tuam collocétur in cælis.

Et ídeo, cum Sanctis et Angelis univérsis, te collaudámus, sine fine dicéntes:

FATHER, all-powerful and ever-living God, we do well always and everywhere to give you thanks.

Your house is a house of prayer, and your presence makes it a place of blessing. You give us grace upon grace to build the temple of your Spirit, creating its beauty from the holiness of our lives.

Your house of prayer is also the promise of the Church in heaven. Here your love is always at work, preparing the Church on earth for its heavenly glory as the sinless bride of Christ, the joyful mother of a great company of saints.

Now, with the saints and all the angels we praise you for ever: Holy...

Communion   Mt 21: 13

D Omus me- a, *do- mus o-ra-ti- ó-nis vo-cá- bitur, di- cit Dómi- nus: in e- a o- mnis, qui pe-tit, ác-ci- pit: et qui quaerit, ínve- nit, et pulsánti ape- ri- é- tur. *T. P.* Alle- lú- ia.

My house will be called a house of prayer, says the Lord; everyone who asks here, will receive, and he who seeks, will find, and to him who knocks, it will be opened.

Or:

Acceptábis sacrifícium, *p. 507.*
Ierúsalem quæ ædificátur, *p. 263.*
Introíbo ad altáre Dei, *p. 451.*
Passer invénit, *p. 502.*
Tóllite hóstias, *p. 551.*
Unam pétii, *p. 480.*

Prayer after Communion
In the dedicated church:

BENEDICTIONIS tuæ, quæsumus, Dómine, plebs tibi sacra fructus repórtet et gáudium, ut, quod in huius festivitátis die corporáli servítio exhíbuit, spiritáliter se retulísse cognóscat.

LORD, we know the joy and power of your blessing in our lives. As we celebrate the dedication of this church, may we give ourselves once more to your service.

Outside the dedicated church:

DEUS, qui nobis supérnam Ierúsalem per temporále Ecclésiæ tuæ signum adumbráre voluísti, da, quæsumus, ut, huius participatióne sacraménti, nos tuæ grátiæ templum effícias, et habitatiónem glóriæ tuæ íngredi concédas.

FATHER, you make your Church on earth a sign of the new and eternal Jerusalem. By sharing in this sacrament may we become the temple of your presence and the home of your glory.

MASSES FOR THE DEAD

The chants of the Funeral Mass can also be used for the various other masses for the dead which follow. The choice of prayers which we propose here is necessarily limited, but the full range of possibilities available can be found in the ritual book. The list of readings is found after the mass prayers, p. 709. Prefaces, p. 65-67.

FUNERAL MASS

Introit   4 Esd 2: 34, 35; Ps 64: 2, 3, 4, 5

VI

Rέquiem * aetérnam dona eis Dómine: et lux perpétua lúceat eis. *Ps.* Te decet hymnus, Deus, in Sion; et tibi reddétur votum in Ierúsalem. *Ant.* Réquiem.

Eternal rest grant unto them, O Lord, and may perpetual light shine upon them. ℣. It is fitting, O God, to sing a hymn unto you on Mount Zion; and our vows shall be carried out for you in Jerusalem.

Or:

Ego autem cum iustítia, p. 497.
Intret orátio mea, p. 586.
Si iniquitátes, p. 566.

Funeral Mass

Opening Prayer

DEUS, Pater omnípotens, cuius Fílium mórtuum fuísse et resurrexísse fides nostra fatétur, concéde propítius, ut hoc mystério fámulus tuus N., qui in illo dormívit, per illum resúrgere lætétur.

ALMIGHTY God, our Father, we firmly believe that your Son died and rose to life. We pray for our brother (sister) N., who has died in Christ. Raise him (her) at the last day to share the glory of the risen Christ.

Gradual   4 *Esd* 2 : 34, 35, ℣. *Ps* 111 : 7

R̊ Equiem * aetérnam dona eis Dómine: et lux perpétua lúceat eis. ℣. In memória aetérna erit iustus: ab auditióne mala non timé- bit.

Eternal rest grant unto them, O Lord, and may perpetual light shine upon them. ℣. The righteous shall be remembered forever; he shall never fear evil tidings.

Or:

Convértere, Dómine, *p. 483.*
Lætátus sum, *p. 548.*
Si ámbulem, *p. 505.*
Unam pétii, *p. 576.*

Alleluia *outside of Lent.* 4 Esd 2: 34, 35

VIII

A- L- le- lú- ia.

℣. Ré- qui- em æ- tér- nam do- na e- is, Dómi-

ne: et lux perpé-

tu- a lú- ce- at e- is.

Eternal rest grant unto them, O Lord, and may perpetual light shine upon them.

Funeral Mass

Or:
De profúndis, p. 593.
In éxitu, p. 563.
Lætátus sum, p. 171.
For a priest or a religious: Ego vos elégi, p. 377.
Tract *during Lent.*

VIII

ABsólve, * Dómine, ánimas ómnium fidélium defunctórum ab omni vínculo delictórum. ℣. Et grátia tua illis succurrénte, mereántur evádere iudícium ultiónis. ℣. Et lucis aetérnae beatitúdine pérfrui.

Deliver, O Lord, the souls of all the departed faithful from all bondage of their sins. ℣. And by your sustaining grace, may they be worthy of escaping the chastisement of judgment. ℣. And partake in the happiness of eternal light.

Masses for the Dead

Or: Ps 129 : 1, 2, 3, 4

VIII

DE profún- dis *clamá- vi ad te, Dómi- ne: Dómi- ne, exáu- di vocem me- am. ℣. Fi- ant aures tu- ae in- tendén- tes in o- ra- ti- ó- nem ser- vi tu- i. ℣. Si in- iqui-tá-tes ob- servá- ve- ris, Dó- mi- ne: Dómi- ne, quis sus- ti-né- bit? ℣. Qui- a apud te pro-pi-ti- á-ti- o est, et propter

le- gem tu- am sustí- nu- i te, Dó-

mi-ne.

Out of the depths have I cried to you O Lord; Lord, hear my voice. ℣. Let your ears be attentive to the prayer of your servant. ℣. If you were to pay heed, O Lord, to iniquities, Lord, who could stand? ℣. But with you there is merciful forgiveness, and because of your law I have awaited you, O Lord.

Offertory

The verse Hóstias can be omitted.

DOmi-ne Ie-su Christe, * Rex gló- ri- ae, lí-be-ra á-nimas ómni- um fi-dé- li- um de-fun- ctó- rum de poenis infér- ni, et de pro-fúndo la- cu : lí-be- ra e- as de o-re le- ó- nis, ne absórbe- at e- as tár- ta-rus, ne cadant in obscú- rum : sed sígni-fer sanctus

Mí- cha- el repraeséntet e- as in lu- cem sanctam :

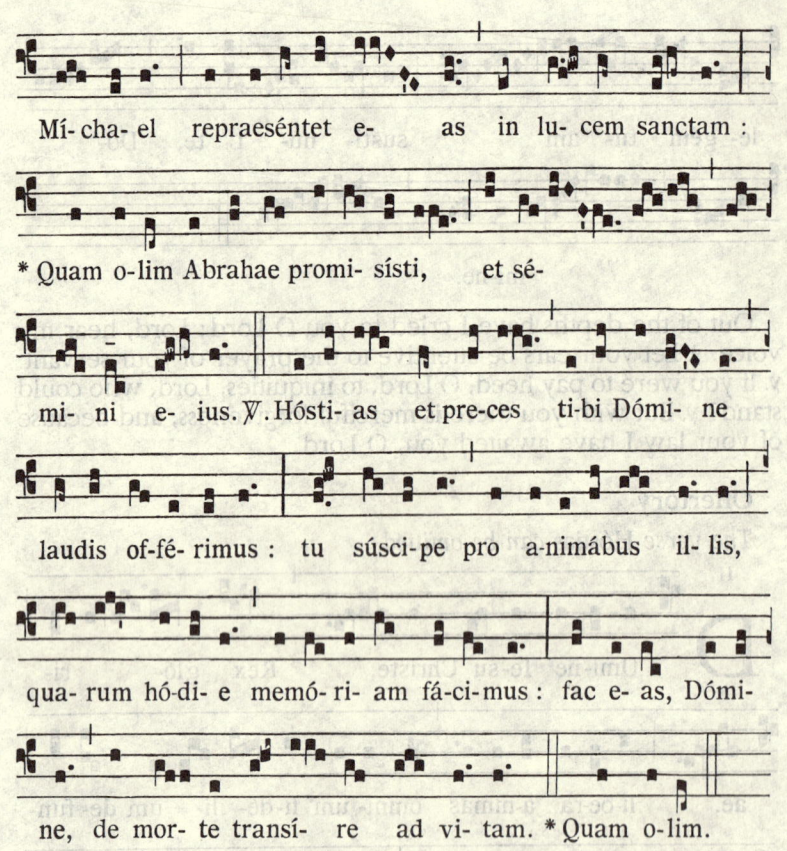

* Quam o-lim Abrahae promi- sísti, et sé-

mi- ni e- ius. ℣. Hósti- as et pre-ces ti-bi Dómi- ne

laudis of-fé- rimus : tu súsci-pe pro a-nimábus il- lis,

qua- rum hó-di- e memó- ri- am fá-ci-mus : fac e- as, Dómi-

ne, de mor- te transí- re ad vi- tam. * Quam o-lim.

O Lord Jesus Christ, King of glory, deliver the souls of all the departed faithful from the sufferings of hell and from the deep pit; deliver them from the mouth of the lion, may they not be swallowed up by hell, may they not fall into darkness; but may Saint Michael, the standardbearer, present them in holy light * as you promised long ago to Abraham and his descendants. ℣. We offer our sacrifices and our prayers to you, O Lord; receive them for the souls that we are remembering today; O Lord, make them pass from death into life * as you promised...

Or:
De profúndis, p. 594.

Funeral Mass

Dómine, convértere, p. 464.
Illúmina óculos meos, p. 475.
Si ambulávero, p. 554.

Prayer over the Gifts

PRO fámuli tui N. salúte hostias tibi, Dómine, supplíciter offérimus tuam cleméntiam deprecántes, ut, qui Fílium tuum pium Salvatórem esse non dubitávit, misericórdem Iúdicem invéniat.

LORD, receive the gifts we offer for the salvation of N. May Christ be merciful in judging our brother (sister) N. for he (she) believed in Christ as his (her) Lord and Saviour.

Prefaces for the dead, p. 65-67.

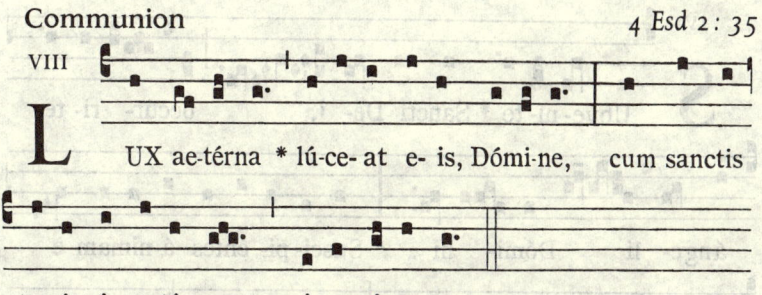

Communion   4 Esd 2 : 35

VIII

LUX ae-térna * lú-ce- at e- is, Dómi-ne, cum sanctis tu- is in aetérnum, qui- a pi- us es.

May eternal light shine upon them, O Lord, in the company of your saints for eternity, for you are full of goodness.

Or:

Amen, dico vobis, quod uni, p. 602.
Dómine, quinque talénta, p. 595.
Dóminus regit me, p. 590.
Illúmina fáciem tuam, p. 445.
Notas mihi fecísti, p. 585.
Panis quem ego dédero, p. 526.
Qui mandúcat, p. 423.

Masses for the Dead

Prayer after Communion

Domine Deus, cuius Fílius in sacraménto Córporis sui viáticum nobis relíquit, concéde propítius, ut per hoc frater noster N. ad ipsam Christi pervéniat mensam ætérnam.

Lord god, your Son Jesus Christ gave us the sacrament of his body and blood to guide us on our pilgrim way to your kingdom. May our brother (sister) N., who shared in the eucharist, come to the banquet of life Christ has prepared for us.

CHANTS FOR THE LAST FAREWELL

Responsory

Subveníte * Sancti Dei, occúrrite ángeli Dómini : * Suscipiéntes ánimam eius : Offeréntes eam in conspéctu Altíssimi. ℣. Suscípiat te Christus, qui vocávit te : et in sinum Abrahae ángeli dedúcant.

Chants for the Last Farewell

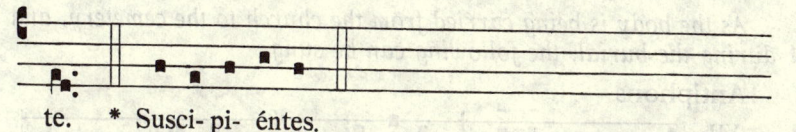

te. * Susci- pi- éntes.

Come to his (her) assistance, O you saints of God, go forth to meet him (her), O you Angels of the Lord; * receive his (her) soul and present it in the sight of the Most High. ℣. May Christ, who called you, receive you, and may the Angels lead you into the bosom of Abraham.

Or:

VIII

Job 19: 25, 26; ℣. 27

Credo * quod Red-émptor me- us vi- vit, et in no-vís- simo di- e de terra surrectú- rus sum: * Et in car-ne me- a vi-dé- bo De- um Salva-tó- rem me- um. ℣. Quem vi- sú-rus sum : e-go ipse, et non á-li- us, et ócu- li me- i con- spe-ctú-ri sunt. * Et in car-ne.

I believe that my Redeemer lives, and that on the last day I shall rise from earth * And in my flesh I shall behold God my Saviour. ℣. I myself shall see him, and not another in my place, and my very eyes will gaze upon him.

Masses for the Dead

As the body is being carried from the church to the cemetery, and during the burial, the following can be sung:

Antiphons

VII

IN pa-ra-dí-sum * dedú-cant te ánge-li : in tu- o advéntu suscí-pi- ant te márty-res, et perdú-cant te in ci-vi-tá-tem sanctam Ie- rú-sa-lem.

May the Angels lead you into paradise; may the martyrs receive you and lead you into the holy city of Jerusalem.

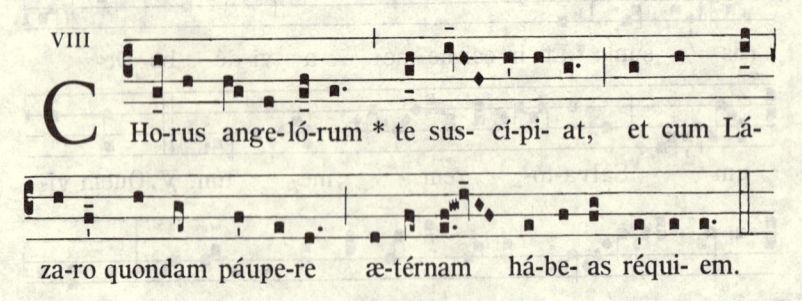

VIII

CHo-rus ange-ló-rum * te sus- cí-pi- at, et cum Lá-za-ro quondam páupe-re æ-térnam há-be- as réqui- em.

May the choir of Angels receive you and, with Lazarus, who was once poor, may you enjoy eternal rest.

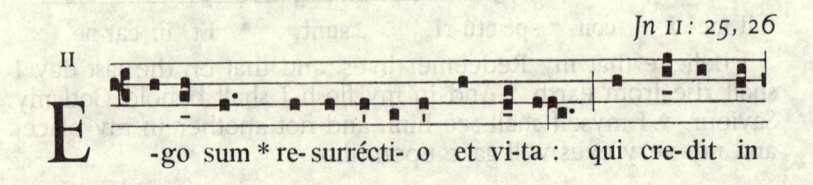

Jn 11: 25, 26

II

E-go sum * re-surrécti- o et vi-ta : qui cre-dit in

me, ét-i-am si mórtu-us fú-e-rit, vi-vet : et o-mnis qui vi-vit et cre-dit in me, non mo-ri-é-tur in ae-térnum.

I am the resurrection and life. He who believes in me, even though he is dead, shall live; and whoever lives and believes in me shall never die.

FUNERAL MASS OF A BAPTIZED CHILD

Opening Prayer

CLEMENTISSIME Deus, qui sapiéntiæ tuæ consíliis hunc párvulum, in ipso vitæ límine, ad te vocásti, preces nostras benígnus exáudi, et præsta, ut cum ipso, quem baptísmatis grátia adoptiónis tibi fílium effecísti, et in regno tuo iam crédimus commoráti, nos étiam ætérnæ vitæ tríbuas esse aliquándo consórtes.

GOD of mercy and love, you called this child to yourself at the dawn of his (her) life. By baptism you made him (her) your child and we believe that he (she) is already in your kingdom. Hear our prayers and let us one day share eternal life with him (her).

Prayer over the Gifts

HÆC MUNERA, tibi, Dómine, obláta sanctífica, ut, quem paréntes a te donátum tibi reddunt infántem, ipsum læti in regno tuo mereántur amplécti.

LORD, make holy these gifts we offer you. These parents return to you the child you gave them. May they have fullness of joy with him (her) in your kingdom.

Prayer after Communion

Corporis, Dómine, et Sánguinis Fílii tui communióne percépta, te fidéliter deprecámur, ut, quos in spem vitæ ætérnæ sacris dignátus es nutríre mystériis, in huius tríbuas vitæ mæróribus confortári.

Lord, hear the prayers of those who share in the body and blood of your Son. Comfort those who mourn for this child and sustain them with the hope of eternal life.

FUNERAL MASS OF A CHILD WHO DIED BEFORE BAPTISM

Opening Prayer

Fidelium tuórum, Dómine, súscipe vota, ut, quos permíttis infántis sibi erépti desidério déprimi, eósdem concédas in tuæ spem miseratiónis fidénter attólli.

Lord, listen to the prayers of this family that has faith in you. In their sorrow at the death of this child, may they find hope in your infinite mercy.

Prayer over the Gifts

Hanc oblationem, Deus, dignáre in nostræ signum devotiónis excípere, ut, qui tuæ providéntiæ consíliis submíttimur confidéntes, tuæ quoque pietátis dulcédine sublevémur.

Father, receive this sacrifice we offer as a sign of our love for you, and comfort us by your merciful love. We accept what you have asked of us, for we trust in your wisdom and goodness.

Prayer after Communion

Corporis, Dómine, et Sánguinis Fílii communióne percépta, te fidéliter deprecámur, ut, quos in spem vitæ ætérnæ sacris dignátus es nutríre mystériis, in huius tríbuas vitæ mæróribus confortári.

Lord, hear the prayers of those who share in the body and blood of your Son. By these sacred mysteries you have filled them with the hope of eternal life. May they be comforted in the sorrows of this present life.

ANNIVERSARY MASS

Opening Prayer

DEUS, glória fidélium et vita iustórum, cuius Fílii morte et resurrectióne redémpti sumus, propitiáre fámulo tuo N., ut, qui resurrectiónis nostræ mystérium agnóvit, ætérnæ beatitúdinis gáudia percípere mereátur.

LORD God, you are the glory of believers and the life of the just. Your Son redeemed us by dying and rising to life again. Our brother (sister) N. was faithful and believed in our own resurrection. Give to him (her) the joys and blessings of the life to come.

Prayer over the Gifts

MUNERA, quæsumus, Dómine, quæ tibi pro fámulo tuo N. offérimus, placátus inténde, ut, remédiis purgátus cæléstibus, in tua glória semper vivus sit et beátus.

LORD, accept these gifts we offer for N. our brother (sister). May they free him (her) from sin and bring him (her) to the happiness of life in your presence.

Prayer after Communion

SACRIS reparáti mystériis, te, Dómine, supplíciter exorámus, ut fámulus N., a delíctis ómnibus emundátus, ætérno resurrectiónis múnere ditári mereátur.

LORD, you renew our lives by this holy eucharist; free N. our brother (sister) from sin and raise him (her) to eternal life.

MASS FOR ONE PERSON

Opening Prayer

DEUS, Pater omnípotens, qui nos crucis mystério confirmásti et Fílii tui resurrectiónis sacraménto signásti, concéde propítius fámulo tuo N., ut, mortalitátis néxibus expedítus,

LORD God, almighty Father, you have made the cross for us a sign of strength and marked us as yours in the sacrament of the resurrection. Now that you have freed our

electórum tuórum aggregétur consórtio.

brother (sister) N. from this mortal life make him (her) one with your saints in heaven.

Prayer over the Gifts

PROPITIARE, quæsumus, Dómine, fámulo tuo N., pro quo hóstiam tibi laudis immolámus, te supplíciter deprecántes, ut, per hæc piæ placatiónis offícia, resúrgere mereátur ad vitam.

LORD, in your mercy may this sacrifice of praise, this offering of peace, bring our brother (sister) N. to the fullness of risen life.

Prayer after Communion

VITALIBUS refécti sacraméntis, quæsumus, Dómine, ut frater noster N., quem testaménti tui partícipem effecísti, huius mystérii purificátus virtúte, in pace Christi sine fine lætétur.

LORD, you give us life in this sacrament. May our brother (sister) N. who received life at your table enter into the everlasting peace and joy of Christ.

MASS FOR MORE THAN ONE PERSON OR FOR ALL THE DEAD

Opening Prayer

DEUS, qui Unigénitum tuum, devícta morte, ad cæléstia transíre fecísti, concéde fámulis tuis (N. et N.), ut, huius vitæ mortalitáte devícta, te conditórem et redemptórem possint perpétuo contemplári.

GOD, our creator and redeemer, by your power Christ conquered death and returned to you in glory. May all your people who have gone before us in faith share his victory and enjoy the vision of your glory for ever.

Mass for a Pope

Prayer over the Gifts

Hostias, quæsumus, Dómine, quas tibi pro fámulis tuis offérimus, propitiátus inténde, ut, quibus fídei christiánæ méritum contulísti, dones et præmium.

Lord, receive this sacrifice for our brothers and sisters. On earth you gave them the privilege of believing in Christ: grant them the eternal life promised by that faith.

Prayer after Communion

Multiplica, Dómine, his sacrifíciis suscéptis, super fámulos tuos defúnctos misericórdiam tuam, et, quibus donásti baptísmi grátiam, da eis æternórum plenitúdinem gaudiórum.

Lord, may our sacrifice bring peace and forgiveness to our brothers and sisters who have died. Bring the new life given to them in baptism to the fullness of eternal joy.

MASS FOR A POPE

Opening Prayer

Deus, fidélis remunerátor animárum, præsta, ut fámulus tuus Papa noster N., quem Petri constituísti vicárium et Ecclésiæ tuæ pastórem, grátiæ et miseratiónis tuæ mystériis, quæ fidénter dispensávit in terris, lætánter apud te perpétuo fruátur in cælis.

God our Father, you reward all who believe in you. May your servant, N. our Pope, vicar of Peter and shepherd of your Church, who faithfully administered the mysteries of your forgiveness and love on earth, rejoice with you for ever in heaven.

Prayer over the Gifts

Quæsumus, Dómine, ut, per hæc piæ placatiónis offícia, fámulum tuum Papam nostrum N. beáta retribútio comitétur, et misericórdia tua nobis grátiæ dona concíliet.

Lord, by this sacrifice which brings us peace, give your servant, N. our Pope, the reward of eternal happiness and let your mercy win for us the gift of your life and love.

Prayer after Communion

Divinæ tuæ communiónis refécti sacraméntis, quæsumus, Dómine, ut fámulus tuus Papa noster N. quem Ecclésiæ tuæ visíbile voluísti fundaméntum unitátis in terris, beatitúdini gregis tui felíciter aggregétur.

Lord, you renew us with the sacraments of your divine life. Hear our prayers for your servant, N. our Pope. You made him the center of the unity of your Church on earth, count him now among the flock of the blessed in your kingdom.

MASS FOR THE DIOCESAN BISHOP

Opening Prayer

Da, quæsumus, omnípotens Deus, ut fámulus tuus N. epíscopus noster, cui famíliæ tuæ curam tradidísti, cum multíplici labóris fructu gáudia Dómini sui ingrediátur ætérna.

All-powerful God, you made N. your servant the guide of your family. May he enjoy the reward of all his work and share the eternal joy of his Lord.

Prayer over the Gifts

Immensam cleméntiam tuam, Dómine, supplíciter implorámus, ut hoc sacrifícium, quod fámulus tuus N. epíscopus noster, dum esset in córpore, maiestáti tuæ pro salúte fidélium óbtulit, ipsi nunc prosit ad véniam.

Merciful God, may this sacrifice, which N. your servant offered during his life for the salvation of the faithful, help him now to find pardon and peace.

Prayer after Communion

Prosit, quæsumus, Dómine, fámulo tuo N. epíscopo nostro misericórdiæ tuæ implorâta cleméntia, ut Christi, in quo sperávit et quem prædicávit, ætérnum cápiat, his sacrifíciis, consórtium.

Lord, give your mercy and love to N. your servant. He hoped in Christ and preached Christ. By this sacrifice may he share with Christ the joy of eternal life.

MASS FOR ANOTHER BISHOP

Opening Prayer

DEUS, qui inter apostólicos sacerdótes fámulum tuum N. epíscopum (cardinálem) pontificáli fecísti dignitáte vigére, præsta, quæsumus, ut eórum quoque perpétuo aggregétur consórtio.

GOD OUR FATHER, may your servant N., who was our bishop, rejoice in the fellowship of the successors of the apostles whose office he shared in this life.

Prayer over the Gifts

SUSCIPE, Dómine, quæsumus pro famulo tuo epíscopo (cardináli) quas tibi offérimus hóstias, ut, cui in hoc sǽculo pontificále donásti méritum, in cælésti regno sanctórum tuórum iúbeas iungi consórtio.

LORD, accept our offering for N. your servant. You gave him the dignity of high priesthood in this world. Let him now share the joy of your saints in the kingdom of heaven.

Prayer after Communion

QUÆSUMUS, omnípotens et miséricors Deus, ut fámulum tuum N. epíscopum (cardinálem), quem in terris pro Christo legatióne fungi tribuísti, his emundátis sacrifíciis, consédere fácias in cæléstibus cum ipso.

ALL-POWERFUL Father, God of mercy, you gave N. your servant the privilege of doing the work of Christ on earth. By this sacrifice free him from sin and bring him to eternal life with Christ in heaven.

MASS FOR A PRIEST

Opening Prayer

PRÆSTA, quæsumus, Dómine, ut fámulus tuus N. sacérdos, quem in hoc sǽculo commorántem sacris munéribus decorásti, in cælésti sede gloriósus semper exsúltet.

LORD, you gave N. your servant and priest the privilege of a holy ministry in this world. May he rejoice for ever in the glory of your kingdom.

Prayer over the Gifts

Concede, quæsumus, omnípotens Deus, ut fámulus tuus N; sacérdos, per hæc sancta mystéria, conspéctu semper claro conspíciat quæ hic fidéliter ministrávit.

All-powerful God, by this eucharist may N. your servant and priest rejoice for ever in the vision of the mysteries which he faithfully ministered here on earth.

Prayer after Communion

Sumptis salutábus sacraméntis, implorámus, Deus, cleméntiam tuam, ut fámulum tuum N. sacerdótem, quem fecísti mysteriórum tuórum dispensatórem in terris, eórum fácias in cælis apérta veritáte nutríri.

God of mercy, we who receive the sacraments of salvation pray for N. your servant and priest. You made him a minister of your mysteries on earth. May he rejoice in the full knowledge of your truth in heaven.

MASS FOR A DEACON

Opening Prayer

Concede, quæsumus, miséricors Deus, fámulo tuo N. diácono felicitátis ætérnæ consórtium, cui donásti in Ecclésia tua cónsequi ministérium.

God of mercy, you gave N. your servant the privilege of serving your Church. Bring him now to the joy of eternal life.

Prayer over the Gifts

Propitiare, Dómine, fámulo tuo N. diácono, pro cuius salúte hoc tibi sacrifícium offérimus, ut, sicut Christo Fílio tuo ministrávit in carne, cum fidélibus servis exsúrgat in glóriam sempitérnam.

Lord, be merciful to N. your servant for whose salvation we offer you this sacrifice. He ministered during his life to Christ your Son. May he rise with all your faithful servants to eternal glory.

Prayer after Communion

Muneribus sacris repléti, te, Dómine, humíliter deprecámur, ut per hoc sacrifícium fámulum tuum N. diáconum, quem inter servos Ecclésiæ tuæ vocásti, a mortis vínculis absolútum, cum iis qui bene ministráverunt partem recípere et in gaudium tuum intráre benígne concédas.

Lord, you fill us with holy gifts. Hear our prayers for N. your deacon whom you counted among the servants of your Church. By this sacrifice free him from the power of death and give him a share in the reward you have promised to all who serve you faithfully.

MASS FOR A RELIGIOUS

Opening Prayer

Præsta, quæsumus, omnípotens Deus, ut fámulus tuus N. qui pro Christi amóre perféctæ caritátis viam percúrrit, in advéntu glóriæ tuæ lætétur, et cum frátribus suis de regni tui beatitúdine gáudeat semptérna.

All-powerful God, out of love for Christ and his Church, N. served you faithfully in the religious life. May he (she) rejoice at the coming of your glory and enjoy eternal happiness with his (her) brothers (sisters) in your kingdom.

MASS FOR RELATIVES FRIENDS AND BENEFACTORS

Opening Prayer

Deus, véniæ largítor et humánæ salútis amátor, quæsumus cleméntiam tuam, ut nostræ congregatiónis fratres, propínquos et benefactóres qui ex hos sæculo transiérunt, beáta María semper Vírgine intercedénte cum ómnibus sanctis tuis, ad perpétuæ beatitúdinis consórtium perveníre concédas.

Father, source of forgiveness and salvation for all mankind, hear our prayer. By the prayers of the ever-virgin Mary, may our friends, relatives, and benefactors who have gone from this world come to share eternal happiness with all your saints.

Prayer over the Gifts

Deus cuius misericórdiæ non est númerus, súscipe propítius preces humilitátis nostræ, et animábus fratrum, propinquórum et benefactórum nostrórum, per hæc sacraménta salútis nostræ, cunctórum remissiónem tríbue peccatórum.

God of infinite mercy, hear our prayers and by this sacrament of our salvation forgive all the sins of our relatives, friends, and benefactors.

Prayer after Communion

Præsta, quæsumus, omnípotens et miséricors Deus, ut ánimæ fratrum, propinquórum et benefactórum nostrórum, pro quibus hoc sacrifícium laudis tuæ obtúlimus maiestáti, per huius virtútem sacraménti a peccátis ómnibus expiátæ, lucis perpétuæ, te miseránte, recípiant beatitúdinem.

Father all-powerful, God of mercy, we have offered you this sacrifice of praise for our relatives, friends, and benefactors. By the power of this sacrament free them from all their sins and give them the joy of eternal light.

READINGS FOR MASSES OF THE DEAD

First reading

* Job 14: 1-3, 10-15: *Hope beyond death.*
  Job 19: 23-27a: *My Redeemer lives.*
* Wis 2: 1-4a, 22-23; 3: 1-9 or 2: 23; 3: 1-6, 9: *The life of man is in the hand of God.*
  Wis 4: 7-15: *In a short time he covered a long road.*
* Is 25: 6a, 7-9: *God shall destroy death.*
* Lam 3: 17-26: *Unshakable hope.*
  Dan 12: 1b-3: *The dead shall awaken one day.*
  2 Macc 12: 43-46: *Prayers for the dead.*

Second reading

Acts 10: 34-43 or 34-36, 39-43: *Our hope will not be disappointed.*
Rom 5: 6b-11: *We shall live with Christ.*
Rom 5: 17-21: *Sin and the abundance of grace.*
* Rom 6: 3-9 or 3-4, 8-9: *To pass through death with Christ.*
Rom 8: 14-17: *We are children of God.*
Rom 8: 18-23: *We are awaiting the deliverance of our body.*
Rom 8: 31b-35, 37-39: *Who will separate us from the love of Christ?*
* Rom 14: 7-9, 10b-12 or 7-9: *Union with Christ in life and in death.*
1 Cor 15: 1-5, 11: *We believe in Christ who has died and has risen.*
1 Cor 15: 12, 16-20: *Christ's resurrection announces our own.*
* 1 Cor 15: 19-24a, 25-28 or 19-23: *We shall all come back to life in Christ.*
1 Cor 15: 51-54, 57: *O death, where is your victory?*
2 Cor 4: 14-5: 1: *To be attached to things eternal.*
2 Cor 5: 1, 6-10: *Our true dwelling place.*
Phil 3: 20-4: 1: *Our dwelling place is in the heavens.*
* 1 Thess 4: 13-14, 17d-18: *We shall always be with the Lord.*
2 Tim 2: 8-13: *We shall live with Christ.*
* 1 Pet 1: 3-8: *Born anew for a living hope.*
1 Jn 3: 1-2: *How God loves us.*
1 Jn 3: 14, 16-20: *Love causes us to pass from death to life.*
* 1 Jn 4: 7-10: *God is love.*
Rev 14: 13: *Blessed are the dead who fall asleep in the Lord.*
Rev 20: 11-21: 1: *Each one shall be judged according to his works.*
* Rev 21: 1-5a, 6b-7: *The new Jerusalem.*

Gospel

   Mt 5: 1-12a: *Authentic happiness.*
* Mt 11: 25-28: *Come to me, all you who labour.*
   Mt 25: 1-13: *The coming of the bridegroom.*
   Mt 25: 31-46: *We will be judged on love.*
   Mk 10: 28-30: *The reward of true disciples.*
* Mk 14: 32-36: *The agony of Jesus.*
   Mk 15: 33-34ac, 37-39: *The Crucifixion.*
   Lk 2: 22b, 25-32: *You can let your servant depart in peace.*
   Lk 7: 11-17: *Jesus raises up the son of the widow.*
   Lk 12: 35-38, 40: *Be ready to receive the Lord.*
   Lk 23: 33-34, 39-46, 50, 52-53: *The good thief.*
   Lk 24: 13-35 or 13-16, 28-35: *The disciples of Emmaüs.*
   Jn 3: 16-17: *God so loved the world.*
   Jn 5: 24-29: *The hour of judgment.*
* Jn 6: 37-40: *Jesus has come so that we may live.*
   Jn 6: 51-58: *The bread of life.*
* Jn 10: 14-16: *The good shepherd gives his life for his sheep.*
   Jn 11: 17-27: *I am the resurrection and life.*
* Jn 11: 32b-45 or 32b-36, 41-45: *Jesus raises his friend Lazarus from the dead.*
   Jn 12: 24-28 or 24-26: *The grain that dies, bears fruit.*
   Jn 14: 1-6: *Jesus has prepared a place for us.*
* Jn 17: 1-3, 24-26 or 24-26: *Jesus prays for his friends.*
* Jn 19: 17ab, 18, 25-30: *Mary at the foot of the Cross.*

At funerals for children, the readings should be chosen from those of the preceding list which are marked with an asterisk, or from the following:

   Eph 1: 3-5: *God chose us before creation.*
   Rev 7: 9-10, 15-17: *The cortege of the Lamb.*
   Mt 18: 1-5, 10: *The greatest in the Kingdom.*

ALPHABETICAL INDEX OF CHANTS

The number preceding each piece designates the mode. The number which follows indicates the page. The chants of the Mass Ordinary are found on p. 73.

Introits

8	Ad te levavi	165	8	Invocabit me	238
7	Adorate Deum	438	8	Iubilate Deo	359
8	Benedicta sit	404	4	Iudica me	265
6	Cantate Domino	368	1	Iustus es	542
3	Caritas Dei	405	1	Iustus ut palma	615
2	Cibavit eos	413	5	Lætare	259
5	Cogitationes	424	2	Lætetur cor	442, 575
1	Da pacem	547	8	Lux fulgebit	193
1	De ventre	631	8	Miserere	537
7	Deus, in adiutorium	516	1	Misereris omnium	229
5	Deus in loco	202, 509	4	Misericordia Domini	364
6	Dicit Dominus: Ego	591	7	Ne derelinquas me	581
4	Dicit Dominus Petro	636	7	Ne timeas	627
1	Dicit Dominus: Sermones	680	4	Nos autem	286
3	Dignus est Agnus	597	3	Nunc scio	641
8	Dilexisti	221	7	Oculi mei	252
5	Domine, in tua	457	6	Omnes gentes	487
2	Dominus dixit	189	3	Omnia	557
2	Dominus fortitudo	481	4	Omnis terra	431
2	Dominus illuminatio	470	7	Populus Sion	169
1	Dominus secus mare	437	4	Protector noster	527
3	Dum clamarem	496	7	Puer natus est	198
8	Dum medium	213	6	Quasi modo	355
3	Dum sanctificatus	391	4	Reminiscere	247
2	Ecce advenit	217	6	Requiem	688
5	Ecce Deus	503	7	Respice, Domine	522
1	Ego autem	497	6	Respice in me	465
3	Ego clamavi	571	4	Resurrexi	349
6	Esto mihi	452	1	Rorate	180
4	Exaudi...adiutor	477	4	Salus populi	552
1	Exaudi...tibi dixit	387	2	Salve, sancta Parens	207
1	Factus est	461	3	Si iniquitates	566
1	Gaudeamus...Mariæ	655	7	Signum magnum	655
1	Gaudeamus...sanctorum	664	2	Sitientes	515
3	Gaudens gaudebo	673	8	Spiritus Domini	396
1	Gaudete	174	1	Suscepimus	492
6	Hodie scietis	185	2	Terribilis est	679
3	In nomine Domini	556	3	Tibi dixit	246
4	In voluntate tua	561	2	Venite, adoremus	446
1	Inclina, Domine	531	7	Viri Galilæi	381
3	Intret oratio	586	3	Vocem iucunditatis	374
			2	Vultum tuum	650

Index of Chants

Graduals

5	Ad Dominum	462
2	Angelis suis	239
7	Audi, filia	657
1	Beata gens	543
7	Benedicam Dominum	517
5	Benedicta es tu	674
4	Benedicta et venerabilis	651
7	Benedictus Dominus	223
5	Benedictus es	406
5	Benedictus qui venit	194
5	Bonum est confidere	528
5	Bonum est confiteri	533
5	Christus factus est	282
7	Clamaverunt	577
5	Constitues eos	642
5	Convertere	483
1	Custodi me	498
5	Diffusa est	209
8	Dilexisti	224
7	Dirigatur	587
2	Dispersit	447
5	Dominabitur	598
5	Domine, Dominus	504
4	Domine, prævenisti	616
2	Domine, refugium	562
1	Dulcis et rectus	426
1	Ecce quam bonum	567
5	Ego dixi	458
3	Eripe me	266
5	Esto mihi	493
5	Ex Sion	170
3	Exaltabo te	472
3	Exsurge	254
5	Fuit homo	176
2	Hæc dies	350
2	Hodie scietis	186
7	Iacta	466
5	In Deo speravit	510
2	In omnem terram	637
7	Lætatus sum	260, 548
7	Liberasti nos	592
5	Locus iste	682
1	Miserere mei	230
5	Misit Dominus	432
7	Oculi omnium	287, 414
5	Omnes de Saba	218
2	Ostende nobis	499
5	Priusquam	632
5	Prope est	181
5	Propitius esto	471
5	Protector noster	478
7	Qui sedes	175
5	Quis sicut	443
2	Requiem	689
5	Respice	523
7	Salvum fac	572
1	Sciant gentes	248
1	Si ambulem	505
3	Speciosus	214
5	Suscepimus	582
2	Tecum principium	190
5	Timebunt	438, 538
1	Timete	665
5	Tollite hostias	448
2	Tollite portas	622
3	Tu es Deus	453
5	Unam petii	204, 576
1	Universi	166
5	Venite, filii	488
5	Viderunt omnes	199

Alleluia verses

7	Adorabo	444
4	Ascendit Deus	382
5	Assumpta est	658
2	Ave, Maria	623
5	Beatus vir	628
5	Bene fundata est	671
8	Benedictus es	410
2	Benedictus qui venit	224
7	Candor est	647
1	Cantate Domino	539
1	Cantate Domino *other*	454
7	Caro mea	415
1	Christus resurgens	370
3	Cognoverunt	360
2	Confitemini...et invocate	553
8	Confitemini...quoniam	339
4	Constitues eos	638
8	Crastina die	187
7	De profundis	593
8	Deus, iudex iustus	467
2	Deus, qui sedes	474
4	Dextera Dei	369
2	Dies sanctificatus	200
1	Domine, Deus meus	463
3	Domine, Deus salutis	518
2	Domine, dilexi	683
7	Domine, exaudi	544
6	Domine, in virtute	479
7	Domine, refugium	524

Index of Chants

8	Dominus dixit	191	1	Tota pulchra es	675
8	Dominus in Sina	383	2	Tu es Petrus	643
2	Dominus regnavit, decorem	195	2	Tu, puer	633
8	Dominus regnavit, exsultet	439	3	Veni, Domine	182
8	Dulce lignum	661	2	Veni, Sancte Spiritus	398
1	Dum complerentur	393	8	Venite ad me	666
1	Ego sum pastor	366	7	Venite, exsultemus	529
1	Ego vos elegi	377	2	Verba mea	459
4	Emitte Spiritum tuum	397	8	Verbo Domini	583
2	Emitte Spiritum tuum	393	2	Vidimus stellam	219
2	Eripe me	506	8	Virga Iesse	625
4	Excita	177			
7	Exivi	376		**Sequences**	
7	Exsultate Deo	511	7	Lauda, Sion	416
8	Felix es	652	1	Veni, Sancte Spiritus	398
4	Gaudete, iusti	205	1	Victimæ pascali	351
7	In die resurrectionis	356			
2	In exitu	563		**Tracts**	
3	In te, Domine	483	8	Ab ortu solis	288
2	Inveni David	225	8	Absolve, Domine	691
1	Lætatus sum	171	8	Ad te levavi	255
8	Lauda, anima mea	573	8	Attende cælum	334
4	Lauda, Ierusalem	578	2	Audi, filia	623
4	Laudate Deum	433	8	Beatus vir	617
2	Laudate Dominum	449	8	Cantemus Domino	330
7	Magnus Dominus	494	8	Commovisti	249
7	Multifarie	210	8	De profundis	692
1	Non vos relinquam	389	2	Deus, Deus meus	278
1	O quam bonus	583	2	Domine, exaudi	302
1	Omnes gentes	488	2	Domine, non secundum	231
4	Oportebat	361	8	Iubilate Domino	328
8	Ostende	167	8	Laudate Dominum	332
3	Paratum cor meum	558	8	Qui confidunt	261
7	Pascha nostrum	351	2	Qui habitat	240
8	Post dies octo	357	8	Sæpe expugnaverunt	268
4	Post partum	210	8	Sicut cervus	336
1	Potestas eius	599	8	Vinea facta est	333
4	Qui posuit fines	588			
1	Qui timent	568		**Offertories**	
7	Quinque prudentes	587	2	Ad te, Domine	167, 501
7	Quoniam Deus	534	8	Angelus Domini	357
2	Redemptionem	365	1	Ascendit Deus	389
1	Regnavit Dominus	388	8	Assumpta est	658
8	Requiem	690	8	Ave, Maria	676
1	Senex	612	8	Ave, Maria...benedictus	183
8	Spiritus est	534	8	Beata es	653
8	Spiritus Sanctus	377	5	Benedic, anima mea	584
1	Surrexit Christus	375	1	Benedicam Dominum	480
7	Te decet	500	2	Benedicite, gentes	378
1	Timebunt gentes	549	3	Benedictus es	455
3	Tollite	426	8	Benedictus qui venit	226

Index of Chants

3	Benedictus sit	411	5	Sicut in holocausto	489
4	Benedixisti	178	3	Sperent in te	468
8	Bonum est	445	1	Stetit angelus	684
4	Confirma hoc	401	1	Super flumina	559
1	Confitebor tibi	269	4	Terra tremuit	353
3	Constitues eos	644	2	Tollite portas	188
2	De profundis	594	4	Tui sunt	200
2	Deus, Deus meus	366	2	Veritas mea	619
8	Deus enim firmavit	196	2	Vir erat	564
3	Deus, tu convertens	172	1	Viri Galilæi	383
2	Dextera Domini	440			
2	Dextera Domini...alleluia	347		**Communions**	
8	Diffusa est	613	4	Acceptabis	507
6	Domine, convertere	464	6	Alleluia	348
6	Domine Deus	672	1	Amen: Quidquid	596
2	Domine Iesu Christe	693	4	Amen: Quod uni	602
6	Domine, in auxilium	540	2	Aufer a me	570
3	Domine, vivifica me	579	1	Beata viscera	654
8	Emitte Spiritum	394	6	Beatam me dicent	660
2	Exaltabo te	236, 512	1	Beati mundo corde	669
5	Exspectans	535	3	Beatus servus	526
1	Felix namque es	211	4	Benedicimus Deum	412
1	Gloria et honore	629, 647	2	Cantabo Domino	464
8	Gressus meos	589	2	Cantate Domino	363
4	Illumina	475	8	Christus resurgens	490
8	Immittet	530	6	Circuibo	486
8	Improperium	428	8	Comedite pinguia	441
8	Improperium...et dederunt	283	1	Data est mihi	385
2	In te speravi	205, 525	6	De fructu	536
5	Intende voci	459	8	Dicit Andreas	435
1	Iubilate Deo	371, 434	6	Dicit Dominus	436
4	Iustitiæ Domini	256, 507	7	Dicite: Pusillanimes	179
1	Iustorum animæ	667	5	Dico vobis: Gaudium	429
4	Iustus ut palma	633	2	Domine, Dominus	575
4	Lætentur cæli	192	8	Domine, memorabor	541
4	Lauda, anima mea	362	4	Domine, quinque	595
2	Laudate Dominum	262	1	Dominus dabit	168
2	Meditabor	250, 574	2	Dominus firmamentum	476
3	Mihi autem	639	2	Dominus regit me	590
4	Oravi	545	5	Domus mea	686
4	Perfice	450, 484	1	Ecce Virgo	184
5	Populum humilem	495	8	Ego clamavi	469
8	Portas cæli	422	2	Ego sum pastor	367
4	Postula a me	600	8	Ego sum vitis	373
8	Precatus est	519	1	Ego vos elegi	380
2	Protege	662	4	Exsulta, filia Sion	197
1	Recordare mei	569	7	Factus est repente	402
5	Reges Tharsis	219	1	Fili, quid fecisti	206
5	Sanctificavit	549	8	Gloriosa	677
8	Scapulis suis	244	3	Gustate et videte	495
8	Si ambulavero	554	8	Hoc corpus	297

Index of Chants

6	Honora Dominum	513	6	Surrexit Dominus	363
4	Ierusalem, quæ ædificatur	263	4	Tanto tempore	372
2	Ierusalem, surge	173	7	Tolle puerum	206
1	Illumina	445	4	Tollite hostias	551
1	In salutari tuo	565	6	Tu es Petrus	645
6	In splendoribus	193	5	Tu mandasti	555
4	Inclina aurem tuam	491	2	Tu, puer	635
8	Introibo	451	5	Ultimo festivitatis	395
7	Ioseph, fili David	620	7	Unam petii	480
2	Lætabimur	580	7	Unus militum	429
6	Lutum fecit	264	8	Venite post me	441
8	Lux æterna	695	1	Videns Dominus	271
4	Magna est	630	1	Viderunt omnes	201
1	Manducaverunt	456	4	Vidimus stellam	221
4	Memento	560	1	Visionem	252, 649
6	Mitte manum	358	2	Vovete	546
2	Multitudo	451			
2	Narrabo	460		**Antiphons**	
8	Nemo te condemnavit	272	6	Adorna	609
5	Non vos relinquam	379	6	Alleluia	348
7	Notas	585	7	Asperges me	70
2	Omnes qui in Christo	227	7	Asperges me *other*	71
8	Oportet te	264	4	Asperges me	71
8	Optimam partem	508	8	Chorus angelorum	698
5	Panem de cælo	521	4	Crucem tuam	310
1	Panis	526	5	Domine, tu mihi	291
6	Pascha nostrum	354	2	Dominus Iesus	290
1	Passer invenit	502	3	Ecce Dominus noster	607
4	Pater, cum essem	390	6	Ecce lignum crucis	309
8	Pater, si non potest	285	2	Ego sum resurrectio	698
4	Per signum crucis	663	7	Hosanna filio David	272
1	Petite	514	1	Immutemur	234
8	Primum quærite	531	7	In hoc cognoscent	292
1	Psallite Domino	386	7	In paradisum	698
3	Qui biberit	258	4	Iuxta vestibulum	234
7	Qui biberit	258	8	Lumen	608
6	Qui manducat	423	3	Mandatum novum	292
3	Qui meditabitur	237	7	Maneant in vobis	293
5	Qui mihi ministrat	270	4	Postquam surrexit	290
1	Qui vult venire	486	1	Pueri...portantes	274
1	Quicumque fecerit	476	1	Pueri...vestimenta	274
5	Quinque prudentes	590	2	Responsum	610
4	Quod dico vobis	485	4	Si ego Dominus	291
8	Responsum	614	6	Ubi caritas	293
1	Revelabitur	188	8	Vidi aquam	71
3	Scapulis suis	245			
6	Sedebit Dominus	602		**Hymns**	
7	Signa	385	7	Benedictus es	407
8	Simile est	513	1	Gloria, laus	275
6	Simon Ioannis	363, 640	3	Pange, lingua...corporis	298
8	Spiritus Sanctus	380	1	Pange, lingua...prælium	318

Responsories			4 Subvenite 696
8 Credo..................	697		
2 Emendemus.............	235		Various
2 Ingrediente.............	277		Improperia................ 311
2 Obtulerunt..............	611		Litany of Saints........... 340

TABLE OF PREFACES

Advent I..................... 49	Ordinary Sundays I............. 59
Advent II.................... 49	Ordinary Sundays II............ 59
Christmas I................... 50	Ordinary Sundays III........... 60
Christmas II.................. 51	Ordinary Sundays IV........... 60
Christmas III................. 51	Ordinary Sundays V............ 61
Epiphany..................... 220	Ordinary Sundays VI........... 62
Baptism of the Lord........... 226	Ordinary Sundays VII.......... 62
Lent I....................... 52	Ordinary Sundays VIII......... 63
Lent II...................... 52	Eucharist I................... 63
Lent III..................... 53	Eucharist II.................. 64
Lent IV..................... 53	Eucharistic Prayer II.......... 29
1st Sunday of Lent............ 245	Eucharistic Prayer IV......... 36
2nd Sunday of Lent........... 251	Presentation.................. 614
3rd Sunday of Lent........... 257	Saint Joseph.................. 619
4th Sunday of Lent........... 263	Annunciation................. 626
5th Sunday of Lent........... 270	Saint John the Baptist......... 634
Palm Sunday.................. 285	Saints Peter and Paul.......... 645
Passion I.................... 54	Transfiguration............... 648
Easter I..................... 55	Assumption 659
Easter II.................... 55	Triumph of the Cross.......... 663
Easter III................... 56	All Saints 668
Easter IV.................... 56	Immaculate Conception........ 677
Easter V..................... 57	Dedication *in the church itself* ... 685
Ascension I................... 57	Dedication *in another church*.... 686
Ascension II.................. 58	For the Dead I................ 65
Pentecost.................... 402	For the Dead II............... 65
Trinity...................... 411	For the Dead III.............. 66
Sacred Heart................. 428	For the Dead IV.............. 66
Christ The King.............. 601	For the Dead V............... 67

TABLE OF CONTENTS

Foreword 5
Order of Mass 7
Eucharistic Prayer I 22
Eucharistic Prayer II 29
Eucharistic Prayer III 32
Eucharistic Prayer IV 36
Communion 41
Prefaces 49
Sprinkling of Holy Water 68
Chants of the Mass Ordinary 73
Liturgical Year 163
Advent 165
Christmas 185
Lent 229
Easter 323
Trinity 404
The Body and Blood of Christ 413
The Sacred Heart 424
Ordinary Time 431
Christ The King 597
Proper of Saints 605
Masses for the Dead 688
Index of Chants 711
Table of Prefaces 716

TABLE OF CONTENTS

Foreword 5
Order of Mass 7
Eucharistic Prayer I 22
Eucharistic Prayer II 26
Eucharistic Prayer III 32
Eucharistic Prayer IV 36
Communion 41
Prefaces 49
Sprinkling of Holy Water 65
Chants of the Mass Ordinary 73
Liturgical Year 103
Advent 105
Christmas 185
Lent 249
Easter 323
Trinity 404
The Body and Blood of Christ 413
The Sacred Heart 424
Ordinary Time 431
Christ The King 507
Proper of Saints 509
Masses for the Dead 688
Index of Chants 711
Table of Prefaces 710

♦ Imprimé en France par Imprimerie Tardy Quercy S.A. Bourges - 16410
Dépôt légal : 1ᵉʳ trimestre 1991

*Music Library
Cathedral of the
Immaculate Conception
Springfield, IL*